Central and Southeast European Politics since 1989

The only textbook to provide a complete introduction to post-1989 Central and Southeast European politics, this dynamic volume provides a comprehensive account of the collapse of communism and the massive transformation that the region has witnessed. It brings together twenty-three leading specialists to trace the course of the dramatic changes accompanying democratization. The text provides country-by-country coverage, identifying common themes and enabling students to see which are shared throughout the area, giving them a sense of its unity and comparability while strengthening understanding around its many different trajectories. The dual thematic focus on democratization and Europeanization running through the text also helps to reinforce this learning process. Each chapter contains a factual overview to give the reader context concerning the region which will be useful for specialists and newcomers to the subject alike.

Sabrina P. Ramet is Professor of Political Science at The Norwegian University of Science and Technology, and Senior Associate of the Centre for the Study of Civil War at the International Peace Research Institute in Oslo (PRIO).

Central and Southeast European Politics since 1989

Edited by

SABRINA P. RAMET

CAMBRIDGE UNIVERSITY PRESS
Cambridge, New York, Melbourne, Madrid, Cape Town, Singapore, São Paulo, Delhi

Cambridge University Press
The Edinburgh Building, Cambridge CB2 8RU, UK

Published in the United States of America by Cambridge University Press, New York

www.cambridge.org
Information on this title: www.cambridge.org/9780521716161

First published 2010

Printed in the United Kingdom at the University Press, Cambridge

A catalogue record for this publication is available from the British Library

ISBN 978-0-521-88810-3 Hardback
ISBN 978-0-521-71616-1 Paperback

For Ola Listhaug,
Kristen Ringdal,
Al Simkus, and
Knut Erik Solem,
friends

Contents

List of figures and maps — *page* x
List of tables — xi
Notes on the contributors — xiii
Preface — xxi
List of acronyms and abbreviations — xxii
Guide to pronounciation of Central and Southeast European words — xxxi

Part 1 Introduction — 1

1 Introduction
SABRINA P. RAMET — 3

2 Post-socialist models of rule in Central and Southeastern Europe
SABRINA P. RAMET AND F. PETER WAGNER — 9

Part 2 Issues — 37

3 The emergence of the nation-state in East-Central Europe and the Balkans in historical perspective
RENÉO LUKIC — 39

4 Central and East European party systems since 1989
ELISABETH BAKKE — 64

5 Economic reforms and the illusion of transition
KARL KASER — 91

6 The War of Yugoslav Succession
MARKO ATTILA HOARE — 111

Part 3 Central Europe — 137

7 Poland since 1989: muddling through, wall to wall
KONSTANTY GEBERT — 139

8 Building democratic values in the Czech Republic since 1989
CAROL SKALNIK LEFF — 162

9 Slovakia since 1989
ERIKA HARRIS 182

10 Hungary since 1989
ANDRÁS BOZÓKI AND ESZTER SIMON 204

Part 4 Yugoslav Successor States 233

11 Slovenia since 1989
DANICA FINK-HAFNER 235

12 Politics in Croatia since 1990
SABRINA P. RAMET 258

13 Serbia and Montenegro since 1989
SABRINA P. RAMET 286

14 Bosnia and Herzegovina since 1990
FLORIAN BIEBER 311

15 Macedonia since 1989
ZACHARY T. IRWIN 328

16 Kosova: resisting expulsion and striving for independence
FRANCES TRIX 358

Part 5 Southeastern Europe 377

17 Romania: in the shadow of the past
LAVINIA STAN 379

18 Bulgaria since 1989
MARIA SPIROVA 401

19 Albania since 1989: the Hoxhaist legacy
BERND JÜRGEN FISCHER 421

Part 6 Former Soviet republics 445

20 The Baltic states
HERMANN SMITH-SIVERTSEN 447

21 Moldova since 1989
STEVEN D. ROPER 473

Part 7 Present and future challenges 493

22 Regional security and regional relations
RICK FAWN 495

23 The EU and democratization in Central and Southeastern Europe since 1989
ULRICH SEDELMEIER 519

24 Facing the twenty-first century: lessons, questions, and tendencies (a conclusion)
AUREL BRAUN 536

Index 553

Figures and maps

Figures

10.1 Unemployment rate (percent of labor force without jobs), Hungary, 1990–2007 *page* 217
10.2 Annual GDP growth, Hungary, 1990–2007 218
10.3 Hungary and East–West migration, 1990–2007 222

Maps

1 Central and Southeastern Europe, 1989 xxxiv
2 Central and Southeastern Europe, 2009 xxxv

Tables

3.1	The age of empires: constitution of nation-states, multinational states, and empires in Central and Eastern Europe and the Balkans, 1800–1918	*page* 46
3.2	Political entities constituting the Versailles System, 1918–38	49
3.3	Nation-states, multinational states, and empires in Central and Eastern Europe and the Balkans under the Nazi System, 1933–45	51
3.4	Nation-states, multinational states, and empires in Central and Eastern Europe and the Balkans under the Yalta System, 1945–89	54
3.5	Nation-states, multinational states, and empires in Central and Eastern Europe and the Balkans after the Yalta System, 1989–2008	56
4.1	Organizational membership	66
4.2	Electoral system, lower house, 2008	69
4.3	Party stability, 2008	74
4.4	Leftist parties in Central and Eastern Europe, by ideology and origin, 2008	76
4.5	Liberal and conservative parties in Central and Eastern Europe, 2008	78
4.6	Third parties in Central and Eastern Europe: agrarian, Green, ethnic, nationalist, 2008	82
4A.1	Institutional set-up	85
5.1	Economic development and share of GDP, private sector, around 1995	93
9.1	Representation of parties and movements in the Slovak National Council and the Federal Assembly, 1990–2	187
9.2	General elections, 1994–2006	187
9.3	Slovakia, overview of important political parties	188
10.1	Hungarian political parties and their ideological positions, 1990–2008	215
10.2	Prime Ministers and their cabinets, 1990–2010	215
10.3	Presidents, 1990–2010	216
10.4	Size of historic and ethnic minorities in Hungary, 2001	223
10.5	Hungarian minorities in neighboring countries, 2001	224
11.1	Results of parliamentary elections in Slovenia, 1990–2008	242
14.1	Election results for House of Representatives, 1996–2006	317
15.1	Phases and events in Macedonian democratization, 1990–2007	334
17.1	Parliamentary elections, 1992 and 1996	384

17.2 Parliamentary elections, 2000, 2004, and 2008 392
18.1 Bulgarian election results, 2005 elections 407
18.2 Bulgarian parliaments and cabinets, 1990–2007 410
18.3 Minority groups in Bulgaria, 2001 412
20.1 Voter support for categories of parties
a Estonian Riigikogu elections, 1992–2007 457
b Latvian Saeima elections, 1993–2006 457
c Lithuanian Seimas elections, 1992–2004 457
22.1 Regional cooperation initiatives 511

Notes on the contributors

Elisabeth Bakke is an Associate Professor of Political Science at the University of Oslo. She wrote her doctoral dissertation on the national question in Czechoslovakia in the interwar period. She is editor of *Sentral-Europa og Baltikum etter 1989*, 2nd edn. (Det Norske Samlaget, 2006) and co-editor (with Håvard Teigen) of *Kampen for språket* (Det Norske Samlaget, 2001). She has contributed articles to various edited volumes and journals, among the latter *Tidskrift for samfunnsforskning*, *Nordisk Østforum*, and *Party Politics*.

Florian Bieber is a Lecturer in East European Politics at the University of Kent, Canterbury. He received his MA in Political Science and History and his PhD in Political Science from the University of Vienna, as well as an MA in Southeast European Studies from the Central European University in Budapest. From 2001 to 2006, he worked for the European Centre for Minority Issues. He is the author of *Nationalismus in Serbien vom Tode Titos bis zum Ende der Milošević Era* (Lit Verlag, 2005) and *Post-War Bosnia: Ethnicity, Inequality and Public Sector Governance* (Palgrave, 2006), and editor or co-editor of four books dealing with Southeastern Europe – among them, *Restructuring Multiethnic Societies: The Case of Bosnia-Herzegovina*, co-edited with Džemal Sokolović (Ashgate, 2001) and *Montenegro in Transition: Problems of Identity and Statehood* (Nomos Verlagsgesellschaft, 2003). His articles have appeared in *Nationalities Papers*, *Third World Quarterly*, *Current History*, *International Peacekeeping*, and other journals.

András Bozóki is a Professor of Political Science at the Central European University. He is the author or co-author of eleven books, among them *Politikai pluralizmus Magyarországon, 1987–2002* (Századvég, 2003), *Migrants, Minorities, Belonging and Citizenship: The Case of Hungary*, co-authored with Barbara Bősze (BRIC, 2004), and *Anarchism in Hungary: Theory, History, Legacies*, co-authored with Miklós Sükösd (Social Science Monographs, 2006). He is also editor or co-editor of twenty-one books, including *The Roundtable Talks of 1989* (CEU Press, 2002). He also translated *The Social System*, by Talcott Parsons and Edward A. Shils into Hungarian, for publication by ELTE in 1988. His articles have appeared in *Comparative Sociology*, *East European Constitutional Review*, *European Political Science*, *Journal of Communist Studies and*

Transition Politics, *East European Politics and Societies*, *Central European Political Science Review*, and *Europaische Rundschau*. During 2003–4, he served as adviser to the Prime Minister of Hungary, and was Minister of Culture in 2005–2006.

Aurel Braun is a Professor of International Relations and Political Science at the University of Toronto. He is the author of *Romanian Foreign Policy since 1965: The Political and Military Limits of Autonomy* (Praeger, 1978) and *Small-State Security in the Balkans* (Barnes & Noble, 1983). He is also editor or co-editor of six books, among them *The Dilemmas of Transition: The Hungarian Experience*, co-edited with Zoltan Barany (Rowman & Littlefield, 1999) and *NATO–Russia Relations in the Twenty-First Century* (Routledge, 2008). He has contributed articles to *Orbis*, *Problems of Communism*, *Millennium*, *Parameters*, *International Journal*, and other journals.

Rick Fawn is Senior Lecturer in International Relations at the University of St. Andrews and past director of its Centre for Russian, Soviet, and Central and Eastern European Studies. He is the author of *The Czech Republic: A Nation of Velvet* (Routledge and Harwood Academic, 2000) and editor or co-editor of seven books, among them *The Changing Geopolitics of Eastern Europe*, co-edited with Andrew H. Dawson (Frank Cass, 2002) and *The Iraq War: Causes and Consequences*, co-edited with Raymond Hinnebusch (Lynne Rienner, 2006). His articles have appeared in *International Affairs*, *Communist and Post-Communist Studies*, *Democratization*, *Journal of Communist Studies and Transition Politics*, *Europe–Asia Studies*, and other journals. He also contributed a chapter to *Kosovo: Perceptions of War and its Aftermath*, ed. by Mary Buckley and Sally N. Cummings (Continuum, 2001).

Danica Fink-Hafner is Professor of Political Parties, Interest Groups and Policy Analysis at the University of Ljubljana and Head of the Centre for Political Science Research at the Faculty of Social Sciences. She is the author or co-author of eight books in the Slovenian and one in the English language, among them *Državljanstvo brez meja/Citizenship* without Borders (Založba FDV, 2007). She is also editor or co-editor of eleven books, among them, *Making a New Nation: The Formation of Slovenia*, co-edited with John R. Robbins (Dartmouth, 1997) and *Democratization in Slovenia: Value Transformation, Education, and Media*, co-edited with Sabrina P. Ramet (Texas A&M University Press, 2006). She is also co-editor (with Mirko Pejanović) of *Razvoj političkog pluralizma u Sloveniji i Bosni i Hercegovini* (Fakulteta za družbene vede, 2006) and editor or co-editor of eight books in Slovenian, among them, *Demokratični prehodi I: Slovenija v primerjavi s srednjeevropskimi postsocialističnimi državami*, co-edited with Miro Haček (Fakulteta za družbene vede, 2000) and *Parlamentarne volitve 2000*, co-edited with Tomaž Boh (Fakulteta za družbene vede, 2002). Her articles have appeared in *Public Administration*, *Journal of Communist Studies*, *Journal of European Public*

Policy, *Canadian Slavonic Studies*, and other journals. She has also contributed chapters to a number of books.

Bernd Jürgen Fischer is a Professor of History and Chair of the Department of History at Indiana University – Purdue University Fort Wayne. He is the author of *King Zog and the Struggle for Stability in Albania* (East European Monographs, 1984) and *Albania at War, 1939–1945* (London: C. Hurst & Co., 1999). He is also editor of *Balkan Strongmen: Dictators and Authoritarian Rulers of Southeastern Europe* (London: C. Hurst & Co., 2007) and co-editor (with Stephanie Schwandner-Sievers) of *Albanian Identities: Myth and History* (C. Hurst & Co., 2001). He received his PhD in History from the University of California, Santa Barbara, in 1982. He served as an Honorary Visiting Fellow at the Albanian Studies Program, School of Slavic and East European Studies, University of London, and in 2006 he was elected a member of the Albanian Academy of Sciences.

Konstanty Gebert is an international reporter and columnist at *Gazeta Wyborcza*, Poland's biggest daily. In the 1970s, he was a democratic opposition activist, and in the 1980s, he worked as an underground journalist (pen name: Dawid Warszawski). He is a frequent contributor to other Polish and international media, founder of the Jewish intellectual monthly *Midrasz*, author of ten books – among them books on Poland's Round Table negotiations of 1989, and on the Yugoslav wars, as well as commentaries on the Torah, and a panorama of the European twentieth century. His latest books, published in 2008, are *Miejsce pod słońcem* (Prószyński) and *Living in the Land of Ashes* (Austeria). His essays have appeared in two dozen collective works in Poland, Japan, the United States, the United Kingdom, Italy, France, and Belgium, and his articles in many newspapers around the world.

Erika Harris is a Senior Lecturer in International Politics and the Director of "Europe in the World Centre" at the University of Liverpool. The author of *Nationalism and Democratisation: Politics of Slovakia and Slovenia* (Ashgate, 2002) and *Democracy in the New Europe* (Palgrave Macmillan, 2006, with Christopher Lord), she is interested in the relationship between identity and democracy. She has contributed articles to *Contemporary European Politics*, *Perspectives*, *Central European Review of International Affairs*, and other journals. Her new projects seek to reflect the increased internationalization of ethnic relations and explore politics beyond the state and between the EU and its periphery. She has recently published *Nationalism: Theories and Cases* (Edinburgh University Press, 2009).

Marko Attila Hoare is a Senior Research Fellow at the Faculty of Arts and Social Sciences, Kingston University, London. He received his BA from the University of Cambridge in 1994 and his PhD from Yale University in 2000. He has been studying the history and politics of the former Yugoslavia since the early 1990s and has lived and worked in Bosnia-Herzegovina, Croatia, and Serbia. He is the author of three books, *The History of Bosnia: From the Middle Ages to the Present Day* (Saqi, 2007); *Genocide and Resistance in Hitler's Bosnia: The Partisans and the Chetniks, 1941–1943* (Oxford University Press, 2006), which won the British Academy Postdoctoral Fellow Monograph Competition in 2004; and *How Bosnia Armed* (Saqi, 2004). His articles have appeared in journals such as *Journal of Genocide Research, European History Quarterly, South Slav Journal,* and *Journal of Slavic Military Studies.*

Zachary T. Irwin is an Associate Professor of Political Science at the Behrend College of Pennsylvania State University in Erie. He received his AB from Hamilton College, his MA from The Johns Hopkins School for Advanced International Studies, and his PhD from Pennsylvania State University. He has contributed chapters to several books edited or co-edited by Sabrina Ramet – among them, *Religion and Nationalism in Soviet and East European Politics*, rev. edn. (Duke University Press, 1989), *Beyond Yugoslavia: Politics, Economics, and Culture in a Shattered Community*, co-edited with Ljubiša S. Adamovich (Westview Press, 1995), and *Democratic Transition in Slovenia: Value Transformation, Education, and Media*, co-edited with Danica Fink-Hafner (Texas A&M University Press, 2006). His articles have appeared in *East European Quarterly, Problems of Communism, South Asia*, and other journals.

Karl Kaser is Professor for Southeast European History at the Karl-Franzens-University of Graz, where he received his PhD in 1980, was promoted to professor 1985 and appointed to full professor 1996. His major work and research projects have focused on historical–anthropological fields such as the history of family, kinship, and clientelism as well as gender relations in the Balkans. Among his major monographical books are *Familie und Verwandtschaft auf dem Balkan. Analyse einer untergehenden Kultur* (Böhlau, 1995); *Macht und Erbe. Männerherrschaft, Besitz und Familie im östlichen Europa (1500–1900)* (Böhlau, 2000); *Freundschaft und Feindschaft auf dem Balkan. Euro-balkanische Herausforderungen* (Wieser, 2001); *Südosteuropäische Geschichte und Geschichtswissenschaft* (Böhlau, 2002); and *Patriarchy after Patriarchy. Gender Relations in the Balkans and in Turkey, 1500–2000* (Lit, 2008).

Carol Skalnik Leff is Associate Professor of Political Science at the University of Illinois at Urbana–Champaign. She is the author of *National Conflict in Czechoslovakia: The Making and Remaking of a State, 1918–1987* (Princeton University Press, 1988) and *The Czech and Slovak Republics: Nation Versus State* (Westview Press, 1997). She has also contributed chapters to numerous edited volumes – among them *Eastern European Nationalism in the Twentieth Century*, ed. Peter F. Sugar (American University Press, 1995), *Resolving Regional Conflicts*, ed. Roger E. Kanet (University of Illinois Press, 1998), and *A Force Profonde: The Power, Politics, and Promise of Human Rights*, ed. Edward A. Kolodziej (University of Pennsylvania Press, 2003). She is currently completing a book, *Elite Transformation in Post-Communist Europe*, for Rowman & Littlefield.

Renéo Lukic is Professor of History at Laval University, Quebec, Canada. He is the author of several books, among them *Les relations soviéto-yougoslaves de 1935 à 1945: De la dependence à l'autonomie et l'alignement* (Peter Lang, 1996) and *L'agonie yougoslave (1986–2003: les États-Unis et l'Europe face aux guerres barxaniques* (Les Presses de l'Université Laval, 2003), and co-author (with Allen Lynch) of *Europe from the Balkans to the Urals: The Disintegration of Yugoslavia and the Soviet Union* (Oxford University Press, 1996). He is also editor of *Rethinking the International Conflict in Communist and Post-Communist States* (Ashgate, 1998) and of *La politique étrangère de la Croatie, de son independence à nos jours, 1991–2006* (Les Presses de l'Université Laval, 2006), and co-editor (with Michael Brint) of *Culture, Politics, and Nationalism in the Age of Globalization* (Ashgate, 2001), and contributed a chapter to *Serbia since 1989: Politics and Society under Milošević and After*, ed. Sabrina P. Ramet and Vjeran Pavlaković (University of Washington Press, 2005). His articles have appeared in *Nationalities Papers*, *Acta Slavica Iaponica*, and other journals.

Sabrina P. Ramet is a Professor of Political Science at the Norwegian University of Science & Technology in Trondheim, Norway, and a Senior Research Associate of the International Peace Research Institute (PRIO) in Oslo. Born in London, she earned her PhD in Political Science from UCLA in 1981. She is the author of twelve books; among these are *Balkan Babel: The Disintegration of Yugoslavia from the Death of Tito to the Fall of Milošević*, 4th edn. (Westview Press, 2002), *The Three Yugoslavias: State-Building and Legitimation, 1918–2005* (Indiana University Press and The Wilson Center Press, 2006), and *Serbia, Croatia and Slovenia at Peace and at War: Selected Writings, 1983–2007* (Lit Verlag, 2008). She is editor or co-editor of twenty-two previous books. Her translation of Viktor Meier's *Wie Jugoslawien verspielt wurde* was published by Routledge in 1999, under the title, *Yugoslavia: A History of Its Demise*. She has contributed more than eighty articles to journals such as *Foreign Affairs*, *World Politics*, *Political Science Quarterly*, *Problems of Communism*, *Problems of Post-Communism*, *Osteuropa*, *Slavic Review*, and *East European Politics and Societies*. She is currently writing a history of the Catholic Church in the United States.

Steven D. Roper is a Professor of Political Science at Eastern Illinois University. His research focuses on constitutional development, conflict resolution, and human rights. He is the author of *Romania: The Unfinished Revolution* (Routledge, 2000), co-author of *Designing Criminal Tribunals: Sovereignty and International Concerns in the Protection of Human Rights* (Ashgate, 2006), co-editor of *Party Finance and Post-Communist Party Development* (Ashgate, 2008), and co-author of *The Development of Human Rights Institutions*

(Palgrave, 2009). His research has appeared in *Comparative Politics, Europee-Asia Studies, Journal of Conflict Resolution*, and *Party Politics.*

Ulrich Sedelmeier is a Senior Lecturer in International Relations at the London School of Economics and Political Science. He is the author of *Constructing the Path to Eastern Enlargement* (Manchester University Press, 2005) and co-editor (with Frank Schimmelfennig) of *The Europeanization of Central and Eastern Europe* (Cornell University Press, 2005), *The Politics of European Union Enlargement* (Routledge, 2005), *Developments in European Politics* (Palgrave, 2006), and *Beyond Conditionality: International Institutions in Post-Communist Europe after EU Enlargement* (Routledge, 2009). His articles have been published in the *Journal of Common Market Studies, Journal of European Public Policy, Politique Européen*, and *West European Politics.*

Eszter Simon earned her PhD in Political Science from the Central European University in 2008. She is a visiting professor at the University of Economics in Bratislava in 2009–10 and an adjunct at King Sigismund College in Budapest. Her areas of specialization include Cold War foreign policy in Britain, theories of foreign policy analyis, and the politics of East-Central Europe (especially Hungary). She has published a chapter on Hungary with András Bozóki in Gerd Meyer (ed.), *Formal Institutions and Informal Politics in Central and Eastern Europe: Hungary, Poland, Russia, and Ukraine* (Barbara Budrich Publishers, 2006).

Hermann Smith-Sivertsen is an Associate Professor of Political Science at the School of Business and Social Science at Buskerud University College, Norway. He received his candidate polit degree in comparative politics from the University of Bergen, and earned his doctorate in political science from the University of Oslo. He authored the chapter 4 on Latvia for *The Handbook of Political Change in Eastern Europe*, 2nd edn., ed. Sten Berglund, Joakim Ekman, and Frank H. Aarebrot (Edward Elgar, 2004). He also contributed a chapter in Frank H. Aarebrot and Terje Knutsen (eds.), *Politics and Citizenship on the Eastern Baltic Seaboard. The Structuring of Democratic Politics from North-West Russia to Poland* (Høyskoleforlaget, 2000). He has published journal articles in both English and Norwegian, among them "Why Bigger Party Membership Organizations in Lithuania than in Latvia 1995–2000?", *East European Quarterly*, Vol. 38, No. 2 (June 2004).

Maria Spirova is a Lecturer in the Department of Political Science at Leiden University, The Netherlands. She earned master's degrees in political science and in Southeast European Studies from the Central European University, Budapest, and her PhD in Political Science from the University of Wisconsin, Milwaukee. Her research focuses on party politics and minority politics and policy in the post-communist world. She is the author of *Political Parties in Post-Communist Societies: Formation, Resistance, and Change* (Palgrave, 2007). Her articles have appeared in *Party Politics, Comparative European Politics,*

Europe–Asia Studies, *Journal of Legislative Studies*, and *Communist and Post-Communist Studies*. She is currently working on a five-country comparative study of party patronage in new democracies.

Lavinia Stan is an Assistant Professor in the Department of Political Science, Concordia University, Montreal, Canada. She is the author of *Leaders and Laggards: Governance, Civicness and Ethnicity in Romania* (East European Monographs, 2003), co-author (with Lucian Turcescu) of *Religion and Politics in Post-Communist Romania* (Oxford University Press, 2007), and editor of *Romania in Transition* (Dartmouth, 1997) and *Transitional Justice in Eastern Europe and the Former Soviet Union: Reckoning with the Communist Past* (Routledge, 2008). Her articles have appeared in journals such as *Europe–Asia Studies*, *East European Politics and Societies*, *Communist and Post-Communist Studies*, *Problems of Post-Communism*, *European Journal of Political Research*, and *Journal of Communist Studies and Transition Politics*.

Frances Trix is a linguistic anthropologist who specializes in Islam in the Balkans. She studied at Prishtina University 1987–8, and received her doctorate in linguistics from the University of Michigan in 1988. She is currently Associate Professor of Linguistics and Anthropology at Indiana University. She is the author of *Spiritual Discourse: Learning with an Islamic Master* (University of Pennsylvania Press, 1993) and *Albanians in Michigan: A Proud People of Southeast Europe* (Michigan State University Press, 2001), and co-editor (with J. and L. Walbridge) of *Muslim Voices and Lives in the Contemporary World* (Palgrave, 2008). She contributed a chapter to *Serbia since 1989: Politics and Society under Milošević and After*, ed. Sabrina P. Ramet and Vjeran Pavlaković (University of Washington Press, 2005) and has published articles in *American Anthropologist*, *Discourse & Society*, *Slavic and East European Information Resources*, *International Journal of Middle Eastern Studies*, and other journals. She is currently working on Rumeli migrant associations in Istanbul and their antecedents in Kosova and Macedonia.

F. Peter Wagner is an Assistant Professor of Political Science at the University of Wisconsin, Whitewater. Prior to coming to Wisconsin, he taught at American University in Bulgaria and at North Carolina State University. He is the author of *Rudolf Hilferding: Theory and Politics of Democratic Socialism* (Humanities Press International, 1996) and co-editor (with Stephen Eric Bronner) of *Vienna: The World of Yesterday, 1889–1914* (Humanities Press International, 1997). He has contributed chapters to various edited collections – among them *Romania since 1989: Politics, Economics, and Society*, ed. Henry F. Carey (Lexington Books, 2004), *Conflicts in a Transnational World: Lessons from Nations and States in Transformation*, ed. Andreas Langenohl and Kirsten Westphal (Peter Lang, 2006), and *Cosmopolitanism and Europe*, ed. Chris Rumford (Liverpool University Press, 2007). He received his PhD in Political Science from Rutgers University in 1993.

Preface

All of the chapters included here were commissioned specifically for this book, except for chapter 12 on Croatia, which was added to the collection when the original contributor contracted to write this chapter dropped out of the project at the last minute. That chapter was originally published, in a somewhat different form, in Sabrina P. Ramet, *Serbia, Croatia, and Slovenia at Peace and at War: Selected Writings, 1983–2007* (Lit Verlag, 2008) and Sabrina P. Ramet, Konrad Clewing, and Renéo Lukic (eds.), *Croatia since Independence: War, Politics, Society, Foreign Relations* (R. Oldenbourg Verlag, 2008). It is reprinted here, in updated form, by kind permission of these publishers.

Until 1989, it was common to use the term "Eastern Europe" to refer to the communist states of Europe outside the Soviet Union. Today, the European Union officially classifies not only the northern-tier countries (Poland, the Czech Republic, Slovakia, Hungary, and Slovenia) but also the Baltic States (Estonia, Latvia, and Lithuania) as belonging to "Central Europe." In a post-1989 context, the term "Eastern Europe" may be taken to include Belarus, Ukraine, and the European portion of Russia, which are not covered in this volume.

I am grateful to the contributors whose work is included in this volume for their excellent work, their attentiveness to the guidelines, their perseverance, and their faith. I am also grateful to the Centre for the Study of Civil War at the International Peace Research Institute (PRIO) in Oslo for providing a subsidy to support the production of this volume. Finally, I wish to express our collective gratitude to John Haslam, Carrie Parkinson, and others at Cambridge University Press for their hard work and professionalism.

Sabrina P. Ramet

Acronyms and abbreviations

AAK	Alliance for the Future of Kosovo
AKR	New Kosovo Alliance
AMN	Party Alliance Our Moldova
ANO	Alliance for the New Citizen (Slovakia)
APL	Albanian Party of Labor
APV Rt	state privatization company (Hungary)
ARBiH	Army of the Republic of Bosnia-Herzegovina
ARD	Alliance for Democratic Reform (Moldova)
ASNOM	Anti-Fascist People's Assembly of Macedonia
Ataka	Attack (Bulgaria)
AVNOJ	Anti-Fascist Council for the People's Liberation of Yugoslavia
AWPL	Election Action of Poles in Lithuania
AWS	Solidarity Election Action (Poland)
AZZZ	Association of Employers, Union and Alliances (Slovakia)
BBWR	Non-Partisan Bloc for Supporting the Reforms (Poland)
BDI	Democratic Party of Integration (Macedonia)
BHT	Bosnia and Herzegovina Television
BiH	Bosnia-Herzegovina
BKP	Bulgarian Communist Party
BMD	Moldova Democratic Bloc
BMDP	Bloc for a Democratic and Prosperous Moldova
BNS	Bulgarian National Union
BPS	Bosnian Patriotic Party
BSEC	Black Sea Economic Cooperation
BSP	Bulgarian Socialist Party/Coalition for Bulgaria
BZNS	Bulgarian Agrarian People's Union
CARDS	Community Assistance for Reconstruction, Development, and Stabilization (EU)
CBSS	Council of the Baltic Sea States

CCM	Joint Constitutional Commission (Moldova)
CDR	Democratic Convention of Romania
CEE	Central and East European
CEELI	Central and East European Legal Initiative
CEFTA	Central European Free Trade Agreement
CEI	Central European Initiative
CEM	Council for Electronic Media (Bulgaria)
CIS	Commonwealth of Independent States
CMEA	Community for Mutual Economic Assistance
COMECON	Council for Mutual Economic Assistance
CPI	Corruption Perceptions Index (Transparency International)
CPSU	Communist Party of the Soviet Union
CSCE	Commission on Security and Cooperation in Europe
ČSSD	Social Democratic Party (Czechoslovakia)
DA	Democratic Alternative (Macedonia)
DEMOS	Democratic Opposition of Slovenia (coalition)
DEPOS	Democratic Movement of Serbia (coalition)
DeSUS	Democratic Party of Pensioners (Slovenia)
DK	Demokršćani (Bosnia-Herzegovina)
DNZ	Democratic People's Alliance (Bosnia-Herzegovina)
DOS	Democratic Opposition of Serbia
DP	Democratic Party (Albania)
DP	Democratic Party (Bulgaria)
DP	Democratic Party (Slovenia)
DPS	Movement for Rights and Freedoms (Bulgaria)
DS	Democratic Party (Serbia)
DSB	Democrats for a Strong Bulgaria
DSP	Democratic Left Party (Poland)
DSR	Democratic Union of Roma
DSS	Democratic Party of Serbia
DÚ	Democratic Union (Slovakia)
DUI	Democratic Party of Integration (Albania)
EBRD	European Bank for Reconstruction and Development
EC	European Community
EEC	European Economic Community
EFGP/EG	European Federation of Green Parties/European Greens
EIDHR	European Initiative for Democracy and Human Rights (EU)
EKA	Opposition Round Table (Hungary)
ELDR	Liberal Democrats in Europe
EPP	European People's Party
EU	European Union

EUFOR	European Union Force
FBiH	Federation of Bosnia-Herzegovina
FDI	foreign direct investment
FDSN	Democratic National Salvation Front (Romania)
Fidesz	Alliance of Young Democrats (Hungary)
FKgP	Hungarian Smallholders' Party
FRG	Federal Republic of Germany
FRY	Federal Republic of Yugoslavia
FSN	National Salvation Front (Romania)
FYROM	Former Yugoslav Republic of Macedonia
G17+	liberal political party in Serbia
GDP	gross domestic product
GDR	German Democratic Republic
GERB	Citizens for a European Development of Bulgaria
GFA	General Framework Agreement (Bosnia-Herzegovina)
GFAP	General Framework Agreement for Peace in Bosnia-Herzegovina
GSP	Generalized System of Preferences
GSP	gross state product
GSS	Civic Alliance of Serbia
GUAM	Georgia, Ukraine, Azerbaijan, Moldova
HDI	Human Development Index
HDSSB	Croatian Democratic Assembly of Slavonia and Baranja
HDZ	Croatian Democratic Union
HDZ BiH	Croatian Democratic Union of Bosnia-Herzegovina
HND	Independent Croatian Democrats
HNS	Croatian People's Party–Liberal Democrats
HR	High Representative in Bosnia-Herzegovina
HSLS	Croatian Social Liberal Party
HSP	Croatian Party of Right
HSS	Croatian Peasant Party
HSU	Croatian Party of Retirees
HVO	Croat Council of Defense
HZDS	People's Party–Movement for a Democratic Slovakia
IBRD	International Bank for Reconstruction and Development
ICFY	International Conference on Former Yugoslavia
ICJ	International Court of Justice
ICTY	International Criminal Tribunal for the former Yugoslavia
IDP	internally displaced person

IDS	Istrian Democratic Assembly
IFC	International Finance Corporation
IFES	International Foundation for Electoral Systems
IFI	international financial institution
IFOR	Implementation Force (UN)
ILO	International Labor Organization
IMF	International Monetary Fund
ISPA	Pre-Accession Structural Instrument
JNA	Yugoslav People's Army
Jobbik	For a Better Hungary
JSO	Unit for Special Operations (Serbia)
KDH	Christian Democratic Movement (Slovakia)
KDNP	Christian Democratic People's Party (Hungary)
KDU–ČSL	Czechoslovak People's Party
Kesk	Center Party (Estonia)
KFOR	Kosovo Protection Force
KGB	Committee of State Security (USSR)
KLA	Kosova Liberation Army
KLD	Liberal Democratic Congress (Poland)
KPN	Confederation for an Independent Poland
KSČM	Communist Party of Bohemia and Moravia
KSS	Communist Party of Slovakia
LCS	League of Communists of Serbia
LDDP	Lithuanian Democratic Labor Party
LDK	Democratic League of Kosovo
LDP	Liberal Democratic Party (Macedonia)
LDP	Liberal Democratic Party (Slovenia)
LDS	Liberal Democracy of Slovenia
LiCS	Liberal and Center Union (Lithuania)
LiD	Left and Democrats (Poland)
LLRA	Lithuanian Poles' Electoral Action
LNNK (TB/LNNK)	For Fatherland and Freedom (Latvia)
LPM	Liberal Party of Macedonia
LPP	First Party (Latvia)
LPR	League of Polish Families
LRLS	Liberal Movement of the Republic of Lithuania
LS	Liberal Party (Croatia)
L′S–HZDS	People's Party–Movement for a Democratic Slovakia
LSDP	Social Democratic Party of Lithuania
LTF	Latvijas Tautas Fronte (Latvia)
LVLS	Lithuanian Peasant Popular Union
LZP	Green Party (Latvia)

LZS	Latvian Farmers' Party/Union
MAAK	Movement for Pan-Macedonian Action
MAP	Membership Action Plan (NATO)
MDF	Hungarian Democratic Forum
MIÉP	Hungarian Justice and Life Party
MKDH	Hungarian Christian Democratic Party (Slovakia)
MP	member of parliament
MSSR	Moldovan Soviet Socialist Republic
MSZMP	Hungarian Socialist Workers' Party
MSZP	Hungarian Socialist Party
NACC	North Atlantic Cooperation Council
NATO	North Atlantic Treaty Organization
NDH	Independent State of Croatia
NDSV	National Movement for Stability and Progress/ National Movement Simeon II (Bulgaria)
NGO	non-governmental organization
NLA	National Liberation Army (Macedonia)
NOD	National Liberation Movement (Bulgaria)
NRSR	National Council (Slovakia)
NRTC	National Radio and Television Council (Bulgaria, later CEM)
NS	New Serbia Party
NS–S	New Union (Lithuania)
NSi	New Slovenia–Christian People's Party
OBN	Open Broadcast Network
ODS	Civic Democratic Party (Czechoslovakia)
OECD	Organization for Economic Cooperation and Development
OHR	Office of the High Representative (Bosnia-Herzegovina)
OKP	"Solidarity" parliamentary caucus
ONS	Union for National Salvation (Bulgaria)
OPEC	Organization of Petroleum-Exporting States
OSAC	Overseas Security Advisory Council
OSCE	Organization for Security and Cooperation in Europe
OZNA	Department for the Protection of the People (the first incarnation of the Yugoslav secret police)
PAA	Agrarian Party in Albania
PC	Center Alliance (Poland)
PC	Romanian Conservative Party
PCRM	Party of Communists of the Republic of Moldova
PCTVL	For Human Rights (in a) United Latvia
PD	Albanian Democratic Party

PDAM	Agrarian Democratic Party of Moldova
PDAR	Agrarian Democratic Party of Romania
PDK	Democratic Party of Kosovo
PD–L	Romanian Democratic Party/Democratic Liberal Party
PDP	Albanian Party for Democratic Prosperity
PDP	Party for Democratic Progress (Bosnia-Herzegovina)
PDP–PDSh	Democratic Party of Albanians
PDSR	Romanian Party of Social Democracy
PES	Party of European Socialists
PF	Popular Front (Moldova)
PfP	Partnership for Peace (NATO)
PGS	Primorsko Goranski Savez (Croatia)
PHARE	Poland and Hungary Assistance for Restructuring of the Economy
PIC	Peace Implementation Council
PiS	Law and Justice (Poland)
PNL	Romanian National Liberal Party
PNŢCD	Christian Democratic National Peasants' Party (Romania)
PO	Civic Platform (Poland)
PPP	purchasing power parity
PPPP	Polish Beer Lovers' Party
PR	proportional representation
PRCM	Communist Party (Moldova)
PRL	People's Republic of Poland
PRM	Greater Romania Party
PSD	Social Democratic Party (Romania)
PSHDK	Albanian Christian Democratic Party of Kosovo
PSL	Polish Peasant Party
PSM	Socialist Party of Labor (Romania)
PSMUE	Internationalist Movement for Unity (Moldova)
PSSH	Albanian Socialist Party
PUNR	Party of Romanian National Unity
PUR	Romanian Humanist Party
PzP	Movement for Changes (Montenegro)
PZPR	Polish United Workers' Party
Rahvaliit/Eme	Estonian People's Party
ROP	Movement for the Renewal of Poland
RRTF	Reconstruction and Return Task Force (OHR)
RS	Serbian Republic (part of Bosnia-Herzegovina)
RSK	Serb Republic of Krajina
RTT	Round Table Talks (Bulgaria)

RzB	People's Party Work for Betterment (Bosnia-Herzegovina)
RZS	Order, Lawfulness, Justice (Bulgaria)
SAA	Stabilization and Association Agreement (EU)
Samoobrona	Self-defense (Poland)
SAO	Serb Autonomous Oblast
SAPARD	Special Accession Program for Agriculture and Rural Development
SAWP	Socialist Alliance of the Working People (all republics of SFRY)
SBiH	Party for Bosnia-Herzegovina
SCD	Slovenian Christian Democrats
SCP	Slovenian Craftsmen's Party
SD	Democratic Party (Poland)
SD	Social Democrats (Slovenia)
SDA	Party of Democratic Action (Bosnia-Herzegovina)
SDE	Social Democratic Party (Estonia)
SDKÚ	Slovak Democratic and Christian Union
SDL′	Democratic Left Party (Slovakia)
SDP	Social Democratic Party (Bosnia-Herzegovina)
SDP	Social Democratic Party (Bulgaria)
SDP	Social Democratic Party (Croatia)
SDP	Social Democratic Party of Montenegro
SDP	Social Democratic Party, renamed Slovenian Democratic Party
SDS	Union of Democratic Forces (Bulgaria)
SDS	Serbian Democratic Party
SDS	Slovenian Democratic Party
SDSM	Social Democratic Party of Macedonia
SDSS	Independent Serbian Democratic Party
SFOR	Stabilization Force (Bosnia-Herzegovina)
SFRJ	Socialist Federated Republic of Yugoslavia
SFRY	Socialist Federated Republic of Yugoslavia
SHIK	post-communist secret police (Albania)
SK	Blue Coalition (Bulgaria)
SKBiH	League of Communists of Bosnia-Herzegovina
SKH	League of Communists of Croatia
SKS	League of Communists of Serbia
SLD	Alliance of the Democratic Left (Poland)
SLS	Slovenian People's Party
SME	small and medium-sized enterprise
Smer–SD	*Smer*–Social Democracy (Slovakia)
SMK	Party of Hungarian Coalition

SMS	Youth Party of Slovenia
SNL	United Independent Lists (Croatia)
SNP	Slovenian National Party
SNS	Serbian People's Party
SNS	Slovak National Party
SNSD	Alliance of Independent Social Democrats (Bosnia-Herzegovina)
SO	Self-defense (Poland)
SOE	state-owned enterprises
SOP	Party of Civic Understanding (Slovakia)
SP	Socialist Party (Albania)
SPM	Party for Economic Renewal (Macedonia)
SPO	Serbian Renewal Movement
SPP (+ SCD)	Slovenian People's Party
SPS	Serbian Socialist Party
SPSEE	Stability Pact for South Eastern Europe
SRJ	Federal Republic of Yugoslavia
SRS	Serbian Radical Party
SRSG	Special Representative of the Secretary General
SRSJ	Alliance of Yugoslav Reform Forces
SSD	Social Democratic Party (Czechoslovakia)
StB	Czech Security Police
SV	Common Choice (Slovakia)
SVK	Serbian Army of the Republic of the Serbian Krajina
SZ	Green Party (Slovakia)
SzDSz	Free Democrats (Hungary)
TB/LNNK	Union for Fatherland and Freedom (Latvia)
TNC	transnational corporation
TO	Territorial Defense (Yugoslavia)
TP	People's Party (Latvia)
TS–LKD	Homeland Union (Lithuania)
TSP	Harmony Party (Latvia)
UD	Democratic Union (Poland)
UDMR	Democratic Union of Magyars in Romania
ULSD	United List of Social Democrats, renamed Social Democrats (Slovenia)
UN	United Nations
UNDP	United Nations Development Program
UNHCR	United Nations High Commissioner for Refugees
UNICEF	United Nations Children's Fund
UNMIK	UN Mission in Kosovo
UNPROFOR	United Nations Protection Force (Bosnia)
USD	Social Democratic Union (Romania)

USKOK	Office for the Suppression of Corruption and Organized Crime (Croatia)
USSR	Union of Soviet Socialist Republics (Soviet Union)
UW	Freedom Union (Poland)
VAT	value added tax
Visegrád/V4	Czech Republic, Slovakia, Hungary, and Poland
VMRO	Internal Macedonian Revolutionary Organization (Bulgaria)
VMRO–DPMNE	Internal Macedonian Revolutionary Organization–The Democratic Party of Macedonian National Unity
VPN	Public Against Violence (Slovakia)
VRS	Army of the Serb Republic
WEU	Western European Union
WTO	Warsaw Treaty Organization (Warsaw Pact)
WTO	World Trade Organization
Zares	Party For Real–New Politics (Slovenia)
ZChN	Christian National Union (Poland)
ZL	opposition joint list (Bosnia-Herzegovina)
ZNG	Assembly of the National Guard (Croatia)
ZRS	Association of Workers of Slovakia
ZSL	United Peasant Party (Poland)

Guide to pronunciation of Central and Southeast European words

Standard vowels (all languages)

a is usually pronounced like the "a" in *ah* (except Hungarian: *see below*)
e is usually pronounced like the "e" in *excellent*
i is usually pronounced like the "i" in *interest*
o is usually pronounced like the "o" in *orchid*
u is usually pronounced like the "oo" in *book*

Special vowels (Hungarian, Polish, Romanian, or Slovak)

a (Hungarian) is pronounced like the "o" in *lodge*
ą (Polish) is pronounced like the "on" in *only*
ă (Romanian) is pronounced like the "a" in *around*
ä (Slovak) is pronounced like the "e" in *velvet*
é (Hungarian) is pronounced like the "a" in *hate*
ę (Polish) is pronounced like the "en" in *Ben*
ó (Hungarian) is pronounced longer than the "o" sound above and like the "o" in *hope*
ö (Hungarian) is pronounced as the "u" in *hurt*
ó (Polish) is pronounced like the "ou" in *you*
ü (Hungarian) is pronounced like the "ü" in the German word *Bühne*

Consonants and consonant combinations

c (Albanian, Bosnian, Croatian, Czech, Hungarian, Serbian, Slovak, and Slovenian) is pronounced like the "ts" in *tsar*
ć (Bosnian, Croatian, Polish, and Serbian) is pronounced like the "ch" in *child*
č (Bosnian, Croatian, Czech, Serbian, Slovak, and Slovenian) is pronounced like the "ch" in *church*
ç with a cedilla (Albanian) is pronounced like the "ch" in *child*
c (Romanian) is pronounced like the "ch" in *child* when it precedes an "e" or an "i", but, when combined with an "h" (as in "che" or "chi"), it is pronounced like the "k" in *kettle*

ch (Czech) is pronounced like the "ch" in the German word *Bach*
cs (Hungarian) is pronounced like the "ch" in *church*
cz (Hungarian) is pronounced like the "ts" in *tsar*
cz (Polish) is pronounced like the "ch" in *church*
d' (Czech and Slovak) captures the "dy" sound as in *dew*
dh (Albanian) is pronounced like the "th" in *that*
dj or đ (Bosnian, Croatian, and Serbian) is pronounced like the "j" in *jury*
dž (Bosnian, Croatian, Serbian, and Slovak) is pronounced like the "dg" in *badge*
dzs (Hungarian) is pronounced like the "dg" in *badge*
ë (Albanian) is pronounced like the "i" in *dirt*
g (Romanian) is pronounced like the "g" in *George*, when it precedes an "e" or an "i", but, when combined with an "h" (as in "ghe" or "ghi"), it is pronounced like the "g" in *spaghetti*
gy (Hungarian) is pronounced like the "j" in *jury*
j (all languages of the region) is pronounced like the "y" in *yodel*, except when it follows a "d" or an "l"
j (Romanian) is pronounced like the "s" in *pleasure*
ł (Polish) is pronounced like the "w" in *tower*
lj (Bosnian, Croatian, and Serbian) is pronounced like the "ll" in *hell* if it comes at the end of a word; otherwise, it should be pronounced as the combination of the two consonants as given in those languages. (English has similar sounds such as the "ky" sound for the first "c" in *cucumber*, or the "my" sound for the "m" in *music*.)
lj has a somewhat different sound in Slovenian, where the "j" adds a "y" sound as in *yodel*, even at the end of words
ly (Hungarian) is pronounced like the "y" in *yes* (the "l" is silent)
ń (Polish) is pronounced like the first "n" in *onion*
ň (Czech) is pronounced like the first "n" in *onion*
ň (in Slovak) is pronounced like the "n" in *nude*; similarly
ny (Hungarian) is a soft "n" like the sound "n" in *news*
ř (Czech) is pronounced like the "s" in *pleasure*
rr (Albanian) is pronounced as a trilled "r"
rz (Polish) is pronounced like the "zh" in *Brezhnev*
s (Hungarian) is pronounced like the "sh" in *bushy;* in all other languages of the region, it is pronounced like the English "s"
š (Bosnian, Croatian, Czech, Serbian, Slovak, and Slovenian) is pronounced like the "sh" in *bushy*
ş (Romanian) is pronounced like the "sh" in *bushy*
sz (Hungarian) is pronounced like the "s" in *sound*
sz (Polish) is pronounced like the "sh" in *bushy*
ś (Polish) is pronounced like the "sh" in *bushy,* only more softly
ţ (Romanian) is pronounced like the "ts" in *tsar*
ť (Czech and Slovakian) captures the "ty" sounds as in the English *tune*

v (Slovenian) is pronounced like the "oo" in *book* when it precedes the letter "š" but like the "v" in *victor* when it precedes a vowel
x (Albanian) is pronounced like the "ds" in *maids*
xh (Albanian) is pronounced like the "dg" in *badge*
w (Polish) is pronounced like the "v" in *victor*
ž (Bosnian, Croatian, Czech, Serbian, and Slovak) is pronounced like the "zh" in *Brezhnev*
ż (Polish) is pronounced like the "zh" in *Brezhnev*
ź (Polish) is pronounced like the "zh" in *Brezhnev,* only more softly
zh (Albanian) is pronounced like the "s" in *pleasure*
zs (Hungarian) is pronounced like the "zh" in *Brezhnev*

Map 1 Central and Southeastern Europe, 1989

Map 2 Central and Southeastern Europe, 2009

Part 1
Introduction

1

Introduction

SABRINA P. RAMET

In January 1989, the countries discussed in this book were all ruled by communist parties. There was considerable variation in the systems operating in these countries, with extensive private agriculture permitted in Poland and Yugoslavia, for example, and collectivized agriculture elsewhere in the socialist bloc. But there were some common features, too, among them the principle that the communist party should rule, censorship of the press, party and state supervision of religious organizations, and close supervision of any ad hoc associations which, typically, were required to register with the police. The Baltic republics – Estonia, Latvia, and Lithuania – as well as Moldova had been annexed by the Soviet Union during the Second World War; the German Democratic Republic (GDR), Poland, Czechoslovakia, Hungary, Romania, and Bulgaria were, as of 1989, all members of the Warsaw Treaty Organization (WTO), a Soviet-led military alliance known colloquially as the Warsaw Pact. Those same countries were also members of an economic organization known as the Council for Mutual Economic Assistance (or COMECON). Albania was active in both the Warsaw Pact and COMECON until 1961, when relations between that country and the Soviet Union cooled. Yugoslavia broke with the Soviet Union in 1948 and maintained an independent course thereafter. In 1955, the country became one of the founding members of the Nonaligned Movement.

Two decades since the Great Transformation of 1989, neither the Warsaw Pact nor COMECON exists. The Soviet Union has broken up into fifteen successor states, of which Russia and Kazakhstan are the largest. Yugoslavia has broken up into seven successor states. The breakup of Czechoslovakia gave birth to the Czech Republic and Slovakia. And the GDR united with the Federal Republic of Germany in 1990, ending forty-one years of separate existence.

Today, most of the states of the region have joined both the North Atlantic Treaty Organization (NATO), thus entering into alliance with the United States, Britain, France, Germany, and other West European states, and the European Union (EU), a political and economic community which, at this writing, unites twenty-seven European states in a single market with common standards for legislation and a common trade policy. As of April 2008, the Baltic states (Estonia, Latvia, and Lithuania), Poland, the Czech Republic, Slovakia, Hungary, Slovenia, Romania, and Bulgaria all joined both NATO and the EU. Croatia and Albania signed accession protocols with NATO in July 2008 and joined that alliance in April 2009. In addition, Croatia is engaged in accession negotations to enter the EU. Macedonia remains interested in joining NATO and there is a general interest within NATO councils in admitting that country; its accession has been held up, however, by Greece's insistence that it holds a copyright to the name "Macedonia" and that that candidate country must change its name if it wishes to join the military alliance. In December 2006, Serbia, Montenegro, and Bosnia-Herzegovina joined NATO's Partnership for Peace, which is generally regarded as a first step on the road to eventual membership in the alliance, and, in April 2008, NATO invited the three states to upgrade their level of cooperation to "intensified dialogue." Also in April 2008, former Soviet republics Ukraine and Georgia were invited to begin negotiations to join NATO, although this provoked a fierce reaction on the part of Russia.

Where candidates for EU membership are concerned, Macedonia is already considered a candidate country, with Bosnia-Herzegovina, Kosovo, Montenegro, and Serbia considered potential candidates; in June 2008, Bosnia-Herzegovina signed a Stabilization and Association Agreement (SAA) with the EU as a first step toward eventual membership. An EU civilian police and justice mission is stationed in Kosovo, which is also the recipient of EU economic assistance.

This tidal change in membership in regional organizations already points to the dramatic change which has taken place in the region since 1989. This change was driven in the first place by discontent with the socialist system and its various constraints (on foreign travel, on internal movement, on associations, on free speech, on the press, on religion, etc.) and by dissident elites who, in many cases, rose to high office after the collapse of communism (the examples of Lech Wałęsa, who became president of Poland, and Václav Havel, who became president first of Czechoslovakia and later of the Czech Republic serve to make the point). But from an early point, local politicians looked to foreign models, studying the constitutions and laws of West European and other countries in drafting new constitutions and laws for their own lands, and inviting foreign organizations, such as the Central and East European Legal Initiative (CEELI) of the American Bar Association, to send delegations to share their expertize. With EU and NATO accession, moreover, have come standards to which candidate countries have had to adapt, and this has served to bring these states into a common framework with West European states.

There continue to be problems in the region, especially in the southeast, where Kosovo and Moldova are Europe's two poorest countries, and where, in Serbia, at the time of writing, the authorities had still failed to arrest the last two war crimes indictees wanted by the International Criminal Tribunal for the former Yugoslavia (ICTY). Corruption is also a problem in many countries of the region, in spite of steady pressure from the international community. According to Transparency International, Slovenia and Estonia – ranked 27th and 28th, respectively, in the organization's 2007 Corruption Perception Index (CPI) – are doing quite well in assuring rule of law and clean government. Hungary, the Czech Republic, Slovakia, Latvia, and Lithuania follow at a distance, but none of the other countries discussed in this book ranked above 61st place, out of 179 countries – or, to put it another way, the remaining post-communist European countries all rank below West European countries, without exception.

This book is intended to serve as an introduction to post-socialist Europe and is divided into seven sections. In chapter 2, the final chapter in part 1, F. Peter Wagner and I explore alternative patterns of post-socialist political development and models of privatization and institution-building, taking into consideration historical legacies and historical memory, and focusing also on the role of corruption, crime, and black market activity in the region, and the struggle against these activities.

Part 2 is devoted to some key issues affecting the region, and opens with a historical retrospective written by Renéo Lukic (chapter 3), by way of tracing the rise of the various states of the region. Elisabeth Bakke in chapter 4 looks at party systems since 1989, examining differences in party membership, electoral systems, and political fragmentation. She contrasts the stability of systems in Central Europe and the Baltics with the changes which were made to several states in southeastern Europe since the mid-1990s. In chapter 5, Karl Kaser examines the challenges which the societies of this region have faced in the economic sector, and notes that the working population accepted the hardships associated with social and economic transformation without significant protest. But, as he also notes, persons who have been economically marginalized in the course of privatization and demonopolization have resorted to such survival strategies as street trading, illegal labor, and petty tax evasion. This section comes to a close with Marko Attila Hoare's chapter 6 on the War of Yugoslav Succession (1991–5). Hoare offers a brief historical overview by way of setting the stage for the war itself, which, as he notes, evolved into a three-sided conflict, pitting Serbs, Croats, and Bosniaks against each other. As Hoare notes, most of the atrocities were committed by Serbian forces.

Part 3 looks at Central Europe or, as it used to be called, "the northern tier." This includes Poland (chapter 7), the Czech Republic (chapter 8), Slovakia (chapter 9), and Hungary (chapter 10). This region has seen the smoothest transition, although there were struggles between president and prime minister for political primacy in all of these states in the first decade after the fall of communism. There have also been controversies about privatization (in all four states), abortion (again, in all four), press freedom (particularly in Poland during Wałęsa's term of office), and gay/lesbian rights – with the Czech Republic and Hungary establishing rights of domestic partnerships for same-sex couples by early 2008. Except for the "velvet divorce" in which the Czech

Republic and Slovakia separated peacefully, the borders in the northern tier have been stable.

Part 4 looks at the Yugoslav successor states, with separate chapters devoted to Slovenia, Croatia, Serbia and Montenegro, Bosnia and Herzegovina, Macedonia, and Kosovo (chapters 11–16). As already mentioned, none of these states existed as independent entities prior to 1991 and there continue to be border disputes among them. The noisiest border disputes involve Kosovo, the independence of which is still being resisted by the Republic of Serbia, and the Republika Srpska, as the (eastern) Serbian half of Bosnia-Herzegovina is called. Many Serbs living in Republika Srpska want to be able to attach their half of Bosnia-Herzegovina to Serbia, while Croats and Bosniaks who dominate the (western) "federation" half of Bosnia-Herzegovina are opposed to a Serbian secession. There is also a still unresolved border dispute between Slovenia and Croatia, especially concerning fishing rights, but this dispute is in arbitration.

The Yugoslav successor states have faced a more difficult transition than societies in the northern tier, because of the effects of war and the UN economic embargo, which contributed to the rise of local mafias and the diversion of such commodities as oil and tobacco into illegal channels. Many people lost their homes to expropriation or saw their homes destroyed, and the process of providing some corrections or compensation for their loss has been a long and complicated process. There have also been controversies about privatization and ethnic minority rights (especially in Croatia, pre-1999 Serbia, and Macedonia).

Part 5 looks at the other states in Southeastern Europe, specifically Romania, Bulgaria, and Albania. The post-communist transition in these states was distinct from the transitions in the northern tier or in the Yugoslav successor states. Unlike the northern tier, where post-communist elites were in place already by the end of 1989, the transition to pluralist systems was more gradual in Romania, Bulgaria, and Albania (chapters 17–19). In Romania, for example, Ion Iliescu took power at the end of 1989 by stepping into the breach; his government, which included many holdovers from the socialist era, won the elections in May 1990 and remained in power until 1996, at which point Romanians elected a government headed by the Democratic Convention (CDR). In Bulgaria, free elections held in June 1990 returned the Bulgarian Socialist Party (BSP) to power and, after losing the next elections, the socialists returned to power in 1995. The BSP remained relatively unreformed until 1995. In Albania, communist leader Ramiz Alia was elected president of Albania in April 1991 and remained in office until April 1992. What this means is that, in these three countries, the initial phase of the post-communist transition was managed by the communists themselves. Moreover, although not afflicted by war, as in the case of the post-Yugoslav region, both Romania and Albania saw some episodic violence – Romania in January, February, and June 1990 and again in September 1991 when, encouraged by Iliescu and his National

Salvation Front, hundreds of miners descended on Bucharest where they ransacked the headquarters of opposition parties and assaulted opposition leaders; and Albania in 1997, when Albanians who had lost money in pyramid schemes set fire to government buildings giving rise to a full-scale rebellion in which insurgents raided weapons depots and ran off with almost a million Kalashnikov assault rifles plus millions of rounds of ammunition, and even a number of tanks, artillery pieces, and surface-to-air missiles. Some of the arms which disappeared in Albania in 1997 later showed up in the arsenal of the Kosova Liberation Army in neighboring Kosovo.

Part 6 is devoted to the former Soviet republics of Estonia, Latvia, Lithuania, and Moldova (chapters 20 and 21). The former three had enjoyed independence from 1918 to 1940 and regained their independence between March 1990 and August 1991. Moldova had been part of Romania from 1918 until 1940 when it was occupied by Soviet forces and subsequently incorporated into the Soviet Union. Moldova declared its independence in August 1991, the same month in which Estonia and Latvia did so. Although these states have confronted many of the same challenges which other post-communist states have confronted, they have also had some specific challenges related to the period of time that they were parts of the Soviet Union, as well as to the presence of Russian minorities, especially in Latvia and in the Transdniestria region in eastern Moldova. Although Transdniestria is formally part of Moldova, it has been *de facto* independent since 1992; a 1,200-strong Russian military contingent stationed in Transdniestria serves to guarantee the region's continued independence of Moldova.

Finally, part 7 looks at present and future challenges. Here, Rick Fawn in chapter 22 examines the network of regional organizations such as the Central European Initiative, the Visegrád group, and, of course, the EU and NATO. And, in the conclusion to this volume, Aurel Braun in chapter 24 looks at some patterns in post-communist development and sums up lessons for the future.

In general, the chapters in this book – and especially those chapters devoted to individual countries – focus on the following themes:

- System rebuilding (institutional transformation and constitutional/legislative transition);
- Politics and governance (including the formation of the party system, the development of rival opinion groupings, and controversies about lustration);
- The role of the media (including its demonopolization);
- Economic issues (including privatization);
- Criminality and corruption; and
- Coming to terms with the communist (and perhaps also pre-communist) past and controversies about the past.

In addition, some of the country chapters also take note of:

- Controversies about religion (including religious instruction in schools, abortion, and the return of confiscated property);

- Migratory movements since 1989; and
- Nationalism and interethnic relations.

The transition from communism has involved an array of simultaneous challenges; in the course of addressing these, the region's post-communist authorities have not only transformed the legal, political, economic, cultural, and social frameworks, but also eliminated some social roles, such as dissident (in the communist-era sense), writer as social witness, and rock musician as political bard, while creating new opportunities and new social trajectories.[1]

Notes

1. See Sabrina P. Ramet, *Social Currents in Eastern Europe: The Sources and Consequences of the Great Transformation*, 2nd edn. (Durham, NC: Duke University Press, 1995); Peter Gross, *Entangled Evolutions: Media and Democratization in Eastern Europe* (Baltimore, Md. and Washington DC: Johns Hopkins University Press and Woodrow Wilson Center Press, 2002); Andrew Wachtel, "Writers and Society in Eastern Europe, 1989–2000: The End of the Golden Age," *East European Politics and Societies*, Vol. 17, No. 4 (Fall 2003), pp. 583–621; *Media Ownership and Its Impact on Media Independence and Pluralism* (Ljubljana: The Peace Institute and the Institute for Contemporary Social and Political Studies, 2004); Frank Schimmelfennig and Ulrich Sedelmeier (eds.), *The Europeanization of Central and Eastern Europe* (Ithaca, NY: Cornell University Press, 2005); Andrew Wachtel, *Remaining Relevant after Communism: The Role of the Writer in Eastern Europe* (Ill. and London: University of Chicago Press, 2006); and Sabrina P. Ramet, *The Liberal Project and the Transformation of Democracy: The Case of East-Central Europe* (College Station, Tex.: Texas A&M University Press, 2007).

2

Post-socialist models of rule in Central and Southeastern Europe

SABRINA P. RAMET AND F. PETER WAGNER*

Throughout the Russian and East European area, the collapse of the communist organizational monopoly and system of rule in the course of 1989–91 raised huge expectations which could not always be fulfilled. There were dreams of overnight prosperity, if not of wealth, of national reawakening, of religious freedom, of the chance to travel. There was also a general and speedy repudiation of the communist past which affected almost all of the countries of the region in one way or the other – all, indeed, except Romania, Serbia, and Montenegro, and even here, the communists survived in power only by redesigning themselves as reformers (as per Ion Iliescu of Romania) or as nationalists (in the cases of Slobodan Milošević and Momir Bulatović of Serbia and Montenegro, respectively). It was a sign of the times that many of those elected as presidents had served time in jail or detention – among them, Lech Wałęsa (Poland), Václav Havel (Czechoslovakia), Franjo Tudjman (Croatia), Alija Izetbegović (Bosnia-Herzegovina), and Zheliu Zhelev (Bulgaria) – and that the biggest controversy in those societies that did not go to war usually centered on the question of which privatization scheme to adopt. But by the mid-1990s, there was growing disenchantment with the new elites who were seen variously as too naïve or too nationalistic or too inexperienced or as simply not effective. Besides, the economies of the post-socialist societies contracted for several years after the collapse of communism, as these states tried to reorient their trade westward, upgrade their technology and production to compete in western markets, and give their currencies a solid foundation (Serbia being an exception to all of these points). By the mid-1990s, former communists in several countries – including Poland, Hungary, Lithuania, and Albania – were gaining new respectability, while in Croatia, Macedonia, Romania, and Moldova former communists had regained power at the end of the 1990s, or at the beginning of the twenty-first century, after local publics lost confidence in conservative parties. (The violence which accompanied the Soviet breakup was, however, neither as pervasive nor as costly, in terms of human life, as that which accompanied the Yugoslav breakup.)

As these societies left communism behind, they were confronted with a number of challenges, among them: revival and privatization of the economy, establishment of a constitutional order to include the rule of law and guarantees for multiparty pluralism, the demonopolization of the media, and the legitimation of the new order. In addition, the post-communist states of the region committed themselves, albeit with varying degrees of seriousness, to the effort to join such organizations as the Council of Europe, the European Community (EC, later, the EU), and NATO.

Yugoslavia, Romania, and Bulgaria, like the Soviet Union, also faced challenges arising from rising ethnic tensions. The Bulgarian communists had unnecessarily stirred up trouble with the indigenous Turks in the 1980s by expelling large numbers of Turks from the country, but the country's post-communist elites, while banning the formation of political parties based on ethnic affiliation, judiciously turned a blind eye to the ethnic aspects of the Movement for Rights and Freedoms – a nominally non-ethnic party which in fact serves as the forum for the country's remaining ethnic Turks. In Romania, after some disquieting signs of trouble in Transylvania, elites were able to keep the lid on tensions – in spite of the trouble-making of Gheorghe Funar (head of the Romanian National Unity Party and mayor of Cluj-Napoca) and Corneliu Vadim Tudor (head of the Greater Romania Party and member of the Senate).

By contrast, Yugoslavia (like the Soviet Union) broke up along ethnic–federative lines – as did also Czechoslovakia, although in the latter case, the dynamics of breakup had more to do with programmatic differences between Václav Klaus, then prime minister of the Czech Republic, and Vladimír Mečiar, then prime minister of the Slovak Republic, who were unable to reach agreement on either a formula for continued union or economic strategy. But while the breakup of Czechoslovakia was accomplished peacefully, coming down in history as the "Velvet Divorce," the breakup of Yugoslavia was violent and bloody.

In building up a new constitutional order, some of the post-communist elites called for "lustration" (purification or cleansing), which has been commonly understood as "the mass disqualification of those associated with the abuses under the prior regime,"[1] which is to say a policy of banning those communists who were considered responsible for abuses from holding office in the new state for a fixed period of time. Lustration was the second big controversy, alongside privatization, to shake the area – among other things because it was in part intended to root out informers who had worked with the secret police, and because of rumors that some of these informers were now holding influential positions in non-communist parties. Lustration was also intended in several countries to force ex-communist politicians out of office. The challenge here was to find the right balance between establishing a sense of accountability on the part of those most responsible for past transgressions and harmful vindictiveness which could prove dysfunctional for society. Even in 2007, nearly twenty years after the collapse of the communist power monopoly, parliaments in the region were still debating initiatives on lustration. In Macedonia, in January 2007, the relevant parliamentary commission unanimously approved a draft bill for lustration, while in Poland, the parliament approved a bill, the same month, to require elected officials, top civil servants, judges, and journalists to obtain a certificate indicating whether they had collaborated with the communist secret police.[2] In Romania, as a lustration bill came up for review by the parliament, there were reports that the careers of many politicians were hanging in the balance.[3]

In Poland especially, but also in other Catholic countries (such as Slovenia), abortion assumed the proportions of nationwide controversy, chiefly because of the energetic efforts by the Catholic Church to have abortion banned. Where abortion was concerned, there were four principal positions: a hardline conservative position (no abortion, regardless of the circumstances), a qualified conservative position (no abortion, except when the mother's life is in danger, or in the cases of rape or incest), an extreme liberal position (abortion on demand), and a qualified liberal position (abortion not only in the cases of endangerment, rape, and incest, but also in the event that the embryo is found to be deformed, in the event that continuing the pregnancy could damage the health of the woman, or in cases of financial difficulties). The Catholic Church's preference was for a complete ban on abortion, without any exceptions, but the Church had to be content with a more qualified success in Poland, while its efforts elsewhere in the region were effectively blocked.

Corruption also proved to be controversial, especially when it turned out that the political elites and their families and cronies were coming into possession of choice real estate and lucrative enterprises, in spite of the absence of any apparent prior wealth on their part, and fattening up their bank accounts. The problem of corruption was the most egregious in Serbia, Bosnia-Herzegovina, Macedonia, Montenegro, Moldova, and Albania (along with Russia and Ukraine), though there were also reports of serious instances of corruption in Poland, Bulgaria, and Croatia. While none of the societies of the region is entirely corruption-free, Slovenia has had the least corruption among the states in the region.[4]

And finally, there have been controversies involved in the War of Yugoslav Succession – some of them stirred up by local elites in order to inflame passions, and others arising from the war itself. At the center of the war was the fundamental question: who should live in the contested lands, and who should rule them. As various observers have noted, the War of Yugoslav Succession was driven, in the first place, by a Serbian strategy to annex land which had belonged to Croatia and Bosnia-Herzegovina and to create a largely homogenous greater Serbian state; because of this goal, the expulsion of non-Serbs from the lands being contested became a central war aim for the government of Slobodan Milošević.[5]

In the following pages, we intend to explore some of these issues, focusing on alternative patterns of post-socialist development, the role of corruption, paths of economic privatization, models of institution-building, and the role of the international community.

Alternative patterns of post-socialist development

By a simple count, the historic "Big Bang" of 1989–91 has resulted at the time of this writing in twenty-nine (more or less) independent national states. This count includes Estonia, Latvia, Lithuania, Poland, the Czech Republic, Slovakia, Hungary, and Slovenia, since 1 May 2004 member states of the EU and Romania and Bulgaria, EU member states since 1 January 2007; the remaining successor states of the defunct Socialist Federated Republic of Yugoslavia (SFRY), with Croatia and the former Yugoslav Republic of Macedonia officially recognized candidates for EU membership as well as Albania; the Russian Federation, Ukraine, Belarus, Moldova, and the still relatively unknown cases of the Central Asian (Kazakhstan, Kyrgyzstan, Uzbekistan, Tajikistan, and Turkmenistan) and the Caucasian national states (Georgia, Armenia, Azerbaijan). In addition, one faces very special cases – countries, regions, and places that are not yet or at least not yet officially recognized as independent, sovereign states: Transnistria, Gagausia, Abkhazia, Adzharia, Southern Ossetia, and still others, most notably Chechnya, in which fighting about its exact status is at the time of this writing still taking place.

In a more general sense, all those countries and places are "newly established" because they are all trying to find and define their way in a new post-socialist European and international order; a general point to which we will return in the conclusion. It is therefore no wonder that today the terms "differentiation" and "variation" best define the development of post-socialist Central and Southeastern Europe. Nevertheless, for all the differences and variations in development, one general fact has also become apparent today: the vast majority of the post-socialist national states, namely twenty out of the twenty-nine, have experienced problems in terms of their political development, and thirteen of those twenty are either borderline autocratic, or feature some variation of autocratic rule or even a new personality cult.

Why have only ten states succeeded so far, whereas the vast majority – including Russia – have failed or have, at any rate, yet to succeed in building and consolidating both a democratic political order and a capitalist free market economy?

The dilemma of synchronicity

As has already been implicitly noted, the aim and tasks of post-socialist development have generally been defined in terms of a "transition" from a dictatorial (party- and/or leader-led) state and its command economy to a liberal-democratic polity and a capitalist free market economy. This perspective, indebted as it is to the Cold War world and its competition of the systems, guided scholars, politicians, and the general public alike, in both West and East, in their initial assessments and hopes. It was quickly noted, however, that the "double transformation" of state and society/economy which such a transition implied was rather unique in recorded history and as such posed a "dilemma of synchronicity" to the actors and their societies. While the political system was to be designed for public input and electoral competition, the social economy was to be designed for private property, (foreign) investment, and market competition. The social hardships that the process of reform would cause in the form of general insecurity, unemployment, and poverty could therefore negatively impact the process of political reform as the democratic mechanisms installed could not help but to provide the access routes also for public disappointment and grievances. Thus, for social–economic concerns, the reformers could and might be voted out of office, and voters might even end up supporting the anti-reformers from the old dictatorial elite. To this systemic, built-in dilemma of reform was even added a third dilemma in all those cases in which the process of reform was in reality beholden to an even larger process: the creation of an independent national state in the first place. The latter process, as the break-up of socialist Yugoslavia and the fighting in other places (Transnistria's split from Moldova, for example) quickly demonstrated, proved to undermine even the very idea of a "transition."

The dilemma of the synchronicity of political and socio-economic reform processes which was seen was of course modeled after the general argument of "democracy against itself." It did work quite well in capturing the central problems that all those national states that were not burdened with border problems or where border problems remained under the threshold of organized violence (note the example of Romania and its neighbors) had to face immediately. Insecurity, for example, was the watchword of the first elections in Bulgaria and Romania, where the ex-communists were democratically elected back into office. Yet even where the anti-communists initially won landslide victories, in the East-Central European cases of Poland, Czechoslovakia, and Hungary, public disappointment with the process of post-socialist development has since led to an electoral invigoration of the so-called socialist successor parties which by the mid-1990s were even beginning to win national elections (Poland in 1993, Hungary in 1994, Albania in 1997 and 2001, and Croatia in 1999). As Rudolf Tökés has remarked in the Hungarian case: "whatever initial advantages Hungary's own brand of 'velvet revolution' might have imparted to the new regime, these were obliterated by the new iron laws of transition between post-totalitarian communism and parliamentary democracy in its part of the world."[6]

Historical legacies and historical memory

The notions of a transition, a double transformation, and the dilemma of synchronicity do not tell us why, despite being general problems every country supposedly had to face, some countries did better than others and some apparently even excelled in their reform process and have since become members of the EU. As the above noted comeback of (some) socialist successor parties already indicates, post-socialism has its own dynamics and has generated its own forms of response. Yet before turning to some of the elements and aspects which have actually constituted the post-socialist changes, an additional dimension deserves our attention at this point: *historical legacies* and *historical memory*.

All cases which are generally accepted as belonging to the best practices category belong to the traditional sphere of East-Central Europe (including here Lithuania, Latvia, and Estonia); the problematic cases can be found mostly in the traditional in-between spaces of Southeast Europe and the post-Soviet, non-EU space, while the worst cases in development are located, with the significant exception of Belarus, in the post-Soviet spaces of the Caucasus and Central Asia. Ukraine, with its political polarization between Russophones (whether Ukrainians or Russians) and Ukrainophones, represents a special case.

This clear geographic pattern in the development of differences, enshrined in fact by the process of EU enlargement, suggests a broad historical–cultural explanation based on what has come to be seen as Europe's traditional internal and external borderlines: North, South, West, East, and a middle space called either East-Central or just Central Europe. East-Central Europe or Central Europe, the historical–cultural space between the Western and the Eastern parts of Europe – that is, between Russia and the far western part of the Germanic lands – was for most of its history actually part and parcel of the historical development that led to the formation of the West. This "in-between space" shared with the West most, if not all, key phases and elements of development: Christianization, Reformation, Renaissance, Enlightenment, the creation of national states, even (to some extent) the double revolutions of industrialization and democratization which characterized the "long nineteenth century" (E.J. Hobsbawm) from the French Revolution to the First World War. By contrast, the traditional East, Russia, its immediate sphere of influence, and parts even further to the East, as well as most of Southeastern Europe, were cut off from and did not experience the central developments that eventually made the West in European history. Exactly this long-standing historical–cultural division appears to have reasserted itself with and in the aftermath of the events of 1989–91. Again, all those countries or national states which can be said to have partaken in the history of Europe's "West" have fared rather well in post-socialist times; the further away a country or national state can be said to have been from that broad historical trajectory of development, the less well it has actually done after 1989–91. In this sense, history and historical memory can be said to have been resources of and for post-socialist development: the famous slogan of the "return to Europe" with which especially the people in East-Central Europe greeted the events of 1989 and the idea of a "revolution of recuperation" put forth by some intellectuals in the (now former) West, most notably by Jürgen Habermas,[7] reflect exactly this larger sense of a historical–cultural belonging and unity.

Although there is considerable truth to such a historical–cultural perspective and explanation, it is at the same time far too general to be able to account for the existing differences and the shades and nuances in post-socialist development. The path from, say, a shared Enlightenment period to a successful consolidation of a liberal-democratic political system and the adoption of a particular constitutional framework in the aftermath of 1989–91 is just too long. This path can, however, be somewhat narrowed and shortened when taking the more recent past, namely, the state socialist period itself, into account. The history of state socialism in Central and Southeastern Europe does account for at least some of the fundamental features which decided the breakdown and shaped the immediate transition period. First, not all countries were to the same extent part of the alliance system (Warsaw Pact and COMECON) dominated by the Soviet Union. Second, besides the obvious question of closeness/distance (political–ideological, and not necessarily geographical) to "Moscow Center" (to use Ken Jowitt's term), one also notes significant differences in the way that the state socialist systems in those countries developed over time. In short, there was a history to state socialism, which a Cold War conception of an "Eastern bloc" simply and completely misses.

Of particular note in this regard is the extent to which some state socialist regimes had already opened themselves up to civil society, even market pressures, or had, at a minimum, developed significant civil society pressures prior to the actual events. The example of Hungary's "Goulash communism" is well known; famous for the development of civil society forces are Czechoslovakia (the "Prague Spring" in 1968, Charta 77) and Poland (Solidarity). Not forgetting the armed resistance to communism in Poland in the first years after the Second World War and the Hungarian revolution in 1956, all three examples here also point to the importance of an organized resistance to state socialist rule at least at some point in history. In all three cases, what has mattered is the internal dynamic unleashed by the events: socialist rule was never the same afterwards. It remained in a fundamental sense *publicly* de-legitimized, and as such (at least in the Hungarian and Polish cases) a contested terrain open to further changes. For that matter, the "Prague Spring" also impacted the western Ukraine, through Ukrainian-language media operating in eastern Slovakia.[8]

Closeness or distance to "Moscow Center" – that is, respective political–ideological allegiances (tight/loose/none) and/or the importance that the Kremlin leadership placed upon a respective country – was equally important. Yet the effect that either closeness or distance could actually have on a country varied considerably. Too much distance, it turns out in retrospect, could be as negative in its impact as too much closeness. Romania and Albania here are two cases in point. For Albania, the birth of the state socialist regime via a war of liberation against the occupation by Fascist Italy already points to a separate trajectory, comparable in this creation with Yugoslavia, with which Albania initially had close ties. Albania under Enver Hoxha was allied with the Soviet Union beginning in 1948. Yet in 1961, Hoxha expelled the Soviet advisers from Albania and associated the country with China; this action came in response to pressures from the Kremlin, and with the Sino-Soviet split functioning as a historical opportunity. Although the creation of a state socialist regime in Romania is comparable to the cases in East-Central Europe – occupation by the Red Army, purges, collectivization – two breaking points can already early on be detected: first when the Romanian leadership under Gheorghe Gheorghiu-Dej successfully resisted the pressures for political reform ("de-Stalinization") in the 1950s and, then again, when it resisted successfully the pressures to integrate into a Soviet Union-centered division of labor (no further industrial development) in the early 1960s.

The radical course of an auto-centric development, begun in earnest in Romania under Nicolae Ceauşescu in the early 1970s and in Albania under Hoxha in the late 1970s, isolated both countries not only from Soviet power, but also from *perestroika* and *glasnost*, as well as from the East European and international systems in general. In Hungary, Czechoslovakia, and Poland state socialism came increasingly under civil society pressure, while movements for national independence in Estonia, Lithuania, and Latvia were able to use the crisis of the Soviet Union and Mikhail Gorbachev's attempts at a fundamental reorientation of the entire system. But in Romania and Albania two leadership-cult dictatorships developed which ended up systematically underdeveloping these two countries. The path of auto-centric independence then also exacted its price during the respective breakdown of the regimes. Both turned out to be violent. Romania's "1989" in fact was the only violent system breakdown at the time, shaped by popular uprising, elite machinations, and fighting involving the military and state security forces (the Securitate) and ended with the summary trial and execution of Nicolae and Elena Ceauşescu. Although it is still not quite clear who might have initiated the fall of the ruling couple, it is clear that members of both party elite and the army used the urban demonstrations which began in the city of Timişoara and spread from there to Bucharest to stage a coup d'état. It is also clear that Romania's independence from the general Soviet military system (there were no Russian troops stationed in Romania) meant that armed forces, regular and paramilitary, were "free" and thus virtually had to be involved in the events. Albania, in turn, did not experience a "1989." The system began to break down in 1990, but it did so without anyone from the elite being able to pick up the pieces and reassemble them. Instead, the country descended into utter chaos – in the wake of the collapse of insolvent pyramid schemes. Many Albanians of working age fled to Western Europe or North America, although the outflux later slowed. In the Baltics, historical legacy can be seen in the fact that the fate of local Russians continues to be a problematic and controversial issue.

At the other end of the scale, namely, at the tight relationship side, one finds the German Democratic Republic (GDR) and Bulgaria. In both cases, the fall of state socialism was as much an intra-elite affair (quasi-coups by members of the Politburo against their leadership) as it was a matter of pressure from below, although one should not underestimate the impact of the anti-regime demonstrations on the streets of Berlin, Leipzig, and Dresden in the autumn of 1989. Obviously, the GDR is here a very special case (and is not part of this chapter, strictly speaking). Yet it should be remembered that in both cases, and Bulgaria being considered in the popular imagination the "GDR of the Balkans," the systems were perceived to be stable virtually until the very end. In the case of Bulgaria, where no popular uprising took place to ring in the changes, the fact that Todor Zhivkov, then the oldest serving state socialist dictator, stepped down (forced to do so 10 November 1989) was a surprise to the Bulgarians themselves. Also in both cases, the intra-elite dissenters could base themselves on the knowledge that Gorbachev had himself declared that the Kremlin would not interfere in what were suddenly deemed strictly internal matters.

Patterns of breakdown and the recreation of political rule

Having identified the general framework of "post-socialism," the simultaneous transition to a liberal-democratic polity and a capitalist free market economy, and keeping mindful of the historical background, several pathways of the breakdown of the state socialist systems and the re-creation of political rule can be systematically identified[9]: transitions from above; negotiated transitions; collapse; and, as a very special trajectory, "fragstruction" (= fragmentation and reconstruction).

The cases of Ukraine, Belarus, the Baltic republics, Romania, and Bulgaria all exemplify the path of the *transitions from above* – as well as the variations in that development. In the cases of Romania and Bulgaria, as already noted, the downfall of state socialism was an intra-elite event, akin to a coup d'état. This does not negate the popular unrest and the heavy fighting in Romania. It does, however, maintain that parts of the old communist party elite played a crucial role in deposing the Ceauşescus (and putting them on trial). The seeming contradiction between the violence of the events and the ability of the old elite to regroup and hold on to power disappears if one simply distinguishes the demonstrations from the ousting of the Ceauşescus (one should also note, as hard as it seems, that for all the TV coverage that the events in Bucharest's University Square elicited, most people in Bucharest and in the rest of the country did stay at home). The pathway of the *negotiated* transition can best be seen when looking at the examples of Hungary and Poland. Hungary is here the example par excellence. Already throughout the 1980s, efforts at reforming the system had been made and those efforts had seen the inclusion of dissident or critical scientists, intellectuals, etc. in a process of negotiation. This process sped up and was in fact radicalized in the second half of 1989. Under considerable public pressure, the Hungarian Communist Party reached, on 18 September 1989, an agreement with the opposition forces on the principles of democratization. A more radical variant is presented by the case of Poland. The Solidarity movement with its charismatic leader Lech Wałęsa had clearly shaken the Polish state socialist system at the beginning of the 1980s. Even after its official dissolution under military law, Solidarity remained a formidable opponent of the military dictatorship of General Wojciech Jaruzelski. Nevertheless, initially also in the Polish case, round table talks were held to reform state socialism. Those talks wound up being radicalized, so to speak, by the electoral results of the semi-free elections of 1989 which led to the formation of the first non-communist government. Obviously, both cases also point us again to the effect that organized opposition had on the unfolding of events.

In keeping with the basic consensus found in the literature, we have labeled another pathway simply *collapse*. Behind this term can be found two quite different cases: Czechoslovakia and Albania. Yet it makes sense at least initially to use the term "collapse" for both because that is in essence what happened to the two state socialist systems. In both cases, the state socialist system ended rather abruptly. This basic fact, however, is also where the two cases part ways. In the case of Czechoslovakia we find that after student protests and mass demonstrations a counter-public actually took over; a different order, but nevertheless an order, quickly took the place of the communist social order. Precisely this did not happen in the Albanian case. Here, the collapse of the regime meant chaos. There was neither a ruling elite nor an opposition (however small and unorganized) that could take the reins. Thus, in the Albanian case, a period of fundamental contestation set in, marked by fighting (armed struggle, more or less organized violence) and the creation of a criminal economy; indeed, the legacy of Albania's criminalized transition is still with us.

The last and very special trajectory of post-socialist development we have labeled "fragstruction," a rather cumbersome neologism constructed out of fragmentation and reconstruction. It, too, comes in two variants: negotiated and contested. The relevant example for the first variant is presented by the Soviet Union, officially: the Union of Soviet Socialist Republics (USSR), itself. The Socialist Federated Republic of Yugoslavia (SFRY) illustrates the contested variant. Obviously, in each case, the actual state entity ceased to exist. Yet it did so under two very different circumstances. In the case of the USSR, the fault line ran along its actual constituent parts *without* leading in large parts (the entire North and East) to armed conflict or even war (this has happened only at the Southern border of the Caucasus, in Tajikistan, and in Transnistria). While the SFRY also fell apart along its constituent fault lines, this fragmentation was achieved and accompanied by armed struggle and war.

In Yugoslavia, Serbia, one of the constituent republics of the erstwhile SFRY, challenged the legitimacy of its borders with Croatia and Bosnia-Herzegovina and sought to annex portions of those two republics, mobilizing local diasporas of ethnic Serbs in support of this cause. Irredentism fueled a four-sided war during 1991–5, involving Croatia, Serbia and its proxies,[10] forces loyal to the Bosnian government, and forces loyal to Fikret Abdić, a maverick businessman who proclaimed the sovereignty of the Bihać enclave in 1993. All told, the war left an estimated 13,538 dead in Croatia and between 100,000 and 215,000 dead in Bosnia-Herzegovina.[11]

Summary

The notion of a transition to a liberal-democratic polity and a capitalist free market economy has animated the discussions about post-socialism, both in the West and in the East. Wherever the old elite has been able to govern the process, and this has especially been the case where it did not even face any political competition to begin with, the processes of reform have been slow and geared more towards the stabilization of political power than to achieving the ends of the reforms themselves. In cases where neither was an old elite able to steer nor was negotiation available (in the absence of an organized opposition), the system simply collapsed. Yet, as history tells us, it could do so in two ways: peacefully and leading towards a reconstruction or radically and leading into instability and chaos. An even more problematic path can be found in all those cases where the political unit itself – the national state, the Republic, the Federation – was at issue. In all those cases, fundamental contestation was what animated the entire process: the struggle for and about political power. The effects of all these alternative paths can further be seen when turning to some fundamental social and economic aspects – corruption and crime, and the vagaries of the privatization process.

The role of corruption, black market activity, and crime

As we have already suggested above, political corruption and black market activity have constituted a dual challenge in the post-communist states. Corruption is multifaceted and includes not only taking bribes, misappropriation of goods, services, and funds, privileged allocation of resources, and falsification of records, but also the use of official channels to extort payments of a strictly illegal nature, overregulation, and selective or false investigations carried out under the auspices of the judicial system. As revealed in surveys conducted among Russian and Polish businessmen in 1997–8, government inspections can have a predatory aspect. Corruption is the inverse measure of the rule of law, which is to say, the more corruption there is, the less a system may be said to function according to the rule of law. Corruption, in turn, breeds cynicism, which erodes the civic sense.

If "corruption thrives on disorganization," as Robert Klitgaard has urged,[12] then systems in transition from one steady state to another are especially vulnerable to corruption. The relationship may also be inverted: disorganization, in turn, is fostered by and thrives on corruption, so that corruption may actually slow down efforts to build a democratic system where an authoritarian system held sway.

Freedom House publishes numerical measures of the levels of corruption in East European societies. These data should be used with caution, since any endeavor to reduce a complex phenomenon to a numerical value inevitably involves some oversimplification; with that caveat in mind, the rankings may be treated as broadly indicative of current trends. Among the post-communist states in Europe, Slovenia is ranked as the least corrupt society in the region, with Russia, Belarus, Azerbaijan, and the Central Asian Republics ranked as the most corrupt.[13] Romania and Bulgaria have been criticized by the EU on several occasions for not combating corruption effectively and, in July 2008, the European Commission announced its intention to block two Bulgarian agencies from using EU funds, by way of signaling the government in Sofia that it had failed to take effective measures to combat corruption.[14] Interpreting the rankings, one may say that Slovenia continues to be unique in the region, with an excellent legal framework and with practices which, for the most part, correspond to basic human rights standards, liberal-democratic norms, and the rule of law (hereafter, "practices which correspond to international norms and the rule of law"). On the other hand, there were persistent criticisms of the government of Prime Minister Janez Janša (who served in that capacity 2004–8) for media censorship; in mid-October 2007, for example, a petition signed by 570 journalists was turned over to parliamentary speaker France Cukjati, accusing Janša of "restricting media freedom."[15] Where press freedom is concerned, Freedom House ranks the Baltic states highest, followed (in order) by Slovenia, the Czech Republic and Slovakia, and Hungary (as of 2007).[16]

Slovenia and Estonia boast very good legal frameworks, with practices which *usually* correspond to international norms and the rule of law. According to Freedom House rankings, Hungary, Latvia, and Lithuania are close behind, followed by the Czech Republic and, slightly behind it, Poland, with good legal frameworks and practices which *often* correspond to international norms and the rule of law.[17] Bulgaria, Romania, and Croatia also have good legal frameworks, but are weaker in terms of practice; in these countries one may speak of *some* practices which correspond to international norms and the rule of law. In Albania, Serbia, and Montenegro, there are good legal frameworks but practices are highly problematic. And in Macedonia and Russia, the legal frameworks have some positive features, but practices are highly problematic.[18]

The situation in Russia, Belarus, and Ukraine is bleak. As Troy McGrath reported in 2003, bribery and corruption are rampant there, in both the government sector and in the private sector.[19] Indeed, in the 2007 CPI prepared by Transparency International, Russia ranked 143rd out of 180 countries surveyed; among European countries, only Belarus ranked lower (tied for 150th).

In Bosnia-Herzegovina, Croatia, and Serbia and Montenegro, the War of Yugoslav Succession seriously aggravated the problem of corruption by providing a setting in which nationalist leaders could exploit the UN-imposed embargo and wartime shortages to take control of trade in key commodities. The largest political parties of all three national groups in Bosnia (Serbs, Croats, Bosniaks) have all engaged in illegal financial transactions and shady dealings, and in April 2001, international authorities placed the Hercegovačka banka, a financial institution used by Bosnian Croat politicians to transfer embezzled funds, under international supervision.[20] But, in spite of this measure, the criminal networks which arose in Bosnia-Herzegovina during the early 1990s in support of political agendas are still in place at this writing.[21] Indeed, the Bosnian Serb prime minister conceded in 2006 that "nothing can be done in this country without corruption and bribery,"[22] and an Overseas Security Advisory Council (OSAC) report issued in March 2007 described the crime rate in Bosnia-Herzegovina as "high," warning that "there is a large organized criminal element" in the country.[23]

All of the societies in the region have some formal mechanism for combating corruption and there has also been growing international cooperation in the fight against organized crime and black marketeering. But in the wake of the collapse of communism, crime rates increased tangibly across the region, giving rise to demands for increasing police powers to conduct surveillance and searches of ordinary citizens, even in the absence of justifiable cause, to tap telephones, to access bank accounts, and so forth.[24] It would be folly, however, to believe that rising crime rates are purely an epiphenomenon of pluralization; on the contrary, crime rates already began to increase in parts of the region in the late 1980s. As of 1991, according to the results of the International Crime Victim Survey, Russia, Poland, and Czechoslovakia recorded respectively the highest, second highest, and third highest rates of crime, with Poland recording the highest rate for pick-pocketing and other "petty" crimes in the region and Czechoslovakia recording the highest rate for burglary in the region.[25] Trafficking in women and girls has also become a serious problem throughout the region; this subject is, however, discussed elsewhere in this volume (see chapters 5, 15, and 19).

Paths of economic privatization

There have been two alternative models of privatization which have been considered in the region: distribution to citizens via coupons or vouchers, and the sale of assets for cash. These two models admit of numerous variations, and have also been affected by additional considerations including claims for restitution registered by those from whom property was confiscated by the communists in the late 1940s, counter-claims by those living in residential property who have been unwilling to vacate their residences to accommodate the claims of persons who had not lived on the premises in half a century, and problems related to the fate of economically unviable enterprises which, if closed, would throw large numbers of employees out of work. To this may be added the complex challenge presented by the claims of the various Churches which, if they had been granted *in toto*, would have resulted in the Catholic Church, in particular, regaining large tracts of land in several countries of the region – lands originally turned over to the Church by royal grants in conditions of feudalism and in a historical context completely different from the situation today. The prospect of the sale of stock to foreign buyers has inevitably been controversial, with advocates viewing this as providing a lifeline for an ailing economy and detractors[26] seeing in it the alienation of the country's capital to foreign ownership.

Privatization was launched in Czechoslovakia soon after the communists had yielded power and, in the Czech Republic, unfolded in three rounds. In the first round, property which had been confiscated by the communists after the coup of February 1948 was returned, as far as possible, to the original owners. Then, in two subsequent rounds, property was put up for sale and, by the end of 1994, 80% of what had been state-owned enterprises (SOEs) had been privatized.[27] In 1991, the government of Czechoslovakia introduced a "voucher system in order to privatize 75% of the state enterprises by the end of 1991 while allowing the populace to participate in the privatization process by buying shares in these enterprises."[28] Voucher privatization continued in the Czech Republic and in Slovakia; some 2.59 million citizens (two-thirds of the adult population) received vouchers in the first round of privatization, 1991–3. A second round was started in Slovakia in 1994, and some 3.4 million vouchers were distributed, but the following year, Prime Minister Mečiar annulled the second round, in spite of the fact that the vouchers had already been distributed, and announced that citizens who had registered for the second round would receive promissory notes redeemable in 2001. The Slovak privatization was characterized by non-transparency during the years 1995–8, which "had negative consequences for the [country's] entire economic development."[29] Bulgaria's privatization was perhaps the slowest in the region, with the state still controlling 85% of industrial production as late as 1996.[30]

Poland adopted yet another path, distinct from both the rapid Czech sell-off and the on-again, off-again Slovak approach. In general, Poland adopted a cautious approach, preferring direct sales and auctions of existing stock, rather than distributing vouchers, although a small number of vouchers were indeed distributed.[31] But estimates of the value of capital stock were unreliable, and the Poles sold off much of their stock to foreign investors at a fraction of its real value. Hungary moved faster than Poland, but not as fast as the Czech Republic, using a mixed scheme involving a combination of restitution (more than in Poland), vouchers, and so-called "spontaneous privatization," in which enterprises were transferred to private ownership via insider deals with outside investors.[32] Estonia rapidly and forcefully privatized, a process organized around the Estonian Privatization Agency, which was modeled after the German *Treuhand Gesellschaft*. Latvia and Lithuania can be placed initially in the camp of the cautious privatizers, and both initially experienced a serious economic downturn; they recovered and developed rather quickly beginning in the mid-1990s. Corrupt privatization was a problem in several countries, as already noted. Privileged information, privileged access, privileged loan terms, and appropriations by dubious means helped to build up private fortunes in much of the former Yugoslavia (as well as Russia). The newly acquired wealth in turn built political influence. Where Russia is concerned, industrial and financial oligarchs enjoyed extensive political influence in Russia during

Boris Yeltsin's second term as president, 1996–9, while the Russian mafia remains a factor even today and has spread its network elsewhere in Europe as well as to the United States.[33]

In Serbia one hesitates even to use the word "privatization" in referring to the Milošević years (1987–2000). As early as 9 July 1992, just three months after the initiation of hostilities in Bosnia-Herzegovina, the Serbian Assembly passed legislation which conferred on President Milošević emergency powers over every facet of the economy; Milošević would use those powers to build a huge private fortune and to aggrandize the coffers of his closest collaborators – all at the expense of ordinary Serbian citizens. But theft is not the same as privatization. Indeed, Milošević was generally hostile to Western-style capitalism and preferred to preside over a corrupt form of socialist economics. Thus, as of 1995, 81.6% of fixed capital in Serbia was still in state hands, another 13.3% was operating under mixed ownership (i.e. a combination of state and private ownership), 2.9% was foreign-owned, and only 2.2% was owned by domestic private entrepreneurs.[34] And while Montenegro prepared a law in 1999 for the distribution of coupons, each worth 5,000 DM to all citizens of the republic, the Serbian parliament took a decision in December 1999, ten months before Milošević's fall, to postpone any decision on privatization for a year.

Finally, in Slovenia, after several abortive privatization plans, Prime Minister Janez Drnovšek was able to push through a compromise plan for privatization in November 1992, under which 20% of each company's stock would be distributed free of charge to the company's employees, another 20% would be distributed free of charge via investment funds, 10% would go into a fund to reimburse people who had lost land and capital stock as a result of communist-sponsored nationalization, 10% would go into a pension fund for all Slovene citizens, and the remaining 40% would be put up for sale.[35] Foreign investors also played a significant role in the privatization of key sectors of the economy in some of these countries, effectively buying up large portions of the local economy. In the autumn of 2008, however, the banking crisis which had begun in the United States and Great Britain quickly spread to Central and Southeastern Europe. Hungary signed an agreement with the International Monetary Fund (IMF) for a $25 billion rescue package, while the Bulgarian stock exchange sank to a two-year low. In Slovakia, industrial output slowed; in the Czech Republic, there was concern that the currency was weakening; in Poland, there was a cautious admission of an economic slowdown; in Albania, there was fear that the local economy could be impacted and preventive measures were taken in the banking sector.

Models of institution-building

If privatization and the battle against corruption and crime marked the transition from state socialist command economy to capitalist free market economy, the creation and adoption of new constitutions and entire new state institutions and functions marked the transition from dictatorial party- or leader-led state to a liberal-democratic polity. One of the choices confronted by the new post-communist elites was the choice between a presidential system and a parliamentary system. What was at stake in the choice between a presidential and a parliamentary system comes down to two things – the stability of the system's democratic character and the quality of its performance. And here, the record of the post-communist systems of Eastern Europe since 1989 is suggestive: Croatia under Tudjman and the Federal Republic of Yugoslavia under Milošević provide examples of presidential systems; Tudjman and Milošević both abused their positions, stoked nationalism, and thrived on corruption. Croatia after Tudjman, Slovenia, Albania, the Czech Republic, Slovakia, Hungary, and Bulgaria provide examples of parliamentary models. Romania, Macedonia, Poland, Slovakia until 1998, and Serbia since the fall of Milošević embody a mixture of presidential and parliamentary *principles*, and have seen episodes of rivalry between president and prime minister. Post-Dayton Bosnia-Herzegovina, in turn, presents a very special case.

As the general considerations in the above already attest, there is more to the issue of institution-building than a clear, formal distinction between a presidential and a parliamentary political system tends to suggest. In addition to the two poles of presidential and parliamentary political systems, one actually finds two mixed systems: the *presidential–parliamentary* and the *parliamentary–presidential* political system. Both are characterized by a double executive: a Head of State (president) and a Head of Government (prime minister, chancellor, etc.). The two mixes are distinguished by the degree of power that either the head of state or the legislative assembly (and its government) has *vis-à-vis* the other. In the presidential–parliamentary model, the president is directly elected and nominates the head of government who, in turn, needs to be approved by vote in the legislative assembly. The head of state retains the right to dismiss the government or even just individual cabinet members without having to rely on parliamentary approval to do so. The legislative assembly, however, does have the right to dismiss the government based on a vote of no-confidence. Nevertheless, in the last instance, even the latter right is undermined by the president's ability to veto such an action, even to dissolve the parliament. By contrast, in the parliamentary–presidential model the head of state does not have the ability to dismiss the government or individual cabinet members without the approval of the legislative assembly.[36] In addition, one also faces nuances of presidential power even within supposedly pure presidential systems.

Parliamentary

Contrary to what one might expect, pure presidential political systems are actually rather rare in Europe's old/new East. In fact, only the newly established national states of Central Asia and the Caucasus opted in the creation of their political systems for this model (in most cases with a weak executive cabinet added). Most of the countries in the Central or Southeast European sphere opted for one or another variation on the parliamentary model, with nine of the independent states under discussion here choosing a unicameral legislature (Albania, Bulgaria, Estonia, Hungary, Latvia, Lithuania, Macedonia, Slovakia, and Serbia) and four of the independent states under discussion choosing a bicameral legislature (Croatia initially, Czech Republic, Poland, and Romania). In March 2001, Croatia abolished the upper house of its legislature, leaving it with a unicameral Assembly. Yet they did so with varying degrees of presidential power. Again, it is important to keep in mind the political continuum that stretches between the purely parliamentary and the purely presidential.

Two factors account for the predominance of the parliamentary model: the essentially *negotiated character of regime breakdowns* and transitions and the *external Western models* that were used in creating the political systems. The link between "negotiations," "external models," and the adoption of a variant of the parliamentary model can clearly be seen when looking again at the cases of Hungary and Poland. In the Hungarian case, the present constitutional arrangements are the result of a set of constitutional reforms undertaken in 1989–90. Some inspiration was taken from the constitution of the German Federal Republic. This can be seen especially in the leading role that the prime minister plays in the cabinet (comparable to the *Richtlinienkompetenz* of the German Chancellor). The president does have a comparatively strong role, but only in a reactive sense. He has a constitutional and a political veto right for proposed legislation. He is, however, elected by the legislative assembly and he can only dissolve the assembly when either a vote of no-confidence against a sitting government has been successful for four times in one year or in the case that within a span of forty days the assembly finds itself unable to vote for a prime ministerial candidate whom the president nominated. In the Polish case, at least in the initial conception one moves closer to a strong president. The obvious models were in this case France and also the United States. Thus, the president is directly elected by the people and in the original conception had the general responsibility for foreign and security policy (advised by a National Security council, which he staffs). However, with the new Constitution (1997), the Polish political system moved from a presidential–parliamentary system to a parliamentary–presidential system: the prime minister and the government have been strengthened and the president has been weakened. The president now has to consult also in foreign and security policy matters with the prime minister. The three Baltic states further illustrate the breadth of institutional arrangements within an essentially parliamentary context. In Estonia, the president is indirectly elected by the parliament and an electoral college (the model being here Germany). The Latvian Saeima with an absolute majority of its members elects the president who then picks a prime minister which, in turn, needs to be approved by the Latvian parliament. In the Lithuanian case, the president is directly elected and is entrusted with solving fundamental issues of foreign policy (Art. 84/1) and signs international treaties (Art. 84/2). Yet in all three cases, the symbolic role of the president as the ideal representative of the nation needs to be stressed.

It is often taken for granted that parliamentary systems are "safer" than presidential systems in containing would-be autocrats. But the example of Slovakia serves as a warning against overly sanguine assumptions about parliamentary systems. Here, Vladimír Mečiar, who served as prime minister for three non-consecutive terms between 1990 and 1998, promoted passage of a language bill which discriminated against speakers of Hungarian, railroaded the privatization legislation passed by his predecessor, undermined the powers of the president, and asserted an inappropriate degree of control over the broadcasting media.[37]

Presidentialism

To stress again a point made above: pure presidential political systems are actually rather rare in Europe's old/new East. We have already encountered this "temptation" in its initial conception in the Polish case. Presidentialism was able to make a stronger impact in all those cases in which political power proved to be continually at stake and democratic principles and practices were not (readily) accepted. The clearest examples of presidentialism, in post-communist Europe, are provided by Slobodan Milošević (first as president of Serbia, 1989–97, later as president of the Federal Republic of Yugoslavia, 1997–2000), Franjo Tudjman (president of Croatia, 1990–9), and Aleksandr Lukashenko (president of Belarus since 1994). In formal terms, Milošević's power was limited and one can point to his use of coalition partners as a reflection of the impact of a multiparty system; but his informal power was considerable, and included the corruption of the political process, the corruption of elections, the corruption of the economy and outright seizure of the bank accounts of private citizens, the serious curtailment of press freedom, and elements of a cult of the personality.[38] The pattern in Croatia was similar, with Tudjman establishing a *democradura* system (democratic in form, authoritarian in nature) in which he abused "state security and intelligence services" to carry out "a secret war against the liberal faction within the HDZ and also against opposition parties."[39] Tudjman and his cronies seized control of the most important media in Croatia, fanned the flames of anti-Serb nationalism, promoted a partial rehabilitation of the *Ustaše* of the Second World War, and oversaw a corrupt privatization in which they were the chief beneficiaries. In Romania, the principles of a parliamentary political system have lived under the shadow of a president as a constitutionally defined "mediator between the powers of the State as well as between the State and society" which has arguably politicized the relationship between president and prime minister, as the political crisis in spring 2007 again demonstrated.

Institution-building in conditions of war

The above discussion quite naturally leads us to a rather different path and model of institution-building, namely, the process of building institutions in conditions of war. For our present purposes, the example which needs to be mentioned here is the case of socialist Yugoslavia and its successor states, specifically Serbia (and Montenegro), Bosnia-Herzegovina, and Croatia. To a certain extent, Albania can also be said to fall under this heading. Slovenia, one of the former Yugoslav Republics, escaped that route because, as the most homogenous among the Yugoslav successor states, there were no ethnic diasporas which could be mobilized against Slovenia; moreover, by September 2007, Slovenia and Croatia had agreed to submit their border dispute to international arbitration,[40] although as of July 2009 the dispute remained unresolved.

Now, what unites these cases is that the transition to a liberal-democratic polity and a capitalist free market economy not only became derailed, but was put on hold from the very beginning. War (Serbia and Montenegro, Bosnia-Herzegovina, Croatia) and disorganized violence (Albania) led to a reliance on a strong leader. The political system that developed around the "strong man" revolves around personal relations (thus, the importance of family or clan) and is as such heavily dependent on the favors and dealings that in word and deed support, in turn, the development of a criminal economy. What distinguishes the above cases from each other is only a matter of degree – and the respective willingness or unwillingness to reform that system of rule.

Indeed, Croatia has experienced a significant political change after Tudjman's death. First, the constitutional changes of November 2000 have led to the introduction of a parliamentary system with the president reduced to representative functions. Second, Stipe Mesić, the first president after Tudjman, has accepted wholeheartedly the new representational role in his daily practice. Finally, the present political leadership has moved forward significantly in addressing the lag in necessary reforms and has also begun to lobby for Croatia's candidacy for EU membership. The positive signs coming out of Croatia at the time of this writing sharply contrast with the situation in Serbia, where the rather obvious Chetnik revival serves as a reminder that many Serbs are still having trouble reconciling themselves to their recent military setbacks. It is not without significance that the strongest party in the December 2003 parliamentary elections in Serbia, with 27.7% of the vote, was the radical-right Serbian Radical Party, headed at the time by Tomislav Nikolić, and that this party was able to expand its vote to 28.7% in elections held in January 2007.[41] While the situation in Bosnia-Herzegovina is in this respect not all that dissimilar, the reasons for it differ. In this case, the continuing inability of the international community to find and implement (!) a solution which might actually let it withdraw only supports and strengthens the ethnic–nationalist differences around which the mix "on the ground" is constructed.

The situation in Albania has improved since 2002, but at the time of this writing it still remains to be seen if that improvement is systemic and lasting. Organized crime, trafficking in drugs and humans, and corruption are still endemic with close ties into the political elite and charges of organized crime and corruption are part of the political power play.

The role of the international community

In the first half of the 1990s, the international community was associated, in the first place, with *inaction* – at least where the War of Yugoslav Succession was concerned. But the role of the international community extended far beyond the imposition of an arms embargo against the warring (and non-combatant) Yugoslav successor states and the impact of this international dimension on the shape of political and economic development in the region since 1989 has been profound.

When, in this context, we write "the international community," we have in mind the UN, the EU, the Council of Europe, NATO, the United States, Russia, Britain, Germany, France, and, on occasion, other states or groups of states. On this understanding, then, we may note that the admission, in 2004, of Estonia, Latvia, Lithuania, Poland, the Czech Republic, Slovakia, Hungary, and Slovenia, alongside Malta and (Greek) Cyprus to the EU (with Romania and Bulgaria following later) entailed the requirement that these states meet various standards, imposing both political and economic criteria on candidate countries. One may mention, in this connection, the requirement imposed on the Slovak government to change its legislation on language use to permit greater use of Hungarian and Romani in public life; the EU also pressured Bratislava to work to reduce discrimination and violence against the Roma population.[42] In the case of Poland, the EU emphasized that the judiciary needed to be reformed and that there was too much corruption in the system generally. The EU also advised Warsaw to reform the pension and social security systems and to overhaul the banking sector. As early as July 1989, Western states agreed at a G7 meeting to set up the PHARE (Poland and Hungary Assistance for Restructuring of the Economy) program, with the mandate to support the economic (and political) transformations which were just beginning in those countries. The PHARE program provided both financial and technical assistance and was later expanded to include other countries as well. PHARE earmarked some 582.8 million ECU for Hungary alone, for the years 1990–5, devoting up to 15% of its budget (after June 1993) to major infrastructure projects in the region.[43] PHARE also provided significant assistance to Poland and, by December 1991, Poland and the EU were sitting down to sign an agreement to establish "a legal framework for multilateral cooperation in economic, political, and cultural sectors."[44] Where economic transformation is concerned, the IMF, the World Bank, and, for that matter, the United States have also been involved, as has the Organization for

Economic Cooperation and Development (OECD) which, for instance, joined the World Bank in demanding (in the years 1993–5) that Romania implement stricter fiscal and monetary policies, accelerate privatization and economic restructuring, and liberalize the economy more generally.

EU requirements have included judicial reform, creation of an independent civil service, improvements in the regulation of financial markets, and ending bailouts of uncompetitive enterprises. But, even though some of the requirements have been difficult to meet, the candidate countries have, for the most part, been determined to meet them, perhaps above all because they have anticipated that admission to the EU will boost the economy by facilitating foreign investment and technology transfers, and by simplifying intra-regional trade. There have also been political pressures – for example, in 1995, when the EU warned Romania that its shift toward nationalist and racist policies could endanger its prospects for EU membership.[45]

The states in post-communist Central and Eastern Europe have also been interested in joining the Council of Europe and NATO, both of which have also asserted their own criteria for membership. Where membership in NATO is concerned, the chief criteria have been stable democracy, the establishment of democratic civil–military relations with a civilian defense minister and political oversight of the military, an upgrading of weapons systems, and a peaceful resolution of territorial disputes; this last criterion provided an incentive for Hungary to reach an agreement with Romania prior to being admitted into the alliance. In 1999, Poland, Hungary, and the Czech Republic were admitted into NATO on the eve of NATO's air operations against the Federal Republic of Yugoslavia (FRY). Romania and Bulgaria, disappointed at having been left out of the first round of admissions to NATO, seized upon the spring 1999 war to demonstrate their enthusiasm for a Western orientation, declaring their support for NATO and making their air space available for NATO aircraft.[46] By March 2004, Romania and Bulgaria were admitted to NATO; in April 2009, Croatia and Albania were admitted into the alliance. Macedonia's entry was postponed because Greece continued to insist that it holds a "copyright" on the name "Macedonia" and that, in order to gain entry into NATO, Macedonia should first change its name. In Serbia, by contrast, some 59% of respondents in an October 2007 poll declared that they were opposed to Serbia's joining NATO, regardless of the outcome of talks concerning Kosovo's future.[47]

Admission to the Council of Europe at times proved to be far more controversial than admission to either the EU or NATO. In Romania, for example, the chief reason for this was the Council's requirement that the Romanian government decriminalize homosexuality. With the Romanian Orthodox Church dead set against any liberalization where homosexuality was concerned, the parliament tried, initially, to find a toothless compromise which would steer a course somewhere between the Council's requirement and the Church's anathemas, producing a draft, in 1996, which would have declared homosexual acts punishable only if they were performed publicly or created a scandal (implying that heterosexuals might copulate in the middle of the intersection without breaking the law) and banning "propaganda or association or any other act of proselytism" intended to "promote" homosexuality among Romanian heterosexuals.[48] But neither the Council nor the Church was satisfied with this bill, albeit for opposite reasons, and the debate dragged on until June 2000, when the two houses of the Romanian parliament finally repealed Art. 200 which had criminalized homosexuality. In the cases of Estonia, Latvia, and Lithuania, the general sentiment was that only by joining the EU and NATO could national independence be secured and further developed.[49]

There have been both European and American initiatives to assist the post-communist region to make the transition to pluralism, as well as initiatives on the part of the UN High Commission on National Minorities and of the Organization for Security and Cooperation in Europe (OSCE). On the European side, there have been initiatives at both the EU and at other levels, among which one may mention the crucial role played by the Institute of East European Law of the University of Leiden in the drafting of a new Russian civil code, as a result of which the civil code in Russia and several Commonwealth of Independent States (CIS) states is based on the Dutch civil code. On the American side, one of the first agencies to become involved with the legislative overhaul of the post-communist states was the Central and East European Legal Initiative (CEELI) of the American Bar Association – which conducted seminars and dispatched teams of jurists, lawyers, and legal experts to countries from Poland to Bosnia to Kazakhstan, to assist local authorities with redesigning their constitutional and legal frameworks, their judicial systems, their legislative operations, and so forth. Although some of those dispatched arrived with no knowledge whatsoever of local conditions, their role has been tangible and their contribution noteworthy.

Returning to the theme of the role of the international community in the War of Yugoslav Succession, it may be noted that while the community was initially disposed to a laissez faire approach which, it was supposed, would allow Serbia to finish off Croatia and Bosnia-Herzegovina in short dispatch, beginning in 1995, the role played by the international community has been robust, defining national boundaries, rounding up indicted war criminals, working to effect the return of refugees to their homes in Bosnia-Herzegovina and Kosovo, and pumping money into both Bosnia and Kosovo. Where Bosnia is concerned, the engagement of the Office of the High Representative and of the Stabilization Force (SFOR), the latter being replaced in December 2004 by the European Union Force (EUFOR), within the framework of the Dayton Peace Accords, should also be mentioned. There were some 42,500 Kosovo Protection Force (KFOR) troops stationed in Kosovo at peak, alongside an additional 7,500 in neighboring Macedonia. Kosovo's ambiguous status, hovering in a twilight zone between independence and reincorporation into Serbia, owed much, if not everything, to the role of the international community, but as of October 2007, Serbia and Kosovo were engaged in "last chance café" negotiations against a 10 December deadline, with the Kosovar Albanians swearing that they would declare independence once that date had passed. On 17 February 2008, having coordinated in advance with the United States and leading West European states, the Kosovar provisional assembly declared the independence of Kosovo. By the end of May 2009, Kosovo's independence had been recognized by sixty-one states. And then there is Montenegro which, under the leadership of President Milo Djukanović (later prime minister of Montenegro), seemed to be pressing forward toward independence during 1999–2001, only to be pressured by Javier Solana, the EU High Representative, into postponing any decision on independence. Given the dysfunctionality of Serbia, however, Montenegrin independence could not be postponed indefinitely and, in the first week of June 2006, the country declared its independence.

Conclusion

It would be nice to be able to state at this point that both the tasks and the hopes of "1989–91" have been met and fulfilled. But this is not the case. The tasks, the creation of liberal-democratic polities and capitalist free market societies, still remain to be accomplished in the vast majority of cases. Yet even where the twin transition has been successfully accomplished and membership status in the EU has been achieved, the price has been high and fundamental problems of development (unemployment, widening gap between rich and poor) have asserted themselves. Indeed, as far as the high hopes engendered by 1989–91 are concerned, they have long since been replaced by disappointment.

However, the reasons for this situation are quite understandable. In the first place, the high hopes did not correspond to the actual tasks and the realities that needed to be faced: the integration of the former East into the new regional and international order that the fall of the East–West divide and conflict had willy-nilly created. Thus, as many critical observers noted from the beginning, the creation of capitalist free market economies would involve more rather than less insecurity and more rather than less social differentiation. The role of criminal networks and corrupt elites is also part of the story, although information on organized crime is, for obvious reasons, fragmentary and incomplete. Yet the mere fact that local elites continue to operate agencies committed to the struggle against organized crime and corruption demonstrates that the problem is far from solved. It would be all too easy to blame "the people" at this point for their disappointments and reactions (including here the electoral rise of nationalist or right-wing, but essentially national–protectionist parties). As we hope to have made clear, if there is anyone to blame, that blame lies squarely with the elites. Instead of seizing the historical moment by taking the high ground, the elites were by and large pursuing a strategy of "divide and rule" aiming to secure their place in the new system. All those societies that had some measure of success in their transition, the new members of the EU and the remaining candidates for membership, fall into either one of the following two categories: they either already had civil society forces that forced the elites to work with them or they later on began to develop a reformist consensus among the elites, who then pushed the necessary reforms (with EU membership clearly being perceived as the major prize in that endeavor among the elites).

This, of course, also sheds some critical light on the value of democracy and the realities of democratization in the process. One measure of democratization is civic engagement – i.e. the extent to which citizens join voluntary associations – which may be viewed as a necessary though not sufficient condition for democratization. The benefits of civic engagement are thought to include not only the potential for citizens to register their views in public and to organize to promote certain views, but also self-education in civic values, increasing competence to assess policies and politicians, and even increasing tolerance of those who are different. Indeed, this analysis is borne out in Romania, where citizens who are active in civic associations are more likely than the inactive to support the rights and equality of ethnic, religious, and sexual minorities.[50]

In the literature on the transition and consolidation of democracy in Eastern Europe, democracy and democratic engagement are at times considered to be problems: the involvement of the people – their voice in elections, in associations, and on the street – is seen as part of the reason why reforms are not moving forward and why anti-reform forces have been able to stage comebacks (including again the rise of nationalist parties). The empirical literature on civic engagement, however, clearly suggests otherwise. Democracy and democratization are not problems. They might indeed be solutions to what ails the societies in the East and the West of Europe. Lack of civic and political engagement and the turn to "radical" political parties and movements are symptoms that point in a clear direction. What ails the people in both the new East and the new West is a lack of democratic venues and a lack of democratic transparency and accountability on the part of the overall political system – and thus the failure of that most noble of promises that "1989–91" harbored: democracy itself.

Notes

* Europe has changed and the Cold War geography of West, Central, and East has virtually lost its meaning. We accordingly use the expression "Central and Southeastern Europe" to refer to the region once known as "Eastern Europe." The authors wish to thank Karl Kaser, Aurel Braun and John Löwenhardt for their detailed feedback on an early draft of this chapter, and Elísabeth Bakke for her comments on a later draft.

1. Eric Brahm, "Lustration," in *Beyond Intractability*, at www.beyondintractability.org/essay/lustration/ [accessed on 14 January 2007].
2. *makfaxonline* (Skopje), 23 January 2007, at www.makfax.com.mk/ [accessed on 27 January 2007]; and AFP (26 January 2007), by subscription.
3. *Nine O'clock* (Bucharest), 13 April 2006, at www.nineoclock.ro/index.php [accessed on 28 January 2007].

4. Transparency International, *2007 Corruption Perception Index*, at www.transparency.org/ [accessed on 17 October 2007].
5. See Sabrina P. Ramet, *The Three Yugoslavias: State-Building and Legitimation, 1918–2005* (Bloomington, Ind. and Washington, DC: Indiana University Press and The Woodrow Wilson Center Press, 2006), chapters 13–15.
6. Rudolf L. Tökés, *Hungary's Negotiated Revolution: Economic Reform, Social Change and Political Succession* (Cambridge: Cambridge University Press, 1996), p. 400.
7. See Jürgen Habermas, "What Does Socialism Mean Today? The Revolutions of Recuperation and the Need for New Thinking," in Robin Blackbourn (ed.), *After the Fall: The Failure of Communism and the Future of Socialism* (London and New York: Verso, 1990), pp. 25–46.
8. For further discussion, see Grey Hodnett and Peter J. Potichnyj, *The Ukraine and the Czechoslovak Crisis* (Canberra: Department of Political Science, Australian National University, 1970).
9. See Juan J. Linz and Alfred Stepan, *Problems of Democratic Transition and Consolidation: Southern Europe, South America, and Post-Communist Europe* (Baltimore, Md. and Washington, DC: Johns Hopkins University Press and Woodrow Wilson Center Press, 1996), pp. 55–65.
10. For documentation, see Sabrina P. Ramet, "Martyr in His Own Mind: The Trial and Tribulations of Slobodan Milošević," in *Totalitarian Movements and Political Religions*, Vol. 5, No. 1 (Summer 2004), pp. 112–38.
11. Davorin Rudolf, *Rat koji nismo htjeli: Hrvatska 1991* (Zagreb: Nakladni zavod Globus, 1999), p. 376; and Vladimír Žerjavić, interviewed in *Globus* (Zagreb), 9 January 1998, p. 24.
12. Quoted in Rasma Karklins, "Typology of Post-Communist Corruption," *Problems of Post-Communism*, Vol. 49, No. 4 (July–August 2002), p. 25.
13. Jeannette Goehring (ed.), *Nations in Transit 2007: Democratization from Central Europe to Eurasia* (New York: Freedom House, 2007), p. 48.
14. *BBC News* (23 July 2008), at newsvote.bbc.co.uk/ [accessed on 23 July 2008].
15. AFP (16 October 2007), from topic@afp.com, by subscription.
16. Goehring (ed.), *Nations in Transit 2007*, p. 45.
17. *Ibid.*, p. 47.
18. Freedom House, *Nations in Transit 2006: Democratization in East-Central Europe and Eurasia* (Washington, DC: Freedom House, 2006) available at www.freedomhouse.org/template.cfm?page=261&year=2006 [last accessed 14 May 2007].
19. Troy McGrath, "Russia," in Adrian Karatnycky, Alexander Motyl, and Amanda Schnetzer (eds.), *Nations in Transit 2003: Democratization in East-Central Europe and Eurasia* (Washington, DC: Freedom House, 2003), pp. 522–3.
20. Florian Bieber, "Bosnia-Herzegovina," in Karatnycky *et al.* (eds.), *Nations in Transit 2003*, p. 173.
21. For a discussion, see Amra Festić and Adrian Rausche, "War by Other Means: How Bosnia's Clandestine Political Economies Obstruct Peace and State Building," *Problems of Post-Communism*, Vol. 51, No. 3 (May–June 2004), p. 27.
22. Quoted in *Mail & Guardian online* (2 January 2006), at www.mg.co.za/ [accessed on 5 November 2007].

23. "Bosnia-Herzegovina 2007 Crime & Safety Report," *Overseas Security Advisory Council (OSAC)*, 5 March 2007, at www.osac.gov/Reports/report.cfm?contentID=63281&print [accessed on 17 October 2007].
24. Ferenc Köszeg, "Introduction," in András Kádar (ed.), *Police in Transition: Essays on the Police Forces in Transition Countries* (Budapest: Central European University Press, 2001), pp. 2, 10.
25. Robert I. Mawby, "The Impact of Transition: A Comparison of Post-Communist Societies with Earlier "'Societies in Transition'," in Kádar (ed.), *Police in Transition*, p. 29.
26. For example, Kazimierz Poznański, *Wielki przekret: Kleska polskich reform* (Warsaw: Tow. Wydnawnicze i Literackie, 2000).
27. Zdenka Mansfeldova, "Die Tschechische Republik," in Anneli Ute Gabanyi and Klaus Schroeder (eds.), *Vom Baltikum zum Schwarzen Meer: Transformation im östlichen Europa* (Munich: Bayerische Landszentrale für politische Bildungsarbeit, 2002), pp. 400–1.
28. Thomas S. Sigel, "Promising Signs in Czechoslovakia," reprinted from *East/West Letter*, Vol. 1, No. 3 (Summer 1992), p. 1, at www.okno.org/ewltr/archive/vol1/czecho-split-v1n3.pdf [accessed on 2 February 2007].
29. Grigorij Mesežnikov, "Die Slowakei," in Gabanyi and Schroeder (eds.), *Vom Baltikum zum Schwarzen Meer*, p. 352.
30. Heinz Brahm and Johanna Deimel, "Bulgarien," in Gabanyi and Schroeder (eds.), *Vom Baltikum zum Schwarzen Meer*, p. 212.
31. Jakob Juchler, "Polen," in Gabanyi and Schroeder (eds.), *Vom Baltikum zum Schwarzen Meer*, p. 296.
32. Keith Crane, "Privatization Policies," in Aurel Braun and Zoltan Barany (eds.), *Dilemmas of Transition: The Hungarian Experience* (Lanham, Md.: Rowman & Littlefield, 1999), pp. 209, 211.
33. See Stephen Handelman, *Comrade Criminal: Russia's New Mafiya* (New Haven, Conn.: Yale University Press, 1995); Phil Williams (ed.), *Russian Organized Crime: The New Threat?* (London and Portland, Oreg.: Frank Cass, 1997); Tanya Frisby, "The Rise of Organised Crime in Russia: Its Roots and Social Significance," *Europe-Asia Studies*, Vol. 50, No. 1 (January 1998); James O. Finckenauer and Elin J. Waring, *The Russian Mafia in America: Immigration, Culture, and Crime* (Boston, Mass.: Northeastern University Press, 1998); and Robert I. Friedman, *Red Mafiya: How the Russian Mob has Invaded America* (Boston, Mass.: Little, Brown, 2000).
34. Laslo Sekelj, "Jugoslawien," in Gabanyi and Schroeder (eds.), *Vom Baltikum zum Schwarzen Meer*, p. 239.
35. Kenneth Zapp, "Compromise in Slovenia Produces a Unique Privatization Process," *Problems of Post-Communism*, Vol. 45, No. 3 (May–June 1996), p. 66.
36. A typology first developed by Matthew S. Shugart and John Carey, *Presidents and Assemblies: Constitutional Design and Electoral Dynamics* (Cambridge: Cambridge University Press, 1992).
37. Details in Sabrina P. Ramet, *Whose Democracy? Nationalism, Religion, and the Doctrine of Collective Rights in Post-1989 Eastern Europe* (Lanham, Md.: Rowman & Littlefield, 1997), pp. 119–28; and Elisabeth Bakke, "Slovakia: Den kronglete vegen til demokrati," in Elisabeth Bakke (ed.), *Sentral-Europa og Baltikum etter 1989* (Oslo: Det Norske Samlaget, 2002), pp. 139–41.

38. See Dušan Pavlović, *Akteri i modeli. Ogledi o politici u Srbiji pod Miloševićem* (Belgrade: Samidzat B92, 2001).
39. Hrvatski Odbor za Ljudska Prava, *CHC Statement No. 81* (Zagreb, 13 November 1998), as quoted in Vjeran Pavlaković, "Between the Balkans and the West: Liberal Democracy in Croatia," in *Modern Greek Studies Yearbook*, Vol. 16/17 (2000–1), p. 364.
40. *Mladina* (Ljubljana), 27 August 2007, at www.mladina.si/dnevnik/102668/ [accessed on 25 September 2007].
41. *Glas javnosti* (Belgrade), 29 December 2003; and AFP (22 January 2007), by subscription.
42. Michael Johns, "'Do As I Say, Not As I Do': The European Union, Eastern Europe, and Minority Rights," *East European Politics and Societies*, Vol. 17, No. 4 (Fall 2003), p. 692.
43. Bennett Kovrig, "European Integration," in Braun and Barany (eds.), *Dilemmas of Transition*, p. 258.
44. Ziya Öniş, "Diverse but Converging Paths to European Union Membership: Poland and Turkey in Comparative Perspective," *East European Politics and Societies*, Vol. 18, No. 3 (Summer 2004), pp. 488–9.
45. Helene Sjursen, "Tilbake til Europa," in Bakke (ed.), *Sentral-Europa og Baltikum*, pp. 217–8.
46. Anneli Gabanyi "Rumänien und die Kosovo-Krise," in Jens Reuter and Konrad Clewing (eds.), *Der Kosovo Konflikt: Ursachen, Verlauf, Perspektiven* (Klagenfurt and Vienna: Wieser Verlag, 2000), pp. 282–3; and Brahm and Deimel, "Bulgarien," pp. 218–20.
47. AFP (3 October 2007), from topic@afp.com, by subscription.
48. Sabrina P. Ramet, "Church and State in Romania before and after 1989," in Henry F. Carey (ed.), *Romania since 1989: Politics, Economics, and Society* (Lanham, Md.: Lexington Books, 2004), p. 290.
49. Ingmar Oldberg, *Uneasy Neighbours: Russia and the Baltic States in the Context of NATO and EU Enlargements* (Trondheim: Trondheim Studies on East European Cultures and Societies, No. 12, 2002).
50. Gabriel Badescu, Paul Sum, and Eric M. Uslaner, "Civil Society Development and Democratic Values in Romania and Moldavia," *East European Politics and Societies*, Vol. 18, No. 2 (Spring 2004), p. 337.

Further reading

Gross, Peter (2002). *Entangled Evolutions: Media and Democratization in Eastern Europe* (Baltimore, Md. and Washington, DC: Johns Hopkins University Press and Woodrow Wilson Center Press)

Mudde, Cas (ed.) (2005). *Racist Extremism in Central and Eastern Europe* (London: Routledge)

Schimmelfennig, Frank and Ulrich Sedelmeier (eds.) (2005). *The Europeanization of Central and Eastern Europe* (Ithaca, NY: Cornell University Press)

Szczerbiak, Aleks (2002). "Dealing with the Communist Past or the Politics of the Present? Lustration in Post-Communist Poland," *Europe-Asia Studies*, Vol. 54, No. 4 (June), pp. 553–72

Vachudova, Milada Anna (2005). *Europe Undivided: Democracy, Leverage, and Integration After Communism* (Oxford and New York, NY: Oxford University Press)

Warren, Mark E. (2004). "What Does Corruption Mean in a Democracy?," *American Journal of Political Science*, Vol. 48, No. 2 (April), pp. 328–43

Weigle, Marcia A. (2000). *Russia's Liberal Project: State–Society Relations in the Transition from Communism* (University Park, Pa.: The Pennsylvania University Press)

Welsh, Helga A. (1994). "Political Transition Processes in Central and Eastern Europe," *Comparative Politics*, Vol. 26, No. 4 (July), pp. 379–94

Part 2
Issues

3

The emergence of the nation-state in East-Central Europe and the Balkans in historical perspective

RENÉO LUKIC

The "*longue durée*" of political history

The emergence of the nation-state appeared as a political process of "*longue durée*" in the political history of East-Central Europe and the Balkans. Alongside this, the multinational states[1] constituted by the USSR, Czechoslovakia, and Yugoslavia, seem to have taken historical detours, lasting seventy-four years for the Soviet Union (1917–91), seventy-five years for Czechoslovakia (1918–93), and seventy-three years for Yugoslavia (1918–91).[2] Much as the division of politics into two camps (left and right) harkens back to the French Revolution and represents the "*longue durée*" of European political history, the appearance of civic nationalism in France and ethnic nationalism in Germany, more or less at the same time (the nineteenth century), represents the ideological source that nourished the creation of new states of East-Central Europe. In this sense, I consider the formation of these nation-states, spread over several centuries, to be of the "*longue durée*," even if this concept is rarely used in political history.[3]

At this point in time it is somewhat surprising that the emergence of nation-states in East-Central Europe and the Balkans, after the fall of the communist regimes, appeared as both extraordinary and undesirable to Western democracies, despite the fact that the nation-state, as François Furet has justly noted, "is the principal form within which modern societies live and the basis upon which they think they should evolve."[4] Jean-Baptiste Duroselle says the same in writing that, in the twentieth century, "every political entity seeks to become a nation-state."[5] Continent-wide revolution in 1848 signaled the emergence of two universal ideologies – nationalism[6] and proletarian internationalism – accompanied by their respective social movements: the movement of nationalities and the first attempts to federalize the socialist revolutionary groups into a single organization called the "First International." The almost simultaneous entrance of both these ideologies into European history left a lasting mark on the relationship between the governed and governing during the nineteenth and twentieth centuries. Proletarian internationalism and nationalism, to use the expression of the French historian Pierre Renouvin, belong to "the deep currents of history," and have profoundly shaped the political mentality of West European citizens. It was in the middle of the nineteenth century that both of these universal ideologies began their political and intellectual migration from Western European politics, where they had been thought out and theorized, to pre-modern Central and Eastern Europe. On the other hand, these politico-ideological transfers to East-Central Europe were made without implementing the rule of law that had been constructed in Western Europe alongside state-building since the advent of the French and English revolutions. The democratic deficit that accompanied these transfers favored the rise of ethnic nationalism in the Balkans which was influenced by its corollary, the "German model" of an ethnic nation, whereas the civic nationalism (or patriotism) of the "French model" of a civic nation had limited influence in Central Europe (being founded chiefly in Hungary). This ideological penetration resulted in the formation of cultural nations in the Balkans where the identifying beacons were ethnic origin, orthodox religion, and language (the famous nineteenth-century Serbian orthographer Vuk Stefanović Karadžić).

The emancipation of nationalities in Europe and their quest for statehood gained momentum with the "Spring of Nations" in 1848. The publication of the brochure, *The Communist Manifesto*, written by Karl Marx and Friedrich Engels, brought to new prominence the revolutionary ideology supposed to liberate the proletariat, the class carrying the torch of universal history. As the proletariat is set free by the advent of the socialist revolution, it should liberate all of humanity at the same time. The establishment of the dictatorship of the proletariat on a worldwide scale would make the category of nation obsolete. For a long time it was believed that the advent of socialism and the creation of an international communist movement with global influence would lead to the gradual withering away of the nation.

The French historian Jean-Baptiste Duroselle noted, with regards to national claims, that "national sentiment renders all forms of foreign domination unbearable and arouses the will of the dominated people to acquire independence, using all means available, such as subversion, violence and war."[7] European enlightenment and modernity fed national movements in East-Central Europe throughout the nineteenth and twentieth centuries, entering the political scene every time the international state system was transforming itself, such as between 1917 and 1920, 1939 and 1945, and in 1989. However, the implementation of the Yalta System constitutes an exception. The international conferences of Moscow (1944), Yalta (1945), and Potsdam (1945), which formed the bipolar Yalta System, did not give significant momentum to national movements for two reasons: first, a certain number of these national movements (such as in Croatia and Slovakia) were seriously compromised by their past alignment with Nazi Germany and Fascist Italy; second, by rapidly establishing its sphere of influence, the USSR – its sphere of influence coincided with the deployment of the Red Army in East-Central Europe (1944–5) – quickly put down all political action aiming to restore national independence. The case of the three Baltic countries, annexed to the USSR in 1940, is particularly instructive here.

Keeping in mind these initial observations, I argue that by observing the evolution of the international system since the nineteenth century in Europe it can be demonstrated that, during the great historical accelerations, the continent found itself profoundly altered on four occasions, to the point where it is preferable to speak of a succession of four distinct European state systems. The international system dominated by European empires and implemented at the Congress of Vienna (1815), was gradually replaced starting in 1917, due to the Bolshevik Revolution and the Versailles System (1919–20).[8] The First World War dismantled and put an end to the multinational empires (Austria-Hungary, the Ottoman Empire, and the Russian Empire), which crumbled in 1917–18 under the weight of military defeats and revolutions, such as the February and October Revolutions in Russia. The Bolshevik leader, Vladimir Ilych Lenin, and the American president, Woodrow Wilson, addressing the issue separately, insisted that the right of peoples to decide their own future applied to the nationalities of the empires in ruins. President Wilson, through his "new diplomacy," thus gave explicit legitimacy to the "principle of nationalities," which served as a basis for the creation of numerous new states. Other great powers (France, Great Britain) acquiesced in Wilson's policy of creating national and multinational states in East-Central Europe. The second modification of the European state system occurred between 1933 and 1945 with the formation of the "New Order" (the Nazi System); the third led to the establishment of the Yalta System (1947–89) in which communist systems took hold in Central and Southeastern Europe; and the fourth is the post-communist system that began in 1989 and still continues today. The formation of each one of these international systems was accompanied by the proliferation of new states. If the great wars seem to have created a historical context favorable to new state formation (as in the past, such as in 1914 and 1939), with the exception of Yugoslavia, the emergence of new states since 1989 has been rather peaceful, unlike the twentieth century's past where diplomatic conferences structured the international system alongside the conquerors and the conquered.

From a geopolitical point of view, East-Central Europe found itself, after 1989, in a similar historical situation to that which had prevailed in 1917–18 when the Bolshevik Revolution and the Peace Conference led to the creation of multiple national and multinational states in East-Central Europe. In 1989, the East–West confrontation ended with the "Tocquevillian" revolution – the revolution of civil society – in East-Central Europe and the breakup of the Soviet Union. This context favored the creation of nation-states from the Balkans to the mountains of the Urals. In East-Central Europe in 1989, the European Community (EC) and the United States assumed the role of hegemonic powers charged with establishing the rules and conditions as a basis for the emergence of new states (in 1919–20 this role was played by the Entente, the United States, and the League of Nations). On 16 December 1991, several days after the signing of the Treaty of Maastricht, the EC, under the pressure of the violent breakup of Yugoslavia, outlined the rules for recognizing the successor states of the communist federations.[9]

In the pages that follow, I will attempt to illustrate this process of European political history's "*longue durée*," which consists of nationalism and nation-state formation. My goal here is not to chronologically reconstruct the history of nationalism and the emergence of the nation-state in East-Central Europe, but rather to trace the general lines of this evolution through the five international state systems that have succeeded each other since the nineteenth century.

The formation of nation-states in the age of empires: the European concert

In 1814–15, as the Napoleonic Wars drew to a close, the reconstruction of Europe began. Even if the great powers wanted a return to the Europe before 1789, the *national* claims that took off throughout the continent following the French Revolution made this idea difficult if not impossible to achieve. However, when the Congress of Vienna opened on 1 November 1814, the representatives of the diverse monarchies had three goals in mind: restoring the political order that had existed before 1789, assuring the legitimacy of hereditary princes, and developing a monarchical solidarity to counter the revolutionary movements. Even though the majority of states controlling European territory were present in Vienna, with the exception of the Ottoman Empire, the majority of the decisions were made by the Great Powers: the Austrian Empire, the Russian Empire, the British Empire, Prussia, and, to a lesser extent, France. Keeping in mind the way in which the discussions were carried out, the Congress of Vienna can be considered to have been "the first great meeting of European diplomacy, this concert of nations, which from that point on would gather together to put an end to tensions and conflicts each time a serious crisis occurred."[10] Even though the Congress of Vienna can be seen as the meeting of those nostalgic for the Old Order, all understood well that Europe could not really return to the past and completely ignore the aspirations that were being expressed following the French Revolution. This is why territorial division, even though it certainly had the objective of containing France, also aimed to put an end to the nascent national claims. The method of remodeling Europe at the Congress of Vienna rested on the principle of establishing a balance of power between the Great Powers and the confirmation of the legitimacy of princes to the detriment of revolutionary ideals. For the most part, the Congress of Vienna achieved stability. The Great Powers kept the peace for nearly forty years.[11] As for national uprisings, they were not really able to come to any sort of fruition until 1848.

Nevertheless, as the "principle of nationalities"[12] continued to progress and attract national movements in the second half of the nineteenth century, the idea of the nation-state[13] made inroads in East-Central Europe. From that moment on, feelings of regional belonging were transformed into national consciousness by political and cultural elites; the nation-state became the main force bringing imperial legitimacy into question. The national movements stemming from the revolutions of 1848 erected "the principle of nationalities" in Europe as a political doctrine questioning the cohesion and legitimacy of the Empires. The Habsburg multinational empire was saved *in extremis* during the 1848 Hungarian national revolution by the intervention of the Russian Imperial Army aided by Croatian troops under the command of Colonel Josip Jelačić. Despite this temporary set-back, national claims inside the Austrian Empire continued to be expressed. In 1867, Hungarians were emancipated from Vienna by signing the "Compromise" (*Ausgleich*), yet without becoming completely independent. From that point on, the Habsburgs were at the head of a dual monarchy, the Empire of Austria and the Kingdom of Hungary, each one possessing its own institutions, administrations, and laws (and having only three common ministries). The following year Croats obtained their own autonomy from Budapest, also called the "Compromise" (*Nagodba*). The "Compromise" between Hungary and the Triune Kingdom (Croatia, Slavonia, Dalmatia) created a new sort of political community. The position of the Triune Kingdom was similar to that of a province within a federal state, for the most part, except that it did not possess the same judiciary functions. The political autonomy of the Triune Kingdom was guaranteed a national autonomous government through the Sabor (Diet), as well as through the recognition of Croatian as an official language and the office of a *ban* (governor). One thing led to another and the Habsburg Empire was dismantled just like the Ottoman Empire. However, the dynamic of the breakup of the Austro-Hungarian Empire was quite different from the progressive weakening of the Ottoman Empire through successive military defeats.

By the first half of the nineteenth century, the Ottoman Empire's military defeats in southeastern Europe had already allowed the creation of nation-states on territory stretching from the Black Sea in the east and the Adriatic Sea in the west. It is yet again the disintegration caused by nationalism that explains the end of the Ottoman Empire in Europe.[14] By declaring their *secession* from the weakened Ottoman Empire, the people of the Balkans were ready to create new states to the former's detriment. In order to justify the creation of new states, national leaders in the Balkans most often invoked their refusal to be governed by an Empire whose state religion was Islam and their desire to be self-governing because they considered the institution of the *millet* (an autonomous confessional community) to be historically outdated. For the moment, let us note that the type of state formed in southeastern Europe was directly imported from the West, which is particularly true for Greece and Serbia whose state models were inspired by France. The Serbian and Greek national leaders imposed the Jacobin state model upon these ethnically heterogeneous collectives.

The domination of the Ottoman Empire over the Balkans was thus contested by diverse national uprisings at the beginning of the nineteenth century. Since the Ottoman Empire had not been represented at the Congress of Vienna, the principles drawn from it, that allowed other European empires to arm themselves in advance against nationalist uprisings, did not apply to the Empire, notably the legitimacy of hereditary monarchs. Moreover, the Ottoman Empire had also been distanced from the Holy Alliance, created on 26 September 1815 on the initiative of Tsar Alexander I. The Holy Alliance brought together the Empires of Austria, Russia, and Prussia. The monarchies of the three empires were joined together through the precepts of the Holy Scriptures and promised mutual solidarity in order to eradicate all nationalist uprisings. If, from the beginning, the Holy Alliance aimed for an "embryonic system of European organization" destined to keep France (still considered the state most likely to upset the European balance of power) in check, it was also a pact among the representatives of Christianity – Catholic emperor, Orthodox tsar, and Lutheran king – aimed at curbing the Muslim Ottoman Empire.[15] France later joined the Holy Alliance in 1818, leaving the Ottoman Empire relatively isolated. The exclusion of the Ottoman Empire from the Holy Alliance explains in part why the Alliance's members did not intervene in the Greek insurrection of 1829–30, which resulted in the creation of the first nation-state in the Balkans – Greece.[16] During the Congress of Vienna, Tsar Alexander I had even encouraged the Greek national movement which at the time was trying to gain independence from the Ottoman Empire. On the other hand, at the time of the Hungarian insurrection in 1848, which followed the same objectives as the Greek insurrection of 1829–30, the ideological and political solidarity of the Russian and Austrian Empires was shown. As I have emphasized, the Russian Empire aided Austria in putting down the Hungarian revolution whose credo was the self-determination of its people and national sovereignty.

The ideological solidarity of the founding members of the Holy Alliance, based upon a respect for the principle of the legitimacy of the hereditary right of monarchs, did not, however, have to encroach upon another pillar upon which the stability of the international system of the Congress of Vienna rested, specifically "the balance of power," the only true guarantee, in the eyes of Metternich, for avoiding a new international disorder similar to the one created by Napoleon I. It was in the name of this principle that England opposed the expulsion of the Ottoman Empire from Europe after Greek independence, fearing that Russia and Austria would profit from it by splitting the Balkans and controlling its straits (a Russian ambition). As a maritime power, England considered Russian control of the straits an unacceptable geopolitical alteration encroaching upon its commercial interests as well as its maritime capacities.

This aside, the principle of nationality in southeastern Europe also benefited from the favorable opinion of Napoleon III who, as we know, gave considerable support to the Italian unification movement. As René Girault explains, due to his cosmopolitan education and his past as a conspirator, Napoleon III understood well the "revolutionary" force of the principle of nationality and the usefulness of nationalist sentiment in altering the European order established at the Congress of Vienna, which remained one of his principal objectives.

Nevertheless, it is necessary to explain the nuances of Napoleon III's role in emancipating nationalities in the Balkans since the emperor paid much less attention to Slavic zones than to the Latin and Arabic ones with regard to this question. This is most likely because the latter two corresponded much more to Mediterranean politics, which Napoleon III sought to keep in the French sphere of influence.[17] The Serbian revolt of 1804 and the conquest of Belgrade in 1806 mark the beginning of the construction of the Serbian nation-state and the re-examination of the presence of the Ottoman Empire in the Balkan Peninsula. The insurrection against Ottoman power had both a national and a religious significance. The Serbian Orthodox Church formed the center of resistance to the Ottoman Empire through its preaching of pan-Serbism, Orthodoxy, and pan-Slavism. In 1832, Serbia obtained complete independence for its church; from that point on the Metropolitan was elected by the Serbian clergy rather than chosen by the patriarch of Constantinople. From one insurrection to another, Serbian independence was recognized in 1878 at the Congress of Berlin.[18] Little Montenegro, a mountainous country bordering the Adriatic Sea, itself managed to resist Ottoman dominion throughout the nineteenth century.[19] Other people of southeastern Europe (Romanians, Bulgarians) followed the Serbs' lead in the nineteenth century so that they themselves could become nation-states. Moreover, Greece had regained its independence after 1830 and its territory continued to grow throughout the nineteenth and twentieth centuries until its modern state was formed in 1947. As for Romania, the principalities of Moldavia and Wallachia were able to obtain their autonomy in 1858; in 1862 they united under a single state to form Romania, whose independence was also recognized at the Congress of Berlin. Also, at the Congress of Berlin in 1878, Bulgaria was defined as a vassal principality of the Ottoman Empire. At the same meeting, a semi-autonomous Eastern Rumelia was created. The two territories united in 1885, and in 1908 Bulgaria rid itself of the last symbolic links attaching it to the Ottoman Empire, thus obtaining its complete independence. In the following years, during the first war in the Balkans in 1912, Bulgaria was again able to expand its territory at the expense of the Ottoman Empire.

During the same period, Macedonian attempts to create their own nation-state were not achieving success, despite their neighbors' victories. In 1903, the "St. Elie" people's insurrection against the Ottomans was violently suppressed, and following this Macedonia became a battleground of Serbia, Bulgaria, and Greece which fought to annex its territories. The Balkan regional powers' competition to conquer Macedonia's territory culminated during the Second Balkan War in 1913. Macedonia had to await the creation of communist Yugoslavia, after the Second World War, in order to acquire its own state and for Macedonians to be recognized as a nation in the Yugoslav Federation.

The Balkan Wars of 1912–13 signified the end of Ottoman domination in the peninsula, the Ottomans having been weakened by the Congress of Berlin in 1878 and through the annexation of Bosnia-Herzegovina by Austria-Hungary

Table 3.1 The age of empires: constitution of nation-states, multinational states, and empires in Central and Eastern Europe and the Balkans, 1800–1918

	Nation-state	Multinational states	Empire
1800–1918: Age of empires	6	0	6
	Greece (1830) Romania (1856) Serbia (1878) Bulgaria (1878 and 1908) Montenegro (1878) Albania (1912)		Russian German Ottoman Austro-Hungarian French British

in 1908. After the end of the First Balkan War in 1912, another nation-state appeared in the region: Albania. The eviction of the Ottoman Empire from the Balkans in 1913, consequently, coincided with the end of the first phase of nation-state formation in the Balkans, which had begun with Greek independence. Further north, toward the end of the First World War and the establishment of the Versailles System, the other empires (Russian, German, and Austro-Hungarian) were able to maintain their rule over the people of East-Central Europe (table 3.1).

The Versailles State System and the Bolshevik Revolution

The people under the rule of the Russian, Austro-Hungarian, and German Empires in East-Central Europe had to await the end of the First World War in order to become nation-states and multinational states. The fall of the Austro-Hungarian monarchy led to the creation of the Hungarian and Austrian nation-states. Furthermore, the Peace Conference gave birth to a multinational state – the Kingdom of Serbs, Croats, and Slovenes founded in 1918 (renamed the Kingdom of Yugoslavia in 1929). Ruled by the Serbian Karađorđević Dynasty, the Kingdom brought together Serbia (which had acquired Kosovo and part of Macedonian territory in 1912–13) and Montenegro as well as Slovenia and Croatia which, up until that point, had been part of the Austro-Hungarian Empire. Bosnia-Herzegovina, which had been militarily occupied by Austria-Hungary since 1878, before being formally annexed to it in 1908, was also integrated into the Kingdom of Serbs, Croats and Slovenes. The same went for Vojvodina in 1918, a province of the Austro-Hungarian monarchy. The political project of uniting the South Slavs, that had been developed principally in Croatian literary and intellectual circles in the nineteenth century, was taking form under the Serbian state.

However, the Croatian, Slovenian, and Serbian union quickly proved to be difficult. Whereas Croats and Slovenes wanted a union based upon the equality of the Kingdom's people, Serbs ran the state in a manner that favored their interests because they formed the dominant nation. The Kingdom of Serbs, Croats, and Slovenes was thus led by the Karađorđević Dynasty as a unitary Serbian nation-state, and not as a multinational state. Serbs ignored, or did not want to recognize that, by annexing new territories during the creation of the Kingdom, they had also annexed the *peoples* who had developed their own national ideologies and their own corresponding political projects since the nineteenth century. This evolution was already in the works well before the unification of South Slavs occurred. Thus, Croats having experienced a certain form of autonomy in the Austro-Hungarian Empire since the sixteenth century, quickly opposed the Serbian centralized state administration. The refusal of this autonomy in the new Kingdom constituted an incommensurable affront. Relations between Serbs and Croats in the Kingdom reached the point of no return in 1928 after the assassination by Serbian Deputy Puniša Račić who opened fire on Croatian deputies in the National Parliament (Skupština), in the capital of the Kingdom of Belgrade. Stjepan Radić, the most prominent Croatian politician at the time, was mortally wounded and later died. Even though Croats began to dream again of an independent Croatian nation-state[20] after Radić's assassination, King Alexander's proclamation of a royal dictatorship in January 1929 prolonged the forced marriage between Serbs and Croats for several years thereafter. Yet this was itself finished in a bloodbath after the creation of the Independent State of Croatia (NDH) in 1941.

Another multinational state, Czechoslovakia, formed by the provinces of Bohemia–Moravia, Slovakia, and Ruthenia, also came into existence through the Versailles System. Much as in Yugoslavia, where the royal government was dominated by Serbs, Czechs reigned over Czechoslovakia's political destiny as the most numerous nation, and imposed their own centralizing policy in the new state, inciting opposition not only from Slovaks, but also from the national minorities that made up the country, such as the German and Hungarian minorities that were concentrated, respectively, in the Sudetenland[21] region and the south of Slovakia. Even though Czechoslovakia was a truly multinational state, Czech politicians considered it to be a nation-state and governed Czechoslovakia as a unitary state between 1918 and 1938.

I compare the two multinational states stemming from the Versailles System – Czechoslovakia and the Kingdom of Serbs, Croats, and Slovenes – in order to emphasize that they were governed as unitary states after having been formed. The two dominant nations, Serbs and Czechs, fiercely resisted the federalization of their respective states. Czechoslovakia, unlike the Kingdom of Serbs, Croats, and Slovenes, responded to pressure from its national communities (Slovaks, Hungarians, and Sudetenland Germans), who sought its decentralization between 1918 and 1938 more effectively, since it was a state with a functioning legal system. In addition, Czechoslovakia was a developed country between the two world wars, with a quality of life comparable to that of West European states. At that time, Czechoslovakia was the fifth most developed state in Europe, even though its wealth was primarily concentrated in Bohemia–Moravia, whereas Slovakia remained much poorer. On the other hand, the Kingdom of Serbs, Croats, and Slovenes was a semi-dictatorship during the 1920s; the following decade it was transformed into a veritable dictatorship with fascist characteristics. The democratization of the Kingdom of Serbs, Croats, and Slovenes did not begin until the end of the 1930s. However, it was too late by that time. The Second World War spread to Yugoslav territory in 1941. Also, unlike Czechoslovakia, the Kingdom was an underdeveloped agricultural country, and the poor living conditions only aggravated national conflicts.

The peace treaties signed between 1919 and 1920, which established the international Versailles System, had the goal of creating a "Europe of nationalities." The fundamental criterion present in the West European states – that the political community has to coincide with the cultural community and, if possible, the ethnic community – was introduced at the Peace Conference (which had the capacity to remodel post-imperial territory in East-Central Europe). In other words, the idea that each nation should be endowed with its own state was omnipresent during the Peace Conference. President Woodrow Wilson outlined his conception of a post-war Europe in his Fourteen Points addressed to the United States Congress on 8 January 1918. The architects of the Versailles System – David Lloyd George, Georges Clemenceau, and Wilson – all accepted that the borders of the newly created states should coincide with concentrations of national groups. Points X, XI, and XIII advocated the "autonomous development" of the peoples of Austria-Hungary, the Balkans (Serbia, Romania, and Montenegro), and Poland. In situations where "autonomous development" was impossible to apply, he recommended special status for minorities (the League of Nations). Granting city-state status to Gdańsk and Rijeka responded to the same need. However, the "principle of nationalities" was not applied to the states that had lost the war. For example, a third of the Hungarian population found itself in three different states (Romania, Czechoslovakia, and the Kingdom of Serbs, Croats, and Slovenes) after the signing of the Treaty of Trianon. The partiality and the imperfection of the application of the "principle of nationalities" represented one of the great faults of the Versailles System. The poor application of the "principle of nationalities" which was associated with the right of peoples to govern themselves, in the spirit of President Wilson, does not, however, render it invalid. This is why the people that were not able to benefit from it in 1919–20 again referred to it in 1989–90.

In this way, the Versailles System gave birth to numerous multinational states and nation-states at the expense of the Ottoman, Austro-Hungarian, Russian, and German Empires. Nevertheless, the multinational states created on this occasion, Yugoslavia and Czechoslovakia, quickly met with difficulties

Table 3.2 Political entities constituting the Versailles System[a] 1918–38

	Nation-state	Multinational states	Empire
1918–38: Versailles System	8	2	2
	Bulgaria (1908) Greece (1830) Romania (1856) Albania (1912) Austria (1918) Germany (1918) Hungary (1918) Turkey (1923)	Kingdom of Serbs, Croats and Slovenes (1918) Czechoslovakia (1918)	French British

Note:
[a] The United States, by refusing to ratify the Versailles Treaty and join the League of Nations after the First World War, essentially remained outside the international system.

due to their inability to manage the national conflicts that existed within them. In fact, majority rule, a fundamental principle of a nation-state under the rule of law, was only perceived as legitimate by the dominant nations, Serbs and Czechs, in these multinational states. This was the source of the dominant nation's politicians' desire to create the "Czechoslovak" and "Yugoslav" nations (an attempt which was primarily seen in Yugoslavia after 1929 and symbolically represented by the changing of the Kingdom's name).

The "principle of nationalities" that was introduced at the Peace Conference in 1919 allowed for the creation of numerous nation-states and multinational states in Central Europe and the Balkans during the interval between the two world wars, to the detriment of the empires that had been defeated during the First World War. By destroying the Russian Empire, the Bolshevik Revolution also provoked the emergence of a number of nation-states in Eastern Europe, but these were almost all annexed to the Soviet Union by 1922. The political map of Central Europe and the Balkans following from the Versailles System was, however, quickly threatened by the emergence of the Nazi movement in Germany and fascism in Italy (table 3.2).

The "New Order": the Nazi System

Hitler came to power in Germany in 1933, carried by widespread protests within the German population over the Treaty of Versailles, and ushering in the ascendancy of the Third Reich over its ruins. The establishment of the Nazi System in Europe initially aimed at getting rid of the multinational states which were, according to Nazi ideologists, without ethnic foundation (*völkisch*), thus "against nature." From this same logic derived the Third Reich's desire to acquire *Lebensraum* (living space) in the east for the "Aryan race." Not forgetting geopolitical considerations, the Nazi New Order sought to replace the "principle of nationalities" as the foundation of the modern state with that of "racial hierarchy." "Inferior races," like Slavs, could have their state removed from them to allow for the expansion of superior races, particularly the "Aryan race."

Starting from 1938, the Nazi System, already consolidated in Germany, began its expansion into Europe by following this racist ideology and another principle dear to Hitler, the reunification of "all Germans into the same state" (the Third Reich), changing the state borders that followed from the Versailles System. It was in the name of this principle that the Nazi regime sought to discredit and defeat Versailles and that Alsace–Lorraine and Austria were annexed. By March 1938, the *Anschluss* was achieved. One of the first new nation-states, Austria, disappeared from the map of Central Europe through its incorporation into the growing Nazi Empire. The same went for the Sudetenland region of Czechoslovakia, where approximately 3 million Germans were living. The Sudetenland territories were annexed to the Reich after the Munich Conference on 29 and 30 September 1938; six months later, on 15 March 1939, what was left of Czechoslovakia was dismembered when German troops entered the country; the creation of the Protectorate of Bohemia–Moravia and an "independent" Slovakia was announced and a puppet government under Nazi control, while formally independent, in fact, directed this new national state. Next, the German Reich set its sight on Poland which it invaded in September 1939, and in doing so started the Second World War. Already, in August 1939, the Non-Aggression Pact signed between Hitler's Germany and Stalin's USSR had sealed the fate of the Baltic states and Poland; the latter was further divided between the two powers after its military defeat against Germany. Two years later, German forces invaded and carved up of the Kingdom of Yugoslavia, creating the "Independent State of Croatia" without a doubt controlled more by the Third Reich than Slovakia was. In the grand scheme, Nazi domination in the Balkans marked, in a way, the return of an empire to the peninsula. Serbia was directly occupied by Germany, Slovenia partially annexed, and the rest of its territory occupied by Italy. Romania, Hungary, and Bulgaria adhered to the Tripartite Pact and thus became satellites of Nazi Germany (table 3.3).

The Nazi System, even though it lasted only for a short period of time, nevertheless had a crucial impact on the formation of the nation-state in East-Central Europe and the Balkans. Nation-states with exclusively ethnic foundations were created in Croatia and Slovakia. Even if they corresponded to the Croatian and Slovak peoples' desire for independence – this does not signify at all that Croats and Slovaks gave majority support to the racist policies practised there – the states were however condemned to disappear after the defeat of Nazi Germany, their ally and protector.

Table 3.3 Nation-states, multinational states, and empires in Central and Eastern Europe and the Balkans under the Nazi System, 1933–45

	Nation-state	Multinational states	Empire
1933–45: Nazi System	5 Hungary Bulgaria Romania Independent State of Croatia (1941) Slovakia (1939)	0	3 Third Reich Italy USSR

Analysis of the Nazi system, particularly the annexation of the Sudetenland by the Reich, is particularly meaningful in understanding the policy of Milošević's regime (1991–2000) leading to the disintegration of Yugoslavia. The events that led to the Reich's annexation of Sudetenland, provoked by Hitler's goal of bringing "all Germans into the same state," form a surprising historical analogy with the policies carried out in Croatia and Bosnia-Herzegovina by Slobodan Milošević and Serbian politicians, starting at the end of the 1980s, with the goal of uniting "all Serbs into a single state."

In fact, the strategies used by Milošević and Serbian politicians to unite Serbs in Croatia and Bosnia-Herzegovina into a "Greater Serbia" call to mind, in several ways, the means employed by Nazis to integrate Sudetenland Germans into the Reich. During the 1930s, Konrad Henlein, the political leader of the Sudetenland Germans, supported the policy of the Nazis aiming to carve up Czechoslovakia. Hitler knew how to exploit the dissatisfaction in this community and used Henlein and his entourage to stir up revolts against the Prague government. The policy of dismembering Czechoslovakia was executed by Nazi Germany in close connection with Sudetenland German leaders. Milošević used the same strategy in Croatia and Bosnia-Herzegovina where he could count on the activism of the Serbian community leaders of these republics. Milošević and his acolytes succeeded in digging up local counterparts of Henlein in Croatia and Bosnia-Herzegovina. These local Serbian leaders, Milan Babić and Radovan Karadžić, applied the policies decided upon by politicians in Belgrade, in their respective republics.

The strategies used by Nazis in Sudetenland and later by Serbian leaders in Croatia and Bosnia-Herzegovina gave comparable results. The Sudetenland region was incorporated into the Reich in 1938–9, in the same way that the pseudo-state consisting of Serbs in Croatia (Krajina) was *de facto* annexed to Serbia between 1991 and 1995. The Serbian republic in Bosnia-Herzegovina (Republika Srpska), during the same time, was itself almost transformed into a province of Serbia and even today they share very close relations. The political adventure of the Sudetenland Germans and the Krajina Serbs both ended in a similar way. After the Second World War, during 1945 and 1947, between 2.5 and 3 million Germans were expelled from the Sudetenland. In the summer of 1995 between 150,000 and 200,000 Serbs fled Croatia following the military defeat of their pseudo-state in Krajina against the Croatian Army. Nazi Germany and Milošević's Serbia both sought to create ethnically pure states whose borders would correspond to the new power relations between them and their neighbours.

The Yalta State System

The Yalta System began with two contradictory diplomatic initiatives in international politics. The first was the restoration of the independence of states in East-Central Europe (though quickly incorporated into the Soviet sphere of influence). The second was the adoption of the Charter of the UN, which for the first time recognized the universal right of a people to self-determination. The Charter of the UN elevated what had simply been a political principle promised by President Wilson during the Peace Conference of 1919 to a norm of international law, which was in time raised to that of *jus cogens*. This defining leap had immense consequences on nation-state formation; first, for the colonies in the Third World and, following this, after 1989, for the states of East-Central Europe, the Soviet Union included.

After the defeat of the Third Reich and the end of the Second World War, several nation-states and multinational states, which had been wiped from the political map in East-Central Europe and the Balkans between 1938 and 1945, reappeared. At the Conferences of Moscow (October 1944), Yalta (February 1945), and Potsdam (July 1945), the new territorial and political reorganization of Europe was decided upon by the three great powers: the United States, the USSR, and Great Britain. The nation-states conquered or dominated by Axis forces during the war quickly regained their independence: Austria (after having been militarily occupied by Allied forces between 1945 and 1955), Poland, and Greece. Hungary, Bulgaria, Albania, and Romania, allies of Germany and Italy, had to renounce their territorial gains of the Second World War after having been liberated by the Allies. On the other hand, the continuity of their states was not questioned in the passing from one international system (Nazi New Order) to another (Yalta). Elsewhere, the two multinational states that had been carved up, Yugoslavia and Czechoslovakia, were reborn. In Yugoslavia, resistance to Nazi Germany and to the fascist *Ustaša* regime of Ante Pavelić came principally from the Yugoslav Communist Party led by Josip Broz Tito. At the end of the Second World War, after its victory over Axis forces, the Yugoslav Communist Party proposed a new multinational arrangement for South Slavs that would this time be based upon a federal system that would have to ensure the equality of all the nations of communist Yugoslavia. As for Czechoslovakia, at the end of the war it regained almost all of its past borders in their entirety, losing only Ruthenia, which was annexed by the USSR in 1945. The problem of the German minority in the Sudetenland region was also dealt with in a radical way; this population was brutally expelled to Germany.[22]

But the Yalta System established after the Second World War also allowed the Soviet Empire to exercise its domination over the countries of East-Central Europe and the Balkans: over Poland, Czechoslovakia, Hungary, Romania, Bulgaria, and the GDR for forty years. The Soviet Union's efforts to assert its dominance in Yugoslavia and Albania failed, however, because of the successful resistance by Tito and Enver Hoxha, the respective leaders of these two countries. Even if these states theoretically preserved their independence, they were all integrated into the Soviet sphere of influence after national front governments created between 1944 and 1949 were dissolved.

In 1968, Moscow formulated the "Brezhnev Doctrine," or doctrine of limited sovereignty, which openly violated a people's right to self-determination, in the same way that the colonial powers had refused this right to the people they dominated. The doctrine was illegitimate because it directly infringed on Art. 1, para. 2, of the UN Charter containing the right to self-determination.[23] The irony is that the USSR and Yugoslavia had both insisted that the principle of the self-determination of peoples be included in the UN Charter. However, the reasons for the pressure exercised by the USSR and Yugoslavia were purely ideological. They hoped that they would favor communist-inspired revolutions in the Third World and that the resulting modification of the balance of power would benefit the communist camp to the detriment of the colonial powers.

From the creation of the Soviet Union in 1922 to the consolidation of communist regimes in Yugoslavia in 1945, and Czechoslovakia in 1948, the peoples constituting these three federations (Czechoslovakia was a federal state after 1968) were never able to exercise their right to self-determination. Inside the communist federations, this right was flouted by the communist parties in power, which never authorized free expression through popular consultations (referenda), but rather exercised a constant control over their constituent peoples.

However, the populations of Croatia, Slovakia, the republics of the Soviet Union, and Yugoslavia definitely constituted peoples in the sense of the UN Charter. It was only through the first free elections in 1989–90 that these peoples began to exercise their right to self-determination. These free elections allowed them to elect their own governments. In the same way, the referenda on independence gave these peoples the choice to establish nation-states, to maintain their federations, or to create another type of state (such as the now-defunct multinational federation of Serbia and Montenegro). The peoples of each of these three communist federations possessed territories (republics) and had a political power in place, which qualified them to create sovereign and independent states, enter freely into union with an independent state, or adopt another political status that they would have chosen of their own free will.[24]

The form that decolonization took in the Soviet Union and in its external empire (the Warsaw Pact) had three dimensions. The first dimension aimed for the Soviet Union to restore the political sovereignty of the states that it had dominated – as such, the end of the "Brezhnev Doctrine." This dimension's immediate result with regard to decolonization was that the satellite states, members of the Warsaw Pact, regained the freedom to act independently on the international stage. The second aspect of decolonization concerned the transferal of political sovereignty from the center to the republics that had formed the Soviet Union.[25] The third dimension concerned restoring the power confiscated from the peoples by the respective communist parties during the time of free elections. With regards to this last point, it was the Soviet Union that guaranteed perennial power to the party-states. This capacity to support the party-states globally (from Vietnam to Cuba) gave the USSR the characteristic of an empire (table 3.4).

As the USSR controlled its sphere of influence militarily and with an iron fist in East-Central Europe and the Balkans, the question of the states' territorial unity was virtually ignored during the Yalta System. The end of the Cold War and national revolts both inside the Soviet Union and on the periphery of its empire (Warsaw Pact) had to occur before a new wave of nation-states came into being (after the decolonization of the Soviet Empire). The end of the Cold War in 1989–90 signified a profound alteration of the balance of power in East–West relations, to the West's advantage. The dissolution of the bipolar international system in Europe was the most important event in international politics, opening the way for the creation of new states in East-Central Europe.

Table 3.4 Nation-states, multinational states, and empires in Central and Eastern Europe and the Balkans under the Yalta System, 1945–89

	Nation-State	Multinational States	Empire
1945–89: Yalta System	9	2	1
	Austria (1955)	Yugoslavia (SFRY) (1945)	USSR
	Albania (1945)	Czechoslovakia (1945)	
	GDR (1949)		
	FGR (1949)		
	Hungary		
	Bulgaria		
	Romania		
	Greece (1945)		
	Poland (1945)		

The end of the communist regimes and the proliferation of new nation-states

This new wave touched the Balkans first. The breakup of communist Yugoslavia was consummated in June 1991, even if it had begun in 1987. During its first wave, it gave birth to three nation-states: Slovenia, Croatia, and the Republic of Macedonia.[26] During the same process, two multinational states were also created: the Federal Republic of Yugoslavia (FRY)[27] and Bosnia-Herzegovina (formed by three constituent nations: Bosniaks, Serbs, and Croats).

In Central Europe, Czechoslovakia sought at first to remain a federal state. The national parliament voted to reaffirm the federal character of Czechoslovakia in 1990. Shortly thereafter, Czechoslovakia disappeared completely, giving rise to two new states: the Czech Republic and Republic of Slovakia. It was during the negotiations held in June and August 1992, that the Czech Prime Minister, Václav Klaus, and the Slovak Prime Minister, Vladimír Mečiar, decided to put an end to the Czechoslovak Federation. The "Velvet Divorce" between the two republics became effective on 1 January 1993.

Likewise, in East-Central Europe, the USSR also broke apart into a multitude of multinational states and nation-states, fifteen in total, at the end of 1991. In resigning from his post on 25 December 1991, Mikhail Gorbachev effectively signed the death warrant of the Soviet Union, which had found itself in a terminal phase since the conservatives' putsch in August. From the ashes of the USSR emerged, of course, the Russian Federation, a multinational state, but also, in the European part of the former Soviet Union, the nation-states of Armenia, Azerbaijan, Belarus, Georgia, Moldavia, and Ukraine. At the same time, the three Baltic countries, Lithuania, Latvia, and Estonia, also regained the independence that they had lost at the signing of the Nazi–Soviet Pact in 1939, and which had been followed by Soviet occupation in 1940. Other nation-states were also created in the same context in Central Asia: Kazakhstan, Kyrgyzstan, Tajikistan, Turkmenistan, and Uzbekistan (table 3.5).

The process of state formation in East-Central Europe and the Balkans after almost two centuries seems to be over. In the Balkans, the FRY, which since February 2003 had been the Union of Serbia–Montenegro, broke up in 2006. Two states emerged: Serbia and Montenegro. Kosovo, formerly an autonomous province of the Socialist Federated Republic of Yugoslavia (SFRY), inhabited primarily by Albanians, became an independent state on 17 February 2008.

During the last decade of the twentieth century in the Balkans, the policies of the Clinton administration allowed the creation – and, above all, the preservation – of Bosnia-Herzegovina. Through the 1994 Washington Accords, which created the Croato-Muslim Federation, the United States was able to assure the survival of the multinational state, Bosnia-Herzegovina. The preservation of Bosnia-Herzegovina was sealed through the Dayton Accords and the Paris Treaty of November and December 1995, where the United States contributed

Table 3.5 Nation-states, multinational states, and empires in Central and Eastern Europe and the Balkans after the Yalta System, 1989–2008

	Nation-state	Multinational states	Empire
1989–2008: Post-Yalta	25	2	0
	Albania (1945)	Russian Federation (1991–2)	
	Romania	Bosnia-Herzegovina (1992)	
	Hungary		
	Bulgaria		
	Greece		
	Austria		
	Poland		
	Unified Germany (1990)		
	Slovenia (1991)		
	Croatia (1991)		
	Macedonia (1991)		
	Czech Republic (1993)		
	Slovakia (1993)		
	Serbia (2006)		
	Montenegro (2006)		
	Kosovo (2008)		
	Nine successor states in the European part of the USSR (1991–92)		
	Georgia		
	Azerbaijan		
	Armenia		
	Estonia		
	Latvia		
	Lithuania		
	Ukraine		
	Belarus		
	Moldavia		

more than anybody else. By assuring the survival of Bosnia-Herzegovina within its present borders, the Dayton Conference and the Accords that came out of it, played a role similar to the Congress of Berlin in the international system of the post-Cold War era. In fact, the great powers (the United States, the EU), by seeking to put an end to the war in Bosnia-Herzegovina while at the same time trying to guarantee the survival of this multinational state, were able to determine rules for the configuration of Yugoslav territory for years to come. The essential rule that came out of the Dayton Accords was that the international community would not accept any forceful border changes in the Balkans. Consequently, the ideas of a "Greater Serbia," a "Greater Croatia," and a "Greater Albania," which could threaten the territorial integrity of certain states in the region, particularly Bosnia-Herzegovina and the Republic of Macedonia, were political projects frowned upon by the international community.

During the twentieth century, the United States played a fundamental role in this part of Europe, not limited to resolving the war in Bosnia-Herzegovina. In 1999, Kosovo was seized from the hands of the FRY by the international community and transformed into a protectorate under the patronage of the UN Security Council after the decisive intervention of NATO. In 2001, the United States and its European allies again aided the Balkans by saving the Macedonian state from Albanian attempts to partition the country.

The influence of the EC and the EU on state formation in East-Central Europe after 1989

At the beginning of the breakup of states in East-Central Europe, the EC took an active part in diplomatic negotiations aiming to contain the effects of a political crisis occurring right at its front door. In this way, the "European concert" reappeared in European international politics in the twentieth century as an international organization whose principal mission was not to juggle political crises – as in the nineteenth century after the Congress of Vienna – but to promote economic integration into Western Europe. This structural limit of the EC considerably diminished its diplomatic effectiveness and its capacity to control the emergence of new states in East-Central Europe.

At first, the EC tried to deter Yugoslav and Czechoslovak leaders from dissolving their respective states and prevent them from creating new states in East-Central Europe. Having failed in its attempt to stop the breakups from happening, the EC next sought to contain the destabilizing effects of the disintegration of the three post-communist federations. The most visible aspect of the EC's activities in 1990–1 was the adoption of rules outlining the behavior that successor states would have to adhere to if they wanted to be diplomatically recognized by the EC. The principal document with which the EC desired to influence the constitutions of the new states was called "Declaration on the Guidelines on the Recognition of New States in Eastern Europe and in the Soviet Union."[28] In this declaration, dated 16 December 1991, the EC and its member states committed themselves to recognizing "subject to the normal standards of international practice and the political realities in each case, those new States which, following the historic changes in the region, have constituted themselves on a democratic basis, have accepted the appropriate international obligations and have committed themselves in good faith to a peaceful process and to negotiations." The obligations defined by the EC with regards to recognition were the following:

> [R]espect for the provisions of the Charter of the United Nations and the commitments subscribed to in the Final Act of Helsinki and in the Charter of Paris, especially with regard to the rule of law, democracy and human rights; guarantees for the rights of ethnic and national groups and minorities in accordance with the commitments subscribed to in the framework of the CSCE; respect for the inviolability of all frontiers which can only be changed by peaceful means and by common agreement; acceptance of all relevant commitments with regard to disarmament and nuclear non-proliferation as well as to security and regional stability; commitment to settle by agreement ... all questions concerning State succession and regional disputes.[29]

After the EC adopted the "Guidelines," it began to consider diplomatic recognition of the Yugoslav republics which had declared their independence. An evolution in this direction had already begun through the creation of the Badinter Commission (after the name of the French judge who presided over it) in August 1991, an organization parallel to the Peace Conference presided over by former Foreign Secretary Lord Peter Carrington, whose role was to provide legal opinions allowing for a political solution to the Yugoslav conflicts. The Badinter Commission, through its stated opinions, established the rules that could have allowed all those involved to arrive at an understanding if they had been respected by all the Yugoslav republics. At first, the Commission ruled that Yugoslavia had already initiated its dissolution. But above all, it stated that republic's borders were inviolable and that only the republics could benefit from the right to self-determination. The Commission's opinion here refuted Serbia's allegations, notably that the borders between republics were only "administrative" and could be changed at will to bring all Serbs living outside Serbia's borders together into the same state. After this reversal, Serbia refused to accept the rulings of the Badinter Commission, including all those that Serbia itself had submitted to the Commission. The work of the Badinter Commission paved the way to the EC's diplomatic recognition of Croatia and Slovenia on 15 January 1992.

The EU returned as a peacemaker in the region only after NATO's military campaign in Kosovo in 1999. After the transformation of Kosovo into an international protectorate governed by the UN, the EU dissuaded Montenegro from separating from Serbia to become an independent state, which would have put an end to the FRY. In 2006, however, Montenegro gained its independence and the EU, which supervised the referendum, had to accept the verdict of Montenegrins, who voted in favor of becoming a completely sovereign state. Soon after, the EU signed the Stabilization and Association Agreement (SAA) with Montenegro in 2007, the first step toward full membership in the EU.

After the independence of Montenegro, the EU and the United States coordinated their policies on recognition toward Kosovo. Thus, Kosovo proclaimed its independence on 17 February 2008. In 1991, the EC was hostile to the creation of new states in East-Central Europe and this attitude only reluctantly changed after Montenegro's independence. However, there is no incompatibility between enlarging the EU and the emergence of new states, provided that human and collective rights are respected (as occurred during the division of Czechoslovakia). Before leaving his position in January 2003, President Havel declared in his last speech of the New Year that "the separation [of the Czech Republic and Slovakia] was probably a good thing despite the bitter aftertaste left over due to the absence of a referendum."[30] The Czech Republic's example accurately shows that there is no incompatibility between a civilized divorce and joining the EU.

Conclusion

In this chapter I have attempted to demonstrate the existence of a long-lasting tendency towards the creation of nation-states in East-Central Europe and the Balkans. It suffices to note that at the beginning of the nineteenth century, no nation-states existed in East-Central Europe, whereas today there are more than twenty. This political process of "*longue durée*," stretching out over approximately three centuries, seemed to come to an end after Kosovo became, in 2008, an independent state. For the time being there is no new candidate in East-Central Europe and the Balkans to claim a status of independent state.

Notes

1. The multinational state is characterized by the existence of two or more nations whose territories are demarcated by internal borders. From a legal standpoint, the multinational state is subject to international law, but not its constituent parts (federal units or provinces).
2. Even if Czechoslovakia and Yugoslavia were dismantled during the Second World War (between 1939 and 1945 for the former, and between 1941 and 1945 for the latter), the Allies (the United States, Great Britain, and the Soviet Union) never recognized their disappearance. As such, these governments continued to treat them in this manner in London during the war.
3. The "*longue durée*" was associated with the social history of the French school: "L'école des Annals."
4. François Furet, *L'atelier de l'histoire* (Paris: Flammarion, 1982), p. 12.
5. Jean-Baptiste Duroselle, *L'Europe: Histoire de ses peuples* (Paris: Perrin, 1993), p. 382.
6. In this study, the poly-semantic concept of nationalism assumes a triple meaning. It represents a political ideology, a social movement, and a primordial identity, the latter as identified by the anthropologist Clifford Geertz.
7. Duroselle, *L'Europe*, p. 383.
8. Even though the Peace Conference was organized in Paris, beginning in January 1919, in this chapter I have opted for the name "Versailles System" in the interest of simplifying the text. Other treaties were also signed close to the Peace Conference: the Treaty of Saint-Germain-en-Laye with Austria on 10 September 1919, the Treaty of Neuilly with Bulgaria on 27 November 1919, and the Treaty of Trianon with Hungary on 4 June 1920.

9. "Declaration on the Guidelines on the Recognition of New States in Eastern Europe and in the Soviet Union," can be consulted in *International Legal Materials*, Vol. XXXI, no. 6 (November 1992), pp. 1486–7.
10. Jean-Claude Caren and Michel Vernus, *L'Europe au XIXe siècle: Des nations aux nationalismes 1815–1914* (Paris: Armand Colin, 1996), p. 23.
11. On the role of the European concert and its capacity to manage the continental crises, see Georges Henri-Soutou, "Le Concert européen, de Vienne à Locarno," in Georges-Henri Soutou and Jean Bérenger (eds.), *L'ordre européen du XVIe au XIXe siècle* (Paris: Presses de l'université de Paris-Sorbonne, 1998), pp. 117–36.
12. According to this principle, "people with the same language, culture, and tradition have the right to political independence if they so desire, provided they occupy a territory that is clearly defined." Henry Bogdan, *Histoire des pays de l'Est* (Paris: Perrin, 1991), p. 124.
13. The nation-state that I refer to here does not correspond to the "French" model. In France, the state was actually created towards the end of the Middle Ages, whereas the French nation appeared much later with the revolution. In this context, the nation includes all those living inside the borders of the state, such that citizenship and nationality coincide. In this specific case, as indicated by Paul Garde, "The nation is based upon the pre-existing borders of the state and every citizen of the state is *ipso facto* a member of the nation … [The] relation between citizenship and nationality is thus innate and given by definition, such that citizens [of national states of the "French" type] have trouble understanding the distinction between these notions. Minorities did not as such exist since every citizen of the state was a member of the nation." On the other hand, in Central and Eastern Europe and in the Balkans, the "German" model of the nation was found; that is to say that the example of Germany in forming nations in these European regions preceded the creation of modern states. This context that resulted in the national state does not always coincide with what is understood by nation; as such members of nations could live outside the borders of the national state which itself encompassed national minorities. In the national states of the "German" type, the concepts of citizenship and nationality were thus distinct, nationality being "a quality inherent in the individual and independent of political vicissitudes [such as citizenship], including language, religion and skin colour, etc." Paul Garde, "National State and Multinational State," in Marie-Françoise Allain *et al.*, *L'ex-Yougoslavie en Europe: De la faillite des démocraties au processus de paix* (Paris and Montreal: L'Harmattan, 1997), pp. 250–1. Here, I understand "nation-state" to be a state that had an identifiable ethnic majority. This does not mean at all that these states are homogenous with regards to their ethnic or national composition, with the exception of Iceland and Portugal. Quite the opposite, the European nation-state is characterized by the presence of national minorities. For example, Latvia is a nation-state even though it possesses a Slavic minority (Russian, Belarusian, and Ukrainian) that totals 42% of the state's population. I make a distinction between nation-state and national state. The national state, or nation-state that I consider a subset of nation-states, is an *ethnic* state that does not recognize, either constitutionally or symbolically, the presence of the Other on its "national" territory. The national state is the product of ethnic nationalism in its racist variant. The independent state of Croatia, formed during the Second World War between 1941

and 1945, and Slovakia, which existed between 1939 and 1945, can be considered to be national states.

14. Jean-Baptiste Duroselle, *Tout empire périra* (Paris: Armand Colin, 1992), p. 306.
15. Jean-Baptiste Duroselle, *L'Europe de 1815 à nos jours*, 7th edn. (Paris: Presses Universitaires de France, 1993), p. 105.
16. Jean-Charles Asselain *et al.*, *Précis d'histoire européenne, 19e-20e siècle* (Paris: Armand Colin, 2000), p. 37.
17. René Girault, *Peuples et nations d'Europe au XIXe siècle* (Paris: Hachette supérieur, 1996), pp. 152–3.
18. In the first half of the nineteenth century Russia tried to increase its influence in the Balkans to the detriment of the Ottoman Empire. Austria-Hungary and England attentively watched over its actions in the region. In 1875, two revolts broke out in the territory of the Ottoman Empire, one in Bosnia-Herzegovina, the other in Bulgaria. The Turks severely crushed both these revolts, but they were quickly followed by uprisings in Montenegro and Serbia beginning in July 1876. Soon after, Russia entered into the game and declared war with the Ottoman Empire on 24 April 1877. Russia left this war victorious and signed the Treaty of San Stefano with the Ottoman Empire on 3 March 1878, which foresaw, amongst other things, the creation of a Greater Bulgaria obviously under Russian influence. Austria-Hungary and England worried about Russia's interference in the Balkans. Austria-Hungary demanded a revision of the Treaty of San Stefano and claimed that it was ready to go to war with Russia to obtain it. Russia, whose armed forces and finances were exhausted by the war, ceded, and the Congress of Berlin met from 15 June to 15 July 1878, to redefine the Balkan map. Greater Bulgaria was dismembered, Austria-Hungary obtained the right to occupy Bosnia-Herzegovina, and other states such as Serbia, Montenegro, and Romania gained their independence. See *ibid.*, pp. 140–3; Bogdan, *Histoire des pays de l'Est*, pp. 199–202.
19. Between 1878 (Congress of Berlin) and 1918, Montenegro was recognized as an independent country by the international community. Petar Petrović Njegoš (1813–51), poet and Prince of Montenegro, released a book in 1847 entitled *Gorski vjenac* (Garland of the Mountains) which, due to its anti-Ottoman and anti-Islamic opinions, became the veritable Bible of Slav (Orthodox) nationalists during the nineteenth and twentieth centuries in their fight against the Ottoman Empire until its expulsion from southeastern Europe.
20. See Renéo Lukic and Allen Lynch, *Europe from the Balkans to the Urals: The Disintegration of Yugoslavia and the Soviet Union* (Oxford and New York: Oxford University Press, 1996), principally chapter 4, "Constants in the Yugoslav Polity, 1918–54," pp. 57–78.
21. According to the census of 1921, Sudetenland Germans numbered 3,124,000 and counted for 22% of Czechoslovakia's population. With the disintegration of the Austro-Hungarian monarchy, Sudetenland Germans, after being incorporated into Czechoslovakia, passed from the status of an imperial nation to a simple national minority, which is why they initially rejected a Czechoslovakian state dominated by Slavs.
22. During the war, the exiled Czechoslovak government often made reference to a forced expulsion of Sudetenland Germans as necessary to deal with the problem that this national minority was raising. It used the Treaty of Lausanne of 1923 as support,

which allowed the transferal of Greek and Turkish populations. The Allies approved this solution, so much so that during the Potsdam Conference in 1945 they sanctioned this population transferral as long as it was "legitímate and appropriate." The expulsion of Germans from Czechoslovakia, as well as Hungarians, began towards the end of the war following the Czechoslovakian government's decrees ("the Beneš Decrees"). In the fall of 1947, the quasi-totality of Sudetenland Germans had been transferred to Germany (around 3 million people). It has been estimated that between 20,000 and 30,000 Germans perished due to their expulsion from Czechoslovakia. Nevertheless, around 200,000 Germans remained in Czechoslovakia and integrated themselves into Czech society. See Norman M. Nairmark, *Fires of Hatred: Ethnic Cleansing in Twentieth-Century Europe* (Cambridge, Mass.: Harvard University Press, 2001), pp. 117–20.

23. Art. 1, para. 2 of the UN Charter defines one of the goals of the organization as: "to develop friendly relations among nations based on respect for the principle of equal rights and self-determination of peoples, and to take other appropriate measures to strengthen universal peace." Another reference to self-determination is found in Art. 55 of the Charter. The UN Charter is available on-line at: www.un.org/aboutun/charter/.
24. "Déclaration relative aux principes de droit international touchant les relations amicales et la coopération entre États conformément à la Charte des nations unies," Annexed to Resolution 2625 (XXV) of the General Assembly of the United Nations, adopted 24 October 1970, as cited in Nicolas Levrat, "D'une exigence de légalité dans les relations internationales contemporaines," in Charles-Albert Morand (ed.), *La Crise des Balkans de 1999: Les dimensions historiques, politiques et juridiques du conflit du Kosovo* (Brussels and Paris: Bruylant/Librairie générale de droit et de jurisprudence, 2000), pp. 263–4.
25. This transfer resulted in the creation of fifteen successor states to the Soviet Union. For a good analysis of the breakup of the Soviet Union along a comparative analysis of the "end of empires," see Robert Strayer, "Decolonization, Democratization, and Communist Reform: The Soviet Collapse in Comparative Perspective," *Journal of World History*, Vol. 12, No. 2 (Fall, 2001), particularly pp. 376–83.
26. The Republic of Macedonia was able to avoid the war with Serbia when it gained its independence, contrary to Croatia and Bosnia-Herzegovina. It was, however, confronted by Greece's hostility, which opposed its name under the pretext that Macedonia was a Greek province and that the name of the new state implied territorial claims on its national territory. Yet it is certain that Macedonia did not carry any territorial claims against Greece and the new state was much too weak to represent any threat to its stability. Nevertheless, due to unjustified incriminations on Greece's part, Macedonia had to wait until 8 April 1993, before obtaining its own seat at the UN under the name of Former Yugoslav Republic of Macedonia (FYROM).
27. The Federal Republic of Yugoslavia (FRY), formed by the republics of Serbia and Montenegro, was a multinational state, since it was composed of two titular nations and numerous national minorities such as Roms, Turks, Bosniaks, and others. Serbs form the titular nation in Serbia, and Montenegrins in Montenegro. As such, Serbs in Serbia and Montenegrins in Montenegro form the majority in their respective republics.

28. "Declaration on the Guidelines on the Recognition of New States in Eastern Europe and in the Soviet Union," can be consulted in *International Legal Materials*, Vol. XXXI, No. 6 (November 1992), pp. 1486–7.
29. "Declaration on the Guidelines," *ibid.*
30. Martin Plichta, "Václav Havel met en scène son départ de la présidence tchèque," *Le Monde* (Paris), 1 February 2003, at www.lemonde.fr.

Further reading

Jelavich, Barbara. *History of the Balkans: Twentieth Century* (Cambridge and New York: Cambridge University Press, 1995)

Jelavich, Charles and Barbara Jelavich. *The Establishment of the Balkan National States, 1804–1920* (Seattle: University of Washington Press, 1977; reprinted, 1993)

Lukic, Renéo. *L'Agonie yougoslave (1986–2003): Les États-Unis et l'Europe face aux guerres balkaniques* (Quebec: Les Presses de l'Université Laval, 2003)

Lukic, Renéo and Allen Lynch. *Europe from the Balkans to the Urals: The Disintegration of Yugoslavia and the Soviet Union* (Oxford and New York: Oxford University Press, 1996)

Roeder, Philip G. *Where Nation-States Come From: Institutional Change in the Age of Nationalism* (Princeton, NJ: Princeton University Press, 2007)

Rokkan, Stein. *State Formation, Nation Building, and Mass Politics in Europe. The Theory of Stein Rokkan: Based on his Collected Works*, ed. by Peter Flora with Stein Kuhnle and Derek Urwin (Oxford: Oxford University Press, 1999)

Smith, Anthony D. *The Ethnic Origins of Nations* (London: Basil Blackwell, 1986)

Zubok, Vladislav. *A Failed Empire: The Soviet Union in the Cold War from Stalin to Gorbachev* (Chapel Hill, NC: University of North Carolina Press, 2008)

4

Central and East European party systems since 1989

ELISABETH BAKKE*

Two decades after the collapse of communism, Central and East European countries have come a long way towards liberal democracy and stable party systems, confounding pessimistic predictions about unstable competition, weak parties, and limited institutionalization.[1] To be sure, party system stabilization has entailed fissure and fusion, producing winners and losers along the way; and some party systems have gone through several restructuring processes, but overall there is surprisingly strong continuity between the parties that are represented in the respective parliaments today and the parties and movements that emerged in the early 1990s. Moreover, not only have ten countries fulfilled the dream of "returning to Europe" by joining the EU – many of the major parties in these countries have also joined European parties such as the Party of European Socialists (PES), the Liberal Democrats in Europe (ELDR), and the European People's Party (EPP), signaling convergence across the old Iron Curtain. And although the left–right dimension initially played a secondary role in many countries, it has gradually come to the fore, as have other, older cleavages. The *tabula rasa* thesis has been thoroughly refuted: communism did not erase all social cleavages – on the contrary, there was "evidence of [a] social basis to party support across the region" already in the early 1990s.[2]

The conditions under which party systems in Central and Eastern Europe developed were nevertheless quite different. The "triple transition"[3] from communism to democracy, from planned economy to market economy, and from multinational federations to independent "national" states shaped party system development. Institutional design, the tempo of the economic reforms, and redistribution were important issues, and the national question played a role in all newly independent states (and most of the "old" states). The new democracies also differ from older democracies in that civil society is still weak, electoral participation is lower (and declining), and parties are often "elite clubs." Moreover, some countries lag behind in the consolidation of democracy as well as party systems.

The first section addresses the status of civil society and party membership. The next section provides an overview of institutional convergence and election laws across the region, while the third and fourth sections are devoted to party system development and party families.

Parties and civil society

"Civil society" in liberal democracies is thought of as an arena for autonomous organized voluntary activity between the state, the market, and the private realm.[4] The state's role is to provide the legal framework for, and sometimes help fund, voluntary organizations. Civil society is believed to be important in liberal democracies, because voluntary organizations serve as schools of democracy, as a safety valve for discontent, and as channels for interest articulation.[5] However, in contrast to Western Europe, where many parties grew out of civil society organizations, most parties in post-communist Europe have been created top-down, and civil society is therefore – with a few notable exceptions[6] – largely irrelevant to party formation.

During Communism, trade unions and other organizations were state-sponsored and under strict party control. Opposition networks were therefore weak, and civic society developed *against* the state. Solidarity in Poland was unique in that it united the opposition in one powerful organization.[7] Besides Poland, only the Czech Republic and Slovenia had developed fairly independent civil societies by 1989, although there were also important independent initiatives in Hungary, Croatia, and even Serbia. In the Baltic states after 1985, local movements for the support of *perestroika* (Gorbachev's program of restructuring) were nominally pro-government, but remained independent, and no communist government had ever welcomed *independent* initiatives in its support.[8]

What is the status of civil society in post-communist Europe today? Although I have not been able to find comparable figures on the proliferation of civil society organizations and political parties for all countries, the data that do exist seem to support the argument that the number of non-governmental organizations (NGOs) has "grown from at best a few hundred per country in 1989 to tens of thousands across the region today."[9] This development has been helped along by Western aid and the internet, as well as by grass-roots activity. However, the number of voluntary organizations is lower than in the West,[10] and according to one of the Western donors many of the established organizations have "evolved into professional intermediaries, i.e. experts and permanent staff with long experience, social security, attractive salaries, self-confidence, little innovation but good delivery of routine operations."[11] As in Western Europe, many NGOs are based on "cheque book participation" rather than large memberships.[12]

There is good reason to doubt the extent of active involvement on the part of ordinary citizens (table 4.1). Marc Morjé Howard points out that post-communist countries score lower than old democracies and post-authoritarian states on membership in all types of voluntary organizations, except trade unions. Moreover, membership has declined after 1989.[13] Low membership can be attributed to the citizens' distrust of organizations, the persistence of private and informal networks that developed under communism, and dissatisfaction with the way the new political and economic system turned out.[14]

Table 4.1 Organizational membership (%)

	Church/ religious	% of these: active	Sports/ recreation	Educational/ cultural	Trade union	Environ- mental	Professional	Charitable	Other	Average	Political party	% of these: active	Average memberships per person
Bosnia	42	16	26	15	33	12	13	13	13	**20.9**	35	6.0	**2.02**
Croatia	55	16	22	14	26	5	15	12	8	**19.7**	9	2.8	**1.65**
Macedonia	18	4	21	14	20	14	14	15	13	**16.1**	21	5.7	**1.50**
Montenegro	13	3	14	14	33	4	13	15	7	**14.2**	23	5.0	**1.35**
Slovenia	30	7	19	9	29	4	12	11	13	**15.6**	5	1.3	**1.30**
Romania	38	15	10	9	21	6	9	6	4	**13.0**	12	5.1	**1.14**
Poland	23	13	14	12	13	8	9	11	15	**13.1**	8	1.2	**1.12**
Slovakia	29	9	22	6	19	5	7	5	13	**13.1**	7	2.2	**1.12**
Czech Republic	17	5	24	9	16	5	9	4	17	**12.4**	7	2.5	**1.07**
Albania	21	5	11	9	9	2	12	3	5	**9.0**	34	13.1	**1.05**
Moldova	33	13	10	9	36	5	4	4	0	**12.5**	3	0.9	**1.03**
Serbia	11	2	14	7	24	2	11	9	6	**10.6**	11	3.0	**0.96**
Hungary	20	9	14	5	12	3	10	6	9	**9.9**	3	2.6	**0.82**
Latvia	13	4	9	10	18	2	9	2	4	**8.4**	3	0.8	**0.70**
Estonia	12	2	14	11	13	2	5	2	3	**7.7**	2	0.6	**0.64**
Lithuania	14	4	7	7	8	2	4	2	1	**5.6**	3	1.1	**0.46**
Bulgaria	3	1	4	4	13	1	2	2	1	**3.7**	6	2.2	**0.35**
CEEC Mean	22.4	7.1	14.8	9.6	20.1	4.9	9.3	7.1	7.8	**12.1**	11.3	3.3	**1.08**
Older democracies	47.2	17.1	40.6	25.0	32.2	13.2	21.1	23.3	22.7	**26.9**	16.6		**2.39**

Sources: World Values Survey 1995_v3 (data collected 1994–9); for Poland, *World Values Survey* 2005_v2008 (data collected 2005), at www.worldvaluessurvey.org. Figures for old democracies are reported in Marc Morjé Howard, *The Weakness of Civic Society in Post-Communist Europe* (Cambridge: Cambridge University Press, 2003), pp. 65–6, 69. The Romanian figures are probably too high; data from 2005 put Romania in the bottom of the list with 0.28 memberships per person.

As in the West, high-income groups, people with higher education, men, and people living in rural areas are more likely to be active in voluntary organizations.

Party membership is also lower in post-communist countries than in older democracies. Very few parties in post-communist Europe come close to the mass parties of the twentieth century,[15] with extensive party organizations, many members, and close links to trade unions, farmers' associations, Churches, etc. In an age of media politics, secularization, and individualism, this was unlikely to begin with.[16] Those that do have many members are former regime parties and early opposition parties. The Croatian Democratic Union (HDZ) reportedly had more than 400,000 members in the 1990s, now reduced to 220,000. Also, the Bulgarian Socialist Party (BSP) with 210,000 members, the Polish Peasant Party (PSL) with 200,000 members, the Albanian Socialist Party (PSSH) and the Albanian Democratic Party (PD) with over 100,000 members each, and the Czech Communist Party (KSČM) with 83,000 members must be regarded as mass parties.[17] The rest of the parties are closer to the elite-dominated cadre parties of the nineteenth century or to the "catch-all" model (broader appeal, smaller organization, fewer members, and stronger leadership). Of the countries for which I have been able to find data, party membership is nominally lowest in Latvia (fewer than 2,000 members per parliamentary party), and highest in Croatia, (average membership 46,500).[18]

Institutions, electoral systems, and political fragmentation

Institutions are interesting, first, because institutional design generally provokes disagreement between political elites and, second, because institutions constrain party system development. As of 2008, institutional *convergence* is evident across the region. All countries except Bosnia-Herzegovina (hereafter Bosnia) are unitary states, all have fairly rigid constitutions, constitutional courts (in Estonia the Supreme Court of Justice) are responsible for constitutional review, human rights are incorporated, and nearly all countries are parliamentary democracies. A majority of the presidents are elected for five years by direct majority vote in two rounds, and no president can be re-elected more than once. The president's constitutional power is in most cases limited to a suspensive veto that can be overturned by majority vote. Exceptions are Lithuania, where the president holds the right of initiative, approves the government's composition, and has certain foreign policy powers, and Poland, where a 3/5 majority is in addition required to overturn a presidential veto. The Polish and Lithuanian systems may therefore be labeled parliamentary–presidential (see chapter 2). Parliaments are unicameral, except for the single federation (Bosnia), the two largest countries (Poland and Romania), the Czech Republic, and Slovenia. Senates are elected by majority vote (the Czech Republic and Poland), indirectly, or in the Romanian case in the same way as the Chamber of Deputies.

In Central Europe and the Baltic states the overall picture is one of institutional *stability*; only Poland made substantial changes in the distribution of power from the "small" 1992 constitution to the final 1997 constitution. In contrast, several Balkan countries changed the actual and/or the formal distribution of power in the mid- or late 1990s, often as part of an effort to rid the country of authoritarian vestiges. In Moldova and Croatia, the constitution was changed to curb presidential powers in 2000 and 2001, respectively; in Bulgaria, Macedonia, Albania, and Serbia, the president's actual power was reduced to comply with the constitution. In the Moldovan case, the parliament's decision to adopt a parliamentary system came in reaction to president Petru Lucinschi's drive to introduce a presidential system.[19] In 2008, Freedom House categorized Kosovo and Moldova as authoritarian regimes, Bosnia as a hybrid regime, while the rest were either labeled consolidated (Central Europe, the Baltic states, and Bulgaria) or semi-consolidated democracies.[20]

From a party systems' perspective, *electoral laws* are particularly important. Majority systems tend to benefit the largest parties and favor strong government over equal representation, while PR systems tend to yield more proportional results. However, the effect of PR systems also depends on district magnitude, the electoral formula, and the presence of electoral thresholds. Overall, there has been a remarkable convergence toward *moderately disproportional* electoral systems across the region:[21] most countries have introduced PR systems, most countries prefer the more restrictive electoral formulas (d'Hondt and Hagenbach-Bischoff methods), and nearly all have electoral thresholds. In Serbia, Montenegro, Kosovo, Moldova, and Slovakia the whole country is one constituency, while the rest vary from five or six big election districts (Latvia, Macedonia) to many small districts (Bulgaria).

As per 2008, three countries had mixed systems: Hungary, Lithuania, and Albania.[22] The Hungarian system is the most complicated, and also the most unforgiving: 176 MPs are elected by majority vote in single-member districts, 152 MPs are elected in 20 multi-member districts, and the last 58 are national compensatory seats. Because the majoritarian part and the PR part of the system are separate, the Hungarian and the Lithuanian systems favor large parties. In Albania, the two parts of the mixed system were connected, but the effect was similar, because the number of single-member districts was much higher than the number of PR seats (100 seats versus 40). A side effect of this is that all the MPs of the two biggest Albanian parties were elected in single-member districts, while the smaller parties won PR seats. As a result, tactical voting in the PR elections was rampant.[23]

Most major changes in electoral systems took place before the second free elections, and where electoral systems have been changed, movement has been away from the extremes.[24] In the first free or partly free elections about half the countries used the communist electoral system – i.e. majority vote in single-member districts, while Bulgaria and Hungary used mixed systems.[25] Moldova, Croatia, and Macedonia then switched temporarily from majority to mixed

Table 4.2 Electoral system, lower house, 2008

	System	No. of districts	PR district magnitude	Electoral formula in first tier	Electoral formula in second tier	Threshold for parties (%)	Threshold for alliances (%)	Preference voting	Effective parties
Hungary	Mixed	176 20	7.6	Majority, 2 rounds Hagenbach-Bischoff	d'Hondt	5	–	No	2.7
Albania	Mixed	100	40	Plurality	Hare	2.5	4	No	2.9
Lithuania	Mixed	71	70	Majority, 2 rounds	Hare	5	7	Yes	5.2
Moldova	PR	1	101	d'Hondt	–	6	9–12	No	2.5
Montenegro[a]	PR	1	81	d'Hondt	–	3	–	No	2.7
Macedonia	PR	6	20.0	d'Hondt	–	–	–	No	3.2
Bulgaria	PR	31	7.7	d'Hondt	–	4	–	No	3.4
Poland	PR	41	11.2	d'Hondt	–	5	8	Yes	3.5
Czech Republic	PR	14	14.3	d'Hondt	–	5	10–20	Yes	3.5
Croatia[a]	PR	10	15.3	d'Hondt	–	5	–	No	3.5
Romania[a]	PR	42	7.9	Hare	d'Hondt	5	8–10	No	3.5
Serbia	PR	1	250	d'Hondt	–	5	–	No	4.3
Slovenia[a]	PR	8	11.3	Droop	d'Hondt	4	–	Yes	4.7
Kosovo[a]	PR	1	120	Hare	–	–	–	No	4.8
Estonia	PR	11	9.2	Hare	Mod. d'Hondt	5	(Illegal)	Yes	4.9
Slovakia	PR	1	150	Hagenbach-Bischoff	–	5	7–10	Yes	5.2
Latvia	PR	5	20.0	St. Laguë	–	5	–	Yes	5.5
Bosnia and Herzegovina	PR	8	5.3	St. Laguë	–	3	–	Yes	6.4

Notes:
Effective parliamentary parties in the latest three elections prior to 1 January 2009. Own calculations, based on the Laakso–Taagepera index.

[a]Romania: 18 seats reserved for minorities. Croatia: 8 minority seats. Slovenia: 2 minority seats. Kosovo: 20 minority seats, of these 10 to Serbs. Montenegro: 5 seats reserved for Albanian minority.

Details on the 2008 Romanian election law were not available in English at the time of writing. The information in table 4.2 is based on the 2004 election law. The new election system is nominally a mixed system, but the effect is highly proportional for the parties that cross the threshold. The forty-two counties are divided into single-member districts, and candidates that win more than 50% of the votes in their district are elected, provided that their party crosses the electoral threshold. Seats that are not distributed this way are proportionally divided; if necessary additional seats are allocated. As before, national minorities are awarded 18 seats.

Source: Election laws accessed through the World Law Guide *Lexadin* at www.lexadin.nl/wlg/

systems, but by the turn of the century all three had switched to PR systems. At the other end of the scale, countries with extremely proportional systems changed the electoral formulas and/or raised the electoral threshold. The most glaring example of a (too) proportional system was the one used in the 1991 Polish election, which led to the "too-many-party-system" of 29 parties.[26]

Electoral laws have been disputed in several countries. In Poland, the governing parties have altered the election law back and forth several times. In Slovakia, the opposition changed the new higher threshold for alliances (5% per party) back after winning the 1998 election. In the Czech Republic, the Constitutional Court stopped an electoral law that was judged to have more disproportional effects than the British first-past-the-post system.[27] There were also complaints that the Croatian Democratic Union (HDZ) had manipulated the election laws to maximize votes. In Macedonia, the Internal Macedonian Revolutionary Organization–the Democratic Party of Macedonian National Unity (VMRO–DPMNE) boycotted the second round of the 1994 elections because it did not feel it had a fair chance under the existing majoritarian system. In Albania, first the ex-communists, and then the Democratic Party boycotted the parliament in the 1996–2002 period; and in Serbia, four opposition parties boycotted the 1997 elections because of a new election law that increased the number of constituencies from 9 to 29, drastically reducing district magnitude.[28]

It is perhaps not very surprising that the countries with the least proportional electoral systems also have the least fragmented party systems, measured in effective parties, and vice versa (see table 4.2), or that countries with large national minorities have more fragmented party systems. However, because electoral alliances are counted as one, the number of effective parties can be deceptive. In the latest elections prior to 1 January 2009, electoral alliances won seats in every country but the Czech Republic, Estonia,[29] and Slovakia. The real number of parties is therefore much higher than the number of effective parties might suggest, especially in Bulgaria and Macedonia; on the other hand, electoral alliances often also cooperate politically.

Party system development in Central and Eastern Europe: an overview

Traditionally, approaches to party system development have been deeply rooted in West European experiences, with emphasis on institutions, cleavages, and civil society.[30] In the old democracies of Western Europe, party systems evolved gradually and "froze" along the cleavages that prevailed when the electoral system was adopted. According to Stein Rokkan, four main cleavages shaped party system development in Western Europe: class conflicts, urban–rural, church–state, and center–periphery conflicts. The relationship among the latter three cleavages accounts for differences among countries, while class conflict explains convergence.[31] It was the latter conflict that produced the left–right dimension that has dominated in many European countries. In contrast to the old democracies in Western Europe, parties in post-communist Central and Eastern Europe emerged in a situation of "instant democracy": universal suffrage was long established and the population fully mobilized when the erstwhile one-party systems opened up to political competition among elites in the early 1990s. The prognosis for early party system stabilization was not good: civil society was underdeveloped, mobilization along traditional cleavages had been discouraged during communism, and scholars expected institutions to be unstable.[32]

Despite their weak civil societies, however, post-communist societies were not akin to a *tabula rasa*,[33] and party system development did not start from scratch. First, although communist regimes had transformed Central and Eastern Europe from peasant societies to urbanized industrial societies, they did not eradicate all historical cleavages. On the contrary, federalization probably helped institutionalize national conflicts in the Soviet Union, in Czechoslovakia after 1968, and especially in Yugoslavia after 1974. Ethnic, religious, and regional cleavages survived the communist regimes, and socio-economic conflicts between the "winners" and "losers" of the economic transition (re-)surfaced. Second, in every country, some parties and movements had a head start. Former regime parties profited from experienced elites, large memberships, newspapers, office facilities, and other property. The popular fronts and forums had superior democratic legitimacy, but initially lacked everything else – from experienced elites to typewriters. The former parties had to come to terms with their past; the latter had to form political platforms and party organizations – and both had to connect to their country's main conflict axis.[34]

Let us first look at the point of departure: who were the players in the various countries' founding elections, and who won? The main issue in the first free elections was of course the transition to democracy, and the main contestants were therefore the former regime parties and opposition movements. Parties formed outside the umbrella movements were successful insofar as they appealed to specific constituencies, such as ethnic minorities or religious groups. In Central Europe, broad *democratic opposition movements* won the founding elections. In Poland, Solidarity won all the contested seats bar one in the first partly free elections in 1989; in Czechoslovakia, Civic Forum and the Public Against Violence triumphed; and in Slovenia, the six-party alliance DEMOS. In Hungary, the Opposition Roundtable broke up before the first free elections in 1990, and the Hungarian Democratic Forum (MDF) became the largest party. In contrast, *communist successor parties* won the first free elections in Albania, Romania, and Bulgaria. In Romania and Bulgaria, the transition to democracy had been orchestrated by communist elites, and the successor parties (the National Salvation Front and the BSP) reaped the benefits in the 1990 elections. The Albanian communists also won the first free elections in 1991, but had to agree to early elections after only a few months.

In the Baltic states, Moldova, and the Yugoslav republics, national independence was a second salient issue besides the transition. In the Baltic states and

Moldova, the popular fronts combined the struggle for democracy with the struggle for independence, and the opposition was therefore democratic *and* national. Former communists split over the question of independence, and the national communists sided with the opposition against Moscow loyalists. The 1990 elections to the republican Supreme Soviets were won by the popular fronts *Rahvarinne* in Estonia, *Tautas Fronte* in Latvia, and *Sąjūdis* in Lithuania. In Moldova, only 101 of the 380 Supreme Soviet deputies were elected on the *Frontul Popular* ballot, but a majority nevertheless supported the Popular Front.[35]

In contrast to Czechoslovakia and the Soviet Union, Yugoslavia never held any democratic elections at the federal level. Under the 1974 constitution, the Yugoslav federal National Parliament (Skupština) was elected through a complicated indirect delegate system,[36] and when the League of Communists fell apart at the 1990 party congress, no Yugoslav institution was strong enough to impose federal elections. In the 1990 elections to the *republican* parliaments, the national question overshadowed the democratic transition everywhere but in Slovenia, and the party or parties that emerged as the main champion of national interests triumphed. In Serbia and Montenegro, the parties in question were ex-communist: the Serbian Socialist Party (SPS) and Montenegro's Democratic Party of Socialists (DPS).[37] In Croatia, the national dissident HDZ won, while opposition parties representing Bosniaks, Serbs, and Croats did best in Bosnia: the (Muslim) Party of Democratic Action (SDA), the Serbian Democratic Party (SDS), and the HDZ. In Macedonia, the VMRO–DPMNE became the largest party, but the government went to the former communists, because of the VMRO–DPMNE's inability or unwillingness to form a coalition with any Albanian party.

By the second democratic elections, a majority of the countries had adopted a democratic constitution, and the three Baltic states, Moldova, and all the Yugoslav Republics but Serbia and Montenegro had become independent states. In Czechoslovakia, independence had not been on the agenda in 1990, but disagreement between the Czech and Slovak winners of the 1992 elections – on the future state form as well as on the tempo of the economic reform – led to the "Velvet Divorce" in 1993. The national question remained salient until the mid-1990s in Estonia and Latvia because of conflicts over citizenship laws, and in the former Yugoslav republics even longer due to the War of Yugoslav Succession. Moreover, conflicts over the "the rules of the game" lingered on. In Slovakia, Croatia, and Serbia the autocratic behavior of the "strongman" leaders – Vladimír Mečiar, Franjo Tudjman, and Slobodan Milošević – led to broad "rainbow coalitions" against them; these coalitions succeeded in ousting Mečiar and Milošević in 1998 and 2000, respectively, while Tudjman's party lost to the opposition in 2000, right after his death. In Romania, Ion Iliescu and the reform communists who had staged the coup against Nicolae Ceaușescu lost against a broad electoral alliance in 1996.

Although some countries lagged behind, by the mid-1990s "stateness" issues and conflicts over the rules of the game had started to fade, and other cleavages gradually took over. First, the effects of the economic reforms started to become noticeable in the early to mid-1990s; post-communist societies saw a sharp decrease in industrial production, Gross Domestic Product (GDP), and exports, and a sharp rise in unemployment and inflation, while wages and pensions lagged behind. Over time, income inequality between the haves and the have-nots increased, strengthening the salience of the socio-economic left–right divide. At the same time, however, the economic crisis hurt government parties all over the region, as the voters tended to vote them out of office. Second, older cleavages came to the fore: countries with national minorities have national minority parties, and Catholic countries have Christian democratic or clerical parties. Territorial or regional divides affect voter behavior, but have not produced many stable parties. In contrast, post-materialism[38] does not seem to be a very salient cleavage, as Green parties have had trouble crossing the electoral threshold.

Let us now turn to the question of party system stabilization. First and foremost, this is a matter of structured competition,[39] but also of reasonably stable party organizations, both of which can be compatible with substantial electoral volatility. At first, the most pessimistic forecasts seemed to be confirmed. The breakup of the opposition movements, usually between the first and second election, led to the emergence of a host of new parties, as did in some cases rifts between communist hardliners and their more reform oriented comrades. New, often short-lived parties (dubbed "divan parties" or "taxi parties" due to the size of their membership), also emerged. Electoral volatility was skyrocketing, especially in the Baltic states, and MP turnover was high everywhere. Anecdotal evidence, later corroborated by more systematic research, showed that MPs wandered between parliamentary caucuses and candidates between party lists like "political nomads."[40]

However, a closer look reveals that many of the early signs of instability have subsided: the tide of new parties has ebbed; the direction of competition has stabilized – in many countries along a left–right dimension; electoral volatility is down – in Hungary and the Czech Republic to West European levels; and as Nick Sitter and I have demonstrated elsewhere, a great majority of the MPs who get re-elected in Central Europe get re-elected for the same party.[41] Rather than looking at the rapid changes in the early 1990s as signs of perpetual party system instability, we should understand this as a restructuring phase, during which diffuse movements gave way to ideologically more cohesive parties, ideologically adjacent parties merged, internally divided parties fought out their differences (sometimes leading to ideological shifts), and party competition changed direction away from the initial pro- and anti-regime pattern. Yet, in cases where broad electoral alliances were formed to oust incumbent elites, as in Poland in 1997 and Slovakia in 1998, the party systems went through a second restructuring phase.

Seen in retrospect, there is surprisingly strong continuity between the parties and movements that emerged during the transition and the present party

Table 4.3 Party stability, 2008 (%)

	Seats 2008		Seats 2008		Seats 2008		Seats 2008
Czech Republic	100.0	Slovenia	87.8	Estonia	57.4	Slovakia	46.0
Hungary	100.0	Albania	80.7	Lithuania	57.4	Poland	18.5
Romania	93.4	Macedonia	75.0	Bulgaria	56.7		
Serbia	92.0	Moldova	66.3	Bosnia and Herzegovina	50.0		
Croatia	90.2	Latvia	59.0	Montenegro	49.4		

Notes:
Table 4.3 shows the percentage of seats won in last elections before 1 January 2009, by parties that had won seats in parliament by the second democratic election. Own calculations. (Kosovo had its first democratic elections in 1997, and is omitted.)

system: in every country, several parliamentary parties have a pedigree that goes back to the early 1990s. In Hungary and the Czech Republic this goes for *all* the parties. Moreover, in a majority of the countries, the largest party is a long-standing party. The exceptions are the People's Party (TP) in Latvia (founded in 1998), the social democratic *Smer*–SD in Slovakia (1999), and the Civic Platform in Poland (2001). However, in several countries new parties have had instant success also after the turn of the century, and the frequent electoral alliances, many of which are "marriages of convenience," are tell-tale signs of unfinished restructuring processes. In Bulgaria, the National Movement Simeon II rose to prominence in only a few weeks before the 2001 election, New Era became the largest party in Latvia in 2002, Res Publica became the second-largest party in Estonia in 2003, and the National Resurrection Party in Lithuania in 2008. In Poland, the two largest parties today – the Civic Platform and Law and Justice – were founded in 2001, admittedly by post-Solidarity elites. This, together with the collapse of the ex-communist party, explains the low percentage of seats won by long-standing parties in Poland (table 4.3).

Party families and origins

The question is then whether Central and East European parties are *sui generis* or belong to recognizable party families. While some parties are admittedly more difficult to categorize than others, most parties fit into the party families defined by Budge *et al.* (socialist, Christian democratic, agrarian, liberal, conservative, "new politics" (i.e. Green), and ethnic/regional/nationalist) and all party families are represented in the region, albeit not in every country.[42] Leftist and center-right parties are the strongest and most numerous, while "third" parties (agrarian, Green, ethnic/regional, and nationalist) are more unevenly distributed. However, while there is a growing body of literature on ex-communist and/or leftist parties,[43] the (center-)right has received less scholarly attention.[44] Following Hanley, I focus mainly on the conservative or liberal parties that "define themselves as (center-) right formations and have been accepted into the main organizations of the European center-right."[45]

Trajectories of the left

Despite the negative association with communism, the "left" was there for the taking for the former communist parties in the early 1990s. Some of the most successful social democratic parties in the region originated in former regime parties, as did a handful of left socialist or communist parties. As a group, leftist parties exhibit the strongest continuity and are by far the most stable of the party families. Two former communist regime parties have retained an orthodox platform and survived as politically relevant parties: the Czech Communist Party (KSČM) and the Moldovan Communist Party (PCRM). The former is politically isolated but has maintained a medium-sized following since the velvet revolution; the latter was re-established after Moldova's ban on communist parties was lifted in 1993 and has been the governing party since 2001.[46] The only other orthodox party to ever win representation is the Slovak Communist Party (KSS), a party formed by former hardliners in 1991.

Insofar as former regime parties reformed and adopted a social democratic platform, they won easy victories over historical social democratic parties in the bid for the left. The Hungarian Communist Party was the first to adopt a social democratic platform, in October 1989, followed by the Lithuanian party in December, and the Polish party in January 1990. All three returned to power in the early 1990s. It is an open question to what extent the Albanian, Romanian, Bulgarian, and Montenegrin ex-communists had reformed when they won the first free elections, and the same can be said about the Macedonian party. However, all these parties have joined the Party of European Socialists (PES) and/or the Socialist International, and can today be regarded as social democratic parties. Less successful, albeit middle-sized, were the ex-communists in Slovakia, Slovenia, and Croatia; however, their fate diverged dramatically after the turn of the millennium: while the Croatian and the Slovenian social democrats won the elections in 2000 and 2008, respectively, the Slovak Democratic Left Party (SDL′) collapsed in 2002. Least successful were the Estonian and Latvian ex-communist parties; they entered the parliament only once, as parts of electoral alliances.

Historical social democratic parties emerged in many countries, but were successful only in two cases: the Czech Social Democrats (ČSSD) and the Serbian Democratic Party (DS). Both parties could make a bid for the social democratic political space without having to compete with reformed

Table 4.4 Leftist parties in Central and Eastern Europe, by ideology and origin, 2008

		Social democratic		
	Communist/left socialist	Ex-communist	Historical	Other
Estonia			SDE	
Latvia	LSP[a]	(LSDSP, merger 1999)		TSP[a]
Lithuania		**LSDP** (merger 2001)		
Poland		**SLD**		(UP)
Czech Republic	KSČM		**ČSSD**	
Slovakia	(KSS)	[SDL′]		***Smer–SD***
Hungary		**MSzP**		
Slovenia		**SD** (merger 1993)		
Croatia		**SDP** (merger 1994)		
Bosnia and Herzegovina		SDP (multiethnic)	SNSD (Serbian)	
Serbia	**SPS**		**DS**	
Montenegro	SNP (pro-Serbian)	**DPS**		
Macedonia		**SDSM**		NSDP
Albania		**PSSH**		PSDSH, LSI
Moldova	**PCRM**			
Romania		**PSD** (merger 2001)		
Bulgaria		**BSP**		

Notes:
[a]Pro-Russian. Ran together in the Harmony Center alliance in the 2006 election.

Parties in parentheses are not in parliament as per 2008, but have received over 5% of the votes in at least one previous election. Parties in square brackets are defunct. Parties that have received more than 20% of the votes in any election are in **bold**.

ex-communists, as the Czech former regime party KSČM remained orthodox, while Slobodan Milošević's Serbian Socialist Party (SPS) combined left-wing socialism with Serbian nationalism. The ČSSD was able to present itself as the major alternative to the center-right coalition in the run-up to the 1996 Czech election, and has been the dominant party on the left since. The DS came to the fore as a part of the Democratic Opposition of Serbia (DOS) which ousted Milošević in the 2000 elections, and has presented itself as a more pro-Western and less nationalist leftist alternative to the SPS. In addition to these two, the Estonian Social Democrats (SDE) admittedly did quite well in their first European Parliament election, after the name change in 2004.

The emergence of separate ex-communist and historical social democratic parties was, to begin with, contingent on the regime cleavage, and once this cleavage started to fade, ex-communist and historical social democratic parties began to merge, first in Slovenia, then in Croatia, Latvia, Lithuania, and Romania. In the Baltic states, merger was preceded by electoral alliances. Such electoral alliances are quite common: in Montenegro the ex-communist party DPS has formed alliances with the miniscule Social Democratic Party of Montenegro (SDP). In Bulgaria, the ex-communist BSP formed the Coalition for Bulgaria with the historical social democrats (and other small parties).[47] And in Poland, the Alliance of the Democratic Left (SLD), itself a merger of the ex-communist party and various regime organizations, allied with small social democratic parties twice.

Nearly all the successful leftist parties are ex-communist or historical social democrats; however, the Slovak social democratic party *Smer*–SD is an exception. *Smer* (Direction) originated as a rather populist centrist party in 1999, and owed much of its initial success to its charismatic founder and chairman Robert Fico.[48] Fico started his career in the ex-communist SDL′, and when his old party fell below the threshold in 2002, Fico moved to fill the social democratic void, presenting *Smer* as the major alternative to the center-right coalition in the run-up to the 2006 elections. *Smer* adopted a social democratic platform, added "social democrats" to its name, joined the PES, and merged with several small social democratic parties (including the ex-communist SDL′ and the historical SDSS).[49]

Liberal and conservative parties

Since post-regime parties in many countries defined the left, the anti-communist opposition often came to define the right and the center-right – with one major exception: Vladimír Mečiar's Movement for a Democratic Slovakia (HZDS).[50] In contrast to the left, most center-right parties in the region are recent formations, and ideologically they combine anti-communism with liberalism or conservatism.[51] However, the exact mix varies over time and across the region, and the parties are therefore not always easy to categorize. When in doubt I have placed market liberal ELDR members in the liberal category, and market liberal EPP members in the liberal conservative category (table 4.5). Overall, conservative parties seem to do better than liberal parties, and the largest post-opposition party is in most cases national conservative. Especially in the early 1990s, liberal conservative parties were few and far between: conservatism in post-communist Europe in 1990 had more in common with the conservatism of the inter-war period, with its strong emphasis on religion and national values, than with the market liberal conservatism of contemporary West European parties.[52]

The region's strongest and most stable *liberal* party in the 1990s was Slovenia's Liberal Democracy (LDS), with showings over 20%, and, until 2004, the kingpin of most Slovenian governments. However, the party collapsed in the 2008 election, after the social liberal wing split off to form *Zares*

Table 4.5 Liberal and conservative parties in Central and Eastern Europe, 2008

		Conservative parties (in EPP)		
	Liberal parties (in ELDR)	Liberal conservative	National conservative and national clerical	Christian democrats
Estonia	Reform, **Kesk**		**Pro Patria and Res Publica**	
Latvia	**[Latvia's Way]**[a]	**JL**	**TP**, *TB/LNNK*	*[LPP]*[a]
Lithuania	NS–S, LiCS, LRLS		**TS–LKD**	[LKD]
Poland	UD/UW/PD	**PO**	***PiS***, *(LPR)*, [**AWS**]	
Czech Republic		***ODS***		KDU–ČSL
Slovakia	(ANO)	SDKÚ		KDH
Hungary	**SZDSZ**		**Fidesz**, **MDF**	KDNP[b]
Slovenia	**LDS**, Zares		**SDS**	(NSi), SLS
Croatia	HSLS, *HNS*		**HDZ**	
Bosnia and Herzegovina	*SBiH*		**SDA**, HDZ, PDP	
Serbia	*LDP*	G17+	DSS	
Montenegro		*PzP*	*NS* (historical)	
Macedonia	LDP, LPM		**VMRO–DPMNE**	
Albania			**PD**	
Moldova	**AMN**			PPCD
Romania	**PNL**	**PD–L**	PUR/PC	PNŢCD
Bulgaria	**NDSV**		**SDS**, DSB, DP	

Notes:
[a]Latvia's Way and Latvia's First Party ran together in 2006, and later merged into one party.
[b]KDNP ran on the Fidesz list in the 2006 election.

Not in EPP/ELDR in *italics*.
Parties in parentheses are not in parliament as per 2008, but have received over 5% of the votes in at least one previous election. Parties in square brackets are defunct. Parties that have received more than 20% of the votes in any election are in **bold**. Some small parties are omitted.

(Party For Real–New Politics) in 2007. The LDS is also unique in that it originated in part in a former regime organization – the Slovenian communist youth movement. In contrast, the less successful liberal parties in the Visegrád countries grew out of the democratic opposition. In the Czech Republic and Slovakia, they failed to cross the threshold in the second election; in Hungary, the Free Democrats (SzDSz) have barely managed to stay in parliament since the flop in 1998; and in Poland, Solidarity's liberal wing fell below the threshold in 2001, after the market liberals left the party.

In the Baltic states, liberalism has been strongest in Estonia, where the market liberal Estonian Reform Party and the social liberal Center Party (Kesk) together polled more than 50% in the 2007 election. In Lithuania the liberals are presently divided among three small parties: the Liberal Movement of the Republic of Lithuania (LRLS), the Liberal and Center Union (LiCS), and the New Union – social liberals (NS–S). In Latvia, the downfall of Latvia's Way, the successor to *Tautas Fronte*, culminated in its merger with Latvia's First Party (LPP) after the 2006 election.

The strongest liberal party in the Balkans in the mid-2000s was the Bulgarian National Movement for Stability and Progress (NDSV), until 2007 known as the National Movement Simeon II. This was the party of the deposed tsar of Bulgaria, Simeon Borisov Sakskoburggotski (English: Saxe-Coburg-Gotha).[53] Other fairly successful parties after the turn of the century were the Party Alliance Our Moldova (AMN), a 2003 merger of several center-left parties, and the Romanian National Liberal Party (PNL), which was the largest party in the victorious Justice and Truth Alliance in the 2004 elections. However, most liberal parties in the Balkans are small, including the Croatian People's Party–Liberal Democrats (HNS), the Croatian Social Liberal Party (HSLS) and the two Macedonian liberal parties, the Liberal Democratic Party (LDP) and the Liberal Party of Macedonia (LPM). The two latter ran in the Coalition for Europe, led by the ex-communist SDSM, in 2008. The PNL and the HNS are the only examples of *historical* liberal parties.

A majority of the region's strongest and most numerous *conservative* parties are *national conservative* – i.e. culturally conservative and nationally oriented. (The *national clerical* parties in Poland are in addition strictly against abortion, same-sex marriages etc.). Several of these parties originated in the umbrella movements or took part in them, and therefore have a pedigree back to the early 1990s. In the Baltic states, the people's fronts disintegrated into various ideological factions, and the national conservative party later merged with other ideologically similar parties. Examples are the Estonian Pro Patria and Res Publica, the Latvian Union for Fatherland and Freedom (TB/LNNK), and the Homeland Union – Lithuanian Christian Democrats (TS–LKD). The Bulgarian umbrella movement, the Union of Democratic Forces (SDS), was originally an alliance of eleven parties, but merged into one party in 1997. In the meantime, the Democratic Party (DP), also a national conservative party, had left the alliance. The third Bulgarian national conservative party, Democrats for a strong Bulgaria (DSB), was a 2003 splinter from the SDS.

Of the Central European countries, only Hungary has national conservative post-forum parties: the MDF, and the Alliance of Young Democrats (Fidesz). The latter party started out as a liberal party, but turned right around 1995. Likewise, the once liberal Romanian Humanist Party (PUR) turned right in 2005 and became the Romanian Conservative Party (PC). The Slovenian Democratic Party (SDS, formerly the Slovenian Social Democratic Party) originated in two of the parties in DEMOS, the Slovenian umbrella. Three of the present national conservative parties in other former Yugoslav Republics were more nationalist in the early 1990s: the HDZ, the Democratic Party of Serbia (DSS), and the VMRO–DPMNE. Of these, only the DSS ran as part of an umbrella movement (DEPOS). In contrast, the Party of Democratic Action (SDA) in Bosnia stressed Bosnia's multi-ethnic nature.[54] The PD in Albania was the first opposition party (1990), and has been the strongest party in Albania besides the ex-communist party.

In Poland, the national clerical parties have roots in the Solidarity movement. Unlike the liberal wing, Solidarity's national clerical wing divided into a number of small parties, most of which failed to cross the 5% threshold in 1993. They then united in the Solidarity Election Action (AWS) in 1997. The present national clerical parties, the Law and Justice (PiS) and the League of Polish Families (LPR, now below the threshold), were both formed in 2001 by AWS elites.

Christian democratic parties in the region are small or medium-sized, and as a group they were stronger in the early 1990s than today. They are largely confined to Catholic countries, and more conservative religiously than the German party. Most of the present parties were separately organized before the first free elections;[55] of these, three were historical parties – the Christian Democratic People's Party (KDNP) in Hungary, the Christian Democratic National Peasants' Party (PNȚCD) in Romania, and the Slovenian People's Party (SLS). The Christian Democratic Movement (KDH) in Slovakia was based on Catholic dissidents, while the Christian Democratic Union – Czechoslovak People's Party (KDU–ČSL) in the Czech Republic originated in a satellite party. The only party that grew out of an umbrella movement is the Christian Democratic People's Party in Moldova. Of the recent parties, Latvia's First Party is defunct and New Slovenia is no big success.

Classical conservative parties of the British or Nordic type were initially few. The Czech Civic Democratic Party (ODS) is the only long-standing liberal-conservative party, and also the most successful of the parties originating in broad opposition movements. (It is a member of the European Democrat Union, but not of the EPP.) All other liberal-conservative parties were founded after the turn of the millennium, except the Romanian Democratic Party (or the Democratic Liberal Party, PD–L, from 2008), a formerly social democratic party that turned right in 2004. The Civic Platform in Poland and the Slovak Democratic and Christian Union both emerged after unsuccessful attempts at merging broad electoral alliances into parties. The G17+ in Serbia and the Movement for Changes (PzP) in Montenegro originated in NGOs staffed by economic experts (the latter was inspired by the former), while the New Era in Latvia[56] ran on a market liberal and anti-corruption platform in 2002.

"Third" parties: agrarian, Green, ethnic, and nationalist

The presence of "third" parties – parties that neither are socialist nor belong to the moderate center-right – differs across the region. Ethnic and nationalist parties thrive on national conflicts between the "state-nation" and the national minorities, while agrarian parties depend on a sizable peasant population. Unlike the left and the center-right, most "third" parties are not members of European parties. The exceptions are three Agrarian parties (the PSL, the HSS, and the BZNS) and three minority parties (the Hungarians in Slovakia, Serbia, and Romania) in the EPP, and three minority parties in the ELDR (the IDS, the Greeks in Albania, and the Turks in Bulgaria).

Most "third" parties originated outside the umbrella movements and regime parties, and most are small or medium-sized. Exceptions are the Movement for a Democratic Slovakia (HZDS), Slovakia's largest party until the 2006 election, and the Moldovan Democratic Agrarian Party (PDAM), the winner of the 1994 Moldovan election. The HZDS originated in the Public Against Violence, but unlike other successful post-forum parties, it remains ideologically diffuse, and cannot be characterized as "rightist" in any conventional sense. It was left-of-center in economic policies, came out as the main champion of Slovak national interests in the 1992 election, and formed governments with other national populist and left-leaning parties until 1998. At the 2000 party congress, the HZDS tried to re-brand itself as a center-right party,[57] only to return to power as a part of Fico's social democratic government in 2006.

Most of the countries were peasant societies with strong *agrarian* parties in the interwar period; but the collectivization of agriculture ruined these parties' potential – except in Poland, where collectivization was reversed. Five of the agrarian parties hark back to historical parties: the Latvian Farmers' Union (LZS), the Polish Peasant Party (PSL), the Hungarian Smallholders' Party (FKgP), the Croatian Peasant Party (HSS), and the Bulgarian Agrarian People's Union (BZNS).[58] Of these, the Polish PSL – also a former satellite party – is the most stable. (The other Polish agrarian party, Self-defense (Samoobrona), crossed the electoral threshold only in 2001 and 2005). The Hungarian party was a medium-sized party in the 1990s, but fell below the threshold in 2002 after factional struggles. The other historical peasants' parties have often entered parliament through alliances, but the Croatian party is the only one with continuous representation. Two agrarian parties were formed by reform communists and dominated by collective farm managers: the PDAM, and the Estonian People's Party (Rahvaliit, formerly called EME), a medium-sized party since the name change in 1999. Finally, the Lithuanian Peasant Popular Union (LVLS) was a 2006 merger of the small Lithuanian Peasants' Party and the New Democratic Party.

Despite the fact that the Green movement was a part of the democratic opposition to communism in several countries, including the Baltic states, Moldova, and Slovakia, *Green parties* have generally been weak.[59] The Greens were admittedly represented in Slovenia in 1990, but entered the Czech and Estonian parliaments on their own only in 2006 and 2007, respectively. In addition, the Latvian Greens are represented in an alliance with the Farmers'

Table 4.6 Third parties in Central and Eastern Europe: agrarian, Green, ethnic, nationalist, 2008.

	Agrarian and Green parties	Ethnic minority parties	Nationalist parties	Other
Estonia	Greens, Rahvaliit	(MKOE, EÜRP)		(Royalists)
Latvia	LZS, Greens	PCTVL		(Siegerist)
Lithuania	LVLS	AWPL		DP, LDP
Poland	*PSL*, (Samoobrona)	German Minority		(PPPP)
Czech Republic	Greens	(HSD–SMS, regional)	(Republicans)	
Slovakia		*Hungarian Coalition Party*	SNS	**HZDS**
Hungary	(FKgP)		(MIÉP)	
Slovenia		+[a]	SNS	DeSUS
Croatia	*HSS*	*IDS* (regional) +[a]	HSP	HSU
Bosnia and Herzegovina			**SDS** (Serbian)	
Serbia		*Alliance of Vojvodina Hungarians*	**SRS**, New Serbia	
Montenegro		Serbian list +[a]		
Macedonia		BDI, [PPD], PDS		
Albania	PAA	*Unity for Human Rights*	National front	
Moldova	**(PDAM)**	(Unitate–Edinstvo)		
Romania		*Hungarian Democratic Union* +[a]	(PRM)	
Bulgaria	*BZNS* (3 parties)	*Movement for Rights and Freedoms*	Ataka, VMRO	**GERB**

Notes:
[a]Seats reserved for minorities – see table 4.2.

Parties in parentheses are not in parliament as per 2008, but have received over 5% of the votes in at least one previous election. Parties in brackets are defunct. Parties that have received more than 20% of the votes in any election are in **bold**. Parties in ELDR or EPP are in *italics*. Table 4.6 is not exhaustive.

Union. The small Environmental Agrarian Party in Albania (PAA), adopted its present name in 2003 and is Green *and* agrarian.

Seen in retrospect, *nationalist* parties have been less successful than many scholars feared in the early 1990s, but they have maintained a presence in countries with sizable minorities, and they have played a part in party system development in many countries. Nationalist parties are anti-Semitic, anti-Roma, anti-minority, and in some cases even irredentist. Parties claiming to defend the interests of the "state-nation' have been strongest in Serbia and the Republika Srpska (in Bosnia): In Serbia, the Serbian Radical Party (SRS), a Greater Serbian party with roots in the Chetnik movement during the Second

World War, won the 2003 and 2007 elections, and in Republika Srpska the SDS was largest until 2006. Historical parties are the medium-sized Croatian Party of Right (HSP) and the Slovak and Slovenian National Party (SNS), both left-leaning in economic policies; and the smaller Internal Macedonian Revolutionary Organization (VMRO) in Bulgaria, which sees the Macedonians as Bulgarians. Irredentist parties besides the Bulgarian VMRO are the Greater Romania Party (PRM), the Albanian National Front, the Hungarian Justice and Life Party (MIÉP), and before 1993, even the Czech Republicans, who wanted to re-unite Czechoslovakia with sub-Carpathian Ruthenia in order to revive Czechoslovakia within its pre-1938 borders.

Ethnic minority parties have the most stable electoral base, provided that the minority's share of the population exceeds the electoral threshold (or minorities are exempt). The Hungarians in Slovakia and Romania have chosen the ethnic "interest group" strategy with great success: the size of both parties roughly corresponds to the Hungarian share of the population. Other examples of small, but fairly stable ethnic minority parties are the Alliance of Hungarians in Vojvodina (Serbia), the German Minority in Poland, and the Election Action of Poles in Lithuania (AWPL). Macedonia is the only country where an ethnic minority (the Albanians) is large enough to form its own party system. In contrast, the Turks in Bulgaria and Russian minorities in former Soviet Republics have chosen the "human rights" strategy. The prime example is the Movement for Rights and Freedoms in Bulgaria; in Latvia, For Human Rights in a United Latvia (PCTVL) is a current example; and in Albania, the Unity for Human Rights is a small, but stable party that serves the Greek minority. (By contrast, Russian voters in Estonia and Moldova have apparently started to support mainstream parties.) Finally, in the Czech Republic and Croatia, *regionalist* parties have won seats; in the Czech Republic only in the early 1990s. In contrast the Istrian Democratic Assembly (IDS) is small but fairly stable. Most major ethnic parties are centrist, and they cooperate to the left as well as to the right.

As for "others" in table 4.6 above, two are pensioners' parties, the Slovenian DeSUS and the Croatian HSU. (Equivalent parties in the Czech Republic and Poland have not been able to cross the threshold.) The rest are examples of parties that do not fit easily into European party families. The most curious is perhaps the Polish Beer Lovers' Party (PPPP), which won 16 seats in the 1991 Sejm. Otherwise, many of the parties in this category are political "one-man-shows," often short-lived parties that are founded to propel their leader(s) into office. There are several examples of this in Slovakia (not in table 4.6): the Party of Civic Understanding (SOP) helped Rudolf Schuster get elected president in 1999, the Alliance for the New Citizen (ANO) served as a vehicle for Pavol Rusko, and *Smer* was the creation of Robert Fico (only the latter made a successful transition to a "normal" party). In Latvia, the German *Bild* journalist Joachim Siegerist founded the People's Union for Latvia (Siegerist party), and in Lithuania, the Russian-born millionaire Viktor Uspaskich founded the Labor Party. The most recent example of a political one-man-show is the Citizens for a European Development of Bulgaria (GERB), founded in 2006 by Sofia's mayor Bojko Borisov, which won the 2007 and the 2009 elections to the European Parliament as well as the latest national election in 2009. The party became member of the EPP in 2008.

Concluding remarks

Party system stabilization is the product of two factors: first, the political party and, second, the patterns of interaction between parties and their competition for executive office. There is surprisingly strong continuity between the *parties* that are represented in parliament as of 2008 and parties that had made it into parliament by the second democratic election. Even in Poland, where the two largest parties were founded in 2001, the elites came from various small post-Solidarity parties. Many of the survivors are former regime parties and parties that originated in broad opposition movements. However, the main *direction of competition* changed at least once in every country, usually from the regime cleavage of the early 1990s, to some variety of left–right competition, except in the former Yugoslav Republics where the national question dominated party competition in the 1990s. Moreover, all party systems went through restructuring processes, and some still have a way to go: signs of unfinished business are the many electoral alliances and in some countries also the presence of several ideologically similar parties.

Alliances are formed for two reasons: they are formed by small and medium-sized parties in order to ensure parliamentary representation, and by larger parties in the quest for executive office. They are less common in countries with higher electoral thresholds for alliances. Three countries in the Balkans stand out: Bulgaria, Macedonia, and Albania.

Finally, most parties in post-communist Europe did not grow out of independent civil society organizations, but were created top-down. However, this does not seem to have the anticipated effect: there is no obvious link between party system stability and the strength of civil society before *or* after 1989. If anything, the very strength of Solidarity impeded party system stabilization in Poland after 1989. First, the long-standing divide between the regime and Solidarity remained the most salient cleavage in Polish politics for almost two decades after 1989. Second, the post-Solidarity elites kept on squabbling, and were unable to produce viable successor parties until the 2001 election. As former Czech Prime Minister Miloš Zeman dryly remarked with regard to Czech dissidents: "he who is efficient at demolition, is not necessarily efficient at building."[60] The good news is that fairly stable party systems can also develop in the absence of a strong civil society.

Appendix

Appendix table 4A.1 Institutional set-up

Country	Constitution adopted	No of MPs, (senators)	Chambers	Presidential election	Presidential age required (years)	Duration (years)	Suspend. veto
Estonia	1992	101	one	2/3 in parliament	40	5	Yes
Latvia	1991	100	one	51 MPs in parliament	40	4	yes
Lithuania	1992	141	one	Majority vote	40	5	yes
Poland	1997	460 (100)	two	majority vote	35	5	yes
Czech Republic	1992	200 (81)	two	141 MPs in both houses	40	5	yes
Slovakia	1992	150	one	majority vote	35	5	yes
Hungary	1989	386	one	2/3 in parliament	35	5	yes
Slovenia	1991	90 (40)	two	majority vote	–	5	No
Croatia	1990	100–160[a]	one	majority vote	–	5	no
Bosnia and Herzegovina	1994	42 (15)	two	majority vote	–	4	no
Serbia	1990	250	one	majority vote	–	5	yes
Montenegro	1992	81	one	majority vote	–	5	yes
Macedonia	1991	120–140[a]	one	majority vote	40	5	yes
Albania	1998	140	one	3/5 in parliament	40	5	yes
Moldova	1994	101	one	3/5 in parliament	40	4	yes
Romania	1991	332 (137)[a]	two	majority vote	35	5	yes
Bulgaria	1991	240	one	majority vote	40	5	yes

Notes:

[a] The number varies from one election to the next. In Romania, the Chamber of Deputies had 334 seats in 2008.

Notes

* I would like to thank Sabrina Ramet, Nick Sitter, Eva Sárfi, and Kjetil Rå Hauge for valuable comments on an earlier version of this chapter.

1. See, e.g. Peter Mair, *Party System Change: Approaches and Interpretations* (Oxford: Clarendon Press, 1997), Richard Rose, "Mobilizing Demobilized Voters in Post-Communist Societies," *Party Politics*, Vol. 1, No. 4 (July 1995), pp. 549–63; and Herbert Kitschelt, "The Formation of Party Systems in East-Central Europe," *Politics & Society*, Vol. 20, No. 1 (1992), pp. 11–12.
2. Geoffrey Evans, "The Social Bases of Political Divisions in Post-Communist Eastern Europe," *Annual Review of Sociology*, Vol. 32 (August 2006), pp. 245–70, at p. 256.
3. This term was coined by the German scholar Claus Offe. See, e.g. Claus Offe, *Varieties of Transition: The East European and East German experience* (Cambridge: Polity Press, 1996).
4. For a discussion of the various meanings of the term, see Krishan Kumar, "Civil Society: An Inquiry into the Usefulness of an Historical Term," *British Journal of Sociology*, Vol. 44, No. 3 (September 1993), pp. 375–95.
5. Natalia Letki, "Socialization for Participation? Trust, Membership, and Democratization in East-Central Europe," *Political Research Quarterly*, Vol. 57, No. 4 (December 2004), p. 666.
6. Apart from the most obvious examples (Solidarity in Poland and the Hungarian Democratic Forum), G17+ in Serbia and Res Publica in Estonia are examples of parties that grew out of NGOs, but these NGOs were themselves elite clubs rather than mass movements. Most closely affiliated with NGOs are the Green parties, but these parties are generally weak.
7. Janina Frenzel-Zagorska, "Civil Society in Poland and Hungary," *Soviet Studies*, Vol. 42, No. 4 (1990), p. 770.
8. Sabrina P. Ramet, "Democratization in Slovenia – The Second Stage," in Karen Dawisha and Bruce Parrott (eds.), *Politics, Power, and the Struggle for Democracy in South-East Europe* (Cambridge: Cambridge University Press, 1997), pp. 189–225 and Sabrina P. Ramet, *Social Currents in Eastern Europe: The Sources and Consequences of the Great Transformation*, 2nd edn. (Durham, NC: Duke University Press, 1995), pp. 55–151.
9. Jonathan Bach and David Stark, *Technology and Transformation: Facilitating Knowledge Networks in Eastern Europe*, Code: PP-TBS-10 (United Nations Research Institute for Social Development, 2003), p. 9 at www.unrisd.org/80256B3C005BCCF9/(httpPublications)/35352D4B078518C0C1256BDF0049556C?OpenDocument&panel=relatedinformation [accessed on 12 February 2008]. See also Marc Morjé Howard, *The Weakness of Civil Society in Post-Communist Europe* (Cambridge: Cambridge University Press, 2003), pp. 50–1.
10. Martin Potůček, "The Uneasy Birth of Czech Civil Society," *Voluntas: International Journal of Voluntary and Nonprofit Organizations*, Vol. 11, No. 2 (2000), p. 114.
11. Rayna Gavrilova's executive letter, February 2007, "Trust for Civil Society in Central & Eastern Europe," at www.ceetrust.org/index.php?ar=1 [accessed on 12 February 2008].

12. Thomas Poguntke, "Political Parties and other Organizations," in Richard S. Katz and William Crotty (eds), *Handbook of Party Politics* (London: Sage, 2006), pp. 396–405, at p. 401.
13. Howard, *The Weakness of Civil Society*, pp. 6, 57.
14. *Ibid.*, pp. 10, 26–30.
15. See, e.g. André Krouwel, "Party Models," in Katz and Crotty (eds.), *Handbook of Party Politics*, pp. 249–69.
16. Zsolt Enyedi, "Party Politics in Post-Communist Transition," in Katz and Crotty (eds.), pp. 228–38, at p. 234. This lack of close links with voluntary organizations goes for all postwar parties, also in the West, Poguntke, "Political Parties," p. 400.
17. Having many members can be a mixed blessing. For instance, only 1.7% of the Czech Communist Party members in 2007 were under forty years of age, while 52.2% were over seventy, and half the members had joined the party between 1945 and 1960! Party membership sources: *HDZ, Hidra*, the Croatian Information Documentation Referral Agency, at www.hidra.hr/strankee/501int2p.htm [accessed on 12 February 2008]; *BSP*, Maria Spirova, "Political Parties in Bulgaria: Organizational Trends in Comparative Perspective," Party Politics, Vol. 11, No.5 (2005), pp. 601–22; *KSČM*, author's interview with PR manager Monika Hoření, *KSČM*, 2 May 2007; *Albanian and Polish parties*, Wolfgang Ismayr (ed.), *Die Politischen Systeme Osteuropas* (Wiesbaden: VS Verlag für Sozialwissenschaften, 2003), pp. 222, 825.
18. Thomas Schmidt, "Das Politische System Lettlands," in Ismayr (ed.), *Die Politischen Systeme*, p. 140; *Hidra*, the Croatian Information Documentation Referral Agency.
19. Since 2001, the president has been elected by the parliament rather than directly. However, Lucinschi's successor Vladimir Voronin remained rather powerful, due to the strong position of the Communist Party. See Klemens Büscher, "Das Politische System Moldovas," in Ismayr (ed.), *Die Politischen Systeme*, pp. 521–22.
20. Democracy Score 2008 Rankings by Regime Type, in *Nations in Transit* (Washington, DC: Freedom House, 2008) at www.freedomhouse.org/template.cfm?page=438&year=2008 [accessed on 28 October 2008].
21. Karen Dawisha and Stephen Deets, "Political Learning in Post-Communist Elections," *East European Politics and Societies*, Vol. 20, No. 4 (2006), pp. 691–728.
22. Albania adopted a new election law for the 2009 election on 18 November 2008, introducing a PR system. See "The electoral code of the republic of Albania," at www.cec.org./2004/eng/indexshqip.htm [accessed on 28 October 2009].
23. In the 2005 election, for instance, the socialists (PSSH) and the Democratic party won 98 of the single-member districts, while the Alliance for Freedom, Justice and Welfare got 18 of the PR seats with 33% of the votes.
24. Dawisha and Deets, "Political Learning," pp. 691–728.
25. Frances Millard, *Elections, Parties, and Representation in Post-Communist Europe* (Houndmills: Palgrave, 2004), p. 30. During communism, normally only one candidate was allowed in each single-member district.
26. For more on electoral systems, see Olga Shvetsova, "A Survey of Post-Communist Electoral Institutions: 1990–1998," *Electoral Studies*, Vol. 18 (1999), pp. 397–409

and Sarah Birch, "Electoral Systems and Party Systems in Europe East and West," in Paul G. Lewis and Paul Webb (eds.), *Pan-European Perspectives on Party Politics* (Leiden: Brill Academic Publishers, 2003).

27. Michal Klíma, "Electoral Reform in the Czech Republic," *Central European Political Science Review*, Vol. 10 No. 3 (2002), pp. 126–47.
28. Laslo Sekelj, "Parties and Elections: The Federal Republic of Yugoslavia – Change Without Transformation," *Europe-Asia Studies*, Vol. 52, No. 1 (2000), p. 61.
29. Estonia banned electoral alliances altogether in 1999. Estonian National Electoral Committee, *Elections and Referendums in Estonia 1989–1999*, section 13.1, www.vvk.ee/english/overview.html#07031999 [accessed on 30 October 2008].
30. For an excellent overview, see Katz and Crotty (eds.), *Handbook of Party Politics*.
31. Stein Rokkan, "Nasjonsbygging, konfliktutvikling og massepolitikkens strukturering," in Stein Rokkan (ed.), *Stat, nasjon, klasse* (Oslo: Universitetsforlaget, 1987), pp. 299, 310, 328.
32. Mair, *Party System Change*, Rose, "Mobilizing Demobilized Voters," pp. 549–63, and Kitschelt, "The Formation of Party Systems," pp. 11–12.
33. Claus Offe, Jon Elster and Ulrich K. Preuss, *Institutional Design in Post-Communist Societies: Rebuilding the Ship at Sea* (Cambridge: Cambridge University Press, 1998), p. 25.
34. For a discussion of the importance of party strategy in Central Europe, see Elisabeth Bakke and Nick Sitter, "Patterns of Stability: Party Competition and Strategy in Central Europe since 1989," *Party Politics*, Vol. 11, No. 2 (2005), pp. 243–63.
35. Helen Fedor (ed.), "The 1990 elections," in *Moldova: A Country Study* (Washington, DC: GPO for the Library of Congress, 1995), at http://countrystudies.us/moldova/34.htm [accessed on 1 February 2008].
36. "Organizacija federacije," in *Ustava Socialistične federativne republike Jugoslavije* (Wikivir, 1974), pp. 291–2, at http://sl.wikisource.org/wiki/Ustava_Socialisti%C4%8Dne_federativne_republike_Jugoslavije_%281974%29 [accessed on 1 February 2008].
37. Sekelj, "Parties and Elections," pp. 59, 63.
38. Ronald Inglehart, *The Silent Revolution – Changing Values and Political Styles among Western Publics* (Princeton, NJ: Princeton University Press, 1977).
39. Mair, *Party System Change*, p. 68.
40. David M. Olson, "Party Formation and Party System Consolidation in the New Democracies of Central Europe," *Political Studies*, Vol. 46, No. 3 (August 1998), pp. 432–46 and Goldie Shabad and Kazmierz M. Slomczynski, "Inter-party Mobility among Parliamentary Candidates Post-communist East-Central Europe," *Party Politics*, Vol. 10, No. 2 (March 2004), pp. 151–76.
41. Elisabeth Bakke and Nick Sitter, "Elite Turnover and Party System Change in Central Europe: Political Nomadism or Political Normalization?," unpublished manuscript.
42. Ian Budge, Kenneth Newton *et al.*, *The Politics of the New Europe: Atlantic to Urals* (New York: Longman, 1997), p. 199; see also Jan-Erik Lane and Svante O. Ersson, *European Politics* (London: Sage, 1996), p. 119 and Francesca Vassallo and Clyde Wilcox, "Party as a Carrier of Ideas," in Katz and Crotty (eds.), *Handbook of Party Politics*, pp. 413–21.

43. See e.g. Lubomír Kopeček (ed.), *Trajectories of the Left: Social Democratic and (Ex-)Communist Parties in Contemporary Europe: Between Past and Future* (Brno: Democracy and Culture Center, MÚ, 2005); Anna M. Grzymała-Busse, *Redeeming the Communist Past: The Regeneration of Communist Parties in East-Central Europe*, (Cambridge: Cambridge University Press, 2002); Vít Hloušek and Lubomír Kopeček (eds.), *Rudí a růžovi: Tranformace komunistických stran* (Brno: MPÚ, 2002); and John T. Ishiyama, "The Sickle or the Rose? Previous Regime Types and the Evolution of the Ex-Communist Parties in Post-Communist Politics," *Comparative Political Studies*, Vol. 30, No. 3 (June 1997), pp. 299–330.
44. But see *Journal of Communist Studies and Transition Politics*, Vol. 20, No. 3 (2004), Special Issue: Center-Right Parties in Post-Communist East–Central Europe; Seán Hanley, Aleks Szczerbiak, Tim Haughton, and Brigid Fowler, "Sticking Together: Explaining Comparative Center-Right Party Success in Post-Communist Central and Eastern Europe," *Party Politics*, Vol. 14, No. 4 (July 2008), pp. 407–34.
45. Seán Hanley, "Getting the Right Right: Redefining the Center-Right in Post-Communist Europe," *Journal of Communist Studies and Transition Politics*, Vol. 20, No. 3 (2004), pp. 9–27, at p. 15.
46. For a discussion of the success of the PCRM, see Luke March, "Power and Opposition in the Former Soviet Union: The Communist Parties of Moldova and Russia," *Party Politics*, Vol. 12, No.3 (2006), pp. 341–65.
47. For the present composition of the Coalition for Bulgaria, see Wikipedia, at http://en.wikipedia.org/wiki/Coalition-for-Bulgaria [accessed on 28 October 2009].
48. Fico is still Slovakia's most trusted politician. Slovak Statistical Office, *Dôvera občanov SR k politikom začiatkom októbra 2008*, at http://portal.statistics.sk/files/Uvvm/y2008/Spravy/no027_m10_y08_Dovera.pdf [accessed on 28 October 2009].
49. For an analysis of *Smer*'s ideological shift see, e.g. Peter Učeň, "Populist Appeals in Slovak Politics before the 2006 Elections," in Martin Bútora *et al.*, *Democracy and Populism in Central Europe: The Visegrád Elections and their Aftermath* (Bratislava: IVO, 2007); or Juraj Marušiak, "Smer – from Pragmatism to Social Democracy? Seeking Identity," in Kopeček (ed.), *Trajectories of the Left*, pp. 165–77.
50. Tim Haughton, "HZDS: The Ideology, Organization, and Support Base of Slovakia's Most Successful Party," *Europe-Asia Studies*, Vol. 53, No. 5 (2001), pp. 745–69.
51. Hanley, "Getting the Right Right," p. 17.
52. George Schöpflin, *Politics in Eastern Europe 1945–1992* (Oxford: Blackwell, 1993), pp. 259–60.
53. A second example of a populist "one-man-show" turned liberal is the Alliance for the New Citizen (ANO) in Slovakia, the vehicle of media-mogul Pavol Rusko (below the threshold).
54. R.J. Crampton, *The Balkans since the Second World War* (London: Longman, 2002), p. 245.
55. This includes the Christian Democratic Party in Lithuania (LKD, now a part of the Homeland Union).
56. Part of the elite left in 2008 to form the conservative Civic Union.
57. Haughton, "HZDS," p. 757.
58. In Bulgaria, three minuscule peasant parties have won seats: the former satellite party BZNS "Aleksander Stambolijski" is part of the BSP-led Coalition for Bulgaria;

the BZNS United ran in the 2005 United Democratic Forces alliance; and the BZNS People's Union ran in the Bulgarian People's Union.

59. March, "Power and Opposition in the Former Soviet Union," p. 348; and Jan Pešek, "Pohľad štátnej moci na disent na Slovensku v ére prestavby," in Jan Pešek and Soňa Szomolányi (eds.), *November 1989 na Slovensku. Súvislosti, predpoklady a dôsledky* (Bratislava: Nadácia Milana Šimečku, 2000), p. 51.
60. Miloš Zeman, *Jak jsem se mýlil v politice* (Prague: Ottovo nakladatelství, 2005), p. 87.

Further reading

Bakke, Elisabeth and Nick Sitter. "Patterns of Stability: Party Competition and Strategy in Central Europe since 1989," *Party Politics*, Vol. 11, No. 2 (2005), pp. 243–63

Birch, Sarah. "Electoral Systems," in Stephen White, Judy Batt and Paul G. Lewis (eds.), *Developments in Central and East European Politics 4* (Houndmills: Palgrave, 2007)

Bútora, Martin *et al. Democracy and Populism in Central Europe: The Visegrád Elections and their Aftermath* (Bratislava: IVO, 2007)

Enyedi, Zsolt. "Party Politics in Post-Communist Transition," in Richard S. Katz and William Crotty (eds.), *Handbook of Party Politics* (London: Sage, 2006)

Evans, Geoffrey. "The Social Bases of Political Divisions in Post-Communist Eastern Europe," *Annual Review of Sociology*, Vol. 32 (August 2006), pp. 245–70

Howard, Marc Morjé. *The Weakness of Civil Society in Post-Communist Europe* (Cambridge: Cambridge University Press, 2003)

Ismayr, Wolfgang (ed.). *Die Politischen Systeme Osteuropas* (Wiesbaden: VS Verlag für Sozialwissenschaften, 2006)

Jungerstam-Mulders, Susanne (ed). *Post-Communist EU Member States: Parties and Party Systems.* (Aldershot: Ashgate, 2006)

Journal of Communist Studies and Transition Politics, Vol. 20, No. 3 (2004), Special issue: Centre-Right Parties in Post-Communist East–Central Europe

Kopeček, Lubomír (ed.). *Trajectories of the Left: Social Democratic and (Ex-)Communist Parties in Contemporary Europe: Between Past and Future* (Brno: Democracy and Culture Centre, MÚ, 2005)

More good articles on party system development in post-communist countries can be found in the journals *Communist and Post-Communist Studies, East European Politics and Societies, Party Politics, Electoral Studies, Europe-Asia Studies, Journal of Communist Studies and Transition Politics*

The latest election results (usually with links to the respective national electoral commissions) are available at Wikipedia (www.wikipedia.org/)

5

Economic reforms and the illusion of transition

KARL KASER

In 2004, the well-known Swiss social anthropologist Christian Giordano at a conference in Sofia stated that the post-socialist transition was over because it had never begun. In his paper he referred to the deep historical roots of dependencies and the economic marginalization of the eastern part of Europe by the core of capitalism in the West. In this long perspective the period of socialism was ephemeral, since it was self-evident that half of a millennium of peripheral status cannot be compensated by any form of economic strategy within a short period of time. How, then, can we talk about a quick spurt from socialist economy to capitalist systems that can be considered equivalent to the regions which invented the original? At its best, said Giordano, the capitalist systems of the East are phenomenological copies of the original. The term "transition," therefore, means nothing other than a transformation from the periphery of the Soviet bloc to the periphery of European capitalism.[1]

What is common between the two forms of hegemony "is the role of external power in setting and enforcing political agendas for the states of the region and thus in influencing domestic political outcomes."[2] The western democracies entered the politics of the region reluctantly and gradually formulated a list of conditions for its inclusion into its institutional framework: copying the West by economic liberalization, opening of the countries to foreign trade, privatization of state-owned assets and the marketization of prices. The present economic relations between East-Central and Southeastern Europe and the West are still patron–clientele or core–periphery relations. Parity with the advanced industrial states of the Atlantic world is not yet visible.[3] Economic reform *per se* could be considered a success; but in several of the countries of the region most of the people are economically not better off than they were in 1989, and for many the standard of living has declined. After a short mini-spurt in the first half of the 2000s, most of the prognoses indicate a stabilization on a relatively low level until 2010 – except for Poland, the Czech Republic, and Slovenia. Was it worth it to suffer the social and economic hardship of so-called transition?

There were good reasons for the assumption that the post-socialist countries would economically follow roughly a similar transitional course. They had had similar experiences with the socialist centralized economy, they began the process of transformation from a similar point of departure, and this was in a period when neoliberalism already had become the hegemonistic economic theory and practice in the West.[4]

Instead of a "transition," a variety of transformations of socialist command economy into neoliberal forms of peripheral capitalism took place. The chosen or imposed form depended on the internal power relations of states, the character of the state and politics of international monetary institutions, the economic internationalization, and involvement or non-involvement in wars after the fall of the communist regimes. Differences had already become visible about a decade after the "transition" processes had begun. Poland's GDP in 1997 was 11% larger than in 1989, whereas that of Bosnia in the same year was slightly more than one-third of its 1989 size. Foreign investment in Hungary accounted for nearly one-third of the foreign investments in the whole region,[5] but decreased to one-fifth in 2008 compared to 1995. Economic data reveal a disastrous economic performance except in Poland and Slovenia. The economically most successful region was the Central-East European states; their economies after a backlash began to grow again in 1993 (table 5.1).[6]

Fifteen years later, Dorothee Bohle and Béla Greskovits distinguish among three pathways into divergent models of global capitalism in Central-East Europe: the state-crafted neoliberalism of the Baltic states, the embedded liberalism of Poland, Czech Republic, Slovakia, and Hungary (the Visegrád countries), and the neocorporatism in Slovenia.[7] The economic reforms of these countries differ significantly from those of South East Europe with their late privatization, late economic recovery, and embedded liberalism. For the social historian, the first crucial question is why different countries embarked upon divergent trajectories leading to diverse market societies starting from a supposedly similar point of departure. The second important question derives from the observation that all post-socialist states sooner or later were included in the processes of internationalization and transnationalization. Why do these processes have different impact on these countries? Third, why have foreign direct investment (FDI) and transnational corporations (TNCs) had a divergent impact on the new market economies? Finally, why does "transition" mean only different ways into capitalistic peripheralization?

Although the divergence of pathways into forms of market liberalism is remarkable, a number of similarities must not be overlooked: a relatively homogenous pressure of international monetary organizations on rapid privatization, a remarkable share of informality of the market and corruption, a bias of economic reforms at the expense of women, high labor migration, the weakness of trade unions, the brain drain, economic integration with the effect of peripheralization, as well as high unemployment rates. The first section will point to key factors for divergences and similarities, the second will discuss the divergence of pathways of post-socialist capitalisms, the third, similarities, and the fourth the results of the economic reform paths taken.

Table 5.1 Economic development and share of GDP, private sector, around 1995

	GNP *per capita*, 1995	Private sector share of GDP, 1995	GDP 1997 (1989=100)	Estimated GDP 2007 (1989=100)	Cumulative FDI inflows *per capita*, US$, 1989–2007
Baltic states					
Estonia	2,860	65	77.9	155	5,756
Latvia	2,270	60	56.8	125	3,447
Lithuania	1,900	55	42.8	116	2,284
CEE States					
Czech Republic	3,870	65	95.8	136	6,128
Hungary	4,120	60	90.4	135	4,915
Poland	2,790	60	111.8	169	2,572
Slovakia	2,950	60	95.6	154	4,325
Slovenia	8,200	45	99.3	149	1,381
Bulgaria and Romania					
Bulgaria	1,830	45	62.8	107	3,824
Romania	1,480	40	82.4	120	1,984
States involved in wars					
Bosnia	765	na	na	86	1,135
Croatia	3,250	70	73.3	111	3,932
Montenegro				80	3,535
Serbia				68	1,599
Peripheral economies					
Albania	670	60	79.1	152	834
Macedonia	860	40	55.3	96	1,103
Moldova	920	30	35.1	51	502

Sources: Valerie Bunce, "The Political Economy of Postsocialism," *Slavic Review*, Vol. 58, No. 4 (Winter 1995), pp. 764–5; European Bank for Reconstruction and Development, *Transition Report Update 2007*, May 2007.

Key factors for the emergence of divergences and similarities

"Economic transition" here is not understood as a teleological transition to matured capitalism, but as a transformation, in which new elements most typically combine with permutations and reconfigurations of existing organizational forms. Therefore, not surprisingly, varieties of pre-capitalism are the result of "transition" processes. These varieties emanate from the level and scope of state ownership, macroeconomic stability, and the degree of integration with western economies. Different paths of extrication from state socialism, together with specific relations between state, economy and society have had an impact, too.[8] We point here to three key factors, which are crucial for the emergence of divergences and similarities: internationalization/transnationalization, the character of transformative state power, and patterns of industrial transformation.

Internationalization and transnationalization

Given that the final goal of economic reform in all post-socialist countries is the full integration into the global and European economy, its different speed results in "packages" of countries. The Baltic countries, the Central-East European countries, as well as Bulgaria and Romania, have already channeled through the basic process. Since 1 May 2005 and 1 January 2007, respectively, Bulgaria and Romania have been EU member states and are represented in all relevant international monetary institutions such as the World Bank, the Organization for Economic Cooperation and Development (OECD), or the World Trade Organization (WTO). Their trade is already mainly with other EU countries and, via foreign investments, they have been incorporated into the global and European economy. However, the export economy throughout the region is under firm foreign control (except in the case of Slovenia); this is especially the case with the banking sector which has been penetrated by foreign capital.[9]

The method of internationalization and export orientation in the first years of transition in Central-East Europe was (and in the Balkan countries still is) outward-processing trade which recalls the times of proto-industrialization. Western firms supplied subcontractors in the region, especially in Central-East European countries, with materials, parts or components to be processed and re-imported afterwards. This enabled Western firms to take advantage of low wages and to reduce production costs. This form of production and relations to Western companies was the engine for exports from the region to the West, especially in the branches of clothing, leather, and shoes. Since about the middle of the 1990s, rising costs and weakened competitiveness resulted in a shift of strategy from outward-processing trade to FDI, which began to shape the manufacturing industry in Central-East Europe and which became strongly linked to the question of EU accession. This question became toxic in the second half of the 1990s; political and economic advantages and disadvantages for the EU-15 were calculated. The following model took shape: the differences in levels of development between Western Europe and the region were significant. Therefore, its integration would be expensive (Cohesion Funds) and could raise tensions and resistance in Western societies. Integration would lead to an increased heterogeneity of the EU market. This should not constitute a disadvantage for the West European economies, because of the labor division already established between the advanced West European economies and those in Central-East and South East Europe. Because of the global wage pressure produced by Asian low-price production in certain branches, West European companies were increasingly forced also to produce in Asia – or in the envisaged accession region, which had geographical advantages and would provide complementary production capacities. The Central-East and Southeast European states were, therefore, not considered rivals on the global market but could support West European competitiveness. The area is a low-wage region with a skilled labor force. Therefore, it constitutes a huge pool of low-cost labor, often low-cost skilled labor. It would make a lot of sense to transfer labor-intensive production (branches such as clothing, leather and shoes, wood, paper, engineering) into new EU countries. This would even permit new production that might otherwise not have been considered. The EU accession process would result in a stable legal and institutional framework with security for investments; higher-wage jobs could be maintained in Western Europe. Those governments in the region which provide infrastructure, skills as well as stable, predictable, and even enforced market rules would succeed. The risk for the countries of the region would be that production organized by Western companies might remain limited to a series of enclaves isolated from the rest of its economies, rather than laying the foundations of broad and sustainable growth.[10]

Weaker and stronger transformative state power

State capacity and its institutional effectiveness in the region are weak compared to its Western counterparts. This discrepancy has deep historical roots, originating in early medieval times. The emerging Western "interventionist" state has been able to set rules and execute them with a firm hand, whereas the Eastern "tributary" state has been lacking power in the form of institutional penetration in order to execute its laws. The socialist era did not change this basic constellation fundamentally; nor has the post-socialist period done so. The Baltic and Central-East European states (including also Croatia) are institutionally more deeply penetrated than the Balkan states, which desperately still lack executive efficiency, although the EU has already invested significantly in building and strengthening institutions. In relation to opening the markets, the decisive question is not whether these states are powerful enough to restrict liberalization but whether they will develop a capability to support the national economy in transforming itself and responding to the constraints of European and global players. Scrutiny of governmental effectiveness and regulatory quality demonstrates that the Baltic and Central-East European states inherited basically functioning governmental and administrative structures, and confirms their superiority to the Balkan systems. The Baltic countries in this respect have been able to catch up with the Central-East European region, including control of corruption, legal security, the rule of law, good governance, and developed state–society relationships.[11] Slovenia proves the most advanced country on this parameter, as well as in achieving political stability through social cohesion, macroeconomic stability, and democratic inclusion. The country has conducted an economic transformation based on national endeavor – by excluding foreign entrepreneurs from key positions – which has almost resulted in a Western type of capitalism – similar to, for instance, the Austrian or German corporatist regime. The country was able to establish an advanced welfare system by the inclusion of trade and economic unions and political parties for stated aims. The government provided macroeconomic stability (low inflation and low budget deficits) and could therefore protect against the short-term capital flows of foreign investors in economic key branches.[12] The rest of the Central-East European countries in this respect were less successful and the Balkan countries have been less successful still.

Industrial transformation

TNCs have had a decisive impact on the reformation of industry. They act according to their own rules, and national governments may or may not support them. Since the countries of the region lack capital, they are highly dependent on FDI. This means that investors decide on the form of industrial reconstruction. Their activities are, of course, profit oriented. Profit maximization depends on various factors such as labor costs, available labor skill, political stability, and the amount of taxes that have to be paid. The performance of the state and its institutions are, therefore, decisive. Minimal standards attract only short-term and low-level investment – for instance, shoe production for Italian companies in Albania. Optimal standards attract capital-intensive foreign investment such as car production in the Czech Republic and in Slovakia. In a comparative perspective, the Central-East European countries have provided the best conditions for foreign investment – not only because they belonged to the belt of industrialized regions under the Habsburg Monarchy. State institutions have been supporting the transformation of inherited industrial structures into new foreign-controlled companies, which mitigated the impact of the liberalization shock. From the very beginning of the transition they attracted foreign capital by providing decisive incentives such as tax exemption regimes and protective regulations. The performance of the Baltic states in this perspective was worse[13] and the performance of the war-shocked republics of former Yugoslavia (FRY) and of the group of countries consisting of Albania, Macedonia, and Moldova was worst again, where de-industrialization could not be stopped by the attraction of foreign investment.

Industrial transformation was the most successful in countries which were already advanced and fairly industrialized before the communist regimes were established and was less successful in countries where industrialization was initiated in communist times. To the first group belong the Czech Republic, Poland, Hungary, and Slovenia; to the latter Slovakia, the rest of FRY, Albania,

Bulgaria, Romania, and Moldova. These countries suffered, except Croatia, greater output collapses (between 27 and 50%, 1994), and greater political turmoil.[14]

Divergences

"Shock therapy" and gradualism

Economic reform was accompanied by debates on gradualism and shock therapy. The idea of gradualism favored a mixed economy consisting of social elements inherited from socialism while transforming the system into a liberal market economy. This idea was soon discarded since those economies with a delay in reforms fared much worse than those conducting a "shock therapy." The methodology of economic transition, although not its outcome, was clear from the very beginning. The sale of state-owned assets and their privatization had already been the defining feature of the global economy since the 1980s. It reached its peak in 1998 when $171 billion of assets were sold in 2,500 transactions worldwide. Besides the fact that, in most economic theories, privatization increases productivity and efficiency, the lending policy of the leading international financial institutions (the International Monetary Fund (IMF) and the World Bank) had an impact on privatization around the world and in the region, too. Countries that borrowed money subsequently privatized significantly. The IMF has included privatization as a standard condition of its structural adjustment lending.[15]

Neoliberal ideology and practice have guided the transitions taking place. The countries went into transition, market liberalization, and privatization at different tempos and opened themselves to FDI. Poland was the first country that applied a "big-bang" strategy at the beginning of January 1990 after initial reforms had been conducted the year before; Czechoslovakia and Hungary (after initial reforms in earlier years) started this process in 1991. These three countries were the fastest in this respect, the Southeast European countries followed at a slower speed. In Yugoslavia (1989) and Bulgaria (1991) shock therapy failed.[16] Speed depended on whether socialist reform parties stayed in power or came into power in the first years after the political transition.

The Polish stabilization program, which began in early 1990, was the first in the region whose objective was to transform a plan-based to a market-based economy. It involved price liberalization, with cuts in subsidies, caps on wages, conversion of the currency, and the reduction of the budgetary deficit. All these objectives were achieved in 1990. On the negative side, however, the stabilization program resulted in a sharp decrease in real incomes, a large increase in unemployment, and a collapse of industrial production. The social costs of the shock therapy were unexpectedly high. In 1994, incomes were 35% less and poverty had risen from an estimated 17% of the population in 1989 to 45% in 1994. The poverty rate more than tripled in all socio-economic groups.[17]

It is hard to determine which of the strategies, shock therapy or gradualism, was more successful, since the potential of the economies in the region differed significantly. The differences in the regions expressed by their GNP were already considerably divergent in 1995. Slovenia's GNP *per capita* with US$8,200 was twelve times higher than Albania's with US$670 *per capita*. On the other hand, a poor country such as Albania had caught up a little bit by 2007 compared to Slovenia, whereas countries such as Moldova or Macedonia had lost ground (see table 5.1).

One of the substantial problems of the transitions and privatizations was that the economic market (capital and investment) was only weakly linked to the social market (values of equality and social justice). Social equality and economic growth did not go hand in hand. Privatization promoted income inequality and undermined public welfare. Economic restructuring occurred at great human cost (low-level security, social exclusion, inadequate social welfare).[18] In Bulgaria, for instance, unemployment was 13% at the end of 1994; the ratio of those looking for work and available positions was 44:1. In 1994 and 1995, the rates of inflation were over 80%. From 1990 to 1994 real wages fell by 50%. In Romania, inflation jumped to 210% in 1992 and to 300% in 1993, the unemployment rate rose from 2.7% in 1991 to 15% in 1994.[19]

Privatization

The tempo of privatization was moderate and slow in countries at war and in the Southeast European countries in general (including Slovenia, but except Croatia). These processes were considerable in the Central European and Baltic countries and most pronounced in Poland and Hungary (see also table 5.1). The approaches to privatization differed. They can be grouped into three methods: small-scale privatization (the transfer of small businesses to individual owners); mass privatization (distribution of the state's assets among the population); capital privatization (the sale of SOEs to individual investors).[20] The second method, for instance, was applied in Czechoslovakia and in Poland on the basis of voucher programs. The advantage of the voucher system was the speed of transfer into private hands. In 1996, 80% of former state companies had been taken over by private agents in the Czech Republic. The disadvantage was that this method did not bring capital and new technology. In less developed economies such as in Bulgaria, which adopted a mass-privatization scheme in 1995, this system was much less successful. Only between 12 and 15% of the assets were privatized in the first wave and fewer in the second wave.[21] The third method was applied in Hungary in 1994–5; a governmental agency sold the right to privatize the biggest state companies to international investment banks and leading consulting firms.[22]

In the middle of the 1990s, the private sector was already responsible for a growing share of the output and the contributions of the public sectors were shrinking in output and employment. Critical observers estimate the rapid privatization of large SOEs as unimportant for economic growth. In their opinion the development of new private firms was much more important.[23] On the other hand, slow privatization tended to foster semi-illegal and illegal practices, and contributed to the survival of highly indebted firms and prevented further economic transformation as in Bulgaria or Romania.

In the Central-East European states, within a few years, economic transformation has changed fundamental aspects of decision-making, production, and the allocation of production throughout the region;[24] in South East Europe economic transformation and privatization took much longer and, in some cases, is still not finished.

Pathways into a global economy

Economic development in East Europe, Central-East, and Southeastern Europe has been triggered by the core of the European economy, geographically situated in the North West and Central Europe. The neighboring belt of post-socialist countries was the first included into the strategies of the core. The more we move from West to East and from North to South, the poorer the economic performance and the more peripheral the integration into the European and global economy. This observation includes factors such as the length and depth of recession following the collapse, the vigor of recovery, and the length of transition; in addition data on income distribution, poverty, social services, the rule of law, and the protection of human rights. Three types of development paths from the socialist into the liberal market economy and integration into the global economy have become visible.

The Baltic states

These are characterized by radically liberalized markets, a market-supporting institutional framework, and a weak welfare system, which was a deliberate decision of their governments which most radically broke with the socialist economy. This was accompanied by a nationalization of the economy in the sense of pushing the ethnic Russian social elite from key positions in the economy. In many cases they were replaced by returning emigrants–entrepreneurs. Economic relations with Russia, however, have not completely ceased, since Russian oil and gas pipelines cross their territories. In addition, the remarkable recovery of Russia's economy since about 2000 exposes their tiny national economies to Russian investors. Their integration into the global economy has been through labor-intensive industries controlled by mobile TNCs and resource-based exports. Their industrial policies are minimalist with low flat taxes.[25] They earn a good part of their living from taxing Russian oil transit, exporting wood and simple wood products, combined with light industry exports.

The Central-East European states

They have also successfully transformed into market oriented liberal economies. Their socio-economic regime, however, differs from that of the Baltic states. They have mitigated the social costs of the initial shock therapy, which was the precondition for a comparatively inclusive democracy. Whereas the Baltic states have so far preserved their traditional industrial structures, the Central-East European states have been successful in industry upgrading. A state-crafted policy of attracting FDI has had priority since the second half of the 1990s after attempts to establish "national" capitalism, pronounced in Poland, have failed. As a consequence, foreign companies dominate their economies. Hungary was the first country exposed to foreign capital because of its huge external debt accumulated in the 1980s.[26] FDI was highly concentrated on Hungary, Poland, the Czech Republic, and Slovakia. Between 1989 and 1995 between 70 and 90% of all regional foreign investment was channeled to these states. Between 1989 and 1996, only $52 *per capita* was invested in Romania, but $130 *per capita* in Hungary and $140 *per capita* in Poland.[27] Slovenia had profited from the SFRY's economic reform course of the 1980s, which strengthened Slovenia's economy by its integration into Western markets. The country stands for a successful combination of industrial upgrading, stability, and social cohesion. It kept away FDI and TNCs.[28]

Southeastern Europe

The region became an area specializing in labor-intensive manufacturing and was the clothing, footwear, and furniture belt of Western Europe. Light industry is combined with a secondary focus on resource-based exports (iron and steel). Export–import activities are fully embedded in the domestic economy; the capacities and workforce of these sectors became incorporated into the supply chains of typically small and medium-size firms. Although foreign firms do sometimes invest, their dominant transborder link is usually not FDI, but intra-firm flows of goods and information based on non-equity forms of control. The most important form is outward-processing trade. This pattern of transnationalization secured access to low-paid but docile and relatively well-trained labor without significant implications for the transfer of capital, or managerial and engineering capacity. Thus, neither significant FDI, nor organization, management, nor marketing skills will be made available to domestic actors, and the national economy at large. The partners function as an extended workbench.

None of the successor states to Socialist Yugoslavia had to begin economic reform under more complex conditions than Bosnia-Herzegovina. The end of the war (1995) was followed by the requirements of war reconstruction; implementing the reforms necessary to create a free-market economy had medium-term priority. A special feature of the country's economic development was and still is the international community (the EU's High Representative). In the first years after the war, the country depended upon international assistance. Until 1998, its focus was on the emergency reconstruction of basic building services. Institution-building and economic reforms were limited by the uncooperative stance of the local political elites. The introduction of a common currency in 1998 provided the precondition of an economic reform agenda and a common economic space. The direct economic losses of the war in 1992–5 are estimated somewhere between $60 and $80 billion. At the beginning of 1996, industrial output was down to 5% of its pre-war level and the unemployment rate was at 70–80% (40% in 2000). In 2002, industrial output was still at only 40% of the pre-war level, which indicates a persistent de-industrialization.[29]

Similarities

Passivity of the workforce

In the early 1990s, many analysts expected protest and violence as a consequence of the social hardship of transformation. But the population accepted its political and economic marginalization without significant protest. Massive strikes have not occurred; the workforce has remained remarkably patient. In the first half of the 1990s, the transformation was much more contentious in Western compared to Eastern Europe. On average in Western Europe almost twice as many strikes were organized. The protest of Hungarian taxi drivers in 1990, the marches of violent Romanian miners to Bucharest, and the Bulgarian foot riots of 1997 were unique events.[30] One of the explanations is that on a discourse level patience was considered a precondition for the way "back to Europe." Another explanation is the weakness of the trade unions and the changeover of unemployed to the informal sector, instead of protesting. Protest has primarily been expressed on voting days,[31] which proved to be just as destabilizing as mass protests.

Informality

The informal market consists in street trading, illegal labor, petty tax evasion, circumvention of state regulations, and informal payments to services. Informality as a survival mechanism is linked to the failure of the formal system: lack of employment and the inability of state institutions to provide adequate health care and education services. When the processes of transition began, large sectors of the population became marginalized. There were no prevention programs and no re-qualification of the labor force. Although already present in socialist times, the informal sector consequently increased, when the official support systems disappeared. The poorer a country is, the higher the unemployment and the informal economy sector. Informality enables the unemployed poor to earn some basic revenues. Research in Romania in 2000 revealed that about 40% of the country's GDP was earned in the informal sector; 80% of the unemployed worked in the informal sector; most informal sector work was in agriculture, construction, trade, and in some service industries. In most of the cases covering health care needs was the reason for going into the sector.

The "suitcase trade" is widespread. People buy goods, food, textile products, jewellery, alcohol or cigarettes from duty-free shops and sell them in the markets or on the streets. Street trading appeared in many cities, towns, and villages, absorbing a range of social groups. The bazaar in Warsaw Stadium that closed in 2007, or the Chinese market in Budapest, had a turnover of millions of Euros. Open-air markets functioned as a substitute for rather than a supplement to the normal retail sector for almost two decades.

A very big source of informal labor is migrant labor. The seasonal migration influences the growth of the informal labor ratio and also the economy of the sending country. People in the native country are living on the money earned abroad; they have casual work and avoid paying taxes. Between 800,000 and 1 million people from Moldova work seasonally or permanently abroad (one-quarter of the population); in Lithuania, the figure is between 300,000 and 400,000.

The informal economy is most widespread in the construction sector; in Lithuania 35% of all undocumented workers are employed in the sector. To provide exact statistical data on informal labor is impossible. Information provided by the trade unions in the region says that 15% of workers are in the informal sector in Estonia, 25% in Lithuania, 27% in Croatia, 30% in Bulgaria, 40% in Serbia, 60% in Moldova, and 80% in Kosovo. The EU average is estimated 9%.[32]

Weakness of labor unions

Characteristic of post-socialist societies is the erosion and dismantling of labor unions, as well as the tardy performance of governments in ratifying the basic conventions of the International Labor Organization (ILO) on labor rights and basic labor conditions.[33] The states in the region did everything to create external economic integration but failed to establish an institutional capacity for the achievement of compromises between capital and labor. The West European post-Second World War compromise between capital and labor has not taken place so far. By 2000, only approximately a quarter of the labor force was represented by trade unions; the few remaining unions are concentrated in the few not yet fully privatized sectors of heavy industries and public services. Whereas the share of workers covered by collective bargaining agreements in the West is 74%, in the East it is only 39%; work conditions in the East are inferior and welfare standards are poor.[34]

Businesses in labor-intensive activities more dependent on labor cost for efficiency are more likely to resist workers' pressure for higher wages and better working conditions. Labor-intensive capital goods industries are most unlikely to offer a stable capital–labor accord. The expected mass consumption of goods, for which workers' purchasing power is important, fuels the acceptance of better living (and expenditure) conditions. For capital-intensive consumer goods industries (e.g. car manufacturing), *the factor of labor is relatively important for production*, but in developed societies it can become a factor of demand. Until the second half of the 1990s those transnationally organized industries that were the least hospitable to a capital–labor accord in post-socialist economies became dominant.[35] The *leading consumer durables industries* were most supportive for the establishment of a West European social contract after the second World War. East European integration into transnational production was via highly labor-intensive production. Most of the consumer goods produced in the East cannot be bought in the East and therefore the consumer goods industries developed as export sectors. Collective action capacities are seriously limited by the ease with which industries can move their production to cheaper locations.[36]

Workers in Slovakia's car production enjoy a privileged position; they are well paid. But attracting capital-intensive investments proves to be very costly for Slovak society, because investors in the car industry require generous incentives. Slovakia delivered both through a flat tax rate – a constant low tax rate of 19% introduced in 2004 – and heavy subsidies for investments. Western labor is using its remaining strength against its European counterparts by restricting their free movement in Europe.[37]

Women and the new economy

There is a wide measure of agreement that women have been among the chief casualties of the shift towards a market economy. They have a disproportionate experience of redundancy, and because of their domestic roles they have suffered the most from the withdrawal of a range of state welfare benefits such as childcare and kindergarten provision.[38] In 1994, in Romania 90% of families with three children and 58% of families with two children lived below the poverty line. State-guaranteed benefits to protect women, families, and children have been drastically cut. In 1994, the state budget for the support of children was 23% of the amount allocated in 1989; social assistance for mothers with several children reached only 3% of its 1989 value.[39]

In Serbia, employment rates decreased by about 800,000 people from 1990 to 2000 – from 2.7 to 1.9 million. Poverty became feminized: in 1998, the overall unemployment rate was 780,436 people, 56.1% of them women.[40] In Bulgaria, too, the general deterioration in living conditions affected women most. In addition, women were less likely to find a job in better-paid private business. Women were and are overrepresented in sectors with low salaries. Work in education and medical care is generally low paid, and these constitute the most feminized professions. Divorced women with children were in an especially disadvantageous position in the late 1990s, because the assistance they received from their ex-husbands for raising the children, if any, was negligible. Employers showed an explicit preference for hiring men. This was possible because Bulgarian labor laws included no provisions against gender discrimination.[41]

The disadvantages of the transition process were even more immediately noticeable in Poland, because the privatization process was more rapid than in the other countries of the region. The various industries, textile and clothing manufactures, and governmental organizations promptly laid off a large proportion of their predominantly female workforces. Thus, women have been the majority of the unemployed; their proportion increased from 53% in 1994 to 56% in 1995. Women are also more numerous among the long-term unemployed; the gap between both sexes is about 10 points.[42]

The brain drain

The migration of highly qualified people constitutes a serious problem for the whole region, but especially for the Southeast European countries. Causes for permanent migration were predominantly war, ethnic and religious persecution, economic difficulties facing countries in transition, and human rights violations. The region is suffering the "backwash effects" caused by mass emigration from the periphery to center. EU enlargement is particularly problematic for new member countries because it is likely that the skilled, relatively young men and women will leave to look for better chances in other EU countries. Estimates put the number of migrants from Yugoslavia, Romania, and Bulgaria at almost a million people since the transitions began. From the post-Yugoslav region alone at least 400,000 people emigrated, 10% of them highly educated. For Albania, the brain drain was devastating: a sixth of the population, including roughly one-third of the country's intellectual elite, was seeking work outside the country in 2001. During the 1990s, almost 40% of lecturers and researchers left. Bulgarian students are among the largest student populations from the region in many European countries; according to official estimates, between 1990 and 1992 around 40,000 Bulgarian scientists emigrated. Some 12,000–15,000 young and highly educated people left Macedonia in the same period of time; some 85% of young Macedonians plan to leave the country after they have finished their studies. Countries with a high standard of living and a knowledge-based economy such as Slovenia are an exception and not concerned by the problem; on the contrary, they attract highly skilled migrants, and some brain drain occurred only at the beginning of the transition process. The inflow of foreign students and highly skilled labor to Slovenia is almost equal to the emigration of highly skilled Slovenians.[43]

Results

The economic reforms of the regions are characterized by the convergence of political and economic institutions and the divergence of economic success compared to Western Europe. By the end of the 1990s the ten future East-Central and Southeast European EU member states were lagging behind any industrialized region of the world. Even Latin American countries surpassed the post-socialist states. Economic backwardness increased in the course of the first half of the 1990s; living standards were deteriorating and poverty was increasing.[44] Since about 2000, however, poverty rates have generally decreased. In Bosnia-Herzegovina, the pattern of aid-dependent development under conditions of decreasing aid had resulted in increasing poverty. In 2001, the percentage of the population below the poverty line reached 19%,[45] but decreased to 4% in 2002–3. In Albania 10% (2004) of the population is still below the poverty line. Albania and Moldova can spend only 7.2% and 7.6% (2003), respectively, of their GDP on social security and social assistance – compared to Bulgaria with 14.5 and Poland with 17.8, respectively.[46] Poverty results in a persistence of the informal market. Losers in the transition processes have included pensioners with their extremely low pensions; those working in agriculture, manufacturing, mining, and in the state sector; ethnic minorities (especially Romanis – in Hungary, 66.7% were below the poverty line in 1996); children; large families; and the less educated. The few winners tend to live in the capital cities.[47]

Absolute poverty (measured as up to $2.25 per person per day) is most notable in Moldova. The country faced the deepest and most prolonged recession among transition countries and is the poorest country in Europe today. After a major economic crisis 1998–2000, the poverty rate jumped from 47% (1997) to 71% (1999), although it decreased to 43% in 2002–3 and to 29.1% in 2005. In small towns the poorest sections face catastrophic falls in consumption; a major portion of the population cannot afford health care and secondary schooling for their children. International migration in search of employment opportunities is an important poverty reduction strategy for many Moldovan households. Migrants are predominantly younger men from rural areas, but approximately 30% are women. Private transfers are substantially larger than social assistance benefits. Most migrants are illegal workers in the host countries, and many of the poorest and youngest females become victims of trafficking in the foreign sex trade.[48]

West European prosperity evidently is maintained *at the expense of* Eastern Europe. Whereas unemployment rates in Western and Eastern Europe in 1993–5 were on a comparable level (9.3% and 10.3%, respectively) in 2000–6 unemployment in Eastern Europe was already almost twice as high as in the West (12.3% versus 6.5%) but should decrease slightly. East European workers must work significantly more, often in less secure jobs, and are paid significantly less (about five times); welfare benefits are much lower in the East than in the West.[49]

Socio-economic reconstruction and transformation led to de-industrialization, the rapid growth of the service sector, and a relatively high portion of population remaining in agricultural production.[50] If we apply a simple categorization of stages into "transitions," the initial stage frequently involves macroeconomic stabilization and a systemic change to start the process of transformation into a market economy, accompanied by substantial falls in economic output. The second stage is characterized by managing the economic transformation through institutional and legal reforms and economic recovery; this needs a competent administration and a strong government. The third stage includes the process of growth and development and catch-up to the Atlantic economic area.[51]

One of the preconditions is a high level of investment and salaries that leaves enough money in the pockets of the employed to be good consumers. Since societies in Central-East and South East Europe lack a strong investment-ready bourgeoisie, only FDI can solve this problem, although creating new problems for the region. The figures in table 5.1 (estimated GDP 2007) indicate that the Baltic states as well as the Central-East European states have recovered since 1993; they are clearly no longer "transition countries." Since about 1998 the Southeast European countries have experienced unprecedented economic expansion after a decade of stagnation and decline. GDP is increasing in every country. Bulgaria, Romania, and Croatia, with a GDP *per capita* of over PPP $8,000 in 2004, are well on the way to recovery; it is expected that their status as EU countries will speed up this process, although the prognoses indicated a deceleration of economic growth until 2006. The rest of Southeastern Europe is still enmeshed in transition problems and not yet economically recovered. Political crisis and conflict have held back economic development, particularly in Bosnia and Herzegovina and Serbia (and Kosovo).[52] The GDP figure for Albania is misleading since the country started at a very low level. The Balkan countries can become the second tier of emerging economies in Europe. Another problem which has to be taken into account is external factors such as the effect of global warming on countries whose GDP relies heavily on summer tourism. This is especially the case with Croatia, with its long and attractive Adriatic coast. The country's service sector accounts for 70% of the GDP and is almost exclusively fed by summer tourism. If the warming continues as predicted, parts of the country (including also Greece, Albania, and Montenegro) may become barren desert and the Scandinavian countries will become primary destinations for summer tourism because only there will the temperature be bearable during the summer months.

If we look at FDI inflows, Estonia, the Czech Republic and Hungary are by far the best positioned, followed by Slovakia and Croatia. Slovenia tries to limit FDI in favor of domestic investment, aiming at strengthening its own market. These six countries have passed the economic transition most successfully and opened their markets most successfully to FDI. The problem, however, is that FDI has a positive effect on wages only in the capital- and skill-intensive sectors, whereas in labor-intensive or unskilled sectors they do not generate any positive effect in terms of higher wages. Moreover, FDI had obviously reached its peak in 2006–7; the forecasts until 2010 predict a serious reduction. The increase of trade with the EU did not lead to positive prospects for wages; the long-term effect is negative at economically significant levels. Therefore, many arguments speak for the peripheralization hypothesis, which says that export orientation will lead to a specialization of the region in low-skill, labor-intensive industries; which will remain in the region only as long as low wages can be paid. The question remains whether this is the way "transition" into matured capitalisms and a catch-up process will ever be achieved.

Notes

1. Christian Giordano, *Die postsozialistische Transition ist beendet, weil sie nie angefangen hat: Zur Archäologie eines gescheiterten Entwicklungsmodells* (Braunschweig: Langenhagen, 2005).
2. Andrew C. Janos, "From Eastern Empire to Western Hegemony: East-Central Europe under Two International Regimes," *East European Politics and Societies*, Vol. 15, No. 2 (Spring 2001), pp. 222–3.
3. *Ibid.*, pp. 236, 247–8.
4. Valerie Bunce, "The Political Economy of Postsocialism," *Slavic Review*, Vol. 58, No. 4 (Winter 1999), pp. 756–8.
5. *Ibid.*, pp. 759–60.
6. *Ibid.*, pp. 763–7.
7. Dorothee Bohle and Béla Greskovits, "Neoliberalism, Embedded Neoliberalism and Neocorporatism: Towards Transnational Capitalism in Central-Eastern Europe," *West European Politics*, Vol. 30, No. 3 (2007), pp. 445–6.
8. Adam Swain and Jane Hardy, "Globalization, Institutions, Foreign Investment and the Reintegration of East and Central Europe and the Former Soviet Union with the World Economy," *Regional Studies*, Vol. 32, No. 7 (1998), p. 588.
9. *Ibid.*, p. 93.
10. John Zysman and Andrew Schwartz, "Enlarging Europe: The Industrial Foundations of a New Political Reality," in John Zysman (ed.), *Enlarging Europe. The Industrial Foundations of a New Political Reality* (Berkeley and Los Angeles: University of California Press, 1998), pp. 1–24.
11. Dorothee Bohle and Béla Greskovits, "The State, Internationalization, and Capitalist Diversity in Eastern Europe," *Competition & Change*, Vol. 11, No. 2 (2007), pp. 94–5.
12. *Ibid.*, pp. 97–112.
13. *Ibid.*, pp. 100–2.
14. Janos, "From Eastern Empire to Western Hegemony," pp. 240–1.
15. Nancy Brune *et al.*, "The International Monetary Fund and the Global Spread of Privatization," *IMF Staff Papers*, Vol. 51 (2004); Nadège Ragaru, "A Balance of Economic Reforms in Central and Eastern Europe," in Hall Gardner (ed.), *Central and Southeastern Europe in Transition: Perspectives on Success and Failure Since 1989* (Westport, Conn. and London: Praeger, 2000), p. 76.
16. Michael Ellman, "The Political Economy of Transformation," *Oxford Review of Economic Policy*, Vol. 13, No. 2 (1997), p. 26.
17. Branko Milanovic, "The Social Costs of the Transition in Poland: 1990–1994," in Demetrius S. Iatridis (ed.), *Social Justice and the Welfare State in Central and Eastern*

Europe: The Impact of Privatization (Westport, Conn. and London: Praeger, 2000), pp. 153–4, 165–6.

18. Demetrius S. Iatridis, "The Social Justice and Equality Contexts of Privatization," in Demetrius S. Iatridis (ed.), *Social Justice and the Welfare State in Central and Eastern Europe: The Impact of Privatization* (Westport, Conn. and London: Praeger, 2000), pp. 3–4.
19. Theodore Katsanevas, "The Effects of Privatization on Employment in Bulgaria, Romania, and Albania," in Demetrius S. Iatridis (ed.), *Social Justice and the Welfare State in Central and Eastern Europe: The Impact of Privatization* (Westport, Conn. and London: Praeger, 2000), pp. 73–4.
20. *Ibid.*, pp. 11–12.
21. Ragaru, "A Balance of Economic Reforms," pp. 78–9.
22. David Stark and László Bruszt, *Postsocialist Pathways: Transforming Politics and Property in East-Central Europe* (Cambridge: Cambridge University Press, 1998), pp. 80–105.
23. Ellman, "The Political Economy of Transformation," pp. 27–8.
24. Stavros B. Thomadakis, "Distributive Institutions, Markets, and Private Governance in Transitional Economies," in Demetrius S. Iatridis (ed.), *Social Justice and the Welfare State in Central and Eastern Europe: The Impact of Privatization* (Westport, Conn. and London: Praeger, 2000), pp. 23–4; Ragaru, "A Balance of Economic Reforms," pp. 79–81.
25. Bohle and Greskovits, "The State," pp. 106, 108.
26. *Ibid.*, pp. 106–7, 109–10.
27. Ragaru, "A Balance of Economic Reforms," p. 82.
28. Bohle and Greskovits, "The State," pp. 107, 109.
29. Vesna Bojičić-Dželinović *et al.*, "Bosnia-Herzegovina: Economic Trends 1998–2002. Problems and Perspectives," *European Balkan Observer*, Vol. 1, No. 2 (2003), pp. 13–17.
30. Béla Greskovits, "The Postsocialist Transformation in Central and Eastern Europe," *Brazilian Journal of Political Economy*, Vol. 22, No. 4 (2002), p. 18.
31. *Ibid.*, pp. 19–20.
32. Endre Sik and Claire Wallace, "The Development of Open-Air Markets in East-Central Europe," *International Journal of Urban and Regional Research*, Vol. 23, No. 4 (1999), pp. 697–714.
33. *Ibid.*, p. 20.
34. Dorothee Bohle and Béla Greskovits, "Capital, Labor, and the Prospects of the European Social Model in the East," Central and Eastern Europe Working Paper, 58, pp. 2–5.
35. *Ibid.*, pp. 6–10.
36. *Ibid.*, p. 26.
37. *Ibid.*, p. 27.
38. Chris M. Hann, *The Skeleton at the Feast: Contributions to East European Anthropology* (Canterbury: Center for Social Anthropology and Computing, 1995), p. 108.
39. Adriana Băban, "Women's Sexuality and Reproductive Behavior in Post-Ceauşescu Romania: A Psychological Approach," in Susan Gal and Gail Kligman (eds.), *Reproducing Gender: Politics, Publics, and Everyday Life after Socialism* (Princeton, NJ: Princeton University Press, 2000), p. 234.

40. Tatjana Đurić-Kuzmanović, "Gender Inequalities in a Nationalist, Nontransitional Context in Serbia, Emphasizing Vojvodina, During the 1990s," in Aleksandar Štulhofer and Theo Sandfort (eds.), *Sexuality and Gender in Postcommunist Eastern Europe and Russia* (New York: The Haworth Press, 2005), p. 36.
41. Krassimira Daskalova, "Women's Problems, Women's Discourses in Bulgaria," in Susan Gal and Gail Kligman (eds.), *Reproducing Gender: Politics, Publics, and Everyday Life after Socialism* (Princeton, NJ: Princeton University Press, 2000), pp. 338–43.
42. Jacqueline Heinen, "The Impact of Privatization on the Female Workforce in Poland," in Demetrius S. Iatridis (ed.), *Social Justice and the Welfare State in Central and Eastern Europe: The Impact of Privatization* (Westport, Conn. and London: Praeger, 2000), pp. 118–20.
43. Vedran Horvat, "Brain Drain. Threat to Successful Transition in South East Europe?," *Southeast European Politics*, Vol. 5, No. 1 (2004), pp. 76–93.
44. Greskovits, "The Postsocialist Transformation," pp. 16–17.
45. Bojičić-Dželinović *et al.*, "Bosnia-Herzegovina," p. 16.
46. *Innocenti Social Monitor 2006: Understanding Child Poverty in South-Eastern Europe and the Commonwealth of Independent States* (UNICEF, 2006), p. 67.
47. Yogesh Atal, "Introduction," in Yogesh Atal (ed.), *Poverty in Transition and Transition in Poverty: Recent Developments in Hungary, Bulgaria, Romania, Georgia, Russia, Mongolia* (New York: Berghahn Books, Unesco Publishing, 1999), pp. 1–31.
48. *Recession, Recovery and Poverty in Moldova* (November 2004), World Bank Report, No. 28024-MD.
49. Bohle and Greskovits, "Capital, Labor, and the Prospects of the European Social Model," p. 2.
50. *Ibid.*, p. 23.
51. Christopher Allsopp and Henryk Kierzkowski, "The Assessment: Economics of Transition in Eastern and Central Europe," *Oxford Review of Economic Policy*, Vol. 13, No. 2 (1997), pp. 2–3.
52. *Innocenti Social Monitor 2006*, p. 12.

Further reading

Aligică, Paul Dragos and Anthony John J. Evans. *The Neoliberal Revolution in Eastern Europe: Economic Ideas in the Transition from Communism* (Cheltenham: Edward Elgar, 2009)

Åslund, Anders. *How Capitalism was Built: The Transformation of Central and Eastern Europe, Russia, and Central Asia* (Cambridge: Cambridge University Press, 2007)

Lorentzen, Anne and Marianne Rostgaard (eds.). *The Aftermath of "Real Existing Socialism" in Eastern Europe, Vol. 2: People and Technology in the Process of Transition* (Houndmills: Macmillan, 1997)

McGee, Robert W. (ed.). *Corporate Governance in Transition Economics* (Berlin: Springer, 2008)

Mitra, Pradeep. *Innovation, Inclusion and Integration: From Transition to Convergence in Eastern Europe, and the Former Soviet Union* (Washington, DC: World Bank, 2008)

Popov, Vladimir. "Shock Therapy versus Gradualism Reconsidered: Lessons from Transition Economies after 15 Years of Reforms," *Comparative Economic Studies*, Vol. 49 (2007), pp. 1–31

Zloch-Christy, Iliana (ed.). *Eastern Europe and the World Economy: Challenges of Transition and Globalization* (Cheltenham: Edward Elgar, 1998)

6

The War of Yugoslav Succession

MARKO ATTILA HOARE

The War of Yugoslav Succession (1991–5) was Europe's bloodiest war since the Second World War. It represented the violent culmination of the political conflict within Yugoslavia of the late 1980s and early 1990s occasioned by the rise of nationalism, particularly within Yugoslavia's Socialist Republic of Serbia; the weakening of the Yugoslav communist regime; the seizure of power by Slobodan Milošević in the Socialist Republic of Serbia in 1987; and his subsequent attempt to overturn the Yugoslav constitutional order. This political conflict pitted Milošević's Serbia against other members of the Socialist Federated Republic of Yugoslavia (SFRJ), in particular the Socialist Republics of Slovenia and Croatia and the Socialist Autonomous Province of Kosovo. Although blood was spilled in the spring of 1989, when the Yugoslav People's Army (JNA) occupied Kosovo, the "War of Yugoslav Succession" properly refers to the armed conflict of 1991–5 in Croatia, Slovenia, and Bosnia-Herzegovina, involving all the Yugoslav republics except Macedonia. By far the bloodiest and most protracted phase of the conflict occurred in nationally heterogeneous Bosnia-Herzegovina in 1992–5. Although the war was primarily fought between JNA and Serb forces on the one hand and Croatian and Bosnian forces on the other, a bitter conflict was also fought between Croat and Bosnian (predominantly Muslim) forces in Herzegovina and Central Bosnia in 1992–4. The War of Yugoslav Succession is the most significant armed conflict to have taken place in Europe since 1945, one that influenced not only the entire course of regional politics and economic development, but also the relations of the major powers (the United States, Russia, and the EU states); global perceptions of the meaning of national conflict, war-crimes and genocide; and the evolution of international justice. It is a pivotal episode in the history of post-Cold War Central and Southeastern Europe. Of course, nowhere was its impact so great as it was upon the Yugoslav successor states themselves.[1]

The term "War of Yugoslav Succession" refers to the fact that the war was fought to determine the new political and territorial order to succeed the moribund SFRJ. The starting date of the conflict is open to interpretation, but the war was definitely ended with the General Framework Agreement for Peace in Bosnia-Herzegovina of 14 December 1995. Although subsequent armed conflicts were fought between Serbian security forces and Kosovo Albanian rebels in 1996–9, between Serbian forces and NATO in 1999 and between Macedonian security forces and Macedonian Albanian rebels in 2001, these were distinct from the War of Yugoslav Succession proper. The latter did, however, involve the international community outside the FRY, above all the United Kingdom, France, the United States, NATO, the EU, and the UN. These states and international bodies dominated efforts to negotiate or impose a peace settlement; their armed forces engaged in clashes with Serb, Croat, and Bosnian forces; and ultimately NATO carried out a small-scale military operation in 1995 to chastize the Bosnian Serbs and coerce them into accepting a peace settlement.

The War of Yugoslav Succession has been variously attributed to "ancient ethnic hatreds," Serbian aggression and expansionism, a civil war between equivalent rival nationalisms, a by-product of the socio-economic collapse of socialist Yugoslavia, and a Western "imperialist" conspiracy. While the first and last of these explanations are nonsense, the others contain at least elements of truth. The war was caused by Serbian expansionism; yet this was catalyzed by socio-economic collapse and by the impact, on relations between the Yugoslav nationalities, of the sudden introduction of multiparty democracy in what had formerly been a one-party state. Serbian aggression went hand-in-hand with elements of civil war. Though the role of outside intervention in the collapse of Yugoslavia has been vastly exaggerated by conspiracy theorists, the course of the war was greatly influenced by external factors. A full understanding requires an examination of the Yugoslavia that produced the war.

The Yugoslav background

Yugoslavia – originally the "Kingdom of Serbs, Croats and Slovenes" – was established on 1 December 1918 through a union of the South Slav lands of the former Austro-Hungarian Empire (then or subsequently known as Slovenia, Croatia, Bosnia-Herzegovina, and Vojvodina, plus parts of present-day Montenegro) with the Kingdom of Serbia. The latter had, earlier that year, annexed Montenegro and in 1912–13 seized present-day Kosovo and Macedonia from the Ottoman Empire. The new state therefore encompassed a multiplicity of peoples with conflicting national ideologies and political traditions. While the Kosovo Albanians, Macedonians, and Montenegrins were subject to harsh repression, the principal division in the new state was between the non-Serb peoples of the former Austria-Hungary, particularly the Croats and Slovenes, and the Serbians (i.e. Serbs of Serbia).[2] The Serbs of the former Austria-Hungary – known as the *prečani* Serbs – played a pivotal role between them, then and later, determining the balance of power between the Serbians and the western Yugoslavs throughout Yugoslavia's history.

Yugoslavia's history, from 1918 until its demise in 1991–2, was dominated by the conflict between the incompatible national projects of its constituent peoples. Equally important was the internal division among the Serbs, divided between proponents of an integral Yugoslav nationalism – with Serbia envisioned as a South Slavic Piedmont – and proponents of an enlarged or Great Serbia, incorporating Bosnia-Herzegovina and much of Croatia. The War of Yugoslav Succession represented the final failure of all attempts by the Yugoslavs to achieve a *modus vivendi*, and the Serbian elite's attempt to impose its preferred settlement by military means, involving its final repudiation of integral Yugoslavism in favor of Great Serbianism.

The politicians representing the Serbs – both Serbians and *prečani* – imposed a centralist constitution on the new state on 28 June 1921, by outvoting the Croats and Slovenes at the constitutional assembly and in the face of their walk-out. This left most state power in Serbian hands, robbing the other Yugoslavs of any autonomy. Non-Serbian resistance to this arrangement – particularly among the Croats but ultimately including even the *prečani* Serbs – ensured a bitter conflict lasting throughout the kingdom's history. In 1929, Yugoslav King Aleksandar attempted to end it by establishing a royal dictatorship and redrawing Yugoslavia's internal map to obliterate traditional regional identities. In 1939, Yugoslav regent Prince Pavle attempted to appease the Croats by granting them autonomy and re-dividing Bosnia-Herzegovina, effectively between Croatia and Serbia. None of these measures succeeded in appeasing the Yugoslavs' conflicting national aspirations. They nevertheless provided the model for the redrawing of Yugoslavia's internal map attempted by Milošević in the 1990s.

From the 1920s, the Yugoslav communists championed the right to self-determination of the Croats, Macedonians, and other Yugoslav nations, against "Great Serbian hegemony." Following the Axis invasion and occupation of Yugoslavia in April 1941, the communists resisted under the combined banners of anti-fascism and self-determination for each Yugoslav land. The communist-led "Partisan" resistance drew its strongest support from western Yugoslavia, particularly Slovenia, Croatia, and Bosnia-Herzegovina. It drew particularly strong support from the Croatian and Bosnian Serbs, on account of the Croatian fascist (*Ustaša*) genocidal persecution of the latter, which literally drove them into the resistance. Yet these Serb Partisans fought under the banners of a free and sovereign Croatia and a free and sovereign Bosnia-Herzegovina within a Yugoslav union of equals. This *prečani* support enabled the communists to establish a federal Yugoslavia, contrary to Great Serbian goals. The latter were upheld in the Second World War by Milan Nedić's Serbian quisling regime and by the Nazi–collaborationist Chetnik movement.[3]

At the Second Session of the Anti-fascist Council for the People's Liberation of Yugoslavia (AVNOJ), which opened on 29 November 1943, the Partisans established Yugoslavia as a federation of six members: Slovenia, Croatia, Bosnia-Herzegovina, Serbia, Montenegro, and Macedonia. This represented a heavy defeat for traditional Serbian nationalism: Serbia definitely lost Macedonia, Montenegro, and all territory in Bosnia-Herzegovina. Furthermore, Serbia lost its hegemony over Yugoslavia, becoming simply one republic among six.

The AVNOJ territorial settlement was to Serbia what the Versailles territorial settlement was to Germany. It was this settlement, in particular the "AVNOJ borders" dividing the Serbs between the republics of Serbia, Croatia, and Bosnia-Herzegovina, against which Serbia rebelled in the 1990s.

Partisan support in eastern Yugoslavia was relatively weak; the Partisan liberation of Serbia and defeat of the Nazi, Nedić, and Chetnik forces there in the autumn of 1944 required massive Soviet assistance. The relatively weak foundations of communist rule in Serbia, and the communists' repudiation of Serb-nationalist claims on Croatia, Bosnia-Herzegovina, Macedonia, and Montenegro, meant they had to compensate Serbian sensibilities elsewhere. Belgrade remained Yugoslavia's capital. Vojvodina and Kosovo were joined to the new People's Republic of Serbia as entities in which, although they were formally autonomous, real power was held by ethnic Serbs and the Serbian security services. To alleviate Serb fears of being divided between different republics, the regime's rhetoric downplayed the republican borders. At the Founding Congress of the Communist Party of Serbia in Belgrade on 12 May 1945, Yugoslav Communist leader Josip Broz Tito stated: "I do not want there to be in Yugoslavia borders that divide; rather, I have hundreds of times stated that I want the borders to be those that join our nations."[4] These concessions to Serbia would prove the weak links in the new Yugoslav chain. Furthermore, for the first two decades of its existence, the People's Federated Republic of Yugoslavia was highly centralized, with power concentrated in Belgrade. This appealed to the strong current of Serbian opinion that favoured integral Yugoslavism.

Serbia nevertheless lost its position of *de facto* first-among-equals in Yugoslavia after July 1966, when Tito purged the conservative Serbian communist strongman Aleksandar Ranković and his supporters. This led to the emancipation of Vojvodina and Kosovo, which now gained real autonomy from Serbia, while power in Kosovo was increasingly transferred to the Albanian majority. These changes were supported by the liberal wing of the Serbian communists, yet they too were purged by Tito in October 1972, further de-legitimizing the regime in Serbian eyes. A new constitution, promulgated in 1974, affirmed the virtual separation of Kosovo and Vojvodina from Serbia and their establishment as *de facto* republics – while they each retained a veto on decisions affecting the Socialist Republic of Serbia as a whole.[5] This completed Yugoslavia's transition to a semi-confederation of semi-sovereign republics and autonomous provinces.

Meanwhile, Yugoslavia's defense system was decentralized, through the establishment of a system of Territorial Defense (TO) parallel to the JNA, placing significant military forces in the hands of the republican, provincial and lower-level communist organizations. The JNA itself was almost federalized: it was organized in six armies corresponding to the five larger republics and Vojvodina, and in an independent corps corresponding to Montenegro. These changes alienated conservative Serbian communists, Serb nationalists, and the JNA high command alike, creating the basis for their tripartite rebellion that took place after Tito's death and that found ultimate expression in the War of Yugoslav Succession.

The Serbian rebellion against Titoism

Serbian opposition to the post-1974 constitutional order came from the ranks of mainstream communists, dissident nationalists, and army officers, and accelerated after Tito's death in 1980. Its leading figure was Dobrica Ćosić, a former communist hardliner purged by the liberalizing Serbian Party in 1968, who then became a nationalist dissident. Serbian intellectual opposition to Titoism was manifested by the Memorandum of the Serbian Academy of Sciences and Arts, excerpts of which were made public in September 1986 and which alleged that the constitutional order denied the Serbs their own state (i.e. a unitary republic), that the western Yugoslav republics were exploiting Serbia economically, and that the regime was acquiescing in the Albanian "genocide" of Serbs in Kosovo, as well as in Croatia's assimilation of its Serb population.[6]

The Serbian communist leadership under Ivan Stambolić, who became President of Serbia in 1986, attempted to win the support of the other Yugoslav republics for constitutional revision at the expense of Kosovo's and Vojvodina's autonomy. The JNA top brass, for its part, began the process of recentralizing military power in Yugoslavia in its own hands in 1981 when, following a Kosovar Albanian popular uprising, it dismantled Kosovo's TO on the grounds of its complicity.[7] In 1987, the semi-federal organization of the JNA was abolished in order to break the influence of the republics over the corps.

It was, however, only after Slobodan Milošević, President of the League of Communists of Serbia (SKS) seized power from Stambolić's faction at the 8th Session of the Central Committee of the SKS on 23 September 1987 that the three groups of Serbian malcontents – communist, nationalist, and military – came together. A hardline communist, Milošević appears to have begun his transition to a populist demagogue on his visit to Kosovo Polje in April 1987 to quell popular unrest. Confronted by a crowd of local Serbs and Montenegrins who complained of having been beaten by the predominantly Albanian local police, Milošević uttered his now infamous words: "No-one is allowed to beat you!," winning the crowd's approval. He appears then to have realized the gains to be made by leading, rather than opposing, the Serbian-nationalist backlash.[8] This was not simply opportunism; Milošević drew upon strong Serbian-socialist traditions of fusing nationalism and socialism.[9] The decline of the Yugoslav economy, increasingly apparent in the 1980s and 1990s and producing widespread strikes and social discontent, catalyzed Milošević's attempt to find new legitimation in nationalism.

Milošević consolidated his power through a populist–nationalist mobilization of the Serbian population, focused on restoring Serbian control of Kosovo: the so-called "anti-bureaucratic revolution." Using the state-controlled media and secret police to mobilize crowds, he overthrew the communist governments of

Vojvodina on 5 October 1988 (the "yoghurt revolution") and Montenegro on 10 January 1989, replacing them with his puppets. A giant rally in Belgrade on 19 November 1988 successfully pressured the Yugoslav parliament to pass legislation restoring Serbian control over Kosovo and Vojvodina. The Kosovo Albanians responded with massive protests. On 28 February 1989, another regime-engineered monster rally in Belgrade pressured the Yugoslav Presidency into authorizing the JNA's suppression of the Albanian protests, which was carried out with some bloodshed. On 23 March the Kosovo assembly was coerced, literally at gunpoint, into accepting the virtual abrogation of Kosovo's autonomy. Milošević became Serbian President on 28 May 1989, crowning his triumphs with a giant rally to celebrate the 600th anniversary of the Battle of Kosovo on 28 June.[10] This popular–nationalist mobilization created a momentum that was difficult for the Milošević regime to control, and that swept it toward war.

Having successfully re-established Serbian control over the autonomous provinces, Milošević next sought to restore the centralized Yugoslav federation of the pre-1966 Ranković era. During 1989, the Serbian leadership campaigned in favor of a new Yugoslav constitution that would drastically strengthen the Federal center *vis-à-vis* the republics. Slovenia opposed this, resulting in conflict with Serbia throughout 1989. Amendments to the Slovenian constitution were passed in September, guaranteeing Slovenian sovereignty within Yugoslavia. Serbia imposed sanctions on Slovenia in December. Parallel to this was the JNA's own struggle against the burgeoning Slovenian democratic opposition, elements of which were, through the Slovenian socialist youth magazine *Mladina*, agitating against the one-party regime, especially the JNA. The arrest of the so-called "Ljubljana Four" in May and June 1988, and their subsequent trial by the JNA, galvanized the Slovenes' push toward democracy and independence; the Slovene communist regime increasingly closed ranks with the opposition against the Serbian–JNA threat.[11] The correct suspicion that the JNA high command viewed its occupation of Kosovo as a model for similar action against Slovenia catalyzed Slovene secessionism.

The Serbian–Slovene struggle culminated at the 14th Extraordinary Congress of the League of Communists of Yugoslavia on 23 January 1990, when Milošević's bloc of delegates attempted to browbeat the Slovenes into submission. The Slovenian and Croatian delegations abandoned the congress in protest, marking the end of a unified Yugoslav political leadership. In April–May 1990, non-communist nationalist parties, which favoured independence for their respective republics and with which the Serbian regime was unwilling to coexist, won elections in both Slovenia and Croatia. The Serbian leadership responded to these developments by abandoning its efforts to recentralize the Federation, and indeed its support for a unified Yugoslavia altogether. It now resolved to establish a Great Serbia (though it avoided this provocative term, preferring to speak of "all Serbs in a single state" – a goal that would be satisfied through the creation of a "new Yugoslavia" comprising those Yugoslav nations that wished to remain in it – i.e. the Montenegrins and Serbs – including those living on

Bosnian and Croatian territory – and possibly the Macedonians and Bosnian Muslims). This meant destroying the Federation while coopting some of its organs – particularly the JNA. Milošević, Yugoslav Defense Secretary Veljko Kadijević and Borisav Jović, Serbia's representative in the Federal presidency, decided on 27–28 June 1990, with regard to Slovenia and Croatia, to "expel them forcibly from Yugoslavia, by simply drawing borders and declaring that they had brought this upon themselves through their decisions," in Jović's words. The JNA was to carry out the "amputation" of parts of Croatia inhabited by Serbs.[12]

1987–90 had seen Serbia rebel against the post-1966 Titoist order; 1990–2 saw it rebel against the entire Titoist order founded at the Second Session of AVNOJ in 1943. The Serbian regime abandoned an all-Yugoslav party; the SKS was reconstituted as the "Socialist Party of Serbia" on 16–18 July 1990. This was immediately followed by the foundation of a Serb nationalist party in Bosnia-Herzegovina, the Serb Democratic Party (SDS). On 28 September 1990, Milošević promulgated a new Serbian constitution, according to which: "The Republic of Serbia determines and guarantees: (1) the sovereignty, independence and territorial integrity of the Republic of Serbia and its international position and relations with other states and international organizations."[13] On 23 October, Serbia imposed customs duties on imports from Slovenia and Croatia. The Milošević regime merged Titoism with Great Serbian nationalism – Titoist in form but Great Serbian in content, a contradictory synthesis that produced a confused, unworkable strategy in the upcoming war.

Armed conflict in Croatia

The shift in Serbian strategy made war inevitable. The Serbian military assault on the western Yugoslav republics began on 14 May 1990, when the JNA General Staff attempted to disarm them by ordering the confiscation of all TO armaments and their storage in JNA depots. This was timed to coincide with the change of regime in Slovenia and Croatia, to minimize the possibility of resistance. The Slovene authorities nevertheless resisted the move, salvaging nearly a third of Slovenia's TO armaments, which provided the basis for the future Slovenian army. The Croatian authorities, however, were caught unprepared and their TO forces disarmed. The new Croatian regime therefore had to create new defense forces from scratch.

The spring 1990 elections in Croatia brought to power the Croatian Democratic Union (HDZ), led by Franjo Tudjman who became Croatian president. This was an initially heterogenous populist–nationalist party committed to Croatian independence. Tudjman had been a Partisan general and JNA officer, and subsequently director of a historical institute in Croatia. In this post, he evolved from an authoritarian communist into a Croat nationalist, leading to his purge in 1967. His nationalist "dissident" path led him, over the following decades, to build links with right-wing Croat émigrés in the diaspora, who would help bankroll the HDZ's electoral victory.[14]

Tudjman sought Croatian independence through a negotiated agreement with Milošević and the JNA. As a former JNA general, he had a long history of collaboration with Belgrade and the JNA and had an exaggerated belief in the latter's military power; and as a historian he was inspired by the Serbo-Croat agreement of 1939, whereby Croatia had achieved autonomy through an agreement with Belgrade, involving the Serbo-Croat partition of Bosnia-Herzegovina. He consistently hindered Croatian military preparations for fear they would provoke JNA military retaliation. Yet his regime behaved insensitively and provocatively toward the Serb minority in Croatia. Shortly after coming to power, the regime drafted a new Croatian constitution, under which the Serbs would lose their status of constituent nation in Croatia alongside the Croats, and be demoted to a national minority. Despite Serb objections, the constitution was eventually ratified on 22 December. This helped to galvanize the Croatian Serb rebellion organized by Serbian intelligence and the JNA.[15]

Although a majority of Croatian Serbs had voted for the Social Democratic Party of Croatia (SDP), which supported Croatian sovereignty, a minority had voted for the nationalist SDS, which spearheaded the Serb revolt, centered on the town of Knin in northern Dalmatia. The rebels overthrew the leaderships of Serb-majority municipalities held by moderates and replaced them with SDS supporters. On 17 August 1990, as the rebels blockaded approaches to Knin – the so-called "log revolution" – the JNA intervened to prevent Croatian security forces from suppressing them. On 30 September 1990, the Serb rebels proclaimed Serb autonomy within Croatia, followed by the establishment of the "Serb Autonomous Oblast [SAO] of Krajina" on 21 December. This was followed by the establishment of the SAOs of Western Slavonia and of Eastern Slavonia, Baranja, and Srem. Thus, the Serb rebels, backed by the JNA, began carving out the borders of a Great Serbian state.

Croatian military resistance was organized by defense minister Martin Špegelj, a former Partisan and JNA general. With the Croatian TO disarmed, Špegelj based the fledgling Croatian military on the forces of the Ministry of Internal Affairs, i.e. the police. He armed them using police and hunting weapons, and sought to import additional weapons from the former Warsaw Pact countries. On 28 May 1991, Croatia formally proclaimed the establishment of the Assembly of the National Guard (ZNG). Yet in the Croatian police inherited from the communist regime, ethnic Serbs had been heavily overrepresented; the HDZ regime's purge of Serb policemen helped fuel the Serb rebellion.

The Yugoslav collective presidency, which was also supreme commander of the armed forces, consisted of one representative from each republic and autonomous province, each of whom was in turn to act as president. Serbia's control over the representatives of Montenegro, Vojvodina, and Kosovo enabled it to paralyze, but not dominate the presidency. The Serbian bloc in the Yugoslav presidency on 9 January 1991 and again on 24–25 January sought presidential authorization for JNA action to disarm the Croatian forces, but this was successfully opposed by the Croatian, Slovenian, and Bosnian representatives.

On 12–15 March, the JNA and the Serbian bloc tried and failed to persuade the other presidency members to authorize emergency measures by the JNA that would have paved the way for a *coup d'etat*. This plan was the brainchild of Kadijević, and was supported with reservations by the Serbian leadership, which preferred an outright campaign to expand Serbia's borders.

Following the failure of Kadijević's plan, and a degree of arm-twisting by the Serbian leadership, the JNA definitely fell in behind the campaign for Serbian expansion. The JNA leadership had its reservations about abandoning Yugoslav unity, but was brought into line by Milošević's threat to replace it with a separate Serbian army. Milošević publicly warned that, if the JNA did not support Serbian policy in Croatia, "That would then be its end."[16] The JNA officers comforted themselves with the euphemism that they were now supporting "a new Yugoslav state of those Yugoslav nations that wanted it, in this phase the Serb and Montenegrin nations."[17] The JNA's readiness to support a "Great Serbia" was made possible by the Serb majority in the officer corps and particularly at the top level: of the four most senior posts in the JNA at this time, three were held by Serbs – the half-Serb, half-Croat, but nevertheless Serb-oriented Kadijević; the Bosnian Serb Chief of Staff Blagoje Adžić; and the Serbian deputy Chief of Staff Života Panić. Serb preponderance in the officer corps was strengthened in this period; by July 1991, the officer corps of the 5th Military District, covering Slovenia and Croatia, was 57% Serb, including its commander; none of its top four officers, nor any of its brigade or corps commanders was Croat.[18]

The war now began in earnest. On 1 March, the SAO of Krajiina declared its independence from Croatia. Milošević effectively declared Serbia's secession from Yugoslavia on 16 March, when he publicly declared that Serbia would no longer recognize decisions of the Yugoslav presidency. He stated further: "We have to ensure that we have unity in Serbia if we want, as the republic that is biggest, that is most numerous, to dictate the further course of events. These are questions of borders, therefore fundamental, state questions. And borders, as you know, are always dictated by the strong, never by the weak. Consequently, what is essential is that we have to be strong."[19] On 31 March, the first blood of the Croatian War was shed, when Serb rebels and Croatian police clashed at Plitvice in central Croatia, leaving one dead on each side. On 2 May, Serb rebels massacred twelve Croatian policemen at Borovo Selo in north-eastern Croatia. On 15 May Serbia's representatives in the Yugoslav presidency refused to allow Croatia's representative to take his turn as president, depriving Yugoslavia of a functioning executive.

The war in Slovenia and Croatia

Slovenia's and Croatia's citizens voted overwhelmingly for independence in referenda on 23 December 1990 and 19 May 1991, respectively; both republics declared independence on 25 June 1991. Slovene police took control of

Slovenia's international borders from their federal counterparts. On the 27 June, the JNA responded by attempting to seize control of Slovenia's international borders and the Ljubljana airport. Tudjman betrayed his military agreement with the Slovenes and refused to come to their assistance, hoping that Croatia could avoid war. Yet the Slovenes had carefully prepared their resistance, and their TO forces inflicted successive defeats on the JNA, which suffered heavier casualties than the Slovenes.[20]

Serbia's leadership viewed the conflict with Slovenia as a formality. With both republics abandoning Yugoslavia, the two had cooperated successfully during 1990–1. Consequently, after the initial limited JNA operations had failed, on 1 July the Serbian leadership rejected the JNA's plan for a full-scale offensive to crush Slovenia, so ensuring the JNA's defeat. Following a cease-fire on 3 July, the JNA's withdrawal from Slovenia was negotiated in the Brioni Accord of 7 July, through the mediation of the EC. Slovenia and Croatia were required to suspend their independence declarations for three months.

Following the end of Slovenia's "ten-day war," Serbia, the JNA, and the Serb rebels embarked on a full-scale war of conquest in Croatia. Since summer 1990, Serb rebels backed by the JNA had already seized approximately one-quarter of Croatia, mostly in the central part of the country (Banija, Kordun, Lika, and northern Dalmatia), but also in western and eastern Slavonia. Serbia now sought to increase and consolidate these conquests. The Serbian–JNA side possessed an incomparably more resolute leadership and an overwhelming superiority in armaments; in 1990, the JNA possessed 1,863 tanks, 3,760 combat vehicles, 1,034 artillery pieces, and 455 combat aircraft.[21]

Rather like Stalin before Operation Barbarossa, Tudjman was both terrified of war with his seemingly mightier neighbour and convinced he could avoid it through avoiding provocation. On 27 December 1990, Tudjman rejected Špegelj's plan for a pre-emptive strike against the JNA in Croatia, to seize its garrisons and armaments and render it incapable of offensive action. On 30 July, after the full-scale JNA assault had already begun, he would again reject such a strike, prompting the exasperated Špegelj's resignation.[22] Tudjman was mesmerized by the precedent of the Serbo-Croat agreement of 1939, lacked all confidence in Croatia's ability to defend itself, and placed all his cards on diplomacy. Unlike the Slovenes, who responded promptly to the JNA assault by besieging its garrisons, Tudjman avoided taking such a step until 14 September 1991. Tudjman's policy was Serbia's strongest trump-card right up to the war's end in 1995.

Serbia's second powerful trump-card was the policy of the international community, in the shape of the EC and UN. The Western states refused to take sides and attempted to negotiate an end to hostilities. This meant attempting to arrange cease-fires and discourage offensive operations, thereby freezing the front lines. This favoured the Serbian side, which already held most of the territory it wanted, and hurt the Croatians, who were seeking to recapture it. The imposition of a UN arms embargo on the combatants on 25 September, at the Yugoslav government's request, hampered the underarmed Croatians' ability to import weapons to redress the imbalance in armaments, while Western pressure on them to lift their blockade of the JNA barracks made it more difficult for them even to recapture their own TO weaponry, confiscated by the JNA in spring 1990; indeed, more difficult to wage war at all.

Nevertheless, the handicaps for the Serbian–JNA side proved to be still greater. The most important of these was a confusion over strategy – an expression of the confusion between an integral Yugoslavist and a Great Serbian orientation that had plagued Serbian leaders since before Yugoslavia's creation, and that Milošević could never quite resolve. Although forced by Milošević to accept a Great Serbian strategy, the JNA high command had nevertheless refused the Serbian leadership's request to withdraw its forces to behind the projected new Serbian borders prior to the start of the conflict. This made it difficult to deploy them for front-line war and left them vulnerable to blockade. Many JNA garrisons and depots indeed fell to the besieging ZNG, enabling the latter to overcome at least slightly its lack of heavy weaponry; of particular significance was the surrender on 22 September of the Varaždin garrison, the second-largest in Croatia. By occupying JNA depots and garrisons in Croatia, the ZNG acquired 250 tanks, 400–500 heavy artillery pieces, about 180,000 firearms and 2 million tons of ammunition and other military hardware, fundamentally altering the balance of forces and preventing realization of the Serbian war aims, according to Špegelj.[23]

The JNA was a multinational conscript army, and non-Serbs – not only Slovenes and Croats, but also Albanians, Macedonians, Muslims, Hungarians, and others to varying degrees – were largely unwilling to fight; so the JNA was plagued with desertions. With Serbia's own war aims unclear in the eyes of its public and even leadership – whether to defend Yugoslavia, establish a Great Serbia, or protect the Croatian Serbs – even Serbs were largely unwilling to fight and die. On 19 September, Serbia's war of conquest became more overt, with JNA forces mounting a large-scale invasion of eastern Slavonia from Serbia. Yet the invaders were rapidly stalemated, in large part due to poor morale in the JNA and the resistance of young Serbs to the draft, something which both Špegelj and Kadijević acknowledge.[24] By the end of September 1991, Kadijević was advocating the JNA's formal transformation into a Serbian army, hoping this would motivate Serb soldiers to fight. But Serbia's leadership rejected this for fear it would alienate the section of its domestic constituency that still viewed it as the supposed upholder of Yugoslavia, and because it would make Serbia appear the aggressor in international eyes.[25]

The Croatian forces, meanwhile, were highly motivated, despite their inferior armaments. The war for eastern Slavonia focused on the town of Vukovar, whose defenders withstood a three-month siege and inflicted massive casualties on the Serb forces. The defense was hampered by international interference; on 13 October, Tudjman ordered a halt to the ZNG's operation to relieve Vukovar under international pressure.[26] The Serbs' conquest of the town on 19 November was nevertheless a pyrrhic victory, as the scale of their losses was such that their offensive power was broken.

Serbia and the JNA increasingly lost the international propaganda war. The statesmen of the EC were from the start hostile to the breakup of Yugoslavia and secession of Croatia and Slovenia; Croatian military retaliation against the JNA was viewed unfavourably. Yet Serbian behavior brought a shift in international opinion. The Brioni Accord had required Serbia to permit Croatia's Stipe Mesić to assume the position of Yugoslav president. Yet on 3 October, the Serbian and Montenegrin members of the Yugoslav presidency carried out a coup, declaring themselves the acting presidency with exclusive control over the JNA, divesting Slovenia, Croatia, Bosnia-Herzegovina, and Macedonia of their rights as federation members. This was followed by the expiration of the three-month moratorium on Slovenia's and Croatia's declarations of independence. At the Hague Conference on 18 October, Serbia unilaterally rejected the proposal of the EC's Lord Peter Carrington for Yugoslavia's reorganization as a confederation of sovereign republics, with autonomy for minorities such as the Serbs in Croatia and the Albanians in Serbia. Serbia was therefore viewed as destroying what was left of Yugoslav unity.

The bulk of atrocities were committed by the Serb forces, an inevitable result of their policy of killing or expelling the non-Serb inhabitants of the areas they occupied so as to render them homogenously Serb and permit their annexation. Although there were Croatian atrocities, particularly the massacre of Serb civilians at Gospić on 16–18 October, these were dwarfed by the scale of Serb war crimes. A notorious early Serb atrocity was the wiping out of the Croat village of Kijevo near Knin on 26 August, but the worst was perhaps the massacre of about 260 civilian prisoners at Ovčara near Vukovar following the town's conquest. At a more symbolic level, the JNA's attack on the Croatian city of Dubrovnik, an internationally renowned UNESCO World Heritage site with no apparent strategic value and a population that was overwhelmingly ethnic-Croat, was a propaganda disaster.

These factors in particular influenced Germany, which had from the start been more sympathetic to the Croatians and Slovenes than had most EC members. Given the apparent pusillanimity of the EC in the face of Serbian obstruction of the peace process, plus the increasing brutality of Serb forces in Croatia, Germany on 15 November resolved in favor of recognizing Slovenia's and Croatia's independence. On 16 December, Germany overcame British, French, and US opposition, leading to an EC invitation to recognize the independence of those Yugoslav republics that so wished, provided they fulfilled conditions specified by the EC's Arbitration Commission. Croatia's fulfilment was only partial; nevertheless Germany recognized Slovenia's and Croatia's independence on 23 December, followed by the other EC countries on 15 January.[27] Serb rebels, meanwhile, proclaimed the "Serb Republic of Krajina" (RSK) on 21 December.

International diplomacy nevertheless rescued the Serbs from defeat. UN representative Cyrus Vance negotiated the so-called Geneva Accord with

Milošević and Tudjman on 23 November, producing a cease-fire and enabling the crumbling JNA to withdraw intact from Croatia, while the Serb rebels retained Vukovar and other conquests. Under international pressure, Tudjman lifted the Croatian siege of the JNA's Zagreb barracks, enabling it to withdraw large quantities of military hardware from the Croatian capital and redeploy it on the front lines against the Croatians.[28] The Geneva Accord permitted the JNA to "withdraw" its forces from Croatia into Bosnia-Herzegovina. This was followed by the Vance Plan to deploy UN peacekeepers to protect Serb-held territory in Croatia. In late November, the ZNG launched a counter-offensive that recaptured about 60% of occupied western Slavonia before Tudjman, under Western pressure, ordered a halt to operations on 26 December. The permanent cease-fire signed by Croatia on 2 January 1992 allowed the JNA to remain in Western and Eastern Slavonia, despite being on the verge of total military collapse.[29] The implementation of the Vance Plan led to the establishment of four UN Protected Areas in Serbian-occupied Croatia. Serbia now prepared to attack Bosnia-Herzegovina.

Serbia's assault on Bosnia-Herzegovina

Serbia's assault on Bosnia-Herzegovina was the next stage in Belgrade's plan of expansionism following the cease-fire in Croatia. This dovetailed with a Bosnian Serb nationalist rebellion against the multinational Socialist Republic of Bosnia-Herzegovina. Bosnian Serbs had been predominant in the Bosnian Partisan movement; in 1945, the fledgling Bosnian republic had a Serb president, prime minister and secretary of the Bosnian communist organization. Serb predominance was particularly strong in the security forces, while Serbs as a whole comprized the largest single Bosnian nationality. Yet this Serb predominance crumbled. The Bosnian Muslims were officially recognized as a nation in 1968 and, thanks to their higher birth-rate and higher Serb emigration, they overtook the Serbs to become the largest Bosnian nationality by the start of the 1970s. The Bosnian Croats, too, were rehabilitated from the late 1960s onward, assuming their share of power in the republic. This loss of hegemony laid the basis for a progressive Bosnian Serb disenchantment with the Bosnian republic, leading eventually to secessionist rebellion.[30]

Free elections in November–December 1990 brought to power an anti-communist coalition of Serb, Croat, and Muslim nationalists – the SDS, the HDZ, and the (Muslim) Party of Democratic Action (SDA). The coalition partners divided up power in the republic amongst themselves. The SDS automatically took power in localities where Serbs formed a majority, giving them control over local councils and police and TO forces. Following their election victory, the SDS began to form regional associations of "Serb municipalities." In September 1991, these associations grew into the SAO of Herzegovina, the Autonomous Region of Krajina, the SAO of Romanija, and, subsequently, the SAOs of Semberia and North Bosnia. So began the Serb campaign to partition

Bosnia-Herzegovina. In October 1991, Mihajlo Marković, deputy president of Milošević's party, stated: "there will be at least three units in the new Yugoslav state: Serbia, Montenegro and a united Bosnian and Knin Krajina."[31]

As Bosnia-Herzegovina, under SDA leadership, drifted toward independence, SDS separatism became increasingly violent. In municipalities where Serbs were in a minority, Serb municipal officials, councillors, policemen, and TO officers abandoned the common Bosnian organs to set up exclusively Serb counterparts in Serb-majority villages, suburbs, or neighbourhoods. A breakaway Bosnian Serb capital was established at Pale, in the suburbs of Sarajevo. When war was launched, the new Serb organs would attempt either to reconquer the abandoned Bosnian centers of power, or to bomb or starve them into submission.

The Bosnian parliament responded to Serbia's hijacking of the federal organs by declaring Bosnia-Herzegovina's sovereignty on 14–15 October. SDS leader Radovan Karadžić on this occasion issued a genocidal threat: "Do not think that you will not lead Bosnia-Herzegovina into hell, and do not think that you will not perhaps make the Muslim people disappear, because the Muslims cannot defend themselves if there is war. How will you prevent everyone from being killed in Bosnia-Herzegovina?"[32] The SDS delegates responded to the parliament's vote by seceding from it to establish a Serb National Assembly. On 9 January 1992 the "Serb Republic of Bosnia-Herzegovina" was proclaimed; it declared independence on 27 March.

A Bosnian Serb army (eventually called the "Army of the Serb Republic" – VRS) was created in this period by the Milošević regime and the JNA. Following the Geneva Accord, they concentrated all Bosnian Serb JNA officers and troops on Bosnian territory, while those from Serbia and Montenegro were largely withdrawn. Thus, by late December 1991, roughly 85–90% of the JNA in Bosnia-Herzegovina was made up of Bosnian Serbs.[33] Having confiscated most of the weapons of Bosnia's TO outside the Serb-controlled areas, the JNA armed the SDS militia and Serb TO, creating a massive military imbalance between Serb and Bosnian republic forces.

Bosnian defense preparations were obstructed at every step by the SDS members of the ruling coalition. The SDS controlled a large part of the Bosnian security services; the Bosnian TO commander, for example, was an SDS supporter. Meanwhile, even many Muslim and Croat officials collaborated with Belgrade and the JNA. This made a unified Bosnian defense policy very difficult; defense preparations were largely left to local Muslim or Croat officials, soldiers or politicians acting on their own initiative. The SDA and HDZ established their own defense forces that bypassed the republic's organs – the Patriotic League and the Croat Council of Defense (HVO), respectively. The HDZ and HVO pursued a separatist policy of their own, establishing the Croat Community of Bosanska Posavina and Croat Community of Herceg-Bosna in November 1991 as autonomous Croat entities equivalent to the SAOs. The SDA, under Bosnian President Alija Izetbegović, increasingly dominated the

Bosnian leadership, but its politicians were unwilling to believe that war would occur and trusted in negotiations with Belgrade and the JNA. This Muslim naïveté helped ensure the crushing Serb victories of the war's early stages.[34]

Bosnia-Herzegovina declared independence on 3 March 1992, following a referendum boycotted by the SDS, in which 63% of the electorate – 99.4% of those voting – voted for independence. This step was taken reluctantly; the Bosnian leadership had opposed Yugoslavia's breakup but feared remaining in a Serbian-dominated rump-state. Bosnia-Herzegovina was recognized by the EU states on 6 April – the forty-seventh anniversary of Sarajevo's liberation from the Nazis. Belgrade and the SDS used international recognition as a pretext for full-scale war, but this had already broken out by the time recognition occurred.

War was launched while the embryonic Bosnian Serb armed forces were still part of or subordinate to the JNA. The conquest of East Bosnia, a Muslim-majority territory, was spearheaded by forces from Serbia: the paramilitary "Tigers" of Željko Ražnatović-Arkan occupied Bijeljina on 1 April; JNA forces, based in Serbia, supported by the Tigers and the paramilitary Chetniks of Vojislav Šešelj, attacked and occupied Zvornik on 8–10 April. Elsewhere, the Herzegovinan capital of Mostar was on 3 April bombarded by JNA forces under the command of Momčilo Perišić, a Serb from Serbia. On the same day, Bosnia's second city of Banja Luka, in the west, where the SDS already controlled the organs of government, was seized by Serbian forces. In south-west Bosnia, JNA forces based in Serb-occupied Croatia, commanded by the up-and-coming Ratko Mladić, captured Kupres from Croat forces on 8 April. Serb forces overran the best part of East Bosnia during April and the northern towns of Brčko, Derventa and Doboj in early May, thereby establishing a corridor linking Serb-held territories in eastern and western Bosnia-Herzegovina. By this point, Serb forces held roughly 70% of the country.

The Serb attempt to establish an exclusively Serb state on territory that was approximately 50% non-Serb was necessarily genocidal. The Belgrade-controlled military and paramilitary forces spearheaded the conquest, while the SDS-controlled civilian authorities acted as adjuncts and were in charge of the actual administrative removal of the non-Serb population.[35] This so-called "ethnic cleansing" involved the systematic massacre, expulsion, detention, torture, and rape of non-Serbs, and the destruction of their civic, religious, and cultural buildings and artefacts. This was intended to destroy the multinational Bosnian republic and end all possibility for coexistence between Serbs and non-Serbs. Perhaps the most notorious atrocities occurred near Prijedor in north-western Bosnia, an area where Serb–Muslim relations had traditionally been particularly good. There, at the concentration camps of Omarska, Keraterm and Trnopolje (particularly in the first two), Muslim and Croat inmates were systematically tortured and murdered on a large scale.[36]

The Serb strategy was nevertheless flawed. The contradictory policy of attempting simultaneously to secede from Bosnia-Herzegovina and conquer it was self-defeating; it involved abandoning Bosnia-Herzegovina's centers of power to the Bosnian leadership. All but one Serb member of the Bosnian TO Staff, including its commander, abandoned it to the Bosnian leadership at the war's start; this Staff became the kernel of the fledgling Bosnian Army. The SDS politicians' flight to Pale left Sarajevo firmly in Bosnian leadership hands. Serb forces brutally besieged Sarajevo throughout the war, but their attempts to conquer or bisect the city were repeatedly repulsed, most spectacularly on 2–3 May. Likewise, the JNA's Tuzla garrison attempted to retreat from Tuzla on 15 May 1992 but was ambushed and destroyed by Bosnian forces; the Tuzla region thenceforth became the strongest bastion of Bosnia-Herzegovina's defense.

The genocide galvanized often initially passive Muslims into a life-or-death resistance; those who attempted to surrender and collaborate, as many local Muslim leaders did, were rewarded by the rapid ethnic cleansing of themselves and their constituents. The Serb rejection of both Muslim collaboration and state organs in non-Serb-majority areas meant that Muslim- and/or Croat-majority cities could only be conquered by their systematic destruction, at a cost in Serb casualties that the SDS leadership was unwilling and unable to pay. The Serbian conquest of Vukovar had cost at least 10,000 casualties; the conquest of Sarajevo, twenty times larger than Vukovar, might have cost the entire VRS. Yet the Bosnian leadership's possession of Sarajevo prevented the complete Serb destruction of the Bosnian state. The Serb blitzkrieg of spring 1992 degenerated into a grinding war of attrition in which the Bosnian side, with its greater manpower reserves, was increasingly at an advantage.

Finally, by establishing an autonomous Bosnian "Serb Republic," Milošević created a Frankenstein's monster that escaped his control, and that prevented him concluding a favourable peace while the Serbs were still winning. Belgrade proclaimed the Federal Republic of Yugoslavia (SRJ) on 27 April 1992, comprising only Serbia and Montenegro, which unsuccessfully posed as the sole successor-state to the old Yugoslavia. The SRJ formally disassociated itself from the war in Bosnia-Herzegovina, and the sections of the JNA comprised of Serbians and Montenegrins were withdrawn from Bosnian territory on 19 May, while those comprised of Bosnian Serbs were merged with the Serb TO and the SDS militia to form the VRS, with Mladić handpicked as commander by Belgrade. Against Milošević's wishes, the Bosnian Serb leadership, dazzled by its early victories, rejected successive peace plans, perpetuating the war until the autumn of 1995. Milošević imposed sanctions on the Serb Republic to coerce it into accepting a peace settlement, but this was largely nullified by his continuing provision of military support to the VRS.

Nevertheless, the Serb rebels benefited from the benevolent policy of the international community. Britain, France, and Boutros Boutros Ghali's UN administration demonstrated a pro-Serb bias that militarily benefited the Serbs.[37] In negotiations at Lisbon in March 1992, international mediators proposed acquiescence in Serb demands for the three-way partition of Bosnia-Herzegovina; this was ultimately rejected by the Bosnians. The UN arms embargo of 1991 was now enforced against Bosnia-Herzegovina, cementing Serb superiority in armaments. Meanwhile, a UN no-fly zone was only weakly enforced, and proved no hindrance to Mladić's use of a helicopter to travel around the war zone.

The presence of UN forces (United Nations Protection Force –UNPROFOR) in Bosnia-Herzegovina increasingly eroded what was left of Bosnian sovereignty. UNPROFOR took over control of Sarajevo's airport from the JNA at the war's start, at the price of effective UN acquiescence in the Serb siege. UNPROFOR enforced Serb-dictated limits on the movement of persons, goods, and services into and out of Sarajevo.[38] Successive UN commanders, especially Satish Nambiar, Lewis MacKenzie, Michael Rose, and Bernard Janvier, displayed a marked hostility toward the Bosnians and preference for the Serb rebels. UN sources went so far as to attribute successive VRS massacres of Sarajevo civilians to the Bosnian authorities themselves, in order to dampen international sympathy for them. The international presence hindered rather than helped Bosnian efforts at self-defense.

The Muslim–Croat conflict

The Serb secession left an uneasy coalition of Muslim and Croat nationalists and non-nationalist Bosnians at the head of the Bosnian state. While the SDA and the non-nationalists sought to consolidate the Bosnian armed forces in the hands of the central authorities, the HDZ, guided by the Tudjman regime in Croatia, increasingly pursued a separatist course, leading eventually to full-scale war between the HVO and the Bosnian army.

At the outbreak of full-scale war in April 1992, the Bosnian leadership formally controlled the armed forces of the Bosnian state, the TO, and the police; the Patriotic League, as the military wing of the SDA; various lesser militias; and, in principle, the Patriotic League's Croat counterpart, the HVO. The Bosnian leadership attempted to weld this disparate collection into a unified Bosnian armed force. On 15 April, the Staff of the TO formally assumed command of all units formed on the political platform of the Patriotic League, marking the official birth of the Army of the Republic of Bosnia-Herzegovina (ARBiH). The ARBiH had a multinational command and composition; just over two-thirds of its troops were Muslims and nearly one-third Croats and Serbs.[39]

HDZ officials held key posts in the Bosnian government, above all the premiership and ministry of defense. Yet they pursued a separate policy. The HVO was a recognized component of the Bosnian armed forces, but rejected integration into the ARBiH. Bosnian defense minister Jerko Doko of the HDZ gave the HVO priority in military procurements. In areas of Bosnia-Herzegovina that fell under its control, the HVO acted as a separate army in the hands of the HDZ. It disputed possession of territories and military facilities with the ARBiH, and in many areas these armed forces rapidly descended into a state of cold war.

The HDZ and HVO were guided by the policy of Tudjman, who staked his cards from the start on a collaborationist policy with the Serbs, involving the Serbo-Croat partition of Bosnia-Herzegovina. This was apparently agreed upon in March 1991, in talks between Tudjman and Milošević at Karadjordjevo. This was followed by a HDZ–SDS meeting at Graz in Austria on 6 May 1992 to delineate their spheres of influence in Bosnia-Herzegovina. Failure to agree on the possession of Mostar led to a Croatian Army offensive that pushed Serb forces back from the Herzegovinan capital on 12–17 June. Yet conflict between Bosnian Serb and Croat forces rapidly subsided in favor of increasingly warm collaboration. The conduit for Croatian support to the Bosnian Croat separatists, bypassing official Croatian government channels, was Tudjman's Bosnian Croat defense minister Gojko Šušak.

Tudjman and Šušak sabotaged the Bosnian defense. The successful joint Croatian–Bosnian defense of Posavina in northern Bosnia was crippled after Tudjman withdrew the Croatian Army, leading to the Serbs' definite securing of the "northern corridor" linking their conquests in western and eastern Bosnia. The town of Bosanski Brod was abandoned by the Croats to the Serbs without a struggle on 8 October 1992. This appears to have been a quid pro quo for the JNA's withdrawal from the hinterland of Dubrovnik in July 1992. The Serb capture of Jajce in central Bosnia on 29 October appears to have been the result of rivalry between the Bosnian army and HVO forces, which prevented a successful coordinated defense. Six days earlier, the first major engagement of the incipient Croat–Muslim conflict occurred, when the HVO drove the ARBiH from the Herzegovinan town of Prozor; the Muslim population was then expelled.

The final push leading to all-out war between the HVO and the ARBiH was provided by the UN's and EU's so-called "Vance–Owen Peace Plan," which assumed its finalized form in January 1993. It proposed dividing Bosnia-Herzegovina into ten cantons, with 43% of Bosnian territory going to the Serbs and 25% each to the Muslims and Croats. The Plan proved a dead letter in the face of Serb rejection. Nevertheless, it was taken by the HDZ as legitimizing its military possession of the three cantons assigned to the Croats. Bosnian Defense Minister Božo Raić of the HDZ responded on 16 January by ordering all ARBiH units in the Croat provinces to submit to HVO command, and all HVO units in the Muslim provinces to ARBiH command, which resulted in fighting as the ARBiH resisted Raić's order.[40] This coincided with the murder on 3 January 1993 of Bosnian Deputy Prime Minister Hakija Turajlić by Serb soldiers with the complicity of French UN forces.[41]

To the world's surprise, the ARBiH, greatly superior in manpower, repeatedly defeated the HVO, driving it from Jablanica and Konjic in the spring of 1993; from Travnik and Kakanj in June; from Bugojno in July; and from Vareš in November. The two armies had existed side-by-side in towns across Bosnia-Herzegovina, and the outbreak of the conflict left the HVO's position in many of them untenable. The HVO and Croatian army attacked and destroyed but failed to capture east Mostar from the ARBiH; the destruction of the world-famous "Old Bridge" brought worldwide condemnation. During 1993 the portion of Bosnian territory under HVO control fell by half, from about 20% to 10%. In the areas it held, the HVO ethnically cleansed the Muslim population and destroyed its religious and cultural heritage in a manner that resembled the behavior of the Serb forces. Large Croat massacres of Muslims occurred at Ahmići on 16 April and Stupni Do on 23 October 1993. The ARBiH was also guilty of large-scale atrocities against Croat civilians, such as at Grabovica on 7–8 September and Uzdol on 14 September.

The Bosnian revival and the road to Dayton

As the Croat–Muslim conflict exploded, Serb forces consolidated their conquests. In April 1993, the UN Security Council declared the East Bosnian enclave of Srebrenica, on the verge of falling to the Serbs, a "safe area"; Sarajevo, Tuzla, Bihać, Žepa, and Goražde were also subsequently declared "safe areas," but the UN made no provisions to render them "safe" in practice; on the contrary, it took steps to disarm the defenders of Srebrenica. The safe area scheme marked a further step in the dismantling of Bosnia-Herzegovina. In August 1993, international mediators issued the finalized version of the Owen–Stoltenberg Peace Plan, amounting to an endorsement of Serbian and Croatian partition proposals: it transformed Bosnia-Herzegovina into a loose "union" of three constituent entities, each with the right to secede. The Serbs were granted approximately 54% of Bosnia-Herzegovina; the Muslims 30% and the Croats 16%; with Sarajevo placed under UN administration. In response, the HDZ proclaimed the Croat Republic of Herceg-Bosna, while the renegade Muslim warlord Fikret Abdić staged an armed rebellion at Velika Kladusa in the north-west and proclaimed the Autonomous Province of West Bosnia. Serb forces at this time captured further territory around Sarajevo. Bosnia-Herzegovina appeared finished.

The Izetbegović regime nevertheless consolidated itself in this period. The independently-minded ARBiH chief of staff, Sefer Halilović was effectively demoted in June 1993 and dismissed in October, after which the army was fully under Izetbegović's control. On 27 September a special "Bosniak Assembly," convened in Sarajevo by Izetbegović, voted to reject the Owen–Stoltenberg Plan, ending the possibility of Bosnia-Herzegovina's formal partition. On 26 October, the regime launched Operation Trebević, the suppression of rogue ARBiH units in Sarajevo that were under the control of gangsters and subverting power in the capital. This was followed by the reconstitution of the moribund Bosnian government, which now became an entirely Muslim-dominated body. The US-brokered Washington Agreement of March 1994 ended the Muslim–Croat conflict; the battered Croats were forced to accept the establishment of a Federation of Bosnia-Herzegovina that would reunite them with the Muslims. The ARBiH was now free to concentrate its forces against the

VRS. The following month saw the first, token, NATO air-strike against Serb forces, at Goražde in east Bosnia.

A certain military equilibrium was reached by mid-1994. Serbian forces held approximately 70% of the country; Bosnian forces 20%, and Croatian forces 10%. However, the ARBiH held the country's economic and demographic heartland, with a population of about 2 million, as against 600,000 for the VRS and 200,000 for the HVO. The ARBiH possessed 110,000 troops organized in six corps with 100,000 reserves, as against 80,000 for the VRS and 50,000 for the HVO. However, the Bosnian army remained seriously handicapped by its lack of heavy weapons: it possessed about forty tanks and thirty armored personnel carriers (APCs), as against 330 and 400, respectively, for the VRS.[42] General Jovan Divjak, Deputy Commander of the ARBiH, stated in February 1995 that out of over 200,000 Bosnian soldiers only 50,000 were armed; "indeed (not one of our units is fully armed because of the arms embargo."[43] The VRS's soldiers, however, suffered from very low morale, poor discipline, and high rates of desertion, even among officers, and were incapable of defending their overextended front lines.

A further shift occurred internationally, where increasing domestic opposition to its policy led the US Clinton Administration to begin to diverge from the Anglo-French policy of appeasing the Serbs. The United States gave the go-ahead for an unlikely ally – Iran – to arm the ARBiH in violation of the arms embargo, and sent a delegation of US army officers to help train the senior staff of the nascent Federation army. The Bosnian Serb rebels, unaware of the extent of their military decline, rejected the latest international peace initiative, the July 1994 Contact Group Plan, which envisaged a 51%–49% division of Bosnian territory between the Federation and the Serb Republic. Continued Serb recalcitrance catalyzed the US policy shift.

The Bosnian resurgence was spearheaded by the ARBiH's 5th Corps under the brilliant commander Atif Dudaković, which covered the north-western corner of Bosnia centered on the town of Bihać, which from the war's start had been wholly surrounded by Serb-held territories. In a string of victories in summer–autumn of 1994, the 5th Corps crushed Abdić's rebel statelet at Velika Kladuša and advanced eastward and southward against the VRS. Although these gains were soon reversed by a VRS counter-offensive, the military weakness of the Serb Republic was revealed. It was 5th Corps resistance, not the pin-prick NATO air-strike of that month, that eventually halted the VRS counter-offensive. In the same period, the ARBiH recaptured much of the territory around Sarajevo taken by the VRS the previous summer. On 3 November, in the first successful joint operation between the HVO and Bosnian Army since the Washington Agreement, Serb forces were driven out of Kupres.

Croatia, since the cease-fire of 2 January 1992, had conducted only token military operations against Serb forces in Croatia, particularly at Maslenica in January 1993 and Medački džep in September 1993. In the autumn of 1994, in response to the shift on the battlefield, the absence of a peace settlement and the change in US policy, Croatia made preparations for the forcible recapture of its Serb-occupied areas. In late November, the Croatian army began a major offensive against Serb forces in south-western Bosnia, in order to encircle the RSK capital of Knin. On 1–3 May 1995, in "Operation Flash," the Croatian army destroyed the SAO of Western Slavonia, revealing the RSK's military bankruptcy.

The Bosnian resurgence experienced repeated setbacks, above all a costly, failed attempt to break the Sarajevo siege in June and July 1995, and the Serb capture of the isolated UN "safe areas" of Srebrenica and Žepa in East Bosnia in July. The capture of Srebrenica involved the Serb massacre of approximately 8,000 Muslim men and boys; a war crime subsequently recognized as genocide by two international courts. The UN authorities rejected the use of air power to prevent the Serb capture of Srebrenica. Serb forces now held all of eastern Bosnia-Herzegovina outside the Tuzla region, except Goražde. Yet they paid a price: US Congressional outrage over the Srebrenica massacre was such that the policy of appeasement now became politically unsustainable for the Clinton Administration, which prepared for a serious military confrontation with the VRS. The accession of Jacques Chirac as French president in place of François Mitterrand in May 1995 brought a parallel change in French policy.[44] The US now encouraged Croatia to take action against Serb forces.

Following the conquest of Srebrenica and Žepa, Milošević turned his attention to the Bihać enclave. The forces of the RSK, under a new commander appointed by Belgrade for the purpose, attacked and seemed poised to overrun the enclave, threatening to win the war against both Croatia and Bosnia with a single knock-out blow. Izetbegović and Tudjman responded by signing an agreement at Split on 22 July for military cooperation, according to which, on the grounds of the "ineffectiveness of the international community," the "Republic and Federation of Bosnia-Herzegovina called upon the Republic of Croatia to extend military and other assistance to their defense against aggression, especially in the Bihać area, which the Republic of Croatia has accepted."[45] On 4–7 August, the Croatian army spectacularly wiped out the RSK (outside of the enclave of Eastern Slavonia), in a campaign called "Operation Storm". Abdić's Muslim–rebel regime in Velika Kladuša, restored with Serb assistance in autumn 1994, was now finally destroyed by the 5th Corps.

This signaled the defeat of the Great Serbian project: international illusions of Serb military superiority were shattered; Croatia had effectively won its war; the 5th Corps was freed from encirclement; and Serb morale was broken. The RSK leadership responded to the Croatian offensive by evacuating the entire Serb civilian population of about 150,000 people from the areas affected, which were abandoned with little struggle.[46] The Tudjman regime helped cement this exodus; hundreds of Serb civilians were killed and Serb homes burned to deter the return of the refugees.

"Operation Storm" was followed by a joint Croatian–Bosnian offensive in western Bosnia in September, which destroyed the VRS's 2nd Krajina Corps.

The Croatian Army took Drvar, Šipovo, and Jajce; the 5th Corps took Bosanski Petrovac, Ključ, and Bosanska Krupa, and the ARBiH 7th Corps took Donji Vakuf. The allies threatened to capture Banja Luka and put an end to the Serb Republic's existence west of the northern corridor. To the east, the ARBiH advanced in Ozren, liberating Vozuća and threatening Doboj. The allied advance was facilitated by NATO air-strikes, beginning at the end of August in retaliation for another Serb massacre of Sarajevo citizens. These disabled the VRS's communications system, leaving it "deaf and blind" and handing a tactical bonus to the allies. The Bosnian Serbs now belatedly accepted the Contact Group Plan. Following a lull in the allied advance brought about by Western diplomatic pressure, the allies resumed their offensive in October, the 5th Corps and the Croatian Army and HVO captured Sanski Most and Mrkonjić-Grad, respectively, on 10 October. These operations made a reality on the ground of the 51%–49% distribution of territory between the Bosnian Federation and Serb Republic specified by the Contact Group Plan. Massive Western pressure, allegedly including a US threat of air-strikes against the ARBiH, induced the Bosnians and Croatians to sign a lasting cease-fire on 12 October. The Izetbegović regime's readiness to sign a cease-fire in its hour of victory, leading to a settlement that treated it as the defeated party, indicated its defeatism, as well as its fear of fighting alongside an unreliable Croatian ally in the face of Western disapproval.[47]

The war in Bosnia-Herzegovina was ended by the Dayton Accord of November 1995, in which the United States pressured the leaderships of Bosnia-Herzegovina, Serbia, Croatia, and the separatist Serbs and Croats to agree to a compromise peace with which none was fully satisfied, and which marked a three-way draw. The Republic of Bosnia-Herzegovina was replaced with a nominal state called Bosnia-Herzegovina consisting of two entities: the (Muslim–Croat) Federation of Bosnia-Herzegovina covering 51% of Bosnian territory, and the Serb Republic covering 49%. The Bosnian Croat nationalists were not treated equivalently to their Serb counterparts; the Croat Republic of Herceg-Bosna was formally abolished and superseded by the Federation, though in practice it remained as a shadow-state. The central Bosnian state was emasculated: most powers were devolved to the entities, including the military and police. A rotating Bosnian presidency was to alternate among members of the three constituent nationalities. The Federation, in turn, was divided into ten cantons and governed by a presidency rotating between the Muslims and Croats. The Federation army was to be united at the corps level and above; below that, it would remain divided between the ARBiH and HVO. Both entities were to be permitted to form independent relations with neighboring states (i.e. with Croatia and the SRJ, respectively).

The Muslims received complete control of Sarajevo and a corridor to the East Bosnian enclave of Goražde; the Serb Republic was compensated by territory taken from the HVO. The Muslim nationalists had achieved a formally unified Bosnia-Herzegovina and complete control of the Bosnian heartland, but the generous amount of territory and autonomy awarded to the Serb nationalists made the latter the principal beneficiaries. Bosnia-Herzegovina was placed under international protection and NATO occupation, in the guise of the Implementation Force. The Bosnian war was formally ended by the General Framework Agreement (GFA) for Peace in Bosnia-Herzegovina, signed at Paris on 14 December 1995 by representatives of the Republic of Bosnia-Herzegovina, the Republic of Croatia, and the Federal Republic of Yugoslavia.[48]

The GFA marked the end of the War of Yugoslav Succession. Just previously, in the 12 November Erdut Agreement, Serb representatives agreed to permit the reintegration of occupied Eastern Slavonia into Croatia, marking a fully successful outcome of the Croatian war of independence. Macedonia, whose people had voted for independence on 8 September 1991 and which had applied for recognition in December, was able to escape bloodshed, thanks to a US warning to Belgrade not to extend the war into this strategically sensitive territory; the JNA peacefully withdrew from Macedonia in November. Yet the GFA ignored the Kosovo question, catalyzing a conflict there in subsequent years, one that would draw in NATO and mark the final defeat of Milošević's hegemonic project.

Notes

1. The impact of the War of Yugoslav Succession on the subsequent politics of Croatia, Serbia, and Bosnia-Herzegovina is analysed in chapters 12, 13, and 14 of this volume.
2. See Ivo Banac, *The National Question in Yugoslavia: Origin, History, Politics* (Ithaca, NY and London: Cornell University Press, 1984).
3. Marko Attila Hoare, *Genocide and Resistance in Hitler's Bosnia: The Partisans and the Chetniks, 1941–1941* (London: Oxford University Press, 2006), pp. 143–56.
4. Josip Broz Tito, *Sabrana djela*, Vol. 28 (Belgrade: Komunist, 1988), p. 34.
5. *Ustav SFRJ i ustavi socijalističkih republika i pokrajina* (Belgrade: Ustavni zakoni registar pojmova, 1974).
6. Bože Čović (ed.), *Izvori velikosrpske agresije* (Zagreb: AC-SK, 1991), pp. 256–300.
7. Branko Mamula, *Slučaj Jugoslavije* (Podgorica: CID, 2000), pp. 40–4.
8. Adam LeBor, *Milošević: A Biography* (London: Polmont and Bloomsbury, 2002), p. 75; and Lenard J. Cohen, *Serpent in the Bosom: The Rise and Fall of Slobodan Milošević* (Boulder, Colo.: Westview Press, 2002), p. 106.
9. Marko Attila Hoare, "Slobodan Milošević's Place in Serbian History," *European History Quarterly*, Vol. 36, No. 3 (July 2006), pp. 452–4.
10. Laura Silber and Allan Little, *The Death of Yugoslavia* (London: BBC Books and Penguin, 1995), pp. 58–73.
11. *Ibid.*, pp. 48–57.
12. Borisav Jović, *Poslednji dani SFRJ* (Belgrade: Politika, 1995), p. 160.
13. *Službeni glasnik Republike Srbije*, Vol. 46, No. 1 (28 September 1990), p. 5.
14. See Darko Hudelist, *Tuđman – biografija* (Zagreb: Profil, 2004).
15. Silber and Little, *The Death of Yugoslavia*, pp. 92–8.
16. *NIN* (Belgrade), 12 April 1991, pp. 40–1.

17. Veljko Kadijević, *Moje viđenje raspada* (Belgrade: Politika, 1993), p. 93.
18. Belgrade Home Service (3 July 1991), trans. in *BBC Summary of World Broadcasts* (4 July 1991); and Yugoslav News Agency (2 July 1991), in *BBC Summary of World Broadcasts* (4 July 1991).
19. *NIN* (12 April 1991), pp. 40–1.
20. Janez Janša, *The Making of the Slovenian State 1988–1992: The Collapse of Yugoslavia*, trans. AMIDAS d.o.o., ed. Aleksander Zorn (Ljubljana: Založba Mladinska knjiga, 1994), pp. 149–212; and Silber and Little, *The Death of Yugoslavia*, pp. 154–68.
21. Branka Magaš and Ivo Žanić (eds.), *The War in Croatia and Bosnia-Herzegovina, 1992–1995* (London: Frank Cass, 2001), p. 111.
22. Martin Špegelj, *Sjećanja vojnika* (Zagreb: Znanje, 2001), pp. 149–58, 247–58.
23. Martin Špegelj, "The First Phase, 1990–1992: The JNA Prepares for Aggression and Croatia for Defense," in Magaš and Žanić, *The War in Croatia and Bosnia-Herzegovina*, p. 34.
24. Špegelj, "The First Phase," pp. 38–9; and Kadijević, *Moje viđenje raspada*, pp. 136–42.
25. Jović, *Poslednji dani SFRJ*, p. 329.
26. Srečko Jurdana, interview with Antun Tus, *Nacional* (Zagreb), 19 November 1997, pp. 17, 48.
27. Michael Libal, *Limits of Persuasion: Germany and the Yugoslav Crisis, 1991–1992* (Westport, Conn. and London: Praeger, 1997), pp. 62–87.
28. Silber and Little, *The Death of Yugoslavia*, p. 186.
29. Norman Cigar, "The Serbo-Croatian War, 1991: Political and Military Dimensions," *Journal of Strategic Studies*, Vol. 16, No. 3 (September 1993), pp. 326–7 and Špegelj, "The First Phase," pp. 35–6.
30. Marko Attila Hoare, *The History of Bosnia: From the Middle Ages to the Present Day* (London: Saqi, 2007), pp. 324–59.
31. Tanjug (9 October 1991).
32. Silber and Little, *The Death of Yugoslavia*, p. 215.
33. Jović, *Poslednji dani SFRJ*, p. 421.
34. Marko Attila Hoare, *How Bosnia Armed* (London: Saqi, 2004), pp. 21–31, 43–64.
35. See, for example, Hannes Tretter *et al.*, *Ethnic-Cleansing Operations in the Northeast-Bosnian City of Zvornik from April through June 1992*, 2 vols. (Vienna: Ludwig Boltzmann Institute of Human Rights, 1994, 1998).
36. Isabelle Wesselingh and Arnaud Vaulerin, *Raw Memory – Prijedor: An "Ethnic Cleansing Laboratory"* (London: Saqi, 2005), pp. 35–65.
37. Hoare, *The History of Bosnia*, pp. 376–9, 393–5.
38. Robert J. Donia, *Sarajevo: A Biography* (London: C. Hurst & Co, 2006), p. 304.
39. Hoare, *How Bosnia Armed*, p. 54.
40. See Marko Attila Hoare, "The Croatian Project to Partition Bosnia-Herzegovina, 1990–94," *East European Quarterly*, Vol. 31, No. 1 (March 1997) and *How Bosnia Armed*, pp. 81–7.
41. Peter Maass, "UN Accused of Blocking Bosnian Slaying Probe: Government Seeks Recall of Two Generals," *The Washington Post* (12 January 1993).
42. *The Military Balance 1994–1995* (London: International Institute for Strategic Studies, 1994), pp. 82–5.
43. Jovan Divjak, interview in *Armija Bosne i Hercegovine 1992.–1995.* (Sarajevo: Ljiljan, 1997), p. 96.

44. Samantha Power, *"A Problem from Hell" - America and the Age of Genocide* (London: Flamingo, 2002), pp. 391–442.
45. "The Split Declaration," *Bosnia Report*, No. 11 (June–August 1995), p. 5.
46. Milisav Sekulić, *Knin je pao u Beogradu*, 2nd edn. (Bad Vilbel: Nidda Verlag, 2001), pp. 178–9.
47. Hoare, *How Bosnia Armed*, pp. 121–128.
48. "General Framework Agreement for Peace in Bosnia and Herzegovina," 14 December 1995, from the website of the Office of the High Representative and EU Special Representative, at www.ohr.int/dpa/default.asp?content_id=379 [accessed on 14 July 2006].

Further reading

Cigar, Norman. *Genocide in Bosnia: The Policy of "Ethnic Cleansing"* (College Station, Tex.: Texas A&M University Press, 1995)

Gow, James. *The Serbian Project and its Adversaries: A Strategy of War Crimes* (London: C. Hurst & Co., 2003)

Hoare, Marko Attila. *How Bosnia Armed* (London: Saqi, 2004)

Judah, Tim. *The Serbs: History, Myth and the Destruction of Yugoslavia* (New Haven, Conn. and London: Yale University Press, 2000)

LeBor, Adam. *Milošević: A Biography* (Polmont and London: Bloomsbury, 2002)

Libal, Michael. *Limits of Persuasion: Germany and the Yugoslav Crisis, 1991–1992* (Westport, Conn and London: Praeger, 1997)

Magaš, Branka and Ivo Žanić (eds.). *The War in Croatia and Bosnia- Herzegovina, 1992–1995* (London: Frank Cass, 2001)

Rohde, David. *Endgame - The Betrayal of Srebrenica* (Boulder, Colo.: Westview Press, 1998)

Silber, Laura and Allan Little. *The Death of Yugoslavia* (London: BBC Books and Penguin, 1995)

Ramet, Sabrina P. *Balkan Babel: The Disintegration of Yugoslavia from the Death of Tito to the Fall of Milošević*, 4th edn. (Boulder, Colo.: Westview Press, 2002)

Thinking about Yugoslavia: Scholarly Debates about the Yugoslav Breakup and the Wars in Bosnia and Kosovo (Cambridge: Cambridge University Press, 2005)

Wesselingh, Isabelle and Arnaud Vaulerin. *Raw Memory - Prijedor: An "Ethnic Cleansing Laboratory"* (London: Saqi, 2005)

Part 3
Central Europe

7

Poland since 1989: muddling through, wall to wall

KONSTANTY GEBERT

Overnight, the poster was plastered on walls all over the country. As Poles on 4 June 1989, went to vote in their first, if semi-free, genuine elections in fifty years, the stern face of Gary Cooper, walking to the showdown in "High Noon" stared at them. But this time, the actor had a bright-red Solidarity badge in his lapel, and in his hand, instead of a gun, was a ballot. Naïve and powerful at the same time, the poster expressed well how Poles felt about the elections: a showdown between the forces of good, armed only with their moral right, and the forces of evil, which finally would have to concede defeat. Though communism was already starting to crumble all around them, Poland would be the first to go.

It had not been easy. Earlier that year, two and a half months of negotiations between the communist military authorities and the independent Solidarity trade union which the coup of December 1981 had driven underground, had produced a compromise. The "Round Table deal" made the union legal again, and allowed it to have its own media: *Gazeta Wyborcza*, daily, which proudly claimed to be "the first free newspaper between the Elbe and Vladivostok," started publishing barely two weeks after the deal was made, capitalizing on the extensive experience of the union's underground press.

More importantly, the country's political make-up was thoroughly revised: elections to the Sejm, or parliament, were to be made partially free for the first time since the communists seized power in the wake of the Second World War. Some 35% of the seats were to be open to entirely free competition, while the remaining 65%, though reserved for the still only legal political forces – the communist party and its two junior, ostensibly non-communist sidekicks, the United Peasant Party (ZSL) and the Democratic Party (SD) – would also be contested, if only by candidates advanced by these parties themselves. Furthermore, an upper house, the Senate, would be established; though its prerogatives were few, elections to this house would be entirely free, permitting a real gauge of voters' preferences.

To compensate for that, a very powerful President – another new institution – was to be elected, by both houses sitting in national assembly. It was assumed that the communists and their allies would easily muster the necessary majority, and that the hitherto military dictator, and party and state leader, General Wojciech Jaruzelski, would be their candidate. Moreover, the union endorsed a government plan of radical economic reform which was to bolster a crumbling state economy, at the expense of the very workers the union – 10 million strong before the coup – claimed to represent.

But Solidarity, born from the great strikes of August 1980, and led by charismatic electrician and Nobel Peace Prize laureate Lech Wałęsa, was much more than just a union. For lack of a better term, it was – given its 10 million membership in a nation of then 37 million – simply the nation organized. Political demands, such as the liberation of political prisoners and a curb on censorship, had been part of the historic "21 Postulates" of the successful August strike. Eventually the union, supported and encouraged by Poland's fledgling political opposition, became more radical in its demands, realizing that the problems resulting from communist misrule could not be solved piecemeal. When, in December 1981, Solidarity demanded free elections for local government, the military struck, even if the coup had been prepared for months. Eight years later, the communists were forced to concede much more. They had run out of options, and Gorbachev's Soviet Union, beset by its own problems, no longer was willing or able to prop up their rule with the ultimate threat of using military force, as it had in Hungary in 1956 or in Czechoslovakia in 1968.

While the deal had the support of an exhausted ruling elite, and of a new class of communist entrepreneurs, already busy privatizing, for their own benefit, the salvageable pieces of the country's decrepit economy, it was viciously opposed by the apparat which – quite correctly, as it turned out – feared that the deal meant the end of communist rule. On the other hand, the opposition within Solidarity argued that communism was dying anyway, and that it would be smarter to wait until it was dead, instead of compromising the union's integrity by making deals. They were particularly outraged that the round table compromise made no specific provisions for punishing those guilty of human rights violations. Some one hundred people had been killed after the coup, and thousands during communist rule before it. The issue of villainy unpunished would continue to fester until the present day.

Union critics of the deal might have been overoptimistic. As it turned out, Poles went to the polls on what was to become Tien An Men Day – and on the next day watched on their TV screens as the Chinese communists murdered opponents by the hundreds – proof, if needed at all, that the system was not all that dead. Had a deal not had been struck, the Polish communists, too, would have been left with a choice of either capitulation or renewed violence, and it is not at all sure they would have preferred the former; several months later, Romania's president, Nicolae Ceaușescu, did not. It might be argued that precisely those elements of the deal that critics considered tantamount to treason – a semi-free election, continued power for Jaruzelski, no revenge, and a union safety net for government economic reform, combined with economic security for communists with their hand in the pot – had in fact pre-empted the violent option. Hard to say, though: Poland was the first to go, and could not, like East Germany, Czechoslovakia, or Hungary later, rely on the experience of others.

The legacy of the past

When Duke Mieszko I embraced Western Christianity in 966, Poland became Europe's remote Eastern borderland. By the sixteenth century, it had become the continent's largest state, stretching from the Baltic to the Black Sea. Home to a dizzying array of nations: Poles, Lithuanians, Ukrainians, Germans, Belorussians, Jews, Armenians, Tartars, and others, it developed a unique political system in which royal powers were counterbalanced by political privileges of the nobility, which made up some 10% of the population. This ensured a climate of political and religious tolerance, furthered the growth of parliamentarism, and made Poland a haven for persecuted groups.

Jews, fleeing pogroms in Western Europe, started settling in Poland in the early Middle Ages, soon developing a parliamentary system of their own (Vaad Arba Artzot). With the transformation of the country into a federation after the union with Lithuania (1569), the passing of the articles of the Warsaw Confederation (1573) guaranteeing religious freedoms, and the introduction of electoral monarchy the same year, when Henri de Valois was briefly elected king of Poland, the basic elements of the system were in place. They guaranteed the political liberties of the nobility (the Polish word for citizen – *obywatel* – means "landed gentleman"), but also a weakness of central authority in the *Rzeczpospolita*, or Noble Republic. *Liberum veto*, the principle of unanimity in parliamentary voting, was to replace the majority vote a century later, making the country virtually ungovernable.

Deprived of natural boundaries, Poland fought on its own territory disastrous wars against (Muslim) Turks, (Orthodox) Russians, and (Protestant) Swedes, earning for itself the moniker of *Antemurale Christianitatis*, but suffering disastrous losses. In particular, the combined wars with Sweden, Russia, Turkey and an internal Ukrainian revolt in the second half of the seventeenth century dealt Poland a blow from which it would never recover. Though the delivery of Vienna from the Turks by King Jan III Sobieski in 1683 was a last hurrah, the country entered its decline, and was unable to prevent its neighbors from occupying parts of its territory. This was not reversed even by the adoption, in 1791, of a constitution, the second in the world after that of the United States. In the late eighteenth century, Russia, Prussia, and Austria, in a series of partitions which met with ineffective military opposition, eventually erased Poland from the map of Europe.

In the nineteenth century, after an abortive attempt to resuscitate Poland in an alliance with France under Napoleon, its integration into the three empires became a fact. In the Russian partition, most oppressive and containing most of the country, Poles fought two major uprisings (1830–1 and 1863), both bloodily defeated. Under Austrian rule, the Polish provinces enjoyed a degree of autonomy and political freedoms, while under the Prussians they were subject to forced Germanization. While Polish lands eventually underwent urbanization, they all remained imperial peripheries, and suffered again disastrously from the destruction wrought by the First World War. Its outcome, however, with the downfall of all three partitioning powers, enabled Poland to reclaim its independence in 1918, after 123 years of foreign rule.

The reborn state had to fight bitter wars over its borders with both Russia (with the Red Army defeated on the outskirts of Warsaw in 1920) and Germany (the Silesian uprisings). A parliamentary republic, its politics driven by intense Polish ethnic nationalism, it refused to accommodate its national minorities, making up one-third of its population. A coup by the father of Polish independence, Marshal Józef Piłsudski, marked the beginning of a slide towards authoritarianism, which was accentuated after his death in 1935. Suspected Ukrainian separatism was brutally combated, while rampant anti-Semitism received official sanction. The economic crisis of 1929 wrecked the economy, which never fully recovered. When the Ribbentrop–Molotov Pact was signed in August 1939, it signaled the death throes of a deeply troubled nation, passionate nonetheless about its independence.

When Germany invaded from the west on 1 September 1939, the outgunned Polish army resisted for five weeks, even when Russia invaded from the east seventeen days later, but the Allies limited their reaction to a declaration of war on Germany not backed by action. German rule in Poland was arguably the most brutal in Europe, while over 1 million Poles were deported from Soviet-occupied territories into Central Asia and Siberia, mostly to die there. Most of the Nazi "Final Solution" occurred in occupied Poland: of its 6 million victims half were Polish Jews, making up also half of Poland's 6 million victims of the Second World War. The underground Home Army, Europe's second largest underground after Yugoslavia, successfully engaged the Germans – but bled itself to death in the Warsaw uprising of August 1944, which followed the Warsaw Ghetto uprising of April 1943. As the Red Army stopped its offensive and did nothing, the Germans pummeled the rebellious city into dust: 200,000 people, mainly civilians, were killed in sixty-three days.

Soviet-liberated Poland, 38% of its national wealth destroyed, was trapped, under the Teheran and Yalta agreements, in Moscow's sphere of influence. Stalin kept the eastern half of Poland he conquered in 1939; rump-Poland was compensated by the Allies by the annexation of former German territories in the north and west. 3.4 million Germans were summarily expelled, while 1.8 million Poles fled from Soviet-annexed areas. As the communists solidified their power after a brief but bloody civil war, the ruined country effectively became a prison. Anti-Semitism, still rife, claimed over 1,000 deaths among the few survivors of the Shoah, while 140,000 Ukrainians were deported from south-eastern Poland, in retaliation for massacres of Poles committed by Ukrainian nationalists in the Second World War.

Mass protests against the regime in 1956 and 1970 were bloodily crushed, but produced limited liberalization; an official anti-Semitic campaign in 1968 forced the emigration of most of the country's remaining Jews. In 1980, a series of strikes on the Baltic sea-coast led to the creation of the "Solidarity" movement, advocating democratic change. Banned after the military coup of 1981, it went underground and led the struggle which eventually ended with the bloodless transition of power in 1989.

Striking a deal

Be that as it may, it is safe to assume that, had General Jaruzelski been able to anticipate the electoral results, he would have thought twice about the deal himself. In the first round, where 50% of the votes were needed to win, Solidarity took 160 of 161 seats in the Sejm allocated to it, as well as 92 of the 100 Senate seats. Probably even more damningly, only 3 of the candidates to the 299 seats allocated to the Party and its allies managed to clear the 50% hurdle: people were delighted to strike all the "Reds" off the ballot. Voters' preferences could not have been more clearly expressed: the Party, which in its heyday, in the 1970s, had 3 million members, was over. In the second round Solidarity easily filled the one remaining Sejm seat, and 7 of the 8 remaining seats in the Senate.

Tellingly, the only non-Solidarity candidate to make it to the upper house was one Henryk Stokłosa, a businessman who had managed to get expelled from the deeply corrupt Communist Party for ... corruption, and had run as an independent, on a "get rich!" program. Just as tellingly, Solidarity barely won another Senate seat, for the industrial town of Radom. Its candidate there, Jan Józef Lipski, was a Second World War hero, former political prisoner, and organizer of aid for victims of communist repression in that town in 1976. Seemingly a shoo-in, he had nonetheless aroused the ire of the local Catholic bishop for being a self-declared democratic socialist and non-believer. The Stokłosa and Lipski campaigns turned out to be the only genuine political contests, and harbingers of things to come; the rest of the elections was in fact a plebiscite.

Not only the communist authorities and their Moscow patrons, but also Solidarity and Western governments were deeply shocked by the outcome. The Polish democratic opposition had not expected that it would have to govern right away; instead, it had looked forward to getting its sea-legs during a transition period before the future, fully democratic elections. In May 1989, US President George Bush had given a major speech in which he stated that the "de-freezing" of the Soviet bloc would move by stages, to avoid uncontrolled developments. Everybody was worried that things might be moving too fast instead.

Or too slowly. In the second round, voter turnout was only 25% this was not surprising, given that in almost all electoral districts the choice was by then only between communists and their allies of different stripes. But in the first round, which had supposedly been a goal the Polish nation had strived for over decades, turnout was barely 62% a full third of the country's citizens had turned their backs on politics itself. This, too, would be a harbinger: in future parliamentary elections turnout would consistently be even lower.

With Solidarity dizzy with its own success, and the communists in deep turmoil, as most of those finally elected had been liberal critics of the party line, and everybody wondering just how long Moscow's forbearance would last, nobody seemed to have a clear idea of what to do next. Writing in *Gazeta Wyborcza* one month after the first round of the elections, Adam Michnik, former political prisoner and leading Solidarity intellectual, as well as the paper's editor-in-chief to this day, suggested a simple, if shocking solution: "Your President, our Prime Minister." In other words, "Solidarity's" acquiescence in Jaruzelski's election, now badly needed but no longer assured, would come with a price: Poland would get a non-communist head of government.

For lack of a better solution, the communists seemingly accepted the deal, and Jaruzelski was elected president by the National Assembly, gaining, in a masterpiece of political choreography by the Solidarity parliamentary caucus OKP, exactly the minimum number of votes he needed, with even some communist parliamentarians voting against him. The party tried nonetheless to ram through its candidate for prime minister – Minister of the Interior and round table negotiator General Czesław Kiszczak – and failed abysmally. A new ruling coalition was needed. Since an alliance between the communists and Solidarity was out of the question for both parties, the only alternative was a coalition between the union and the party's former sidekicks: the ZSL and the SD. Once this became a political reality, President Jaruzelski gave former political prisoner and Solidarity advisor Tadeusz Mazowiecki, a prominent Catholic intellectual, the mission of forming the government.

While Moscow did not react with outrage, the Polish party was not so sanguine; it issued a statement saying that "the takeover of full State power by 'Solidarity' bears great threats for the Polish State," and Ceauşescu lobbied for a Warsaw Pact intervention.[1] The party's – if not the Romanians' – fears were finally assuaged by the inclusion of five communist ministers in the new government, including the previous ministers of the interior and of defense, two generals. Together with Jaruzelski, the military–communist trio was to guarantee that things would not get too much out of hand. But when the new government was almost unanimously voted in by the Sejm on 12 September, the economy – not internal politics – was to be its first concern.

A clean break: I

The departing communist government of Mieczysław Rakowski had not only allowed for a privatization of state assets which was tantamount to robbery, but had set inflation loose. As goods disappeared from the market, this government then liberalized foodstuff prices, sending them skyrocketing. The dollar rose as steeply, and so did the budget deficit, as enterprises delayed tax payments, and eventually also the payment of salaries. The country descended into economic chaos, and a social explosion loomed. Had not international aid stepped in, a disaster would surely have occurred, but in the fall the new government, which had also inherited an exorbitant foreign debt, received credit assurances of 1.5 billion dollars from the World Bank and 700 million dollars from the IMF. This gave it the breathing space for the preparation of radical political reforms, designed by the liberal deputy prime minister Leszek Balcerowicz. He was to initiate his "shock therapy" on 1 January 1990.

In the meantime, however, matters just as urgent called for the government's attention. As other Eastern bloc countries started following in Poland's footsteps and shaking off communist rule, and the Soviet Union showed the first signs of disintegrating, Poland had to redefine its foreign policy. Though feelings of anti-communist solidarity with democratic opposition movements elsewhere in the bloc, as well as a legitimate loathing of Soviet domination, ran deep in the new government, the stark fact was that Poland now needed the USSR. With the Berlin Wall tumbling down and German reunification looming, the country felt that its Western border might be threatened.

As compensation for wartime damages and for the 50% of pre-war Polish territory the Soviet Union had swallowed up under the Ribbentrop–Molotov Pact of 1939 and would not return, the Big Three had allocated to Poland in Potsdam, after the fall of the Third Reich, previously German areas east of the Oder and Neisse river, making up one-third of the country's post-war territory; their population had been expelled to the west, and the territories resettled by Poles fleeing from the now-Soviet east. Though first East Germany, and then, in 1970, the Bundesrepublik, had formally recognized the Oder–Neisse line, the West German Constitutional Court had ruled that Germany still existed within the borders of 1937, and Chancellor Helmut Kohl, fearing to lose the votes of the expellees, refused to pledge recognition of Poland's western border in the name of a future united Germany. Under such circumstances Mazowiecki, who – like Jaruzelski and many other members of the Polish political elites, old and new – had personal memories of the Second World War, preferred to play it safe and count on Moscow to dissuade possible German revanchism.

This meant not only that Poland would not immediately pressure Moscow to withdraw its troops stationed on Polish soil, but also that Poland would tread cautiously around Soviet red lines, which then included recognition of independence movements in the republics of the USSR. Poland's foreign ministry, led by the very able Krzysztof Skubiszewski, a respected academic specialist in international law with no previous overt political affiliations, decided to follow a two-track policy, by cultivating democratic movements, and soon democratic governments in Central Europe, without alienating Moscow or supporting opposition to its rule within the USSR too closely. In those heady months, however, most emerging democracies were too busy with internal politics and the economy to have much time for foreign policy.

The strategy eventually paid off, but at the risk of alienating Poland's emerging eastern neighbors, especially Lithuania and Ukraine, which in the past had had stormy relations with the Poles, ruled over territories which had been Polish until the Second World War, and were just as unsure of their western borders as Poland was. When Lithuania complained that Iceland, not Poland, had been the first to recognize its independence in 1991, a Polish diplomat replied: "If we had the kind of land boundary with the USSR as Iceland has, we would have been delighted to be the first."[2] When, however, Ukraine declared its independence in 1991, Poland this time was the first to recognize it; the German threat had been put to rest, and the USSR was no more. Support from London and Paris had allowed Poland to sit on the "2+4" negotiations (they became "2+4+1"), in which the Allies discussed their reunification with the two Germanies. Poland's original fears proved to be groundless.

Another looming breakthrough – with Israel – was stymied by a remark made by the then Israeli Prime Minister Yitzhak Shamir, who commented that "Poles suckle anti-Semitism with their mothers' milk." Together with other Eastern bloc members, except Romania, Poland had broken off relations with Israel after the Six Days War in 1967; a vicious anti-Semitic campaign then followed in 1968. Though anti-Semitism was still largely present in Poland, including also within Solidarity itself, there also existed a powerful feeling of guilt and sympathy towards Jews and the Jewish state. Poland, which had accepted to be a transit country for Soviet Jews in the fall, after Hungary backed off under terrorist threat, wanted to be the first former communist country to re-establish relations with Jerusalem. Shamir's words – he had lost relatives, murdered by Polish peasants in occupied Poland in the Second World War – had made that difficult, and Czechoslovakia became the first country; Poland followed as the second one in early 1990.

Settling accounts

Though the economy was the first concern of Mazowiecki's government, and the German threat temporarily loomed large, the government had to come to terms with the legacy of the decaying system Solidarity had, somewhat to its own surprise, managed to topple, bloodlessly. In his parliamentary exposé, the new prime minister had declared: "we are cutting the past away with a thick line."[3] By this he meant that his government bore no responsibility for the deeds and misdeeds of its communist predecessors, and was to be judged on its accomplishments alone. Many, however, understood it to mean a policy of leniency towards the crimes of the previous regime, and their perpetrators. Though only a hundred had been killed under martial law, thousands had gone to jail, and thousands had been beaten on the streets, during brutally repressed demonstrations. Furthermore, thousands had been killed in the past, when the regime had been more repressive. All this called for justice – especially in the face of the fact that many former communists had done well, while most of the population lived precariously.

But there was a feeling among the new elites that the country had to tread cautiously, and that the fact that the communists had bloodlessly negotiated away their power must morally, if not politically or legally, limit retribution from the victors. The Communist Party formally disbanded in January 1990, spawning a successor organization – the Social Democracy of the Polish Republic, led by two politicians: Aleksander Kwaśniewski and Leszek Miller – who were to become in the years to come, respectively, president and prime minister. The communists' former peasant sidekicks broke free of them and reformed into a new party – the Polish Peasant Party (ZSL) – while the other sidekick – the Democratic Party – (SD) which had targeted the intelligentsia, rapidly became irrelevant. In March, a Solidarity deputy minister was finally named to the ministry of the interior: he was to replace General Kiszczak only in July, more than a year after the elections of 1989; the minister of defense was also then replaced, by a supposedly apolitical admiral. Apart from that, the army, for all its role in crushing the democratic movement throughout the 1980s, remained largely untouched by the transformation.

The security service was also purged only in the spring of 1990. Almost half of its functionaries resigned on their own and did not seek re-employment, but most of those who decided to stay passed the test and remained in their jobs. In the meantime, the service had been busy destroying its files. The courts were not purged, in deference to judicial independence. The party/state media monopoly was broken up, but the government to this day keeps 49% of the shares of a major daily newspaper, and state broadcast media, especially TV, are totally subservient to whatever government is in power, making a mockery of their stated mission as public media. Censorship was swiftly abolished, however, and private media flourished. This was especially true of *Gazeta Wyborcza*, owned originally by its own journalists, which had become not only an opinion leader but a political force to be reckoned with.

The most important changes occurred in the economy. Balcerowicz's "shock therapy" plan, implemented on 1 January 1990, basically froze wages (by taxing their growth) and liberated prices (by cutting state subventions for energy production). The cost of bank credit was raised to the expected level of inflation. These measures effectively curbed inflation – from 76% in January to barely 6% in March, but at very high social cost: uncompetitive state businesses closed down, and unemployment – hitherto unknown – grew exponentially. Even though the devaluation of the zloty to market levels and deregulation of foreign exchange both abolished the currency black market and boosted Polish exports, farmers were still not able to compete with subsidized foodstuffs imported from the EEC. People started to massively convert from seeking state employment to doing business on their own, mainly in retail trade. The new Polish middle class was to arise from among the dozens of thousands selling Chinese T-shirts and similar things from folding beds on sidewalks.

But fortunes were already beginning to be made. As incomes started sharply to differentiate in what used to be an egalitarian society (privileges of the nomenklatura were hidden from the public eye), a backlash against the rich started to build up. The first strikes and protests started barely months after Balcerowicz's plan was introduced, much too early for it to show much success. Furthermore, most of the new rich were correctly suspected of not having come to their fortunes through legitimate enterprise: legal loophole abuse, corrupt privatization, and outright fraud were rampant. The perception of the rich as dishonest bloodsuckers was to stick, and play a role in future politics. Another consequence was the growth of crime, including organized crime, and corruption, as ill-paid officials found themselves making economic decisions which would affect million-dollar fortunes. Both crime and corruption would continue to adversely impact the country's development.

The return of politics

While the former ruling bloc disintegrated and re-formed, so did the Solidarity movement. The trade union recovered barely 2 million of its erstwhile 10 million members, and was increasingly unhappy about the liberal policies it was expected to support. Politically, too, the movement was splintering. A new party, the Christian National Union (ZChN), was created in the fall of 1989 with the full support of the Catholic Church, seemingly a guarantee of success in a nation which was 95% Catholic. Wałęsa, re-elected Solidarity chairman, remained a loose cannon, wielding great power but having no place in the new power system. He soon declared his aspirations to the presidency, at a time when many Solidarity leaders – including such figures as Bronisław Geremek and Michnik – thought he would be too divisive, something they saw as a threat to the unity of the movement which they wanted to maintain at all cost. But politics eventually reasserted itself; as Wałęsa declared for the presidency, the Solidarity movement splintered into a rapidly shifting array of political parties. Jaruzelski, formally elected for a four-year term, obligingly announced that he would resign; the new president would be elected by universal suffrage. To counter what they saw as Wałęsa's dictatorial ambitions, Solidarity intellectuals supported Prime Minister Mazowiecki for the presidency.

Their fears were not groundless; Wałęsa used to ride roughshod over union democracy, and did not change once the battle had been won. When *Gazeta Wyborcza* refused to endorse him, he forbade it to use the Solidarity logo – a gesture which, though traumatizing at the time, effectively enabled the paper to become independent. The union leader promised a "war on the top," i.e. among elites, to avoid a "war on the bottom," i.e. civil strife. Facing the prime minister of a government whose popularity had fallen, from an incredible 90% in January 1990 to just half of that eight months later, the trade union leader and national legend could not lose. In fact, in the first round of the elections, held on 25 November 1990, Wałęsa got 40% of the vote, Mazowiecki just 18%.

But Mazowiecki's expected defeat was not the most important result of these elections. The prime minister came not second, but third – beaten not only by the mustachioed hero, but also by Stan Tymiński, a mysterious returnee from Canada, who combined Stokłosa's "get-rich" rhetoric with social populism, a hint of mysticism, and a lot of conspiracy theory. He attracted 23% of the vote, and challenged Wałęsa in the second round, actually improving his performance by an additional 3%. Though the "Party X" he then set up quickly disappeared from Polish politics, his performance indicated the existence of an electorate thoroughly distrustful of both the old regime (though a post-communist candidate scored well, at 9%) and the new. This electorate would reassert itself in the future.

Wałęsa was inaugurated in a moving patriotic ceremony to which the departing Jaruzelski had not been invited. The new president took the insignia of power not from him, but from the last president of Poland's Second World War government-in-exile, flown in from London for the occasion. Thus, the new head of state stressed the continuity between the new democratic Poland and its pre-war predecessor, the Second Republic, leaving the communist "People's Republic of Poland" (PRL) as just a name for Soviet domination. The debate on what the PRL had exactly been – an occupation regime or an expression of Polish sovereignty, albeit severely limited – was to bedevil Polish politics for years to come.

Mazowiecki, in the wake of his embarrassing electoral defeat, promptly resigned as prime minister, and went on to create in 1991, out of his electoral base, a new party – the center-left Democratic Union (UD). The new president therefore had to scramble to create a new government – even if, under the country's new provisional "small constitution" passed by the Sejm this was not strictly speaking his job. But Wałęsa, as it turned out, loved playing politics; in the long run, this would prove to be his undoing. After toying with a number of candidates, he finally selected Jan Krzysztof Bielecki, the leader of the small Liberal Democratic Congress (KLD); the government he set up included key personalities of the previous cabinet and enjoyed wide support in the Sejm. It essentially continued the policies of its predecessor, scoring a major success when foreign creditors agreed to cancel half of Poland's foreign debt. It was increasingly clear, however that, like Jaruzelski, the Sejm, born in semi-legitimate circumstances, also would have to go. After a series of bitter clashes between the Sejm and the president, essentially about the limits of the head of state's powers – he saw next to none – a date was set for October 1991.

Wałęsa in power

In the meantime, Wałęsa set out to build a parallel center of executive power in the Belvedere – the presidential office and residence. Its main players included the twin Kaczyński brothers – Lech and Jarosław – who had been instrumental at the round table and at the brokering of the government compromise in the summer of 1989, and now were the leaders of a small party, the Center Alliance (PC). Another key, but extremely shady personality was Mieczysław Wachowski, a former Wałęsa driver and bodyguard, who had by now become his closest advisor and a policy-maker in his own right.

The president's first foreign policy test came in August, during the abortive coup against Gorbachev, carried out by hardliners in Moscow. Wałęsa seemed to believe the putsch would succeed, and was tardy in expressing his condemnation. As the coup disintegrated, former interior minister and architect of Jaruzelski's successful coup of 1981, General Kiszczak, was asked by Polish TV for his opinion on the development. "I would have done it differently" he replied with a straight face.

As the Soviet Union, in the wake of the failed coup, started falling apart, Poland – once the German bogeyman was buried, Bielecki and Chancellor Kohl having signed a friendship treaty – started demanding that Soviet troops stationed there leave. Poland turned decisively west, securing membership in the Council of Europe in late 1991, and signing an association agreement with the European Economic Community (EEC). In a ground-breaking visit, President Wałęsa traveled to Israel – the first ever Polish leader to do so – and gave a powerful speech in the Knesset, recognizing past wrongs committed by Poles against Jews, and asking forgiveness.

Though Poles were still struggling under the new and often brutal economic system, and getting more and more fed up with the fractiousness of their political life, the Pope's two visits in 1991 were celebrated as major spiritual events by most of the population. A growing minority, however, was beginning to question the Church's growing influence on Polish public life – from state patronage of religious ceremonies, through the bishops' overt support for the ZChN, down to their frequent, unofficial but effective, vetting of candidates for public service. Such criticism, unthinkable under Communism when the Church was persecuted by the government, was seen as treason by a substantial Catholic fundamentalist fringe. This conflict, too, would grow in time.

But the parliamentary elections of October 1991, run under a rigidly proportional system, produced a much more confused and variegated result. Not less than twenty-nine parties entered the Sejm, led by the largest vote-getter, Mazowiecki's UD, which won 12.3% of the vote, closely followed by the post-communist Alliance of the Democratic Left (SLD) with 12%. The Catholics, the Peasants, and the Kaczyńskis' PC garnered about 10% each. It was clear that such a badly divided parliament would have a hard time cobbling together a government coalition, let alone confronting a growingly assertive president. It was also clear that the bishops' bid for the public vote had failed – their party got fewer votes than the seemingly utterly compromised ex-communists. Their powerful return testified to the strength of the "biological" vote they could muster, among people who had done well in the PRL – but also to the level of discontent with liberal economic reform, fractious politics, and Church influence in public life. But the SLD, and its successors, had a hard time deciding whether they represented the past, or the present. In the meantime, they could, as the biggest opposition party, watch from the side-lines as their ex-Solidarity adversaries fought bloodily among themselves.

This they proceeded to do with gusto. After protracted negotiations a five-party coalition was cobbled together, led by right-wing politician Jan Olszewski, and excluding both the SLD and the UD, suspected of being "pink." It was also met with criticism by President Wałęsa, who had in the meantime broken with the Kaczyński brothers, whose PC was in the coalition. Bitter infighting ensued, until late May 1992, when the government disclosed to the Sejm a list of supposed agents of the former communist secret police, who occupied now high-ranking positions in the state. The list included the names of President Wałęsa and Sejm Speaker Wiesław Chrzanowski. Based on flimsy evidence (communist-era archives were depleted and of limited trustworthiness), and immediately leaked, it provoked public outrage. For many this was an example of malign political slander – for others, the beginning of the final purge of enemies of the nation. After a dramatic debate, the Sejm recalled the Olszewski government. A fundamental divide was thus created, between the partisans of further "lustration," or vetting state positions for suspected former agents, and its opponents, who believed the evidence flimsy and the procedure undemocratic.

After a brief transitory government led by PSL leader Waldemar Pawlak, a new coalition of eight parties was set up under Hanna Suchocka, Poland's first woman prime minister, this time supported by the president and giving the UD a leading role. This government was paralyzed by political infighting and though it included "Solidarity," it was unable to contain growing social protest, as unemployment grew to 14% and wages did not rise. Another confrontation arose in the spring of 1993 around the role of the Church in public life, as the Sejm passed a law, still in force, banning abortion, hitherto legal, except in cases of rape, incest, or threat to the life of the mother and the fetus. Other laws made it mandatory for public media to "respect the Christian system of values" and formalized religious instruction, introduced already in 1990 and officially non-mandatory, into public schools. These developments followed the signing by Poland of a concordat with the Vatican, and were seen by a large segment of public opinion as examples of unacceptable Church interference in public life. This issue, too, continued to rankle, with opponents of lustration also usually opposed to such interference; their adversaries would brand them as "pinkos."

While conflict raged at home, Poland scored some successes abroad. Presidents Wałęsa and Boris Yeltsin negotiated an agreement on withdrawing former Soviet troops from Poland in two years, and a friendship treaty was signed with Russia, as well as with all the other European former Soviet republics, now independent states. Poland's stated aspiration to join NATO, however, was received with outrage in Moscow, an early acquiescence by Yeltsin notwithstanding, and coolly by the West. Former Prime Minister Mazowiecki was appointed US Special Rapporteur on Human Rights in the Former Yugoslavia, a role he fulfilled with distinction for three years, until he quit in disgust with the UN after the Srebrenica massacre. A major crisis in

Christian–Jewish relations over the continuing presence of a Carmelite convent on the site of the former death camp at Auschwitz was finally defused after the nuns moved out in 1993, at the Pope's request.

The former communists return: I

The economy, bolstered somewhat by a growing private sector, including foreign investments, was still flagging, and the GNP remained below 1989 levels, while the budget deficit grew to an alarming 6.5%, which led to spending cuts which were met with social protest. Inflation continued to fall, however, but this was not enough to curb mounting outrage at social cuts. In May 1993 Solidarity introduced a motion of no-confidence in the government, intended to intimidate it. Supported both by the post-communists and the right-wing opposition, it passed by one vote. The Sejm was dissolved, and new elections called for the fall.

In these elections voter turnout, if marginally better than two years earlier, still barely hovered over the 50% mark, indicating a deepening alienation of half of Polish society from political life. Not surpringly, since the former Solidarity camp had thoroughly compromised itself by infighting and by alienating its trade union base, it was triumphantly won by the former communists, who took 20.4% of the vote, while the barely reformed PSL got 15.4%. The UD scored acceptably at 10.6%, while a new party, the Union of Labor, which tried to unite the non-communist left, attracted just 7.3% of the vote. Of the remaining post-Solidarity parties, only the nationalist KPN and the pro-presidential Non-Partisan Bloc for Supporting the Reforms (BBWR)[4] managed to enter Parliament. 30% of the vote was wasted on small right-wing parties which did not manage to cross the 5% threshold.

The SLD and PSL set up their government, again under Pawlak. Even though it was the first parliamentary return to power by the post-communists in the former Eastern bloc, the government was to be one of continuation, not of a return to the past. Key ministries – internal affairs, foreign affairs, and defense – required presidential approval. Enjoying massive social support, it followed the main lines determined by the previous Solidarity governments, and strove hard, if with little success, to obtain the president's support. Coalition leaders even apologized publicly for the sins of the communist past. On the other hand, sectors of the state economy returned to party control, a purge was conducted in the foreign service and in the new secret service, and a number of legal proceedings against former dignitaries, including General Jaruzelski, were shelved. The process of decentralizing the state administration and granting substantial powers to local self-government was also stopped. President Wałęsa, the remaining state authority from the Solidarity movement, fought hard against the government of the former Sejm speaker Józef Oleksey (SLD), who replaced Pawlak, in particular defending his prerogatives in foreign policy and defense, guaranteed under the interim "small" constitution.

The defeated opposition started rebuilding its ranks, with the UD merging with the liberal KLD into the Freedom Union (UW), while the right, after unsuccessful attempts, remained badly splintered. Only in 1997 would all its strands unite in an electoral bloc called Solidarity Electoral Action (AWS). The union, though defeated in the elections, recovered influence as a social force, organizing successful strikes. Church–state relations deteriorated, as the left-wing coalition tried to roll back some of the earlier changes, only to encounter an insurmountable presidential veto. Early in 1995, the president forced a change of prime minister, which is when Oleksy assumed that office. Nothing much would change, however, until the Presidential elections scheduled for the fall of 1995. In a dizzying field of hitherto unknown candidates, only two really counted: the incumbent, running for re-election on a strongly anti-communist platform, and his post-communist challenger Aleksander Kwaśniewski, capitalizing on the wave of popular discontent from the previous year. On 5 November 1995, each of them took about a third of the vote, with veteran dissident leader Jacek Kuroń (UW) scoring 9.2%. In the runoff, Kwaśniewski, opposed now by all tendencies of the post-Solidarity spectrum, scrambled through with 51.7% of the vote. The country was deeply polarized.

As Wałęsa was about to leave the presidential palace in December 1995, independent Poland's biggest political crisis exploded. Interior minister Andrzej Milczanowski, a former underground Solidarity activist and political prisoner, accused his boss, former communist apparatchik and prime minister, Józef Oleksy, of being a Russian spy. Though an outraged Oleksy denied the accusation, and the evidence was inconclusive (he was to be exonerated years later), he was forced to resign in early 1996. In the wake of this affair, the Sejm would one year later pass a law on lustration. It was to affect only top state positions, presumption of innocence maintained, and statements about having, or not having, been an agent, were to be publicized, together with the results of their judicial verification. There was no penalty for false statements. Seeing Solidarity MPs vote for it (under the previous regime, the secret police was forbidden to recruit Party members, so the SLD was safe, but former anti-communists not) the head of the SLD caucus and future prime minister Leszek Miller quipped: "I've never seen carp vote for Christmas before"[5] (carp is a traditional Polish Christmas dish).

While a new government, again one of continuation, was set up in February 1996 under the ostentatiously non-partisan, if post-communist, Włodzimierz Cimoszewicz, President Kwaśniewski emerged as a growing alternative center of power. Having distanced himself from his SLD, he initiated an opening to centrist post-Solidarity forces, especially the UW. As the Cimoszewicz government continued to bring back former communists into public service, reopened the abortion debate and – in a symbolic gesture – decided to privatize the Lenin Shipyards in Gdańsk, the cradle of Solidarity, former underground leader Barbara Labuda spectacularly became a minister in the president's office.

The main battle was fought over the new constitution, especially its preamble, where the right wanted to see a clear reference to God. The president, supported by moderate UW politicians such as Geremek and the Catholic Mazowiecki, wanted a more inclusive formula, mentioning both the religious and the non-religious, as well as defining Poland as a civic, as opposed to an ethnic, state. Solidarity, now solidly right-wing Catholic, called this a "constitution of national treason" – but the law, still binding, was passed in May 1997 by referendum, if with a majority just over 50% and a turnout of little over 40%. It also made dismissing governments much more difficult.

Solidarity strikes back

The referendum was the opening battle of parliamentary elections scheduled for the fall of 1997. Fear of a post-communist monopoly of power, opposition to the liberal and secular policies of the Cimoszewicz government, the continuing social cost of economic reform, and gross mismanagement by the government after a disastrous flood in the summer – all this boded ill for the ruling coalition. When the results came in on 21 September 1997, however, the SLD had actually increased its score to 27.1%, though its PSL ally lost as much as the SLD gained, and was reduced to 7.3%. Most importantly, however, the AWS emerged victorious with 33.8% of the vote, while the UW was stable at 13.4%. Apart from the big four, only a small right-wing party – the Movement for the Renewal of Poland (ROP), a short-lived party – crossed, just barely, the 5% electoral threshold. The country was in for another about turn.

Though quite dissimilar in their political program (economic and political liberalism for the UW, social conservatism and state interventionism for AWS), the two parties, bonded by the shared experience of the anti-communist struggle, soon set up a coalition government under a moderate if unknown professor, Jerzy Buzek (AWS). Balcerowicz (UW) returned as deputy prime minister in charge of the economy, while two other UW politicians: Bronisław Geremek and Janusz Onyszkiewicz took over, respectively, foreign affairs and defense. The new government purged the secret services of suspected SLD sympathizers, and introduced a controversial law on lustration, albeit restricted to top state positions, governed by due process, and penalizing only false statements. It also spearheaded an ambitious project of devolution of powers to local government, and undertook a shake-up of the country's creaky public health care and welfare systems. It failed to address growing social discontent, however, and as strikes and social conflict increased, the popularity of the SLD grew again, soon to rival that of the AWS.

In a fundamental international breakthrough Poland finally joined NATO in 1999, and immediately endorsed the Alliance's war in Kosovo. EU accession negotiations continued apace, with the Nice summit of 2000 deciding to allocate to Poland, once it joined, as many votes in the Council as Spain had. An attempt to set up a regular mechanism for Polish–German–French consultations, the Weimar Triangle, proved impractical, however. Relations with Russia and Belarus deteriorated, but those with other Central European states, and especially with Lithuania and Ukraine, which had incorporated large swathes of formerly Polish territory, flourished.

Though the SLD, through its control of the public broadcast media, continued in its stark opposition to the government, President Kwaśniewski sought to distance himself from it, and moved closer to the liberals of the UW, themselves in an increasingly difficult relationship with their coalition partners. This helped to promote the president as a non-partisan arbiter, but was detrimental to the UW, criticized both for the government's failures, and for its ties – too cozy to many – with the former communist head of state. Especially on Church and state issues, the UW was closer to the president than to the heavily Catholic AWS – and the Church was playing a very active role in Polish politics, especially since the country ratified the concordat with the Vatican in 1998, allowing, for example, for religious instruction in schools. The emergence of Radio Maryja, a fundamentalist broadcaster run by the powerful Redemptorist monk, Father Tadeusz Rydzyk, galvanized the national and religious Right, while a new conflict at Auschwitz, around the crosses erected at the site of the former Carmelite convent by rightist militants, criticized by international Jewish organizations, brought forth displays of anti-Semitism. This issue became central in 2000, with the publication of Jan T. Gross' *Neighbors*, a slim volume documenting the wartime massacre of the Jewish inhabitants of Jedwabne, a small Polish town, by their Christian neighbors.[6] Though eventually Polish public opinion admirably accepted the findings, once confirmed by the Institute of National Remembrance, a state historical and prosecutorial body, the extreme right found a new lease on life by attacking "nefarious Jewish influence" in Poland. Finally, growing cronyism inside the government and internal political clashes between the different tendencies within the AWS also undermined the government's popularity. In 2000, the UW left the government, leaving the AWS to govern without a majority.

The former communists return: II

Given this situation, Kwaśniewski's re-election in the first round of the presidential elections of the fall of 2000 was easy to predict; he won with 53.9% of the vote. A liberal candidate – Andrzej Olechowski – without much political backing managed to get 17.3%, while AWS leader Marian Krzaklewski came third with only 15.6%. Lech Wałęsa, who also ran, attracted barely 1%, while a populist peasant leader, Andrzej Lepper, scored 3%. With defeat looming, the AWS started to splinter, and finally disintegrated. As expected, the SLD (in coalition with a smaller left-wing party), won 40.1% of the vote, while a newly founded liberal party, the Civic Platform (PO) led by Donald Tusk emerged second, with 12.7%. Three other newcomers, Lepper's populist Self-defense (SO), the conservative Law and Justice (PiS) of the Kaczyński twins Jarosław and Lech, and the extreme-right League of Polish Families (LPR), heavily supported by Radio Maryja, scored respectively 10.2%, 9.5%, and 7.9%. The PSL maintained a toe-hold, but the UW did not even manage to cross the electoral threshold of 5%, and disappeared from Polish politics, though some of its top leaders would eventually be elected to the European Parliament.

From 2001 to 2005 both the government and the presidency thus remained in the hands of the post-communist SLD, allied with the PSL. Though the badly splintered opposition was hardly a threat, and the new extremist parties: the SO and the LPR much more hostile to democracy than the SLD, this continuous rule brought political corruption and incompetence to new levels, dwarfing even the distressing record of the AWS government. The economy slumped, and social conflicts continued unabated, with unemployment reaching 19%. In 2002, *Gazeta Wyborcza* revealed that it had been solicited, in the name of "those in power," for a $17.5 million bribe in return for the passing of a law which would allow the paper to buy a TV station it wanted to purchase.[7] This led to parliamentary investigation into government sleaze, the traces leading to the office of Prime Minister Leszek Miller. As it had been the case with the AWS government, the SLD's junior partner PSL eventually withdrew in 2003. The government's sole, if predictable, success was the positive result of a referendum on EU accession, effective one year later. More contentiously, Poland sent troops to fight together with the Americans in the second Gulf War.

Continuing investigations into government sleaze led to the discovery of links between organized crime and some SLD personalities. This led to a sharp increase in the popularity of the opposition, including the dangerous populists of the SO. As both parliamentary and presidential elections loomed, the PO and the PiS established an alliance, promising to govern together, while contesting both elections separately. But when, contrary to expectations, the PiS outdistanced the PO in the parliamentary elections by 27% to 24% of the vote, and its leader Lech Kaczyński defeated Donald Tusk in the second round of the presidential elections by 55% to 45%, the PiS's appetite increased. As coalition negotiations broke down, the triumphant conservatives went on to produce a minority government. After its failure, the PiS entered in a coalition with the SO and the LPR, appointing the extremist parties' leaders as ministers and deputy prime ministers.

A clean break: II

What followed was a bizarre and frightening episode in Polish political history, with the government engaging in fundamentalist right-wing policies at home, and alienating all allies abroad. An attempt to extend lustration to cover entire professions, such as academic lecturers and journalists, without due process, was eventually thrown out by the Constitutional Court, but not without generating a division inside Polish society deeper than anything since 1989. The government turned to Radio Maryja for support while waging war on the "liberal media." The LPR, running the education ministry, tried to rid the schools of "anti-national influences," while waging an overt war on homosexuals, including incitement to physical violence. As SO staffed entire segments of the government with its cronies, its leaders continued to ignore judiciary proceedings against them, including fraud, extortion, and rape. In foreign affairs, the government opened a hysterical cold war with Germany over supposed revanchism in Berlin, alienated the EU with anti-European declarations, and dramatically increased political confrontation with an already hostile Russia. On almost all fronts, it was a political disaster. Such successes as existed – a marked drop in unemployment to 10% and an economic boom – were due to EU membership, which allowed mass migration of Poles seeking jobs in the West, and poured massive structural funds into the country's economy.

When in the summer of 2007 the coalition imploded, as a police provocation against Deputy Prime Minister Lepper was uncovered, and the government set out to arrest, over supposed leaks, its own minister of the interior and chief of police, early elections became a necessity. These were won overwhelmingly by the PO, which obtained an unprecedented result of 41.5% of the vote, while PiS scored well at 32.1%, and LiD (Left and Democrats, an SLD-based coalition including some former UW leaders) did poorly at 13.5%. The PO leader Donald Tusk, in coalition with PSL (8.9% of the vote), set up a new government, intent to undo the damage created in the Kaczyński biennium. The new government enjoyed huge popularity, but had from the beginning to contend with the hostility of the remaining twin, President Lech Kaczyński, whose turn in office runs out in 2010. Crises paralyzed foreign policy: the president enthusiastically supported the US missile defense shield, which was to be set up in Poland, about which the government is skeptical, and long refused to sign the Lisbon Treaty, which Poland had ratified. In internal affairs, a book alleging that Lech Wałęsa had been a police informer in the early 1970s, and had been manipulated by his masters ever since, created a major scandal, with the Kaczyńskis endorsing these findings, and the government (as well as Wałęsa himself) rejecting them as secret police fabrications. The era of contentious politics is apparently not over.

Timeline 1989–2007

6 April 1989	Round table negotiations between communist government and delegalized Solidarity end with deal on semi-free elections
8 May 1989	First legal independent daily, "*Gazeta Wyborcza*," starts publishing
18 June 1989	Second round of elections gives Solidarity its allocated 35% of seats in Lower House and 99% of seats in Upper House, for which elections were free
19 July 1989	General Wojciech Jaruzelski elected president by parliament
24 August 1989	Tadeusz Mazowiecki appointed first non-communist Prime Minister since 1945
1 January 1990	Deputy Prime Minister Leszek Balcerowicz's "shock therapy" economic reforms come in effect

27 January 1990	Communist Party (PZPR) disbands
14 March 1990	Yearly inflation rate hits all-time high of 1360%
12 April 1990	Censorship abolished
9 December 1990	In second round of first free universal elections since 1945, Solidarity leader Lech Wełęsa elected president
31 March 1991	Military structures of Warsaw Pact abolished
8 April 1991	Visa-free travel between Poland and most Western European countries
22 July 1991	On former communist holiday, stock exchange opens in former Communist Party Central Committee building in Warsaw
27 October 1991	First democratic parliamentary elections since 1945; fifteen parties in Parliament
26 November 1991	Poland joins Council of Europe
1 January 1992	Income tax introduced
8 November 1992	Last Soviet units leave Poland
5 December 1992	First private TV starts broadcasting
7 January 1993	New law severely limits abortion rights
24 May 1993	Carmelite nuns leave Auschwitz site, ending four-year long bitter Christian–Jewish conflict
19 September 1993	Post-communists win parliamentary elections
19 November 1995	Post-Communist Aleksander Kwaśniewski wins presidential election
21 December 1995	Post-communist Prime Minister Józef Oleksy accused of being a Russian spy; eventually resigns, and later is cleared
2 April 1997	New constitution adopted
19 September 1997	Post-Solidarity bloc wins parliamentary elections
23 February 1998	Concordat with Vatican signed
12 March 1999	Poland joins NATO
28 May 1999	Soldiers remove 500 crosses planted by fundamentalists at Auschwitz site, ending another Christian–Jewish crisis
16 March 2000	Poland sends first troops to Afghanistan
15 April 2000	Jan T. Gross' book *Neighbors* published, launching frank wide-scale debate about Polish–Jewish relations
8 October 2000	Kwaśniewski re-elected president
23 September 2001	Post-communists win parliamentary elections
27 December 2002	*Gazeta Wyborcza* scoop opens country's biggest corruption scandal, the Rywin affair
20 March 2003	Polish troops participate in Second Iraq War
1 May 2004	Poland joins the EU
25 September 2005	Right-wing PiS under Jarosław Kaczyński wins parliamentary elections
23 October 2005	PiS candidate Lech Kaczyński, Jaroslaw's twin brother, wins presidential elections
5 May 2006	Populist Samoobrona (SO) and extreme-right League of Polish Families join minority PiS government
19 July 2006	PiS leader Jarosław Kaczyński becomes prime minister

7 January 2007	Newly appointed Warsaw archbishop Staniłlaw Wielgus resigns after having been denounced as former communist agent
15 March 2007	Sweeping lustration law enters in effect
13 May 2007	Constitutional Court throws out most of lustration law
21 October 2007	Early elections, called after protracted political crisis, bring defeat to PiS and victory to center-right Civic Platform; for the first time, post-communists fail to capitalize on unpopularity of non-communist government
16 November 2007	Civic Platform leader Donald Tusk becomes prime minister
21 December 2007	Poland joins Schengen free-travel zone

Fact sheet

Area	312,685 sq km^2
Population (July 2007 estimate)	38,518,241
Urban population (2001)	67%
Below the poverty line (2003)	17% of population
Unemployment rate (2007)	12.8%
GDP *per capita* (2007)	$16,200
GDP growth (2007)	6.5%
Inflation (2007)	2.1%

Sources: Urban population, Main Statistical Office (Warsaw); all other data, CIA, *The World Factbook*, at www.cia.gov/library/publications/the-world-factbook/geos/pl.html/ [accessed on 2 February 2008].

Parties in parliament (results of the 21 October 2007 election)

Party	% of the vote	Number of deputies elected
Lower house (Sejm)		
Civic Platform (PO)	41.51	209
Law and Justice (PiS)	32.11	166
Left and Democrats (LiD)	13.15	53
Polish Peasant Party (PSL)	8.91	31
German minority		1
Upper house (Senate)		
Civic Platform		60
Law and Justice		39
Independent (unaffiliated)		1

Sources: Agence France Presse (23 October 2007), from topic@afp.com, by subscription; and *The Warsaw Voice* (24 October 2007), at www.warsawvoice.pl/ [accessed on 2 February 2008].

Short biography of Lech Wałęsa

From peasant son with only a trade school education to creator and leader of the world's biggest trade union ever, Nobel Peace Prize winner and president of Poland, Lech

Wałęsa's career was meteoric. Born in 1943, he achieved world fame as the leader of the communist world's most successful strike, in the Lenin Shipyards in Gdańsk, in August 1980. When in 1981 the regime cracked down on his 10 million strong Solidarity union, Wałęsa, interned, refused to cave in, and continued to lead the underground opposition, earning the Nobel Prize in 1983 for his non-violent resistance. Elected president in 1990, after the fall of communism, he proved bitterly divisive as a leader, lost his re-election bid in 1995 to a former communist, and has played no role in political life since. In 2008, inconclusive allegations that he had been a police informer in the early 1970s resurfaced, generating a nationwide scandal.

Notes

1. Wojciech Roszkowski, *Najnowsza historia Polski 1980–2006* (Recent Polish history 1980–2006, in Polish) (Warsaw: Świat Książki, 2006), p. 123
2. Personal communication.
3. Parliamentary exposé (24 August 1989).
4. The name of this party was chosen with an eye to generating the acronym BBWR, which resonated with the earlier BBWR, the Non-Partisan Bloc for Cooperation with the Government, established by Marshal Pilsudski in 1928.
5. Parliamentary debate (11 April 1997).
6. Jan Tomasz Gross, *Neighbors: The Destruction of the Jewish Community in Jedwabne, Poland* (Princeton, NJ: Princeton University Press, 2001).
7. *Gazeta Wyborcza* (27 December 2002).

Further reading

Castle, Marjorie. *Triggering Communism's Collapse: Perceptions and Power in Poland's Transition* ((Lanham, Md.: Rowman & Littlefield, 2003)

Chodakiewicz, Marek Jan, John Radziłowski, and Dariusz Tołczyk (eds.). *Poland's Transformation: A Work in Progress* (New Brunswick, NJ: Transaction Publishers, 2006)

Kurski, Jaroslaw. *Lech Walesa: Democrat or Dictator?* (Boulder, Colo.: Westview Press, 1993)

Lukowski, Jerzy and Hubert Zawadzki. *A Concise History of Poland*, 2nd edn. (Cambridge: Cambridge University Press, 2006)

Michnik, Adam. *The Church and the Left*, trans. David Ost (Chicago Ill.: University of Chicago Press, 1993)

Millard, Frances. *Anatomy of the New Poland: Post-Communist Politics in its First Phase* (Aldershot: Edward Elgar, 1994)

Polish Politics and Society (London and New York: Routledge, 1999)

Osa, Maryjane. *Solidarity and Contention: Networks of Polish Opposition* (Minneapolis, Minn.: University of Minnesota Press, 2003)

Roszkowski, Wojciech. *Najnowsza historia Polski 1980–2006* (Recent Polish History 1980–2006, in Polish) (Warsaw: Świat Książki, 2006)

Staar, Richard F. (ed.). *Transition to Democracy in Poland* (New York: St. Martin's Press, 1993)

Szczerbiak, Aleks. *Poles Together? The Emergence and Development of Political Parties in Post-Communist Poland* (Budapest and New York: Central European University Press, 2001)

Tworzecki, Hubert. *Parties and Politics in Post-1989 Poland* (Boulder, Colo.: Westview Press, 1996)

Zubrzycki, Geneviève. *The Crosses of Auschwitz: Nationalism and Religion in Post-Communism Poland* (Chicago, Ill.: University of Chicago Press, 2006)

8

Building democratic values in the Czech Republic since 1989

CAROL SKALNIK LEFF

In the run-up to the "Velvet Revolution" of 1989 that overthrew communism, Czechoslovakia was routinely and accurately styled one of the "Gang of Four" most repressive regimes in the Soviet bloc. Juan Linz and Alfred Stepan's typology of communist regimes assigned the country to the category of "frozen totalitarianism," in which "despite the persistent toleration of some civil society critics, ... almost all the other control mechanisms of the party state stay in place and do not evolve" except by decay.[1] Despite this inauspicious starting point, and the prompt dissolution of Czechoslovakia in 1992, the new Czech Republic successfully democratized, marketized, and integrated into the complex of European institutions. Of the OECD countries, only Poland and Slovakia showed more robust growth in 2007,[2] and the Bertelsman Transformation index of 2008 ranked the Czech Republic as the leading consolidated democracy in the region.[3]

In this chapter, I shall explore the evolution of the Czech post-communist regime in three stages. First, I will unpack some important historical legacies of the multiple regimes the Czech Republic experienced in the twentieth century – parliamentary democracy in the interwar First Republic, the Nazi "protectorate" in the Second World War, and the communist state. I will then examine the institutional framework for democratic decision-making. The final step will be to analyze the broad political process under this system, emphasizing some of the distinctive dynamics that have created accountability problems in Czech politics and left some key transition problems still unresolved.

Historical legacies

Grigore Pop-Eleches has made a forceful case for the dominance of historical–cultural legacies in determining the outcome of post-communist regime change.[4] He compiles a multi-item index to capture some important legacy indicators (history of statehood and democracy, ethnic and religious identity, proximity to the West, type of communist regime), and finds that these are more powerful predictors of democratic success than some of the more widely studied factors such as well-designed institutions. This is a timely reminder that all studies of regime change need historical context.

The Czech Republic has a distinctive historical legacy because it can fairly be called a re-democratization. Like most other states in East-Central Europe, Czechoslovakia was founded as a democratic republic after the First World War when the major regional empires collapsed in defeat. The new state brought together the Czech lands from the Austrian part of the Habsburg empire and Slovakia from the Hungarian half. Despite the complexities of unifying two formerly separate territories, the interwar Czechoslovak First Republic was alone in the region in maintaining a functioning parliamentary system based on free and competitive elections from 1918 up to the Munich Accords, imposed as a result of pressure from Nazi Germany in 1938. The democratic system was undeniably flawed, notably in its closed elite and its dealings with the state's multiple minorities. Nonetheless, under the iconic presidential leadership of sociologist and moral philosopher Tomáš Masaryk (1850–1937), the political system remained open to competing views, even permitting a legal communist party to contest elections, a marker of tolerance echoed nowhere else in the region. Moreover, despite the travails of the global depression, interwar Czechoslovakia ranked as one of the top ten industrial economies in the world.

What is most important, however, is the resonance this period retained for future generations. For the communists, Masaryk was anathema, but the Masaryk legacy was invoked in each subsequent period of political liberalization, notably the "Prague Spring" of 1968 and the "Velvet Revolution" of 1989; Masaryk was the subject of one of the first post-communist exhibitions (entitled simply "TGM") at the National Museum in Prague, and the university in Brno was renamed after him. The first post-communist president, dissident playwright Václav Havel (b. 1936), was repeatedly cited as an intellectually appropriate successor to the president Liberator of the First Republic.[5] Citizens marked the interwar democratic interlude as one of the most important periods in their history. Czechs had a historical reference point for democracy. This experience in turn anchored a broader identification with the West that novelist Milan Kundera captured in a famous essay – an identification perceived to have been ruptured, he argued, by the experience of being "kidnapped by the [Soviet] East."[6] A return to a Europe without adjectives "East" or "West" seemed an appropriate aspiration, encapsulated in the logic of joining European institutions.

Masaryk's Czechoslovakia was also an institutional reference point for regime change; the core political institutions of the post-communist Czech republic replicated the First Republic in its key democratic features: a bicameral parliament with proportional representation for elections to the lower house and directly elected Senators, and a presidency elected by legislature. The appropriateness of this model remains contested, as we shall see.

The legacies of the communist regime are complex, for the Communist Party (KSČ) took power in the February revolution of 1948 after decades of participation in a functioning parliamentary system, where it consistently gained more than 10% of the vote, and had won a relatively free and fair election in 1946 to lead the governing coalition. Prolonged democratic exposure in the First Republic, however, ironically ushered in one of the harsher and more rigid communist regimes. Not only were there extensive purges in the Stalinist 1950s, but the reform currents within the party that emerged afterwards were extinguished by the purges that followed the Soviet invasion of 1968. It was frequently claimed, although hyperbolically, that during the post-invasion normalization there were more ex-communist party members than active ones.[7] The highest leadership was essentially frozen until 1989, and with it the policy agenda.

An exhaustive study of post-communist party systems by Herbert Kitschelt and his colleagues argued that more economically advanced communist states such as Czechoslovakia possessed greater state capacity and bureaucratic efficiency and a well-mobilized working-class base that proved resistant both to severe corruption and to reform; such a regime was necessarily repressive, because more advanced societies were prone to rebel.[8] Kitschelt's depiction does seem to account for the government repression of Czech dissident movements such as Charter 77 and for the pattern of mass protest that challenged and defeated the regime in 1989 once repression was unable to stem the tide.[9]

The systemic failure to reform or liberalize meant that the KSČ could contribute much less to the transition than its more flexible communist counterparts in Hungary and Poland. Indeed, the Czech public manifests an enduring allergic reaction to the communist era. Czechs consistently register the least positive evaluation of the former communist regime of any of the new EU members, by a wide margin. In the 2001 New Europe Barometer, only 31% of Czechs evaluated the communist period positively; the next most negative state was Lithuania, where 54% of the public accorded a positive rating to the former regime. By contrast, Czechs gave the highest positive rating of all ten states to the present era, tied with Hungary.[10]

Perhaps the clearest negative policy response to the *ancien régime* was the early embrace of "lustration" – a term Czechs coined to describe the purging of the former communist elite from sensitive political positions. Not only did the government enact legislation in 1991 to bar leading communist functionaries, security officials, and informants from a number of public positions (although not from holding electoral office), for five years, but the ban was extended indefinitely in 2000.[11]

In an analysis of statistical results of the lustration program, political scientist Kieran Williams has found only limited evidence of a widespread impact on actual dismissals,[12] although several ministerial careers ended after a positive vetting. Yet the program was deeply polarizing from its inception. Critics questioned the level of due process, the dubious validity of relying on the accuracy and completeness of security police records to identify informants, and the politicization of the process. Ironically, dissidents were highly vulnerable to collaboration charges, for it was they whom the security police (StB) monitored and attempted to blackmail into cooperation.

The most sensational and protracted case involved Foreign Minister Jan Kavan, whose dissident activity abroad during the communist period was shadowed by allegations of StB collaboration. Although Kavan was eventually cleared, the broader controversy persisted over the moral logic of destroying reputations of vigilant regime opponents for an isolated or even inadvertent incident of contact with the police.[13] Lustration throughout the region also aroused EU concern, because the policy's problematic elements of retroactive justice were seen as a deviation from the rule of law.

Despite lustration, the entrenched and unrepentant elite of the communist period had an impact on coalition-building after the collapse of communism. Anna Grzymala-Busse noted that a reform wing of the KSČ vainly attempted to emulate the widespread move in neighboring countries to rename the party and democratize its agenda. She attributes the failure of the Czech initiative to the party's decentralized structure, which left the fate of renewal in the hands of the party's regional bureaucracy, who defiantly refused to accommodate to the democratized regime.[14] As a result, an unreformed Communist Party of Bohemia and Moravia (KSČM) survived to contest for leftist voters with the moderate and more typically "European" Social Democratic Party (ČSSD).

The most prominent historical legacy of the twentieth century, however, was undoubtedly the unresolved question of Czech–Slovak statehood. This fundamental democratic question – Who are the people? – was in effect resolved in 1992 by creating two separate states. Czechoslovakia had emerged after the First World War as a hasty product of the collapse of the Habsburg Empire and the post-war treaty-making process. Czechs at that time cited security grounds for a centralized unitary state, while Slovaks thought they had been promised regional autonomy. This set up a permanent tension between Czechs and Slovaks over appropriate institutions of governance – a dispute that erupted each time successive regimes faltered and were rebuilt (most dramatically in the interregnum of the Second World War Slovak state under Nazi tutelage, but also in 1945 and the "Prague Spring" reforms of 1968). Unresolved, these periodic confrontations bred a legacy of Czech–Slovak distrust. Rather belatedly, the state had federalized in 1969 – the major reform of the "Prague Spring" to survive the Soviet invasion.

After the collapse of communism, all parties to the Czech–Slovak controversy readily acknowledged that communist federalism was not "authentic" because it was imbedded in an authoritarian regime. Thus, negotiations over the appropriate democratic expression of a common Czech and Slovak state became an immediate priority – indeed, no new constitution was possible without resolving this issue. Scholars have paid considerable fruitful attention to the fatal bargaining failure that ensued – an elite deadlock that had created, by mid-1992, a paradoxical decision to separate despite the fact that majorities of both Czechs and Slovaks continued to favor staying together. The inherited constitutional process for reaching a revised ethno-federal bargain, some argue, was booby-trapped because of the veto power accorded each republic's representatives.[15] Other scholars emphasize the interests of key political actors – most notably Czech Prime Minister Václav Klaus (b. 1941), whose central focus on economic transformation was only impeded by Slovak resistance, and Slovak Prime Minister Vladimír Mečiar (b. 1942) who, in trying to consolidate his power within Slovakia, may have miscalculated by overestimating Klaus' commitment to the Czechoslovak project.[16]

The public also assigned a hefty share of the blame for the state dissolution to power politics.[17] Yet the citizens themselves were dramatically polarized, not on the continuance of the state, but on the form it should take; Czechs favored a unitary state or centralized federalism, while the Slovaks preferred a looser federation or confederation. Ultimately, however, what may have been most important about public opinion was the low-level intensity of commitment to the existing state. The elite decision to separate might otherwise have generated massive mobilization; instead, lacking the focal point of a popular referendum on the issue, the new two-state dispensation emerged without much resistance or public protest.

What is perhaps most interesting about the dissolution of the state is the relatively mild trauma inflicted – in many respects it was truly, as it was styled at the time, a "Velvet Divorce." After some skirmishing in the spring of 1993, an equitable allocation of assets was adopted. Most Slovaks resident in the Czech Republic capitalized on a relatively simple process to acquire Czech citizenship.[18] Relations between the two new countries remained fairly amicable, and both economies underwent a successful capitalist transition.

A retrospective evaluation of the split conducted ten years afterwards, in February 2003, showed a near-reversal of sentiment on its desirability: 59% of Czechs polled supported state dissolution, compared to 55% *opposed* at the time.[19] The EU had resisted the split, and insisted on the renegotiation of the Europe Agreements signed by the common state. Ironically, however, the prospect of future EU membership seems to have helped fuel the divorce. The transactional costs imposed by new borders would ultimately be mitigated by inclusion in the larger common European space. A 1992 political cartoon showed a Czech and Slovak shaking hands as they parted, with the valediction "See you in the European Union!"

An additional ethnic legacy was the controversy over the so-called Beneš decrees which had authorized the expulsion of 3 million Sudeten Germans from Czechoslovakia in response to the wartime Nazi occupation of the Czech "protectorate." The Czechs firmly supported the expulsion to resolve a troubled Czech–German relationship that had rankled since the Czech lands had been incorporated into the Austrian Habsburg empire after defeat at the battle of White Mountain in 1620. However, the imposition of collective guilt on a whole group, and the deaths and suffering incurred by those who were expelled, assured an eventual reckoning with the German government.

All discussion of this episode was suppressed in the communist period, but it became a volatile issue immediately after the "Velvet Revolution." Deportee families in Germany had kept the question alive, and pressured the German government to incorporate it into the post-communist foreign policy agenda governing relations with the Czechs. Czechs vocally resented the perceived German attempt to create an equivalency between the deportations and the wartime behavior of Nazi Germany. There were also practical fears of German demands for property restitution in the former deportation zones – a key reason why successive Czech prime ministers had also refused to revoke the Beneš decrees even though they no longer had active legal meaning.

Nonetheless, unified Germany was economically and politically powerful in Europe; the Czech–German relationship was an important one. Indeed, Germany was a primary gatekeeper for membership in the EU, and the German government framed the "Sudeten" question in European terms of fairness and rule of law. It would be 1997 before a formal declaration on mutual relations could finally be approved in both parliaments – a document in which both countries expressed carefully calibrated regret for the previous behavior of their governments, concluding with the hopeful assertion that "Both sides agree that injustice inflicted in the past belongs in the past, and will therefore orient their relations toward the future."

The declaration hardly resolved the issue; deportee families continued to press for revocation of the Beneš decrees on human rights grounds, and Austrian Chancellor Wolfgang Schüssel called for revocation of the decrees as a criterion of EU membership as late as 2002. However, the European Court of Human Rights refused to hear the legal cases because the protocols that guide the court's judicial rulings had not been in place at the time of the decrees.[20] After commissioning three legal scholars to examine the issue and considerable internal discussion, the EU concluded that revocation of the Beneš decrees need not be a requirement for Czech accession, because the human rights mandates governing membership eligibility related to current behavior, not past wrongs.[21]

A final distinctive identity legacy is that of religion. The Czech Republic is decidedly atypical for a nominally Catholic country, and the Church has no resonance in politics comparable to that in Poland or Slovakia. Analysts are fond of quoting from the World Values Survey that more Czechs believe in UFOs than in God! The Counter-Reformation reimposed Catholicism in response to the Bohemian Protestant Hussite movement at the same time that the Czech lands lost their sovereignty to the Habsburgs; thus, the nexus between religion and identity carried a rather negative valence. The communist era further eroded the ties, with the Vatican and the government so deadlocked that most bishoprics were vacant in 1989. The Church then experienced marked difficulty in restoring its position in the post-communist state, with a fierce restitution battle over the control of the St. Vitus cathedral next to the "Castle" (*hrad*), the Czech president's residence.

Religious organizations have limited impact on public opinion even on values issues that are highly emotional elsewhere. Over a presidential veto and concerted objections from ten Churches, parliament passed a civil union bill in 2006 that afforded same-sex partners some of the same rights and obligations as married couples. This was the first and most extensive law on same-sex partnerships to be enacted in post-communist countries, and was notable for the support of some 62% of the public.

Designing a capitalist democracy

As previously noted, the institutional architecture of the new Czech state resembled that of the interwar republic. In this section, we shall see that these particular institutional choices do not meet with broad popular support, despite emphatic support for the broader logic of democracy.

The Czech constitution of 1992 mandated a bicameral parliament and elected regional governments, but this democratic infrastructure was slow to develop. As a unit within the larger Czech and Slovak Federated Republic, the Czech Republic had been unicameral and had lacked a president, a Senate, and regional assemblies. Prime Minister Václav Klaus was in no hurry to implement the necessary changes. To be sure, Václav Havel moved from the federal presidency, which he had resigned amidst the breakup of Czechoslovakia, to the Czech presidency in January 1993. The Klaus government, however, delayed enacting the legislative framework for the Senate and regional governments – alternate power centers that would challenge his party's dominance of politics. Klaus also resisted the establishment of an ombudsman to monitor government operations.[22] Elections for the Senate did not occur until 1996 and for regional governments until 2000; in the meantime, the checks on the power of the government were attenuated.

Once in operation, however, the full constitutional framework lacked a strong consensus. A series of recurrent controversies centered in particular on the method of presidential selection, the functionality of the constitutionally mandated proportionality of electoral rules, and the logic of the Senate's role in policy-making. None of these debates has engendered successful institutional redesign; so the controversies linger.

Direct presidential election has been a publicly approved norm in post-communist states. Only Hungary and Estonia share with the Czech Republic a presidency selected by the legislature. This is not a popular alternative with Czechs; supporters of direct election outnumber supporters of the existing system by almost three to one,[23] and the issue re-animates itself with each successive presidential selection, most recently in the fall of 2007. In September of that year, the Senate held a conference on the question that exposed ongoing partisan divisions on the issue. The ČSSD supports a constitutional change to direct presidential election, but the governing Civic Democratic Party (ODS) is split on the issue and ODS Prime Minister Mirek Topolánek favors the current system, which he describes as "traditional" in the Czech Republic, as indeed it was in interwar Czechoslovakia.

The situation is still more complex because re-opening the selection method would also re-open the issue of presidential power. The ČSSD proposal would confer a popular mandate while significantly paring back presidential appointment and dissolution powers, as well as the incumbent's immunity from prosecution and barriers to removal from office. Previous two-term President Václav Havel long chafed under the limited presidential leverage and had argued fruitlessly for enhanced power. There appears to be no parliamentary constituency for a more powerful office, but equally no consensus on revising the existing functions. Given the popularity of incumbent President Václav Klaus, and the high standing of the presidential institution (which ranks first in opinion surveys among all constitutional institutions, at some 75%), there is no urgency to resolve this staple item on the institutional agenda.

The Czech Senate, however, has been a stepchild from its inception, like the indirectly selected presidency a relic of the interwar republic, but far less revered. Like the interwar Senate, it was designed to harbor "elder statesmen" (the minimum age is forty compared with twenty-one in the lower chamber) as a deliberative but limited check on the Chamber of Deputies. It was born in controversy; the initial concept was to transfer the suddenly jobless federal Czechoslovak MPs to a new Senate when Czechoslovakia dissolved in 1993, but parties unrepresented or underrepresented in the federal parliament blocked that initiative.

The Senate is less popular (around 25% support) than any other constitutional institution.[24] Voter turnout reflects this tepid response – the high point was a mere 30% in the inaugural 1996 elections – and has decreased ever since. Each time Senate elections record miserably low turnouts, there are calls for its abolition. Less radical critics and even its friends suggest a reform of its functions. Three-time Senate Chair Petr Pithart has defended the Senate with an argument from the American constitutional tradition: "The continuity of the chamber that changes one third every two years is a stabilizing element in our fragile democracy."[25] But even he appears to favor a rethinking of the Senate's function to tie it more closely to regional governments.

The final institutional component – the electoral system – has arguably had the most profound effect. Post-communist electoral systems have generally been subject to scrutiny and frequent, though modest, revision.[26] By the late 1990s, the Czech system, from the outset quite proportional in its effect, came under fire for failing to generate stable parliamentary majorities. I will address this problem in depth in the following section, but here it is important to note that resolution of this problem proved politically and legally difficult.

Not surprisingly, the largest parties – the ČSSD and the ODS – despite ideological differences, agreed on the need to move toward a more majoritarian electoral system favoring larger parties in order to reduce partisan fragmentation – and, not incidentally, to enhance their own political clout. Smaller parties of all ideological colorations were understandably less enthusiastic. Nonetheless, the larger parties were able to push through an electoral law that increased the number of electoral districts to 35 – the greater the number of districts, the fewer the seats awarded in each district, and the less proportional the system. In the end, only a modest electoral change was possible, because the principle of proportionality is constitutionally protected under the suffrage provisions of Article 18 of the constitution;[27] the courts ruled the law too disproportional to meet the constitutional standard. A more moderate proposal did pass muster with the court. Even so, the smaller parties have continued to contest the constitutionality of the revised legislation; the Green Party lodged a constitutional challenge after the 2006 elections, arguing that a system that translated their 6% of the vote into 3% of the seats was clearly not proportional.[28]

The Czech media has faced the same challenges prevalent throughout the region: professionalization of reporting standards, ownership and control, and relationship to the government. Complaints of interference by Václav Klaus in programming decisions at Czech Television led to a major journalists' strike in 2000–1, culminating in the resignation of the director, who was seen as too responsive to government pressure. In general, however, international monitoring organizations have given the Czech Republic fairly high marks, and so does the Czech public. The media (radio, television, and newspapers) have consistently garnered the highest levels of trust of any post-communist political or governmental institution.[29]

The final set of institutional choices involved the marketization strategy. The distinctive Czechoslovak privatization plan – voucher or coupon privatization– had its roots in a desire to rapidly transform a 97% state-controlled economy in a manner that might prove legitimate with a public that more enthusiastically embraced democracy than capitalism. Because Czechoslovakia was unburdened by the massive international debt that plagued neighboring Poland and Hungary, the privatization strategy was less encumbered by the need to raise revenue. Accordingly, the key thrust of the privatization process was to create citizen participation by offering all adults the opportunity to purchase coupons redeemable for shares in reorganized state enterprises at a minimal price – about a week's wages – designed to cover only the administrative costs of the program. At a stroke (or, more accurately, in two waves, in 1992 and 1993), a stock market and a private sector would emerge, and citizens would become stakeholders in the new market economy.

This at least was the plan, one that appealed sufficiently to find wide imitation elsewhere. In practice, however, voucher privatization had its pitfalls. It did indeed "privatize" the economy rapidly. By the end of the second wave, the government had paid off its IMF loans and Economic Minister Karel Dyba was triumphally rejecting the "emerging economy" label for his country: "Forget it. We've already emerged."[30]

On the other hand, coupon privatization had some unfortunate consequences. Initial public hesitancy to embrace the unfamiliar concept was reversed when brash young entrepreneur Vladimír Kožený burst upon the scene with his Harvard Investment Fund that promised to deliver breathtaking profits from the voucher privatization "in a year and a day" – a fairy tale phrase – provided that citizens entrusted their coupons to him to invest in the new market. Using western ad campaigns and attractive women to sell his service, he soon cornered a share of the coupon market that alarmed the government and prompted legislation to control the concentration of vouchers in any of the new Investment Privatization Funds.

This episode had two consequences. First, Kožený's own role in the process soon tainted the program's legitimacy, as his financial dealings proved murky and indeed actionable, leading to his prudent self-exile to the Bahamas. His was only the most visible case of fraudulent or incompetent fund management. Second, and more important structurally, the state-owned banking sector ended up creating the bulk of the funds that held and invested vouchers. This created a non-transparent accountability structure in which the banks were both lenders to new private enterprises in one role and guardians of their stockholders' interests in another, all while being themselves among the last institutions to face privatization.[31] In the event, banks proved hesitant to call in bad loans and force bankruptcy that would have thrown people out of work; it has been widely recognized that bank-owned funds did not safeguard shareholder interests. In short, voucher privatization did not resolve the corporate governance problem; indeed, it created incentives for "tunneling" out corporate assets.[32]

In economist János Kornai's term, "soft budget constraints" continued to operate in the Czech economy. Wage growth failed to match lagging productivity, unemployment remained artificially low. Thus, the Czech economy hit a wall in 1996 and 1997; growth, trade, and investment stagnated, GDP slumped, and unemployment rose. The Czechs had to cede their standing as the bloc "tiger" to Slovakia, whose economy started to flourish in the late 1990s. The Czechs spent another decade righting the ship, to the detriment of Czech enthusiasm for the market. Joseph Hraba, in analyzing the trends in popular support for post-communist institutions in the Czech Republic, argues that support for economic reform tended to follow performance, while democratic attitudes remained more stable.[33] The latter point is fortunate for, as we shall now see, Czech democracy has some performance problems.

Political dynamics: the dilemma of unstable parliamentary majorities

The Czech Republic clearly *is* a democracy. Elections were from the outset adjudged to be free and fair. Moreover, the first two Czech governments (1990–2, 1992–6) were also very stable by regional standards; they functioned from election to election without a government crisis. The first Prime Minister, Klaus, served over five years, from June 1992 to December 1997 – a regional record then exceeded only by Slovenian Prime Minister Janez Drnovšek.

This positive beginning had given way to greater instability by the mid-1990s. Ironically, the greatest problem was a party that had never served in a Czech cabinet government, the unreconstructed communist party (KSČM), staunchly supportive of the old system and long the only electorally successful party in the region to retain the designation "Communist" in its name.[34] From 1990 through 2006, through six elections, the KSČM always boasted the second or third largest parliamentary delegation, even after the ČSSD supplanted them as the largest party of the left. At its peak performance, in 2002 the communists claimed 18.5% of the vote and 41 seats, and were placed second in the European elections of 2004.

In a multi-party parliament, a delegation the size of the communist fraction would normally be an eligible partner in any potential coalition government, but its "uncoalitionability" as an unreformed remnant of a hard-line regime meant that the party's electoral strength was overmatched by far greater voter repugnance.[35] Even in KSČM's successful 2002 election performance, for example, between 39 and 45% of opinion poll respondents reported that they would never under any circumstances vote communist, almost twice the number who rejected any other party. Voters did not reject the left in general; only 3–4% of the respondents in the same survey rejected the ČSSD.

The enduring electoral power of the KSČM has had several effects. The first was the delay in developing a viable governing party on the left. Ex-communist successor parties in most neighboring countries reformed and won the largest share of left voters.[36] With the pariah KSČM partially colonizing the left, it was only in the third elections (1996) that a separate Czech Social Democratic Party gained sufficient strength to act as the primary left alternative. Until that time, the right wing, and particularly the ODS of Václav Klaus, faced no viable opposition.[37]

The emergence of the ČSSD created a bimodal party system with basically moderate electoral centers in the ODS on the right and the ČSSD on the left. Such a pattern is typically European. Elsewhere, however, government coalitions have generally rotated in power. But in the Czech Republic it remained difficult to create parliamentary majorities because the communists continued to poll strongly and soak up too large a bloc of parliamentary seats. The survival of the KSČM has therefore had a second and more durable impact on parliamentary arithmetic – from 10 to 18% of the parliamentary seats have not been available for government formation, and politics has not normalized around shifting center-left and center-right majorities.

Minority governments or cabinets with wafer-thin majorities have accordingly been the norm since 1996, to the detriment of both stability and accountability. No elections since 1992 have produced stable majority governments. Maxmilián Strmiska has neatly summarized the "reproduction of seemingly stalemate post-electoral situations, manifestations of governmental and political instability and, for the most part, abortive alternation of governmental parties and the tendency of important sectors of Czech party elites towards non-standard semi-consociative solutions" after 1996.[38]

The Klaus government installed after the June 1996 elections was a minority government "tolerated" by the runner-up ČSSD. This shaky government collapsed in late 1997, amidst a serious economic slowdown and multiple corruption scandals. No parliamentary majority could form after the 1998 elections either. In both 1996 and 1998, then, the result was a minority government with significant dependence on its major partisan rival – a somewhat fractured accountability mechanism.

The ČSSD bargain to gain power in 1998 warrants further elaboration. Lacking a majority and in need of guarantees to stay in office, ČSSD party leaders forged the so-called "opposition agreement" with the rival ODS. In exchange for parliamentary posts, the ODS agreed not to topple the government with a no-confidence vote and not to scuttle the budget. Otherwise, each party was free to pursue divergent policy objectives. The remainder of the opposition agreement provided the most striking departure from routine cabinet politics. The two major forces on the left and right agreed to use their initial supermajority in parliament for a constitutional revision that would create an electoral system favoring larger parties (like themselves!) and hence more probable majority governments.

As Kaare Strøm has demonstrated, minority governments are not uncommon or dysfunctional in Western Europe, particularly in Scandinavia.[39] But in the post-communist setting, they have not worked as well. The "opposition agreement" to keep minority government afloat was very unpopular, particularly since the ODS and the ČSSD had each made pre-election promises not to cooperate with the other. By the end of the electoral cycle, polls showed that respondents accepted that the opposition agreement had stabilized the government, but judged the policy results to be negative.[40] It is not coincidental that the mass protests of the 1999 "Thanks, now leave" campaign occurred in this period. Echoing the "Velvet Revolution" of 1989, these protests targeted the post-communist elite as corrupt and unresponsive.

After the 2002 elections, the ČSSD was able to build a temporary governing majority by including the so-called Coalition Parties of the center-right. But the results were very fragile, with three different cabinet governments from 2002 to 2006, a majority eventually eroding into a minority government. After the most recent election (June 2006), the parliament split perfectly down the middle, with the left (ČSSD, Communists) and the right (ODS, Christian Democrats, Greens) each garnering 100 seats. The government did not achieve a parliamentary investiture vote until January 2007; six months after the elections, indeed that fragile government crashed, embarrassingly, right in the middle of the Czech EU Presidency in the spring of 2009. The chronic governance problem continues.

The communists have thus been a permanent tax on parliamentary governance in the constriction of coalition-building. Other parties are hesitant to be seen in public with them, and the seats that they occupy as a thus-far permanent opposition have absorbed just enough of the available parliamentary seats to undercut stable majorities. The ČSSD must repeatedly pledge not to seek a ČSSD–KSČM coalition. And, in turn, the right-wing ODS itself has resorted to tactical cooperation with the communists when it suited them – the two making common cause in protecting the Beneš decrees, and in delivering the parliamentary basis for Klaus' election to the Czech presidency in 2003.[41] The problem is likely to continue, since public opinion surveys have shown continued high levels of polarization – strong support for the communists coupled with strong antagonism to them. Nonetheless, the communists scored a breakthrough from their isolation in November 2008, when they were included in a *regional* government for the first time with the ČSSD following the fall regional elections.

The protracted period of fragile governments has contributed to at least four unfortunate consequences for Czech politics: popular alienation, corruption, economic performance failures, and underachievement in the EU accession process. I have already noted the public's aversion to the current practice of politics, further evident in declining voter turnout.

Second, shaky governance has impeded response to the problem of transitional corruption that Czech politics shares with its neighbors. Although corruption in party finance was the central issue in the collapse of the minority Klaus government in 1997, widely publicized corrupt partisan practice has been too pervasive to make it a decisive electoral issue between the two major parties.[42] Indeed, resort to the "opposition agreement" after 1998 only amplified the problem, since no loud and powerful opposition voice existed to challenge government behavior. By the end of the ODS–ČSSD interlude of collaboration in 2002, the Corruption Perceptions Index (CPI) published annually by Transparency International, ranked the Czech Republic 52nd, at the bottom of the entering group of new EU members, and behind several post-communist Balkan countries still awaiting the call.[43] In 2002, on the eve of the formation of the first majority government since 1996, the opinion journal *Respekt* expressed hope that the absence of the ODS in government would "automatically cut away the tentacles of connections and favors such as necessarily develop during a long period of control over the executive."[44] There is some evidence that this has occurred; corruption as measured by Transparency International peaked in the era of the "opposition agreement," and has modestly improved thereafter.

The Czech economic trajectory is the third area in which the distinctive Czech governance patterns may have contributed to problems. Mitchell Orenstein's study of the post-communist economic reform process emphasizes the importance of democratic policy alternation for correcting policy errors; in the Czech case, he argues that the extended policy stability of the Klaus era was inimical to optimal reform, allowing for "the continuation of mistaken policies, such as mass voucher privatization, and enabling special interests to become entrenched around erroneous or partial reforms."[45] Lax accountability therefore contributed to the lack of rigor in the economic reform process and set the stage for the economic slowdown and mid-term governmental collapse in 1997, as well as pervasive corruption problems. Commentators on the Czech economic scene frequently link the soaring budget deficits of the ODS–ČSSD cohabitation period with the lack of opposition constraint on the government.

Finally, the complex partisan alignment slowed the process of accommodation with the EU's membership requirements and presented Europe with a peculiar form of Czech Euro-skepticism, one that was ill-aligned with the preferences of the electorate. Above all, the linkage between political elites and voters was distorted by the outlying position of ODS leader Václav Klaus, who repeatedly defined joining the EU as a mere "marriage of convenience," and a long-term necessity rather than a cherished dream.

Klaus' indictment of the EU, first enunciated when he was prime minister, and continuing through to his presidency during the final stages of EU accession, was of the EU as a bureaucratically overregulated leviathan with a federalist agenda that threatened Czech economic autonomy. His twin mantras were "A Europe of Nations" and "A Liberal Europe." As president, he chided the ČSSD government's one-sided "ANO" (Yes) campaign in the run-up to the country's accession referendum of 2003 as a vision through "rose-colored glasses," and coyly refused to say how he had voted in that referendum.[46] What is striking about this posture is that he lent a strongly Euro-skeptic coloration to a right-of-center party whose electorate strongly *supported* accession. Milada Vachudova and Liesbet Hooghe deemed the ODS to be the only right-of-center party to be openly antagonistic to the EU[47] – an exaggeration driven by Klaus' high profile.

There was a less dramatic mismatch between voters and leaders on the left. The ČSSD, leading incumbent governments during the accession negotiations, worked relentlessly to overcome the legislative deficits accrued during the mid-1990s in the face of lukewarm interest among the party's electoral base. The communists reserved their firepower for NATO.

President Klaus' reservations about Europe continue to mark the political atmosphere surrounding EU membership. Public trust in the EU spiked upward in the wake of accession to nearly two-thirds support in 2004, but by 2007 had receded to about 50% of the population.[48] The Czechs have joined Europe, but perhaps as jaded "old" Europeans with a suspicious eye on Brussels.

Conclusion

In the spring of 2008, the Czech Republic commemorated the fortieth anniversary of the "Prague Spring" and the Soviet invasion by entering the Schengen space of borderless travel. A refurbished Golden Prague attracts most of the over 6 million tourists who visit the country each year. Borders are open, and so is debate. Czech citizens sustained an ongoing and vigorous "No to Bases!" protest campaign against government plans to host US radar bases in West

Bohemia as part of the Bush administration's now-suspended missile shield project. Plans are under consideration to sell to developers the aging Pankrac Prison, where both Nazi and communist regimes had jailed opponents – including then-dissident Václav Havel. There may be flaws in Czech democratic capitalism, but the radical change in opportunity and citizen efficacy is hard to miss.

Timeline 830–2004

830–907	Great Moravian Empire
11th–14th century	Premyslid dynasty
15th century	Hussite Period – Czech reformation
1620	Battle of White Mountain final Czech loss of sovereignty to Habsburgs; Counter-Reformation
19th century	Czech national revival
1918–38	Czechoslovakia's First Republic established after collapse of Habsburg dynasty
1938	Partition of Czechoslovakia by Hitler after Munich Accords
1939–1945	Czech lands occupied under Nazi protectorate
1946	Czechoslovak Communist Party wins national elections
1948	Communist takeover in "February Revolution"
1968	"Prague Spring" reform movement ended by Warsaw Pact invasion
1989	"Velvet Revolution" topples communist regime; Czechoslovak state dissolves into independent Czech and Slovak Republics
1999	Czech Republic joins NATO
2004	Czech Republic joins EU

Fact sheet

Area	78,866 km^2
Population (July 2009 estimate)	10,211,904
Czech	90.4%
Moravian	3.7%
Slovak	1.9%
Other (2001 census)	4%[a]
Urban population (2008)	73%
Major cities	
Prague	2 million
Brno	380,000
Ostrava	316,000
Below the poverty line (2001 estimate)	4.3% of population
Unemployment rate (31May 2009)	7.9%
GDP *per capita* (2008 estimate)	$26,100
Higher education (OECD 2005)	12.3% of population
Literacy rate	99% of population

Note: *a* No minority larger than 4%.
Sources: CIA, *The World Factbook – Czech Republic,* at www.cia.gov/library(publicationsd-the-world-factbook/geos/EZ.html [accessed on 11 July 2009]; and "Information on Unemployment in the Czech Republic by May 31, 2006," at www.mpsv.cz/files/clanky/7135/textang10509.pdf [accessed on 11 July 2009].

Parties in the Czech Parliament

President: Václav Klaus elected 2003
Prime Minister: Mirek Topolánek (ODS) in coalition with KDU and Green Party

Parliamentary representation after 2006 Election	Seats
Civic Democratic Party (ODS)	81
Czech Social Democratic Party (ČSSD)	74
Communist Party of Bohemia and Moravia (KSČM)	26
Christian Democratic Union (KDU-CSL)	13
Green Party	6

Short biography of Václav Havel

Václav Havel (1936–) was a lifelong dissident who served as Czechoslovakia's only president before state dissolution (1990–2) and two subsequent terms as Czech president (1993–2003). Born in Prague into an affluent family in 1936, he experienced a childhood of Nazi occupation followed by communist rule. His family's bourgeois intellectual background barred him from university study in the humanities, but even though politically marginalized he forged an internationally visible career as a dramatist and essayist. His essays, most notably "The Power of the Powerless," offered a critique of the moral corrosion of communism as well as potent appeals to speak truth to power. Havel served multiple jail terms in the communist period for political activism in the Czech dissident movement Charter 77. After the Soviet invasion, his plays and essays could only be published and performed abroad, but his intellectual and moral credentials made him an effective choice to serve as the head of a new democratic state that needed international recognition and support. A jazz fan who was also attracted by the Western counter-culture in his youth, Havel made good copy as a somewhat unconventional leader who hung out with rock musician Frank Zappa and meditated with the Dalai Lama. His popularity eroded somewhat over time, in part because the presidential office was too weak to meet public expectations, but also in part some of his moral positions (against the death penalty, criticism of the Beneš decrees, against harsh retribution against communists) were themselves unpopular.

Notes

1. Juan Linz and Alfred Stepan, *Problems of Democratic Transition and Consolidation: Southern Europe, South America, and Post-Communist Europe* (Baltimore, Md. and Washington, DC: Johns Hopkins University Press and Woodrow Wilson Center Press, 1996), p. 42.

2. OECD, Main Economic Indicators, November 2007, http://www.oecd.org/dataoecd/43/20/35827900.pdf.
3. *Deutsche Welle*, 19 February 2008.
4. Grigore Pop-Eleches, "Historical Legacies and Post-Communist Regime Change," *Journal of Politics*, Vol. 69, No. 4 (November 2007), pp. 908–26.
5. See, for example, H. Gordon Skilling, *Czechoslovakia's Interrupted Revolution* (Princeton, N.J.: Princeton University Press, 1976) and Ladislav Holy, *The Little Czech and the Great Czech Nation* (Cambridge: Cambridge University Press, 1996).
6. Milan Kundera, "The Tragedy of Central Europe," *The New York Review of Books*, 26 April 1984.
7. Using elite mobility surveys, Gil Eyal argues that many of the purged were able to "correct trajectory"; he accepts lower official estimates of the number purged. See Gil Eyal, *The Origins of Post-Communist Elites: From Prague Spring to the Break-up of Czechoslovakia* (Minneapolis, Minn.: University of Minnesota Press, 2003), pp. 40–7.
8. Herbert Kitschelt, Zdenka Mansfeldova, Radoslav Markowski, and Gabor Toka, *Post-Communist Party Systems* (Cambridge: Cambridge University Press 1999), p. 28.
9. Rasma Karklins and Roger Petersen, "Decision Calculus of Protesters and Regimes: Eastern Europe 1989," *Journal of Politics*, Vol. 55, No. 3 (August 1993), pp. 588–614.
10. Richard Rose, "Advancing into Europe? The Contrasting Goals of Post-Communist Countries," in Adrian Karatnycky, A. Motyl, and A. Schnetzer, (eds.), *Nations in Transit 2002* (New York: Freedom House, 2002), pp. 39–48.
11. Slovak governments abandoned the program after independence.
12. Kieran Williams, "A Scorecard for Czech Lustration," *Central European Review*, 1 November 1999, http://tc2tc.mojolingo.xuite.net/m2m-0400/www.ce-review.org/99/19/williams19.html. See also Kieran Williams, "Lustration as the Securitization of Democracy in Czechoslovakia and the Czech Republic," *Journal of Communist Studies and Transition Politics*, Vol. 19, No. 4 (December 2003), pp. 1–24.
13. See Tina Rosenberg, The *Haunted Land: Facing Europe's Ghosts after Communism* (New York: Random House, 1996).
14. Anna Grzymala-Busse, *Redeeming the Communist Past: The Regeneration of Communist Parties in East-Central Europe* (Cambridge: Cambridge University Press, 2002).
15. For this and other perspectives, see Michael Kraus and Allison Stanger (eds.), *Irreconcilable Differences?: Explaining Czechoslovakia's Dissolution* (Lanham, Md.: Rowman & Littlefield, 2000).
16. See, for example, Abby Innes, *Czechoslovakia: The Short Goodbye* (New Haven, Conn.: Yale University Press, 2001). The Innes argument is more complex than this, but the contingency of the situation and responses of elite actors are at the center of her analysis.
17. Carol Skalnik Leff, *The Czech and Slovak Republics: Nation Versus State* (Boulder, Colo.: Westview Press, 1997), p. 138.
18. Czech Republic, Ministry of Interior, "Nabytí státního občanství České republiky některými slovenskými státními občany," at www.mvcr.cz/rady/zakladni/stat_o11.html.
19. "Názory na rozdělení Československa," Centrum pro výzkum veřejného mínění, Press release, 17 February 2003, at www.cvvm.cas.cz/upl/zpravy/100180s_po30217.pdf.
20. The Czech Constitutional Court ruled the decrees valid in 1995.

21. Euractiv, "The Beneš Decrees: Implications for EU Enlargement," 26 June 2002, at www.euractiv.com/en/enlargement/benes-decrees-implications-eu-enlargement/article-110130; "European Parliament, Directorate-General for Research Legal Opinion on the Beneš Decrees and the Accession of the Czech Republic to the European Union," Working Paper prepared by Professor Dr. Dres. h.c. Jochen A. Frowein, Professor Dr. Ulf Bernitz, and The Rt. Hon. Lord Kingsland QC, October 2002, at www.europarl.europa.eu/studies/benesdecrees/pdf/opinions_en.pdf.
22. The Social Democratic government elected in 1998 fulfilled a campaign pledge to install an ombudsman.
23. See, for example, the polling analysis in "Občané o způsobu volby, pravomocích a postavení prezidenta republiky," Centrum pro výzkum veřejného mínění, 30 May 2002, at www.cvvm.cas.cz/index.php?lang=1&disp=zpravy&r=1&shw=100057.
24. "Důvěra k ústavním institucím a spokojenost s politickou situací v dubnu 2007," Centrum pro výzkum veřejného mínění, 20 April 2007, at www.cvvm.cas.cz/index.php?lang=1&disp=zpravy&r=1&shw=100678.
25. Senate of the Czech Republic. Casopis 1/2001, at www.senat.cz/cgi-bin/sqw1250.cgi/new/web/casopis.sqw?CID=37.
26. See especially Karen Dawisha and Stephen Deets, "Political Learning in Post-Communist Elections," *East European Politics and Societies*, Vol. 20, No. 4 (Fall 2006), pp. 691–728, who note that changes tend to converge toward the middle, with highly proportional systems becoming less so and more majoritarian systems becoming more proportional.
27. Article 18 mandates that "Elections to the Chamber of Deputies shall be ... according to the principles of proportional representation," at www.servat.unibe.ch/law/icl/ez00000_.html.
28. *Radio Prague*, 14 June 2006.
29. Centrum pro výzkum veřejného mínění, "Důvěra ve vybrané instituce v ČR a dalších zemích visegrádské čtyřky," Press Report, 16 January 2007, at www.cvvm.cas.cz/upl/zpravy/100642s_po70116.pdf.
30. Cited in Leff, *The Czech and Slovak Republics*, p. 187.
31. See especially Karla Brom and Mitchell Orenstein, "The Privatised Sector in the Czech Republic: Government and Bank Control in a Transitional Economy," *Europe-Asia Studies*, Vol. 46, No. 6 (1994), pp. 893–928. The second wave of 1993 occurred after the state's dissolution and did not include Slovaks. See also the appraisal of privatization in *OECD Economic Surveys 1997–1998: Czech Republic* (Paris: OECD, 1998).
32. In Czech parlance, "tunneling" was the process by which an irresponsible new owner stripped a company of assets; the image is of an enterprise being emptied out of value, leaving an empty shell. For a discussion of this problem, see Robert Cull, Jane Matesova, and Mary Shirley, "Ownership and the Temptation to Loot: Evidence from Privatized Firms in the Czech Republic," *Journal of Comparative Economics*, Vol. 30, No. 1 (2002), pp. 1–24.
33. Joseph Hraba *et al.*, "Trends in Czech Attitudes toward the Market and Democracy," *Journal of Political and Military Sociology*, Vol. 29, No. 2 (Winter 2001), pp. 200–20.
34. For an analysis that clarifies the KSČM links to its past, see Stanislav Balk, "KSČM a jeji vztah k vlastni minulosti," *Stredoevropsky politicke studie*, at www.cepsr.cz/clanek.php?ID=200.

35. For an excellent policy-based analysis of the communists' outlaw position, see Victor Gomez, "Cramped Spaces: The Making of the Czech Political Party System after 1989," Paper prepared for a conference on "Light in Shadows, Czechoslovakia 1968," University of Toronto, 8 October 2008.
36. As many scholars have noted by now, the so-called "regime divide" has complicated coalition-building, and communist parties tend to be excluded unless they are sufficiently large to act as the dominant coalition partner.
37. Although voters for left parties tend to be older and less educated than voters for right parties, since 1998 the ČSSD have attracted the younger and better-educated segment of the left electorate. See Blanka Rehakova, "Volebni chovani ruznych skupin volicu v predcasnych parlamentnich volbach v roce 1998," *Socialni trendy*, Working Paper 2/1998.
38. Maxmilián Strmiska, "Czech Multipartism in the Late 1990s," *Stredoevropske politicke studie/Central European Political Studies Review*, Vol. 2, No. 2 (Spring 2000), at www.cepsr.com/clanek.php?ID=121 [last accessed on 2 December 2008].
39. Kaare Strøm, "Minority Government," *Comparative Political Studies*, Vol. 17, No. 2 (July 1984), pp. 199–228.
40. See survey report, "Reflexe stranickeho systemu a opozicni smlouvy," polling period January 2002, CVVM, Sociologicky ustav AV CR, at www.cvvm.cas.cz/upl/zpravy/100042s_PV20220b.doc.
41. In 2002, *Respekt* cheekily called them "natural allies." *Respekt* (18:2002), at www.respekt.cz. Interestingly, the communists supported the election of Václav Klaus because the ČSSD nominee was deemed too soft on the Sudeten German issue.
42. See Hilary Appel, "Corruption and the Collapse of the Czech Transition Miracle," *EEPS*, Vol. 15, No. 3 (Fall 2001), pp. 528–53.
43. www.transparency.org/surveys/index.html#cpi.
44. *Respekt On-line*, 27/02, at www.respekt.cz/English/clanek_detail.php?f_id=69; Corruption Perceptions Index, Transparency International, at www.transparency.org/policy_research/surveys_indices/cpi/2007.
45. Mitchell A. Orenstein, *Out of the Red: Building Capitalism and Democracy in Post-Communist Europe* (Ann Arbor, Mich.: University of Michigan Press, 2001.
46. *Mlada fronta dnes*, 14–15 June 2003.
47. Milada A. Vachudova and Liesbet Hooghe, "Postcommunist Politics in a Magnetic Field: How Transition and EU Accession Structure Party Competition on European Integration," *Comparative European Politics*, Vol. 17, No. 2 (July 2009), pp. 179–212.
48. Centrum pro výzkum veřejného mínění Důvěra a spokojenost Čechů s OSN, "EU a NATO," Press release, 12 March 2007, at www.cvvm.cas.cz/upl/zpravy/100665s_pm70312.pdf.

Further reading

Deegan-Krause, Kevin. *Elected Affinities: Democracy and Party Competition in the Czech Republic and Slovakia* (Stanford, Calif.: Stanford University Press, 2006)

Demetz, Peter, *Prague in Black and Gold: Scenes from the Life of a European City* (New York: Hill & Wang, 1997)

Golan, Galia. *The Czechoslovak Reform Movement: Communism in Crisis 1962–1968* (Cambridge: Cambridge University Press, 1971)

Reform Rule in Czechoslovakia: The Dubček Era 1968–1969 (Cambridge: Cambridge University Press, 1973)

Holy, Ladislav. *The Little Czech and the Great Czech Nation: National Identity and the Post-Communist Transformation of Society* (Cambridge: Cambridge University Press, 1996)

Leff, Carol Skalnik. *National Conflict in Czechoslovakia: The Making, and Remaking of a State 1918–1987* (Princeton, NJ: Princeton University Press, 1988)

Williams, Kieran. *The Prague Spring and Its Aftermath: Czechoslovak Politics 1968–1970* (Cambridge: Cambridge University Press, 1997)

9

Slovakia since 1989

ERIKA HARRIS

Introduction: from nationhood to statehood

The story of post-communist Slovakia tends to be a story of political turmoil, ethnic mobilization, and a cautiously declared success. Slovakia has been a difficult case of post-communist transition, always hovering on the verge of regression to authoritarianism; every election was "critical" to the continuation of democracy,[1] despite the fact that Slovakia managed to enter the EU in the first wave of eastern enlargement in May 2004, after having had only two years to complete the negotiation process. Currently, Slovakia is one of the most successful examples of "Europeanization" both politically and economically and shows impressive levels of foreign investment into the country.[2] The question that begs to be answered, though, is whether the effects of Europeanization are longer lasting than the effects of the communist and pre-communist past, which I have argued elsewhere[3] constitute an accumulation of negative conditions for the process of democratization.

The Slovak national question, 1918–89

Slovakia came into existence on 1 January 1993 as a result of the breakup of Czechoslovakia which split under the pressure of anxiety about the pace of economic transformation on the Slovak side and what in the turmoil of the early post-communism appeared to be an irreconcilable difference in cultural and historical understanding of the common Czechoslovak state from both sides – the Czech and the Slovak.[4] The Czech lands (Bohemia and Moravia) had a markedly different past from Slovakia.[5] The Czechs could boast a glorious medieval and Renaissance past with Prague as one of the most beautiful cities in Europe, while Slovaks ruled for centuries by Hungary had little national past. After the Austro-Hungarian compromise (1867), the monarchy changed into two nearly sovereign states with different nationality policies and different consequences for Czechs and Slovaks. The Slovaks were subjected to the modernization policies of Hungary, degenerating into increasingly intensified "Magyarization" which amounted to a national state built "on an extremely chauvinistic principle," as was admitted at that time by the Hungarian leading politician Baron Desiderius Bánffy.[6] In practice, that meant an attempt to annihilate the Slovak nation – eventually all Slovak secondary schools and cultural organizations were closed and prohibited. On the other hand, the Czechs under Austrian rule enjoyed a growing autonomy and a pre-eminent participation in the industrialization of Central Europe. As far as Budapest was concerned, Slovakia did not exist, and Slovaks were merely Slav-speaking peasants in the rural upper (Northern) Hungary. If the first-ever appearance of Slovakia on the map of Europe within the newly established Czechoslovakia (1918) was an answer to the centuries of Hungarian domination, the dissolution of the common state (1992) was to be a final answer to the "Slovak question."[7] The latter came to signify at times perceived, but mostly legitimate, concerns about national, political, economic, social, and cultural relations between themselves and their larger, mightier, and more cultivated partner.

The interwar Republic of Czechoslovakia (popularly known as *Prvá Republika*, the "First Republic") championed liberal thought in its minority and language policies (the Constitution of 1920 made both the Slovak and Czech languages official and guaranteed cultural autonomy for all minorities), but its centralized institutions and its economy disadvantaged the less numerous Slovaks. The Slovak preoccupation with their inferior position was exacerbated by the lack of middle classes and educated elites who, if not Hungarian, German, or Jewish, were supplemented by Czechs helping to run the new Slovakia. This led to increasing calls for political and cultural autonomy advocated by the cleric Andrej Hlinka. The influence of the Slovak People's Party, hitherto led by Hlinka, grew steadily and incorporated a number of growing and mutually complementary trends within Slovak society – the influence of the Catholic Church, the conservative population, and nationalist inclinations towards a national conception of democracy. Seven decades later the state, still marred by the revival of these trends, yielded to their weight.

In 1939, when Hitler declared the "Protectorate of Bohemia and Moravia," Slovak autonomist aspirations were answered in the form of a clericalist, authoritarian Slovak state (*Slovenský štát*, 14 March 1939) led by the new leader of the Hlinka Party, father Dr. Jozef Tiso.[8] The first-ever independent Slovak state was Hitler's puppet; whether willingly or not, the regime collaborated in the deportation of Jewish citizens into the concentration camps and established its own form of National Socialism which stood for discrimination against all non-Catholics and non-Slovak citizens. Whether Slovak non-collaboration with Hitler would have changed the course of the Czech tragedy is doubtful, but the dramatic events of 1939 left a bitter taste of betrayal among Czechs and seriously damaged the image of Slovak nationalism. The humiliation and limitation of independence under Hitler's patronage became painfully obvious when Hitler's bigger and more important ally – Hungary – annexed parts of eastern Slovakia and the southern belt, events that to this day complicate the Slovak–Hungarian relationship.

Slovakia entered the war on the side of Germany, but ended it in an abortive insurrection against the German rule (*Slovenké Národné Povstanie*, August

1944). This was politically a significant event: Slovakia was no longer viewed as an enemy, but a partner in negotiations about the restoration of the common state which was sealed, in the presence of the Moscow leadership and the Czechoslovak Communist Party (KSČ), in 1945 (*Košický Vládný Program*). If the Slovak leadership harbored any hopes about Slovakia's constitutional position in the newly reconstituted Czechoslovakia, this was not the time to resolve them. The chain of events and power struggles led to a communist takeover in February 1948. The early years of the communist regime were marked by the repression of all non-communist identities and Church leaders, including purge trials, imprisonment, and executions of some leading Slovak and Czech communists labeled "bourgeois nationalists." In the notorious *Slánský trial* (1952), involving Rudolf Slánský, the General Secretary of the Party, which was planned in Moscow but carried through by President Klement Gottwald, eleven out of fourteen accused of treason, Zionism, and bourgeois origins were executed and three were condemned to life imprisonment.[9]

Despite some acknowledgment of past injustices, Czechoslovakia remained in the grip of the rigid Stalinist elite, led by Antonín Novotný, into the early 1960s. The protest against the zero growth economy and increasingly more centralized government led from about 1963 onwards to the emergence of a reform movement culminating in January 1968 in the election of the new leader of the Communist Party – Slovak Alexander Dubček – who ushered in a period known as the "Prague Spring." The new reformist Action Programme (April 1968) sought economic decentralization, the greater openness of public discussion, and crucially, a federal solution to Slovak dissatisfaction with centralized government.[10] The committees were still working on constitutional mechanisms for parallel legislative and executive organs in the two republics when, in August 1968, the Warsaw Pact armies crushed all hopes for Dubček's communism with a "human face." The only reform from the Action Programme that was implemented was the federalization of Czechoslovakia. In another absurd twist in Czechoslovakia's sad history, Dubček was in 1969 replaced by another Slovak – Gustáv Husák who, after being imprisoned as one of the "bourgeois nationalists," now presided over the "normalization" period. The newly declared federal state was a federation in name only; the Czechs were hurt by a perceived Slovak betrayal and Slovaks were disappointed by Husák's centralization policies.

The Czecho-Slovak split

In the first days after the "Gentle Revolution" (November 1989), the Czechs and Slovaks found themselves united in a struggle against totalitarianism, similar to 1968. The unity, however, did not last long and all the problems hidden by the Husák regime came out in the open with the national question leading the agenda in Slovakia. Nevertheless, in the first free elections in

1990, the only openly disintegrative political party, the Slovak National Party (SNS), shared third place with the Communist Party of Slovakia (KSS), after the Public Against Violence (VPN) and Christian Democratic Movement (KDH).

The odd alliances that were built against the common communist enemy, in the absence of it, began to disintegrate in both the Czech Republic and Slovakia. In the Czech Republic, the architect of the "Gentle Revolution," the Civic Forum, split and its dominant faction led by the "privatization" guru Václav Klaus became the Civic Democratic Party (ODS), a party in favor of capitalism with a harsh face for which there was little support in Slovakia; Czechs and Slovaks came to democracy with divergent expectations and experience. The Slovak counterpart of the Civic Forum, the VPN, split, too, for similar reasons. The winner of this split was Vladimír Mečiar and his HZDS (Movement for a Democratic Slovakia). Mečiar was not a nationalist; in fact he was a reformist communist and above all an instinctive politician with a great talent for seizing the moment – the moment was political turbulence, societal insecurity, the rising Hungarian voice in fear of the Slovak rising sense of nationalism, and the Czech economic nationalism ready to ditch Slovak interests. Mečiar took up the national question which to the majority of Slovaks seemed to be, if not the main question, then certainly a question that in some way concerned democracy. In June 1992 Mečiar won elections with 37.26% of vote. The fate of the country was in the hands of two ambitious leaders, Klaus and Mečiar, with incompatible ideas about the future, while the respective populations, convinced of the need for a solution, but lacking in political ideas and experience, resigned themselves to their own prime ministers.

The split of Czechoslovakia was legal in terms of complicated and rushed legislation passed by the government which enabled the reluctant Federal Assembly deputies to end the state to which they swore allegiance. Whether the split was legitimate we will never know because, in the absence of a referendum, it is impossible to judge whether the population actually wanted to split the country – all subsequent polls suggest that this may not have been the case.[11] It is reasonable to argue that the split of Czechoslovakia was a case of "chance and circumstance"[12] which produced the result some may have dreamed of, but nobody actively sought.

The rest of this chapter is divided into two parts. The first is concerned with the analysis of the political transformation, governance, and "Europeanization" in independent Slovakia. The second offers a socio-political analysis of society, including the controversies about the past, the role of the Church, criminality, and the media. The conclusion, while drawing together the principal issues, such as the instability of the party system, the speed of reforms combined with historical legacy, and ambiguities surrounding national issues, argues that the democratization process in Slovakia has been largely successful, but by no means completed.

Democratization, regression, restoration, and Europeanization of Slovakia

In conveying the realities and complexities of Slovak transition from communism to democracy it is suggested here that Slovakia's transition from communism to democracy went – is going? – through several "transitions" that affect one another, but nevertheless have distinct characteristics within the main post-communist transition. There are at least three clearly distinguishable phases. The ***first*** phase (1989–93), still within Czechoslovakia, ended with the dissolution of the state. The discontinuation of the first phase in both political and constitutional terms bears directly on the subsequent second stage: two historically and ideologically different processes, nation-building and state-building became in an unprecedented way compressed into one process – the democratization process.[13] The sudden and controversial attainment of independent statehood meant that political and cultural elites established on the back of the nationalist politics of the first phase continued to mobilize on national issues, but their new target became the largest and historically most sensitive Hungarian minority. Democratic state-building became secondary to the continued nation-building which characterized the first and second phases of Slovakia's transition.

The ***second*** phase (1994–8) was the most notorious period in Slovakia's transition dominated by Mečiar's administration. Its hallmarks were the ambivalent attitude to liberal democracy and relations with the West and strong nationalist leanings exemplified by hostility to all things non-Slovak. The general elections in September 1998 brought a victory of political parties committed to the restoration of democracy and the reversal of Slovakia's much-diminished chances of European integration. It must be argued that 1998 signaled a new, ***third*** phase (1998–2004) of post-communist politics in Slovakia, and that within this third transition liberal democracy was considered to be consolidated enough for the country to accede to the EU in 2004. The main characteristic of this third phase has been the almost complete synchronization of the democratization process with "Europeanization." The present political analysis concludes with the 2006 elections. The presence of nationalists and Mečiar in the post-2006 government points to the limitation of "Europeanization," but evidence below also stresses its robustness for the continuation of democratic politics (tables 9.1–9.3).

From the examination of tables 9.1–9.3, we can make a number of significant observations about the Slovak party system: (1) the continued inter-party fragmentation and amalgamation (table 9.3); (2) ethnic divisions in party structures (table 9.2); (3) the overwhelming success of charismatic leaders (Mečiar/HZDS and Fico/*Smer*); and, finally, (4) the formation of broad government coalitions across the left–right political spectrum.

There is a sense of instability in Slovak politics whereby each consecutive government tends to be an experiment to redeem the disappointment with the

Table 9.1 Representation of parties and movements in the Slovak National Council and the Federal Assembly,[a] 1990–2

Parties	1990		1992	
	(%)	Seats	(%)	Seats
VPN	29.34	**48**[b]	8.88	–
KDH	19.20	**31**	**7.93**	**17**
SNS	13.94	22	14.7	9
KSS/SDL'/SV	13.34	22	7.42	18
MKDH/Egy.	8.66	14		17
DS	4.39	**7**		–
SZ (Greens)	3.48	6		–
HZDS		–	**37.26**	**74**

Notes:

[a]For more detail on Political Parties, see table 9.3.

[b]**Bold type** denotes coalition parties

Table 9.2 General elections, 1994–2006 (parliamentary parties only)[a]

Party	1994		1998		2002		2006	
	(%)	Seats	(%)	Seats	(%)	Seats	(%)	Seats
ANO		–		–	***8.0**	**15***		–
DÚ	8.5	15		–		–		–
HZDS	***34.9**[b]	**61***	27.0	43	19.5	36	***8.79**	**15***
KDH	10	17		–	***8.2**	**15***	8.31	14
KSS		–		–	6.3	11		–
MK	10.1	17		–		–		–
SDK		–	***26.3**	**42***		–		–
SDKÚ		–			***15.9**	**28***	18.35	31
SDL'		–	***14.6**	**23***		–		
Smer		–			13.4	25	***29.14**	**50***
SMK		–	***9.1**	**15***	***11.1**	**20***	11.68	20
SNS	***5.4**	**9***	9.0	14		–	***11.73**	**20***
SOP		–	***8.0**	**13***		–		–
SV	10.4	18		–		–		–
ZRS	***7.3**	**13***		–		–		–

Notes:

[a] For more detail on Political Parties, see table 9.3.

[b] **Bold type** with asterisk denotes coalition parties.

Table 9.3 Slovakia, overview of important political parties

ANO	Alliance of a New Citizen/Aliancia Nového Občana, founded by the owner of the TV Markíza Pavel Rusko. (formed for 2002 elections)
DS	Demokratická strana/Democratic Party
DÚ	Demokratická Únia /Democratic Union (breakaway factions from HZDS and SNS)
	Együttéllés (hung.) Spolužitie /Coexistence
HZDS	Hnutie za demokratické Slovensko/Movement for Democratic Slovakia (splinter group of the VPN)
KDH	Kresťanskodemokratické hnutie/Christian Democratic Movement
KSS	Komunistická strana Slovenska/Communist Party
MK	Maďarská koalícia/Hungarian Coalition
MKDH	Maďarské kresťansko demokratické hnutie/Hungarian Christian democratic movement
SDK	Slovenska Demokratická Koalícia/Slovak Democratic Coalition (coalition of five parties: KDH; DS; SDSS (Social Democratic Party); SZS (Green Party); DÚ (Democratic Union) (1998))
SDL'	Strana demokratickej ľavice/Party of the Democratic Left
SMK	Hungarian Coalition an amalgam of three parties: MKDH, MOS – Hungarian Civic Party, and Coexistence (1998)
SNS	Slovenská národná strana/Slovak National Party
SOP	Strana Občianského Porozumenia (1998)/Party of Civic Understanding
SV	Spoločná voľba/Common Choice
SZS	Strana zelených na Slovensku/Green Party
VPN	Verejnosť proti násiliu/Public Against Violence
ZRS	Združenie robotníkov Slovenska/Association of Workers of Slovakia
SDKÚ	Slovenská Demokraticka Kresťanská Únia/Slovak Democratic Christian Union (the rump of the SDK, without the KDH) (2002))
Smer	Direction (*breakaway from the SDL*) (2002))

previous one. The stability of the party system is permanently undermined by the mobilization of voters' support, exacerbating the already fluid electoral base that tends to be attracted often by new and sometimes ephemeral parties that disappear after one electoral period (ANO, SOP, ZRS, see below). In the same vein, one ought to question the ideological profile of "movements" and "coalitions" that have become characteristic of Slovak politics: starting with Verejnosť Proti Násiliu (VPN), most obviously Mečiar's Movement for a Democratic Slovakia (HZDS), the Christian Democratic Movement (KDH) and currently, the incredibly successful *Smer* (Direction).

The second transition 1994–8

By 1994, Mečiar's confrontational political style combined with the public's loss of interest in Czecho-Slovak relations led to many defections from the HZDS and the nationalist SNS. Following the vote of no-confidence and a short interlude (March–October 1994) when the government was led by the ex-foreign minister Jozef Moravčík and consisted of the new DÚ (formed by the defectors from the HZDS and SNS) aided by SDL′ and KDH, Mečiar and his HZDS emerged victorious in October 1994. Mečiar's third victory began with a legendary all-night session of the Parliament (3–4 November 1994) where the opposition was decimated and the newly reinvigorated HZDS was joined by the newly formed workers' party ZRS and the right-wing SNS. If Slovak democracy was fragile before, after the 1994 elections it descended even lower. The HZDS attempted to defy the Constitutional Court which to its credit continued to challenge the government[14] and completely excluded opposition parties from any participation in bodies overseeing state functions, e.g. broadcasting, scrutiny of the Slovak Intelligence Service, and representation on parliamentary committees. Slovakia's international reputation was further damaged by the hostile relationship between President Kováč and Prime Minister Mečiar which culminated in the abduction of the president's son in August 1995 in Bratislava, in which the Slovak Information Service was implicated. Moreover, the government orchestrated the failure of a referendum proposed by the opposition about the direct election of the president in May 1997.[15] When Kováč's term ended in March 1998 the fragmented elites failed to reach a consensus to elect a new head of state and presidential powers were, in the absence of the president, transferred to Mečiar. His administration thrived on the preservation and exacerbation of conflicts deriving from ethnic and social divisions and this second stage of Slovak transition can be characterized by attempts to consolidate political and economic power by any, if necessary, undemocratic, means.

The third transition, 1998–2002

The "critical" general elections in September 1998 brought a victory of a wide "coalition of coalitions" of four parties, of which three were new and two encompassed a number of parties: the leftist SDL′, the new center-right SDK (Slovak Democratic Coalition of five parties), the new center-right SMK (the Party of Hungarian Coalition embracing three parties) and the newly formed pro-business and pro-integration SOP (a Party of Civic Understanding, mostly comprising technocrats and many ex-communists). In actual fact, the four-party coalition led by the Prime Minister Mikuláš Dzurinda (SDK) encompassed ten political parties, and one of its problems proved to be the maintenance of its unity because of the plurality of the political streams and personal and party interests it embraced. The fragility was further compounded by the dire economic situation it inherited after years of decreased foreign investment, opaqueness of privatization, and the misuse of political power in preventing a proper economic competition. Dzurinda's government's immediate steps to help the ailing economy were particularly aimed at assuring greater transparency in privatization processes.[16]

The combination of the fear of constitutional crisis, the dismay at the political and financial corruption, the embarrassment of disqualification from European integration, together with a successful mobilization of voters by the opposition (turnout 84.2%) meant that Mečiar faced opponents who, if not united among themselves, were united in new hostility toward him. His HZDS won the highest number of votes (the situation to be repeated in the 2002 elections), but was unable to form a government.[17]

The unity of the leading party SDK, as expected, was short-lived and the inter-party and inter-coalition fractiousness and further proliferation of parties continued. Among new "alternatives" the most significant was the splinter party of the SDL′, *Smer* (*Direction*). This vehicle for the very ambitious Robert Fico whose main platform, anti-corruption and order, spiced up with a careful but persistent exploitation of the "national" issue, became the new ideologically ambiguous movement to dominate Slovak politics. This was, however, not to be in the 2002 elections, in which the main issue became European integration. Robert Fico won in 2006 when the EU's political conditionality ceased to exercise influence on Slovakia's democratization.

Democratic consolidation or Europeanization?

After the 2002 elections one could have argued that Slovakia's democracy seemed to have been stabilized and rescued from extreme elements that sought an alternative to liberal democracy which some commentators termed "post-communist authoritarianism."[18]

The lesson of European history is that democracy depends on more than democratic forces within the state: crucially it depends on an international system for its reinforcement. European democracy, whether swept away before 1945, rescued from the outside, reinforced in the west as part of the Cold War competition, or submerged in the east as part of the same competition, and then universalized to most of the continent after 1989, has always been a story of international relations, as well as of politics within the state. In that sense, communism, post-communism, and Europeanization have a common denominator: "the role of external power in setting and enforcing political agendas for the states of the region and thus influencing domestic political outcomes."[19]

Europeanization has become a very "fashionable" concept which at times suffers from "conceptual stretching,"[20] but among its many meanings it is best understood as "a process of transformation of domestic structures of a state by European frameworks, norms and rules."[21] Domestic structures entail the formal institutions of the state and its national legal system and administration, but also the perception and public discourses about national and ethnic identity and the meaning of citizenship, the role of the state, and political traditions. In post-communist states, the adaptation to economic, social, and political changes had to be in accordance with the Copenhagen criteria (1993)[22] by which the conditions for entry into the EU were made explicit.

Democratic conditionality is the "core strategy" of the EU to "induce candidate states to comply with its human rights and democracy standards."[23] This strategy operates on two levels: explicit and implicit. The explicit strategy is reinforced by reward in the form of full membership in the EU, and its success depends on candidate states' calculations of domestic political costs and compliance. The conditionality strategy assumes that the Community's common ethos and the "density of interaction" will in the longer-term create a self-sustaining environment of international democratic norms.[24] Notwithstanding the many limitations associated with the internationalization of domestic politics, I have argued elsewhere[25] that, on balance, the EU's democratic conditionality linked to membership intensifies the democratization process from beyond the state more effectively and concretely than other strategies of other international organizations.

It must be argued that the EU's scrutiny of the 2002 elections contributed to pro-democracy government and, hence, to the continuation of the third, restorative transition stage in the face of domestic opposition. The Dzurinda government's election campaign made the issue of the accession into Euro-Atlantic structures (both the EU and NATO were making their decisions in the autumn of 2002) central to its re-election by stressing that "the integration of Slovakia" was not merely a question of foreign policy, but a "paramount domestic issue."[26] It seems that the EU's appeal to Slovak citizens that, if they wanted Slovakia "to become a member of the EU," they "should do something about it"[27] brought dividends. The 2002 coalition that emerged from a surprisingly short two-week period of negotiations dominated by SDKÚ included also the SMK, the KDH, and the new ANO and was seen to characterize both the continuation and consensus in Slovak politics[28] despite the fact that the only one of the four parties that made up the 1998–2002 government (the SMK) returned in 2002; the other two "continuing" parties were splinter parties of the SDK. Mečiar's HZDS repeated its victory in the percentage of votes gained, but failed again to form the government. The fact that maintaining the course of democracy was an issue at all in the 2002 elections – the fifth since the fall of communism – indicated the fragility of Slovakia's transition.[29]

A new "Direction"?

"Critical" may be a description of the latest June 2006 elections, too. As indicated already, the new post-accession Slovak governing coalition is led by *Smer*'s Robert Fico who, following what can only be described as bungled post-election coalition-building negotiations by the opposition, chose the HZDS and SNS as his coalition partners. If there ever was an argument about the limits of political conditionality for the purpose of accession, the return to power of two parties from the 1994–8 establishment, Mečiar's HZDS and the nationalists, must be it. This reward-based strategy by the EU to stabilize political changes and promote liberal-democratic norms was initially, in the pre-accession period, very effective in Slovakia,[30] but lost its influence and domestic rationality very soon after accession.

The June 2006 election, similarly to all previous ones, was also accompanied by a degree of nationalist rhetoric and the usual inter-party haggling, but the inclusion of the SNS appears to be questioned not only by minorities, but also by ordinary citizens.[31] The combination of (1) a relatively low turnout (54%, 71% in 2002), (2) release of the EU's political conditionality, and (3) overall dissatisfaction with the government's neoliberal policies, amplified by the lack of transparency and economic abuse of power brought victory to the *Smer* party which then proceeded to form a government of least resistance. How should this new government in Slovakia be evaluated, and where does this leave Slovak transition? Is "Europeanization" a force robust enough to sustain the continuation of democratic politics in the presence of an extreme nationalist party and the previously unacceptable Mečiar's HZDS? Are we looking at a fourth phase of the transition?

Some of these questions were partially clarified in my interviews with Slovak politicians and practitioners in June 2007.[32] There is no doubt that a degree of "regression" must be acknowledged. The concentration of power in the hands of *Smer* in the new government is overwhelming; out of sixteen Cabinet posts, eleven are from *Smer* and the remaining five are shared between HZDS and SNS (provocatively, the Ministry of Education has been given to the nationalist SNS) (interviews with Kukan and Nagy, see p. 200). It is often argued by the current opposition that *Smer* serves as a front for three main streams that remain prevalent in Slovak politics: big entrepreneurs who since 1998 realized that they need a new champion to replace Mečiar, nationalists, and old and new communists (Csáky and Mesežnikov).

On the other hand, the post-2006 government has inherited a very good economy (8–9% growth) and presides over one of the most Europhile populations (80% of the population supports the membership of the EU) among the new EU members (Csáky, Kukan). In terms of foreign policy, the adoption of the Euro went ahead in January 2009 and Slovakia supports the accession of Turkey and has ratified the Constitutional Treaty (Zala).[33] Most importantly, the new government maintains a status quo with the Hungarian minority and, given the presence of nationalists in the government, the expected "catastrophic scenarios" have not materialized (Nagy).

The more detailed analysis of the Fico government's economic policies (i.e. changes in the Labor Law in favor of less harsh redundancy notice for short-term contracts and part-time employment, reversal of some privatization projects, reduction in doctors' and hospital fees) suggests that the Fico government is seeking to combine the maintenance of the pragmatic policies of the previous administration while creating a more "caring" image of itself which seems to satisfy the majority of the population. It would appear that little has changed and that, while Slovakia's tenuous democracy is not being strengthened, its continuation is not in jeopardy – which indicates that a degree of consolidation has been achieved.

Post-communist Slovakia: socio-political analysis

The early years of Slovakia's transformation were marred by anti-liberal tendencies, a strong national orientation, toleration of lawlessness by state authorities, high expectations from the state combined with egalitarianism and a general misunderstanding about how these tendencies affected long-term prospects. It is beyond the remit of this chapter to elaborate on vague concepts such as political culture,[34] but there is some relevance in reiterating three important factors connected to the lack of democratic tradition and independent statehood if one seeks to grasp the political tradition in post-communist Slovakia.

First, insecure nationhood feeds off insecure democracy and vice versa. There is a deep-rooted tradition in Slovakia which understands politics only as a struggle for national realization and confuses political solidarity with ethnic solidarity. This naturally leads to the misinterpretation of statehood as "ownership" of the state by the majority population and creates an ongoing tension in the majority–minority relationship (14–18% of the population declares itself non-Slovak). This is one of the reasons why the Hungarian Coalition, while in the government between 1998 and 2006, achieved only minor compromises on some issues but no major victories and no constitutional guarantees for the protection of minorities.[35]

The second point relates to this belated nation-building. One of the most important, and I would argue most damaging, characteristics of communism was its control of information and attempts to curb any independent intellectual thought; inevitably, history, too, became the subject of the regime's official ideology – a kind of "organized forgetting."[36] Nation-building is also an ideology, but an ideology that relies on historical memory in which there is some continuity, even if always somewhat distorted. In the present case, the void of the non-existence first filled by the too short and too confusing interwar period, then wiped out by the wartime fascist state and then totally manipulated by communism, left Slovaks without any moral or historical compass by which to navigate yet another complete overhaul of their identity and normative framework. The society was looking to build a democratic state, but the necessary ingredients – such as historical self-criticism and knowledge, tolerance, civic engagement and political responsibility – were all lacking.

The third point relates to the modernization of Slovakia. It adds to the idiosyncrasy of this transition that the very late, post-Second World War industrialization of Slovakia reached its peak in the 1980s – thus, the standard of living was rising markedly throughout the communist period and the majority of the population did not feel that the communist economy needed radical changes. Moreover, industrialization under communism was rapid and, while accompanied by rapid urbanization, the huge housing estates were built in rural and very traditional settings and traditional ties, networks, and ways of life persisted for a long time. This type of modernization rather amounted to the "ruralization" of the cities than the urbanization of the countryside.[37] Hence, the pre-industrial traditionalism augmented by the communist destruction of the country, cities, and history and the persistence of undemocratic regimes begins to explain something about the society's lack of trust in institutions and in the rule of law and the appeal of nationalism and charismatic leaders. It is reasonable to argue that this unfortunate historical legacy will exhaust its appeal with time.

The role of the Church since 1992

The oldest polarization of society was along religious lines, between Catholics (69% of the population) and Protestants. The most important anchors in the Slovak national development were priests – from the nineteenth century onwards, through the interwar period, and the wartime Slovak state. Later, this particular stream of national consciousness combined with many émigrés from abroad formed a strong opposition to the communist regime. Some Catholic dissidents suffered greatly in the struggle for religious freedom under the communist regime and many of those are currently leading members of the KDH – most famously, Ján Čarnogurský, the founder of the KDH and one-time prime minister (April 1991–June 1992). Ján Čarnogurský's family had a direct connection to the wartime Slovak state (his father was a member of the parliament during that time) and unusually they were not imprisoned. The communist regime found it easy to persecute Church leaders, for example the Bishop of Nitra Ján Korec who, as many KDH leaders, was a supporter of the anti-communist nationalist ideology. Korec was elevated to the College of Cardinals in 1991.

Despite the significant rise of religious identity post-1989, it cannot be argued that in the present situation Catholicism has a strong influence on the politics of Slovakia; the KDH remains an important party, mostly due to its coalition-building efforts, but has never won a significant electoral victory (even in the first democratic elections in 1990 it came second to the purely civic VPN). The major controversy over the Catholic Church remains its wartime history because, despite many publications claiming that many priests had tried to save Jews,[38] the facts are that the Slovak state was led by a cleric Dr. Jozef Tiso and that out of 90,000 Jews living on the territory of the Slovak state (plus some 40,000 in the territories annexed by Hungary, 130,000 in total) only 12,000 returned from the camps. The Church has sought Tiso's rehabilitation and blamed his execution in 1945 for crimes against humanity on communist propaganda. The KDH leadership, while denouncing the deportation of Jews, found it always difficult to deny the Church's role in allowing for these deportations. On the other hand, even if there is a connection between certain strains of Slovak nationalism and the early post-communist period, it is erroneous to seek any deeper linkages in contemporary politics to that regrettable period.[39]

The Church in Slovakia is among the most trusted institutions, but there is no clear legislative arrangement to regulate the state–Church relationship. It seems that the Church's main concern now is moral decay, issues of ethics, culture, abortion, and other usual concerns of clergy everywhere in Europe. While bishops openly supported the post-Mečiar government in the 1998 elections, they remain reserved on the issue of European integration. Currently, the post-2006 government shows little interest in the Church and its role in politics has declined.

Corruption and criminality

The cases of proved and suspected corruption at the government level, particularly during the Mečiar administration, are convincing and well documented. The second wave of voucher privatization was terminated in favor of "direct sales" of state property (1995), regulated by a body beyond government control (Fond Národného Majetku/National Property Fund), but with direct links to the government. The sales, if not to unknown companies, could be traced in some instances to members of the government. The most revealing in this respect is the interview with the former Minister for Work, Social Affairs, and Family in the 1994–8 government, Olga Keltošová in *SME*.[40] In this interview she admits to having been offered the spoils of privatization and explains in some fairly apologetic terms the corrupted atmosphere in the government. Some further examples of clientelist politics of that period are: the largest steel works *VSŽ* were sold to the Minister of Telecommunications Andrej Rezeš, in the government until 1997; the government revoked the licence of the largest investment corporation *Sporofond*, involving some 40,000 investors, in the second wave of privatization in defiance of a Supreme Court ruling; 49% of shares in *Nafta Gbely* were sold to an unknown company despite higher offers from other investors, at an estimated loss of 100 million USD to the Slovak treasury. Noteworthy was the influence of ex-managers of ex-state-owned enterprises (SOEs), organized in the Association of Employers, Union and Alliances (AZZZ), whose members helped to formulate the government's privatization philosophy and often became the new owners of the newly privatized enterprises. The list of clientelist structures and connections to organized economic crime is beyond the present brief and does not add to the fact that the close connection between politics and business interests[41] plagues Slovak politics to this day. Many analysts argue that despite the current government's declaration of a "social state," there is no other social democratic party in Europe with such close personal links to the business community as the supposedly social-democratic *Smer* (Mesežnikov).[42]

Overall, the dynamics and structures of crime in contemporary Slovakia are comparable to other countries in the EU and even show slight signs of improvement.[43] The overall crime committed on Slovak territory in 2006 did not differ significantly from previous years and while violent crimes dropped, the "other crime" – i.e. property crime, the ever-more sophisticated economic crime, people smuggling and drug-related crimes, have increased.

Media

The development of the mass media during the transformation can also be divided into three, partially overlapping, phases[44] which correlate roughly to the phases of transition as described already. In the first phase (1989–92), the mass media, freed from the political monopoly of the state, enjoyed wide activity and a fairly strong influence on politics and society. The early 1990s was used by politicians to "enlighten" the public about new "truths"; they debated, analysed, persuaded, and explained, even if the general comprehension of the new political vocabulary (i.e. federalism, national sovereignty, free markets, etc.) was often imprecise and the understanding of what constitutes a political argument was at times depressingly low and reminiscent of the communist "black and white" style of moralizing. One of Mečiar's greatest assets was that he was media-savvy in the "old" style, which gave the public a false impression of democracy but within the recognizable style of language and attitude. In the second phase (1992–4), many new periodicals became victims of poor distribution and ultimately declining revenues. Overall, the radicalization of politics in this period led to the increase of state control of the media, but on the whole their role in shaping public opinion was not significant. The increased professionalism of journalists in the third phase (1994–8) was, however, matched by the increased political pressure from the government and new owners and led to a form of self-censorship, particularly in television. This in turn impinged on the media's public authority, which remains low to this day.

The media–society relationship in Slovakia suffers from the population's tendency to trust personalities rather than informed critical analysis of political developments – a situation that can be attributed to the long history of communist propaganda, less developed critical abilities, and low levels of political education, augmented by the recent history of "strong" personalities in Slovak politics. The media are not very popular with the present government. Prime Minister Fico pushed through a controversial media bill (April 2008) in order to "increase the responsibility of press editors and owners of other media" which extends the existing "right of response" clause to the "right of correction and response" by anybody, based on any minor factual error that is not necessarily related to personality rights; in addition, unusually, the length and placement of correction can be equivalent to the original text[45] and non-compliance can cost the newspaper up to $10,000 in fines. The editors responded to the bill and the possible limitation of their independence by publishing newspapers with blank front pages on two occasions during the debate, but failed to prevent the adoption of the bill.

Today as everywhere else, politics in Slovakia is a matter of image and politicians' "spontaneity" is a well-rehearsed reproduction of their most rewarding image in terms of voters' popularity. It is said that Prime Minister Fico's *Smer* party is not an ideological party, but a "party of opinion polls"[46] and that, in a manner similar to Mečiar, he engages in populist rhetoric as the defender of ordinary people.[47] If this is the case, as it indeed appears to be because the policies of this government are far less populist than its rhetoric, then we are probably observing the "normalization" of the role of the media in Slovak politics.

Consolidated democracy? A conclusion

"Democracy requires a distinctive set of political values and orientations from its citizens: moderation, tolerance, civility, efficacy, knowledge, participation."[48] Concluding this study of Slovakia, I would argue in sum that democracy in Slovakia has been slow in coming and remains slow in consolidating because consensus on its substance has not yet fully developed. On the other hand, the reversal of democracy to some form of a hybrid between democracy and authoritarianism represents an unlikely scenario. More likely, Slovakia will settle into a perennially somewhat turbulent European democracy, economically more developed than politically. While all electoral competition thus far appeared "critical" to either the existence of the state (1990 and 1992 within Czechoslovakia), democracy (1994, 1998, and 2006), or European integration (2002), this trend is likely to subside. On the other hand, the readiness with which ethnicity re-emerges as a political tool every time political elites vie for voters' attention should tell us something about the entrenchment of an ethnic division in conceptualizing the relationship between "the nation" and the state. Slovak experience with pluralist politics is historically limited; all processes that mature democracy requires – i.e. political and reasonable economic development, secure nationhood and statehood and the resolution of the majority–minority relationship – were in Slovakia synchronized into one rapid and tightly compressed process accelerated further by European integration. Viewed from this perspective, Slovakia's transition from communism to democracy has been relatively successful and still ongoing.

Timeline 1989–2006

17 November 1989	Beginning of the "Velvet Revolution" (in Slovakia often referred to as "Gentle Revolution"), leading to collapse of communist regime

December 1989	Václav Havel becomes President of Czechoslovakia
June 1990	Vladimír Mečiar becomes Prime Minister of Slovakia within newly renamed Czech and Slovak Federal Republic
March 1991	Mečiar forms Movement for a Democratic Slovakia
April 1991	Mečiar replaced by Ján Čarnogurský
June 1992	Federal Assembly elections take place, but no federal government formed; instead, Mečiar and Klaus become Prime Ministers in Slovakia and the Czech Republic, respectively.
September 1992	Slovak National Council declares Slovak sovereignty and adopts constitution of the Slovak Republic
November 1992	Federation dissolved
January 1993	Slovakia becomes independent state
March 1994	Second Mečiar government falls
December 1994	Mečiar government returns for third time
1995–6	Slovakia applies to join EU, but is plagued by diplomatic démarches, connected to treatment of opposition.
August 1996	Alleged government involvement in abduction of President Kováč's son
	Before the Slovak–Hungarian Treaty can be ratified, the Language Law is introduced and relationship with the Hungarian minority deteriorates
May 1997	Referendum on the direct election of the president demanded by the public disrupted by the government
December 1997	EU rejects Slovakia from the first wave of post-communist enlargement
September 1998	Parliamentary elections: Mečiar's third government defeated and Mikuláš Dzurinda becomes prime minister; new government includes Party of Hungarian Coalition (SMK)
	President Kováč finishes term. In the absence of agreement on his successor parliament amends the election law
May 1999	Rudolf Schuster becomes head of state in direct election
February 2000	Accession negotiations with EU begin
December 2000	Slovakia joins OECD
	Parliament agrees on eight regional government competencies
December 2001	First regional elections held
September 2002	Second Dzurinda government voted in
	Ivan Gašparovič replaces Schuster as president after defeating Mečiar in the second round
May 2004	Slovakia joins EU
June 2006	Parliamentary elections: Dzurinda government defeated; Robert Fico and his winning party *Smer* form a governmental coalition with HZDS and the Slovak National Party (SNS)

Source: Erika Harris, *Nationalism and Democratisation: Politics of Slovakia and Slovenia* (Aldershot: Ashgate, 2002); Erika Harris, "Europeanization of Slovakia," *Comparative European Politics*, Vol. 2, No. 2 (August, 2004), pp. 85–211; Karen Henderson, *Slovakia: The Escape from Invisibility* (London and New York: Routledge,

2002), pp. vii–xiii; Shari J. Cohen, *Politics without a Past* (Durham, NC: Duke University Press, 1999), pp. ix–xiii.

Fact sheet

Area	49,035 km^2
Population (July 2009 estimate)	5,463,046
Hungarian (2001 census)	9.67%
Moravian	3.7%
Combined Czech, German, Polish, Jewish, Ukrainian, Ruthenian, and Roma	5%[a]
Major cities	
Bratislava	452,288
Košice	241,606
Prešov	93,147
Nitra	87,569
Žilina	86, 811
Below the poverty line (2005)	20% of population
Unemployment rate (April 2009)	10.92%
Total GDP (2008 estimate)	$100.6 billion
GDP *per capita* (2008 estimate)	$29,900
Real GDP growth (2008 estimate)	6.4%
Inflation (2008)	4.6%
Higher education (2006)	12% of population
Literacy rate	99.6% of population
Percent urbanized	56%

Note:
[a] Some unofficial estimates put the number of Roma at 8%.
Sources: Martin Bútora, Grigorij Mesežnikov, and Miroslav Kollár (eds.), *Slovakia 2006* (Bratislava: Institute for Public Affairs, 2007), pp. 17–18. *Financial Times*, Special Report Slovakia (London, 20 February 2007), p. 1, at www.slovakia.org/society.htm; http://en.wikipedia.org/wiki/List_of_countries_by_literacy_rate#endnote_1; http://migration.ucdavis.edu/MN/more.php?id=3164_0_4_0; www.statistics.sk/pls/elisw/vbd [all accessed on 26 July 2007]; *The Slovak Spectator* (20 May 2009), at www.spectator.sk/ [accessed on 11 July 2009].

Parties in the Slovak Parliament

The current government was formed in July 2006 by three political parties: SMER–Social Democracy (*Smer*–SD), the Slovak National Party (SNS), and the People's Party-Movement for a Democratic Slovakia (L'S–HZDS).

The National Council – *Národná rada Slovenskej republiky* (NRSR) – has 150 deputies, elected by proportional representation subject to 5% threshold.

President: Ivan Gašparovič (since June 2004)

Prime Minister: Robert Fico (since July 2006)

Composition of the parliament (as of 31 December 2006)			
SMER–SD	50	SNS	19
SDKÚ–DS	31	L'S–HZDS	16
SMK	20	KDH	14

Short biography of Vladimír Mečiar

Vladimír Mečiar (1942–), the most dominant personality in Slovakia's post-1989 politics, was born on 26 July 1942 in Zvolen, and trained as a lawyer. As a reformist, he was expelled from the Communist Party in 1970 and joined the pro-democracy movement Verejnosť Proti Násiliu (VPN, the Public Against Violence) in 1989. In January 1990 he became the minister of the interior and in June 1990, after the first free parliamentary elections, prime minister of Slovakia. In March 1991 he formed the Movement for a Democratic Slovakia (HZDS) and in April 1991 was deposed and replaced by Jan Čarnogurský. In June 1992, following his party's victory in the second parliamentary elections Mečiar again became prime minister. His election, combined with the election of his Czech counterpart, Václav Klaus, resulted in the dissolution of the Czechoslovak federation. In March 1994 Mečiar was unseated and replaced by Jozef Moravčík, only to return as prime minister in October 1994 for two further electoral terms. Between 1998 and 2006 his party remained in opposition. After the 2006 elections his HZDS joined the governmental coalition. In 2004, he lost the presidential race in the final round.

Interviews: Bratislava, June 2007

Dušan Čaplovič	Deputy Prime Minister of the Slovak Republic for the Knowledge Based Society, European Affairs, Human Rights and Minorities
Pál Csaky	Leader of the Party of Hungarian Coalition (SMK)
Alexander Duleba	Director of the Slovak Foreign Policy Association
Eduard Kukan	Member of the Parliamentary Foreign Relations Committee
Grigorij Mesežnikov	Director of the Institute for Public Affairs
László Nagy	Chairman of the Parliamentary Committee on Human Rights, National Minorities and the Position of Women
Boris Zala	Chairman of the Parliamentary Foreign Affairs Committee

Notes

1. Geoffrey Pridham, "The Slovak Parliamentary Election of September 2002: Its Systemic Importance," *Government and Opposition*, Vol. 38, No. 3 (July 2003), pp. 333–56.
2. Slovakia joined the Eurozone on 1 January 2009 (the only other country from the 2004 enlargement is Slovenia). FDI into Slovakia for 2008 was expected to be about

$2.7 billion (Jan Cienski, "A Confident Place at Europe's Top Table," *Financial Times* (London, 23 July 2008), at www.ft.com/slovakia.

3. Erika Harris, *Nationalism and Democratisation: Politics of Slovakia and Slovenia* (Aldershot: Ashgate, 2007), p. 218.
4. For the history of Czechoslovakia and its breakup, see Harris, *Nationalism and Democratisation*, chapter 3. For a detailed account of the actual breakup, see Eric Stein, *Czecho/Slovakia: Ethnic Conflict, Constitutional Fissure, Negotiated Breakup*, (Ann Arbor, Mich.: University of Michigan Press, 1997).
5. Tony Judt, *Postwar: A History of Europe since 1945* (London: Pimlico, 2007), pp. 659–64. See also Carol Skalnik Leff, *The Czech and Slovak Republics: Nation Versus State* (Boulder, Colo.: Westview Press, 1997).
6. Cited in Ľubomír Lipták, *Slovensko v 20.storočí* (Bratislava: Kalligram, 1998), p. 44.
7. Rudolf Chmel (ed.), *Slovenská otázka v 20.storočí* (Bratislava: Kalligram, 1997).
8. Ivan Kamenec, *Tragédia politika, kňaza a človeka* (Bratislava: Archa, 1998).
9. Judt, *Postwar: A History of Europe since 1945*, pp. 185–6.
10. Harris, *Nationalism and Democratisation*, p. 84 and Leff, *The Czech and Slovak Republics*, p. 57.
11. As late as April 1992, 77% of respondents in Slovakia agreed with the statement that despite all disagreements the ties between the two nations should not be broken, while roughly half of the population claimed to want to maintain the common state (Czech Republic 53%, Slovak Republic 42%). Z. Bútorová, "Premyslené 'Áno' zániku ČSFR," *Sociologický Časopis* XXIX, No. 1 (March 1993), pp. 88–103, at p. 91.
12. Judt, *Postwar: A History of Europe since 1945*, p. 664.
13. Harris, *Nationalism and Democratisation*, chapter 2.
14. C. Mudde and P. Kopecký, "Explaining Different Paths of Democratization: The Czech and Slovak Republics," *Journal of Communist Studies and Transition Politics*, Vol. 16, No. 3 (Summer 2000), pp. 63–84, at p. 67.
15. See Grigirij Mesežnikov and Martin Bútora (eds.), *Slovenské Referendum '97* (Bratislava: IVO, 1997). See also Harris, *Nationalism and Democratisation*, pp. 103–4.
16. Olga Reptová and Martin Strieborný, "Privatizácia," in Miroslav Kollár and Grigorij Mesežnikov (eds.), *Slovensko* (Bratislava: IVO, 2001), pp. 493–511, at pp. 494–5.
17. Martin Bútora, Grigorij Mesežnikov, and Zora Bútorová (eds.), *Kto? Prečo? Ako? Slovenské voľby '98* (Bratislava: IVO, 1999).
18. Kevin Deegan Krausse, "Slovakia's Second Transition," *Journal of Democracy*, Vol. 14, No. 2 (April 2003), pp. 65–79, at p. 65.
19. Andrew C. Janos, "From Eastern Empire to Western Hegemony: East-Central Europe under Two International Regimes," *East European Politics and Societies*, Vol. 15, No. 2 (March 2001), pp. 221–49, at p. 223.
20. Johan Olsen, "The Many Faces of Europeanisation," Arena Online Working Papers, WP02/January 2002, at www.arena.uio.no/publications/working-papers2002/papers/02_02.xml [accessed on 2 October 2008], and Claudio Radaelli, "Whither Europeanisation? Concept Stretching and Substantive Change," *European Online Papers*, Vol. 4, No. 8 (July 2000), at http://eiop.or.at/eiop/texte/2000-008a.htm [accessed on 2 October 2008].
21. Erika Harris "Europeanization of Slovakia," *Comparative European Politics*, Vol. 2, No. 2 (August 2004), pp. 85–211, at p. 186.

22. For details see Christopher Lord and Erika Harris, *Democracy in the New Europe* (Houndmills: Palgrave Macmillan, 2006), pp. 92–3.
23. Frank Schimmelfennig, Stefan Engert, and Heiko Knobel, "Costs, Commitment and Compliance: The Impact of EU Conditionality on Latvia, Slovakia and Turkey," *Journal of Common Market Studies*, Vol. 41, No. 3 (June 2003), pp. 495–518, at p. 495. See also Frank Schimmelfennig *The EU, NATO and the Integration of Europe: Rules and Rhetoric* (Cambridge: Cambridge University Press, 2003).
24. Lord and Harris, *Democracy in the New Europe*, p. 91.
25. Lord and Harris, *Democracy in the New Europe*, p. 92.
26. *SME*, 8 July 2002, p. 1.
27. Pat Cox, the Speaker of the European Parliament in his address to the Slovak parliament, in Mesežnikov and Butora, *Slovenské Referendum '97*, p. 197.
28. Harris "Europeanization of Slovakia," p. 195.
29. Lord and Harris, *Democracy in the New Europe*, p. 105; Tim Haughton "We'll Finish What We Have Started: The 2002 Slovak Parliamentary Elections," *Journal of Communist Studies and Transition Politics*, Vol. 19, No. 4 (Winter 2003), pp. 65–90; Harris, "Europeanization of Slovakia," p. 195.
30. For EU conditionality as both a concept and as practice, see Schimmelfennig, and Frank Schimmelfennig, "European Regional Organizations, Political Conditionality, and Democratic Transformation in Eastern Europe," *East European Politics and Societies*, Vol. 21, No. 1 (February 2007), pp. 126–41, and Lord and Harris, *Democracy in the New Europe*, chapter 5.
31. Zora Bútorová, "Nová vláda nemá podporu väčšiny verejnosti," Bratislava, IVO, 2006, at http://ivo.sk/buxus/docs/vyskum/subor/produkt_2351.pdf [accessed 11 March 2007].
32. For the list of interviewees, see p. 200.
33. Tim Haughton and Darina Malová, "Emerging Patterns of EU Membesrhip: Drawing Lessons from Slovakia's First Two Years as a Member State," *Politics*, Vol. 27, No. 2 (June 2007), pp. 69–76.
34. But see Sabrina P. Ramet and Danica Fink-Hafner (eds.), *Democratic Transition in Slovenia: Value Transformation, Education, and Media* (College Station, Tex.: Texas A&M University Press, 2006). See also Vladimír Krivý, Viera Feglová, and Daniel Balko, *Slovensko a jeho regióny* (Bratislava: Média, 1996).
35. Erika Harris, "Moving Politics Beyond the State? The Hungarian Minority in Slovakia," *Perspectives: The Central European Review of International Affairs*, 28/2007 (Summer), pp. 43–62.
36. Shari J. Cohen, *Politics without a Past* (Durham, NC: Duke University Press, 1999), p. 38.
37. In 1960, only 30% of the population lived in the cities; now, it is just above 55%, while 43% lives in localities of fewer than 5,000 inhabitants: Harris, *Nationalism and Democratisation*, n. 36, p. 127. See also the Fact sheet on p. 199.
38. *Zamlčaná Pravda o Slovensku*, published in 1996 by Friends of President Tiso in Slovakia and abroad (Partizánske: Garmond), consists of contributions of a number of revisionist historians defending the Church and its role in deportations of Jews.
39. For example, Nadya Nedelsky "The Wartime Slovak State: A Case Study in the Relationship between Ethnic Nationalism and Authoritarian Patterns of Governance," *Nations and Nationalism*, Vol. 7, No. 2 (April 2001), pp. 215–34.

40. www.sme.sk/c/3379003/Olga-Keltosova-HZDS-mi-ponukalo-privatizovat.html [accessed on 30 October 2007].
41. Ivan Mikloš, in Martin Bútora and Peter Hunčík (eds.), *Slovensko 1995* and Martin Bútora, *Slovensko 1996* (Bratislava: IVO, 1996 and 1997, respectively).
42. Interview with the author; and Grigorij Mesežnikov in an interview with Tom Nicholson, "Who is Really Benefiting from Fico's Politics?," at www.ivo.sk/buxus/docs/publicistika/subor/Mes [accessed on 11 March 2007].
43. Květoň Holcr and Jaroslav Holomek, "Criminality," in Martin Bútora, Grigorij Mesežnikov, and Miroslav Kollár (eds.), *Slovensko 2006* (Bratislava: IVO 2007).
44. Andrej Školkay, "Transformácia Masmédii," in Soňa Szomolányi (ed.), *Slovensko: Problémy konsolidácie demokracie* (Bratislava: Slovenké združenie pre politické vedy, 1997), p. 171.
45. *Prague Post*, at www.praguepost.com/articles/2008/04/23/support-for-slovak-media-righst.php [accessed on 1 October 2008].
46. Interview with the author, July 2007.
47. "Mocenská zmena na Slovensku: dôsledky and súvislosti," *Parlamentný kuriér*, February 2007, at www.ivo.sk/buxus/docs/publicistika/subor/PK_februar2007.pdf [accessed on 11 March 2007].
48. Larry Diamond (ed.), *Political Culture and Democracy in Developing Countries* (Boulder, Colo. and London: Lynne Rienner, 1993), p. 1.

Further reading

Baker, Edwin. *Minority Conflict in Slovakia and Hungary?* (The Hague: University of Groningen, 1997)

East European Politics and Societies, Vol. 21, No.1 (February 2007), an issue devoted to post-communist transitions

Haughton, Tim. *Constraints and Opportunities: Leadership in Post-Communist Europe* (Aldershot: Ashgate, 2005)

Kirschbaum, Stanislav. *A History of Slovakia*, 2nd edn. (Houndmills: Palgrave Macmillan, 2006)

Leff, Carol Skalnik. *The Czech and Slovak Republics: Nation Versus State* (Boulder, Colo.: Westview Press, 1997)

Mannová Elena (ed.). *A Concise History of Slovakia* (Bratislava: Historický ústav, 2000)

Marcinčin, Anton and Miroslav Beblavý. *Economic Policy in Slovakia 1990–1999* (Bratislava: Center for Social and Media Analysis, Slovak Foreign Policy Association, Institute for Economic and Social Reforms, 2000)

Salner, Peter. *Prežili Holocaust* (Bratislava: Veda, 1997)

Schöpflin, George. "Nationalism and Ethnic Minorities in Post-Communist Europe," in R. Caplan and J. Feffer, *Europe's New Nationalism* (New York and Oxford: Oxford University Press, 1996)

Skilling, Harold Gordon. *Czechoslovakia's Interrupted Revolution* (Princeton, N.J.: Princeton University Press, 1976)

Williams, Kieran. *The Prague Spring and its Aftermath: Czechoslovak Politics 1968–1970* (Cambridge: Cambridge University Press, 1997)

10

Hungary since 1989

ANDRÁS BOZÓKI AND ESZTER SIMON

Located in East-Central Europe, Hungary has often found itself at a crossroads of political influences of greater powers as well as of different cultures. Although Hungary enjoyed independence for centuries in its early history, the experience of foreign domination over the last five centuries is one of the defining features of Hungarian public consciousness. Most notably, Hungary was under the control of the Ottoman Empire in the sixteenth and seventeenth centuries the Habsburgs in the eighteenth, nineteenth and the beginning of the twentieth centuries and the Soviet Union from 1945 until the regime change in 1989. Therefore, Hungarians had to master the techniques of survival under foreign domination.[1] They learned how to operate informally, under and within formal, rigid rules, which represented the interests of the dominant foreign power.

Nonetheless, during its twentieth-century history, Hungary made some genuine albeit short-lived attempts to achieve democracy. First, there was the brief liberal-democratic government of Count Mihály Károlyi in late 1918. A second attempt was made during the semi-democratic coalition government between 1945 and 1947. Finally, Hungary operated as a democracy for twelve remarkable days during the anti-totalitarian revolution of October 1956. The Hungarian revolution was internally successful but was crushed by the intervention of the Soviet Red Army. These shining moments of recent Hungarian history cannot hide the fact that throughout the twentieth century Hungary enjoyed democracy for one decade only, the 1990s.

Pre-history

Nomadic Hungarian tribes settled in the Carpathian basin in 895. When founding the Christian state in 1,000, King (Saint) Stephen (997–1038) did not only ensure the survival of his people in a Christian environment but also expressed a desire to belong to Western Europe as he chose Western Christianity over the authority of the Byzantine Empire and the Orthodox Church. With an iron hand, he transformed Hungary into a strong Christian feudal state.[2]

Hungary encountered the first major shock of foreign occupation when the Mongols (Tartars) invaded much of Europe in 1241–2. The Mongol forces left a ruined country behind them and a succession of weak kings followed. King Andrew II had to make concessions to the nobility in 1222 when he issued the Golden Bull, which gave Hungarian noblemen the right to resist the king if he acted against the law.

After the death of King Stephen's last descendant in 1301 and a short period of interregnum, the foreign Angevin dynasty consolidated their power. Of the Angevin kings, the reign of Louis I (1342–82) brought significant territorial expansion. In the post-Angevin period, King Matthias (1458–90) was the most notable ruler, the son of a war lord who had been fighting successfully against the increasingly threatening Ottoman Empire. Hungary experienced unprecedented prosperity during the reign of Matthias, and a vivid cultural life characterized his renaissance court.

In 1541 Hungary could no longer contain the expansion of the Ottoman Empire. As a result, the country was broken into three parts. The central areas fell under Turkish rule for 150 years, the Eastern areas (Transylvania) remained independent but at the price of being the vassal of the Ottoman Empire. Western Hungary was under Habsburg authority. In 1686, Christian forces led by the Habsburgs started to liberate the country from Turkish occupation, only to replace it with Habsburg domination.

In the Habsburg era, there were two major rebellions for independence. The Rákóczi War of Independence took place between 1703 and 1711. When the uprising was crushed, its leader Ferenc Rákóczi was forced to emigrate to Rodosto (in Turkey). The next major attempt at independence came in 1848 after two decades of reforms that were initiated by Hungarian noblemen with the reluctant compliance of the Habsburgs in order to transform the backward and still largely medieval country into a modern prospering nation. The revolutionary fervor that swept through Europe in 1848 did not leave Hungary untouched. Revolutionary demands were first accepted by the ruling Habsburgs and the first Hungarian government under the leadership of Lajos Batthyány was elected. Later the Habsburgs retracted the concessions, which resulted in a year of war. With the help of Russia, Austria crushed the Hungarian uprising in August 1849.

A wave of retaliation and authoritarian rule followed, to which Hungarians reacted with passive resistance. After a decade and a half, a series of internal and external problems forced a more conciliatory attitude on Austria, which culminated in the Great Compromise of 1867 that made Hungary an equal part of the Dual Monarchy with Austria. The era of Dualism brought liberal constitutionalism and economic prosperity until the outbreak of the First World War.[3]

The late 1910s and early 1920s were a period of turmoil. In the wake of defeat in 1918, the Austro-Hungarian Empire collapsed.[4] A short period of democratic governance took place under the leadership of Count Mihály Károlyi in

1918–19. After his resignation, Béla Kun and the Communist Party grabbed power for a few months. Finally, conservative–nationalist forces managed to solidify and hold on to power for the remainder of the interwar period.

As a defeated power in the First World War, Hungary lost two-thirds of its territory as a result of the Treaty of Trianon in 1920, which placed a large part of the ethnic Hungarian population outside the country's borders. The shock of territorial loss fueled nationalism as well as revanchism. In the interwar years this led Hungary to tighten relations with Hitler's Germany in the hope of regaining its lost territories.[5] Hitler's promise of returning the lost territories, threat of military occupation, and economic pressure made an unenthusiastic Hungarian government comply with the introduction of a series of restrictions on the rights of Jews from 1938 onwards. However, the Hungarian government withstood pressure to send Jews to concentration camps until March 1944 when Nazi Germany invaded its reluctant ally and took control of the country. A year later Hungary was liberated from Nazi rule as a result of a bitter fight between German and Soviet troops.

Large parts of the population treated liberation with reservations, since the country did not regain full independence: German occupation was simply replaced with Soviet domination. Thus, Hungary became an occupied country although it could hold free elections in the autumn of 1945 despite the presence of the Red Army. In vain did the center-right Independent Smallholders' Party win the election with an absolute majority, because as a result of strong Soviet pressure all major parties were forced into a grand coalition with the communists, and the parliament was left with virtually no opposition.[6] The years 1945–7 can be characterized as semi-democracy at best, in which the country was forced to move slowly but surely towards a Stalinist type of dictatorship. The multi-party system was eliminated by 1948 as parties were banned, and opposition politicians were imprisoned, killed, or forced into emigration. In foreign policy, Hungary was not allowed to receive any funds from the Marshall Plan, which significantly contributed to the post-war economic reconstruction of Western Europe.

The three epochs of communist rule

Between 1948 and 1989 the Hungarian political regime was a one-party dictatorship of the communists, and the country belonged to the Soviet bloc.[7] It is important to note that it was not the country but the *regime* that could be labelled "communist." 10% of the population belonged to the communist party but the 90% of non-party members were seen as potential enemies of the regime. Every fourth Hungarian family had a member in jail in the early 1950s. The communist leader of the time, Mátyás Rákosi, who ruled the country until 1956, was proud to call himself the "best pupil" of Stalin.

Nevertheless, these decades were by no means uniform. One can differentiate between three epochs of communist rule in Hungary: totalitarianism, post-totalitarianism, and regime disintegration. Between 1948 and 1962 the regime was a classic totalitarian regime:[8] totalitarian propaganda, the arbitrary powers of the secret police, and (until 1956) the personality cult of the communist leader created unbearable communist terror, controlled and sometimes softened externally by the Moscow leadership, which was the real holder of power in the Soviet Empire. Communism was an international regime, in which nothing could happen against the will of the Moscow leadership. Following the death of Stalin, the toughest measures of terroristic rule were temporarily lifted in 1953–4, but re-Stalinization took place in 1955–6.

Re-Stalinization provoked resistance. First, it provoked a protest among intellectuals and students who formed a discussion circle. Later, they moved beyond this and organized peaceful mass demonstrations in October 1956, which led to the outbreak of the revolution on 23 October. This uprising is widely seen as the first anti-totalitarian (anti-communist but not necessarily anti-socialist) revolution in history. A reform oriented communist leader, Imre Nagy, took over as prime minister and he reorganized the cabinet on a coalition basis by inviting representatives of the Peasant Party, the Smallholders' Party, and the Social Democratic Party (MSZDP) to join him. The new cabinet declared that Hungary was leaving the Warsaw Pact (the joint military organization of the Soviet bloc) and planned to follow the example of Austrian neutrality. In the domain of internal politics, freedom of speech and press had been restored, and the self-established Workers' Councils took over the state-owned factories.[9] They advocated a kind of socialism that meant the ownership of producers over the means of production rather than the centralized ownership of the state by a small elite.

However, the democratic surge was short-lived. On 4 November, Soviet troops invaded Hungary, and entered for a few days into a bloody fight with younger people on the streets of Budapest. Imre Nagy and his revolutionary cabinet were removed from power and replaced with the puppet of the Soviet Union, János Kádár.[10] In November–December 1956, 200,000 mostly young and educated people used the opportunity provided by the lack of border control and emigrated to the West. Imre Nagy and his fellow politicians were imprisoned. They were executed in June 1958.

While Kádár had cemented his power by means of terror, in the early 1960s he softened the harshness of his rule, when he declared that "those who are not against us are with us." By accepting or even endorsing the neutrality of citizens, the regime moved away from classic totalitarianism to post-totalitarianism. Permanent political mobilization was replaced by political demobilization and neutralization. Forced political activity was replaced by recommended political passivity. Amnesty was granted to political prisoners, others received passports to travel abroad, and young people of non-working-class ("bourgeois") background were again allowed to enter universities. In addition, cultural life became more colorful, non-Communist books were translated, and jazz and rock music were tolerated.

The post-totalitarian decades shaped Hungarian political culture in a significant way. People learned that collective resistance could not work so they had to find informal, individual, non-political ways of interest representation and survival. The regime that existed between 1962 and 1985 was similar to a classic authoritarian one, for it preferred the pacification and atomization of the society, maintaining the political monopoly of the Communist Party in exchange for higher living standards, decentralizing reforms in the economy, and relatively greater space for people in their private sphere:[11] it was the era of "Goulash communism." The aim was to make people forget the tragedy of 1956 through more relaxed social and economic policies and a more tolerant cultural life. This made Kádár and his regime ("Kádárism") relatively popular, as citizens welcomed de-politicization after years of aggressive Communist propaganda.[12]

However, "Goulash communism" became increasingly difficult to maintain after the second half of the 1970s. The comparatively acceptable living standards were financed by foreign loans in the 1960s and early 1970s, but led to high foreign debt. The aging communist leadership could not cope with external and internal challenges for long, and the first signs of dissent appeared both inside and outside the party. By the 1980s the compromise between the communists and the society to which economic development was a fundamental benefit came to an end. Between 1976 and 1986 production and living standards declined steadily in Hungary, provoking increasing public criticism and occasionally resistance.

The impact of Solidarity's "self-limited revolution" in Poland,[13] and the rise of Mikhail Gorbachev to power in the Soviet Union, marked the end of the epoch of post-totalitarianism by the mid-1980s. The period between 1985 and 1989 witnessed the long erosion and disintegration of the communist regime. Civil society started to organize itself, critical intellectuals became active in discussion forums and organized new political associations and parties. At the same time, reform oriented lawyers and economists questioned the foundations of the regime. This process of disintegration can also be described positively as the start of the democratization process.

Democratization, 1987–90

From 1990 onwards Hungary has enjoyed, for the first time in its history, a fully free, liberal democratic political regime, where elections were considered free and fair and there was a competitive multi-party system. The revolutionary changes of 1989 in Hungary can be characterized by elite-driven negotiations and non-violence. Touched by the shocking memory of 1956 when thousands of young people died in street fights, all political actors were concerned to avoid violence. Instead of trying to reform the communist state, which had proven impossible to regenerate, opposition groups aimed at organizing civil society. They were thus able to demonstrate their public support and become a legitimate negotiating partner for the communist leadership. Organizing civil society proved to be a key factor for the success of the negotiated exit from communism. Opposition groups wanted to achieve a revolutionary outcome without using traditional revolutionary means.

The Hungarian transition to democracy was characterized by non-violence and round table talks between the communist powerholders and the organizations of the emerging opposition. Agreement was possible among the elites by upholding the fiction of legality; legal security was put before justice. Upholding the procedural legal continuity, the negotiating parties – at least in relation to the principal laws – managed to avoid continuity with the dictatorship regarding their content. In order to avoid being divided and to unify their strength, the opposition parties decided to form an Opposition Round Table in March 1989. There were three parties to these talks: the Communist Party (MSZMP), the Opposition Round Table (EKA, with nine organizations), and the so-called Third Side (seven organizations), which were satellite organizations of the MSZMP and were invited by them to the talks. The real discussion took place between the MSZMP and EKA while the Third Side basically accepted their compromise.[14]

The trilateral National Round Table Talks occurred mostly in the summer of 1989 and resulted in a change of the Constitution and the declaration of a democratic Republic on 23 October 1989. The unresolved issues (Party organizations in workplaces, the paramilitary force of the Communist Party, the status of the president, and the accounting for communist wealth) were settled in a referendum on 26 November 1989. The transition came to an end in the March–April parliamentary elections (won by the center-right MDF "Hungarian Democratic Forum," whose leader, József Antall, became prime minister), and by the local elections of October 1990 (won largely by the biggest opposition party, the liberal SZDSZ (Free Democrats)). Analyzing the Hungarian case, we should also stress the importance of the split within the communist party between the reformers and the hardline representatives of the old guard, which greatly contributed to the success of peaceful transition.[15] No true hardliners were represented in the National Round Table Talks, since they had already been marginalized before the talks began.

Many realized only afterwards that informal structures of the old regime that were contrary to – or, at least, did not follow from – democratic principles persisted in the new regime. Since in Hungary it was not so much a *return* to democracy, but was the first time that democracy was being fully built, it was uncertain whether these informal practices could be seen only as the heritage of the communist regime, or whether they were deeper, more fundamental – that is, the heritage of previous centuries. Negotiated revolution meant an informal way out of state socialism, but did not necessarily mean a way out of previously learned practices of informality.[16]

Failed reforms might lead to revolutions while failed revolutions might lead to reforms. The latter happened in Hungary during the long interval of

1956–89. Opposition strategies of democratic transition were based on experience that had been rooted in the previous historical processes and events. The Hungarian constitutional revolution was also a result of such a learning process.[17]

Changes in Hungary cannot be understood without the influence and heritage of the earlier freedom fights of the societies in the region. International factors played a role in the success of democratization: internal pressure and external support for the Western democratic community – and, above all, the Gorbachev factor[18] – were highly significant. While in Poland a quite homogenous civil society that was organized into one "umbrella" organization (Solidarity) won over the state party, in Hungary divided opposition organizations were even competing with each other to bring the regime down. In short, in Poland democracy existed before pluralism, while in Hungary pluralism came into being before democracy.

Political values and visions of 1989

The most highly esteemed political value among the participants of the Round Table Talks was the idea of *freedom*, in both its liberal and democratic senses. On the one hand, liberal freedoms – the exercize of human rights and civil liberties – were advocated. In the ideal political community people could talk freely and openly both in private and public, the press was free, and the freedoms of assembly and party formation were guaranteed as inalienable rights of every citizen. At the time, freedom was understood in a *negative* rather than a positive sense,[19] as independence *from* the state (the Party, the police, the military, and the government as a whole). It was freedom *from* something – freedom from the intervention and paternalism of the state. The goal was individual freedom – that is, the opportunity for individuals to pursue their activities free of harassment, interference, and control. This concept of freedom was the cumulative outcome of two major sources of influence: the legacy of dissent that valued highly human rights and equal human dignity, and the dominant Western neoliberal ideology.

On the other hand, freedom as a democratic value was identified with *popular sovereignty* – that is, the idea of a political community created by the will and consent of the people. However, this assumes the existence of an independent political community, which was not the case in Soviet-dominated, post-war Hungary. For more than four decades the physical presence of Soviet advisors and the Red Army influenced – even if not always determined – the political steps that the Hungarian communist leadership could take. Therefore, it was not by chance that the withdrawal of Soviet troops became an important demand as the prerequisite for building a democratic society.

Democracy was understood as a *representative* government, wherein people exercized their constitutional powers indirectly through their elected representatives. Democracy was defined in terms of existing competition, participation, and civil liberties; among these, Hungarians emphasized the first and third and ignored the second. This was the consequence of an aversion from the forced, non-voluntary, demonstrative participation of the masses during communism. Since people were distrustful of political mobilization initiated at the top, the democratic opposition came to embrace a liberal, "non-participatory" democracy. They laid stress on getting rid of the paternalism of the state and put an emphasis on independent political action instead of republican public behavior based on active participation of citizens in public life.

One reason why regime change in Hungary was carried out so smoothly was the participants' mutual insistence on peaceful means. *Non-violence* was highly valued and taken seriously by all sides: at times, non-violence was prized as highly as freedom. The participants' commitment to non-violence, and their genuine desire to reach consensus through negotiations, is one of the important legacies of 1989.[20] The preference of the democratic opposition for non-violence was primarily based on their evolutionist strategy, but was also motivated by the awareness that ordinary people had no wish to repeat the revolution of 1956. The communists, still in power, also wished to get out of the crisis without resorting to violence. Non-violent conflict resolution was ensured by the then-still-living legacy of self-limiting political action. Even the so-called radical opposition was quite moderate in comparison.

The legacy of the Polish self-limiting revolution of 1980–1 was a real starting point for the negotiating process in Central Europe.[21] In Hungary, regime change based on an agreement between the powerholders and the opposition was a difficult and tedious process, which raised the value of consensus: *consensual* democracy came to be seen as the ideal form. The negotiators agreed that certain institutions of the transition, such as bills passed with a two-thirds majority, continue to exist after the transition, thereby allowing those institutions to become established as integral parts of the new democracy. Later this consensual behavior was heavily criticized by the radical right, which wanted tougher lustration laws and a more sweeping change in the power relations of the elite: lustration, or "decommunization," became a marginal demand. Legislation on this issue, limited as it was, has not been approved by the Constitutional Court.

The ideal of consensus did not manifest itself only in the negotiations between the powerholders and the democratic opposition, but also characterized the internal dynamics of the EKA. Their achievement was that they successfully realized the dream of a united front. Although it can be described as internally divided and conflict-ridden, the EKA succeeded as a cooperative, consensus oriented body of the opposition. Beyond stressing their difference from the MSZMP, their identity was built around the value of consensus that the institution of the veto right forced upon them. Civil society was often identified with democratic social movements that were fighting for "true democracy" against the existing institutions; until 1989, many activists and some theorists believed that political parties and governmental institutions were inherently non-democratic,[22] and should be substituted by the unwritten, non-institutionalized, self-evident general consensus of civil society.

Even if it soon became clear that the old concept of a unified civil society belonged to the past myths of anti-totalitarian movements rather than to a future of any viable democracy, it was difficult to accept that democracy was about *conflicts* – that is, conflicting values and interests that are openly expressed and must be institutionally regulated. Conflicts are not dysfunctional in a democracy but are the very essence of it.[23] In the process of Round Table-type transitions, it was not easy to understand that the point was not to eliminate conflicts in the name of consensus, but to channel them through functioning democratic institutions. The participants of the Round Table talks wanted to establish a moderate, smoothly functioning democratic regime. Thus, when political conflicts sharpened, they tended to condemn each other as the "enemies of democracy," all convinced that only their interpretation of democracy was correct.

An important element of the political visions of the opposition was their insistence that Hungary must *return to Europe*. For a time, "Finlandization" served as a model for how Hungary might overcome its past, and the example of Austria's development was repeatedly raised as well. Both examples suggested a neutral military status for Hungary. Only from 1990 did some politicians begin to raise the possibility of joining NATO, which started to gain public support after the August 1991 coup in Moscow and, more visibly, after the eruption of war in Yugoslavia.

The aspiration to join the EC also played an important role in Hungary's return to Europe. From the beginning, the idea of membership in the EC (later, EU) was more popular within Hungarian society than the proposal to join NATO, because of the former's identification with the ideal of social welfare. However, the commitment to EU membership was not equally strong across the political spectrum. The Hungarian Left regarded "Europeanization" as a process – as a project of political and economic modernization. In this, the EU could easily serve as a reference point. On the other hand, the Right argued that the major common cultural heritage of Europe was Christianity, which Hungary had already shared. Consequently, "Europe" for them was not a program but a status that Hungary had automatically regained after the collapse of Communism.

Since 1989, the desire to return to Europe has gradually become a reality. Hungary joined the European Council in 1991, the Partnership for Peace in 1994, NATO in 1999, and the EU in 2004. Most recently, on 1 January 2008, Hungary became part of the Schengen zone within the EU.

This regime change created an unprecedented historical situation in Hungary in which the political elite could create the institutional framework of democracy without bloodshed. Whatever our definition of "change" may be, it is beyond doubt that the changes of 1989–90 represent the dividing line between dictatorship and democracy. The old regime collapsed and the institutions created in the negotiations of 1989 prevailed. However, the tone-setting political and economic groups, mentalities and practices, and the popular perception of regime change evolved much more slowly.

Political and electoral systems

Hungary is a parliamentary democracy where the parliament is the center of democratic politics. The president's functions are largely ceremonial and (s)he is elected by the parliament. The unicameral parliament elects the prime minister but ministers are responsible to the prime minister directly, as members of his/her cabinet, and not to the parliament. The parliament elects the members of the Constitutional Court (for nine years), and the ombudsmen (for six years). Their independence, and that of the National Bank, is guaranteed constitutionally.[24]

The electoral system of Hungary is extremely complex due to the compromise reached at the Round Table negotiations. The 1989 "Act on Elections" established a three-level electoral system which combines single-member districts with regional and national party lists. The election consists of two rounds, and in ordinary circumstances is held every four years.[25]

Of the 386 seats in the Parliamentary Assembly, 176 are filled through elections in single-member districts. Only the candidate who can collect the signatures of 750 eligible voters may compete in the elections. In the first round, a 50% voter turnout is required. If the required level of voter turnout is met without any of the candidates obtaining an absolute majority, all the candidates who received at least 15% of the votes, but no less than three, advance to the second round. If the voter turnout does not reach the required 50% in the first round, all candidates regardless of the results may compete in the second round. In the second round there is a requirement of a 25% voter turnout and the candidate who receives a relative majority is elected. If the 25% limit is not met, the seat is filled through a by-election at a later time. In reality, the first round is rarely successful, and by-elections are seldom needed.

A maximum of 152 seats are distributed on the basis of regional party lists. In the first round of the elections voters also cast a vote for regional party lists and so in practice have two votes. The country is divided into twenty regional districts where the number of seats is between 4 and 28, depending on the size of the population of each district. Only those parties that are able to nominate candidates in at least one-quarter of the single-member districts in that region may put forward lists in a given region. If voter turnout reaches 50%, seats are distributed after the first round – otherwise the second round decides. However, in order to win seats on the regional list a party must win at least 5% of all votes countrywide.

A minimum of 58 seats are distributed on the basis of the national or compensation lists. National lists can be put forward by parties that have regional lists in at least seven counties. In addition, no party failing to meet the 5% threshold may receive seats through the national list. Seats are distributed on the basis of votes which either do not result in winning a seat in single-member districts or that remain after the distribution of regional seats.

Up until 2006, successive governments always lost elections. Center-right coalitions took office in 1990 (MDF, KDNP, FKGP) and in 1998 (Fidesz, MDF, FKGP), whereas in 1994 and 2002 the MSZP and SZDSZ formed left-liberal coalitions. In 2006, the MSZP–SZDSZ coalition was the first ruling coalition that managed to win re-election. The re-elected center-left government is also a record holder in other respects. Hungary's first-ever minority government came into being on 30 April 2008 when SZDSZ, the smaller governing party, decided to withdraw from the coalition. The country also saw the first successful vote of no-confidence when Gordon Bajnai replaced Ferenc Gyurcsány as prime minister on 14 April 2009. The Bajnai government regards itself as a caretaker, intending to stay in office until the elections scheduled for the spring of 2010. The election turnout of the voters has been generally low, for various reasons. First, the political culture reflects the pessimism that is characteristic of Hungarians. On the other hand, the high expectations of each incoming government, and the subsequent disappointment in their performance, may also contribute. Furthermore, the respect for parties is very low. This also has the consequence that about 40% of the voters are uncommitted between elections.

Political parties

Political parties are the formative actors in the Hungarian political field. According to their origin we can speak of historical, successor, and new parties. "Historical parties" are those that existed prior to the communist regime: the Hungarian Smallholders' Party (FKGP) and the Christian Democratic People's Party (KDNP). By a "successor party" we mean the heirs of the Communist Party: the Hungarian Socialist Party (MSZP). "New parties" are those that emerged during or after the regime change: the Hungarian Democratic Forum (MDF), the Free Democrats (SZDSZ), the Alliance of Young Democrats (Fidesz), and the Party of Hungarian Justice and Life (MIÉP). The major parties of Hungary may also be placed on left–right axis: MSZP is a center-left party; SZDSZ is left-liberal; and Fidesz, that used to be a right-liberal party, is the main force in the center-right today. The MDF and the KDNP share the right side of the political spectrum with Fidesz; MIÉP is on the extreme right (table 10.1).

Among the far-left parties, the Workers' Party represents the old Kádárist left, while the Communist Party is a mix of Kádárism and anti-capitalist anti-globalism. Both are minor parties outside parliament. The MSZP is a dominant

Table 10.1 Hungarian political parties and their ideological positions, 1990–2008

Far left	*Socialist*	*Liberal*	*Conservative*	*Far right*
Workers' Party	MSZP	SZDSZ	Fidesz	MIÉP
Communist Party	MSZDP		MDF	Jobbik
			FKGP	
			KDNP	

Table 10.2 Prime Ministers and their cabinets, 1990–2010

Year	Prime Minister	Party
1990–3	József Antall	(MDF–FKGP–KDNP)
1993–4	Péter Boross	(MDF–KDNP)
1994–8	Gyula Horn	(MSZP–SZDSZ)
1998–2002	Viktor Orbán	(Fidesz–FKGP–MDF)
2002–4	Péter Medgyessy	(MSZP–SZDSZ)
2004–9	Ferenc Gyurcsány	(MSZP–SZDSZ; since 2008: MSZP minority government)
2009–10	Gordon Bajnai	(MSZP)

player in the Hungarian left, which has been represented in parliament consistently since 1989 and has been the governing party for ten of those years. The Socialists elected four prime ministers (Gyula Horn, Péter Medgyessy, Ferenc Gyurcsány, and Gordon Bajnai, see table 10.2). Horn, Medgyessy, and Gyurcsány represented contradictory tendencies of old social democracy, Kádárist nostalgia, pro-privatization modernization and Blairist "Third Way" policies,[26] whereas Bajnai is a non-party member technocrat. The Hungarian Social Democratic Party (MSZDP) is an extra-parliamentary force led by a former communist minister who is a billionaire today, but the party plays no significant role in Hungarian politics. The Alliance of Free Democrats (SZDSZ) is a social-liberal parliamentary party, the heir of the democratic opposition of the 1980s, which recently adopted a more neoliberal economic stance. It used to be a big party, achieving 20–22% in the first two elections, but since 1998 it has been struggling to enter parliament by achieving 5–8% of the votes.

As for the political right, Fidesz is the leading force represented in parliament since 1990. At the time of regime change Fidesz was a small liberal party, only to become a center-right conservative party by the mid-1990s. Fidesz produced one prime minister (Viktor Orbán) and engineered the election of two center-right presidents (Ferenc Mádl and László Sólyom, see table 10.3). The Hungarian Democratic Forum (MDF) is a parliamentary party which used to be the biggest conservative force and the winner of the first election. It was the

Table 10.3 Presidents, 1990–2010 (elected by parliament)

Year	President
1990–2000	Árpád Göncz
2000–5	Ferenc Mádl
2005–10	László Sólyom

largest leading member of the first governing coalition, producing two prime ministers (József Antall and Péter Boross). However, it lost significance after 1994 and is now a minor conservative-liberal party in opposition, increasingly supporting neo-conservative economic policies.

The Independent Smallholders' Party (FKGP) used to represent the countryside and, thus, agrarian interests. It was a medium-sized party and a member of two center-right governments (1990–2 and 1998–2001). However, it failed to gain any representation in parliament in 2002 and has no impact on Hungarian politics today. The Christian Democratic People's Party (KDNP) is a Christian-socialist party and has been in parliament as a minor party since the first free elections. It combines culturally right-wing policies with an economically leftist agenda. On the far right, the Party of Hungarian Life and Justice (MIÉP) was created by the former MDF politician István Csurka in 1993. The party spent four years in parliament (1998–2002), formally in opposition but often voting together with the center-right government. Since 2002, MIÉP has been outside parliament with no significant impact on politics, its agenda mainly taken over by Jobbik (For a Better Hungary), an extra-parliamentary party composed of younger, more militant extreme right supporters who speak for order and patriotic values with racist overtones. While the size of its support base has not yet been tested domestically, the general dissatisfaction with the left not only resulted in the overwhelming victory of Fidesz, but also brought about a third-place finish for Jobbik, which won 15% of the vote in the 2009 election for the European Parliament.

Economic development

Long-term economic recession was already plaguing Hungary during the 1980s and the double need of a transition to a market economy and a necessity for seeking new markets after the collapse of the Community for Mutual Economic Assistance (CMEA) at the beginning of the 1990s only added to the crisis. Of these, the finding of new markets appears to have been easier, the EU emerging as Hungary's largest export market. While in 1989 only one-quarter of exports were directed toward the EC, in ten years the ratio had tripled to three-quarters. In the transition to a market economy, the EU's role was also significant in providing financial aid (PHARE, SAPARD, ISPA programs), setting clear

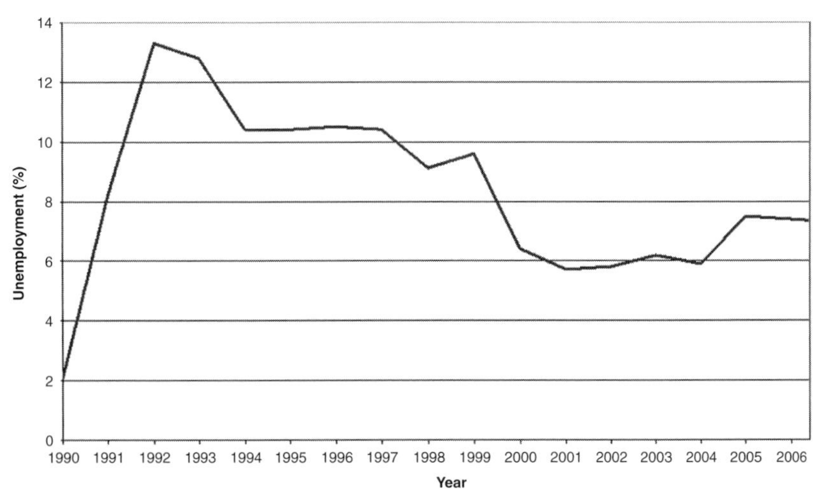

Figure 10.1 Unemployment rate (percent of labor force without jobs), Hungary, 1990–2007
Source: György Csáki and Gábor Karsai (eds.), *Evolution of the Hungarian Economy 1848–2000: Hungary from Transition to Integration* (Boulder, Colo.: Social Science Monographs, 2001); CIA, *The World Factbook 2008*, at www.cia.gov/library/publications/the-world-factbook.

criteria for EU membership, and constantly tightening cooperation with Hungary.[27]

In the early 1990s, Hungary faced a choice between a quick but painful or a slow but, hopefully, less painful transition to a market economy. The first democratically elected government opted for the latter when it promised to create a social market economy. This meant that the government initiated no major reforms, despite serious economic problems such as skyrocketing inflation and unemployment, sliding living standards, negative economic growth rates, a thriving shadow economy, and large-scale smuggling (figure 10.1). However, it could not avoid raising petrol prices so that they came closer to their market value, which shattered the public's illusion of a painless transition and resulted in the blocking of major roads by taxi drivers in protest (figure 10.2).

Major economic reforms were initiated by the Horn government in 1995. Austerity measures – the so-called "Bokros package" – were introduced in 1995: social welfare benefits were cut, tuition fees in higher education introduced, taxes raised, the range of free medical services narrowed, the Hungarian currency devalued by 9%, and an additional crawling-peg devaluation announced. While some of the social welfare payment cuts were later declared unconstitutional, the remaining changes were severe enough to bring favorable macroeconomic results, culminating in the declaration of the convertibility of the Hungarian currency (the forint) and the realization of a credit agreement with the IMF and the acceptance into the OECD in 1996.[28]

The economy boomed until 2001 in spite of the Asian and Russian economic crises, but economic recession in the wake of 9/11 made itself felt in Hungary as well. In addition, the Orbán government abolished some of the reforms such as

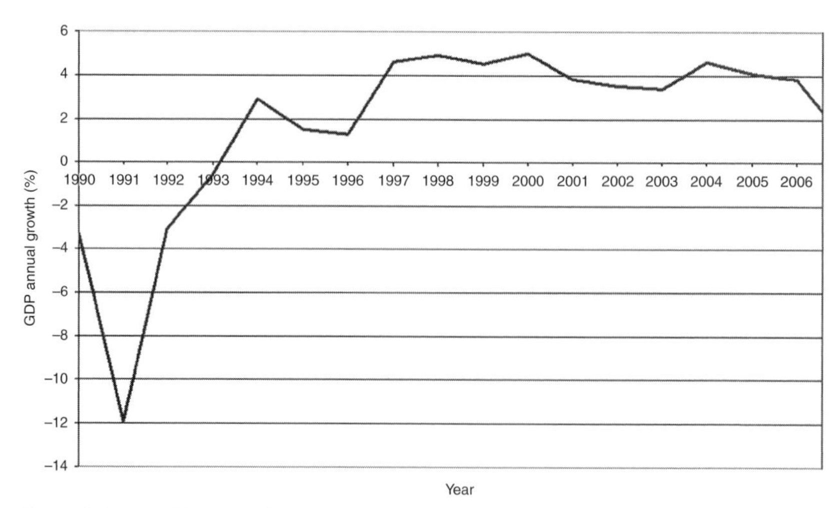

Figure 10.2 Annual GDP growth, Hungary, 1990–2007
Source: Gygörgy Csáki and Gábor Karsai (eds.), *Evolution of the Hungarian Economy 1848–2000: Hungary from Transition to Integration* (Boulder, Colo.: Social Science Monographs, 2001); CIA, *The World Factbook 2008*, at www.cia.gov/library/publications/the-world-factbook.

tuition fees for higher education and, despite worsening macroeconomic figures, increased welfare spending and the minimum wage. On the positive side, the government started large-scale highway and real estate development.[29] Extensive welfare spending was continued by the Medgyessy government that delivered on its campaign promises and raised pensions and wages in the public sphere – in health care and education.[30]

As a consequence, plans to introduce the Euro in Hungary were publicly abandoned and an unpopular economic package was introduced in 2006. After fifteen years of procrastination, major reforms of the pension and health care systems were finally initiated. In 2006, the government decided to begin the privatization of the health care system, which the opposition sought to block through a referendum, but low participation prevented the referendum from being valid. The following reforms brought growing health care costs for citizens, public confusion, and the plan for a health insurance scheme that was the result of political compromise between the coalition parties; as such, it combined the private and state health insurance concepts and, potentially, their disadvantages.[31] The next referendum campaign was successful and required the government to revoke some of the reforms. However, the largest governing party, the MSZP, went further and backed off any kind of privatization of the health care system that had been advocated by its minor coalition partner (SZDSZ). Irrevocable differences over health care reform, Gyurcsány's loss of credibility with the public, and the taint of corruption finally made the MSZP–SZDSZ coalition untenable. Economic reforms petered out at a time when global recession made such changes imperative. Reforms were finally introduced by Bajnai's caretaker government, which enjoys a parliamentary majority with the outside support of SZDSZ and which procured a substantial loan from the IMF and the EBRD. Reforms, including the revocation of the thirteen-month pension, the introduction of a property tax and incentives for companies to preserve jobs, have also been on the government's agenda.

Unquestionably, privatization was the greatest success story of the economic transition. The liquidation of state assets and the creation of private property were important elements of the process of replacing a centrally planned economy. It was also a response to Hungary's large public debt, which successive governments hoped to reduce by quick, market-based transition. The process of privatization gave the opportunity for FDI to enter the country. As a result, one-third of FDI entered through privatization. In eight years, most sectors of the economy had been entirely or largely privatized and by 2006, 85% of the GDP was produced by the private sector.[32] However, privatization also created several problems. Large multinational companies entered the country in the process, draining capital away from small and medium-sized companies (SMEs). The latter have as a consequence not only been short of capital but are also rather inefficient and small in number.

Issues of corruption

Privatization and other state projects, especially highway construction tenders, were fertile fields for corruption. Corruption, links to organized crime, grey and black money, and creative accounting practices have also tainted the reputation of both the political elite and the parties.[33] The lack of adequate state funding – the hypocritically low limits of legally allowed campaign costs – and small party membership necessitate financial creativity and corrupt political practices. As a result, parties are usually found to operate correctly, but all of them are surrounded by a network of friendly client companies that, in exchange for preference in state tenders, willingly comply with party needs and spend some of their profits on party projects.

Scandals revealing the close ties between the political and economic elites surface from time to time. In 1996, the Tocsik affair originally erupted over the incredibly high premium money (about $3 million) that the contracted lawyer, Marta Tocsik, received for negotiating advantageous deals for the State Privatization Company (APV Rt.). Tocsik's statement before a parliamentary committee revealed that local governments were required to kick back a part of their profit from the privatization of local government assets to governing parties.[34] More recently, a Socialist politician, János Zuschlag, was arrested after being accused of fraud relating to funds obtained from the Ministry of Sport and local government sources.

Not only does the polarization of economic interests along party lines hinder the development of the economy, national interests are likely to suffer as well. It was not by chance that when, in 2007, the usually bickering parties almost unanimously approved more lenient measures for the privatization of strategic industries, concerns were raised that the protection of interests of the political–economic oligarchy was taking precedence over the country's more general interests.[35] In the wake of the Zuschlag scandal, Prime Minister Gyurcsány vowed to make party financing transparent, launched a referendum campaign, and proposed a new party-financing law. It became clear, however, that there was no political will to implement a more transparent regulation. Similar efforts to cut down on such practices in the heavily corrupt traffic police and health care system have already been made; they have proved successful in the former case but with regard to the health care system the results are yet to be seen.

Hungarian investigative journalism does a good job of revealing some outrageous cases of corruption but the political and economic elites are increasingly immune to the scandals. Ideally, scandals should be healthy signs of democratic accountability, but they are meaningless in Hungary because the relevant authorities do not follow up the leads. It is not by chance that Hungary is sometimes ironically described as "a country without consequences"– i.e. there is a lack of political accountability that demoralizes both the public and those who are expected to defend public interests.

Education

Fee-paying in higher education has been one of the most politicized areas of education policy, which is curious in the light of the sweeping changes that have taken place in the field of education since 1989. The Education Law of 1993 started the transformation of a centrally planned and financed education system into one of the least centralized systems in the EU. The role of the state was limited to the definition of learning aims and the skills that students needed to acquire at a certain age and accreditation of the framework curricula that broke these aims down by content and subject field. Schools are free to choose among these framework curricula and adapt them to their local needs.

However, the results of liberalization have been mixed. On the one hand, it saw a broadening of educational choice by the appearance of private and faith-based schools. On the other hand, the traditional structure of schooling – eight-year primary and four-year secondary education – was supplemented with schools working with 4–8 or 6–6 models, which limited students' choice, because the different curricula made it extremely difficult for students to move from a school working with one model to a school working with another. Moreover, selection of students has been moved back from age 14 to age 10, discriminating against students maturing later. Similarly, while liberalization saw an expansion of choice in textbooks, this often happened to the detriment to textbook quality. Such problems were dealt with by increasing attention to quality control in the second half of the 1990s.

The second half of the 1990s also revealed decreasing student performance in international comparison, which resulted in a change from content-based learning to skill acquisition after 2000. EU directives after 2000 stressed competitiveness, lifelong learning, and the harmonization of education systems. The last of these resulted in the most comprehensive change in higher education, namely the replacement of the traditional 4–5 year undergraduate education with the Bologna criteria of three-year BA and two-year MA programs.

As for the financing of education, despite the fact that the state was channeling increasing proportions of the GDP into education, the general economic depression of the early 1990s saw a decrease in the funds in real terms. Demographic changes also led to a sizable shrinkage in the number of school-age children, which led to the closing of schools and growing unemployment amongst teachers. Today, schools are being closed or merged to enhance financial efficacy and reduce burdens on the state and local government budgets. The state provides a fixed amount of funding for each student, which make up about 65–70% of the financial support for public schools, and the local governments are supposed to provide the rest of the money. The state provides both the head quotas and the supplementary amount for faith-based schools. While higher education has seen some expansion, the number of state-financed places at public universities is shrinking and with the introduction of fees even these students will be required to pay for a part of their education.

Gender issues

Concerning gender, there is a wide gap between what the dynamics of education would predict and actual reality. Women make up the majority of students at higher education institutions, but they are still not well represented in important leading and managerial positions. The problems are similar in the area of politics, which is by and large a men's profession despite the fact that in the late 1990s several parties made some room for women on their party lists. In November 2007, the government introduced a bill whereby in national and European elections women should have every second place on party lists. Support was high, but the bill failed to pass because almost half of the MPs abstained during the voting.

Women earn lower wages in similar positions to men, and there appears to be a hidden discrimination against women. Discrimination against the middle-aged hit men and women alike, but companies avoid employing young women who do not yet have children or have young children. Although women on maternity leave are legally protected against being fired, in practice this provides little protection: they are often fired after the end of the protection period or upon their return are relegated to unfulfilling positions which they decide to leave voluntarily.

These developments are the result of market forces, but allow much of the duality of communism toward gender issues to survive. Communism had elevated women to equal status and required them to become a part of the workforce. The state provided day care for children but women still had to shoulder domestic chores. Today women are free theoretically to choose if they wish to work, but since two incomes are needed to provide for a family, this choice is rather restricted. Moreover, they are not spared domestic duties, since even most middle-class families cannot afford to employ domestic help.

Migrants, minorities, and interethnic relations

Discrimination against minorities is, in general, not an acute problem, largely due to the fact that although the Hungarian minority law recognizes thirteen historic and ethnic minorities, these make up a very small proportion of the population. While Hungary was targeted by several waves of migration after 1989 such events did not substantially change the size of these minorities, for two reasons. First, the largest number of immigrants arrived from Romania between 1988 and 1991 and most of these were of ethnic Hungarian origin. Second, while a more substantial number of refugees – about 62,000 – arrived in 1991 and 1992 from the FRY as a result of the war in the Balkans, they did not remain in Hungary. Some sat out the war and then returned home, others soon left for Western Europe.

Similar to refugees from the FRY, many refugees and migrants who arrive in Hungary treat it as a transit country and not the final destination of their journey. Illegal migration and human trafficking has since 1996 created additional problems and cause a major headache for Western Europe, while the feared exodus of Hungarians after accession to the EU did not happen. Those Hungarians who decided to leave for the West have primarily targeted Austria and Germany but

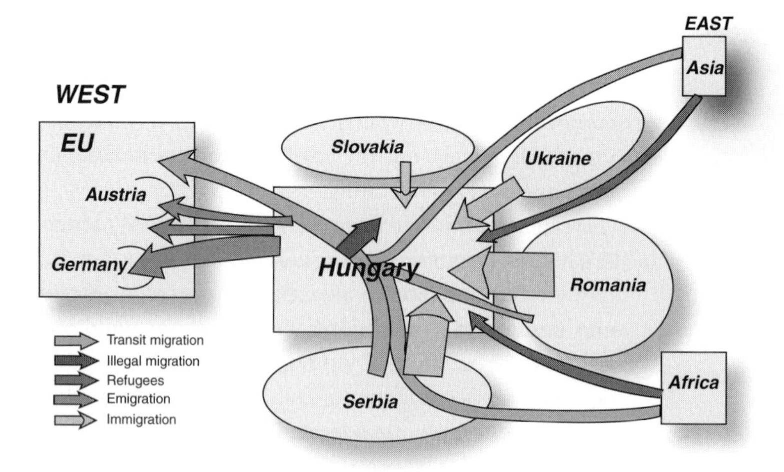

Figure 10.3 Hungary and East-West migration, 1990–2007
Source: Zoltán Dövényi, at foldrajz.ttk.pte.hu/magyarorszag/letoltes/keletnyugat.ppt.

Table 10.4 Size of historic and ethnic minorities in Hungary, 2001 census data

Rank	Minority	Minority membership	% of total population
1	Roma	190,046	1.88
2	German	62,233	0.62
3	Slovak	17,692	0.18
4	Croatian	15,620	0.15
5	Romanian	7,995	0.08
6	Ukrainian	4,070	0.04
7	Serbian	3,816	0.04
8	Slovenian	3,040	0.03
9	Polish	2,962	0.03
10	Greek	2,509	0.02
11	Bulgarian	1,358	0.01
12	Ruthenian	1,098	0.01
13	Armenian	620	0.01

Source: ec.europa.eu/education/policies/lang/languages/langmin/euromosaic/hu_en.pdf.

their number is rather small, since Hungarians in general do not move easily even within their own country, and least of all abroad (figure 10.3).[36]

Despite their small number (see table 10.4), the thirteen recognized national and ethnic minorities enjoy extensive rights.[37] One aspect of minority relations has, however, been unresolved since 1994, when the Constitutional Court declared that minorities must win representation in parliament. Differences among parties, irreconcilable demands from the minorities, democratic dilemmas (2 votes for minority members at elections versus 1 vote for the general population), and the fact that the thirteen minority representatives may bring down any government, have hindered the realization of minority representation in parliament.[38]

In spite of generally good interethnic relations, this issue is still on the political agenda because of the problematic situation of the Roma minority and the large number of Hungarians living in neighboring countries. The number of the Roma population is estimated to be at least double if not triple the official figures. Transition hit the Roma especially hard: the industries where most of them worked collapsed first and many of them lived in small villages where unemployment was also generally high. One out of every four Roma is registered as unemployed and even if they are employed, available jobs are often temporary or seasonal. The general level of education among the Roma is also very low. The consequences are inadequate sanitary conditions, housing problems, and difficulty in breaking out of the situation. The problem is further aggravated by migration and, thus, the concentration of the Roma in the poorest regions of the country.[39]

An equally pressing matter is discrimination toward the Roma in every area of life, most prominently in employment, education, and the perceptions of the police.[40] To improve the situation, the government initiated several programs in the second half of the 1990s. In 1997, the "medium-term package of measures to improve the living conditions and social position of the Roma in Hungary" was accepted. It aimed at improving the conditions of the Roma while maintaining their cultural and linguistic heritage. The participation of (Roma) civil organizations and cooperation with the Roma community were essential parts of the program. In addition, the government joined into the effort of nine countries in the region to further the inclusion of the Roma in the 2005–15 period and accepted the corresponding action plan in 2004.[41]

To overcome the lack of parliamentary representation, parliamentary parties and the Roma community established close ties: for example, the MSZP has a Roma organization and in 2002 Fidesz offered one of the Roma organizations, Lungo Drom, two places on the party's national list. Fidesz has also delegated one representative of Roma origin to the European Parliament who, by lobbying for the opportunity for, and then submitting a report on, the situation of Roma women to the European Parliament introduced the problem at that forum.

Interethnic relations are also important because of the large Hungarian communities living in neighboring countries, particularly in Romania, Serbia, and Slovakia. The most conservative estimates put the total number of Hungarians living in neighboring countries at above 2.5 million – more than a quarter of the population of Hungary. As a result, policies toward Hungarian minorities abroad are as much a domestic as a foreign policy concern, and attitudes and actions toward them strongly correlate with the degree of nationalism exhibited by the parties. Although parties of all shades agree in providing support for ethnic Hungarians abroad, not surprisingly parties on the right are not only more nationalistic but treat the advancement of such Hungarians as an important part of their identity. This leads them to pursue more confrontational policies toward neighboring countries (table 10.5).

József Antall, the prime minister of the first democratically elected, center-right government, caused quite a stir both abroad and in certain circles at home when he stated that he wished to be the prime minister of 15 million

Table 10.5 Hungarian minorities in neighboring countries, 2001 census data

Minority	Population	Data year
Romania	1,447,544	2002
Slovakia	520,528	2001
Serbia	295,370	2001
Ukraine	155,600	2001
Austria	90,000	2001
Croatia	16,505	2001
Slovenia	6,500	2002
Total	2,532,047	

Source: Government Office for Hungarian Minorities Abroad, at www.hhrf.org/htmh/en.

Hungarians – a number that included the Hungarians outside Hungary. Moreover, the government's move away from a centrist policy line and its insistence on a minority protection clause stalled the conclusion of the Basic Treaty with Romania. The Basic Treaty with Romania and Slovakia was finally signed by Gyula Horn's Socialist-led cabinet: Horn believed that the cause of Hungarians abroad would be best served by developing cordial relations with the countries where they lived.

The center-right Fidesz government followed in office from 1998. Domestically, it wished to reserve membership in the nation only for those who shared its ideological views and by 2002 had made some alarmingly rightist statements. The four years between 1998 and 2002 also saw a short-term nationalistic revival when István Csurka's extreme right and revisionist party, MIÉP, won 14 mandates in parliament.

At the same time, the government institutionalized the protection of Hungarian minorities abroad and legally defined their status in a Status Law. The Status Law aimed at granting extensive rights – passport and citizenship – to Hungarians outside the borders. This caused vehement protest among the foreign governments concerned and the EU also expressed a negative opinion about it. Finally a watered-down version of the plan was accepted, granting only cultural and economic benefits to Hungarians abroad. Péter Medgyessy's Socialist government modified the law further, abolishing those parts that neighboring governments objected to most. In December 2004 a binding referendum was held about dual citizenship for ethnic Hungarians abroad, although more people voted for dual citizenship than against it, participation was too low to make the results valid.

Religion

Transition to democracy brought not only liberal minority policies but also religious freedom. Religion was generally disapproved of and discouraged under communism, but practice was not impossible. The changes in 1989 brought a short-lived increase in religious fervor. But by 2001, only 58% of the people declared themselves to be "believers" and only 15% of them attended church regularly. Most belonged to the Catholic Church, but the Reformed and Lutheran Churches also had a small following: 78% of the population identified with the Catholic, 15% with the Reformed, and 3% with the Lutheran Church, 1% of the population declared itself to belong to the fourth historical religion, Judaism. There is also a substantial Greek Catholic community (15%) and the rest of the population are either unaffiliated or belong to other Christian groups, Orthodox, Buddhist, or Islamic communities.

The appearance of religious freedom has seen a dramatic increase in the number of registered churches. To be registered, a religious body has to provide 100 signatures of its followers and any local court may then register the church. As a result there are about 150 registered churches in Hungary. Religious education is not part of the school curriculum, but students are allowed to register for extracurricular religious courses that members of the various churches teach in schools. All religious bodies are given the right to engage in extracurricular educational activities but the bulk of the task is carried out by the historic Churches.

Although historically the Hungarian state had close ties to Catholicism, there is no state religion in Hungary. Religious denominations are legally equal even if several factors undermine this in practice. The media law gave airtime on the public service-state channels to historical Churches, but not others. Amongst both the general population and government circles an attitude of suspicion prevails concerning the smaller newly established religions.

Relations with the Catholic Church are directed by the 1997 State Treaty with the Vatican. Critics claimed that the treaty discriminate positively in favor of the Catholic Church, but the conditions stipulated in the Treaty are also applied to other denominations. Thus, the state has agreed to return most property confiscated under communism. The state also ensures financial support of Church-run schools and universities, museums, and Church-owned social services. It allows for citizens to donate 1% of their income to religious communities and receive tax exemption. In addition, the state also devotes additional funds from tax revenues to religious bodies. Not everyone is satisfied with such extensive state support; of political parties, the Free Democrats question the scheme, believing that Churches should draw the cost of their operations from among their members. This is, however, difficult to achieve not only because of customary practice but also because the culture of making donations is absent in Hungary.

The relationship of politics and religion shows a division along party lines. If the Free Democrats are critical toward the state financing of churches, the right maintains close ties to the traditional churches, especially the Catholic Church. Originally the Catholic Church aligned itself with the Christian Democrats, but when they ceased to become an important force in politics churches switched their allegiance to the largest conservative party, Fidesz. Church involvement in politics is apparent through participation in collecting signatures for referenda or in support of the policy positions of the political right in church sermons.[42]

Conclusions

By all international standards, Hungary can be regarded as a consolidated democracy. In the first two decades after the regime change, there was no need for early elections, which substantially contributed to political stability. Hungary is also a country where governments are generally known to lose elections, which could be seen as a healthy sign of a functioning democracy. In the long run, the future of Hungary is closely tied to the EU. Frequent exchange programs and study-abroad programs speed up the process of intercultural learning, dialog and mutual understanding among university students and young and middle-aged professionals. However, as of 2009 Hungary is still in a sober mood of post-accession trauma. Politicians and opinion-makers still need to realize that the EU in itself is not the solution for Hungary but can be a framework for several solutions. People learned under the old regime that solutions come from outside and that they could not significantly contribute to their own fate. This passive role of the onlooker may be an obstacle to internal innovation.

Moreover, formal political stability has its costs. The choice for voters is increasingly limited, political parties lose elections but they do not disappear or flexibly transform themselves to satisfy their potential voters' needs. Even if parties are widely discredited, they simply do not vanish; rather, they seem to stay "forever." Voters at elections base their voting decision on the negative strategy of choosing the least bad alternative, which reflects the low and steadily declining reputation of the whole political elite. The inflexibility of the political regime in offering opportunities for new parties, the unwillingness of existing parties to ease the entry regulations for newcomers, and the deeply divided constituencies are all obstacles to further structural reform[43] and may be a recipe for the unexpected eruption of popular political protest.

Current Hungarian democracy reminds one of a "partyocracy," where democracy is largely reduced to the activities of political parties.[44] Due to the relative weakness of independent civil society (social movements, watchdog groups, NGOs, think tanks, trade unions, and the media), almost all democratic channels are subjects of increasing influence from, if not occupation by, the political parties. Even if people are sick of "partyocracy," they are still not strong enough to organize themselves collectively. The political regime has changed to a democracy but the political culture of passive individualism, which was characteristic feature of the post-1956 decades, seems to survive. This passive–negative, distrustful popular attitude to institutions, and the "colonization" of democracy by the dominant political parties, negatively influence the quality of democracy in Hungary.

Timeline 1989–2008

March 1989	Formation of Opposition Round Table
June–September 1989	National Round Table talks
23 October 1989	Proclamation of the third Hungarian Republic
March–April 1990	First free elections: center-right MDF election victory
September–October 1990	First free local elections
October 1990	Taxi-drivers' blockade
1994	Return to power of communist successor party (MSZP)
1995	Introduction of economic austerity package
1998	Election victory of center-right Fidesz
1999	NATO membership
2002	Election victory of center-left MSZP
2004	EU membership
2006	Governing party re-elected for the first time

September–October 2006	Violent clashes on streets between anti-government protesters and police
2008	First minority government (MSZP)

Fact sheet

Area	93,030 km[2a]
Population (July 2008 estimate)	9,930,915[b]
Major cities[c]	
Budapest (2007)	1,696,128
Debrecem	204,124
Miskolc	172,637
Szeged	164,883
Below the poverty line (2007)	15.9% of population[d]
Unemployment rate (2007 estimate)	7.3%[e]
GDP ***per capita*** (2007 estimate)	$19,000[f]
Higher education (2001)	9.4% of population[g]
Literacy rate (2003 estimate)	99.4% of population[h]

Notes:

[a] Including % of minorities over 10% of population. CIA, *The World Fact Book 2008*, at www.cia.gov/library/publications/the-world-factbook/ [accessed on 13 September 2008].

[b] CIA, *The World Fact Book 2008*.

[c] Hungary [City Population: Cities, Towns, Counties and Provinces, Statistics and Maps] 2007, available at: www.citypopulation.de/Hungary.html#Stadt_gross [accessed on 24 July 2007].

[d] UNDP, *Human Development Report 2007/2008*, at http://hdr.undp.org/en/media/HDR_20072008_EN_Complete.pdf [accessed on 13 September 2008].

[e] CIA, *The World Fact Book 2008*.

[f] CIA, *The World Fact Book 2008*.

[g] Census data 2001, at www.nepszamlalas.hu/hun/kotetek/18/tables/load1_24.html [accessed on 25 July, 2007].

[h] UNDP, *Human Development Report 2007/2008*.

Parties in the Hungarian parliament

Party	Deputies
Hungarian Socialist Party (MSZP)	189
Alliance of Young Democrats (Fidesz)	141
Christian Democratic People's Party (KDNP)	23
Alliance of Free Democrats (SZDSZ)	20
Hungarian Democratic Forum (MDF)	11
Independent	1

Source: "Magyar Országgyűlés," at www.parlament.hu [accessed on 24 July 2007].

Abbreviations

EKA	*Ellenzéki Kerekasztal*/Opposition Round Table
Fidesz	*Fiatal Demokraták Szövetsége*/Alliance of Young Democrats
FKGP	*Független Kisgazdapárt*/Independent Smallholders' Party
Jobbik	*Jobbik Magyarországért*/Movement For a Better Hungary
KDNP	*Kereszténydemokrata Néppárt*/Christian Democratic People's Party
MIÉP	*Magyar Igazság és Élet Pártja*/Party of Hungarian Justice and Life
MSZDP	*Magyar Szociáldemokrata Párt*/Hungarian Social Democratic Party
MSZP	*Magyar Szocialista Párt*/Hungarian Socialist Party
NKA	*Nemzeti Kerekasztal-tárgyalások*/National Round Table Talks
SZDSZ	*Szabad Demokraták Szövetsége*/Alliance of Free Democrats

Short biography of Árpád Göncz

Árpád Göncz (1922–) was the first president of the third Hungarian Republic. He served two terms as president between 1990 and 2000. While his activist approach to the office during his first term generated a few political controversies (e.g. exceeding his constitutional powers as commander-in chief, he ordered the military to avoid intervention during the taxi-drivers' blockade in the fall of 1990), by triggering some Supreme Court decisions, it also helped clarify constitutional ambiguities about the division of competencies between the various government institutions of the newly established democratic regime. Despite losing the constitutional battle, he remained active in politics, taking advantage of his most powerful constitutional tool, the right to speak out effectively on political questions in the media or parliament.

In 1990, Göncz was elected by the support of Conservative and Liberal fractions in parliament, while in 1995 he was re-elected by the support of Socialist and Liberal fractions. In his second term he became much less active in shaping internal politics and focused mostly on fulfilling his ceremonial duties. His popularity as a politician remained high throughout his terms and his conduct in office also won general respect and popularity for the presidency.

Due to his activity in the 1956 revolution Göncz spent five years in prison in 1958–63. In the 1980s, he was known as an author and literary translator of the works of numerous British and American authors. In 1988–90 he served as Chairman of the Hungarian Pen Club. In 1988, he was a funding member of the Alliance of Free Democrats. His daughter, Kinga Göncz, served as minister of social affairs (2004–6), and was Hungary's first female foreign minister (2006–9).

Notes

1. Cf. Paul Lendvai *Hungary: The Art of Survival* (London: I. B. Tauris, 1988).
2. For further details on Hungarian history, see Miklós Molnár and Anna Magyar, *A Concise History of Hungary* (Cambridge: Cambridge University Press 2001) and Paul Lendvai and Ann Major, *The Hungarians: A Thousand Years of Victory and Defeat* (Princeton, N.J.: Princeton University Press, 2004).

3. For a general overview, see Andrew C. Janos *The Politics of Backwardness in Hungary, 1825–1945* (Princeton, NJ: Princeton University Press, 1982).
4. Oscar Jászi *The Dissolution of the Habsburg Monarchy* (Chicago, Ill: University of Chicago Press, 1929).
5. For more details, see Peter F. Sugar (ed.) *Eastern European Nationalism in the Twentieth Century* (Washington, DC: The American University Press, 1995).
6. Béla Zhelitski, "Postwar Hungary, 1944–1946," in Norman Naimark and Leonid Gibianskii (eds.), *The Establishment of Communist Regimes in Eastern Europe, 1944–49* (Boulder, Colo.: Westview Press, 1997), pp. 73–92.
7. Charles Gati, *Hungary and the Soviet Bloc* (Durham, NC: Duke University Press, 1986).
8. Hannah Arendt, *The Origins of Totalitarianism* (Cleveland OH: Meridian Books) 1958; and Carl Friedrich and Zbigniew Brzezinski *Totalitarian Dictatorship and Autocracy* (Cambridge, Mass: Harvard University Press, 1956).
9. Bill Lomax, *Hungary, 1956* (London: Allison & Busby, 1976).
10. Paul E. Zinner, *Revolution in Hungary* (New York: Columbia University Press and Freeport, NY: Books for Libraries Press, 1962).
11. William F. Robinson, The *Pattern of Reform in Hungary: A Political, Economic and Cultural Analysis* (New York: Praeger, 1973).
12. William Shawcross, *Crime and Compromise: János Kádár and the Politics of Hungary since the Revolution* (London: Weidenfeld & Nicholson, 1974).
13. Jadwiga Staniszkis, *Poland's Self-Limiting Revolution* (Princeton, N.J.: Princeton University Press, 1984).
14. For detailed analyses see Rudolf L. Tőkés, *Hungary's Negotiated Revolution* (Cambridge: Cambridge University Press, 1996); and András Bozóki (ed.), *The Roundtable Talks of 1989: The Genesis of Hungarian Democracy.* (Budapest: CEU Press, 2002).
15. Patrick H. O'Neil, *Revolution from Within: The Hungarian Socialist Worker's Party and the Collapse of Communism* (Cheltenham: Edward Elgar, 1998).
16. Cf. József Böröcz "*Social Change by Fusion*," PhD dissertation (Budapest: MTA, 1992), mimeo; Hans-Joachim Lauth, "Informal Institutions and Democracy," *Democratization*, Vol, 7, No. 4 (2000), pp. 21–50.
17. Cf. Joseph Held, (ed.), *The Columbia History of Eastern Europe in the Twentieth Century* (New York: Columbia University Press, 1992); Joseph Rothschild, *Return to Diversity: A Political History of East-Central Europe Since World War II* (New York: Oxford University Press, 1993); and Grzegorz Ekiert, *The State Against Society: Political Crises and Their Aftermath in East-Central Europe* (Princeton, N.J.: Princeton University Press, 1996).
18. Archie Brown, *The Gorbachev Factor* (Oxford: Oxford University Press, 1996).
19. For more details on the conceptual difference, see Isaiah Berlin, "Two Concepts of Liberty," in Michael Sandel (ed.), *Liberalism and Its Critics* (New York: New York University Press, 1984), pp. 15–36.
20. See the minutes of the negotiations, in András Bozóki *et al.*, (eds.), *Kerekasztal-tárgylások 1989-ben* [Roundtable Talks in 1989] Vols. 1–4 (Budapest: Magvető 1999), and *Kerekasztal-tárgylások 1989-ben* [Roundtable Talks in 1989], Vols. 5–8 (Budapest: Új Mandátum, 1999–2000).
21. For the documents of the Gdańsk negotiations, see Anthony Kemp-Welch (ed.), *The Birth of Solidarity: The Gdańsk Negotiations, 1980* (New York: St. Martin's Press, 1983).

22. Especially influential was George (György) Konrád, *Antipolitics* (London: Methuen, 1984).
23. Lewis Coser, *The Functions of Social Conflict* (New York: Free Press, 1959); and Albert Hirschman, "Social Conflicts as Pillars of Democratic Market Society," *Political Theory*, Vol. 22 no. 2 (May 1994), pp. 203–18.
24. For more details, see András Körösényi, *Government and Politics in Hungary* (Budapest: CEU Press, 1999).
25. György Fábián and Imre László Kovács, *Voksok és mandátumok* [Votes and Mandates] (Budapest: Villányi Úti Könyvek, 1998), pp. 72–5.
26. András Bozóki, "The Hungarian Socialists: Technocratic Modernizationism or New Social Democracy," in A. Bozóki and John Ishiyama (eds.), *The Communist Successor Parties of Central and Eastern Europe* (Armonk, N.Y.: M.E. Sharpe, 2002), pp. 89–115.
27. György Csáki and Gábor Karsai (eds.), *Evolution of the Hungarian Economy 1848-2000. Hungary from Transition to Integration* (Boulder, Colo.: Social Science Monographs, 2001), pp. 336–96.
28. *Ibid.*, pp. 34–54.
29. Hungary, "Britannica Books of the Year, 1998–2006," *Encyclopædia Britannica Online* (28 August 2007), at www.britannica.com/eb/.
30. *Ibid.*
31. János Kornai, "Kávé és tea" [Coffee and Tea], *Népszabaság* (22 October 2007), at www.nol.hu.
32. Csáki and Karsai, *Evolution of the Hungarian Economy*, pp. 171–225.
33. *Ibid.*
34. Open Society Institute (OSI), *Monitoring the EU Accession Process: Corruption and Anti-Corruption Policy 2002: Country Reports* (Budapest and London: OSI 2003), pp. 268–72.
35. Zoltán Kovács, "Az ételt visszaküldik" [The Food Is To Be Sent Back], *Élet és Irodalom* (October 19 2007), at www.es.hu.
36. Zoltán Dövényi, "Kelet és nyugat között: Magyarország a nemzetközi vándolrás áramlataiban" [Between East and West: Hungary in the Flows of International Migration], Open University lecture (25 April 2007), at foldrajz.ttk.pte.hu/magyarorszag/letoltes/keletnyugat.ppt.
37. European Commission, "The Euromosaic study on Regional and Minority Language Use, Hungary" (28 August 2007), at ec.europa.eu/education/policies/lang/languages/langmin/euromosaic/hu_en.pdf.
38. Project on Ethnic Relations, "Parliamentary Representation of Minorities in Hungary. Legal and Political Issues" (25 May 2000), at www.per-usa.org/Reports/HungaryRep42501.pdf; Beáta Balogh, "Újra porondon a kisebbségek: A megoldást a parlamentbe jutás jelenti?" *Hírszerző* (26 August 2007, at www.hirszerzo.hu/).
39. Mária Neményi and Júlia Szalai (eds.), *Kisebbségek Kisebbsége: A magyarországi cigányok emberi és politikai jogai* (Budapest: UMK, 2005); András Bozóki and Barbara Bősze, *Migrants, Minorities, Belonging and Citizenship: The Case of Hungary* (Bergen: BRIC, 2004).
40. Lukács György Róbert, "Roma munkerő-piaci programok és környezetük," in Neményi and Szalai, *Kisebbségek Kisebbsége*, pp. 94–9.
41. Open Society Institute (OSI), "Monitoring the EU Accession Process: Minority Protection: An Assessment of Selected Policies in Candidate States," Vol 1

(Budapest and London: OSI, 2003), pp. 245–97; "Decade of Roma Inclusion 2005–2015" (1 September 2007), at www.romadecade.org/
42. Zsolt Enyedi and Joan O'Mahony, "Churches and the Consolidation of Democratic Culture: Difference and Convergence in the Czech Republic and Hungary," *Democratization*, Vol. 11, No. 4 (August 2004), pp. 171–91.
43. Cf. András Bozóki, *Politikai pluralizmus Magyarországon* [Political Pluralism in Hungary] (Budapest: Századvég, 2003); István Schlett, Csaba Gombár, András Bozóki *et al.*, *Merre tovább, Magyarország?* [Where to Go, Hungary?] (Budapest: Palatinus, 2008).
44. Cf. András Bozóki, "Partocracy and Reform," *Figyelő* (10 April, 2008).

Further reading

Andor, László. *Hungary on the Road to the European Union: Transition in Blue* (Westport, Conn.: Praeger, 2000)

Bátonyi, Gábor. *Hungary* (London: Routledge, 2009)

Böröcz, József. "'Fox and the Raven': The European Union and Hungary Renegotiate the Margins of 'Europe'," *Comparative Studies in Society and History*, Vol. 42, No. 4 (October 2000), pp. 847–75

Bozóki, András (ed.). *The Roundtable Talks of 1989: The Genesis of Hungarian Democracy* (Budapest and New York: Central European Union Press, 2002)

Bozóki, András, András Körösényi, and George Schöpflin (eds.). *Post-Communist Transition: Emerging Pluralism in Hungary* (London: Pinter and New York: St. Martin's Press, 1992)

Bozóki, András and and Eszter Simon. "Formal Institutions and Informal Politics in Hungary," in Gerd Meyer (ed.), *Formal Institutions and Informal Politics in Central and Eastern Europe: Hungary, Poland Russia, and Ukraine* (Opladen and Farmington Hills, Mich.: Barbara Budrich, 2006), pp. 14–94.

Enyedi, Zsolt. "The Role of Agency in Cleavage Formation" *European Journal of Political Research*, Vol. 44, No. 5 (27 July 2005) pp.697–720

Hanák, Péter and and Joseph Held. "Hungary on a Fixed Course: An Outline of Hungarian History," in Joseph Held (ed.), *The Columbia History of Eastern Europe in the Twentieth Century* (New York: Columbia University Press, 1992), pp. 164–227

Korkut, Umut. "The 2006 Hungarian Election: Economic Competitiveness versus Social Solidarity," *Parliamentary Affairs*, Vol. 60, No. 4 (6 August 2007), pp. 1–16.

Körösényi, András. *Government and Politics in Hungary* (Budapest and New York: Central European University Press, 1999)

Rainer, János. *Imre Nagy: A Biography* (London: I. B. Tauris, 2009)

Renwick, Alan. "Anti-Political or Just Anti-Communist? Varieties of Dissidence in East-Central Europe and Their Implications for the Development of Political Society," *East European Politics and Societies*, Vol. 20, No. 2 (2006), pp. 286–318

Romsics, Ignác. *Hungary in the Twentieth Century* (Budapest: Corvina & Osiris, 1999)

Schiemann, John W. *The Politics of Pact-Making: Hungary's Negotiated Transition to Democracy in Comparative Perspective* (New York: Palgrave Macmillan, 2005)

Tőkés, Rudolf L. *Hungary's Negotiated Revolution* (Cambridge: Cambridge University Press, 1996)

Part 4
Yugoslav Successor States

11

Slovenia since 1989

DANICA FINK-HAFNER

During the last twenty-five years, Slovenia has experienced deep social changes involving an economic and political transition from a socialist system, the creation of an independent state with a market economy, a liberal-democratic type of political system, favorable socio-economic trends as well as the successful integration of the new state into the world system and even into the EU regional political system. This former Yugoslav Republic, which took a risk by declaring its independence and seeking international recognition in 1991, presided over the EU in the first half of 2008. Slovenia's idiosyncratic success has resulted from various factors, with the key ones including relatively open borders to the West during the socialist regime including strong economic ties with West European countries, which contributed to lively economic and social modernization and a sounder socio-economic base than was found in many other post-socialist countries during the transition and the consolidation of a new regime; gradualism in social, economic, and political reforms; the very cautious taking of advice from international financial organizations; the relatively homogenous ethnic structure; and no substantial damage from the war in the Balkans in the 1990s.

Slovenia before 1989–90

The history of the Slovenian nation has usually been portrayed as the history of a relatively small, primarily culturally defined community living for a long time under a variety of larger, predominant nations in the framework of multinational states. Certain experiences living within the framework of the Habsburg Empire and the two Yugoslavias (1918–41 and 1945–91) influenced Slovenian society, politics, and culture. First settled as early as 250,000 BCE, Slovenia was incorporated into the Roman Empire around 10 BCE, and was invaded by Huns and Germanic tribes around 500 CE. The Duchy of Carantania flourished in the area which is today Slovenia from about 600 to roughly 1,000 CE, but in 1335 the region came under Habsburg rule. In spite of invasions by Ottoman Turks during 1408–15 and again during 1450–1550, Slovenia remained part of the Habsburg Empire from 1335 until 1918, with a brief interruption during 1809–13, when it was incorporated into the Illyrian province, a Napoleonic satellite state. A Slovenian political program was adopted on 20 April 1848, during the revolution which swept much of Europe. From 1918 to 1941, Slovenia was part of the Kingdom of Serbs, Croats, and Slovenes (renamed the Kingdom of Yugoslavia in October 1929), and was occupied by Germany and Italy during the Second World War. From 1945 until 1991, Slovenia was one of six constituent republics of socialist Yugoslavia.

In spite of the more recent socialist past, it was nineteenth-century politics which were revived to an important extent in the emergence of political cleavages during the transition (the division between the conservative–Christian democratic, liberal and social-democratic political clusters). Unlike all the other post-socialist countries joining the EU in 2004, Slovenia (then part of socialist Yugoslavia) distanced itself from Moscow in 1948 as well as from economic, military, and political alignments with the Eastern bloc. On the contrary, it participated in the creation and leadership of the Nonaligned Movement. While criticizing the Eastern bloc countries for not having a proper democracy, it developed its own socialist self-management system featuring the leading role of the Communist Party, while opening up its borders to the West.

More recent social developments which have directly contributed to the current characteristics of Slovenia are closely linked to the deep economic and political crisis of the Yugoslav socialist system in the 1980s and the conflicts arising from differences between the then-socialist Republic of Slovenia and other units of the Socialist Federated Republic of Yugoslavia (SFRY) over solutions to the Yugoslav economic and political crisis. The Republic of Slovenia, as the economically most developed federal unit, which also had very open borders to the West, together with the largest share of exports to the West (compared with the other federal units) had experienced a more lively change of values and political preferences during the 1980s. Oppositional civil society in the form of social movements (such as peace, ecological, gay and lesbian, feminist, for a different psychiatry,[1] writers' association) emerging on the basis of subcultural movements (especially punk) demanded the introduction of a democratic political system, while the economic elite started to favor market economy reforms. Political pressures stemming from opposition social movements were not only targeting the political elite in the Socialist Republic of Slovenia, but they were also indirectly or directly challenging the federal Yugoslav political and military elite. One of the biggest controversies at that time was the initiative launched by the Slovenian peace movement to legalize conscientious objection to military service in the Yugoslav army (compulsory at that time). This initiative, together with the heavy criticism in the oppositional political weekly magazine *Mladina* of the leading generals of the Yugoslav People's Army for their misuse of positions for private gain and the later advocacy of a territorial organization of the military (in the framework of socialist republics) sharpened frictions between Slovenia and Serbia. As a reaction to Serbian nationalism came the publication, in 1987, of a new Slovenian national program drawn up by a group of intellectuals associated with the *Nova revija* magazine. This only contributed further to provoking federal political and military criticism of the Slovenian political elite due to its alleged "softness" in tolerating oppositional movements; these frictions and mutual suspicions culminated in the subsequent military trial of Janez Janša (a member of the peace movement and one of *Mladina*'s leading journalists at the time) and three collaborators. Slovenians were outraged that the trial, held in Ljubljana, was conducted in the Serbo-Croatian language; this not only triggered the creation of a strong oppositional movement inspired by liberal-democratic values but also evoked a nationalist response. Both the economic and political transition had been taking place in a gradual, legalistic way. As noted in the chapter in this volume by Marko Attila Hoare, Slovenia did not take a lead in changing the character of the federal Yugoslav state. In fact, Slovenia (by adopting amendments to the constitution of the Republic of Slovenia during the 1989–90 period) merely reacted to the 1988 amendments to the federal Yugoslav constitution (introducing even more centralization), and to the Serbian constitution adopted in 1990.[2] By 1990, the market economy as well as political pluralism had become the basis of a new social and political system in Slovenia at a time when, in the rest of socialist Yugoslavia, political elites could not agree either on transitional changes in the whole federal state or on an asymmetrical federation which would have allowed Slovenia to continue with its systemic changes within the framework of the federal state (as proposed by the Slovenian political elite). Since such a political agreement could not be achieved, Slovenia continued toward its independence (in concert with Croatia). That decision was legitimated by a plebiscite held on 23 December 1990 in which 88.2% of all Slovenian voters voted for independence. Still, it was only possible to fully implement the country's independence after a ten-day war and a period of several months of "cooling-off" (as demanded by the EC). In this historical context, Slovenia and Croatia agreed to maintain country borders as of 25 June 1991. However, since the whole border was not marked in detail in the context of the former Yugoslavia, disagreement about sections of it remains an important populist issue in both countries. Since at the end of 2008 Slovenia demanded that Croatia exclude all the documents determining the (otherwise not yet agreed) border from Croatia's official documentation presented to the European Commission as part of the full EU membership negotiations, this has been presented to the Croatian public as Slovenia blocking Croatia's joining the EU, while at the same time not revealing serious Commission criticism concerning Croatia's failure to fulfil EU membership preconditions in the field of judiciary, public administration, the fight against corruption and organized crime, the promotion of minority rights, refugee return, the pursuit of war criminals, and ICTY access to documents.[3]

Institutional transformation and constitutional and legislative transitions

Two major transformations have taken place along with the accompanying constitutional and legislative transitions. The first included the building of a new national socio-political system within the framework of the new independent state. The second involved bringing about the national institutional system's and actors' adaptation to Slovenia's integration with the EU. As for the first-mentioned institutional transformation, Slovenia can serve as a "textbook example" not only in terms of favorable pre-conditions and factors working in favor of a gradual and successful transition to a democracy and successful economic developments, but also in terms of the main political actors' decisions. These include a decision on a legalistic approach to the formation of a new system and a new state, opting for a parliamentary system and proportional electoral rules.

The legislative transition was gradual, starting in 1988 after a series of events in Belgrade which were perceived as a threat to Slovenia. The key events involved the federal Military Council (a mixed party and army body) meeting in Belgrade where it defined the situation in Slovenia as a special war against the Yugoslav People's Army and discussed the possibility of a military intervention in Slovenia; a secret session of the presidency of the League of Communists of Yugoslavia which discussed the possibility of repressing the opposition in Slovenia; the election of Milošević as president of the Central Committee of the League of Communists of Serbia; the arrest of Janez Janša and (together with Ivan Borštner, Franci Zavrl and David Tasić) his indictment by the military prosecutor; and the proposal by the federal government of a 133% increase in the federal budget for 1989. The Slovenian authorities first reacted to threats of the diminishing position of republics within socialist Yugoslavia by adopting the 1988 amendments to the Constitution of the Socialist Republic of Slovenia that obliged the Republican Assembly to protect the constitutional position of the Republic (according to the 1974 federal and republics' constitutions, under which the republics had been granted important political, cultural, and legislative autonomies) when and if the federal organs interfered with decisions contrary to their constitutionally (Yugoslav) regulated competencies. The Slovenian Assembly proclaimed the right to nullify federal decisions and adopted a provision that a state of emergency could not be decreed without its own agreement. The amendments which followed in the 1988–90 period were adopted not only to allow careful progression in the building of the new economic and political system, but also in order to guarantee that the transition had sound bases and to minimize any possible external challenges to its validity. Even when the 96th amendment was adopted in October 1990, asserting the priority of Slovenian law over federal law, the continuation of federal law was allowed in fields where the establishment of a new Slovenian legal order was not yet in place (provided that it was not in conflict with laws in the Republic).

The new set of politically pluralist elites (also involving part of the successfully transformed old elite) opted for a parliamentary constitutional system and proportional electoral rules. Due to the power relations between the transformed parts of the old political elites and newly emerging oppositional elites, only a limited and less radical practice of lustration or purging of former communists took place in Slovenia.[4] At the same time, however, the new constitutional provisions of 1991 limited the role of the president of the Republic. Specifically, at the time the new Constitution was being written, the most popular politician with a realistic chance of being elected president was Milan Kučan – a former president of the transformed League of Communists of Slovenia. Although the president of the Republic is elected directly, it is a largely ceremonial post which confers on its holder the merely formal title of commander-in-chief of the Armed Forces; the president also proposes candidates for some important institutional roles in the parliament and protocol duties. The period of Milan Kučan's two presidential mandates and the long-term prime ministership of Janez Drnovšek (president of the center-left Liberal Democracy of Slovenia) did not see any conflicts between the two officeholders. But this changed after Janez Janša assumed the office of prime minister in November 2004, and the years 2004–7 saw a conflict between Janša's center-right government (Janša, from the beginning of the 1990s, was a leader of the anti-communist Social Democratic Party of Slovenia that in 2003 was renamed the Slovenian Democratic party) and Janez Drnovšek (elected president for the 2002–7 mandate). Drnovšek had temporarily taken on the role of oppositional critic at a time when the center-left parties were still coping with their big 2004 electoral loss. By doing so, he triggered a general discussion of the role of the president in the national political system, which also continued in the context of some relatively bold decisions made by President Danilo Türk (presidential candidate of the center-left) elected at the 2007 presidential elections – especially his denial of support for several candidates proposed to hold the position of ambassador by the outgoing center-right government in the autumn of 2008. So far, the legal interpretation of very limited presidential powers has prevailed.

Given the relatively weak powers granted to the president, Slovenian political elites – like the political elites of most Central European post-socialist countries – stressed the role of the national parliament. Besides the lower chamber (the National Assembly) the Slovenian Constitution of 1991 also established an upper chamber (the National Council) based on a mixture of representation of local communities (22 seats) and some elements of corporatism (18 seats are reserved for functional representation, the largest share being reserved for the representatives of employers' organizations and trade unions). In practice (apart from some instances when it has asked the National Assembly to reconsider a piece of legislation) the National Council does not play an important part in law-making. That is why the Slovenian parliamentary system is described as a "one-and-a-half" system, and why there have been some publicly expressed doubts about the need to keep it (especially on the part of the center-right Slovenian Democratic Party) or to transform it into a chamber representing "Slovenian regions in the making."[5]

Already in the mid-1990s, the Slovenian political system began to adapt to EU standards. At first this involved adaptation to EU policy-making procedures (negotiations with the EU and adoption of the *acquis* in the Slovenian legal system). Later, the national political system had to adapt to a new role – taking part in EU policy-making. Europeanization[6] in Slovenia not only has been reflected in the adoption of EU law in the pre-accession stage but has increasingly affected institutional settings as well as the functioning of the national political system. As in other accession countries, it was the executive which started to adapt by creating new institutions and procedures, as well as by adding EU-linked tasks to the national government and public administration. European integration also facilitated institutional changes to Slovenia's political system: (a) the amendment to the Constitution of 7 March 2003 (amending Articles 47 and 68 of the Slovenian Constitution of 1991) allowing the National Assembly to transfer the implementation of some sovereign rights of Slovenia to international organizations on the basis of an international agreement ratified by the Slovenian parliament, provided these international organizations were based on the respect of human rights and freedoms, democracy and the principles of the rule of law (Article 3a of the Constitutional Law); and (b) the Law on Cooperation between the National Assembly and the Government on EU Matters, which was based on the above constitutional amendment and on certain Scandinavian solutions.

The National Assembly first created a new parliamentary body (for European affairs) and adapted statutory rules in order to enhance adoption of the *acquis* in national law. Only later (in preparation for its role in full Slovenian EU membership) did it face a more radical adaptation. On the basis of the change in the national legal system as well as the adaptation of its statutory rules, the National Assembly shifted the execution of some of its law-making to the EU and to the national executive.[7] A special Law on Collaboration between the National Assembly and Government on European Union Matters (adopted on 25 March 2004) defines the government as an actor which represents and asserts positions on behalf of the Republic of Slovenia in EU institutions. The first years of Slovenia's full EU membership have shown that, in spite of a relatively important formal role of the National Assembly, the practice of managing EU affairs reflects the growing power and secrecy of governmental activities in EU policy-making when compared to the transparency and important role of the National Assembly during Slovenia's accession negotiations (the policy-taking stage). It seems that some warnings that full EU membership might bring about the "import of the EU's democratic deficit" do have some validity, not only in the weakening of the practical role of parliament, but also in the decline in the inclusion of interest groups (either through discussing EU matters in parliamentary working bodies or their participation in the preparation of Slovenian negotiating positions in the Slovenian executive).

Unlike the National Assembly, political parties do not seem to be strongly affected by the Europeanization processes. The Liberal Democracy of Slovenia (linked with the European Liberal Democrats, ELDR) and the predecessor of the Social Democrats (linked to the Party of European Socialists, PES) gained associate member status during the 1990s, while the Slovenian Democratic Party (linked to the European People's Party, EPP), the Slovenian People's Party (linked to EPP), New Slovenia (also linked to EPP), and the Youth Party of Slovenia (SMS), later linked with the European Federation of Green Parties/ European Greens (EFGP/EG) followed the trend at the beginning of the first decade of the twenty-first century. While the majority of Slovenian parties which are members of their European counterparts incorporated some of their general orientations or values into their party manifestos, most of them have introduced no organizational party changes or they have been quite minor.[8] Still, in the post-accession period Slovenian MEPs from all parties have occasionally used the EU arena to influence domestic policy issues.

Politics and governance

There were some oppositional social movements which applied critical pressure to the Slovenian political elite to allow a more liberal public space during the 1980s. While oppositional civil society was one of the main sources of the newly emerging political opposition (the first oppositional political organization was established in 1988), a cluster of oppositional movements and "proto parties" either ceased to exist or were transformed into more institutionalized political parties or into various interest groups such as NGOs after the first free elections. The further democratization and consolidation of democracy were more based on: (a) an interest group system – partly transformed civil society organizations already existing within the socialist system and partly newly developing interest groups; (b) some remains of socialist-type corporatism involving not only functional representation in the self-management and delegate system but also the systemic role of trade unions and the employers' organization (the Slovenian Chamber of Commerce even had the right to initiate new legislation under the old system); and, more than anything else, (c) the role of a newly developed and still very dynamic party system.

Given the institutional setting of the proportional electoral system (at first including only a three-mandate parliamentary threshold and, since 2004, a 4% threshold) and the rules for converting the percentage of votes garnered into a percentage of seats in the Assembly, the Slovenian party system has remained relatively fragmented (institutional rules encourage political parties to compete individually and create coalitions only after the elections) and open to the entry of new small parties (table 11.1). Since 1992, seven–eight parties have gained parliamentary seats in the elections. As the party system was maturing, parties gaining support close to 30% or more began after 2000 to change certain characteristics of the party system (the Liberal Democracy of

Table 11.1 Results of parliamentary elections in Slovenia, 1990–2008

Party		1990[a]	1992[b]	1996[b]	2000[c]	2004	2008
Liberal Democratic Party (LDP); since 1994 Liberal Democracy of Slovenia (LDS)	no. of votes	156,843	278,851	288,783	390,797	220,848	54,771
	% of votes	14.49	23.46	27.01	36.21	22.80	5.21
	no. of seats	12	22	25	34	23	5
	% of seats	15	24.44	27.77	37.77	25.55	5.56
Social Democratic Party (SDP), renamed Slovenian Democratic Party (SDP)	no. of votes	79,951	39,675	172,470	170,541	281,710	307,735
	% of votes	7.39	3.34	16.13	15.80	29.08	29.26
	no. of seats	6	4	16	14	29	28
	% of seats	7.5	4.44	17.77	15.56	32.22	31.1
United List of Social Democrats (ULSD) renamed Social Democrats	no. of votes	186,928	161,349	96,597	130,268	98,527	320,248
	% of votes	17.28	13.58	9.03	12.07	10.17	30.45
	no. of seats	14	14	9	11	10	29
	% of seats	17.5	15.56	10	12.22	11.11	32.2
Slovenian Christian Democrats (SCD)	no. of votes	140,403	172,424	102,852			
	% of votes	12.98	14.51	9.62			
	no. of seats	11	15	10			
	% of seats	13.8	16.66	11.11			
Slovenian People's Party[a] (SPP)	no. of votes	135,808	103,300	207,186	102,817	66,032	54,809[a]
	% of votes	12.55	8.69	19.38	9.53	6.82	5.21
	no. of seats	11	10	19	9	7	5
	% of seats	13.8	11.11	21.11	10	7.78	5.56
New Slovenia–Christian People's Party (NSi)	no. of votes				94,661	88,073	35,774
	% of votes				8.76	9.09	3.40
	no. of seats				8	9	
	% of seats				8.89	10	
Slovenian National Party (SNP)	no. of votes		119,091	34,422	47,251	60,750	56,832
	% of votes		10.02	3.22	4.38	6.27	5.40
	no. of seats		12	4	4	6	5
	% of seats		13.33	4.44	4.44	6.65	5.56
The Greens of Slovenia (GS)	no. of votes	95,640	44,019	18,853	9,712	6,703	5,367
	% of votes	8.84	3.70	1.76	0.90	0.69	0.51
	no. of seats	8	5				
	% of seats	10	5.56				
Democratic Party of Pensioners (DeSUS)	no. of votes			46,152	55,696	39,150	78,353
	% of votes			4.32	5.16	4.04	7.45
	no. of seats			5	4	4	7
	% of seats			5.56	4.44	4.44	7.78
Party For Real	no. of votes						98,526
	% of votes						9.37
	no. of seats						9
	% of seats						10.0
Democratic Party (DP)	no. of votes	102,931	59,487	28,624	8,102	2,670	
	% of votes	9.51	5.01	2.68	0.75	0.28	
	no. of seats	8	6				
	% of seats	10	6.67				

Table 11.1 (cont.)

Party		1990[a]	1992[b]	1996[b]	2000[c]	2004	2008
Party of the Youth	no. of votes				46,719	20,174	54,809[a]
	% of votes				4.33	2.08	5.21
	no. of seats				4		0
	% of seats				4.44		
Slovenian Craftmen's Party (SCP)	no. of votes	38,269					
	% of votes	3.54					
	no. of seats	3					
	% of seats	3.8					
Socialist Alliance of the Working People (SAWP)	no. of votes	58,082	32,696				
	% of votes	5.37	2.75				
	no. of seats	5					
	% of seats	6.3					

Notes:
[a] On 15 April 2000, the Slovenian People's Party and the Slovenian Christian Democrats united in a new party, the SPP+SCD – Slovenian People's Party. Just before the 2000 parliamentary elections a group, mostly from the former SCD, left the party and competed at the elections as a new party, New Slovenia. At the 2008 national elections, the Slovenian People's Party and the Party of the Youth competed together, but no Party of the Youth candidate actually gained any parliamentary seats after the joint lists successfully entered parliament.
(a) Parliamentary elections in April 1990, Socio-political Chamber, proportional system, number of seats: 80 (78 for parties, plus 2 for the representatives of (Italian, Hungarian) national minorities. (b) Parliamentary elections in December 1992 and November 1996, National Assembly, proportional system (d'Hondt system), number of seats: 90 (88 for parties, plus 2 for representatives of (Italian, Hungarian) national minorities).
(c) Parliamentary elections in October 2000, partial change of the electoral system: introduction of a 4% threshold and the Droop formula.
Sources: Uradni list Republike Slovenije: 17/90; 60/92; 65/96; 98/2000, compiled by Alenka Krašovec and Tomaž Boh, in Danica Fink-Hafner and Tomaž Boh (eds.), *Parlamentarne volitve 2000* (Ljubljana: Fakulteta za družbene vede, 2002).

Slovenia's gain of 36.21% of the votes and 37.77% of the seats in 2000 has so far not been matched, though). In this context, ideologically relatively heterogeneous government coalitions began to be replaced by more ideologically coherent coalitions. The center-right government (2004–8) led by the Slovenian Democratic Party (having received 29.08% of the votes and 32.22% of the seats in 2004) was replaced by the center-left government led by the Social Democrats in 2008 (having received 30.45% of the votes and 32.2% of the seats). The biggest oppositional party gain of 29.26% of the votes and 31.1% of the seats at the 2008 national elections (the Slovenian Democratic Party) hints at a continuation of this new pattern of party competition in the future.

The typical European "ideological rainbow" without strong extremes on the left or right is present, currently ranging from the Liberal Democracy, the Social Democrats, and the Party For Real–New Politics (*Zares*) on the center-left with the Slovenian Democratic Party, the People's Party and the New Slovenia–Christian Democratic Party on the center-right. The Slovenian National Party, and especially its individual politicians, embrace a leftist evaluation of events and actors in the Second World War including the role of the Partisans, and are extremely critical of the Catholic Church, while at the same time espousing nationalism and extreme right positions concerning social minorities. Party competition is basically bi-polar, involving center-left and center-right clusters of parties. Among the main cleavages already rooted in the nineteenth century is the liberal–conservative cleavage, which is reflected above all in differences concerning the status and influence of the Catholic Church. More recent history provides for additional cleavages related to opposing interpretations of the Second World War, the socialist system, and the role of the communist party. The center-right parties stress the misuse of communist power in the creation of a revolutionary system even during the Second World War, the post-war massacres among the opponents of the socialist regime immediately after 1945, and the anti-democratic character of the socialist regime; by contrast, the center-left parties stress that the Second World War cannot be interpreted differently from the way it is in other countries, stressing that the war was a struggle between Nazism and Fascism on one side, and anti-fascists on the other. Within that framework, they are very critical of the collaboration of leading high-ranking Catholic clergymen with the occupation forces and are strongly against their rehabilitation (especially Bishop Gregor Rožman, who has been accused of collaboration with Axis occupation authorities). They do not agree with the center-right parties in their stress on traditional values related to the family, the social roles of women, and conservative views on a variety of social minorities and their rights. Since most citizens expect a relatively strong role of the state in social policies, and strong trade unions fought against liberalization, the conservative political orientation of the Slovenian Democratic Party has become much milder as the Janša's government's term has continued.

Among the parliamentary parties represented in parliament throughout the 1992–2008 period only the Slovenian National Party has never been in any coalition governments, yet it has succeeded in winning electoral support (among other ways) by employing a populist critique of all the other parties. Similarly, a new political party (The Party For Real–New Politics, *Zares*, see above) was also established on the basis of criticism of the predominant party politics about a year before the national elections, and gained up to 10% of the votes at the 2008 national elections, the first elections in which it competed. In general, Slovenian voters have been very critical of political parties – the political institutions with the least trust in the Slovenian political system. Although since 1990 some parties have occasionally gained a more significant share of votes, coalition governments have been ideologically mixed most of the time. With the exception of the 1990 and 2004 elections, the governments created have been led by the center-left Liberal Democracy of

Slovenia (Janez Drnovšek being its president and the Slovenian prime minister). While the first (1990) government coalition included former anti-regime political parties, it was ideologically relatively heterogeneous. That is why it lasted for only a short period; furthermore, many of the newly established parties at that time subsequently split into left and right streams with various degrees of electoral success. The second center-right coalition built directly on the basis of election results (the 2004–8 mandate) represented center-right parties from the Slovenian ideological spectrum as well as the small center-left Democratic Party of Pensioners (DeSUS) – in order to ensure a parliamentary majority. The 2008 electoral result also represented a milestone in the consolidation of the party system – the first democratically elected government led by a successor to the reformed League of Communists named Social Democrats (Socialni demokrati, SDK).

Among the constants of political developments in Slovenia several issues have involved critical relationships between political parties and other political institutions (especially the public administration), on the one hand, and the mass media, on the other. Since the transition period, the question of whether the mass media in Slovenia are pluralist enough (implying that they are too supportive of those transformed political parties with roots in the old regime) has remained on the agenda. The center-right political actors who emerged in opposition to the old regime have argued that the mass media have been ideologically unbalanced (too center-left oriented) and, when in power have tried to employ a variety of instruments including a special fund for pluralization of the mass media to "correct" the situation. This was true particularly at the beginning of the 2004–8 term, when they interfered in the mass media's cadre policy and ownership structure. The recently created center-left government has made the depoliticization of the mass media one of its priorities. Media experts have shown that the early media deregulation and liberalization in Slovenia were accompanied by privatization in the process of democratization, although the state has continued to be a major media shareholder. Since journalists and media companies' employees did not retain ownership and control of the media, as was possible according to the Slovenian media privatization model (they sold their shares when their value increased), they have become even more vulnerable to political pressures as well as to pressures from advertizers.[9] Protests by journalists (especially intense and internationalized during 2007) served to challenge the legitimacy of political pressures on the mass media, but at the same time a growing segment of the newly emerging economic elite is taking on an ever bigger role.

When looking at party–state relations it should be noted that the institutionalization of the young party universe in Slovenia, as in other post-socialist systems, has been relatively weak, and the socialist legacy of the strong role of politics in relation to other social spheres has persisted. There are at least three important aspects to these relationships. First, in the context of the slow privatization and the relatively limited party membership (only around 5% of

Slovenian citizens are members of political parties), parties agreed early on to legalize the state financing of political parties. Second, socialist legacies have also persisted in politico-administrative relations: politico-ideological change in power has also been accompanied by a change in personnel. Third, political parties in government have tended to treat the ministerial fields as their "feudal territories" and have not remained immune from clientelistic relations, occasionally being exposed by the mass media. Still, various data including the Freedom House ranking have shown that the level of corruption in Slovenia is not very high. According to a longitudinal Slovenian public opinion survey, fewer than 30% of Slovenian citizens believe that corruption is a big problem. The most efficient actors in fighting corruption are perceived to be the mass media and the National Anti-Corruption Commission. As declared in public opinion surveys in the 2002–6 period, corruption related to state institutions has been personally experienced by around 6% of those surveyed in the case of police procedures and a similar proportion in relation to procedures at the local community level. The biggest corruption problem seems to be the problematic health care reform, including privatization – some 14.5% of those surveyed in the 2002–6 period declared that they had personal experience with corruption when they tried to see a physician.

As in the case of corruption, where Slovenians are in the middle of a transformation and the partial persistence of regarding corruption as part of social normality is still widespread, in other aspects of political culture we can also see a mixture of several value streams – traditional, modern, as well as some postmodern. Sociological analysis[10] has revealed inconsistencies in the transformation of political culture in Slovenia. Politically relevant attitudes have been changing gradually and the emergence of broad support for the democratic political system during the transition period (the end of the 1980s and the beginning of the 1990s) has not been paralleled by other important shifts in values and attitudes. This is especially the case with ethnocentrism and xenophobia. In fact, the democratization processes did not exclude the coexistence of general support for democratic rules and the endorsement of discriminatory measures toward ethnic and other minorities. At least partially, political parties are tied to important segments of voters they can count on when playing the nationalist card on some policy issues: as the 2004 parliamentary election campaign showed, mobilization regarding these issues in the context of a low turnout of more liberal voters can bring about an important difference in election results.

Slovenian patterns of political participation include a mixture of old (traditional subordinate political culture pattern involving participation at elections as a citizen's duty), modernized collective participation in interest group activities, and new, more individualized, organizationally untied activities related to specific issues, accompanied by a not (yet) very openly expressed new political individualism and protest potential among youth. The only politician who has so far sensed this change and challenged the predominant type of politics is Janez Drnovšek. In 2006, he (at that time the acting president of the Republic) attracted attention as the founder of a new social movement (*Gibanje za pravičnost in razvoj*, Movement for Justice and Development). This movement has espoused new views beyond conventional politics and beyond strict national borders. The Movement's main activities are based on one key goal – to "make the world a better place." Its more specific political value orientations include ecology, conflict resolution, a decent life for everyone, a more just world order, opposing violence in all forms, the better treatment of animals, elevating humanity's level of consciousness, and "preventing our decline due to rising natural, religious and social inequalities." In just a short period of time the Movement has become very popular. After criticism of Janša's government was posted on the Movement's homepage (signed by Janez Drnovšek, albeit as a private individual), his dual political role as president of the Republic and as leader of this Movement was heavily criticized by the main governmental parties and some members of the public, who argued that the dividing line between Drnovšek's activities as a statesman and his activities as leader of the Movement was unclear. This duality ended when Drnovšek resigned his leadership position in the Movement. On 15 April 2007 Stane Pejovnik was elected president of the Movement (officially registered as a voluntary citizens' association, *Združenje Gibanje za pravičnost in razvoj*, on 6 March 2006). With Drnovšek's death on 23 February 2008 the Movement lost its public visibility, although it has retained his philosophy. Some of its ideas have also found their place in the newly established (in 2007) party "Party For Real–New Politics" (*Zares*) led by Janez Drnovšek's former close collaborator Gregor Golobič. Among them are criticism of the older parliamentary political parties' shallow politics, a new type of politics (transparent, inclusive, self-restricting) involving active citizenship, civil society, and to a limited extent also internationally relevant policies (primarily related to ecology). The party scored a relatively big success at the 2008 parliamentary elections, winning 9.37% of the votes and 10% of the parliamentary seats as well as joining the center-left coalition government.

Controversial policy issues

The continuous process of transition and democratic consolidation in favorable socio-economic preconditions and the conservative change of social/state ownership have allowed gradualism in the pursuit of some big reforms in the fields of social policy, health care and pension reform. A gradual and very slow, three-stage privatization process, including a mass privatization in the first stage, gave not only a rather important role to politics due to a continuously significant share of state property and reluctance toward dealings with foreign investors,[11] but also a rather moderate change in the social structure. According to the official Slovenian statistics based on Eurostat methodology, inequality of income distribution has remained among the lowest in the EU and the proportion of inhabitants living below the poverty line is comparatively low – to an important extent also due to a continuity of social transfers. Criminality has not been high, although there has been growth in some internationally linked illegal activities (people and drug smuggling). Still, in spite of being a mainly non-problematic and quite a safe country, Slovenia has had several persistent ideologically and politically important issues on its agenda.[12] The key big political themes have included the interpretation of the Second World War and the socialist regime, political control of the mass media (as mentioned on p. 245), the treatment of some interethnic issues linked to xenophobia and nationalist sentiments, privatization and denationalization affairs as well as Church–State relations.

Education has been one of the most fragile political and policy fields, and there has been controversy about history curricula and textbook reform. Rewriting the earlier textbooks for use in a pluralist Slovenia has reflected the left–right cleavage in Slovenian society, especially visible in controversies on treating certain figures and events in the Second World War, especially the role of anti-communist forces (including some leading clergymen from the Catholic Church), and the massacres perpetrated by the communists after the war. Charges of genocide pressed against Mitja Ribičič (a high-ranking officer of the secret police *Odbor za zaščito naroda, OZNA*) during the center-right government term (2005–6) before the court in Ljubljana (at least 217 unlawful civilian killings in the spring of 1945) has shown the liveliness of that cleavage. After Ribičič's appeal at the Higher Court the process was halted for lack of evidence. Among those policy issues which have proven especially controversial are policies related to social minorities (refugees from the Yugoslav war zone, "the erased" (see below), Roma, women, homosexuals). During the transition to a democracy and the process of gaining independence in Slovenia nationalism was predominantly portrayed as "defensive"; it gained a less polite face during the first half of the 1990s when the war raging in Croatia and Bosnia-Herzegovina brought a large number of refugees from other former socialist republics (some from Croatia, most from Bosnia-Herzegovina).[13] The Slovenian policy on refugees reflected a gap between the democratic and human rights standards, as defined in the new Slovenian constitution of 1991, and practical measures when referenced to international authorities and standards. The still influential remains of nationalism are visible in the treatment of a special group of people who lived in the territory of Slovenia at the time of the country's independence, but did not apply for Slovenian citizenship by the legally defined deadline. While more than 170,000 individuals gained citizenship without having to relinquish their previous citizenship, the status of those who did not apply in time vanished overnight: they were erased from the register of permanent inhabitants of Slovenia in a controversial procedure, even though they had been living in the country for a long time. This "erasure" has remained controversial up to the time of writing. Moreover, although the policy regarding this group has so far been amended several times, this has been challenged by the actions of political parties supporting extreme right attitudes which demanded a referendum on implementing the revised law of 2003 and even misused it in pre-election struggles in 2004 on behalf of the center-right parties. The 2004–8 center-right government was accused of maneuvering around the Constitutional Court of the Republic of Slovenia's ruling of 4 March 2003 by accepting a proposal to make changes to the constitutional law[14] which were too restrictive to be able to gain the prescribed two-thirds parliamentary majority. The new center-left government appointed on 21 November 2008 has put respect of the Constitutional Court's ruling among its priorities. After Katarina Kresal, leader of Liberal Democracy of Slovenia, took over at the Ministry of the Interior, the number of the "erased" has been double-checked and on 23 February 2009 additional decrees began to be issued to those who had already sorted out their status (having already gained the right to residence or citizenship). For that reason and by stressing the expected costs for Slovenia's budget of possible demands for financial compensation by the "erased," the opposition, led by Janez Jansa's Democratic Party, started its interpelation on 23 February, but due to the governing coalition support did not succeed.

Many controversies have been directly or indirectly related to the agenda of the Catholic Church. In education there have been especially persistent controversies about religion (including religious instruction in schools), in the fields of defense and police (the introduction of clergymen paid by the state to take care of patients in hospitals, soldiers, police force members and their family), the social role of women, and issues related to demographic policy (such as the Catholic Church's desire to link women primarily to their families, especially their children, and to eliminate the legal possibility of abortion). What seems to have created an aversion to the Catholic Church more recently has been the return of property confiscated after 1945 (without imposing on the Church an obligation to pay taxes even though the state is paying for clergymen's pensions). Three state properties on the Lake Bled island were granted to the Catholic Church as well as a forty-five-year free lease of the island at the very end of the center-right government's term, in spite of a controversial Constitutional Court ruling of 2007 and without parliamentary approval. There were also the Church's growing investments in various social subfields (especially education, mass media, economic and financial organizations) while at the same time it was revealed as a morally double-standard institution (especially pedophile affairs; internal Catholic Church dispute over the investment into T3, a TV network making money especially by offering pornographic programs; and a delayed implementation of the Slovenian Bishops' Conference decision on selling Maribor organizational units' share in T3). The newly elected center-left government stressed the need to respect the constitutional division between the Church and the State as well as to show more respect for equality among Churches and religions in Slovenia – leaving the space for an interpretation that its policy will lead toward a decline in the Catholic Church's monopoly.

Apart from these highly politicized issues, there have been others demonstrating first of all the mixture of traditional, modern, and post-modern values in Slovenian society. In the case of homosexuals, policy change has only been very slow and limited (Slovenia has a law on the registration of same-sex couples, but they are not given all the rights of heterosexual couples as regulated in the family law). The Constitutional Court of the RS unanimously ruled (concerning the case presented on behalf of Mitja Blažic and Viki Kern) that the National Assembly needed to correct the law on registration of the same-sex partner community within six months, so that the rules regarding inheritance between same-sex partners would be the same as in the case of married couples (currently in Slovenia such partners may only be heterosexual).[15] The Constitutional Court ruling has been interpreted as paving the way for equalization of other rights as well. On the contrary, the still stubborn sexism[16] shown in social values, social positions, and the roles of women has not only been limited by the national gender equality legislation, but has recently begun to be guided by the EU law based on the gender mainstreaming principle and monitored by European institutions.

Conclusions

Slovenia is a success story when compared to other post-socialist countries. Still, it is a society in transition with social, economic, and political problems. When compared internationally, in many social and political aspects the country finds itself between the richest and most consolidated democracies in the world (the so-called "First World") on one hand and the former socialist world (the "Second World") on the other. Among the still very important values are social equality and an expectation that the state should provide the minimal preconditions for a decent life for each citizen. When looking at foreign examples the most common ideal is a "Scandinavian model" combining capitalism, democracy, and a social state (the latter ideal was even included in the 1992 Constitution). In spite of the fact that Slovenia has been developing into an ever-more open society (including quite common travel abroad and a rather broad spread of new technologies among households), for Slovenians living in Slovenia with a reasonably good living standard has remained so important that it has led toward a positive net migration (immigration is bigger than emigration). It remains to be seen to what extent the delayed impact of the 2008 world economic crisis will impact Slovenia's economic, social, and political development.

Timeline 1988–2008

1988–90	Amendments to Slovenian Constitution of 1974 gradually introduce new economic and political system and at end also precedence of Slovenian law over federal law

April 1990	Election of non-communist government
25 June 1991	Slovenian National Assembly proclaims "Declaration of Independence and the Basic Constitutional Charter on the Autonomy and Independence of the Republic of Slovenia"
October 1991	Last Yugoslav People's Army troops leave Slovenia
23 December 1991	New "Slovenian Constitution" adopted Slovenia's admission to OSCE
15 January 1992	EC countries officially recognize Republic of Slovenia
13 April 1992	Diplomatic relations between Republic of Slovenia and EC established
May 1992	Slovenia's admission to UN
5 April 1993	"Cooperation Agreement between the European Community and the Republic of Slovenia" signed
1 September 1993	"Cooperation Agreement" comes into force
7 December 1993	Pursuant to "Cooperation Agreement," Republic of Slovenia and EC begun explorative discussions on signing "Europe Agreement"; first serious problems, including question of real estate ownership (problems relating to Italy) Slovenia admitted to WTO
15 March 1995	Negotiations begin to sign "Europe Agreement"
19 May 1995	Negotiations to sign the "Europe Agreement" concluded
10 June 1996	The "Europe Agreement" signed; on the same day, Slovenia formally applies for EC/EU membership
11 November 1996	The "Interim Agreement on trade and trade-related matters between the European Community, the European Coal and Steel Community and the European Atomic Energy Community, of the one part, and the Republic of Slovenia of the other part" was signed; the "Interim Agreement" was in force from 18 May 1997 until the "Europe Agreement" came into effect on 1 February 1999
3 July 1997	Leaders of Slovenian parliamentary political parties sign a special agreement on cooperation during Slovenia's accession to the EC/EU
13 July 1997	Slovenian National Assembly amends Art. 68 of the Constitution as required by the EC/EU (the so-called "real estate clause") as precondition for signing the "Europe Agreement"
15 July 1997	Ratification of the "Europe Agreement" in the Slovenian National Assembly
16 July 1997	European Commission sets out its opinion on Slovenia's EC/EU membership application in Agenda 2000
September 1997	Government of the Republic of Slovenia adopts the "Strategy of the Republic of Slovenia for Integration into the European Union"
31 March 1998	Accession negotiations officially opened

1 February 1999	The "Europe Agreement" comes into force, the delay due to the slow ratification procedures of member states
May 1999	Government of the Republic of Slovenia adopts "The Republic of Slovenia's National Programme for Adoption of the *Acquis* by the end of 2002'
November 2002	Slovenia invited to join NATO
13 December 2002	Negotiations on the Republic of Slovenia's accession to EU completed
25 March 2003	Publication of preliminary official results on the EU referenda held in Slovenia on 23 March (89.61% in favor; 60.31% turnout).[a]
March 2004	Slovenia becomes first transition country to graduate from borrower status to donor partner status at World Bank
29 March 2004	Slovenia becomes full member of NATO
1 May 2004	Slovenia becomes full member of EU
2005	Slovenia takes over OSCE presidency
1 January 2007	Slovenia (first post-socialist country to do so) joins Eurozone
Night 20/21 December 2007	Slovenia joins Schengen zone together with eight other EU 2004 member states and Switzerland
January–June 2008	Slovenia (first post-socialist country to do so) holds EU presidency

Notes:

[a] Official information was published in *Delo*, 25 March 2003, p. 1. The preliminary official information does not include votes cast by Slovenian citizens abroad. With respect to the share of this kind of voters in the total body of voters, there was no substantial change in the final official result: 84% in favor in a 60.44% turnover (www.duk.gov.si/referendum200302/on1poroculoeu.html) [last accessed on 20 July 2009].

Fact sheet

Area	20,273 km^2
Population (2007, 2008)	2,019,406, 2,032,362[a]
Slovenian	163,137 (83.06%)
Serb	38,964 (1.98%)
Croat	35,642 (1.81%)
Bosniak	21,542 (1.10%)
Hungarian	6,243 (0.32%[b]
Roma	3,246 (0.17%)[c]
Italian	2,258 (0.11%)[b]
Urban population	
Settlements with 4,999 or fewer inhabitants	61.6%

Settlements with 5,000–49,999 inhabitants	20.4%
Settlements with more than 50,000 inhabitants	18%[d]
Major cities	
Ljubljana (31 December 2005)	266,941[e]
Maribor (31 December 2005)	111,073[e]
Below the poverty line (2004)	12.1% of population[f]
Unemployment rate (2005)	5.8%[g]
GDP *per capita* (2007)	17,076 Euros, USD 23,403[h]
Agriculture (1995, 2007)	2.7%, 1.2%[i]
Real GDP growth (PPP, 2005)	79.8%[j]
Inflation (2008)	5.7[k]
Higher education	7.9% of population[l]
Literacy rate	99.7% of population[m]

Notes:

[a] 2007: Slovenian figures 2008 (www.stat.si/doc/pub/slo_figures_08.pdf) [last accessed on 17 July 2009]; 2008: www.stat.si/doc/pub/PSP/00-PS-912-0906.pdf [last accessed on 17 July 2009]. Net migration per 1,000 population increased from 1.3% in 2000 to 7.1% in 2007 (www.stat.si/doc/pub/slo_figures_08.pdf) [last accessed on 17 July 2009]. The total ethnic population (2002 census) was 196,404.

[b] Officially recognized ethnic minority, 1 MP in National Assembly.

[c] Officially recognized ethnic minority on local level, representatives in some local councils.

[d] www.stat.si/doc/pub/slofigures08.pdf [last accessed on 17 July 2009]; 50% of the total population is urban and urban settlements include 13.4% of the total land area (www.un.org/esa/population/publications/2007_PopDevt/Urban 2007.pdf) [last accessed on 19 July 2009].

[e] www.stat.si/letopis/2006/31_06/31-02-06.htm?jezik=si.

[f] EU average 16% (Statistical Office of Slovenia, www.stat.si/novica.prikazi.asp[x?id=708).

[g] ILO (Slovenian figures 2006). After joining the EU, the unemployment rate declined from 6.5% in 2005 to 4.4% in 2008. The delayed economic crisis came in 2009: at the beginning of the year the unemployment rate increased to 5.4% (www.stat.si/doc/pub/PSP/00-PS-912-0906.pdf) [last accessed on 17 July 2009].

[h] UMAR/IMAD predict a 4% decrease in GDP in 2009 (www.umar.gov.si/en) [last accessed on 17 July 2009]. Euros and USD figures from www.stat.si/doc/pub/slo_figures_08.pdf [last accessed on 17 July 2009].

[i] www.sta.si/vest.php?id=1395804 [last accessed on 19 July 2009].

[j] % of EU-25 (Slovenian figures 2006).

[k] www.umar.gov.si/fileadmin/user upload/publikacije/eo/2008/og1208/sem1208.pdf. [last accessed on 17 July 2009], decreasing below 1% in 2009 (www.stat.si/novica_prikazi.aspx?id=2461) [last accessed on 17 July 2009]. UMAR/IMAD predict average inflation to be 0.4% in 2009 (www.umar.gov.si/en) [last accessed on 17 July 2009].

[l] Slovenian figures 2006.

[m] CIA, *The World Factbook*, www.cia.gov/library/publications/the-world-factbook/geos/si.html [accessed 29 November 2009].

Short biography of Milan Kučan

Milan Kučan's political career started in the socialist youth organization during the 1960s. In the framework of the old system it peaked in 1986 when he was elected president of the Slovenian League of Communists, symbolizing the victory of a liberal stream of a young generation of politicians. Although having held many political positions in Ljubljana and Belgrade he has been closely associated with the old political elite's adaptation in the transition to a democracy in Slovenia. The military trial of the *Mladina* journalist Janez Janša in Ljubljana (as part of a Slovenian conflict with the Yugoslav political and military leadership) has been, among other things, interpreted as Kučan sacrificing Janša and the primary source of their later political conflicts. Still, Kučan's political career continued in the democratized system even in symbolically high political positions. Voters rewarded Kučan's political leadership by giving most votes to the reformed communist organization as an individual party in 1990 and Kučan, while "freezing" his party membership, won the elections to become president of Slovenia as well as two subsequent presidential elections for five years after the end of his term of office, Kučan had the right to the Office of the Former President of the Republic of Slovenia. This had ended on 22 December 2007, on the expiration of President Janez Drnovšek's term of office. The institution "Former President of the Republic of Slovenia" is new, established on the basis of a law (Zakon o zagotavljanju pogojev za opravljanje funkcije predsednika republike Slovenije, adopted on 28 January 2003 and becoming valid at the beginning of March[17]). This determines the rights of the former president after the end of his or her mandate – the right to the title "Former President of the Republic of Slovenia," the right to an office for the period of five years and two staff, as well as the right to participate at state events in line with the rules of protocol.

Notes

1. Since 1988, the movement has been based on a criticism of the official psychiatry and on offering an alternative social understanding of madness and its social inclusion. See more at www.altra.si [last accessed on 27 January 2008].
2. Sabrina J. Ramet notes in her article "Slovenia's Road to Democracy" (*Europe-Asia Studies*, Vol. 45, No. 5 (1993), pp. 869–86) that it was Serbia which first constituted itself as independent by adopting the Serbian Constitution in September 1990, ending Serbia's subordination to the federal government.
3. http://ec.europa.eu/enlargement/pdf/press.corner/key-documents/reports nov 2008 strategy paper mcl country conclu.en.pdf [last accessed on 19 July 2009]; http://ec.europa.eu/enlargement/pdf/press.corner/key-documents/reportsnov2008/croatia progressreporteu.pdf [last accessed on 19 July 2009].
4. Janez Pečar, "Changes in Adaptations of Formal Control," in Danica Fink-Hafner and John R. Robbins (eds.), *Making a New Nation: The Formation of Slovenia* (Aldershot, Brookfield Vt., Singapore, and Sydney: Dartmouth, 1997), pp. 94–105.

5. On 20 June 2006 the Constitution of 1991 was amended to make regions obligatory, but the additional laws needed for the establishment of regions have not yet all been adopted by the National Assembly.
6. The all-encompassing definition of Europeanization by Claudio Radaelli, "The Europeanization of Public Policy," in K. Featherstone and Claudio M. Radaelli (eds.), *The Politics of Europeanization* (Oxford: Oxford University Press, 2003) has been too broad for analyzing Slovenia's adaptation to European integration processes until very recently. For the purpose of this chapter, "Europeanization" is defined as the assimilation of legal norms and procedures previously adopted by the EU as well as the top-down adaptation of national political system institutions, actors, and political processes to promote European integration.
7. Danica Fink-Hafner, "Ensuring Democratic Control over National Government in European Affairs – The Slovenian Experience," in Gavin Barrett (ed.), *National Parliaments in the European Union* (Dublin: Clarus Press, 2008), pp. 393–414.
8. Alenka Krašovec and Damjan Lajh, "Have Democratization Processes been a Catalyst for The Europeanization of Party Politics in Slovenia?," *Journal of South East Europe and the Balkans*, Vol. 10, No. 2 (August 2008), pp. 183–203.
9. See, e.g. Sandra Bašić Hrvatin, "Media Liberalism," in Sabrina P. Ramet and Danica Fink-Hafner (eds.), *Democratic Transition in Slovenia: Value Transformation, Education, and Media* (College Station, Tex.: Texas A&M University Press, 2006), pp. 168–86.
10. See, e.g. Ivan Bernik, Brina Malnar, and Niko Toš, "Slovenian Political Culture: Paradoxes of Democratization," in Fink-Hafner and Robbins (eds.), *Making A New Nation*, pp. 56–82; Ola Listhaug and Kristen Ringdal, "Slovenian Values in a European Context," in Ramet and Fink-Hafner (eds.), *Democratic Transition in Slovenia*, pp. 55–71; and Mitja Hafner-Fink, "Values of the Slovenian Population: Local and Collective or Global and Individual?," in Ramet and Fink-Hafner (eds.), *Democratic Transition in Slovenia*, pp. 127–47.
11. See more in Jože Mencinger, "Privatization in Slovenia," *Slovenian Law Review*, Vol. 3, No. 1–2 (December 2006), pp. 65–81.
12. An annual overview of the most important institutional changes and policy issues in Slovenia has been available in the *European Journal of Political Research Political Data Yearbook* since 2003 (contributions by Danica Fink-Hafner).
13. Marjeta Doupona Horvat, Jef Vershueren, and Igor Ž. Žagar, *Pragmatika legitimizacije. Retorika begunske politike v Sloveniji*, 2nd edn. (Ljubljana: Peace Institute, Media Watch, 2001), at http://mediawatch.mirovni-institut.si/edicija/seznam/09/mediawatch09.pdf [last accessed on 20 July 2009].
14. Information published on behalf of the Government of Slovenia, at www.altra.si and http://www.vlada.si/index.php?&i1=UVI&i2=slo&i3=1&i4=sjv&i5=ter_dvl_021&i10=artic&i12=E464B3E502E8DEECC12573840050D614&i15=on_Gnovica&j1=utf-8&j2=content&j3=gids&j4= [accessed on 31 October 2007].
15. Constitutional Court ruling, http://adlocitve.us-rs.si/urs/os-odl.usf/015EC.66748A09c70A4C.12575EF00211108 [(last accessed on 19 July 2008)].
16. Maca Jogan, "The Stubbornness of Sexism in the Second Part of the Twentieth Century in Slovenia," in Niko Toš and Karl H. Müller (eds.), *Political Faces of*

Slovenia: Political Orientations and Values at the End of the Century (Vienna: Edition Echoraum, 2005), pp. 297–313.

17. http://www.up-rs.si/uprs.nsf/dokumentiweb/C7F384270C527977C12570350047 B7FF?OpenDocument [last accessed on 17 July 2009].

Further reading

Fink-Hafner, Danica. "Slovenia," in annual contributions to *Political Data Yearbook, European Journal of Political Research*, published since 2003

"Slovenia: Between Bipolarity and Broad Coalition-building," in Susanne Jungerstam-Mulders (ed.), *Post-Communist EU Member States: Parties and party systems* (Aldershot and and Burlington, Vt.: Ashgate, 2006), pp. 203–31

Fink-Hafner, Danica and Damjan Lajh. *Managing Europe from Home: The Europeanization of the Slovenian Executive* (Ljubljana: Znanstveno in publicistično središče, 2003)

The 2008 Slovenian EU Presidency: A New Synergy for Europe? A Midterm Report (Stockholm: Swedish Institute for Policy Studies, 2008)

Fink-Hafner, Danica and John R. Robbins (eds.). *Making A New Nation: The Formation of Slovenia* (Aldershot, Brookfield, Vt., Singapore, and Sydney: Dartmouth 1997)

Radaelli, Claudio. M. "The Europeanization of Public Policy," in K. Featherstone and Claudio M. Radaelli (eds.), *The Politics of Europeanization* (Oxford: Oxford University Press, 2003), pp. 27–56

Ramet, Sabrina P. *Serbia, Croatia, and Slovenia at Peace and at War: Selected Writings, 1983–2007* (Berlin and Münster: Lit Verlag, 2008)

Ramet, Sabrina P. and Danica Fink-Hafner (eds.). *Democratic Transition in Slovenia: Value Transformation, Education, and Media* (College Station, Tex.: Texas A&M University Press, 2006)

Rizman, Rudolf Martin. *Uncertain Path: Democratic Transition and Consolidation in Slovenia* (College Station, Tex.: Texas A&M University Press, 2006)

Toš, Niko and Vlado Miheljak (eds.). *Slovenia Between Continuity and Change, 1990–1997* (Berlin: Sigma, 2002)

Toš, Niko and Karl H. Müller (eds.). *Political Faces of Slovenia: Political Orientations and Values at the End of the Century* (Vienna: Edition Echoraum, 2005).

Internet sources

Electoral Commission of the Republic of Slovenia (*Republiška volilna komisija*), at www.rvk.si

Government Office of the Republic of Slovenia for Growth (*Služba vlade Republike Slovenije za razvoj*), at www.svr.gov.si

Human Rights Ombudsman of the Republic of Slovenia (*Varuh človekovih pravic Republike Slovenije*), at www.varuh-rs.si

National Assembly (*Državni zbor*), at www.dz-rs.si

National Council (*Državni svet*), at www.ds-rs.si

OGRS – Official Gazette of the Republic of Slovenia/*Uradni list Republike Slovenije*, at http://zakonodaja.gov.si

President of the Republic of Slovenia (*Predsednik Republike Slovenije*), at www.up-rs.si

Slovenian Government website – Slovenia, at www.gov.si

Statistical Office of the Republic of Slovenia (*Statistični urad Republike Slovenije*), at www.stat.si

12

Politics in Croatia since 1990

SABRINA P. RAMET*

Croatia's post-communist transition cannot be discussed apart from the dramatic impact of the War of Yugoslav Succession, fought on the territory of Croatia for four-and-a-half years (1991–5). Like all the other Yugoslav successor states, the breakup of the Socialist Federated Republic of Yugoslavia (SRFJ), of which Croatia had been a constituent federal unit, disrupted established trade patterns. The war itself destroyed much of Croatia's infrastructure, and also encouraged nationalistic responses in which the rights of Serbs and other non-Croats living in Croatia were viewed, by some, as obstacles to the achievement of a Croatian national state, or even as illegitimate. Yet, in spite of the war, Croatia, in the era of Franjo Tudjman (who served as the country's president from 1990 to 1999), achieved a measure of pluralism, albeit a limited pluralism, as the regime's encroachments upon media freedom (to be detailed below) make obvious.

Croatia could look back to an earlier tradition of statehood. The site of Celtic settlements as early as the fourth century BCE, the region which today comprises Croatia was incorporated into the Roman Empire around 10 BCE. Slavs arrived on the territory of present-day Croatia in the early seventh century CE, and in 803 Croatian tribes accepted the rule of Charlemagne, converting soon after to Christianity. The Croatian medieval state grew during the years 840–80, and, during the reign of King Tomislav (910–28), fended off Hungarian invasions. Croatia expanded in the eleventh century but after the death of the last Croatian King in 1097 King Kálmán of Hungary was crowned King of Croatia, creating a political union between Croatia and Hungary. After 1526, Croatia was divided between the Ottomans and the Habsburgs and in 1527 Ferdinand I of the Habsburg dynasty was crowned King of Croatia. Later, under the Treaty of Karlowitz (1699) previously Ottoman-ruled parts of Croatia were assigned to the Habsburg Empire. From then until 1918, Croatia remained part of the Habsburg Empire, except for the years 1809–13, when it was incorporated into the Illyrian province, a Napoleonic satellite state. In 1867, the Habsburg Empire was divided into two autonomous zones; Dalmatia was assigned to the Austrian half of the empire, with the rest of Croatia assigned to the Hungarian half.[1] From 1918 to 1941, Croatia was part of the Kingdom of Serbs, Croats, and

Slovenes (renamed the Kingdom of Yugoslavia in October 1929),[2] and, in rearranged borders, functioned as an Axis satellite during the Second World War.[3] After the war, Croatia was one of the six constituent republics of socialist Yugoslavia (1945–91), re-emerging as an independent state only in June 1991.

In this chapter, I shall focus on four themes: the corruption of the political process, the impact of the war, the development of the political system and political parties, and policies toward the media.

Corruption of the political process

Franjo Tudjman (1922–99) seemed larger than life. It was not so much that he had served as a colonel in the Partisans, rising to the rank of general after the war, or that he had subsequently earned a doctorate in history and headed the Institute for the History of the Workers' Movement, or even that he had been a prominent dissident figure from the 1960s until being elected president of Croatia in May 1990. What made Tudjman seem larger than life was his self-concept as the Father of his country and the way in which he projected that self-concept. His Tito-like poses before the camera, for which he sometimes donned white uniforms reminiscent of those worn by Tito, were a part of this. More important, however, was the way in which he treated other people – solicitous and ready to listen to advice, but always looking down from his balcony, as it were.

Tudjman's self-concept is, I would argue, an important reason – though not the only one, of course – why the political process became corrupted in the early years of independence. In Tudjman's mind, it was he himself who could best be trusted to know what should be done, what was in Croatia's interest, and where the rules should be bent. Just as the father in the family may set rules for his children to which he himself is not subject (such as bedtime or attention to homework), so too Tudjman, as Father of his country, could preside over a system in which he (and his inner circle) could be exempt from the rules and laws which applied to other people. There are numerous examples which may be cited. For example, during Tudjman's years as president, his party – the Croatian Democratic Union (Hrvatska Demokratska Zajednica, or HDZ) – apparently "raised most of its funding through 'racketeering' schemes in which government contractors would be paid only in return for substantial contributions to party coffers."[4] Where party funding is concerned, other sources of corruption include the fact that Croatian political parties derive 75% of their funding from state subsidies, distributed according to a disbursement schedule determined by the ruling party or parties, and the non-existence of laws providing for public disclosure of such disbursement.

As Mate Granić notes in his memoirs, "Tudjman had complete control over the ministries of defense, foreign affairs, and police, as well as over the information services, and for a while he also controlled the Ministry of Finance."[5] Some of his power was formal and institutionalized, some was informal, even personal. He dominated the HDZ, he bestowed favors on his hangers-on, and he even diverted government funds to the traditionalist Croatian Population Movement, run by retired priest, Don Anto Baković, whose objective was to increase the birthrate.[6]

As president, Tudjman abused a provision in the constitution which allowed him to set up agencies and other bodies to assist him in discharging his duties, in order to establish formally legal entities such as the Presidential Council for National Security, which made it possible for him to by-pass the *Sabor* (parliament) on certain issues.[7] Tudjman applied the same formula in the economic sphere. The result was the emergence, during Tudjman's years in office, of "a virtual parallel government covertly displacing legitimate constitutional bodies."[8] But Tudjman's authority also had its roots in the constitution and laws themselves. Article 101 of the 1990 constitution, for example, granted the president of the Republic the authority to "pass decrees with the force of law and take emergency measures in the event of a state of war … or when government bodies are prevented from regularly performing their constitutional duties."[9] Another provision, adopted at the time the constitution was being written, ordained that no person elected to the office of mayor could assume office without confirmation by the president. At the time, this provision was regarded as a safety measure given the secessionist proclivities of some of the Serbian politicians in municipalities with local Serb majorities.[10] In the winter of 1995–6, however, when an opposition coalition won the mayoral race, Tudjman used this provision to veto the installation of four opposition candidates, one after the other, and installed his own candidate instead.

Corruption, cronyism, and nepotism went hand in hand in Tudjman's years in office, and the privatization process was deflected to transfer large chunks of socially owned property into the pockets of members of the Tudjman family, and various HDZ politicians and their cronies. Corruption extended to the judiciary as well, and this has remained a problem in the post-Tudjman era.

Ironically, however, what seemed to bother some Croats most – at least the sports fans – was Tudjman's decision to change the name of Zagreb's popular soccer team, "Dinamo," to "Croatia" (in English). The Bad Blue Boys, as the team's fans called themselves, revolted against this intrusion of political power into their world and protested loudly. Tudjman seemed to have difficulty understanding how anyone could prefer the name "Dinamo" to the name of country and, in a speech to the Fourth General Convention of the HDZ on 21 February 1998, he blamed agitation for the restoration of the name "Dinamo" on "certain foreign centres" allegedly seeking to undermine HDZ rule.[11] That said, Tudjman remained clearly the most popular politician in Croatia during his years in office. In 1996, for example, the weekly magazine *Globus* asked 1,000 Croats whom they would choose for president if elections were held then; 40.6% declared Tudjman to be their favorite, placing him far ahead of second-place Dražen Budiša, who attracted only 17.9% in support.[12] Tudjman's popularity survived his death, as borne out by another *Globus* poll, conducted in 2002, which showed that 41% of respondents rated Tudjman's conduct of office in "positive" or "very positive" terms, with only 21.9% rating his political role in "negative" or "very negative" terms. In the same opinion poll, some 20.0% of respondents declared that Tudjman was "the most important Croatian statesman in history."[13]

Impact of the war

The War of Yugoslav Succession lasted almost forty-four months, if one counts the war as starting with the attack by Serbian insurgents on the Plitvice National Park at the end of March 1991 and ending with the Dayton Peace Accords in November 1995. But the die had already been cast in mid-March 1991, when the Executive Council of the self-declared Serbian Autonomous District declared the Serbs' secession from Croatia. The first casualties of the war occurred in Borovo Selo on 1 May, when Serb insurgents killed twelve Croatian police, wounding twenty more,[14] but 1 July marked the first day of uninterrupted fighting between the two sides. Backed by the Yugoslav Army and Air Force, Serb insurgents quickly took control of about 30% of Croatian territory, expelling local inhabitants who were not Serb and killing between 6,000 and 10,000 Croats. By the end of 1991, more than 400,000 citizens of Croatia were homeless, 40% of Croatia's industry had been destroyed, gross industrial production had plummeted by 28.5%, and tourism had predictably slipped by more than 80%.[15] Unemployment rose, inflation gathered steam, and net income declined. According to figures cited by President Tudjman, there were some 13,500 persons killed in Croatia during the years 1991–5, and another 35,000 wounded, with another 20,000 Croats killed in Bosnia-Herzegovina and 50,000 wounded during those same years.[16] In those areas which had been occupied by Serb insurgents, more than three-quarters of Catholic churches and monasteries had been destroyed by the end of the war; by contrast, only 2.5% of Serb Orthodox churches were destroyed in those areas which the Croatian Army recovered from insurgent control in the course of 1995.[17]

A number of misconceptions have arisen concerning Tudjman's policies and the role played by Croatia's Serbs in the years 1990–1. The first is the notion that the red-and-white checkerboard found on the post-1990 Croatian coat of arms represented a restoration of a symbol previously used during the era of the fascistic Independent State of Croatia (NDH) in 1941–5. Quite apart from the fact that the checkerboard has a long history, going back at least as far as the fifteenth century,[18] to constitute a "restoration" it would have to have been removed during the intervening years of socialism and would have to be identical with that used in the NDH. Neither is the case. In fact, the red-and-white checkerboard was used on the Croatian coat of arms throughout the socialist era, with a red square placed on the upper left, to distinguish the socialist version from the NDH version, which placed a white square in that position. Post-1990 Croatia has preserved the socialist arrangement of squares. Thus, the claim which one may read in some American and British newspapers that local Serbs were angry because the Tudjman regime allegedly restored the old fascist checkerboard is based on a myth.

A second misconception – one may even say, a myth – is that local Serbs were acting autonomously, and that Milošević played little role in stoking up the conflict in Croatia. In fact, the Serbian president exerted influence over the Serbs of Croatia from the beginning. Already in 1990, when the newly elected President Tudjman offered the vice-presidency to Jovan Rašković, head of the local Serbian Democratic Party, together with cultural autonomy (which is to say, guarantees for the use of ekavian and the Cyrillic alphabet), Rašković consulted with Milošević before taking a decision; egged on by Milošević, Rašković declined the offer and called for a boycott of the parliament by deputies from his party. Moreover, as I have noted elsewhere,[19] the Serb paramilitaries set up on the Serbian president's authorization not only benefited from JNA training, transfusions of JNA equipment, and infusions, throughout the war, of funding from Belgrade, but also reported directly to the Yugoslav Army.

Finally, there is a third misconception – that President Tudjman's alleged dismissal of local Serbs from positions in the police and administration somehow "justified" the effort by Serbs to secede from Croatia and the atrocities which Serb paramilitaries would commit against Croats. The standard account inverts the actual chronology, however. What happened is that, as early as the spring of 1990, local police in Knin (mainly Serbs) were operating as if they were an independent force, i.e. not responding to orders from the government in Zagreb which was paying their salaries. By mid-August 1990, Knin police were taking the side of the growing Serbian insurgency and it was in response to that situation that Zagreb removed the ringleaders of the rebellion from the payroll. Those removed from the payroll *ipso facto* lost their right to their state-issued apartments.[20] This result has come down as the "firing of Serbs" but, as this chronology makes clear, the outcome was the result of the actions taken by the Serb police and not the result of prejudice on Tudjman's part. In any event, as we know from the diaries of Borisav Jović, among other sources, Milošević was already bent on war by spring 1990[21] and the refusal of Croatian Serb police to respect the chain of command figured as merely one element in this escalation to war. Still, whatever the truth of the matter, Belgrade was able to turn this case of insubordination into anti-Croat propaganda by casting the blame on Tudjman for a result chosen by the Serbs themselves.

Thanks to the diplomatic quarantine of Croatia, which lasted to the end of 1991, and the arms embargo imposed by the UN Security Council in September 1991, alongside Croatia's incomplete preparations for independence,[22] close to one-third of Croatia's territory was quickly lost.[23] As insurgents continued to take more land, the Croatian government reversed its earlier stand on autonomy and offered the Serbs of Krajina not merely cultural autonomy, but *full* autonomy – i.e. administrative autonomy.[24] This *might* have been enough to cool local tempers back in 1989, before Tudjman was president, but it would not have been enough even in summer 1990, let alone a year later.

In early October 1991, the Yugoslav Army ratcheted up its campaign, opening up a fresh offensive all along the front lines, and bringing, once again, not only tanks and heavy artillery into combat against the underarmed Croats, but also ground attack aircraft and naval bombardment. Then, that month, the East Slavonian town of Vukovar (pre-war population of about 50,000) fell to the Yugoslav Army after the last few civilian defenders of the city ran out of ammunition. The Army and Serb insurgents then took control of what was left of Vukovar, executing those males who did not manage to escape, and plundering its museums, shipping their contents back to Belgrade. In the course of the war, sixty-six museum buildings in Croatia were destroyed and forty-five museums and galleries were plundered. According to a statement made in 1999 by Ivan Šimonović, then Croatian ambassador to the UN, some 6,551 works of art went missing from Croatia during the war, another 1,430 were destroyed, and 728 were damaged.[25] The artworks confiscated from Vukovar were returned to Croatia only ten years later.[26]

After the war, Croatian authorities began the unearthing of mass graves, and by June 1999 had discovered some 117, in which Serb troops and paramilitaries had buried their victims, and had exhumed 2,955 bodies.[27] But the Croatian side also committed atrocities. Among the places associated with massacres for which Croatian forces have been blamed are Gospić and Pakračka Poljana in Croatia, and Ahmići and Stupni Do in Bosnia-Herzegovina. After the war, those held responsible for the killings at Gospić were put on trial. According to Ivan Dasović, a witness at the trial of the "Gospić group," when he talked with Tudjman about the liquidations of Serbs he was given to understand that "everyone" in the leadership had known about them at the time.[28] Then there was the case of the 100 Serbs who disappeared from Sisak in autumn 1991 – presumably killed.[29]

But what might have unfolded as a war pitting forces loyal to Belgrade and Pale (where the Bosnian Serbs made their wartime capital), on the one side, against forces loyal to Zagreb and Sarajevo on the other, evolved into a three- and even four-sided war. In addition to those forces loyal to Belgrade/Pale and Zagreb, there were also those forces loyal to the Sarajevo government headed by Alija Izetbegović, whose term of office was supposed to expire in 1992,[30] and also forces loyal to Fikret Abdić, a successful businessman from Velika Kladuša, who set up an enclave in and around Bihać, trading with both Bosnian Serb and Bosnian Croat forces.[31] Abdić sold foodstuffs to the Krajina Serbs and purchased oil and other goods from Croatia, reselling much of the oil to the Krajina Serbs and Bosnian Serbs, as well as to Serbia itself.[32] In what has remained one of the murkier chapters in the war, President Tudjman traveled to Karadjordjevo for a meeting with Serbian President Milošević on 25 March 1991 – reportedly to discuss the possible partition of Bosnia-Herzegovina between Croatia and Serbia.[33] According to current President Stjepan Mesić,

Tudjman hoped to restore to Croatia the boundaries of the short-lived banovina (1939–41), which included portions of what is now Bosnia-Herzegovina. The following month, groups of Croatian and Serbian scholars and "political experts," authorized by Presidents Tudjman and Milošević, met in Tikveš near Osijek, to continue the discussion of matters of mutual interest.[34] There were disagreements among the Croats, however, and there were no further meetings of experts. Indeed, those aborted discussions yielded no fruit. All the same, the notion of a partition of Bosnia-Herzegovina was no mere whim, as was obvious from the publication that same year of Anto Valenta's book, *Podjela Bosne i borba za cjelovitost*. In this work, Valenta advocated an exchange of populations, with 194,000 Serbs from the central Muslim areas to be swapped for 194,000 Muslims who were to leave areas to be assigned to Serbia. A similar exchange between Croatia and the Muslim entity would have involved 170,000 persons on each side.[35]

Although Milošević's sincerity in meeting with Tudjman at Karadjordjevo is open to question, Tudjman's biographer, Darko Hudelist, contends that, with the collapse of Socialist Yugoslavia, Tudjman expected that the Croatian lands, including not only Croat-inhabited areas of Bosnia-Herzegovina but also the Srijem and Bačka regions of Vojvodina and Boka Kotorska in Montenegro, would join the emergent Croatian state. In accord with this expectation, according to Hudelist, Tudjman made the expansion of Croatia an explicit strategic goal and directed his policies toward the achievement of that aim.[36] Ivica Radoš casts doubt on this assessment, however, portraying Tudjman as playing a defensive role and, where it concerns the disputed meeting at Karadjordjevo, claims that there is no proof that Tudjman and Milošević agreed on a division of Bosnia.[37] And even if they did, it is clear that Milošević did not behave subsequently as if he had an agreement with Tudjman. Moreover, whatever Tudjman may have thought concerning Bosnia-Herzegovina after the Karadjordjevo meeting, he made no secret of his determination to retrieve the entire territory of Croatia and, as early as October 1991, expressed confidence that, even with the UN arms embargo in place, Croatia would prove to have the arms necessary to defend itself.[38]

Although originally on friendly terms, the governments of Zagreb and Sarajevo fell out by the latter half of 1992 and, from October 1992 to February 1994, Muslim forces loyal to Izetbegović and reinforced by *mujahedin* volunteers from several Islamic countries battled against Bosnian Croat forces backed by the Croatian Army.[39] An autonomous Croatian Community of Herceg-Bosna had been proclaimed already in November 1991, though it was emphasized at the time that the intention was not to secede from Sarajevo's jurisdiction but merely to establish a legal basis for local self-administration; at the time, the authorities of Herceg-Bosna added that they would respect the government headed by President Izetbegović as long as it remained independent "of the former and every kind of a future Yugoslavia."[40] Only later, in July 1992, did Bosnian Croat leader Mate Boban (installed by Tudjman in place of the more moderate Stjepan

Kljuić) and his associates proclaim the establishment of the Croatian Republic of Herceg-Bosna, signaling an end to respect for the sovereignty of the Sarajevo government. Meanwhile, in a conversation with Bosnian Croat leaders in late December 1991, President Tudjman had shared his opinion that "from the perspective of sovereignty, Bosnia-Herzegovina has no prospects" but that Croatian policy should nonetheless be one of "support for the sovereignty [of Bosnia-Herzegovina] until such time as it no longer suits Croatia."[41] A transcript of Tudjman's conversation on 22 October 1993 confirms that the Croatian president had given express instructions to Defense Minister Gojko Šušak and Army Chief-of-Staff General Janko Bobetko on that occasion to shore up Herceg-Bosna in a belief that "the future borders of the Croatian state are being resolved there."[42] By 2003, having combed through various documents and having heard relevant testimony, the International Criminal Tribunal for the former Yugoslavia (ICTY) concluded that the Croatian government of Franjo Tudjman had played a crucial role in "the organization, planning, and coordination of military operations which took place during the conflict between the HVO [the Bosnian Croat forces] and the Army of BiH [the Bosnian army], and that [the record] conclusively proves how the Republic of Croatia and the Croatian Community of Herceg-Bosnia had a single goal – to incorporate the 'Croatian provinces' into a united Croatian state."[43] Moreover, according to *The Washington Post*, at peak the flow of Croatian funds into the coffers of Bosnian Croat forces exceeded $500,000 per day.[44]

There were also negotiations with both Bosnian President Izetbegović and Bosnian Serb leader Radovan Karadžić during the war concerning possible partition plans. In January 1994, for example, Izetbegović offered Tudjman two alternative plans for a partition of Bosnia within the space of ten days – both of them rejected.[45] Later that year, Ivić Pašalić, a key adviser to President Tudjman, led a three-man delegation to a town near Banja Luka to negotiate with Karadžić, on Tudjman's behalf, about the partition of Bosnia-Herzegovina. Significantly, this meeting occurred several months after the Washington Agreement which supposedly reconciled Zagreb and Sarajevo, thus giving the lie to claims that Croatian irredentism ended in February 1994. Karadžić used the occasion to propose an exchange of territories and populations and, according to a report published in the Rijeka daily *Novi list* somewhat later, Tudjman was very interested in Karadžić's ideas.[46] Although the details of these contacts and of Zagreb's support for Herceg-Bosna were not known at the time, it was generally understood that Zagreb was playing a double game in Bosnia. This in turn provoked protests – among others, on the part of Stjepan Mesić, who resigned from the HDZ in protest, to form his own political party, and Ivo Banac, professor of history at Yale University, who was already writing a regular column for *Feral Tribune* and who would later lead the Liberal Party (LS) for about a year.

Tudjman failed to achieve his territorial objectives in Bosnia-Herzegovina, but he succeeded in defending the territorial integrity of Croatia, and in this regard could legitimately claim to have led Croatia to victory in "the Homeland War." The military operations which restored western Slavonia and the Krajina to Zagreb's jurisdiction were conducted in May ("Operation Flash") and August ("Operation Storm") 1995, respectively. Although Serbs continue to criticize these operations even today, especially "Operation Storm," the Croatian position is that since the international community had recognized Croatia within its socialist-era boundaries, it followed that the Serbian occupation of portions of Croatia was *illegal under international law*, which in turn meant that it was legal for Croatia to adopt such actions as would end the illegal occupation of portions of its territory.

In any event, the war had significant demographic and economic consequences for Croatia. Since many Serbs either fled Croatia during the war or were driven out, the number of Serbs living in Croatia declined so that, while Serbs had accounted for just over 12% of the population in 1991, they constituted just 4.54% of the population in 2001, according to official census results. At that time, 89.63% of the population was Croat out of a total population of 4,437,460.[47] As of 2000, there were some 230,000 Serb refugees from Croatia – 200,000 of them living in Serbia and Montenegro, and another 30,000 living in Bosnia-Herzegovina, most of them in the Republika Srpska.[48]

Development of the political system and political parties

The transformation of the political system from communist one-party rule to a pluralist system took place, thus, under adverse conditions. At the time this process began, Croatia operated with a bicameral legislature – a system which policy-makers were determined to change. There were other features of the communist system which needed to be changed as well. But for the time being, the question was whether to hold elections first or draft a new constitution first. Following the more common model, Croatia held elections first, deferring the drafting of a new constitution until after the elections. Under the Law on Elections adopted at the time and intended to apply only to the spring 1990 elections, a majority system was adopted, rather than one of proportional representation. The League of Communists of Croatia (SKH) expected to emerge with the largest number of votes, and the majority system would in turn enhance its strength in the post-election legislature. That, at least, was the scenario as imagined by the SKH. But the HDZ, which had been established only on 28 February 1989,[49] scored an upset victory at the polls and, under the electoral scheme which had been adopted, its 43% plurality was converted into an absolute majority of 69% in the socio-political chamber, which was the determinative chamber and the nucleus of the future *Sabor*.

On coming to power, Tudjman – the communist general turned anti-communist historian turned nationalist politician – endeavored to transform his party, the HDZ, into a broad front capable of attracting votes across a broad spectrum. To achieve this, he needed to be fuzzy on program and diffuse in symbolic politics. The fact that a street named for Andrija Hebrang, Tito's old nemesis, ran into Tito Square in downtown Zagreb, and that there were streets named for Mile Budak, the NDH minister, in various towns already suggested an embrace of all of Croatia's history – as did, for that matter, the restoration of the equestrian statue of Ban Josip Jelačić to Zagreb's main square. When it came to Ante Pavelić, who had headed the collaborationist NDH during the Second World War, Tudjman repeatedly expressed himself in ways guaranteed to generate controversy. In 1996, for example, in the course of urging that Pavelić's last remains be returned (from Madrid) to Croatia, Tudjman claimed that "*Pavelić's idea of creating a Croatian state contained positive things*, but it must also be acknowledged [that] he made terrible mistakes in the implementation of his policy."[50] Whether or not the debilities of Ustašism can be reduced to "mistakes," Tudjman struck a different note two years later. On that occasion, addressing a gathering of HDZ cadres, Tudjman would claim that his

> programme, the HDZ programme for the reconciliation of the divided Croathood has provided a way out of the historical vicissitudes and hardships due to our geo-political position and international forces, but also to internal disunion …
>
> With our programme of reconciliation of Croathood … we prevented a civil war in Croatia in the days of the collapse of the former Yugoslavia and the communist system.
>
> With our reconciliation programme focused on the achievement of Croatian freedom and of our democratic State, we prevented the confrontation between the Domobrani (Home Guardsmen) and the Partisans, the Ustashi and the Communists. Such a confrontation would have directly jeopardized the very existence of the Croatian people.[51]

In that same speech, having seen for himself how some people in the West had been taken in by Serbian wartime propaganda which depicted the new Republic of Croatia as some sort of reincarnation of the NDH, Tudjman took time to condemn the NDH for its atrocities and persecutions "not only against Jews, Serbs and communists, but also against Croatian anti-fascists and democrats," for having ceded land to Italy, and for having agreed to foreign occupation, among other things.[52]

If diverse viewpoints were to be reconciled, however, a key sticking point was whether to define Croatia as a *national state* – which is to say as the state of Croats, implying thereby that the educational and cultural systems would be attuned to the notion of Croatian primacy within their state – or as a *citizens' state*, based on the principle that all citizens are equal and should enjoy equal rights and prerogatives. The solution was a compromise, and, in the constitution adopted on 22 December 1990, Croatia is defined as "the national state of the Croatian people and the state of the members of other peoples and minorities, who are her citizens."[53] As already noted, the constitution established a semi-presidential system; this included establishing the right of the president to appoint and dismiss the prime minister and deputy prime minister, as well as other ministers. Under the rules adopted with the revision to the socialist constitution, Tudjman had become president on the basis of a vote in the *Sabor*, but Article 95 of the 1990 constitution established that henceforth the president would be elected by direct popular vote.[54] The constitution also set a limit of two five-year terms for any president. Tudjman handily won popular elections in 1992 and 1997, and there were rumors in 1999 that he was contemplating having the constitution amended in order to permit him to run for re-election in 2002.

Aside from the HDZ, the other major political parties to emerge were: the Social Democratic Party (SDP) (as the Communist Party eventually renamed itself), headed by Ivica Račan; the Croatian Social Liberal Party (HSLS), established in May 1989 under the leadership of Dražen Budiša; the Croatian Peasant Party (HSS), resurrected in December 1989 as the reincarnation of the party of Stjepan Radić and Vladko Maček; the Croatian People's Party (HNS), founded in October 1990 by Savka Dabčević-Kučar; the Croatian Party of Right (HSP), set up in February 1990 and looking back to the tradition of Ante Starčević, headed initially by former dissident Dobroslav Paraga; the Istrian Democratic Assembly (IDS) formed in February 1990 to defend the interests of the people of Istria; and the Serbian People's Party (SNS) founded in May 1991 and led by Milan Djukić until his death in October 2007. Stipe Mesić and Josip Manolić originally joined the HDZ but, in 1994, protesting against Tudjman's policies in Bosnia, they resigned from the party to form their own opposition party, the Independent Croatian Democrats (HND). Three more parties were formed later, as a result of splits. The first of these was the Croatian Party of Right 1861 headed by Paraga, which resulted from the takeover of his party by Anto Djapić, who proceeded to transform the HSP into a satellite of the HDZ. The second was the Independent Democratic Serbian Party, formed in March 1997 and headed by Milorad Pupovac. The third was the Liberal Party (LS), which resulted from the disaffection of more cosmopolitan-minded liberals within the HSLS with the nationalist orientation of party boss Budiša. Vlado Gotovac led the cosmopolitans out of the HSLS, forming the LS, which Banac would later lead briefly. The HSLS and the LS reunited as a single party in February 2006, electing Djurdja Adlešić as president of the reconstituted HSLS. That same month saw the birth of yet another political party – the United Independent Lists (SNL), headed by Tatjana Holjevac, who committed herself to work for allocating 40% of the national budget to regional projects to be determined at the regional level.[55] In May 2006, yet another political party was born – the Croatian Democratic Assembly of Slavonia and Baranja (HDSSB), established in order to defend regional interests. Kresimir Bubalo, the prefect of Osijek-Baranja County, was elected party president, at a session also attended by Anto Djapić, Mayor of Osijek.[56] Taken in tandem, the creation of these two parties suggests a more general mobilization at the regional level. (In addition to the foregoing more prominent or more recently established parties, there are a number of other political parties operating in Croatia, among them a party committed to defending the interests of pensioners.)

But the HDZ was able to maintain its dominance of the *Sabor* so effectively throughout Tudjman's years in office that there was never any need until after his death for the HDZ to enter into a coalition with any other party. Curiously, each of the first six parliamentary elections in Croatia (1990, 1992, 1993, 1995, 2000, 2003) was conducted according to a different electoral law and a different set of rules.[57] As Srđjan Vrcan notes, this practice could serve political purposes. The electoral law passed just before the 1995 elections, for example, annulled certain rights granted to Croatia's Serb minority under the 1990 constitution and, accordingly, reduced the number of parliamentary seats reserved for them to three. Even more tellingly, after the votes in that election had been cast and results started to come in, the HDZ saw that its sister party, the HSP, was not going to pass the threshold of 5% necessary to obtain parliamentary representation. But a solution was found on the spot. Instead of computing the threshold on the basis of votes cast, the electoral commission started to count only those votes treated as "valid."[58]

The fifth round of parliamentary elections, held in January 2000, resulted in the formation of a coalition government headed by the SDP, whose president, Ivica Račan, became prime minister. Other parties in his coalition were the HSLS, the HNS, the HSS, the LS, and the IDS, although the IDS later left the coalition. Račan and Budiša had entered into a pre-election alliance, under the terms of which Budiša would support Račan for prime minister and Račan would, in turn, support Budiša's candidacy for the presidency. Among the several presidential candidates, however, was Stjepan Mesić, considered rather a dark horse. People with whom I spoke in the run-up to that election were convinced that Mate Granić, the candidate of the HDZ, would win the elections, and if Croatia had had an electoral law similar to that in the United States – i.e. no run-off election – perhaps he might have won. But with the option of the run-off, people could vote with their heart in the first round, without worrying that they were "throwing their votes away," as the shibboleth has it. In fact, Mesić emerged as the front-runner in this upset election, taking 41.1% of the vote. Budiša placed second, with 27.7%, and Granić, the supposed favorite, trailed in third place with just 22.5% of the vote. With this, the stage was set for a run-off election, which Mesić won with 56.9% of the vote.

Račan's plan, prior to the election, had been to convert Croatia from a semi-presidential system to a parliamentary system, in effect stripping the presidency of most of its powers. Mesić signaled his agreement with this program, and in the course of amendments passed in 2000 and 2001 the office of the president was downgraded and the office of prime minister became the most powerful political office in Croatia. Račan announced the establishment, in October 2001, of the Office for the Suppression of Corruption and Organized Crime (USKOK) and that same month, Croatian police took into custody twenty-one people who were suspected of embezzlement from the state budget. They were subsequently released, however, because the Zagreb County State Attorney in charge of the case refused to sign a court order to authorize their continued detention; this provoked a huge scandal.[59] In fact, the fight against corruption has not gone well and even four years later, Transparency International (the international agency concerned with fighting corruption) concluded that the Croatian authorities had not succeeded in building public trust in the implementation of the anti-corruption program.[60] The inception of Croatia's accession to the EU, however, has exerted pressure on the authorities in Zagreb to deal more effectively with corruption and on 31 March 2006 the *Sabor* adopted a National Anti-Corruption Program for 2006–8, pledging "to reduce corruption to a level that would not obstruct Croatia's economic, social, political and other development."[61] Commenting on the bill, Justice Minister Ana Lovrin admitted that problems of corruption have been especially acute in the judiciary (as well as in the medical sector) and that "a closer supervision of the spending of budgetary funds allocated to local government units" was indicated.[62]

In addition to the judiciary and the public health sector,[63] the office for privatization and the Zagreb land registry have also been accused of corruption and, in December 2007, twenty-two people at the land registry were arrested on charges of graft and corruption.[64] Moreover, although the fight against corruption stagnated during 2005–6, by the end of 2007, under pressure from the EU, there seemed to be a new resolve on the part of Croatian authorities. Olli Rehn, the EU Commissioner for Enlargement, indicated that Croatia could be in the EU by 2010, provided that it dealt effectively with corruption.[65]

Meanwhile, in the wake of Tudjman's death, a power struggle for leadership of the HDZ developed between Ivić Pašalić, formerly Tudjman's chief adviser rumored to have been involved in some surveillance scandals, and Ivo Sanader, who had become president of the HDZ upon Tudjman's death. Pašalić did not seek the leadership of the party for himself directly, but tried to promote his own candidate, Andrija Hebrang (the son of the Andrija Hebrang who had challenged Tito in Croatia half a century earlier).

In the event, it was Sanader who emerged victorious in this struggle and Sanader who, succeeding in coming across as less stridently nationalist than the HDZ had seemed to many in the 1990s, would lead the HDZ to a decisive electoral victory in November 2003. Where 53 parties had contested the parliamentary elections in 2000, some 58 parties fielded candidates in the elections held on 23 November 2003.[66] Sanader's HDZ emerged as the big winner, capturing 66 seats in the *Sabor*, against 34 for the SDP. The HNS and its coalition partner, the PGS, together commanded 11 mandates. The HSS garnered nine seats in the *Sabor*. Libra (a fraction of the HSLS which had broken away from the party in the summer of 2001 when Budiša created a scandal by demanding that the government reject ICTY chief prosecutor Carla Del Ponte's demand for the extradition of two generals) and the LS together captured one seat each. The IDS won four seats.[67] With this, Sanader took over the office of prime minister, promising to take steps to resolve the problem of Serb refugees who had lost their homes. Deputies from the Samostalna demokratska srpska stranka (Independent Serbian Democratic Party, SDSS) signed an agreement for cooperation with deputies of the HDZ the following month, and party president Pupovac highlighted the importance of this agreement, saying that the HDZ had accepted nearly all of his party's demands. Among other things, the HDZ promised to return confiscated property to institutions of the Serbian community. Moreover, by the end of 2004, the government committed itself to assure the return of occupied homes to their original owners and to provide compensation for such private property as had been destroyed, so that it might be rebuilt.[68] According to the authors of *Politička upotreba izbjelica: 1990–2005*, it would cost the Croatian government about 4.5 billion Euros to compensate Serb refugees for their losses.[69] Two years later, however, Croatia's Serbs remained dissatisfied, alleging that the number of suspected war criminals was unrealistic. Human Rights Watch offered some confirmation of Serb complaints, reporting in September 2006 that, with the notable exception of the reconstruction of houses damaged in the war, the living conditions of Croatia's Serbs had not improved in the years that Sanader had been prime minister.[70]

The Sanader government has not been without its problems, among them a scandal concerning the government's transfer of majority ownership of the Liburnia Riviera Hotel to SN Holding and Dom Holding, resulting in the dismissal of Damir Ostović as president of the Croatian Privatization Fund, and a crisis over the budget, which developed in early 2004 when it turned out that it was not adequate to enable Sanader to keep all of his campaign promises. To secure Serb support, Sanader had promised to pay for the renovation of 7,000 Serb homes which had been destroyed or seriously damaged during the war, and he had also promised to halt a review and revision of benefit payments to veterans and to increase benefits to mothers. Moreover, while Tudjman had bequeathed his successors a foreign debt of US$16 billion, Sanader inherited (from the SDP-led government) a foreign debt of US$25 billion.[71] Where corruption is concerned, the Liburnia scandal was not the Sanader's government's only headache. In 2005 USKOK suffered a setback when Nevenka Tudjman, the daughter of Croatian's first president, was acquitted on charges of having abused her connections to obtain contracts for businessman Igor Knezević, receiving kickbacks in return.[72] USKOK appealed the decision, however, and in August 2005, the Croatian Supreme Court "partly" upheld the appeal. Also of note is the alleged involvement of Hrvoje Petrac, a Croatian tycoon, in kidnapping the son of a former Croatian deputy prime minister, holding the child for ransom.[73] Meanwhile, presidential elections were scheduled to be held in early January 2005, with several candidates running. In the first round, incumbent Stjepan (Stipe) Mesić won 49.03% of the vote, failing by less than 1% to secure a first ballot victory. Mesić's chief rival, Jadranka Kosor, the HDZ candidate, came in second with about 20% of the vote. In the run-off elections held two weeks later, Mesić cruised to an easy victory, winning about 65% of the vote, in the initial tally.[74]

On 11 April 2007, sixty-two-year-old Ivica Račan, battling with cancer, stepped down as head of the opposition SDP; less than three weeks later, he was dead. The SDP elected forty-one-year-old Zoran Milanović, a former diplomat, to take the reins of the party, and it was under his leadership that the party contested new parliamentary elections on 25 November 2007, with former economics minister, Ljubo Jurčić as its candidate for prime minister. Sanader's HDZ emerged as the biggest vote-taker, winning 66 seats, but the SDP finished a strong second with 56 seats.[75] By 1 December, however, Sanader had been confirmed as the prime minister-designate and, two weeks later, completed negotiations with the HSS and HSLS to form a coalition government.[76]

Policies toward the media

Without independent and critical news media it is impossible to sustain, let alone build, a liberal democratic system. It is in recognition of this fact, as well as of the power of the press to shape the policy agenda and national debate, that the media are sometimes called the "fourth branch" of the government. It is, however, in this sphere that the record of the Tudjman regime is perhaps particularly problematic, although the situation has improved since 1999. There were, to begin with, issues of ownership. Directly or indirectly, the HDZ took control not only of the state television station, which commanded a stable audience of about 55% of the population throughout the 1990s,[77] but also of the influential daily newspapers *Vjesnik*, *Večernji list*, *Slobodna Dalmacija*, and *Glas Slavonije*. Early in its reign, the HDZ carried out a purge of the journalists who had been working at Croatian Television, replacing them with younger, less experienced but politically more reliable journalists. Among the four papers acquired by the HDZ or its allies, the big prize was *Večernji list*, with a circulation of 180,000 – more than double that of the other three newspapers combined. The independent media included the daily newspaper *Novi list* from Rijeka, with a circulation of 60,000, and the weeklies *Globus*, *Nacional*, and *Feral Tribune*. As Boris Buden notes, *Globus* got off to an impressive start, but gradually lost readers and influence as a result of its sensationalism and misinformation.[78]

The highly respected weekly magazine, *Danas*, was critical of Tudjman's early moves, but was subsequently taken over by the regime only to be abandoned by its experienced journalists, who launched a rival magazine, *Novi Danas*. The regime succeeded in suffocating the new magazine within a month, while the HDZ-run incarnation of *Danas* hobbled along for a couple of years, with a weak circulation of between 5,000 and 6,000, before expiring for lack of interest.

For those periodicals which insisted on maintaining an independent line, there were other measures available, including drafting the editor into the army and bringing libel suits against the offending publication. All told, about 1,000 libel suits were brought against various media in the years 1990–2000, for the most part by government ministers or other politicians. 56% of these suits involved *Globus*, *Novi list*, and *Nacional*.[79] In addition, the independent weekly *Feral Tribune* was regularly in the dock for publishing articles, photo montages, and even captions which offended Tudjman or others in the HDZ regime. In fact, as of April 1999, about eighty court proceedings and appeals were in process involving *Feral Tribune* alone.[80] But the judiciary continued to enjoy an independence from the authorities, in spite of a certain amount of corruption, and, as a result, acquitted Viktor Ivančić, editor of *Feral Tribune*, and Marinko Čulić, a journalist for the same publication, in 1996 on charges of defamation of the president and, two years later, cleared Davor Butković, the former editor-in-chief of *Globus* of charges of having slandered and insulted Prime Minister Zlatko Mateša and his cabinet.[81] About the same time as Butković was getting a clean slate, Božidar Balenović, editor-in-chief of the fortnightly *Otok* (based in Ivanić Grad) was also cleared of similar charges. (In June 2008, *Feral Tribune* closed down because of financial problems, after fifteen years of publication.)

Such treatment of the media inevitably came to the attention of the Council of Europe and other international organizations, which suggested to Zagreb that its media policy did not meet European standards. In the wake of this criticism, though not necessarily in response to it, the government presented its draft laws on the establishment of private mass media and the allocation of frequencies in December 1993. But problems continued even after this ostensibly promising initiative. In 1996, the regime had in mind to take over the independent radio station, Radio 101. Mass demonstrations in Zagreb at the end of that year stopped the regime in its tracks and, in 1997, the station was granted a concession to broadcast from Zagreb.[82]

It is also a matter of some interest that the Croatian secret police, known more formally as the Service for the Protection of the Constitutional System, followed the work of the Alternative Information Network (Alternativna Informativna Mreža, or AIM) for years, bugging the telephones of its editor and journalists and keeping them under surveillance. (AIM, now defunct, was an online news service largely funded by the EU and covering the Yugoslav area, written by highly qualified, independent journalists, with its editorial offices in Paris.) Agents of the secret police actually compiled dossiers on 126 journalists working for AIM, and, in a 1994 speech, Tudjman incongruously accused it of seeking to restore a united Yugoslavia.[83]

After the transfer of power to the SDP-led coalition in 2000, journalists hoped for better times. But these hopes were dashed. In the years 2001–4, for example, at least five journalists received jail sentences for libel, although their sentences were suspended after the payment of fines. At one point in 2003, there were more than 800 cases against Croatian journalists pending in the courts, although many of these dated back to the Tudjman era.[84] There were also charges, in 2005, that the Counterintelligence Agency headed at the time by Franjo Turek had tapped the telephones of five Croatian journalists during 2003 and 2004, "because they were suspected of participating in a media-intelligence campaign against Croatia."[85] But for all that there has been a liberalization of the legal system, including as regards the press, since 1999, which has resulted in an increase in foreign investment in the Croatian media. Then, in 2003, "the ownership restrictions in broadcasting were lifted for both domestic and foreign owners."[86] At the same time, the new law on the media introduced anti-monopoly provisions for the mass media. The following year, changes to the criminal code reduced the threat of libel suits for journalists. Politicians continued to try to influence the content of national television programming;[87] in October 2006, and again in March 2007, Croatian journalists complained about lack of professional freedom.[88] Perhaps it is not surprising, in such conditions, that an opinion poll taken among Croats in July 2007 found that only 27% of respondents trusted the local media.[89]

Conclusion

In the 1990s, foreign observers were fond of drawing comparisons between the Milošević regime in Serbia and the Tudjman regime in Croatia. Both regimes, so the story went, were corrupt, both relied on nationalism to generate public support, both sought to control the key media and to stifle independent voices in the press, both were hostile to feminism, and both confronted hostile minorities (Albanians in Kosovo, Serbs in the Krajina). But there were also important differences. In the first place, Milošević had planned and orchestrated an aggressive war intended to expand the borders of Serbia; there was no fighting on the territory of the Republic of Serbia during the years of the War of Yugoslav Succession. Tudjman, by contrast, neither planned nor orchestrated the war. In Croatia, the Zagreb authorities fought what was clearly a defensive war, while, in Bosnia, from Tudjman's perspective, the war was likewise a defensive one, intended to secure the lives and property of Croats who were threatened by a war which they themselves had not started.[90] Secondly, Milošević's Socialist Party of Serbia was the successor party to the old League of Communists of Serbia, and continued to reflect some of the old socialist attitudes – e.g. as regards private property. Tudjman's party, the HDZ, was an opposition party, committed to an anti-communist program. And, thirdly, Milošević used the police to beat and jail some of his political opponents (such as Vuk Drašković in 1993) and, by failing to acknowledge opposition victories in 1996, kindled street protests that dragged on for nearly eighty days. Tudjman, by contrast, refrained from strong-arm tactics against opposition politicians, was generally more successful in maintaining popular confidence in his rule (as indicated by the approval ratings cited above), and even his blockage of the opposition victory in the mayoral contest in Zagreb never generated protest even remotely comparable to what was seen in Belgrade.

Tudjman died in December 1999 and Milošević was ousted by a popular revolt in October 2000, after he attempted to falsify the results of the presidential election which Vojislav Koštunica, a legal scholar, had actually won. In the years since the end of their respective terms of office, Croatia has edged forward in the direction of a more open, more liberal society, eventually adopting, in the face of resistance from the Catholic Church, an anti-discrimination law in July 2008, which banned discrimination on the basis of racial, ethnic, political, religious, or sexual criteria.[91] By contrast, Serbia has slipped backwards, basking in revanchist Chetnik nationalism and engaging in the most offensive historical revisionism concerning the number of victims to die at the Jasenovac concentration camp.[92] Until December 2005, the fact that Croatia could not deliver the fugitive general, Ante Gotovina, to the ICTY constituted an obstacle on the country's path to inclusion in the EU. But with the apprehension of Gotovina (on Spanish soil) on 7 December, thanks to active cooperation between Croatian and Spanish police,[93] the path was cleared for Croatia's admission to the European club. Less than two weeks later, the US Senate adopted a resolution recommending that Croatia be admitted to NATO without further delay.[94] In subsequent months, Croatia's armed forces were gradually brought up to NATO standards and, at the end of December 2006, as a token of its commitment to military cooperation with the Western alliance, the Croatian parliament voted to increase the Croatian military contingent in Afghanistan from 150 to 300.[95] By March 2007, Great Britain, Italy, and Hungary, among others, had joined the United States in endorsing Croatia's admission, with the US Senate voting (in November 2006) to earmark US$3 million in military aid for Croatia[96]; on 3 April 2008 the Croatian government received a formal invitation to join NATO,[97] joining the alliance a year later. As for entrance into the EU, in spite of conflicting reports about the struggle against corruption,[98] the European Parliament declared itself satisfied (in February 2007) with Croatia's progress in adapting its legislation to EU standards, fighting corruption, and carrying its share of the burden of war crimes trials in its national courts, projecting Croatia's admission as the 28th member state of the EU.[99] There was also praise from the European Parliament in February 2008 for Croatia's efforts in assuring propitious conditions for the return of Serb refugees; of the 280,000 Serbs who took flight from Croatia during 1991–5, about 130,000 had returned by that date.[100] In spite of a broad consensus within the EU that Croatia had made satisfactory progress toward meeting the conditions for accession, Slovenia blocked negotiations with Croatia concerning accession chapters dealing with regional policy, justice, freedom and security, the environment, and the free circulation of capital, because of bilateral issues in contention.[101] In May 2009, the Croatian *Sabor* agreed to the draft agreement proposed by the European Commission as a basis for the resolution of the border dispute with Slovenia. But on 18 June the Slovenes broke off talks with Croatian representatives after Croatian Prime Minister Sanader offered two new proposals and the Slovenian side rejected them. On 24 June, in the wake of this setback, Brussels called off accession talks with Croatia. A week later, Sanader stepped down as prime minister, declaring that "The EU and [the] project of European integration have no chance if the principle of blackmailing is accepted as a principle of acting within the EU."[102] Sanader's erstwhile deputy, Jadranka Kosor, was quickly confirmed as his successor as prime minister and signaled that overcoming the economic crisis and gaining entry into the EU would be the highest priorities for her government.

I have suggested in this chapter that democratization should be understood as involving the establishment of the rule of law, political pluralism, an independent judiciary, and a free press. If one adds liberalism to the equation, with the idea that the system being developed should be not just any kind of democracy but specifically a liberal democracy, then the inculcation of liberal values becomes of critical importance, and here the contents of textbooks, newspapers, and films can make a key difference. And, judging by the changes to the history textbooks since 1999,[103] there is reason to hope that liberal values, too, are gaining ground in Croatia.

Timeline 925–2009

925	Establishment of the Kingdom of Croatia, with King Tomislav reigning as the first king
1102	Croatia forced into union with Hungary, ruled by the King of Hungary
1527	Croatia enters union with Austria
1699	Treaty of Karlowitz ends Austro-Turkish war and settlies Croatia's southern borders
1809–13	Croatia incorporated into Province of Illyria, part of Napoleon's empire
1867	Signing of the *Ausgleich*, dividing the Habsburg Empire into an Austrian half and a Hungarian half; Croatia divided between the two, with Dalmatia assigned to Austria, and the rest of Croatia assigned to Hungary
December 1918	Establishment of the Kingdom of Serbs, Croats, and Slovenes
20 June 1928	Assassination of Stjepan Radić, head of the Croatian Peasant Party
October 1929	Kingdom renamed the Kingdom of Yugoslavia
26 August 1939	Signing of the Sporazum, establishing the autonomous banovina of Croatia
1941	Proclamation of Independent State of Croatia, an Axis state headed by Ante Pavelić; the country occupied by German and Italian troops
May 1945	End of the Second World War; Yugoslavia re-established with the communists in the leading positions
1946	Passage of the first communist constitution for Yugoslavia; trial of Zagreb's Archbishop Alojzije Stepinac
1953	Passage of the Basic Law, usually counted as the second constitution for communist-era Yugoslavia

1963	Passage of the third constitution for communist Yugoslavia
1967–71	Liberal politicians in power in Slovenia, Croatia, Serbia, and Macedonia
1974	Passage of the fourth constitution for communist Yugoslavia
May 1980	Death of Yugoslav President Josip Broz Tito
May 1990	Croatian Democratic Union (HDZ), led by Franjo Tudjman, a retired army general-turned-historian, wins parliamentary elections; Tudjman subsequently elected president of Croatia
June 1991	Croatia and Slovenia declare disassociation from defunct Socialist Federated Republic of Yugoslavia
December 1991	EU announces it will extend diplomatic recognition to Croatia and Slovenia
1991–5	War of Yugoslav Succession
November 1995	Dayton Peace Accords (formally signed on 14 December)
7 August 1996	Presidents of Croatia and Serbia agree to establish diplomatic relations
15 January 1998	Eastern Slavonia is reintegrated into Croatia; it had been seized by the Serbs in 1991
3 October 1998	Pope John Paul II beatifies Alojzije Cardinal Stepinac
10 December 1999	Death of Croatian President Franjo Tudjman
2000	Social Democratic Party, led by Ivica Račan, wins parliamentary elections; Račan becomes prime minister; Stjepan Mesić elected president of Croatia
December 2001	Federal Republic of Yugoslavia returns artworks looted from the city of Vukovar in 1991
February 2003	Croatia applies for membership in the EU
23 November 2003	HDZ, led by Ivo Sanader, wins parliamentary elections; Sanader becomes prime minister the following month
July 2005	Montenegro agrees to pay Croatia $460,000 in war damages for cattle seized by its troops in June 1991
October 2005	EU gives green light for accession talks with Croatia to begin
7 December 2005	Arrest of former General Ante Gotovina on war crimes charges
25 November 2007	HDZ, led by Ivo Sanader, wins parliamentary elections, allowing Sanader to stay on as prime minister
9 July 2008	NATO allies sign accession protocols with Croatia
April 2009	Croatia admitted into NATO

Fact sheet

Area	56,542 km^2
Population (July 2009)	4,489,409
Croat (2001 census)	89.6%
Serb (2001 census)	4.5%
Other (2001 census)	5.9%
Urban population (2008)	57%

Below the poverty line (2007)	11% of population
Unemployment rate (2008)	14.8%
GDP ***per capita*** (2008)	$16, 100
Real GDP growth (2008)	4.8%
Inflation (2008)	6.3%

Sources: CIA, *The World Factbook*, www.cia.gov/library/publications/the-world-factbook/geos/hr.html [accessed on 2 November 2008 and on 12 July 2009]; and unicef–Croatia, www.unicef.org/infobycountry/croatia_statistics.html [accessed on 8 March 2008].

Parties in the Croatian *Sabor* (results of 25 November 2007 elections, showing only results for those parties with deputies in the *Sabor*)

Party	percent of the vote	Number of deputies elected
Croatian Democratic Union (HDZ)	36.6	66
Social Democratic Party (SDP)	31.2	56
Green–Yellow Coalition (five parties)	6.5	8
Croatian People's Party–Liberal Democrats	6.8	7
Istrian Democratic Assembly	1.5	3
Croatian Democratic Assembly of Slavonija and Baranja	1.8	3
Pensioners' coalition (two parties)	4.1	1
Independent Democratic Serbian Party		3
Party of Democratic Action (minority list)		1
Other national minority representatives		4

Source: "Croatian parliamentary election, 2007," Wikipedia, at en.wikipedia.org/wiki/Croatian_parliamentary_election,_2007 [accessed on 8 March 2008].

Short Biography of Franjo Tudjman

Franjo Tudjman was the first president of the Republic of Croatia, serving in that office from May 1990 until his death in December 1999. Born on 14 May 1922 in Veliko Trgovišće, a village in the Zagorje region of Croatia, he joined Tito's Partisans during the Second World War, rising to the rank of colonel during the war. In 1945, he took a post in the Ministry of Defense in Belgrade, subsequently rising to the rank of major-general. He left army service in 1961 and, having earned a PhD in history from the Zadar branch of the University of Zagreb, he founded the Institute for the History of the Workers' Movement of Croatia, serving as its director from 1961 to 1967. In 1972, he was found guilty of ideological subversion and given a two-year prison sentence, but he was released after nine months. He was tried again in 1981, for having given a frank interview to Swedish television, in which he discussed the situation of Croats in Yugoslavia. He received a three-year sentence but was released after he had served eleven months in prison. During the 1980s and into the beginning of the 1990s Tudjman, always a prolific writer, produced several books, among them: *Nationalism in Contemporary Europe*

(1981), first published in English and later published in Croatian translation under the title, *Nacionalno pitanje u suvremenoj Europi* (1990); *Bespuća povijesne zbiljnosti: Rasprava o povijesti i filozofiji zlosilja*, 2nd edn. (1989), later published in English translation under the title, *Horrors of War: Historical Reality and Philosophy*, rev. edn. (1996); and *Hrvatska u monarhističkoj Jugoslaviji, 1918.–1941.*, 2 vols. (1993). In the course of 1989, he organized a political party, the Croatian Democratic Union (Hrvatska Demokratska Zajednica, HDZ) and, in May 1990, his party won the first multi-party elections in Croatia in more than half a century. He subsequently served as president of Croatia from 30 May 1990 until his death on 10 December 1999. The Serbian insurgency broke out in March 1991 and by July 1991 Croatia found itself in a full-scale war against Serb insurgents who enjoyed the support of the Yugoslav Army. By the end of 1991, about 30% of Croatian territory has been occupied by Serb insurgents. Tudjman nonetheless rallied the Croats and eventually succeeded in quashing the insurgency, restoring Croatia's pre-war boundaries. During his years in office, he won praise for winning the war and has been lauded as a master strategist. But he stirred controversy because of allegations of corruption of the media and in connection with the role of the Croatian Army in Bosnia-Herzegovina during the war years.

Notes

* This is an abridged and updated version of a chapter first published in Sabrina P. Ramet, *Serbia, Croatia, and Slovenia at Peace and at War: Selected Writings, 1983–2007* (Berlin and Münster: Lit Verlag, 2008) and also in Sabrina P. Ramet, Konrad Clewing, and Renéo Lukic (eds.), *Croatia since Independence: War, Politics, Society, Foreign Relations* (Munich: R. Oldenbourg Verlag, 2008), reprinted with the kind permission of Lit Verlag and of Konrad Clewing.

1. For a discussion, see Robert A. Kann and Zdeněk V. David, *The Peoples of the Eastern Habsburg Lands, 1526–1918* (Seattle and London: University of Washington Press, 1984).
2. See Sabrina P. Ramet, *The Three Yugoslavias: State-Building and Legitimation, 1918–2005* (Bloomington, Ind and Washington, DC: Indiana University Press and Woodrow Wilson Center Press, 2006), chapters 2–3.
3. See Sabrina P. Ramet (ed.), *The Independent State of Croatia 1941–45* (London and New York: Routledge, 2007).
4. Michael Pinto-Duschinsky, "Financing Politics: A Global View," *Journal of Democracy*, Vol. 13, No. 4 (October 2002), p. 73, as quoted in Zdravko Petak, "Financing Political Parties in Croatia: Parliamentary Elections 2003," *Politička misao: Croatian Political Science Review*, Vol. 40, No. 5 (2003), p. 69.
5. Mate Granić, *Vanjski poslovi. Iza kulisa politike* (Zagreb: Algoritam, 2005), p. 29.
6. Concerning Baković, see Ramet, *The Three Yugoslavias*, p. 589.
7. Zoran Kusovac, "The Prospects for Change in Post-Tudjman Croatia," *East European Constitutional Review* (Summer 2000), p. 58.
8. *Ibid.*, p. 58.
9. *The Constitution of the Republic of Croatia* [1990] (Zagreb: Narodne Novine, 1993), Article 101, pp. 125–6.
10. Kusovac, "The Prospects for Change," p. 61.

11. Franjo Tuđman, *The HDZ – The Core Party of Democratic Croatia* (Zagreb: Ivan Valent, March 1998), p. 48.
12. "HDZ-u i HSP-u raste popularnost u hrvatskom biračkom tijelu," *Globus* (Zagreb), 26 January 1996, p. 79.
13. Vlado Vurušić, "Tuđmanov život nakon smrti," *Globus*, No. 627, 13 December 2002, p. 35.
14. Ivo Perić, *Povijest za IV. razred gimnazije*, 3rd edn. (Zagreb: ALFA d.d., 2003), p. 231.
15. These figures are drawn from my *Balkan Babel: The Disintegration of Yugoslavia from the Death of Tito to the Fall of Milošević*, 4th edn. (Boulder, Colo.: Westview Press, 2002), p. 163.
16. Tuđman, *The HDZ*, p. 51.
17. *Reuter News Service* (1 October 1995), on *Lexis-Nexis Academic Universe.*
18. Slavko Granić, "The Croatian Coat of Arms: Historical Emblem or Controversial Symbol?," *Journal of Croatian Studies*, Vol. 34–35 (1993–4), p. 9.
19. See my "Martyr in his Own Mind: The Trial and Tribulations of Slobodan Milošević," *Totalitarian Movements and Political Religions*, Vol. 5, No. 1 (Summer 2004), pp. 112–38.
20. See in particular Nikica Barić, *Srpska pobuna u Hrvatskoj 1990–1995* (Zagreb: Golden Marketing, 2005), pp. 78–9, 81, 126.
21. Borisav Jović, *Posledni dani SFRJ – izvodi iz dnevnika* (Belgrade: Politika, 1995).
22. On this point, see Viktor Meier, *Yugoslavia: A History of Its Demise*, trans. by Sabrina P. Ramet (London and New York: Routledge, 1999).
23. For an alternative account of the reasons for Croatia's military travails, see Martin Špegelj, *Sjećanja vojnika*, ed. Ivo Zanić (Zagreb: Znanje, 2001).
24. *The Toronto Star* (1 August 1991), p. A1, on *Lexis-Nexis Academic Universe.*
25. *Croatia Weekly* (Zagreb), 23 December 1999, p. 13.
26. *Vjesnik* (Zagreb), 12 December 2001, at www.vjesnik.hr [accessed on 17 December 2001].
27. *Croatia Weekly* (10 June 1999), p. 3.
28. *Vjesnik* (6 February 2002), at www.vjesnik.hr [accessed on 6 February 2002].
29. *Vjesnik* (12 March 2004), at www.vjesnik.hr [accessed on 14 March 2004].
30. On this point, see Ramet, *The Three Yugoslavias*, chapter 15.
31. Branko Mamula, *Slučaj Jugoslavija* (Podgorica: CID, 2000), p. 250.
32. Tim Judah, *The Serbs: History, Myth and the Destruction of Yugoslavia* (New Haven, Conn.: Yale University Press, 1997), p. 245.
33. Stjepan Mesić, president of the SFRY collective presidency for a few months during 1991 and, since 2000, president of Croatia, in interview with SPR, Zagreb, 30 July 1997. See also Igor Lasić, "Odnosi Hrvatske i BiH: Veliko ništa," *Dani* (Sarajevo), No. 216 (27 July 2001), p. 20.
34. *Tanjug* (10 April 1991), trans. in *BBC Summary of World Broadcasts* (13 April 1991), on *Lexis-Nexis Academic Universe.*
35. As summarized in Cathie Carmichael, *Ethnic Cleansing in the Balkans: Nationalism and the Destruction of Tradition* (London and New York: Routledge, 2002), p. 36. Anto Valenta, *Podjela Bosne i borba za cjelovitost* (Vitez: HKD "Napredak," 1991).
36. Darko Hudelist, *Tuđman: Biografija* (Zagreb: Profil, 2004), pp. 672, 682.
37. Ivica Radoš, *Tuđman izbliza: Svjedočenja suradnika i protivnika* (Zagreb: Profil, 2005), p. 94.

38. Franjo Tuđman, *Hrvatska riječ svijetu: Razgovori sa stranim predstavnicima* (Zagreb: Hrvatska Sveučilišna Naklada and Hrvatski Institut za Povijest, 1999), pp. 171–3 (from *Der Spiegel*, 12 August 1991) and pp. 177–80 (from *Komsomolskaia pravda*, 9 October 1991).
39. For a discussion of this fighting, see Charles Shrader, *The Muslim–Croat Civil War in Central Bosnia: A Military History, 1992–1994* (College Station, Tex.: Texas A&M University Press, 2003).
40. *Dossier: Crimes of Muslim Units Against the Croats in BiH 1992–1994* (Mostar: Centre for Investigation and Documentation, 1994), p. 10.
41. President Franjo Tudjman, in conversation with representatives of the HDZ's Bosnian branch, Zagreb, 27 December 1991, according to the official transcript reprinted in Ciril Ribičič, *Geneza jedne zablude: Ustavnopravna analiza nastanka i djelovanja Hrvatske zajednice Herceg-Bosne* (Zagreb, Sarajevo and Idrija: Naklada Jesenski i Turk, Sejtarija and Založba Bogataj, 2000), pp. 129, 166.
42. As quoted in Sergej Abramov, "Tuđman '93: U Herceg-Bosni se rješavaju buduće granice RH," *Novi list* (Rijeka), 3 April 2003, at www.novilist.hr [accessed on 3 April 2003].
43. *Ibid.*
44. *Washington Post* (13 June 2000), as cited in Mirna Solić, "The Tudjman Tapes," in TOL (Prague), 10 July 2000, at archive.tol.cz/itowa/jul00cro.html [accessed on 13 February 2004].
45. Granić, *Vanjski poslovi*, as summarized in *Večernji list* (18 August 2005), at www.vecernji-list.hr [accessed on 18 August 2005].
46. Jelena Lovrić, "Pašalić je bio Tuđmanov pregovarač s Karadžićem," *Novi list* (3 April 2002), at www.novilist.hr [accessed on 3 April 2002].
47. *Večernji list* (18 June 2002), at www.vecernji-list.hr [accessed on 21 June 2002].
48. Siniša Tatalović, "Human Rights in Croatia – The Burden of the Ethnic Minorities Problem," in Dragica Vujadinović *et al.* (eds.), *Between Authoritarianism and Democracy – Serbia, Montenegro, Croatia*, 2 vols. (Belgrade, Podgorrica, and Zagreb: CEDET/CEDEM/CTCSR, 2005), Vol. 2, p. 508.
49. "Hrvatska Demokratska Zajednica Inicijativni Krug," *Bilten (za članstvo)*, Vol. 1, No. 1 (June 1989), p. 1.
50. Quoted in the *Independent* (London), 24 April 1996, p. 10, on *Lexis-Nexis Academic Universe*, my emphasis.
51. Tudjman, *The HDZ*, p. 16.
52. *Ibid.*, p. 21.
53. Quoted in Nenad Zakošek, "Das politische System Kroatiens," in Wolfgang Ismayr (ed.), with the assistance of Markus Soldner and Ansgar Bovet, *Die politischen Systeme Osteuropas* (Opladen: Leske Budrich, 2002), pp. 644–5.
54. *Ibid.*, p. 647.
55. HINA (27 February 2006), *World News Connection*, Accession number 222000743.
56. HINA (8 May 2006), *World News Connection*, Accession number 225550414.
57. Srđan Vrcan, "Elections in Croatia: A Symptomatic Case or an Anomaly?," in Dragica Vujadinović *et al.* (eds.), *Between Authoritarianism and Democracy – Serbia, Montenegro, Croatia*, 2 vols. (Belgrade, Podgorica, and Zagreb: CEDET/CEDEM/CTCSR, 2005), Vol. 1 p. 243.
58. *Ibid.*, p. 247.

59. Predrag Bejaković, "Corruption in Croatia: Institutional Settings and Practical Experiences," *Politička misao: Croatian Political Science Review*, Vol. 39, No. 5 (2002), p. 137.
60. *Novi list* (1 June 2005), at www.novilist.hr [accessed on 29 July 2005].
61. HINA (31 March 2006), in *BBC Monitoring Europe – Political* (31 March 2006), on *Lexis-Nexis Academic Universe*.
62. HINA (29 March 2006), in *BBC Monitoring Europe – Political* (29 March 2006), on *Lexis-Nexis Academic Universe*.
63. *Glas Slavonije* (Osijek), 22 September 2006, at www.glas-slavonije.hr/ [accessed on 22 September 2006]; and *Večernji list* (6 December 2007), at www.vecernji.list/ [accessed on 30 December 2007].
64. *Javno.org* (Zagreb), 11 December 2007, at www.javno.com/ [accessed on 31 December 2007].
65. *Jutarnji list* (Zagreb), 28 April 2007, at www.jutarnji.hr/ [accessed on 1 May 2007].
66. Mirjana Kasapović, "Coalition Governments in Croatia: First Experience 2000–2003," *Politička misao: Croatian Political Science Review*, Vol. 40, No. 5 (2003), p. 54.
67. *Vjesnik* (25 November 2003), at www.vjesnik.hr [accessed on 30 March 2004]. In preliminary results, the HDZ was reported to have won 62 seats.
68. *Novi list* (20 December 2003), at www.novilist.hr [accessed on 26 September 2004]. See also *Vjesnik* (26 March 2004), at www.vjesnik.hr [accessed on 26 March 2004]. For an update on the situation regarding refugees, see HINA (31 March 2006), in *BBC Monitoring Europe – Political* (31 March 2006), on *Lexis-Nexis Academic Universe*.
69. As cited in *Večernji list* (18 August 2005), at www.vecernji-list.hr [accessed on 18 August 2005].
70. Davor Konjikusić, "Croatian Serbs Question Deal with Government," *Institute for War & Peace Reporting* (19 October 2006), at www.iwpr.net/ [accessed on 27 October 2006]; and *Human Rights Watch*, as summarized in HINA (5 September 2006), at www.hina.hr/ [accessed on 5 September 2006].
71. Drago Hedl, "Croatia: Budget Crisis Threatens Sanadar," in *Institute for War & Peace Reporting*, BCR No. 482 (26 February 2004), at www.iwpr.net [accessed on 4 March 2004].
72. "Supreme Court Upholds USKOK's Appeal against Acquittal of Nevenka Tudjman," HINA (17 August 2005), at www.hina.hr [accessed on 18 August 2005].
73. Petrac was taken into custody in August 2005. See *Vjesnik* (1 September 2005), at www.vjesnik.hr [accessed on 27 December 2005].
74. *The Independent* (3 January 2005), at news.independent.co.uk [accessed on 3 January 2005]; and *Guardian* (London), 17 January 2005, at www.guardian.co.uk [accessed on 18 January 2005].
75. *Vjesnik* (27 November 2007), at www.vjesnik.hr/ [accessed on 27 November 2007]; and AFP (26 November 2007), from topic@afp.com, by subscription.
76. AFP (26 November 2007), from topic@afp.com, by subscription; and *Vjesnik* (1 December 2007), *Vjesnik* (4 December 2007), and *Vjesnik* (17 December 2007) – all at www.vjesnik.hr/ [accessed on 31 December 2007].
77. Boris Buden, "Croatia," in Hannes Grandits, Siegfried Gruber, Karl Kaser, Robert Pichler, and Christian Promitzer (eds.), *Education and Media in Southeast Europe: Country Reports* (Graz: Center for the Study of Balkan Societies and Cultures, 1999), p. 37.

78. *Ibid.*, p. 38. The point about *Globus'* sensationalism is confirmed by Lino Veljak, "Civil Society and Politics in Croatia," in Vujadinović *et al.* (eds.), *Between Authoritarianism and Democracy*, Vol. 2, p. 335.
79. Zrinjka Peruško, "Media and Civic Values," in Sabrina P. Ramet and Davorka Matić (eds.), *Democratic Transition in Croatia: Value Transformation, Education, and Media* (College Station, Tex.: Texas A&M University Press, 2007), p. 234.
80. Milivoj Djilas, "Attack on the Media in Croatia," *AIM Press* (28 April 1999), pp. 1–2.
81. The evidence against Butković was an article bearing the headline, "Croatian government corrupt and greatly influenced by organized crime." See Igor Vukić, "Verdicts in Favour of Freedom of the Media," *AIM Press* (28 April 1998), at www.aimpress.an/dyn/trae/archive/data/199702/70202-003-trae-zag.htm.
82. On this point, see Igor Vukić, "Concession Granted to Radio 101," *AIM Press* (2 February 1997), p. 1.
83. Drago Hedl, "Croatian Secret Services Spied on AIM," *AIM Press* (23 December 2001), pp. 1–2.
84. Anna McTaggart, "Croatian Minister Pays Up to Keep Journalists Out of Jail," *Institute for War & Peace Reporting*, BCR No. 509 (30 July 2004), at www.iwpr.net [accessed on 25 January 2005], pp. 2–3.
85. HINA (7 February 2005), *BBC Worldwide Monitoring* (7 February 2005), on *Lexis-Nexis Academic Universe.*
86. Peruško, "Media and Civic Values," p. 232.
87. Barbara Peranić, "Croatia," in Jeannette Goehring (ed.), *Nations in Transit 2006: Democratization from Central Europe to Eurasia* (New York: Freedom House, 2006), p. 209.
88. *Vjesnik* (24 October 2006), at www.vjesnik.hr/ [accessed on 24 October 2006]; and *Vjesnik* (24 March 2007), at www.vjesnik.hr/ [accessed on 29 March 2007].
89. *Jutarnji list* (28 July 2007), at www.jutarnji.hr/ [accessed on 19 August 2007].
90. Whatever one makes of Croatian Serb claims that they were threatened in Croatia, it was nonetheless they who started the war there.
91. AFP (9 July 2008), from topic@afp.com, by subscription.
92. If Serb claims are accepted at face value, then 70percent of all those who lost their lives in the Yugoslav region through unnatural causes during the Second World War were Serbs killed at one location – Jasenovac – and if that were true, then the Second World War should truly be seen as having been not only a horrific war but also a very strange war.
93. *Glas Slavonije* (9 December 2005), at www.glas-slavonije.hr [accessed on 9 December 2005]; and *Večernji list* (13 December 2005), at www.vecernji-list.hr [accessed on 13 December 2005].
94. HINA (22 December 2005,) at www.hina.hr [accessed on 23 December 2005].
95. Regarding adaptation, see "Croatian Parliament on Armed Forces Status," *Javno*.org (28 March 2007), at www.javno.com/en/croatia/clanak.php?=id=30421 [accessed on 31 March 2007]; regarding the contingent in Afghanistan, see Agence France Presse (AFP), 8 December 2006, at topic@afp.com, by subscription.

96. HINA (17 November 2006), at www.hina.hr/ [accessed on 19 November 2006].
97. *Jutarnji list* (3 April 2008), at www.jutarnji.hr/ [accessed on 2 August 2008].
98. The Zagreb daily newspaper *Vjesnik* reported in July 2006 that corruption had been "tangibly reduced" while another Zagreb daily, *Jutarnji list*, citing the annual report of Transparency International, claimed that Croatia was at more or less the same place in the international ranking of levels of corruption as it had been the previous year. See *Vjesnik* (27 July 2006), at www.vjesnik.hr/ [accessed on 27 July 2006]; and *Jutarnji list* (6 November 2006), at www.jutarnji.hr/ [accessed on 26 November 2006].
99. HINA (28 February 2007), at www.hina.hr/ [accessed on 1 March 2007]; and *Vjesnik* (28 March 2007), at www.vjesnik.hr/ [accessed on 29 March 2007].
100. AFP (7 February 2008), from topic@afp.com, by subscription.
101. AFP (30 October 2008), from topic@afp.com, by subscription.
102. Quoted in AFP (1 July 2009), from topic@afp.com, by subscription.
103. On this point, see Magdalena Najbar-Agičić and Damir Agičić, "The Use and Misuse of History Teaching in 1990s Croatia," in Ramet and Matić (eds.), *Democratic Transition in Croatia*, pp. 193–223.

Further reading

Bartlett, William. *Croatia: Between Europe and the Balkans* (London and New York: Routledge, 2003)

Fisher, Sharon. *Political Change in Post-Communist Slovakia and Croatia: From Nationalist to Europeanist* (New York: Palgrave Macmillan, 2006)

Goldstein, Ivo. *Croatia: A History*, trans. by Nikolina Jovanović (London: C. Hurst & Co., 1999)

Hofman, Nila Ginger. *Renewed Survival: Jewish Community Life in Croatia* (Lanham, Md.: Lexington Books, 2006)

Ilišin, Vlasta and Furio Radin (eds.). *Youth and Transition in Croatia* (Zagreb: Institute for Social Research, 2002)

Lukic, Renéo and Allen Lynch. *Europe from the Balkans to the Urals: The Disintegration of Yugoslavia and the Soviet Union* (Oxford and New York: Oxford University Press, 1996)

Magaš, Branka. *Croatia through History: The Making of a European State* (London: Saqi, 2007)

Magaš, Branka and Ivo Žanić (eds.). *The War in Croatia and Bosnia-Herzegovina, 1991–1995* (London: Frank Cass, 2001)

Ramet, Sabrina P. *The Three Yugoslavias: State-Building and Legitimation, 1918–2005* (Bloomington, Ind. and Washington, DC: Indiana University Press and Woodrow Wilson Center Press, 2006)

Ramet, Sabrina P., Konrad Clewing, and Renéo Lukic (eds.). *Croatia since Independence: War, Politics, Society, Foreign Relations* (Munich: R. Oldenbourg Verlag, 2008)

Ramet, Sabrina P. and Davorka Matić (eds.). *Democratic Transition in Croatia: Value Transformation, Education, and Media* (College Station, Tex.: Texas A&M University Press, 2007)

Tanner, Marcus. *Croatia: A Nation Forged in War* (New Haven, Conn.: Yale University Press, 1997)

Vujadinović, Dragica, Lino Veljak, Vladimir Goati, and Veselin Pavićević (eds.). *Between Authoritarianism and Democracy - Serbia, Montenegro, Croatia*, Vols. 1–2 (Belgrade, Podgorica, and Zagreb: CEDET/CEDEM/CTCSR, 2003, 2005)

13

Serbia and Montenegro since 1989

SABRINA P. RAMET

On 5 October 2000, angry Serbs stormed the parliament building in downtown Belgrade, as smoke poured out of the open windows. Protesting against the attempted theft by Slobodan Milošević (1941–2006) of the presidential election he had called, the protesters effectively ended thirteen years of rule by Milošević and his Socialist Party of Serbia. The events of that day inspired many Serbs with hope. They hoped that the corruption associated with the Milošević era would end. They hoped that the Serbian economy would improve radically, and that the poverty of those least well off would be eased. They hoped for political stability and, as the successful presidential candidate, Vojislav Koštunica (b. 1944), put it, for a normal life.

These hopes have been only partially satisfied. While Serbia still has problems with corruption, Ivica Dačić, the Minister of the Interior since July 2008, immediately took steps to deal with the problem. Although, according to Transparency International's Corruption Perceptions Index (CPI), it has improved its rating – in from 106th place in 2003 (the first year that Serbia was rated) to 85th place in 2008 (tied with Montenegro) – *Nations in Transit* reported in 2006 that nearly every political party in the parliament had lost deputies to other parties as a result of bribes, and that "the fight against corruption has not been a high priority of post-Milošević governments, despite rhetorical commitments" with the result that "corruption remains deeply entrenched at all levels."[1] On the positive side, poverty was cut from 13.4% of households in 2002 to 6.6% of households in 2007, according to official government figures, although Radio B-92 has since reported that 10.7% of the population in central Serbia lived below the poverty line as of October 2007.[2] But on the negative side of the tally, having lost Montenegro in 2006, Serbia lost Kosovo as well less than two years later, with uncertainties about the future of the Albanian-inhabited enclaves within Serbia itself (in spite of assurances by the EU) and fears of the outbreak of war, fanned in 2008 by Moscow-based newspapers. Among the post-communist states of Europe, Serbia's situation perhaps most closely resembles that of Macedonia, which is to say, economically among the less prosperous countries of Europe and on a slow track in terms of entry into the EU, although the only major obstacle to the initiation of EU accession talks at this writing is the Serbian government's failure to apprehend Ratko Mladić and Goran Hadžić, who were indicted in 1995 and 2004, respectively on charges of war crimes. Montenegro's prospects for gaining membership in the EU seem better and, on 19 October 2007, some sixteen months after independence, the constitutional parliament of Montenegro adopted a new constitution for that republic, replacing the constitution of 1992. In terms of the economy, Serbia has the more diversified economy, while Montenegro's is heavily dependent upon tourism.

Before Milošević

Serbia and Montenegro existed as medieval states; Serbia lost its independence to the Ottomans in 1459, while Montenegro lost its independence in 1499. Unlike Serbia, however, Montenegro enjoyed limited autonomy within the Ottoman Empire. Both states regained their independence in the course of the nineteenth century and were recognized internationally in 1878, as part of the settlement of the Congress of Berlin. Both states made territorial gains in the Balkan Wars of 1912–13, with the Serbian army annexing the regions known today as Kosova and Macedonia. In 1918, Serbia and Montenegro joined the new Kingdom of Serbs, Croats, and Slovenes (renamed the Kingdom of Yugoslavia in October 1929), combining with lands which had belonged to the Austro-Hungarian Empire. The Kingdom was invaded by Axis forces in April 1941 and divided up into occupation zones. Serbia was occupied by German forces, with a local puppet government, headed by Milan Nedić, the former minister of war who was installed in office in August 1941 and whose government received arms and money from Berlin. Montenegro was occupied by Italian forces.

Communist-led Partisans offered resistance to the Axis occupation; their leader, Marshal Josip Broz Tito (1892–1980), would later become prime minister, and still later, president of socialist Yugoslavia. Dragoljub "Draža" Mihailović (1893–1946), a colonel in the Yugoslav army, organized Chetnik forces to resist the occupation. But by the end of 1941, the Chetniks slid into a pattern of collaboration with any partner willing to give them arms to use against the Partisans. Among others, the Chetniks collaborated with Germans, Italians, and Bulgarian forces, and even with local Croatian fascists (*Ustaše*) in joint military ventures against the Partisans.[3]

After 1945, Tito successfully defied the Soviets, resulting in Yugoslavia's expulsion from the Soviet-led Cominform and a Soviet bloc economic blockade. Tito turned to the West for aid, and later went on to co-found the Nonaligned Movement, consisting of states which were neither part of the Soviet bloc nor affiliated with any Western alliance. Four constitutions were passed in Tito's era, but, at the time of his death in May 1980 the system was already under strain, with a growing foreign debt and rising rates of unemployment and inflation. Criticism of the policies of Tito and his immediate successors grew steadily, beginning in the late 1970s; within Serbia itself, there were communists who had never reconciled themselves to the fourth constitution, passed in 1974, which had expanded the autonomy and status of Kosovo and Vojvodina, two provinces lying within Serbia and which were now defined as "federal units." Anti-Belgrade riots throughout Kosovo in April 1981 provoked a Serbian backlash, manifested, *inter alia*, in an appeal by the Serbian Orthodox Church to protect the holy shrines of the Serbian people in Kosovo. Then, in 1985, members of the Serbian Academy of Sciences and Art agreed to draft a memorandum expressing their discontent with socialist Yugoslavia. An incomplete draft was leaked to the Belgrade daily newspaper, *Večernje novosti*, in September 1986 and was published in the 24–25 September 1986 issue. With its claims that Serbs had been treated unjustly throughout the Tito era, were "endangered" in Croatia, and were being subjected to "physical, political, legal, and cultural genocide" in Kosovo,[4] the memorandum electrified the Serbian public and raised the political temperature. At the time, Milošević condemned the memorandum as an example of "nothing else but the darkest nationalism,"[5] but by the following year he himself had embraced nationalism and staged a coup within the League of Communists of Serbia (LCS), ousting his political mentor and erstwhile friend, Ivan Stambolić, from power. Although he came to power illegally, behind-closed-doors conversations about confronting him and restoring legality in Serbia came to nothing.[6] By May 1989, in addition to being president of the LCS, Milošević was also president of Serbia.

The Milošević era: before the war

Upon first coming to power, Milošević tried to appeal to both non-Serbs and Serbs, albeit with contradictory messages. His appeal to Serbs was nationalistic and his dramatic helicopter landing at Kosovo field on 28 June 1989, for the commemoration of the 600th anniversary of the battle in which medieval Serbia was reduced to an Ottoman vassal (before being annexed outright seventy years later), was a dramatic gesture. His appeal to non-Serbs rested on his promotion of what he and his advisers called the "anti-bureaucratic revolution," while he sought to reverse the processes of decentralization begun in the 1960s and recentralize government in Belgrade. His early steps included a purge of Stambolić's allies from power, a purge and taming of the Serbian press, and, by spring 1989, the reduction of the autonomy of the provinces of Kosovo and Vojvodina, in spite of their status as federal units. Then, on 1 July 1990, a referendum was held in Serbia, on Milošević's initiative. The referendum asked Serbian voters to endorse changes to the constitution to eliminate virtually all remaining vestiges of provincial autonomy. The Kosovar Assembly replied the following day by declaring Kosovo a "republic" – separate from Serbia but still a constituent part of socialist Yugoslavia.[7] In response, the Serbian parliament suspended the provincial assembly and the provincial executive council, thereby eliminating the chief organs of self-government in this no longer self-governing province. Belgrade also dismissed the editors of the principal Albanian-language newspapers and the station managers of radio and television stations.

Meanwhile, by 1988 the Belgrade media began to publish anti-Croat and anti-Muslim propaganda. Among other things, the Belgrade media alleged (in 1989) that the reason that Tito had moved some factories from Serbian lowlands to more mountainous areas in Slovenia and Croatia after Yugoslavia's expulsion from the Cominform was to weaken Serbia; the Belgrade media dismissed the idea that the factories would be safer in the more mountainous regions of those other republics, in the event of a Soviet invasion. The Serbian propaganda probably contributed to the victory of Franjo Tudjman, a retired general and historian, in the presidential elections in Croatia in May 1990.

In fact, according to the diaries of Borisav Jović, who served as president of the collective presidency of socialist Yugoslavia from May 1990 to May 1991, he and Milošević talked about war as early as the spring of 1990.[8] Arms were imported from the Soviet Union and stockpiled in Serbia. As this was being done, the Yugoslav People's Army confiscated the arms consigned to the territorial defense forces in Slovenia, Croatia, and Bosnia-Herzegovina. This confiscation was in violation of the Yugoslav constitution and laws but was a crucial step in the preparation for war on Serbia's part.

Serbian agitation for cultural autonomy within Croatia began in summer 1989, more than six months before Tudjman's election and at a time when the Croatian communists still expected to hold onto power.[9] Immediately after his election, Tudjman met with Jovan Rašković, president of the recently founded Serbian Democratic Party in Croatia, and offered him the post of vice-president in the government; he also offered to extend cultural autonomy to Croatia's Serbs, thus meeting a demand registered the previous year. But Rašković consulted with Milošević before replying to this offer and, on the advice of the Serbian president, declined the offer and called for members of his party to boycott sessions of the Croatian parliament.[10] Instead of joining the government, members of the Serbian Democratic Party collaborated with the Milošević regime in setting up Serb militias in Croatia and Bosnia-Herzegovina, outside established channels; Serbs began receiving (illegal) arms transfusions from the army. In October 1990, five months after Tudjman's election, an ad hoc body, calling itself the Serb National Council, declared the autonomy of Serb-inhabited areas of Croatia. That same month, Serbs in Croatia raided police stations to "arm themselves, set up barricades (often felling trees across roads), and mined sections of railway lines leading into the districts of greatest Serbian concentration."[11] Serbs in Belgrade gathered in front of the parliament building demanding weapons so that they might invade Croatia.[12]

As Serb–Croat tensions escalated, the federal government of socialist Yugoslavia increasingly experienced financial problems. Already in November 1990, Slovenia, Serbia, and Vojvodina announced that they would not remit any further taxes to the federation. The following month saw the Serbian government take out a loan of $1.8 billion from the national bank. Insofar as this would clearly not be repaid, this "theft," as it came to be known, produced a crisis of confidence and led directly to Slovenia and Croatia announcing that they would not recognize any further debts incurred by the federation. The federal government was, by then, operating at 15% below budget and had laid off about 2,700 federal officials.[13]

Meanwhile, the political landscape of socialist Yugoslavia was changing as one republic after the other adopted electoral laws allowing for multiparty elections. In July 1990, the League of Communists of Serbia (SKS) reconstituted itself under a new name, the Socialist Party of Serbia (SPS). In September 1990, the Serbian Assembly adopted a new constitution in which the president of Serbia, not any officer or body of socialist Yugoslavia, was declared to be commander-in-chief of all armed forces on the territory of Serbia. In December, elections were held in Serbia, bringing victory to Milošević, who handily won re-election as president of Serbia with a hefty 80.5% of the vote. During the final six months of the SFRY, negotiations were conducted among the leaders of the country's six republics. When these led to no result, Slovenia and Croatia declared independence on 25 June 1991.

Years of war, 1991–5

From June 1991 to November 1995, war raged in the lands which had formerly comprised socialist Yugoslavia. Serbia had no ambitions in Slovenia and the ten-day war fought between the Yugoslav People's Army (JNA) and Slovenian forces resulted in 17 dead and 149 wounded on the Slovenian side, and 37 dead and 163 wounded among JNA troops.[14] By October 1991, Slovenia had achieved its independence, which was recognized by the major Western states in December. The major fronts of the war were in Croatia and, beginning in April 1992, Bosnia-Herzegovina (hereafter, Bosnia), and initially pitted Serbs against non-Serbs, although, as Marko Attila Hoare notes in his chapter in this volume, Croatian and Muslim (Bosniak) forces, which were initially allied against Serbs in Bosnia, later came to blows, resulting in a three-sided (and briefly even four-sided) conflict.

After Slovenia, Croatia, Bosnia-Herzegovina, and Macedonia had declared their disassociation from Yugoslavia, Serbia and Montenegro proclaimed the creation of a new state on 27 April 1992 – the Federal Republic of Yugoslavia (FRY). Serbia continued to operate under its September 1990 constitution, while Montenegro adopted a new constitution in October 1992. The constitution established a bicameral parliament with a Chamber of Republics, consisting of 20 deputies from Serbia and 20 from Montenegro, and a Chamber of Citizens, with 108 deputies from Serbia and 30 from Montenegro. Montenegro's allocation of deputies in the Chamber of Citizens was generous, given that that republic accounted for only about 5% of the population of the FRY but, in spite of that, the center of gravity of power in the system lay in Serbia, specifically with the SPS.[15]

The war strengthened Milošević's power. As early as 9 July 1992, the Serbian Assembly passed legislation granting him emergency powers over the economy. Some 15,000 students protested in downtown Belgrade, but their protest had no effect. Meanwhile, the Serbian economy shrank by 8.2% in 1991, 26.2% in 1992, and a further 30.3% in 1993, relative to the previous year. Both Serbia and Montenegro underwent a "massive criminalization of all state structures, from which the virus of corruption spread" throughout Serbian society.[16] The public health service was destroyed through plundering by officials and their cronies, who stole expensive medical equipment and sold it on the black market. Hospitals and pharmacies also suffered from shortages of medicines and pharmaceuticals during the war years, since the regime gave priority to supplying troops fighting for an enlarged Serbia. The economic sector was transformed not through privatization but through a combination of embezzlement, plunder, illegal transfer of stock, and manipulation, from which Milošević's cronies and supporters benefited. The economic mismanagement was associated with galloping inflation which reached a rate of 313,563,558% in December 1993–January 1994.[17] With such a high rate of inflation, pensions were reduced to nothing, workers were forced to take their wages and spend everything on the day they were paid (since the value of their earnings would evaporate by the end of the day), and those beneficiaries of the Milošević system who had taken out loans under preferential conditions in order to purchase economic enterprises or lavish houses were able to pay off their loans at a small fraction of their original value.

Although the war did not spread to Serbian territory, Serbia was deeply involved. To begin with, it was Milošević who appointed the commanders of the Serbian Army of the Republic of the Serbian Krajina (SVK, or the Croatian Serb army), assigning JNA officers to assume command. Milošević paid the salaries of the officers of both the SVK and the Army of the Bosnian Serbs (VRS) throughout the war, and coordinated with the commanders of both armies about strategies and tactics; indeed, as of late 1993, more than 1,800 officers and NCOs of the VRS were on Belgrade's payroll.[18] Milošević also sent supplies of various kinds to those forces throughout the war.

The war impacted Serbia and Montenegro in various ways. First of all, although the old socialist system had been one in which shortages of various goods were commonplace, the combination of war and the UN-imposed economic embargo resulted in shortages becoming more serious and therefore in promoting a black market. This in turn promoted the growth of organized crime in these two republics. Second, the propaganda generated in Belgrade built up tendencies toward dysphoric rumination, exaggerated perceptions of conspiracy, sinister attribution error, and hypervigilant social information processing.[19] Third, the war created a context in which only political parties prepared to remain completely marginal could dare to oppose it.

The leading opposition politicians – Zoran Djindjić (1952–2003), head of the Democratic Party (DS), Vuk Drašković (b. 1946), head of the Serbian Renewal Movement (SPO), and Vojislav Šešelj (b. 1954), head of the Serbian Radical Party – all supported the war, with Drašković and Šešelj even founding units of volunteers to fight in Bosnia. And, fourth, the war resulted in a massive hemorrhaging of the population, with young people and persons with higher education in particular seeking refuge abroad; it has been estimated that up to 200,000 people left Serbia alone during the war years.[20]

Some people fought back, rejecting the regime-promoted nationalism and the war itself. Given the war fever which gripped much of Serbia in those days, this took courage. Among those who opposed the war was a group called Women in Black, based in Belgrade, who protested against both compulsory mobilization and ethnic cleansing, among other things.[21]

After the war

Milošević joined Croatian President Tudjman and Bosnian President Alija Izetbegović in negotiating a peace agreement at the Wright–Patterson Air Force Base near Dayton, Ohio, in November 1995. The Dayton Peace Agreement, as it is sometimes known, was formally signed in Paris on 14 December 1995. At this point, *per capita* income in the FRY stood at less than $1,500 per year, less than half of what it had been four years earlier. Inflation had been moderated but was still running at 119% annually.[22] In January 1996, Drašković, Djindjić, and Vojislav Koštunica, head of the Democratic Party of Serbia (DSS), formed an electoral alliance at the local level in Kragujevac. This was a portent of things to come, for Drašković and Djinjić would soon build bridges with Vesna Pešić, head of the Civic Alliance of Serbia (GSS) (a non-nationalist party) and, in early September 1996, announced the formation of the "Zajedno" (Together) coalition consisting of their three parties. It was with this coalition that they contested local elections across Serbia in November. Zajedno candidates took the lead in fourteen cities including Belgrade and the coalition held a victory celebration on Belgrade's Square of the Republic on 18 November 1996. However, at Milošević's orders, the electoral commission refused to confirm these results and subsequently annulled Zajedno victories in Niš, Jagodina, and Kraljevo. Then, on 24 November, authorities annulled the victories of some thirty-three Zajedno candidates for offices in and around Belgrade, announcing that a third round of voting would be held three days later. Protests against Milošević's manipulations had begun on 19 November but these now spread, with as many as 100,000–200,000 participants taking part on some days. The third round went ahead, in spite of opposition protests, with the regime now claiming to have won a resounding victory at the polls. But instead of giving up, outraged Serbian citizens took to the streets for seventy-eight days, defying rain, snow, and cold. Milošević's attempt at suppressing the protests by force failed, and the regime's (temporary, as it turned out) closure of Radio B-92 backfired. Milošević appealed to the Organization for Security and Cooperation in Europe (OSCE) to send a team to Belgrade and verify the results. He hoped that the OSCE team would endorse his version of the elections, but instead of doing that the OSCE mission filed a report in which it concluded that Zajedno had won the elections in all fourteen disputed towns, including Belgrade. Milošević finally conceded defeat in these elections in what was an early sign of his declining popularity.

Meanwhile, Milošević's second term as president of Serbia was expiring and, under the constitution, he was not allowed to seek re-election to that office. Milošević took several steps to maintain his hold on power, however. The first step was to rein in Serbia's media. He pushed through a new law on the broadcast media in mid-March 1997, as a result of which the Serbian authorities shut down fifty-five small radio and television stations in July. Until 1994, Milošević had been content to control Radio–Television Serbia, and the newspapers *Politika* and *Politika ekspres*. But in late 1994 his regime had assumed control of the daily newspaper *Borba*, and newspapers which were critical of the president came under pressure. The second phase of Milošević's new media policy came in October 1998, with the publication of a new law on the media.[23]

Milošević's second step was to arrange for the constitution to be amended, so that some of the powers hitherto assigned to the president of Serbia would be transferred to the office of the president of the FRY. With that accomplished, Milošević arranged for his installation as president of the FRY on 23 July 1997. After a chaotic series of four rounds of voting for his successor as Serbian president in the latter months of 1997, Milan Milutinović, a protégé of Milošević's, was declared the winner and installed as president of Serbia; by now, however, this office had largely ceremonial functions.

The period January 1998–October 2000 was dominated by the Kosovo crisis (described by Frances Trix in her chapter in this volume), by a rash of gangland killings on the streets of Belgrade and Novi Sad, as well as an attempted assassination of Vuk Drašković while the opposition leader was vacationing in Budva, Montenegro, in June 2000, and by a growing estrangement between Montenegro and Serbia. A striking sign of this estrangement came during NATO's war with the FRY over Kosovo, when Montenegro, although a constituent unit of the FRY, declared itself "neutral"! Montenegrin President Milo Djukanović also called on NATO to remove Milošević from power, signaling that Montenegro's "neutrality" was assuming an anti-Milošević dimension. "Significantly, the first protest of any kind in Montenegro during the campaign came only on 21 May when 1,000–3,000 inhabitants of the town of Cetinje demonstrated against the deployment of Yugoslav army reinforcements in the area."[24] After the war with NATO ended, the Montenegrin government drafted a plan to redesign the FRY as a confederation of two equal states, with separate foreign ministries, separate currency systems, and separate defense systems.[25] In November 1999, the Montenegrin government adopted the DM as its official currency, jointly with the dinar, in a bold step toward asserting economic independence from Belgrade. In response to Djukanović's increasingly maverick policies, a battalion of military police was formed, loyal to federal prime minister Momir Bulatović (a Montenegrin supporter of Milošević). The United States urged Djukanović to be cautious but gave him $7 million in grant aid on top of a previous grant of $8 million, to be used to promote judicial and local government reform.

By March 2000, Serbia had imposed a blockade of supplies of medicine to Montenegro and rumors of war were reported in the press. Montenegrin Vice President Dragiša Burzan told the Croatian daily *Slobodna Dalmacija* about this time that Montenegrin independence was "unavoidable."[26] By late May 2000, some 65% of Montenegrins were reported to favor independence and in July 2000 fewer than 10% of Montenegrins were said to trust Belgrade. Within Serbia itself, an underground resistance movement called "Otpor" (Resistance) appeared, with a youthful membership.

Under the existing constitution, Milošević's term of office would expire in 2001 without any legal provision under which he could run for either of the two presidential offices he had held. He therefore set out to change the constitution, which he succeeded in doing by July 2000, in spite of opposition by Djukanović as well as by opposition leaders within Serbia. Under the amended constitution, the election of the president of the FRY would be referred to popular election, and re-election of the incumbent would be allowed. Ivan Stambolić, Milošević's political mentor, was by now becoming increasingly outspoken against Milošević, and on 25 August he was kidnapped in broad daylight and killed; much later, it would be documented that the murder had been carried out on Milošević's orders. By early 2000, however, there was a new determination among some of Serbia's opposition leaders to challenge Milošević's hold on power. Opposition parties, except for Vuk Drašković's SPO, decided to rally around a single candidate and chose Vojislav Koštunica as the candidate best situated to defeat Milošević. After the presidential elections were finally held, on 24 September 2000, the Federal Electoral Commission announced that Koštunica, candidate of the Democratic Opposition of Serbia (DOS) had won 48.22% of the vote against 40.23% for Milošević, with the remainder of the votes dispersed among three other candidates; the commission called for a second round of voting to take place on 8 October. The opposition, however, which had conducted exit polls, claimed that Koštunica had won 54.6% of the vote and that there was no need for a run-off election. Hundreds of thousands of protesters now descended on Belgrade, in a move coordinated by opposition leaders. Schools, factories, theaters, restaurants, and coal miners went on strike to protest Milošević's attempted theft of the election, with bus services in Belgrade and Niš also shut down. On 5 October, as demonstrators stormed the building of the federal Assembly, the police initially responded with stun grenades and tear gas, but later gave up their defense of

Milošević and, in some cases, even defected to the opposition. By the end of the day, the Federal Electoral Commission admitted that it had made a "mistake" and confirmed Koštunica as the duly elected president of the FRY. On the following day, Milošević addressed the Yugoslav public on television and admitted his defeat, congratulating Koštunica. The Milošević era was over.

Koštunica versus Djindjić

During Milošević's rule, the FRY had become a pariah state, but immediately after his fall, it was reintegrated into the international community, being admitted to the UN and welcomed into the Balkan Stability Pact. The first order of business for the victorious DOS coalition was to schedule parliamentary elections, in order to complete the process of transition from rule by the SPS (still headed by Milošević). The elections were duly held on 23 December and brought the coalition 65% of the vote, or 178 of the 250 seats in the Serbian Assembly. With this, Djindjić became Serbian prime minister. Koštunica soon fired many of the top brass in the Army, although not Chief-of-Staff Nebojša Pavković. Rade Marković was removed as head of the State Security Service on 26 January, but not until after he had managed to destroy various incriminating documents.

Milošević had been indicted by the International Criminal Tribunal for the former Yugoslavia (ICTY) in May 1999 on charges of war crimes and the government now found itself under international pressure to turn the fallen Serbian leader over to the tribunal. Koštunica at first resisted, arguing that Milošević should be tried under Yugoslav law, not under international law. But the United States used a combination of bribes and threats of a cut-off of aid to obtain Milošević's arrest, which took place, finally, on 1 April 2001. While Prime Minister Djindjić pressed for the surrender of Milošević to the international authorites, President Koštunica continued to obstruct any such action until 28 June 2001, when Milošević was put on a helicopter and flown to The Hague, where the ICTY had its seat. But the feuding between Koštunica and Djindjić over Milošević was only the first of a series of feuds between the two men.

As I have written elsewhere,

> Most of the major problems confronting the Koštunica–Djindjić duumvirate – such as endemic organized crime, rampant petty crime, widespread lawlessness and corruption, widespread poverty, high unemployment, Albanian secessionism in Kosovo, Montenegrin separatism, and Vojvodinan resentment at the loss of autonomy – were parts of Milošević's legacy. But what they added was a division of power at the top and intramural squabbling which seemed to have the potential to paralyze policymaking. Where Milošević had kept politicians, criminals – those two categories involving some of the same people – police, and army in his pocket, Koštunica and Djindjić were at war with each other, vying for control of the police, and targeting each other's protégés.[27]

Among other things, where Djindjić wanted to cooperate with the international community in remanding indicted war criminals to the custody of the ICTY and enjoyed the loyalty of Dušan Mihajlović, the Minister of the Interior, and the police forces under his jurisdiction, Koštunica wanted to defy the ICTY and enjoyed the loyalty of the so-called Red Berets (or more formally, the Unit for Special Operations, or JSO), originally established in 1991 as a paramilitary force but incorporated into the State Security Service in 1996. This conflict came to a head in early November 2001, when Mihajlović ordered the JSO to arrest two brothers on ordinary criminal charges. After they had arrested the two men and turned them over to Mihajlović, the Red Berets discovered that they were wanted by the ICTY. The Red Berets now set up roadblocks and demanded the release of the two brothers, passage of a law to regulate cooperation with the ICTY, and the resignation of Mihajlović. This was nothing less than a revolt but Koštunica chose to characterize it as a legitimate protest, thereby revealing the depth of his rivalry with the prime minister.[28] The protest lasted for a week, ending with Djindjić's apparent victory: Mihajlović retained his post, while Goran Petrović, chief of state security, and Zoran Mijatović, his deputy, who had supported the Red Berets, were forced to resign. That this revolt had wider dimensions than a mere disagreement about cooperation with the ICTY may be seen in the fact that the JSO had links with organized crime.[29]

For Montenegro, the fall of Milošević created problems for its drive toward independence since the United States and Western Europe, which had supported its aspirations for independence as long as Milošević was in power, now supported a unified FRY. One expression of this came in December 2001 when, in a state visit to Belgrade, French President Jacques Chirac declared that, even if Montenegrin independence were approved by a majority of Montenegrins in a free and fair referendum, they could not count on recognition from members of the EU. Subsequently, Javier Solana, the EU High Representative for Common Foreign and Security Policy, made repeated trips to Belgrade in order to exert pressure on the Montenegrins and Serbs to come to an agreement. On 14 March 2002, an agreement in principle was reached to replace the FRY with a new state to be called the Union of Serbia and Montenegro.

With the FRY consigned to the scrap heap and the office of FRY president dissolving, Koštunica decided to run for president of Serbia. In the first round of voting on 29 September 2002, Koštunica, appealing to Serbian nationalist sentiments, emerged with 30.89% of the vote, not far ahead of second-place Miroljub Labus, a liberal, who garnered 27.36% of the vote. A run-off conducted on 13 October failed when fewer than 50% of the electorate bothered to vote and in the third round Labus withdrew from the race, allowing Vojislav Šešelj, who had placed third in the first round, to re-enter the race. When this vote also failed for lack of participation, Nataša Mićić, the president of the Serbian parliament, assumed the post of interim president of Serbia, as mandated under the constitution of that time.

Then, on 12 March 2003, a month after the formal proclamation of the State Union of Serbia and Montenegro (as the successor state to the FRY), Zoran Djindjić was gunned down on the streets of Belgrade, by Zvezdan Jovanović, deputy commander of the JSO. He was succeeded in the office of prime minister by Zoran Živković, hitherto one of Djindjić's closest confidants. There was a huge outpouring of grief, and some half a million persons attended Djindjić's funeral, including delegations from more than seventy countries. Nearly five years later, Milorad "Legija" Ulemek and eighteen members of his Zemun clan were sentenced to a total of 465 years in prison for the murder of Djindjić and Stambolić and the attempted murder of then opposition leader Vuk Drašković. Ulemek himself received a forty-year sentence.

Koštunica returns to power

In mid-November 2003, the government announced that parliamentary elections would be held the following month, a year earlier than required. This time, about 80% of eligible voters took part. The biggest share of the vote (27.7%) went to Šeselj's Serbian Radical Party (SRS), by then headed by Tomislav Nikolić, since Šešelj was facing trial in The Hague for war crimes. Running in a distant second place was Koštunica's Democratic Party of Serbia (DSS), with 18%, following by the Democratic Party (DS), Djindjić's old party, now headed by Boris Tadić (b. 1958), with 12.6% of the vote and the G17+ Party headed by Miroljub Labus, with 12.6% of the vote. These were followed in turn by the Socialist Party and a coalition of Drašković's SPO and the New Serbia Party (NS) headed by Velimir Ilić. With no party ready to enter into a coalition with the SRS, it fell to Koštunica to put together a coalition. He fashioned a minority government by forging an alliance with the SPO–NS coalition and Labus' G17+, assuring himself of the support of 109 of the 250 deputies in the Assembly.

Assuming office as prime minister of Serbia on 3 March 2004, Koštunica called a halt to some of the economic reforms launched by Djindjić, revoked certain reforms in education and in the justice system, and downgraded most of the key figures in charge of Operation Saber, the anti-crime initiative launched after the assassination of Djindjić. All of these represented a repudiation of Djindjić's policies and legacy and were followed by the publication of books denigrating the dead prime minister. In particular, "Djindjić's attempt to purge the Army and the police was brutally curbed,"[30] while, for the interim, his assassination put cooperation with the ICTY on hold. Meanwhile, Montenegro, which had been forced into the State Union by the EU – in a political "fixed marriage" – announced in April 2004 that it intended to stage a referendum on independence as early as March 2005. EU pressure forced the government in Podgorica to postpone the referendum for a year. In the meantime, Serbian presidential elections were scheduled for 13 June 2004. SRS candidate Nikolić came out as the frontrunner in the first round of elections but in the run-off later that month Boris Tadić of the DS captured 52.1% of the vote, edging out Nikolić. Tadić would prove to be less nationalistic than Koštunica and more inclined to cooperate with the ICTY.

The question of cooperation with the ICTY would dominate the headlines, but corruption was a no less serious issue. A publication of the Center for Liberal-Democratic Studies in Belgrade in 2003 declared boldly that "since our state is one of the most corrupt in the world, it is certain that our police could not have been left untouched" and noted that those at "the top of the police hierarchy (or their families) could not have grown [as] rich as they were from [the] salaries they received."[31] Moreover, as the authors noted, corruption of the police force reduces its ability to carry out its duties; as a result, it both reflects and reinforces corruption elsewhere in the system.

In October 2005, the Assembly of the State Union of Serbia and Montenegro ratified the UN Convention Against Corruption but left other international conventions on anti-corruption measures hanging. Meanwhile, the extensive corruption in Serbia was scaring away potential foreign investors,[32] allowing goods to enter Serbia through illegal channels,[33] and obstructing privatization. A study carried out by the Heritage Foundation of Washington, DC concluded that "Serbia's power structure remains in the grip of what it calls war criminals, corrupt security chiefs and ultra-nationalist politicians."[34] At the end of December 2006, after the dissolution of the Union of Serbia and Montenegro, the Serbian cabinet belatedly adopted a plan to fight corruption, forwarding it to the Assembly for consideration. But, even as the plan went forward, the liberal daily newspaper *Danas* gloomily lamented that "the government of Serbia is the center of both power and corruption."[35] Even in 2007, corruption was said to be "endemic in Serbia," to absorb 20% of GDP,[36] and to have penetrated even the educational system.[37] Moreover, an opinion poll taken at the end of 2007 revealed a severe lack of confidence in Serbia's justice system. Of the 4,838 people who had taken part in the poll as of 26 December, 2,200 (45% of the total) thought that the justice system protected criminals and persons guilty of malpractice and abuse of the system, while another 2,312 people (48%) thought that the system was unjust, problematic, and inefficacious. Only 222 persons (5%) had nice things to say about the system, while 104 persons (2%) did not know what to say about the system.[38] This lack of confidence has, moreover, extended to the entire political system which, according to 27% of respondents in a 2005 poll, is run by criminals. Another 19% of respondents thought that the international community controlled Serbia, while only 13% of respondents thought that the government governed Serbia.[39]

When Milošević was first ejected from power, the sentiment among both EU leaders and the political mainstream in Serbia was that Serbia should be placed on the same track into the EU and other European organizations as other post-communist states. For all the post-communist countries the EU imposed conditions for membership, involving adaptations to the institutional and legal framework. But, in Serbia's case, as also in the case of Croatia, there were additional conditions – specifically, cooperation with the ICTY in the arrest of indicted war criminals and a purging of nationalism from the school textbooks and from official discourse. Koštunica's government dragged its feet on all these conditions, whether one thinks of the struggle against corruption or the reform of the textbooks or cooperation with the ICTY. School textbooks continued, for example, to laud Milan Nedić (1878–1946) and Draža Mihailović, both of whom collaborated with the Axis during the Second World War, representing them as Serbian heroes, while in December 2004 the Serbian Assembly adopted a law equating the status and rights of the collaborationist Chetniks with those of the anti-fascist Partisans. Deploring this action, the anti-fascist war veterans' associations denounced the law as an offense to the nation, adding that Serbia was "the first country in Europe to declare a quisling movement as being liberating and anti-Fascist."[40]

In the years following the end of the War of Yugoslav Succession in 1995, the ICTY gradually succeeded in bringing most of those indicted for war crimes to The Hague to stand trial. By April 2008, only four indictees remained at large – all of them Serbs: Ratko Mladić (b. 1942), who had commanded the VRS during the war; Radovan Karadžić (b. 1945), the wartime Bosnian Serb leader; Goran Hadžić, who served as prime minister of the Republic of Serbian Krajina from February 1992 until December 1994; and Stojan Župljanin, who had commanded the Bosnian Serb police during the war. After years of denial that they had any knowledge of Mladić's whereabouts, Serbian government officials eventually admitted that he had been under military protection until mid-2002, that Koštunica and other high-ranking officials had known where he was, and that he had been receiving a state pension until December 2005.[41] In April 2006, Belgrade "guaranteed" that Mladić would be apprehended and turned over to the ICTY by the end of that month, and in October of that year Serbia's war crimes prosecutor announced that the fugitive would be arrested "within a matter of days."[42] In the meantime, the G17+ Party quit the coalition in protest at the authorities' failure to arrest the fugitive. For the EU, the arrest of Ratko Mladić remains a key precondition for Serbia's admission to its membership. However, on 1 October 2006, even as European pressure on Serbia to allow the people of Kosovo to choose their own future intensified, the Serbian Assembly voted overwhelmingly (242 deputies in favor, 8 absent) to approve a new constitution for the country, subject to popular referendum. In a key clause, the constitution proclaimed that Kosovo, by then having a 90% Albanian majority, was an "integral" and inalienable part of Serbia. For the Albanians of Kosovo, however, this constitution served only to deny them their self-determination and to preserve what they viewed as the last colony in Europe. The Serbian government, however, "excluded the Kosovo Albanians ... from voting in the referendum"[43] and, by excluding those with the most to lose, succeeded in winning a bare majority of 52.3% in favor.[44] The fact that more than 47% were opposed to the constitution serves to indicate that it was highly controversial even among Serbs. An opinion poll taken a year later found that 41% of Serbs would rather forgo EU membership than relinquish the Serbian claim to sovereignty in

Kosovo, with 37% prepared to break off diplomatic relations with nations recognizing a declaration of independence by the parliament of Kosovo.[45] In this regard, the Serbian parliament showed itself to be more hardline than the people of Serbia, with 220 deputies out of 250 voting, on 26 December 2007, to break diplomatic relations with the United States and any European countries which might recognize the independence of Kosovo. Koštunica had boldly declared, the previous May, that history afforded no examples of European states being compelled to give up 15% of their territory "for any kind of concessions or prizes."[46] More than half a century earlier, however, the French government had declared Algeria an integral and inalienable part of France and yet, at the end of a bloody war fought over eight years (1954–62), was forced to give up what amounted to more than 78% of what it had considered integral to France. But, for France, there were no "prizes" on offer to compensate for its loss.

An independent Montenegro

As already noted, Montenegro, which had been brought into union with Serbia in 1918 without consultation with the legal government of Montenegro and against the wishes of a large proportion of Montenegrins,[47] was growing increasingly alienated from Serbia in the final years of the Milošević era. Moreover, even after Milošević had been removed from power, leading Montenegrin politicians such as Milo Djukanović remained intent upon restoring Montenegrin independence. The eventual achievement of independence was anticipated in 1993 by the restoration of the autocephalous Montenegrin Orthodox Church, which had been suppressed in 1920, and by the decision taken in March 2006 that Montenegrin state bodies, rather than bodies of the Union of Serbia and Montenegrin, would command the armed forces in Montenegro.[48] Finally, on 21 May 2006, Montenegrins took part in their much-delayed referendum on independence, with 55.4% of voters endorsing independence. On 3 June 2006, Montenegro formally declared independence; the government of Serbia immediately accepted this outcome.

In the follow-up elections held in September, Djukanović's pro-independence coalition achieved a strong victory, capturing 41 of the 81 seats in the national assembly. Two months later, Djukanović, basking in his successes, stepped aside as prime minister, and Željko Sturanović succeeded him in that office. In the following months, Montenegro signed an agreement on the transit of NATO troops across the territory of Montenegro, entered into a military partnership with the United States, and, in April 2007, initialized the Stabilization and Association Agreement with EU representatives; the agreement was subsequently signed six months later. In domestic affairs, the adoption of a new constitution for the Republic of Montenegro on 19 October 2007 was a landmark, notwithstanding the opposition of pro-Serbian deputies.[49] In the wake of the passage of the constitution, Montenegro set up a Fund for Minorities to assist them in preserving their languages, religious customs, and cultures. Having served as Montenegrin prime minister in 1991–8 and as president of Montenegro in 1998–2000, Djukanović returned to the prime minister's office in January 2003, with Filip Vujanovic inheriting the presidency. Djukanović stepped down in November 2006 but won re-election in February 2008. The Coalition for a European Montenegro, headed by Djukanović, won an absolute majority of seats in the parliamentary election held in March 2009, returning him for his sixth term as prime minister.

Serbia loses Kosovo and elects a new government

On 3 February 2008, Boris Tadić, the head of the DS, narrowly edged out the pro-Russian Tomislav Nikolić, the candidate of the Serbian Radical Party (SRS), to win re-election as president of Serbia. Satisfied with the results of the election, the EU wasted no time in offering Serbia a political accord. However, Koštunica and his DSS ministers quickly lined up against the agreement, claiming that if the Serbian government were to sign the agreement it would be indirectly recognizing Kosovo's right to establish itself as an independent state.[50] With this, the agreement died on the table.

Scarcely a week and a half later – on 17 February 2008 – the Kosovar parliament unanimously endorsed a declaration of independence from Serbia. Serbian Prime Minister Koštunica immediately denounced Kosova as a "phoney state," while Foreign Minister Vuk Jeremić declared that Belgrade would not maintain normal ties with any countries that recognized the independence of Kosova. But within four days of the declaration of independence, fifteen states recognized the new state – among them, the United States, Turkey, Britain, France, Germany, Italy, Denmark, and Albania. Other states quickly followed suit, although Slovakia and Romania (bearing in mind their forcible annexation of portions of Hungary after the First World War), Spain (bearing in mind its secessionist Basques), and Russia (hoping to build an alliance with Serbia) took Serbia's side.

Meanwhile, the Serbian government, which had "annulled" Kosova's independence three days in advance, now formally protested the EU's decision to send 2,000 police and jurists to help Kosova set up its state, and filed criminal charges against Kosova's Albanian leaders on charges of having "committed a serious criminal act against the constitutional order and security of Serbia."[51] Serbian Assistant Defense Minister Dušan Spasojević offered that Serbia did not "see it as a military problem. It's a political problem," he continued, adding ominously, "for the time being."[52] But on 21 February, in an anti-Western riot which the Viennese newspaper *Die Presse* claimed had been organized by Koštunica and his chief of office, Aleksandar Nikitović,[53] some 800 young hooligans went on a violent rampage attacking the embassies of the United States, Britain, Belgium, Turkey, and Croatia. Since Croatia had not yet recognized Kosova, the attack on the Croatian embassy seems to have been motivated by other considerations.

But while Koštunica declared defiantly that the EU would have to choose between Kosova and Serbia, Bulgarian Prime Minister Sergei Stanishev advised the Serbian government that, on the contrary, "Serbs have to decide now between looking towards the past ...[and] looking towards the future and the European perspective."[54] Hoping to expand his electoral base, Koštunica called for snap elections on 11 May. But, to Koštunica's dismay, Tadić's pro-European bloc emerged in first place with 38.4% of the vote, winning 102 seats in the 250-seat parliament. Koštunica's DSS trailed in third place with a meager 11.6% of the vote. Tadić's DS formed a coalition with the SPS (formerly the party of Slobodan Milošević) and three smaller parties, naming Mirko Cvetković, the erstwhile Minister of Finance, as prime minister. This new government immediately signaled its two top priorities – membership in the EU and regaining control of Kosovo – even though these two objectives seemed to be mutually exclusive, and persuaded the UN General Assembly to refer the question of Kosovo's independence to the International Court of Justice (ICJ). Foreign Minister Vuk Jeremić issued a statement pledging that Serbia would "accept any opinion that comes from the ICJ."[55] About the same time, it was announced that, in the thirty months since April 2006, district courts in Serbia had rehabilitated 694 persons, including Slobodan Jovanović (1869–1958), who had served as prime minister in the Yugoslav government-in-exile from January 1942 to June 1943.[56]

Under sustained pressure from the EU, the Serbian authorities arrested war crimes indictees Stojan Župljanin in June 2008 and Radovan Karadžić in July 2008, remanding them to the custody of the ICTY. At that point, two war crimes indictees remained at large – Goran Hadžić and Ratko Mladić – but, as of early November 2009, neither of these fugitives had been apprehended.

The war continues to cast a dark shadow over Serbia. In February 2006, the ICJ opened proceedings in a claim of genocide brought by the government of Bosnia-Herzegovina against Serbia. A year later, the court cleared Serbia of responsibility for the slaughter of 8,000 men and boys at Srebrenica in July 1995, in a landmark case hailed by the Serbian authorities and media. It emerged later, however, that the Serbian government, in sending its archives to The Hague, had obtained the tribunal's permission to keep some of the contents from reaching the fifteen judges who were to rule on the case.[57] When this information was revealed, there were howls of protest, especially from Bosniaks, but it was by then too late to do anything about it, since the ICJ does not provide for any system of appeal. This decision, if anything, reinforced tendencies toward denial of responsibility among Serbs for the tragedy of the War of Yugoslav Succession or for the atrocities in Kosovo; and while many Serbs are undoubtedly innocent of direct involvement in the atrocities, or even of supporting political parties which were culpable in some way, some Serbs are clearly implicated in the horrors of the past two decades.

But the issue of responsibility for war crimes has not gone away. In November 2008, Croatia lodged a claim of genocide against Belgrade before the ICJ, and the Bosnian federation declared its intention to refile its claim of genocide, on the argument that the withholding of key documents from the court earlier had rendered its judgment null and void.[58] However, in spite of Serbia's failure to arrest Hadžić or Mladić, the IMF agreed to extend a $518 million line of credit to Serbia, to help the country weather the global financial crisis.[59]

Conclusion

Yet, even a decade after Dayton, ethnic minorities in Serbia were still experiencing hardship, with neo-Nazis, for example, beating up Hungarians in the Vojvodina. According to the Hungarian news agency MTI, "violent acts against Serbia's Hungarian minority became a frequent phenomenon" after Koštunica became prime minister in early 2004; moreover, József Kasza, chairman of the Alliance of Vojvodina Hungarians, claimed that "economic discrimination and unemployment for the Hungarian minority was an even bigger problem than violent acts."[60] In October 2005, Human Rights Watch released a report criticizing the Belgrade government for not doing enough to protect members of minority groups and noting that Hungarians in the Vojvodina had been "the most frequent target of the attacks," although "members of the Slovak, Croat, and Muslim minorities have been targeted as well."[61]

Nor can Serbia boast of a free press. NGOs such as the Humanitarian Law Fund, the Helsinki Committee for Human Rights in Serbia, and the Youth Initiative for Human Rights, and journalists associated with B-92 Radio, the daily newspaper *Danas*, the weekly magazine *Vreme*, and the newspaper *Novine vranjske* have been variously threatened (sometimes with death threats), assaulted, slurred in graffiti, or, in the case of the last-mentioned newspaper, served a lawsuit because of the cover of its New Year's edition in 2005.[62] In February 2008, as already noted, Boris Tadić was re-elected president of Serbia. Three months later the electoral bloc he led won a plurality of the vote in parliamentary elections and subsequently formed a coalition government with the Socialist Party. Mirko Cvetković, a former minister of finance, took office as prime minister, and Ivica Dacić, leader of the Socialist Party, became deputy prime minister and minister of the interior. The new government promised to arrest Mladić and Hadžić, the two remaining war crimes indictees, by the end of 2009 and remand them to The Hague. At this writing, their arrest is the last major hurdle for Serbia to cross before it can begin negotiations for EU admission. For Montenegro, the path into the EU is somewhat less complicated.

Timeline 1389–2008

1389	Battle of Kosovo between a Christian army led by Serbian Prince Lazar and an Ottoman army led by Sultan Murad
15th–19th centuries	Serbia ruled by the Ottoman Empire

1817	Serbia gains autonomy
1878	Serbian independence recognized internationally
1918	Establishment of Kingdom of Serbs, Croats, and Slovenes
1929	Kingdom is renamed Kingdom of Yugoslavia
1941–4	Serbia occupied by German troops and puppet government headed by General Milan Nedić collaborates with the Axis
May 1945	End of the Second World War; Yugoslavia re-established with the communists in the leading position
1946	Passage of first communist constitution for Yugoslavia
1953	Passage of Basic Law, usually counted as second constitution for communist-era Yugoslavia
1963	Passage of third constitution for communist Yugoslavia
1967–71	Liberal politicians in power in Slovenia, Croatia, Serbia, and Macedonia
1974	Passage of fourth constitution for communist Yugoslavia
May 1980	Death of Yugoslav President Josip Broz Tito
1981	
April 1987	Provincial-wide riots in province of Kosovo
September 1987	Eighth Session of the League of Communists of Serbia; Slobodan Milošević seizes power within Serbia
1989	Milošević suppresses autonomy of Kosovo and Vojvodina, in violation of the constitution of 1974
June 1991	Slovenia and Croatia declare disassociation from defunct SFRY
1991–5	War of Yugoslav Succession
April 1992	Proclamation of FRY, consisting of Serbia (with Kosovo and Vojvodina) and Montenegro
November 1995	Dayton Peace Accords
July 1997	Milošević is elected president of FRY
1998	Launching of rebellion against Serbian rule by Kosova Liberation Army
24 March 1999	Beginning of a seventy-eight-day war between NATO and Serbia, over treatment of Albanians of Kosovo
October 2000	Milošević forced to acknowledge his defeat in previous month's election; Vojislav Koštunica becomes president of FRY; Zoran Djindjić becomes prime minister of Serbia
28 June 2001	Milošević remanded to the custody of the International Criminal Tribunal for the former Yugoslavia (ICTY) in The Hague
February 2003	FRY scrapped and replaced by new Union of Serbia and Montenegro
March 2003	Assassination of Djindjić
March 2004	Koštunica becomes prime minister of Serbia
March 2006	Milošević found dead in his cell in The Hague
June 2006	Montenegro declares independence
October 2006	Serbian voters approve new constitution which declares that Kosovo is an inalienable part of Serbia
December 2006	Serbia admitted to NATO's Partnership for Peace program

February 2007	UN envoy Martti Ahtisaari announces his plan for an independent Kosovo
17 February 2008	Kosovo declares independence as the Republic of Kosova

Fact sheet

Serbia	
Area	77,474 km^2
Population (2009)	7,379,339
Urban population (2007)	52.6%
Below the poverty line (2007 estimate)	6.5% of population
Unemployment rate (2007)	18.8%
GDP *per capita* (2008)	$10,900
Real GDP growth (2008)	5.6%
Inflation (2007)	6.8%

Sources: factiva (Reuters), at www.alertnet.org/ [accessed on 13 February 2007]; AFP (27 December 2007), from topic@afp.com, by subscription; and CIA, *The World Factbook*, at www.cia.gov/library/publications/the-world-factbook/geos/rb.html [accessed on 29 March 2008 and 9 July 2009].

Fact sheet

Montenegro	
Area	13,938 km^2
Population (July 2007)	684,736
Urban population (1998)	c. 60%
Below the poverty line (2007)	7% of population
Unemployment rate (2007)	14.7%
GDP *per capita* (2005)	$3,800
Real GDP growth (2007)	6%
Inflation (2007)	3.9%

Sources: Montenet, at www.montenet.org/people/people.htm; US Department of State, *Background Note: Montenegro*, at www.state.gov/r/pa/ei/bgn/70949.htm; SEEbiz (18 December 2007) at www.seebiz.eu/en/macro/montenegro/montenegro-has-3.9%25-inflation-rate,4604.html [accessed on 8 March 2008]; and CIA, *The World Factbook*, at www.cia.gov/library/publications/the-world-factbook/geos/mj.html [all last accessed on 8 March 2008].

Parties in the Serbian parliament (results of 21 January 2007 election)

Party	percent of the vote	Number of deputies elected
Serbian Radical Party (SRS)	28.7	81
Democratic Party (DS)	22.9	64
Democratic Party of Serbia (DSS)	16.7	47
G17+ Party	7.1	19
Socialist Party of Serbia (SPS)	5.9	16
Other parties	18.7	23

Parties in the Montenegrin parliament (results of 10 September 2007 election)

Party	percent of the vote	Number of deputies elected
Coalition for a European Montenegro	47.7	41
Serbian People's Party (SNS)	14.4	12
SNP–NS–DSS Coalition	13.8	11
Movement for Changes (PzP)	12.9	11
Liberals and Bosniak Party	3.7	3
Albanian minority	3.1	3

Short biography of Slobodan Milošević

Born in 1941 in Požarevac, Serbia, Slobodan Milošević rejected the strict religiosity of his father and became involved in communist party activities in 1959, while still in high school. His father committed suicide in 1962; his mother did likewise a decade later. He studied law at the University of Belgrade, but after graduation took a position as economic adviser to the Mayor of Belgrade. He married Mira Marković in 1965, obtaining a job, three years later, at Tehnogas, where his friend Ivan Stambolić was already employed. Stambolić helped Milošević to become head of Beobanka, at the time one of Yugoslavia's largest banks, in 1978. On 16 April 1984, he was elected president of the Belgrade communist party organization and, two years later, thanks to Stambolić's support, he became president of the League of Communists of Serbia (LCS). The following year, at the Eighth Session of the LCS, he turned against Stambolić, marginalizing him and seizing power for himself. Stambolić was removed from office on 14 December 1987. Milošević served as president of Serbia from 8 May 1989 to 23 July 1997 and as president of the FRY from 23 July 1997 to 5 October 2000. During the years 1990–91, he prepared the ground for war against Croatia and Bosnia-Herzegovina, illegally establishing Serb militias in those republics, arming them, and authorizing the Yugoslav army to train them. He faced repeated anti-war opposition during his years in power, especially within Belgrade, but weathered the protests of March 1991, July 1992, and June 1993, thanks to the loyalty of the army and the police and to support in the countryside. He failed to achieve his military objectives in the War of Yugoslav Succession (1991–5) but he used the nationalism stirred up by the war to stay in power for nearly thirteen years. During the years 1989–98, he carried out a policy discriminating against Albanians in Kosovo; in December 1998, he launched "Operation Horseshoe" in Kosovo, with the result that some 80,000 Albanians were driven from their homes by mid-March 1999. On 24 March, NATO began a seventy-eight-day air campaign against Serbia, forcing Milošević to agree to the deployment of an international peacekeeping force in the province. On 27 May 1999 he was indicted by the ICTY on charges of war crimes in Kosovo; subsequently, he was also indicted on charges of war crimes in Croatia and in Bosnia-Herzegovina. Remanded to the custody of the Tribunal on 28 June 2001, he was put on trial but died on 11 March 2006 of apparent heart failure.

Notes

1. Florian Bieber, "Serbia," in Jeannette Goehring (ed.), *Nations in Transit 2006: Democratization from Central Europe to Eurasia* (New York: Freedom House, 2006), pp. 519, 529.
2. "Poverty in Serbia Reduced by Half in the Period 2002–2007," Poverty Reduction Strategy of the Serbian Government (29 November 2007), at www.prsp.sr.gov.yu/engleski/vest.jsp;jsessionid=969E84155C7A20C1A2565B263D15E346?id=383 [accessed on 23 December 2007]; and "20% of Serbians Live in Poverty - Study," B-92 (18 October 207), at www.b92.net/eng/news/ [accessed on 3 November 2007].
3. For documentation of the Chetniks' collaboration with Axis forces, see Branko Latas, compiler, *Saradnja Četnika Draže Mihailović sa okupatorima i ustašama (1941–1945): Dokumenti* (Belgrade: Društvo za istinu o antifašističkoj narodnooslobodilačkoj borbi (1941–5), 1999).
4. *Memorandum of the Serbian Academy of Sciences and Art* (1986), trans. Dennison Rusinow with Aleksandar and Sarah Nikolić and reprinted in Dennison Rusinow, "The Yugoslav Peoples," in Peter F. Sugar (ed.), *Eastern European Nationalism in the Twentieth Century* (Washington, DC: American University Press, 1995), pp. 341, 338.
5. Quoted in Tim Judah, *The Serbs: History, Myth and the Destruction of Yugoslavia* (New Haven, Conn.: Yale University Press, 2000), p. 160.
6. Details in Branko Mamula, *Slučaj Jugoslavija* (Podgorica: CID, 2000), pp. 115–16.
7. *Vjesnik* (Zagreb), 3 July 1990, p. 1.
8. Borisav Jović, *Posledni dani SFRJ - izvodi iz dnevnika* (Belgrade: Politika, 1995).
9. *Vjesnik* (28 August 1989), p. 5; *NIN* (Belgrade), No. 2018 (3 September 1989), pp. 17–23; *Slobodna Dalmacija* (Split), 11 September 1989, p. 4; and *NIN*, No. 2020 (17 September 1989), pp. 18–20.
10. Christopher Bennett, *Yugoslavia's Bloody Collapse: Causes, Course and Consequences* (Washington Square, NY: New York University Press, 1995), p. 129.
11. Sabrina P. Ramet, *Balkan Babel: The Disintegration of Yugoslavia from the Death of Tito to the Fall of Milošević*, 4th edn. (Boulder, Colo.: Westview Press, 2002), p. 58.
12. *Tanjug* (1 October 1990), trans. in FBIS, *Daily Report* (Eastern Europe), 2 October 1990.
13. *Borba* (Belgrade), 26 December 1990, p. 3; and *Tanjug* (3 March 1991), trans. in FBIS, *Daily Report* (Eastern Europe), 5 March 1991, p. 56.
14. Nicole Janigro, *L'Espolsione delle Nazioni: Il caso Jugoslavo* (Milan: Feltrinelli, 1993), p. 21.
15. Renéo Lukic, "From the Federal Republic of Yugoslavia to the Union of Serbia and Montenegro," in Sabrina P. Ramet and Vjeran Pavlaković (eds.), *Serbia since 1989: Politics and Society under Milošević and After* (Seattle: University of Washington Press, 2005), pp. 58–9.
16. Maja Miljković and Marko Attila Hoare, "Crime and the Economy under Milošević and His Successors," in Ramet and Pavlaković (eds.), *Serbia since 1989*, p. 195.
17. *Ibid.*, p. 198.
18. *New York Times* (9 April 2007), at www.nytimes.com/ [accessed on 9 April 2007]. See also Sabrina P. Ramet, "Martyr in His Own Mind: The Trial and Tribulations of Slobodan Milošević," *Totalitarian Movements and Political Religions*, Vol. 5, No. 1 (Summer 2004), p. 121; Davorin Rudolf, *Rat koji nismo htjeli: Hrvatska 1991*

(Zagreb: Globus, 1999), p. 67; and Louis Sell, *Slobodan Milošević and the Destruction of Yugoslavia* (Durham, NC: Duke University Press, 2002), pp. 232–3.

19. See Sabrina P. Ramet, "Under the Holy Lime Tree: The Inculcation of Neurotic and Psychotic Syndromes as a Serbian Wartime Strategy, 1986–95," in Ramet and Pavlaković (eds.), *Serbia since 1989*, esp. pp. 126–30.
20. James Gow and Milena Michalski, "The Impact of the War on Serbia: Spoiled Appetites and Progressive Decay," in Ramet and Pavlaković (eds.), *Serbia since 1989*, p. 153.
21. "Reakcije prolaznica/prolaznika na protest Žena u crnom," in *Žene za Žene* (Belgrade: Žene u crnom, 1994), p. 15. See also Žarana Papić, "Women in Serbia: Post-Communism, War, and Nationalist Mutations," in Sabrina P. Ramet (ed.), *Gender Politics in the Western Balkans: Women and Society in Yugoslavia and the Yugoslav Successor States* (University Park, Pa.: Pennsylvania State University Press, 1999), pp. 153–69.
22. *Deutsche Presse-Agentur* (22 December 1995), on nexis.com.
23. "Zakon o javnom informisanju Republike Srbije," *Politika* (Belgrade), 22 October 1998, p. 21–2.
24. Ramet, *Balkan Babel*, p. 347.
25. "Montenegrin Government Adopts Platform Redefining Relations with Serbia," *Tanjug* (6 August 1999), at www.freeserbia.net/News.html.
26. As reported in Montenegrin Information Ministry website (Podgorica), 16 March 2000, in *BBC Summary of World Broadcasts* (18 March 2000), on *Lexis-Nexis Academic Universe*.
27. Sabrina P. Ramet, *The Three Yugoslavias: State-Building and Legitimation, 1918–2005* (Washington, DC and Bloomington, Ind.: Woodrow Wilson Center Press and Indiana University Press, 2006), p. 527.
28. Davor Pašalić, "Ratko Mladić živi u ulici Blagoja Parovića u Beogradu," *Nacional* (Zagreb), No. 316 (4 December 2001), p. 36.
29. Details in Ramet, *The Three Yugoslavias*, pp. 528–9.
30. Sonja Biserko, "Concept of Human Rights Denied," in Sonja Biserko (ed.), *Human Rights and Collective Identity – Serbia 2004* (Belgrade: Helsinki Committee for Human Rights in Serbia, 2005), p. 20.
31. Boris Begović and Boško Mijatović (eds.), *Corruption in Serbia* (Belgrade: Center for Liberal-Democratic Studies, 2003), posted at pdc.cell.her/archive/0000396/01/corruption_five_years_later.pdf [accessed on 13 July 2009].
32. *Danas* (Belgrade), 19 February 2004, at www.danas.co.yu/ [accessed on 9 October 2007].
33. "Serbian Prosecution Indicts 28 Customs Officers with Corruption," *Makfax vesnik* (Skopje), 28 May 2007, at www.makfax.com.mk/ [accessed on 3 December 2007].
34. "Anti-Corruption Fight Moves Slow[ly] in Serbia," in *Wood Report – Voice of America* (6 August 2005), at www.voanews.com/english/archive/ [accessed on 20 January 2007].
35. *Danas* (28 December 2006), at www.danas.co.yu/ [accessed on 9 October 2007].
36. *Southeast Europe Net* (3 January 2007), at www.seeurope.net/?q=node/3998 [accessed on 20 January 2007].

37. *Danas* (7 March 2007), at www.danas.co.yu/ [accessed on 9 October 2007]; and *Danas - Vikend* (1–2 September 2007), at www.danas.co.yu/ [accessed on 9 October 2007].
38. *Glas javnosti* (Belgrade), 26 December 2007, at www.glas-javnosti.co.yu/ [accessed on 26 December 2007].
39. Zoran Stojiljković, *Partijski sistem Srbije* (Belgrade: Službeni glasnik, 2006), p. 338.
40. Quoted in HINA news agency (Zagreb), 21 December 2004, infoweb.newsbank.com. See also "Četnički zakon," *Republika*, No. 348–349 (1–31 January 2005), at www.republika.co.yu/ [last accessed on 12 July 2005].
41. AFP (27 September 2006), from topic@afp.com, by subscription; and *Kurir* (Belgrade), 2 December 2006, at www.kurir-info.co.yu/Arhiva/ [accessed on 12 December 2006].
42. *Daily Telegraph* (London), 27 April 2006, at www.telegraph.co.uk/ [accessed on 3 September 2006]; and Vladimir Vukčević, as quoted in AFP (12 October 2006), from topic@afp.com, by subscription.
43. AFP (28 October 2006), from topic@afp.com, by subscription.
44. AFP (30 October 2006), from topic@afp.com, by subscription.
45. AFP (3 October 2007), from topic@afp.com, by subscription.
46. AFP (19 May 2007), from topic@afp.com, by subscription.
47. Šerbo Rastoder, "A Short Review of the History of Montenegro," in Florian Bieber (ed.), *Montenegro in Transition: Problems of Identity and Statehood* (Baden-Baden: Nomos Verlagsgesellschaft, 2003), p. 129; and Branislav Grigorijević, *Kralj Aleksandar Karadjordjević*, Vol. 1: *Ujedinjenje Srpskih zemalja* (Belgrade: Beogradski izdavačko-grafički zavod, 1996), pp. 421–3.
48. MINA news agency (21 March 2006), in *BBC Monitoring - International Reports.*
49. Regarding the opposition of pro-Serbian deputies, see Igor Jovanović, "Pro-Serbian Parties Oppose Montenegro Constitution," *Southeast European Times* (24 October 2007), at www.setimes.com/ [accessed on 22 December 2007].
50. *The Independent* (7 February 2008), at www.independent.co.uk/ [accessed on 8 February 2008].
51. AFP (18 February 2008), from topic@afp.com, by subscription.
52. Quoted in AFP (20 February 2008), from topic@afp.com, by subscription.
53. *Die Presse* (Vienna), 26 February 2008, at diepresse.com/ [accessed on 2 March 2008].
54. Quoted in AFP (20 February 2008), from topic@afp.com, by subscription.
55. Quoted in AFP (15 August 2008), from topic@apf.com, by subscription.
56. *Danas* (27 October 2008), at www.danas.rs/ [accessed on 28 October 2008].
57. *New York Times* (9 April 2007), at www.nytimes.com/ [accessed on 9 April 2007].
58. AFP (11 November 2008), from topic@afp.com, by subscription; and *Vjesnik* (26 November 2008), at www.vjesnik.hr/ [accessed on 27 November 2008].
59. AFP (18 November 2008), from topic@afp.com, by subscription.
60. Both quotations: Hungarian News Agency (MTI), 16 February 2005, on *Lexis-Nexis Academic Universe*. See also *Glas Slavonije* (Osijek), 11 December 2005, at www.glas-slavonije.hr/ [accessed on 11 December 2005]; and *Glas Slavonije* (19 July 2007), at www.glas-slavonije.hr/ [accessed on 29 December 2007].
61. HINA news agency (10 October 2005), in infoweb.newsbank.com.

62. AFP (3 May 2007), from topic@afp.com, by subscription; Tanja Matić, "Serbia: Don't Mention the War" (28 October 2005) and Nikola Lazić, "Media Intimidation in South Serbia" (14 October 2005), both in *Institute for War & Peace Reporting*, at www.iwpr.net/ [both accessed on 31 December 2005].

Further reading

Bieber, Florian (ed.). *Montenegro in Transition: Problems of Identity and Statehood* (Baden-Baden: Nomos Verlagsgesellschaft, 2003)

Judah, Tim. *The Serbs: History, Myth and the Destruction of Yugoslavia* (New Haven, Conn.: Yale University Press, 2000)

LeBor, Adam. *Milošević: A Biography* (Polmont and London: Bloomsbury, 2002)

Listhaug, Ola, Sabrina P. Ramet, and Dragana Dulić (eds.). *Civic and Uncivic Values in Serbia: The Post-Milošević Era* (forthcoming from Central European University Press)

Lukic, Renéo and Allen Lynch. *Europe from the Balkans to the Urals: The Disintegration of Yugoslavia and the Soviet Union* (Oxford and New York: Oxford University Press, 1996)

Morrison, Kenneth. *Montenegro: A Modern History* (London: I. B. Tauris, 2009)

Ramet, Sabrina P. "The Denial Syndrome and its Consequences: Serbian Political Culture since 2000," *Communist and Post-Communist Studies*, Vol. 40, No. 1 (March 2007), pp. 41–58

The Three Yugoslavias: State-Building and Legitimation, 1918–2005 (Bloomington, Ind. and Washington, DC: Indiana University Press and Woodrow Wilson Center Press, 2006)

Ramet, Sabrina P. and Vjeran Pavlaković (eds.). *Serbia since 1989: Politics and Society under Milošević and After* (Seattle: University of Washington Press, 2005)

Sell, Louis. *Slobodan Milošević and the Destruction of Yugoslavia* (Durham, NC: Duke University Press, 2002)

Thomas, Robert. *Serbia under Milošević: Politics in the 1990s* (London: C. Hurst & Co., 1999)

Vujadinović, Dragica, Lino Veljak, Vladimir Goati, and Veselin Pavićević (eds.). *Between Authoritarianism and Democracy – Serbia, Montenegro, Croatia*, Vols. 1–2 (Belgrade/Podgorica, and Zagreb: CEDET/CEDEM/CTCSR, 2003, 2005)

14

Bosnia and Herzegovina since 1990

FLORIAN BIEBER

Bosnia and Herzegovina (hereafter, Bosnia) only reluctantly became an independent country as Yugoslavia dissolved in 1991–2. Bosnia emerged the most weakened of all states from the wars over Yugoslavia's dissolution. Not only was it physically destroyed, around 100,000 Bosnian citizens were dead and half of the population displaced, but also a third of the population which identified as Serbs and many Croats (less than a fifth of the population) had little commitment to the state and saw their future in neighboring Serbia and Croatia. Bosnia survived only as a weak state which gave predominance to ethnoterritorial units carved out during the war through ethnic cleansing and mass murder. In order to survive the immediate post-war period, Bosnia could only exist with limited sovereignty and a strong international presence. Thus the post-communist period in Bosnia was overshadowed by the aftermath of the war and debates were unlike those in most other countries in Central and Eastern Europe. Ethnicity often took precedence over democratization, fragmentation over economic reform, and international imposition over domestic state-building.

This chapter on the deeply divided Bosnian polity will first explore the aborted democratization process before the war and the impact of the war itself. It will then turn to the political system and the development of the country's party system. Subsequently, it will discuss the nature and impact of EU integration processes and economic liberalization. Examining the media and efforts of dealing with the past, the chapter will highlight the impact of the divisions in Bosnian society on post-war reform and democratization.

Bosnia before the war

Within the context of post-Tito liberalization in Yugoslavia, the League of Communists of Bosnia (SKBiH) remained one of the more dogmatic republican parties and began opening the political space to opponents only in 1989–90. During the 1980s a series of political trials targeted nationalist dissidents, most prominently Alija Izetbegović, later to become the first democratically elected president of Bosnia, and Vojislav Šešelj, leader of a paramilitary formation during the war and president of the nationalist Serb

Radical party in Serbia. While these emerged as key figures in the 1990s, the main difficulties the League of Communists faced were a series of scandals and the economic crisis of Yugoslavia, rather than nationalist challengers. In 1987, the party was shaken by the *Agrokomerc* scandal. This agricultural company based in Northwestern Bosnia, had grown through protection of the SKBiH and the issuing of promissory notes without adequate financial backing. Its collapse discredited the party and demonstrated the intense connection between the party and corruption in the republic. The most prominent Bosnian communist official Hamdija Pozdarac, a Bosnian member of the Yugoslav presidency, had to resign, as did dozens of others. These resignations brought to power a more liberal party leadership in Bosnia. At the same time, the nationalist mobilization in Serbia was being felt in Bosnia. In Serbia, Slobodan Milošević had come to power in 1987 and began channeling and organizing nationalist protests in favor of a centralized Yugoslavia and abolition of the autonomy of Kosovo and Vojvodina.[1]

Following the collapse of the League of Communists of Yugoslavia during the last party congress in January 1990, the individual republics began organizing multiparty elections. Bosnia was one of the last republics to hold elections in November–December 1990. Initially ethnic parties were banned from competing in elections, but this prohibition was lifted by the constitutional court, opening the door to the formation of the Muslim Party for Democratic Action (SDA), the Croat Democratic Community (HDZ) and the Serb Democratic Party (SDS). The last Yugoslav prime minister, a Bosnian Croat businessman, Ante Marković, established the only major multiethnic alternative to the reformed League of Communists, the Alliance of Yugoslav Reform Forces (SRSJ). While opinion polls suggested a victory of the multiethnic parties, the three nationalist parties won an overwhelming victory, gaining control of all key republican institutions and winning the elections in most municipalities. This surprise was not only due to the new experience with multiparty politics and unpredictable polls. By forming a pre-election alliance the nationalist parties presented themselves as the main anti-communist bloc. Second, the voting dynamics for the nationalist parties followed the pattern of a classic prisoners' dilemma with many voting for the party for the fear that members of other ethnic groups would vote for "their" party, giving them a decisive political advantage. Finally, increased polarization of the political climate throughout Yugoslavia benefited the nationalist parties. Winning more than three-quarters of the seats in parliament, the distribution of power among the three nationalist parties thus closely reflected the population distribution among the three dominant ethnic groups.[2]

The institutional set-up reflected the importance of ethnicity with a seven-member Presidency, granting two seats for Muslims, Serbs, and Croats each and one for other communities. Similarly the election law required that the parliamentary representation of ethnic groups mirror the population census. Following their electoral success, the three nationalist parties formed a coalition, which secured Alija Izetbegović the position of president of the presidency, the HDZ representative Jure Pelivan the post of prime minister, and the SDS representative Momčilo Krajišnik the position of president of the parliament. Beyond replacing the League of Communists in power, the new coalition held few common positions. In fact, on the future of Yugoslavia and Bosnia's role, the parties were deeply divided. As a result, no reforms were possible beyond eliminating the word "Socialist" from the name of the republic. The SDS under the leadership of Radovan Karadžić received active support from Slobodan Milošević and Serbia, including arms to prepare for conflict. The party supported close ties to Serbia and the preservation of Yugoslavia, whereas the HDZ argued for close links with Croatia and received support from its sister party which had gained power in Croatia under Franjo Tudjman. The SDA supported Yugoslavia, but was wary of Bosnia remaining in Yugoslavia if Croatia left the federation and Yugoslavia would become dominated by Serbia.

Bosnia during the war

As the war in Croatia began in the summer of 1991, following declarations of independence by Slovenia and Croatia in June 1991, the prospects of Yugoslavia surviving appeared dim. With an HDZ and SDA majority, the Bosnian parliament voted in October 1991 to declare the republic's sovereignty. Following the vote, the SDS began withdrawing from joint institutions and began forming the Serb Republic. Following a request from the EC, Bosnia organized a referendum on the republic's independence from Yugoslavia in February–March 1992. While most Serbs followed the call for a boycott by the SDS, the participating voters overwhelmingly endorsed Bosnian independence. The war in Bosnia began in early April 1992, as Bosnia declared its independence.[3]

Already in the fall and winter 1991–2 the Croatian war occasionally crossed into Bosnia, but the Bosnian war began in earnest in April 1992. In a massive campaign of "ethnic cleansing" and territorial conquest, the self-declared Serb Republic rapidly established control over 70% of Bosnian territory in the course of 1992. It received financial and military support from the newly founded Federal Republic of Yugoslavia (FRY, Serbia and Montenegro) and the Bosnian Serb Army remained fully integrated with the Yugoslav Army. The Serb Republic sought to secede from Bosnia and join neighboring Serbia together with the self-declared Serb Republic of Krajina in Croatia. The Muslim–Croat coalition in Bosnia fell apart in 1993, resulting in a three-way war, which increased pressure on the underequipped Bosnian government forces. The HDZ-controlled Croat forces (HVO) sought to carve out "Herceg Bosna" in Herzegovina to join neighboring Croatia. This war ended with the US-brokered Washington Agreement in 1994 and paved the way to a joint Croat–Bosnian offensive in the summer of 1995 that managed to reverse some of the territorial gains of the Bosnian Serb army. In July that year, the Bosnian Serb forces conquered the eastern Bosnian town of Srebrenica and killed some

8,000 men and boys in the largest single massacre in Europe since 1945, an act which has been described as genocide by the International Criminal Tribunal for the former Yugoslavia (ICTY). During the summer of 1995 the military balance of power shifted with the advances of the Croatian and Bosnian forces and NATO bombardment of Bosnian Serb positions, leading first to a cease-fire followed by peace talks. These negotiations were held in Dayton, Ohio, under the auspices of the Contact Group (United States, key EU members, and Russia) and resulted in the General Framework Agreement for Peace in Bosnia and Herzegovina (GFAP), initialed in November in Dayton and formally signed in Paris in December 1995.

The GFAP was not only a cease-fire agreement, but it also established the post-war political order, establishing the country's constitution and key principles for state-building. With the arrival of the NATO-led implementation force (IFOR) in December 1995, the war came to an end after three-and-a-half years of fighting.

Governance and international intervention after the war

The Dayton Peace Agreement established a uniquely complicated political system, based on a constitution (Annex 4 of the GFAP) written in English and without an official translation. The constitution was primarily based on the principle of interethnic accommodation and compromise between the wartime parties, rather than democratization. At its core, the new constitution and the GFAP were schizophrenic and often ambivalent, by both endorsing and seeking to reverse "ethnic cleansing." The GFAP recognized the ethnoterritorial autonomies carved out during the war, while simultaneously making Bosnia party to all key European and international human rights conventions and establishing the unconditional right to return for refugees and internally displaced persons (IDPs) as a principle of post-war justice. The inherent tensions between these approaches in the peace agreement was a source of contradictions, as well as an opportunity for overcoming some of the rigid forms of ethnic autonomy during the post-war period.

The political system established at Dayton recognized two entities established during the war, the Serb Republic (*Republika Srpska*, RS) and the Federation of Bosnia and Herzegovina (*Federacija BiH*, FBiH). The RS was created in 1992 as a secessionist unit to join Serbia, while the Federation was created in 1994 to end the Bosniak–Croat war, comprised of ten cantons under a weak federal roof, and has served as a model for the state-level constitutional set-up. Of the ten cantons, three had an overwhelming Croat and five a large Bosniak[4] majority, whereas the remaining two cantons had a "mixed" Bosniak and Croat population. With each ethnic group enjoying significant autonomy, joint institutions in the Federation and at state level were constitutionally weak and implementation of these institutions was undermined by nationalist Croat and Serb politicians who sought to preserve their communal autonomy. Originally, the joint state had only three ministries (Foreign Affairs, Foreign Trade, Civil Affairs) while all key powers, including control of the police and army remained in entity (and cantonal) control. Reflecting Yugoslav traditions, the head of state is a three-member rotating presidency, with one Serb elected in the RS and one Bosniak and Croat elected in the Federation. As a system of power-sharing, all three nations have to be represented in government. In addition, all three ethnic groups in the government and the Parliamentary Assembly (composed of the 42-member House of Representatives and the 15-member House of Peoples) hold extensive veto rights.[5]

By linking ethnic and territorial affiliation, many citizens were in fact excluded from the political process (i.e. Serbs from the Federation could not be elected to the state presidency or be represented in the House of Peoples) and the primary importance of ethnicity was further consolidated. After the war, the political system, in combination with the social divisions, effectively prevented the emergence of a statewide party.

The first elections in September 1996, only nine months after the end of the war, were organized by the Organization for Security and Cooperation in Europe (OSCE), which was charged with this task and with democratization more generally. The elections were intended to allow for a rapid transfer of authority from international peacekeepers to domestic authorities. However, as they reaffirmed and legitimized the nationalist parties in power, they ushered in an extended international presence and more than a decade of diminished sovereignty as international actors became increasingly engaged in the governance of the country.[6]

A central role fell to the Office of the High Representative (OHR), an ad hoc body formed to oversee the civilian aspects of the implementation of the GFAP. Originally equipped only with a weak mandate and small staff, it could do little besides monitoring the lack of implementation by the political elites in Bosnia. In December 1997, at a conference in Bonn, the Peace Implementation Council (PIC) that oversees the peace process and is composed of fifty-five countries and organizations, granted the High Representative (HR) powers to impose legislation and dismiss officials for obstructing the implementation of the GFAP or for their wartime involvement. These powers, known as the "Bonn powers," have been used by subsequent HRs[7] to dismiss more than 100 officials from public office, ranging from members of the state presidency and presidents of the entities, down to mayors and local police officials. Similarly, hundreds of laws and amendments have been imposed by the HR, including laws on state symbols (flag, anthem), far-reaching changes to the entity constitutions, and voting mechanisms in the state government.

While formally a fully independent country, Bosnia has lacked full sovereignty since the Dayton Peace Accords due to the strong role of international actors. Thus Bosnia has been described as a "semi-protectorate," a "controlled democracy" or even a "European Raj."[8]

Political pluralism and fragmented spheres of political competition

At the end of the war, the three nationalist parties held a near-monopolistic control over their respective communities. Only in the regions controlled by the Bosnian government at the end of the war did some ethnic and political diversity exist. Thus, in 1996, Bosnia was a multiparty state without genuine democratic competition. The post-conflict phase ushered in a gradual liberalization of the political space. Political alternatives to the dominant three nationalist parties slowly began to emerge after 1996. The frequent elections (1996, 1997, 1998, 2000, 2002, 2006), however, had only limited impact in encouraging moderation. No party has been able to successfully cater to a cross-ethnic, cross-entity electorate. Instead, party pluralism has largely emerged within each of the three ethnic groups and the entities. Among the Bosniak electorate, and to some degree among Serbs and Croats in the central Bosnian cities (Sarajevo, Tuzla), the Party for Bosnia and Herzegovina (SBiH) and the Social Democratic Party (SDP) have successfully challenged the predominance of the SDA, especially in 2000 and 2006. All three parties advocate a more centralized Bosnia and consider the Serb Republic illegitimate. While the SDP emerged from the League of Communists and is probably the most diverse party in terms of the ethnic background of the party leadership and electorate in Bosnia, the SBiH of former Bosnian Prime Minister Haris Silajdžić split off from the SDA in 1996 and has often advocated a more radical platform, without formally catering to Bosniak voters alone. Among Serb parties, the main challenger to the SDS has been the Alliance of Independent Social Democrats (SNSD), which first came to power in the RS in 1997 through international support. The SNSD, under the leadership of Milorad Dodik, has often been Social Democratic in name only and since its return to power in 2006, has supported a more uncompromising position in regard to protecting the autonomy of the Serb Republic than the SDS. Among the Croat electorate, the dominance of HDZ came under serious threat in 2006 when the dominant party split into two wings (HDZ and HDZ 1990) over constitutional reform in Bosnia (table 14.1).

The power-sharing arrangement requires the participation of Bosniak, Croat, and Serb, and representatives from both entities in government. Thus, coalition formation has been difficult and governing coalitions are not based on a convergence of parties which favor similar policies. At the state level, the three nationalist parties have been in power until 2001 and again in 2003. Since 2006 the SDS has become an opposition party at the state level and in the RS, but the SDA and HDZ have remained in government.

While some parties have crossed entity boundaries, they only campaign to their own core electorate, mostly to be found among displaced persons, who have the right to vote in their pre-war homes, which explains the strong performance of the SDA in the RS in the first post-war elections. As the electoral and political system and social structures do not encourage cross-ethnic and cross-entity

Table 14.1 Election results for House of Representatives, 1996–2006, %

Party	1996	1998	2000	2002	2006
FBiH					
Party of Democratic Action (SDA)	57.1	47.9	27.0	32.4	25.5
Croat Democratic Community (HDZ)	28.6	19.7	19.3	15.9	8.0
Croat Democratic Community 1990 (HDZ 1990)	–	–	–	–	6.1
Social Democratic Party (SDP)[a]	7.1	14.5	27.3	16.2	15.4
Party for Bosnia and Herzegovina (SBiH)	7.1	–	15.6	16.2	23.0
RS					
Serb Democratic Party (SDS)	64.3	21.0	39.7	33.7	19.4
Party of Democratic Action (SDA)	21.4	16.6	7.4	7.3	3.7
Alliance of Independent Social Democrats (SNSD)	14.3	27.7	10.6	22.4	46.9
Party for Democratic Progress (PDP)	–	–	15.2	10.4	5.1

Notes:
[a] SDP was part of the opposition joint list (ZL) in 1996. SDA and SBiH ran together in 1998 (with other smaller parties). SNSD was part of coalitions in 1996 and 1998. HDZ and HDZ 1990 ran in 2006 with other smaller Croat parties.

political parties, parties have remained ethnically divided. In particular, the fact that the fundamental organization of the state remains contested makes issue oriented and non-ethnic political campaigns difficult. More centralization and stronger state-level institutions, while rejecting an autonomous Serb Republic, have been favored by parties with a strong Bosniak electorate, which makes these unelectable among most Serb and Croat voters. These fundamental differences have prevented the emergence of a Bosnian-wide opposition or interest groups of any kind which are able to draw on broad support across the ethnic divide.[9]

The system of government has been in constant flux since 1996, as international intervention sought to strengthen the weak dysfunctional state established at Dayton. In addition to the abolition of the entity-based armies, the state government increased from three ministries to nine, although some remain embryonic. At the same time, the power of the entities has declined and both had to tone done their claim to represent only one or two ethnic groups in Bosnia to the disadvantage of others. These changes have been ad hoc and imposed or coerced by the OHR. An attempt to reform the Dayton constitution in order to formalize *de facto* changes and to further streamline and simplify decision-making procedures narrowly failed in the Bosnian parliament in 2006.

European integration and limitations of conditionality

European integration did not emerge on the agenda before 1999, when the EU outlined a prospect of integration through the instrument of the Stabilization and Association Process, which was offered to all countries of the Western

Balkans, including Bosnia. Even with this perspective, EU integration featured lower on the list of Bosnian priorities than in other countries, such as Croatia and Macedonia, which had signed Stabilization and Association Agreements (SAAs) with the EU in 2001. The feasibility study of the European Commission in 2003 listed a number of reforms necessary for Bosnia to even begin negotiating an SAA. The requirements of the EU extended beyond the conditionality employed elsewhere in Central Europe. In addition to cooperation with the ICTY the EU required that Bosnia reform and streamline its system of government, including its police forces. Similarly the Venice Commission of the Council of Europe called for a streamlining of the system of government and linked the end of international intervention in the form of the OHR to the reform of the institutional structure.[10] A key aspect of the increased role of the EU in Bosnia has been the "Europeanization" of international organizations in the country, with the EU taking over the police mission from the UN in 2003 and the peacekeeping force from NATO in 2004. At the same time, the HR has been simultaneously the EU's Special Representative (EUSR) since 2002. Negotiations over the conclusion of an SAA, however, did not begin until 2005 and were signed only in June 2008 following protracted delays over police reform.

As EU integration has appeared as a distant prospect in Bosnia, Europeanization has not been able to unfold the transformative dynamic it has had in other countries in Central and Eastern Europe. In addition, the fact that the EU and other international actors are intrinsically involved in the governance of Bosnia and the state-building process has further complicated the impact of Europeanization. In fact, the conditions imposed by the EU have been considerably more detailed and far-reaching than elsewhere, as conditionality has been employed to transform Bosnia's system of government and to replace the direct intervention of the HR. While EU integration is possibly the only unifying political project of the Bosnian elite and voters, the commitment of political elites to EU integration has been wavering, as ethnopolitical mobilization still appeared to trump Europeanization.

The fragmented political and social space exacerbates this dynamic, as it prevents the emergence of a Bosnian-wide political or social debate.

Delayed economic reforms

The war interrupted both the democratic and the economic transformation. Considering that no privatization or any other substantial economic reform had taken hold before the war, the nationalist parties were able to secure control of the economic sector. In addition, the war created new elites close to the nationalists, who had benefited from the conflict and the monopolistic control of the nationalist parties. Furthermore, the war enriched new businessmen, who became rich through sanction-busting, arms deals, and the black market. These business elites not only were often key financiers of indicted war criminals, but also succeeded in securing their monopolistic control in the post-war period.[11]

Economic reform was further complicated by the widespread destruction of factories and infrastructure, as well as loss of documentation and otherwise unclear ownership structures. During the war, industrial production declined by 90% and the economy as a whole by 75%. By 2006, the GDP of Bosnia had reached only 85% of its pre-war levels.

The Dayton Peace Accord paid scant attention to the economy, allowing for the fragmentation of the economic space. In the first post-war years, legal trade and business across the entity boundary was nearly impossible. A common currency, the convertible Mark (KM), was introduced only in 1998 and value added tax (VAT) became the first statewide tax collected not exclusively at the entity level in 2006. Still, more than a decade after the war, Bosnia has no economy or finance ministry and remains a fragmented economic space.[12] The multilayered administration, with more than 140 ministries and 14 governments at state, entity, and cantonal levels took up 70% of the budget in 2006, limiting the ability of the governments to stimulate economic development or address unemployment, which hovers around 20%.[13]

The privatization of the socially owned enterprises posed difficulties encountered elsewhere in Central and Eastern Europe. As in other spheres, the privatization process was largely driven by international actors, while the political elites long resisted and obstructed the process. When the first wave of privatization took place in the late 1990s, many companies ended up under the control of supporters of the governing nationalist parties. A key industry in Bosnia, the aluminum smelter in Mostar, was partially privatized to a Croatian company, funding the HDZ and employing exclusively Croats.[14] This example is representative for other companies in Bosnia. Voucher privatization, promoted by Western donors, was utilized in both entities, resulting in local businesspeople purchasing companies at low cost from citizens who were unfamiliar with the process. The format of the privatization and the timing, only a few years after the end of the war, meant that few companies were sold to foreign investors. As a result, privatization did not promote new business practices, nor did it secure a much-needed infusion of new investments.[15] A second wave of privatization in 2006–7 was more successful in the RS, but has been largely seen as continuing to be driven by political considerations. For example, the Serbian state-owned *Telekom Srbije* bought the RS *Telekom Srpske* in a controversial privatization in 2006, which was widely viewed as an effort to consolidate links between the RS and Serbia.[16] The recent privatization efforts in the Federation have been slower and yielded fewer results than in the RS.

Altogether economic reform has been first about reconstruction and only later been focused on liberalization and privatization. As the economy did not fall under the mandate of the international presence, international organizations have focused less on creating the pre-conditions for economic liberalization.

Fragmented media

The media sphere was fragmented along ethnic lines during the war, as was the political and economic system. Whereas prior to the war there were no Serb, Croat, or Muslim media, after the war few media outlets reached out to other communities. During the war itself, TV and radio broadcasters, in particular in the RS, were key pillars of the war effort and engaged in hate speech and misinformation that contributed significantly to the conflict.[17]

After the war, the media scene was marked by ethnic division and an anarchic plurality of media outlets, with over seventy TV and over 2,000 radio stations operating in Bosnia by 2000. In addition, many Serbs and Croats turned to their kin states for print media and television. The Communication Regulatory Agency reduced the number of broadcasters through a licensing procedure aimed at increasing the professionalism of the media. As a result, a number of strong private TV stations emerged, such as *TV Hayat* in the Federation and *Pink*, which is the only private station with countrywide programming, linked to the Serbian TV empire *Pink*, championing folk music and light entertainment.

The first international effort to loosen the stranglehold of nationalist media by establishing the Open Broadcast Network (OBN) in 1996 had run out of international funding by 2001 and became a regular commercial station. More successful was the reform of the public broadcast system in 2004–5. The reforms, partly imposed by the OHR, placed the two entity broadcasters under one roof and Bosnia and Herzegovina Television (BHT) as a countrywide public station. The reform sought to establish an independent broadcaster modeled on the BBC, which increased the professionalism of public television, but the entity broadcasters have continued to favor particular parties.

The daily newspaper *Oslobodjenje*, which received global attention for continuing publication during the siege of Sarajevo, declined in terms of its reach and quality after the war and was eclipsed by the tabloid *Dnevni Avaz* as the main newspaper for readers in the Federation. In the RS, the independent daily *Nezavisne novine* emerged as the prime challenger to the entity-controlled *Glas Srpske*. The paper's founder, Željko Kopanja, lost both legs in a car bomb attack in 1999, linked to the paper's reports on war crimes and organized crime. Its attempt to become a Bosnian-wide daily failed, signaling the continued fragmentation of the media space. As a result, print runs are small, with no newspaper exceeding 100,000 copies per day, and dailies have remained susceptible to political pressure due to their financial vulnerability.[18]

Generally, the level of professionalism has increased dramatically since the war, when hate speech was an integral part of most media outlets. Still, the media remain largely separate, catering to different audiences and possessing mutually exclusive loyalties. While soap operas and entertainment shows are popular throughout Bosnia without a political or ethnic bias, news and political analysis largely fail to penetrate entity and ethnic boundaries.

Dealing with the past

Bosnia has been struggling with the dual legacy of authoritarianism and the war. Whereas the war overshadows the communist past as a source of contention, it has not been dealt with in terms of debates within Bosnian society. For most of the post-war period, the primary institution addressing wartime events has been the ICTY. Pursuing war criminals since 1993, the ICTY has been the key institution investigating and documenting war crimes. The court has indicted key suspected criminals, including the political and military commanders of the Bosnian Serb forces, Radovan Karadžić and Ratko Mladić. In a series of important decisions, the commanders of the siege of Sarajevo and of the genocide in Srebrenica have been sentenced to long prison sentences. In addition to Bosnian Serb war criminals, the ICTY has also sentenced Bosnian government officials and Bosnian Croat commanders for war crimes. The possibly most important trial, however, came to an inconclusive end in March 2006 when the former Yugoslav and Serbian president Slobodan Milošević died in prison in The Hague while standing trial for war crimes in Croatia, Bosnia, and Kosovo. The arrest of Radovan Karadžić on 12 July 2008 in Belgrade, and his subsequent extradition to the ICTY, marked an important step in bringing one of the key culprits for the war to court. Following his arrest, the most senior indicted war criminal at large remained Ratko Mladić, who commanded the Bosnian Serb army during the war. The tribunal has often come under attack by local authorities for supposed bias in its work. Similarly international actors in Bosnia have often hesitated to cooperate with the ICTY for the fear of triggering open resistance, leading to more instability.[19] Being based in the Netherlands, the tribunal has also been geographically removed from Bosnia, diminishing its impact in the country in terms of dealing with the past. One key reason for the creation of the ICTY by the UN Security Council was the assumption that local courts would be biased in hearing war crimes cases, or simply unable to do so. In recent years, this has changed when the Court of Bosnia and Herzegovina was established and began hearing war crimes cases, including some which were handed to the court by the ICTY.

In addition to the ICTY, the International Court of Justice (ICJ) has been involved in examining the war. After fifteen years, the ICJ ruled in February 2007 that Serbia was not guilty of having committed genocide in Bosnia, but it was guilty of not preventing genocide in Srebrenica. While authorities in the RS and Serbia celebrated the judgment as a "victory," it was seen by many Bosniaks as confirming that genocide took place in Bosnia, mirroring the conflicting views of the past.[20]

A key institution in dealing with the wartime past has been the Research and Documentation Center in Sarajevo, a state institution created in 2004. The center has been documenting war crimes and, possibly most importantly, investigating the number of victims of the war. Considering that the controversies over the number of victims during the Second World War was a key ground for nationalist mobilization in the 1980s and 1990s, the establishment of a precise historical record is considered to be of key importance. According to preliminary figures released in 2006, the Bosnian war had 97,826 victims, 66.11% of whom were Bosniaks, 25.54% Serbs, and 7.85% Croats.[21] A separate Srebrenica Commission was established by the RS government on the basis of a binding decision of the Human Rights Chamber. The Commission's report, acknowledging that between 7,000 and 8,000 Bosniaks were killed by the Bosnian Serb army in July 1995, was adopted by the RS government, which also issued a formal apology.[22] These efforts have, however, not translated into a broad social debate. Efforts by some NGOs to establish a Truth Commission on the basis of the South African model have been stalled by both international actors and Bosnian institutions.

In practical terms, the greatest impact in undoing some of the effects of the war has been the unconditional right to return to refugees and IDPs guaranteed in the Dayton Peace Accord. At first, only a few refugees returned to areas that were now controlled by another ethnic group. This was the consequence of fear of persecution, lack of any employment opportunities, and the fact that properties had been re-assigned during the war and were often now occupied by other refugees or cronies of the local political elite. After the OHR established the Reconstruction and Return Task Force (RRTF) in 1997 to secure refugee return and local authorities were pressured to secure the refugees' rights to their pre-war homes, refugee return accelerated significantly. Thus, by 2004 1 million, or half of all refugees and IDPs, had returned to their pre-war homes, close to half of them being returnees to areas where they were no longer in a dominant position. Much of the return was not permanent and often refugees merely sold their property to settle in their new homes in parts of Bosnia where their community dominates or in neighboring Croatia and Serbia. Nevertheless, previously largely homogeneous regions, which had seen large-scale ethnic cleansing during the war, regained some of their diversity.

Conclusions

In the first post-war decade, many of the visible traces of the wartime destruction have been eliminated, the infrastructure reconstructed and a million refugees and IDPs returned home. Nevertheless, a quarter of the population has not returned to their pre-war homes, the country is estimated to have half a million fewer inhabitants than it had before the war, and GDP has still not reached the pre-war level.

Bosnia after the war has become a deeply divided society with little space to cross ethnic and entity boundaries. While the historical experience suggests that "ethnic belonging" is likely to remain an important factor in social and political life, the particular post-war system of government has institutionalized a link between ethnicity and territory and given predominance to ethnicity which has rendered democratization difficult, if not impossible.[23] The weak state, in combination with complicated decision-making processes and limited commitment of parts of the political elite to the state or the post-Dayton political system, has created a dependency on international intervention which further undermines the quality of democratic governance.[24]

During the first four–five years of post-Bosnia, most international efforts were focused on reconstruction and peacekeeping. It was only around 2000 that state-building and economic reforms took a front seat in the reform process. By 2005–6 this phase had come to an end, as the internationally driven reforms reached their limits. During this period state institutions, such as a joint army, some crucial ministries, and a joint border police, began emerging. At the same time, the absolute power of the nationalist parties steadily eroded, allowing for more intra-ethnic pluralism. The third post-war phase began in 2005–6 with the transition from externally driven state-building to greater sovereignty. Reforms of the existing institutional set-up by Bosnian elites, in combination with a replacement of the OHR and other international organizations by the EU and the process of EU conditionality have been the key features of this phase. This transition has been marred by set-backs which highlight the difficulties of moving from post-conflict state-building to European integration. European integration embodies high requirements of state capacity and coherence, which a weak state like Bosnia struggles to fulfill. At the same time, the draw of EU integration as a motivator and socialization tool for political elites offered a too-distant time horizon and too few immediate rewards. Consequently, domestic reforms have been repeatedly stalled and the withdrawal of the OHR has been post-poned several times. Democratization and the Europeanization of Bosnia remain more conditional on its neighbors than is the case in most other Central and East European countries, as a majority of Bosnian citizens seek to maintain close contacts with their kin states Croatia and Serbia. While Croatia abandoned predatory designs on Bosnia after 2000 in exchange for accelerated integration into the EU, Serbia has not yet made such a commitment, which continues to plague Bosnia's stability. Thus, the future of democratization in Bosnia and the stability of the state does not exclusively depend on the country alone, but in large degree to the neighborhood it finds itself in.

Timeline 1990–2007

18 November and 16 December 1990	First multiparty elections held in Bosnia
25 June 1991	Slovenia and Croatia declare independence from Yugoslavia
29 February and 1 March 1992	Referendum on independence in Bosnia
6 March 1992	Bosnia declares independence from Yugoslavia

4 April 1992	Beginning of war in Bosnia
7 April 1992	International recognition of Bosnia by United States and EC
11 July 1995	Srebrenica falls to Bosnia Serb forces, resulting in killing of 8,000 men and boys
26 November 1995	The General Framework Agreement for Peace in Bosnia and Herzegovina (GFAP) signed in Dayton, Ohio
20 December 1995	NATO-led Implementation Force (IFOR) stationed in Bosnia
14 September 1996	First post-war elections in Bosnia
21 December 1996	IFOR replaced by Stabilization Force (SFOR)
9–10 December 1997	Peace Implementation Council enhances power of the High Representative (HR) at the Bonn conference
2 December 2004	EU-led EUFOR mission Althea replaces SFOR peacekeepers
6 June 2006	Armies of the Serb Republic (RS) and of the Federation integrated into the army of Bosnia and Herzegovina.
1 October 2006	First entirely Bosnian-organized elections
4 December 2007	Bosnia and EU sign the Stabilization and Association Agreement (SAA)

Fact sheet

Area	51,197 km^2
Population (2008 estimate, Agency for Statistics of Bosnia and Herzegovina, www.bhas.ba/new)	3,842,265
Major cities	
Sarajevo	304,075
Banja Luka (2005 estimate)	165,000
Tuzla	131,393
Zenica	127,713
Below the poverty line (2004 estimate, PRSP[a])	19.5% of population
Unemployment rate (2008, Agency for Statistics of Bosnia and Herzegovina, www.bhas.ba/new)	23.4%
GDP *per capita* (2008, Agency for Statistics of Bosnia and Herzegovina, www.bhas.ba/new)	1,933 Euros
Literacy rate (1999–2007, UNICEF, http://hdrestats.undp.org/en/countries/data_sheets/cty_ds_Bltt.html)	3.3% of population

Note: [a] PRSP = World Bank, Poverty Reduction Strategy Papers

Census result, 1991

Group	(percent)
Muslims/Bosniaks	43.5
Serbs	31.2
Croats	17.4

Parties and coalitions in the House of Representatives of Bosnia and Herzegovina, 2006–

Party of Democratic Action	(SDA)	9	Serbian Democratic Party	(SDS)	3
Party for Bosnia and Herzegovina	(SBiH)	8	Croat Community	(HDZ 1990, HZ, HSS, KDU, HDU, DK)	2
Alliance of Independent Social Democrats	(SNSD)	8	Bosnian Patriotic Party	(BPS)	1
Social Democratic Party	(SDP) (BiH)	5	Democratic People's Alliance	(DNZ)	1
Croat Democratic Party	(HDZ)	3	People's Party Work for Betterment	(RzB)	1
			Party for Democratic Progress	(PDP)	1

Short biography of Alija Izetbegović

Alija Izetbegović (1925–2003) was the first president of the Bosnian presidency elected in 1990 (1990–6) and re-elected after the war in 1996 to the new presidency, which he first chaired (1996) and later belonged to as Bosniak member until his resignation in 2000. As president of the Bosniak Party of Democratic Action (SDA), he was the undisputed leader of the Bosniak/Muslim community and shaped Bosnian politics until his death in 2003. Izetbegović, a lawyer by training, was a dissident to communist rule, arrested in 1983 for Muslim nationalism and alleged fundamentalism as author of the controversial 1970 Islamic declaration. After serving five years in prison, Izetbegović was one of the founders of the SDA in 1990, which captured the Muslim (later Bosniak) vote. As president of the state presidency, Izetbegović at first favored a reformed Yugoslavia and only reluctantly took Bosnia towards independence. Leading Bosnia during the war, he continued to advocate a multiethnic centralized Bosnia, but also pursued a narrow Bosniak nationalist agenda. The SDA moved from a broad movement to a more nationalist party in the course of the war and the post-war period. Izetbegović participated in all the peace negotiations for Bosnia and reluctantly agreed to the Dayton Peace Accords in 1995. He continued in the first years of post-war Bosnian and Bosniak politics as member of the new state presidency in 1996 until his resignation due to ill-health in 2000.

Notes

1. Neven Andjelić, *Bosnia-Herzegovina: The End of a Legacy* (London: Frank Cass, 2003), pp. 56–75.
2. See Suad Arnautović, *Izbori u Bosni I Hercegovini '90: Analize izbornog procesa* (Sarajevo: Promocult, 1996).
3. See Marko Attila Hoare's chapter in this volume.
4. A congress of Muslim intellectuals adopted the name "Bosniak" for Muslims in 1993. This chapter will thus use the term "Muslim" until 1993 and "Bosniak" for the ethnic group afterwards.
5. See Florian Bieber, *Post-War Bosnia: Ethnicity, Inequality and Public Sector Governance* (Houndmills: Palgrave, 2006), pp. 40–62.

6. On the first elections, see Paul Shoup, "The Elections in Bosnia and Herzegovina: The End of an Illusion," *Problems of Post-Communism*, Vol. 44, No. 1 (January–February 1997), pp. 3–15.
7. The post of HR has been held by Carl Bildt (1996–7), Carlos Westendorp (1997–9), Wolfgang Petritsch (1999–2002), Paddy Ashdown (2002–6), Christian Schwarz-Schilling (2006–7), Miroslav Lajčak (2007–9), and Valentin Inzko (2009–).
8. The latter draws parallel to the British colonial rule in India. Gerald Knaus and Felix Martin, "Travails of the European Raj, Lessons from Bosnia and Herzegovina," *Journal of Democracy*, Vol. 14, No. 3 (July 2003), pp. 60–74.
9. Bieber, *Post-War Bosnia*, pp. 90–107.
10. Venice Commission (European Commission for Democracy through Law) (2005), Opinion on the Constitutional Situation in Bosnia and Herzegovina and the Powers of the High Representative, CDL-AD (2005) 004, 11 March, available online at venice.coe.int.
11. Michael Ehrke, "Bosnien: Zur politischen Ökonomie erzwungenen Friedens," Friedrich-Ebert-Stiftung, *Internationale Politik-Analyse*, 2002, at http://library.fes.de/pdf-files/id/01456.pdf.
12. Tim Donais, *The Political Economy of Peacebuilding in Post-Dayton Bosnia* (London: Routledge, 2005), pp. 99–100.
13. *Frankfurter Allgemeine Zeitung* (Frankfurt, 4 December 2006), p. 12. Official unemployment numbers are above 40% (44.2% in 2007), but these underestimate the significant grey and black sector. European Commission, Bosnia and Herzegovina – Economic Profile, at http://ec.europa.eu/enlargement/bosnia_and_herzegovina/economic_profile_en.htm.
14. International Crisis Group, *Bosnia's Precarious Economy: Still Not Open for Business*, 7 August 2001, pp. 25–6, at www.crisisweb.org.
15. Donais, *The Political Economy of Peacebuilding*, pp. 114–27.
16. *Balkan Insight* (26 June 2007), at www.birn.eu.com.
17. See Mark Thompson, *Forging War: The Media in Serbia, Croatia and Bosnia-Herzegovina* (London: Article 19, 1994); Kemal Kurspahić, *Prime Time Crime: Balkan Media in War and Peace* (Washington, DC: USIP, 2003).
18. Bosnia and Herzegovina, Nations in Transit, Freedom House, Reports 2005, 2007, at www.freedomhouse.org/template.cfm?page=17&year=2006.
19. Florence Hartmann, *Paix et châtiment* (Paris: Flammarion, 2007).
20. *Neue Zürcher Zeitung* (28 February 2007), at www.nzz.ch.
21. *Globus* (Zagreb, 2 February 2007), quoted from *Bosnia Report*, No. 55–56 (January–July 2007).
22. B92 Vesti (Belgrade, 11 June 2004); Republika Srpska Government, *The Events in and around Srebrenica between 10th and 19th July 1995*, (Banja Luka, 1994).
23. On the nature of the political system in an ethnically divided system, see Mirjana Kasapović, *Bosna i Hercegovina: podijeljeno društvo i nestabilna država* (Zagreb: Politička kultura, 2005) and Florian Bieber, "After Dayton, Dayton? The Evolution of an Unpopular Peace," *Ethnopolitics*, Vol. 5, No. 1 (March 2006), pp. 15–31.
24. Within Bosnia and in academic and policy debates, there is much controversy whether the international intervention itself is the problem, as argued by David Chandler, *Bosnia: Faking Democracy after Dayton* (London: Pluto, 1999) and the European Stability Initiative, or whether international intervention is necessary to

control nationalist elites which seek to destroy the state, as argued by the International Crisis Group and many Bosnian scholars, such as Nerzuk Ćurak, *Geopolitika kao sudbina: Slučaj Bosna* (Sarajevo: Fakultet političkih nauka, 2002).

Further reading

Bieber, Florian. *Post-War Bosnia: Ethnicity, Inequality and Public Sector Governance* (Houndmills: Palgrave, 2006)

"After Dayton, Dayton? The Evolution of an Unpopular Peace," *Ethnopolitics*, Vol. 5, No. 1 (March 2006), pp. 15–31

"Bosnia-Herzegovina: Slow, Progress towards a Functional State," *Southeast European and Black Sea Studies*, Vol. 6, No. 1 (March 2006), pp. 43–64

Bose, Sumantra. *Bosnia after Dayton: Nationalist Partition and International Intervention* (London: C. Hurst & Co., 2002)

Bougarel, Xavier, Elissa Helms, and Ger Duijzings (eds.). *The New Bosnian Mosaic: Identities, Memories and Moral Claims in a Post-War Society* (Aldershot: Ashgate, 2007)

Caspersen, Nina. "Good Fences Make Good Neighbours? A Comparison of Conflict-Regulation Strategies in Postwar Bosnia," *Journal of Peace Research*, Vol. 41, No. 5 (2004), pp. 569–88

Chandler, David (ed.). *Peace without Politics? Ten Years of State-Building in Bosnia* (London: Routledge, 2005)

Divjak, Boris *et al.*, *National Integrity Study BiH 2007* (Banja Luka: Transparancy International Bosnia and Herzegovina, 2007), at www.ti-bih.org/documents/20-02-2007/National_Integrity_System_Study_2007.pdf [law accessed on 22 July 2009]

Dizdarevic, Srdjan *et al.* (eds)., *Democracy Assessment in Bosnia and Herzegovina* (Sarajevo: Open Society Fund Bosnia and Herzegovina 2006), at www.soros.org.ba/images_vijesti/Istrazivanje%20demokratije/Democracy%20Assessment%20in%20Bosnia%20and%20Herzegovina.pdf

Donais, Timothy. *The Political Economy of Peacebuilding in Post-Dayton Bosnia* (London: Routledge, 2005)

Further links

Bosnia Institute, at www.bosnia.org.uk/default.cfm

European Stability Initiative, at www.esiweb.org/index.php?lang=en&id=17

International Crisis Group, at www.crisisgroup.org/home/index.cfm?id=1242&l=1

Nations in Transit, Freedom House, at www.freedomhouse.org/template.cfm?page=17&year=2006

Office of the High Representative, at www.ohr.int

15

Macedonia since 1989

ZACHARY T. IRWIN

Macedonia, an independent state since September 1991, has a long and controversial history. The first recorded states on the territory of today's Republic of Macedonia were the Thraco-Illyrian Kingdom of Paionia and the Kingdom of Macedon. Alexander the Great, who ruled as King of Macedon 336–323 BCE, built a huge empire, which extended as far as present-day Afghanistan but after his death his empire fell apart. The region became part of the Roman Empire in 146 BCE, and after the division of that Empire in 285 CE was part of the Eastern Roman (or Byzantine) Empire.

Slavs came to the region of present-day Macedonia in the 580s CE. In the tenth century, the region came under Bulgarian rule, but the Byzantines had reasserted control by 1018. In the fourteenth century, the region of Macedonia fell under Serbian control but by 1395 Macedonia had become part of the Ottoman (Turkish) Empire. Macedonia remained under Ottoman rule until the Balkan Wars of 1912–13, when it was annexed by Serbia. After the First World War, Macedonia was incorporated into the Kingdom of Serbs, Croats, and Slovenes, renamed the Kingdom of Yugoslavia in October 1929.

During the Second World War, most of Macedonia was occupied by Bulgarian forces. But after the war when the communists took over Yugoslavia, Macedonia was incorporated as one of six constituent republics and, over time, its autonomy expanded. The ruling communists classified Macedonia as an underdeveloped republic and earmarked special funding to bring the economy close to the Yugoslav average. The program did not realize its intended results, however, and the Macedonian social product per worker – an important measure of economic development – actually shrank as a percentage of the Yugoslav average between 1975 and 1986. Moreover, by 1987, unemployment in Macedonia stood at 26.7% – the highest rate of unemployment among the country's six republics.[1]

Three months after Slovenia and Croatia declared their secession from Yugoslavia, in June 1991, Macedonia followed their lead, adopting a new constitution in November of that year. Kiro Gligorov (b. 1917), a seventy-four-year-old Macedonian politician who had held various high posts in socialist Yugoslavia, including as member of the state presidency, had been elected president of Macedonia in January 1991. He remained president after the declaration of independence, serving in that office until 1999. His successor was Boris Trajkovski (1956–2004), a Methodist and member of the nationalist Internal Macedonian Revolutionary Organization–Democratic Party for Macedonian National Unity (VMRO–DPMNE), who was elected at the age of forty-three. After Trajkovski was killed in a helicopter crash in February 2004, Branko Crvenkovski, a center-left politician who had been serving as prime minister (1992–8 and 2002–4), was elected president of the republic. On 6 April 2009 Georgi Ivanov, candidate of the right-wing VMRO–DPMNE, won the presidential election, succeeding Crvenkovski in that office.

Macedonia in an international context

As one of the less developed successor states to Socialist Yugoslavia, Macedonia has confronted fundamental challenges to its status as an independent state. Poor and landlocked, Skopje endured a Greek blockade through 1995 as a consequence of its claim to the name "Macedonia." Official Bulgaria does not recognize Macedonian as a nationality distinct from Bulgarian. Relations between Macedonia's Albanians (who make up 25% of the country's population) and its ethnic Macedonians (64% of the country's population) have been burdened by destabilizing events, including the influx of about 300,000 Albanian refugees from Kosovo and virtual civil war in the spring of 2001 between government forces and Albanian insurgents.[2] The recent stalemate concerning Kosovo's independence and Serbia's response indicates a potential crisis. Prolonged involvement in Macedonian politics by the United States and EU indicates that Macedonian instability is perceived to threaten the entire region. In 2006, Elizabeth Pond opined that "if" the country "had lost its reputation as a tinderbox, it owes its escape both to the inattention of history and to the intensive attention of the European Union."[3]

The role of NATO and the EU in Macedonian affairs has involved support for democratic reform and mediation and peacekeeping among Macedonian citizens, whether ethnic Macedonians or ethnic Albanians. Officials have offered EU membership as an incentive for democratic stability. Popular support for such an outcome enables exertion of what is described as "passive and active leverage" in Macedonian political choices. The latter concerns "the deliberate conditionality exercised in the EU's pre-accession process" and the former the "attraction of EU membership" for formerly communist countries with its "tremendous geopolitical, socio-cultural, and economic benefits."[4] The EU has formalized its agreement with Macedonia through the Framework Stabilization and Agreement and the Community Assistance for Reconstruction, Development, and Stabilization (CARDS), affirmed by the 2000 Zagreb Summit and the 2003 Thessaloniki Agenda, among others.[5] The goal of these agreements is eventual inclusion in the EU, and for Macedonia they include implementing reforms in the 2001 Framework Agreement (Ohrid Accord) ending the Albanian insurgency. The document specifies amendments to the constitution, the 115th amendment emphasizes decentralized government, along with political and financial authority.[6]

European involvement has extended into policy areas through both the UN Development Program and the Council of Europe. In 2006, the Council's Parliamentary Assembly outlined its recommendations, acknowledging "substantial progress" in development since the country's accession.[7] In 2006, the Macedonian authorities jointly authored a detailed "Blue Ribbon Report" that reflected a mix of economic and political achievements. The findings confirmed those of earlier UNDP citizens' focus groups that criticized the abuse of political patronage in the civil service. The report insisted that public administration and services needed to "demonstrate political neutrality, legitimacy and accountability to democratic government [elsewhere affirming that] ... citizens value not just the public services, but the 'procedural' aspects of how they are delivered – especially participation, fairness, equity, and probity."[8] A 2007 meeting between Macedonia's Minister of Local Government, Abdurrahaman Memeti, and the EU Ambassador to Macedonia expressed satisfaction on the process of devolution.[9]

Implementation of the Amendment on Local Government and the corresponding law, part of the Ohrid Agreement, have been associated with economic development and improvements in the Human Development Index (HDI). Higher levels of resources available to local communities have impacted standards of living more than the same amounts consumed by the central government. Although Macedonia's HDI overall ranks 69th out of 177 states, its score of 0.81 approximately ties with Albania at 0.78; yet the difference in *per capita* GDP ($7,200 versus $5,300) between the two indicates a potential to improve overall Macedonian HDI exclusive of greater wealth.[10] HDI differences within Macedonia are associated with urban and rural populations and with a "weak, but statistically significant" difference between areas inhabited mostly by ethnic Macedonians and those areas with predominantly ethnic Albanian populations.[11] These and similar studies associate ethnic relations, economic growth, and political reform with foreign sources of reform.

Despite the positive consequences of this tutelage, there are legacies of corruption, ethnic conflict, and poverty that burden development. On the eve of independence, Macedonia's *per capita* gross state product (GSP) was 36.6% lower than the Yugoslav average, and despite average annual federal transfers of 6% of the Republic's GSP, its position had declined consistently compared with the developed republics.[12] The World Bank reports that despite a 3% increase in growth in 2003, poverty remained at 22% of the population, a condition attributed to "stagnant" levels of inequality, a "lack of good jobs," and "inadequate restructuring of the economy."[13] In 2005, unemployment remained at 37.2% and growth at 3.8%. Structural economic rigidity, endemic corruption, and low foreign investment represent pre-independence legacies from the former Yugoslavia. Some areas, however, suggest improvement. Transparency International's Corruption Perceptions Index for Macedonia improved between 2006 and 2007 from 105th/163 to 84th/179.[14] International involvement is clearly a factor in anti-corruption efforts.

Before independence

Independent Macedonia confronted the problems of institutional accommodation of a large minority, a late (1913) and fragmented liberation, and a dysfunctional political legacy among the majority Slavs. Unlike other post-communist regimes, Macedonia could not easily redeem its pre-communist nationalist legacy for a multiparty system. The country's national intelligentsia confronted the division of Macedonian territory among Yugoslavia, Greece, and Bulgaria. During the interwar period, an anti-Yugoslav terrorist Internal Macedonian Revolutionary Movement (VMRO) movement on the right was coopted by revisionist forces in Italy and Bulgaria, while the Comintern-dominated left sought unification within a "Balkan communist federation."[15] Socialist Yugoslavia became the paladin of national expression through the wartime Anti-Fascist People's Assembly of Macedonia (ASNOM) and its assurance of federated statehood. Macedonia's founding President, Kiro Gligorov, had been a member of ASNOM. Socialist Yugoslavia repudiated Serbia's denial of a Macedonian nationality and defended Macedonia's status as constituent nation and founding republic in relations with Greece and Bulgaria.[16] Non-communist dissent was virtually absent.

State identity linked socialist and independent Macedonia through an emerging political culture. Bertsch's 1974 survey found that, among Yugoslav nations, Macedonians were most supportive of the regime's "universal" values of socialism and ethnic tolerance.[17] The study determined that the regime's efforts at "mobilization" in Macedonia directly promoted values of "modernism" and "universalism," unlike respondents in other republics. The difference may reflect the greater traditionalism among Macedonians, but it also is consistent with higher levels of trust between citizens and their leadership. In the early 1980s, the authorities tolerated both cultural pluralism and the assertion of Macedonian Orthodoxy. Considering the political strictures on Serbian Orthodoxy and Roman Catholicism, greater tolerance of Macedonian Orthodoxy implied a policy of promoting national identity through creation of an autocephalous (self-governing) Church in 1967. On the fortieth anniversary of that event, Metropolitan Kiril recalled the event as the restoration of "the honor, dignity, and pride of the Macedonian nation [that] mended the great historic injustice of 1767, when our Ohrid Archbishopric was abolished in a non-canonical way."[18] Kiril added that the Serbian Orthodox Church's refusal to recognize Macedonian autocephaly betrayed the goal "of ultimately eliminating us as a nation [and] as a state." Asserting continuity between the tenth-century Ohrid Patriarchy and Macedonian Orthodoxy was central to refuting Serbian Orthodox claims that the Macedonian Church was "in schism," and without basis for its separation from the Serbian Church.[19]

Traditionally, autocephaly reinforced national identity. Macedonian Orthodoxy has expressed political views supporting the independent state's legitimacy, including rights of the Macedonian diaspora.[20] The governments of both socialist and independent Macedonia have supported the construction of a large Orthodox Cathedral in central Skopje, along with promoting Macedonian culture and language and industrial subsidies. In a spirit of consensus, the republic's party leadership sought to lead, rather than oppose, greater social pluralism in the late 1980s. President Gligorov symbolized continuity between socialist and independent Macedonia, but his popularity did not resolve the challenges of democratization.

Democratization

Understanding the significance of relations between Macedonia's Slavs and Albanians for "democratic values" is as challenging as interpreting political attitudes. The 2001 Framework Accord established a common agenda for political reform that links Europeanization and democratization. The Accord's implementation became a basis for integrating more than 25% of the population. Since its independence, successive governments have included an Albanian coalition partner, but some observers might have taken exception to Prime Minister Nikola Gruevski's remarks (in 2007) that the country was a "contemporary model of multi-ethnicity, observing human rights, especially those of minority communities in the country … [T]heir just representation in public and state institutions is the essence of the national strategy." Gruevski stated that Macedonia would enter NATO based on its progress in "the rule of law, the boost in institutions [*sic*], and improvement in the rights of minority communities."[21] Apart from the coalition's satisfaction with prospects of NATO–EU membership, the situation was less favorable from the viewpoint of democratization.

Political parties serve to represent interests, forming responsible government, and organizing opposition. We shall examine Macedonian political parties below, but their development indicates a general feature of Macedonian politics. Unexpected circumstances have compelled adaptation through improvization. President Gligorov transformed the Macedonian League of Communists into the Social Democratic of Macedonia Party (SDSM), and sought legitimacy through competitive elections and an Albanian coalition partner. The nationalist VMRO–DPMNE also demonstrates the importance of improvized change. Initially, the party emerged from Macedonia's first non-communist nationalist movement, the Movement for Pan-Macedonian Action (MAAK) under the leadership of Ljubčo Georgievski. He precluded cooperation with Albanian parties because "Macedonia can be only the national state of the Macedonian people" and because of the "aggression of the Albanian nationalists."[22] After winning a plurality of 38 of 120 seats in Macedonia's first parliamentary election, the party refused to enter into a coalition. Party spokesman Dosta Dimovska reinforced the ideological character of VMRO–DPMNE's program, claiming that "we are successors of the historical VMRO and I cannot see anything wrong in following historical traditions."[23] She added that the VMRO–DPMNE had "a special economic program that would stop the merciless destruction [of] state companies," wreaked by the SDSM government's Law on Privatization, and that the party would reject the "impossible demands from the Albanian minority."

Nevertheless, VMRO–DPMNE won a plurality of 43 seats in the 1998 parliamentary elections. This result and the precedent of the SDSM coalition with the Albanian Party for Democratic Prosperity (PDP) enabled Georgievski to re-evaluate his opposition to a coalition with an Albanian partner. The opportunity for such a coalition, distinct from the previous government, emerged when Arben Xhaferi and Menduh Thaçi left the PDP in 1997 and merged with a smaller Albanian party to form the Democratic Party of Albanians (DPA–PDSh), winning 10 seats in 1998. Along with Vasil Tupurkovski's Democratic Alternative (DA), the three parties governed with a 62-seat majority. Xhaferi spoke of the "great accordance of stances regarding some requests of the Albanians" within the new coalition.[24] The cleavage of the Albanian parties and VMRO–DPMNE's altered view towards a coalition government contributed to create a stable alternative to the Social Democrats.

Elite values: periods and events

I have chosen to examine Macedonian development over several periods since independence (table 15.1). The distinction among these categories and the periods loosely conform to areas of state concern. The period 1990–2 was one of achieving independence and institutional foundation; 1993–2001 marked a period of consolidation and acculturation; the period since 2001 was distinguished by negotiating the Ohrid Accord and its consequences. EU and/or NATO, one might identify a fourth period. Categories of "events" within the periods are understood as "systemic–national," "procedural–democratic," and "executive–normative." "Systemic–national" events involve questions such as independence and the constitution, the orientation toward the EU, and the Albanian uprising. The "procedural–democratic" category includes electoral probity, judicial decisions, and the legal environment. The "executive–normative" group includes decisions of state actors and political parties that encompass rule-making, articulation, and aggregative functions. These categories describe institutions, practices, and events that express sustainable democratic values within an evolving context. In each period, certain unresolved issues in each category create the basis for a transition to the next period.

The "systemic–national" category is important in this respect. The decision to direct the country toward the EU, confirmed in the Stability Agreement for South Eastern Europe in 1997, took on a new meaning with the 1991 Ohrid Accord in the third period, yet one prefigured by the admission of UN Observers in 1991 during the first period. In each period, foreign institutions

Table 15.1 Phases and events in Macedonian democratization, 1990–2007

Event	1990–2	1993–2001	2001–7
Systemic–National	Independence Referendum	NGO involvement Europeanization	Albanian uprising
Legal–Procedural	Constitution	Electoral system and reform	Ohrid Framework Accord
Executive–Normative	Coalition Government	Party system coalition	Decentralization of legal reform Anti-corruption

moved from a source of democratic incentive to direct participation in Macedonian politics. Macedonia's leadership has sought to rationalize foreign demands in ways consistent with their claim to defend national interest. A single category of issues may create unresolved problems: some, like human rights issues in the "executive–normative" category, have persisted over time.

Macedonia, 1991–3: referendum, constitution, and elections

As already mentioned, VMRO–DPMNE won a plurality of parliamentary seats in the 1991 elections held concurrently with the election of Kiro Gligorov as president. As Yugoslavia's situation deteriorated, he formed a "Government of Experts" from all major parties, the Federation's collapse and war vindicated his decision. The referendum for independence followed in September. Ljubčo Georgievski (VMRO–DPMNE) accepted the post of deputy prime minister, only to resign in protest against positions awarded to Albanians. The elections also established a pattern of aggregation that has remained relatively constant – one of two major Slavic parties and an Albanian party remained within the government despite major unresolved issues. However qualified, a divided vote among both Macedonia's Slavs and the country's Albanians offered incentives for coalition-building and Albanian cooperation.

A successful referendum on 8 September 1991, endorsing independence, offered the leadership a legitimacy beyond the presumption of self-determination. Independence was a "reluctant" national goal, as Sabrina Ramet notes, and the consequences of a successful referendum were perilous.[25] Yugoslavia's dissolution presented a variety of threats. Macedonian officials sought to prevent Yugoslavia's destruction by potential claims from an independent Serbia or Greece. Despite Gligorov's emphasis that the rights of the Albanian citizens could not be "overemphasized" after independence, the Albanian political leadership called for a boycott of the referendum and independence itself. Nevzat Halili, president of the Albanian PDP, demanded that Albanians receive equal national status with Slavic Macedonians as a constituent nation, warning that in the absence of such recognition they "would hold a separate referendum, involving not only Macedonians, but also Kosovo Albanians."[26] The question of the status of Macedonia's Albanians in the constitution was not fully addressed until 2001, and although the threat of a separate referendum was not realized, the problem of the legitimacy of the referendum and the constitution remained.

The constitution proclaimed a democratic parliamentary state with safeguards against authoritarianism. For example, the directly elected president was limited to two terms "at most" rather than two consecutive terms (Art. 80). Some form of "cohabitation" on the French model was anticipated, since the president and the Assembly were elected separately and the president was obligated to appoint a "government from the party or parties which has/have a majority in the parliament" (Art. 90). Constitutionally enumerated powers limited those of the government and the president. Beyond familiar rights, citizens were guaranteed the right to leave and return to their homeland and protection to "exile or extradition" (Art. 27); an absolute prohibition against the death penalty (Art. 10); *habeas corpus* and the prohibition of *ex post facto* laws (Arts.12, 14); and unfettered "public expression of thought" and "the right to protect the source of information in the mass media" (Art. 16). Moreover, the Assembly established that "state of [national] emergency" is limited to "an epidemic or natural disaster" (Art. 125). The Constitutional Court, responsible for the "protection of constitutionality and legality," would maintain its mandate "for the duration of the state of war or emergency" (Art. 128). The phrase "as defined by law" limited the right of "nationalities" to be educated in their native language to primary and secondary levels, and thus limited the right of "nationalities to express, foster and develop their identity and national attributes" (Arts. 48–49). The constitution appears to be directed toward fulfilling the criteria for recognition established by the European Commission.

In November 1991, two months after the parliament had declared Macedonia's independence, it adopted the constitution. For Albanian delegates, the phrase "national state of the Macedonian People" implied second-class status and justified abstention. Nevertheless, the constitution became a focus for democratic reform. In tandem, the constitution and the independence referendum were sufficient to convince the EU's Badinter Commission to advise the International Conference on Former Yugoslavia (ICFY) that Macedonia had fulfilled the conditions necessary for recognition. The government accepted the advice of the ICFY Working Group on Ethnic and National Communities in 1993 to include the Serbian community among recognized nationalities. Subsequently, constitutional amendments have disavowed any "territorial pretensions" I(1) and proclaimed non-interference in foreign domestic affairs II(1).

Such unusual constitutional provisions demonstrate what I have called the "improvized" nature of Macedonian change. The "name conflict" with Greece was elevated to a constitutional issue although such policy issues seldom have such significance. Macedonian sources consider that Greece's claim to the name reflects the non-recognition of a "large ethnic Macedonian minority in Greece."[27] In 1995, the UN and United States brokered an "interim accord" between Athens and Skopje, by which Athens abandoned the blockade and Skopje agreed to end its use of the sixteen-pointed "Star of Vergina" on its flag and to use provisionally the designation "Former Yugoslav Republic of Macedonia" (FYROM) in international fora such as the UN. In contrast, Albania proper had little involvement in Macedonia's constitutional accommodation with its Albanian minority. Efforts by smaller Albanian parties in the 1994 elections, appealing for constitutional revision on a consociational, or federal basis, such as that of Belgium, were unsuccessful and have remained so.[28]

It was in this initial period that one of the first delegations of foreign observers came to Skopje to discuss "democratic development" in Macedonia. In the fall of 1992, a Helsinki Commission delegation visited Macedonia and met with President Gligorov and the entire government. The group heard several complaints concerning the absence of Albanian in education and identity cards, as well as discriminatory "gerrymandering" in legislative districts.[29] The delegation also noticed the "varying degrees" of Albanian objections to government policy. President Gligorov acknowledged the "excesses of nationalism" in apparent reference to VMRO–DPMNE and the difficulty of achieving a "democratic system" under the conditions of the Greek blockade. The complaint about parliamentary representation notwithstanding, there was no claim that the Albanians were being politically repressed as such. The status of the constitutionally mandated Council on Inter-ethnic Relations, which had been created in 1992, was resolved in 2007, although it has not been a significant actor in intercommunal relations.

Of course, there were other opinions. In connection with its political asylum practices, the US Department of Justice sent a human rights study delegation to Macedonia in 1994, and reported that "the fact that ethnic Albanians are reasonably well represented in the Parliament and the Government does not eliminate this [anti-Albanian thinking] or prevent discriminatory treatment and sometimes repressive government policies from being followed, particularly at the local level."[30] The report also pointed to "fairly widespread incidents of police brutality," gerrymandering, alleging undercounting in the 1990 and 1994 census, and a fifteen-year residency requirement for voting in the 1992 citizenship law. Albanians, able to move between Kosovo and Macedonia in socialist Yugoslavia, objected to the latter requirement.

Macedonia, 1994–2001: precarious foundation: NGOs, reforms, and coalitions

Macedonia's "Albanian problem" was not solved by the simple contrivance of inclusion of one of their parties in a coalition government. The gap between policy outcomes sought by less advantaged Albanian citizens and the policy preferences of the Slavic majority has resulted in practices which have diverged from formal standards of democratic procedure. If all Macedonians sought tangible benefits in a political democracy, Macedonia's Albanians compounded that sentiment with a sense of collective discrimination. Prior to 2001, a gap in perceptions of democracy between *ethnic* Albanians and the government emerged, and became apparent when the coalition was unprepared for the 2001 insurgency. More specifically, as the fighting spread to the city of Tetovo, DPA–PDSh spokesman Menduh Thaçi advocated force, apparently underestimating the support for the insurgency. He remarked, "If there is no possible political solution, the next step is obvious … the territorial integrity of Macedonia must be protected by the state armed forces." On 3 March 2001, Thaçi added, "We did communicate with the National Liberation Army … But at a certain point, they refused to talk with us anymore. They are saying that they lost patience with us, and I added that we are Albanians too [and that] we can lose patience with them as well."[31] Albania's prime minister was less hesitant: "We [should] punish the extremists in Macedonia and support [the country's] territorial integrity."[32] The threat to "territorial integrity" elicited a prompt response from the EU, the United States, and other NGOs.

Cooperation with international economic agencies was of great benefit to the government in providing important resources in difficult circumstances. In 2000, the International Monetary Fund's (IMF) Director for Macedonia, J. de Beaufort Wijnholds, commended Macedonia's "increasing transparency," the quality of its "continuing dialogue" with international agencies, and its willingness to publish staff reports.[33] He also acknowledged the "relentless efforts" of the international community to assist Macedonia during the "very difficult circumstances" of the 1999 Kosovo crisis. The assistance confirmed a continuing pattern of support. Between 1993 and 2001, commitments from the International Bank for Reconstruction and Development (IBRD) alone totaled about $500 million. Actual disbursements were $347 million, including $90 million to help manage the Kosovo crisis. Lending by the International Finance Corporation (IFC) has amounted to $61 million for eight projects, leaving Macedonia with "one of the highest *per capita* exposures worldwide."[34] Economic cooperation did not encompass the much greater challenge of economic growth. Closure of the Greek port of Thessaloniki to Macedonia meant that about 80% of Macedonian exports passed through the FRY. Macedonia's high trade:GDP ratio (78.5% in 2003) meant that the blockade impacted both exports and growth before 1995, but by 1998 growth had reached 3.8%. The 1999 Kosovo crisis was expected to create a 5% decline in output, but its early resolution led in fact to a decline of only 2.7% in 1999.[35]

Nevertheless Macedonia's efforts at privatization were scarcely more successful than those of other formerly socialist countries. A 1993 Law on the Transformation of Social Capital was adopted in order to promote privatization; seven years later, an IMF Working Paper found that "Some 60% of all privatization (weighed either by total number of employees or total equity) went to insiders while strategic investors accounted for less than 20% of all privatizations."[36] Corruption of privatization meant little new investment, profit, or improved productivity, a fact whose consequences were noted by the IMF report which revealed that 60% of the firms in existence in 1994 had ceased to exist by 2000, while two-thirds of the firms in 2000 had started after 1994. Prospects for foreign investment remained poor. In Southeastern Europe, Macedonia ranked near Albania and Moldova at the bottom of the list of countries receiving foreign direct investment (FDI) despite its adherence to the Stabilization and Association Accord (SAA) allowing tariff-free exports to EU countries.[37]

NGO cooperation was also important in promoting reform in the electoral process. The VMRO–DPMNE opposition refused to take part in the 1994 second round of parliamentary elections, claiming fraud. At the time, British observers found the boycott to be "unjustified" despite the existence of "regrettable technical irregularities."[38] Four years later, parliamentary elections marked a marginal improvement. The US-sponsored Commission on Security and Cooperation in Europe (CSCE) encountered "no significant problems" in the first round of elections, but a "notably more negative and tense atmosphere in the second round." The ad hoc distribution of voter identification cards became a "potential for fraud."[39] Similarly, the second round of presidential elections in 1999 was marred by serious fraud and was rescheduled. According to OSCE observers, the government bore responsibility for irregularities at local polling locations in Albanian areas.[40] Despite such incidents, the period 1994–2001 marked a stage of important development in the party system.

Both policy and personal differences distinguish the two major Slavic parties but Albanian party differences appear to relate to coalition involvement. The coalition parties opposed the creation of a federation through a referendum in Albanian-inhabited areas. Nevertheless, the PDP supported broad autonomy for Albanian areas and, more recently, diplomatic recognition of Kosovo, a decision that could have provoked Serbia. The party consistently pressed for Albanian language and educational rights and investigation of police abuse. The PDP and the government also disagreed over the length of residency requirements for Albanian refugees in the citizenship law. Coalition conflict led to the PDP's division and the DPA's emergence as a more "radical" Albanian party and its merger with the People's Democratic Party (PDSh).

In November 1993, nine Macedonian Albanians, including two deputy ministers, were arrested for allegedly organizing paramilitary units to prepare an armed uprising.[41] Although the accused may have been involved in arms smuggling, the charge of subversion was unsubstantiated. The DPA–PDSh split from the PDP when the latter decided to remain within the government after the accusations were published.[42] Nevertheless, the DPA–PDSh found a basis to enter a coalition with VMRO–DPMNE after the 1998 elections, and its decision was rewarded with portfolios in Justice, Labor and Social Policy, and Local Government. Although extending beyond the period under consideration, the PDP threatened to boycott the second round of parliamentary elections scheduled for 2002, alleging fraud. An OSCE observer delegation of over

800 members established that the electoral conditions were "in line with European standards," despite some allegations of violence.[43] Arguably PDP electoral skepticism *vis-à-vis* the election may have resulted from its poor prospects against the newly formed (Albanian) Democratic Party of Integration (DUI).

Besides electoral regularity, the electoral system itself had been a matter of concern before 2001. Albanian spokespersons maintained that a system of proportional representation should replace the system of 85 majoritarian and 35 proportionally chosen seats,[44] an electoral system burdened by malapportionment. In testimony to the International Foundation for Electoral Systems (IFES) and the Helsinki Watch, PDA–PDSh, President Arben Xhaferi claimed that the municipality of Bitola, with a population of 96,000 voters, 85% of whom are Slavic, had the same number of representatives as Tetovo, with 136,000 voters who are 85% Albanian.[45] Such a situation violated Art. 18 of the electoral law, which set precise limits on the size of districts. President Trajkovski was responsive and took part in an IFES-sponsored seminar with representatives from the Albanian parties in the fall of 2000. As a result, a "Working Group on Electoral Reform" was created with the IFES and the Ministry of Justice in order to recommend reforms. The work of the IFES in this area was superseded by the Framework Accord and ultimately achieved the reform of electoral districts in 2002.

More general efforts to improve the political system and its policy output were undertaken by the Stability Pact for South Eastern Europe (SPSEE). The Pact organized conferences under a "parliamentary troika" of the European Parliament, the OSCE, and the Council of Europe. Annual discussions included common policy and procedural matters in the region, such as combating contraband and cross-border cooperation.[46] SPSEE's "core objective" of "managing and stabilizing population movements" became especially important for Macedonia during the 1999 crisis in Kosovo and in assisting refugee resettlement from areas affected by the 2001 insurgency.[47] SPSEE established a precedent for later cooperation with other multilateral organizations and for bilateral cooperation.

Despite its qualifications concerning police abuse and minority representation in state administration, the UN Special Rapporteur for Human Rights noted in 1997 that Macedonia had made considerable "progress" in the protection of human rights since independence.[48] Attila Agh's study of democratization in Central Europe and the Balkans concluded that pressure from NGO organizations, including the OSCE, the EU, and NATO, had promoted both the sovereignty and the legitimacy of transitional democracies throughout the region.[49] All have been deeply involved in Macedonia's evolution. Agh associates the process of Europeanization with democratic institutions of press freedom, human rights, free migration, and minority rights. In Macedonia, assessments of these democratic components varied, but NGO relations established before 2001 marked subsequent progressive outcomes. For example,

Freedom House's measure of "press freedom" registered a 10% improvement in 2006 as a result of reformed laws on freedom of information and imprisonment for libel.[50]

However, NGOs appear to have had little impact on Macedonia's Parliamentary Assembly. The parliament's dysfunction was evident in the area of bureaucratic supervision and effective government–opposition relations. After the 1998 elections, the opposition Social Democratic Party of Macedonia (SDSM) provided conclusive evidence that Macedonia's intelligence agencies, responsible to the Ministry of Justice, had illegally wiretapped elected officials, journalists, diplomatic personnel, and other citizens.[51] The episode embarrassed the government and the Parliamentary Commission responsible for supervising Macedonia's two intelligence agencies. The opposition accused the Justice Ministry of having ordered the practice, while the Minister blamed "old structures in these departments politicized by the [former governments of the] SDSM."[52] Government–opposition animosity prevented parliamentary investigation. At various times, Prime Minister Georgievski accused the opposition of obstructing legislation, bribing delegates, and fabricating scandals.[53]After the defection of five MPs from the Democratic Alternative (DA) in the summer of 2000 and the ensuing uproar, *Nova Makedonija* observed that parliament had become a sort of "national entertainment."[54] Somewhat earlier, a sample of Macedonian opinion had revealed that 55% of adults were "dissatisfied" with "democracy" and 37% "satisfied."[55] Parliamentary debate did little to improve the impression.

Parliament's Committee on Inter-Ethnic Relations was unable to consider the problem of police abuse, despite its charge to protect constitutional rights. In its 1996 report on Macedonia, Helsinki Watch registered "many violations of basic human rights carried out by the police."[56] It blamed the situation on "irresponsible and non-professional behavior" of officials in the Ministry of the Interior and, more precisely, on a "system of colleagueship [allowing] the overstepping of authority." The report considered that neither citizens nor local authorities could exercise control. By mid-2000, the situation had not greatly improved. Reports of police abuse remained serious and numerous. Reports by Helsinki Watch, the US Department of State, and Amnesty International have reported the ill-treatment of detainees, excessive force, and illegal detention. An especially serious episode occurred in January 2000 when several police were murdered in the largely Albanian town of Aračinovo. The police responded with collective force.[57] Shortly afterwards, an Albanian detainee died in police custody, as did a second detainee several months later. In spite of the recommendations of an ombudsman and the reaction of international human rights organizations, there was little governmental response. Continued violations appeared to have little impact on the parliament – a Standing Committee of Inquiry for the Protection of Citizen Rights and Freedoms was no more effective than the Parliament Committee on Inter-Ethnic Relations.

Generally, Slavic–Albanian relations stagnated under the VMRO–DPMNE–DPA–PDSh coalition along with relations between the Albanian parties. Arben Xhaferi, head of the DPA–PDSh, claimed that his co-nationals still suffered from discrimination, marginalization, and cultural disinheritance, but he also insisted that Albanians were "attached to the integrity of Macedonia where they intend to establish their identity on a political and legal basis."[58] The opposition PDP advanced the idea of a publicly funded Albanian University in Tetovo, while the DPA and its ruling Slavic partners supported a private university. Ultimately, foreign support for the institution left the dispute unresolved, but differences in the Albanian leadership increased with the post-insurrection amnesty and the emergence of Ali Ahmeti's Party of Democratic Integration (DUI) in the following period.

Macedonia, 2001–7: From the insurrection to the gates of the EU

The Albanian insurgency confirmed conclusively the assertion that relations with Slavic Macedonians had become the country's "defining feature."[59] Prior to the insurgency the government depended on formality rather than substance in meeting the challenge of integration. Constitutional guarantees "to express, foster, and develop their national identity" (Art. 48) did not address Albanian objections that defined the state as "the national state of the Macedonian People." Art. 48 imitated phrasing from an OSCE meeting of the Conference on the Human Dimension.[60] The coalition government sought to appoint commissions on ethnic relations in areas with mixed populations; in such areas, disputes could be investigated by an ombudsman or appealed to the Supreme Court, and languages other than Macedonian could be accorded official status. Whether such procedures were effective remains uncertain, like the outcome of EU–Macedonian discussions for the creation of a National Council for Interethnic Relations.[61] Nationality relations at the local level conveyed an impression of segregation and resentment. Moreover, for Albanians, their bleak economic situation aggravated political discontent. I have mentioned independent Macedonia's initial poverty, its high unemployment, and the consequences of the Greek embargo and Yugoslav sanctions. The absence of regional data limits comparison of poverty among Macedonians versus Albanians, but two facts are suggestive. Rural domestic product amounted to only 10% of income, but rural population exceeded 40% of the total.[62] The refugee burden from Kosovo in Macedonia fell disproportionally on some 8,000 rural Albanian families.[63]

The 2001 insurgency started in the rural village of Tanuševci bordering Kosovo. A Macedonian television program depicting the village as a center of lawlessness and contraband had prompted reinforcement of local police to seal the border.[64] Because of this, several Macedonian police were killed. Fighting may have started owing to an agreement between Skopje and Belgrade on border delineation unfavorable to the Albanians. The insurgent National Liberation Army (NLA) brought its offensive to Tetovo on 13 March and reached Aračinovo outside Skopje in early June. According to the International Crisis Group's report, the government's counter-offensive destroyed ten villages, created some 42,700 Macedonian Albanian refugees who fled to Kosovo, and displaced about 50,000 citizens.[65] Prior to the fighting, the report notes that the VMRO–DPMNE–PDA–PDSh coalition had "reached an informal understanding regarding spheres of [governing] influence."[66] Accordingly, Slavic Macedonian police had not been present in Albanian-inhabited parts of the country in early 2001. Excepting a report of rioting in the mixed city of Bitola, ethnic relations remained tense but generally stable in areas outside the fighting. More immediately, the international community sought to persuade the Macedonian government to abandon any plans to defeat the rebellion and, instead, to create a four-party coalition suitable for a political settlement.

On 27 March 2001, NATO Secretary General George Robertson and Javier Solana, EU Representative for the Common Security and Foreign Policy, met with the leaders of the major Macedonian parties and President Boris Trajkovski. DPA–PDSh leader, Arben Xhaferi, remarked that "Macedonia as a state should finally gain stability to enter the EU and NATO, and in that process … the process of [peace] talks [ought] to go ahead."[67]Although it is unlikely that the talks touched on so distant a contingency as EU–NATO membership, they reached a consensus about a need for a political settlement respecting the country's territorial integrity. Western interests were represented by Robert Frowick, Special Envoy of the OSCE. Matters moved slowly. A cease-fire was not attained until May, but it followed intensive negotiations among the leaderships of Albania, Kosovo, and Macedonia as well as insurgent leader Ali Ahmeti.[68]An unpublished negotiating document reportedly pledged to realize most Albanian political demands as well as "full rehabilitation and reintegration of all members of the National Liberation Army (NLA)."[69]

Ahmeti ultimately became the founder of the DUI in 2002 and a coalition partner. He was born in Macedonia, but became politically involved in Kosovo as a student at the University of Priština, graduating in 1983, and spending periods in exile in Switzerland.[70]Ahmeti organized protests and the miners' strike against the Serbian regime of Slobodan Milošević and in 1986 assumed responsibility for relations between the Albanian diaspora and the National Movement for the Liberation of Kosovo. His skill as a military leader brought him to lead military formations in Kosovo and, in 2001, the NLA in Macedonia. Ahmeti's career demonstrates the interconnection between Kosovo and the Albanian community in Macedonia and the European diaspora, and it indicates that this relationship did not imply political unity. Secession from Macedonia was not on the agenda at Ohrid.

The Ohrid Accord became the basis for a comprehensive settlement, the political agenda for the coming years, and a centerpiece of democratization and constitutional revision. Representing the EU, Javier Solana undertook the negotiations. A "breakthrough" followed on an agreement to expand ethnic Albanian membership in the police force, declaration of Albanian as an "official language" in areas where the minority's population exceeded 20%, and a deployment of NATO forces to assist in decommissioning insurgent weapons.[71] The Ohrid Accord is not easily summarized.[72] Relevant portions speak of "securing the future of Macedonia's democracy and … permitting … closer and more integrated relations between the Republic of Macedonia and Euro-Atlantic Community." Details about the police, local government, municipal boundaries, public employment, language, and judicial reform were derived from the principles of "preserving and reflecting the multi-ethnic character of Macedonia's society … in public life" and "complete respect" for "the principle of non-discrimination and equal treatment under the law."

Speculation about the Accord's balance in recognizing Slavic and minority interests is inappropriate, for several reasons. Certain provisions are incommensurate with respect to the beneficiaries. Albanians remained committed to a unitary state, while all nationalities recognized its "civic" rather than national character. Second, had the insurgency and the Accord never happened, its minority provisions might eventually have become conditional for EU entry. Finally, the document included open-ended constitutional amendments, such as 69(2) concerning the adoption of "laws that directly affect culture, use of language, education, personal documentation, and use of symbols." The latter required a "double majority" or Badinter majority – i.e. one requiring both a parliamentary majority and a majority among Albanian delegates. Disputes concerning which legislation would require such a majority were to be resolved by a broadly charged parliamentary "Committee for Inter-Community Relations." In fact, the "double majority" was seldom necessary, although membership on the Parliamentary Committee became contentious. In 2006, the Democratic Party of Integration (BDI) advocated a constitutional amendment that would have regulated which parties could form the government. The double majority system was intended to protect the interests of the Albanian minority.[73] The post-Ohrid constitution became a fulcrum of "democratic values."

Late in 2003, the government published the 2002 Census, the results of which recorded that ethnic Albanians constituted 25.17% of the population. In the context of the Ohrid Accord the percentage was significant since the agreement recognized as "official" a language whose speakers constituted 20% or more of the municipal or the national population. The reform has not been implemented widely in areas that qualify; one 2008 report referred to "technical, financial and personnel" obstacles to its realization.[74] Both international monitors, and the coalition's Deputy Premier Ali Ahmeti, accepted the census as accurate.[75] While not ending all dissent over the census, the episode resolved a long-standing issue intersecting persistent national distrust, public administration, and foreign involvement. In 1991, Albanians had boycotted the census, alleging that the government had sought to diminish their political influence by undercounting the actual numbers. Because of an Albanian boycott, the 1991 Census estimated Macedonia's Albanian population at 21.7% based on a statistical projection. A PDP spokesman claimed that the Albanian population was closer to 40%, a share beyond a constitutional "minority." In response after Macedonian independence, Ambassador Geert-Hinrich Ahrens, Head of the Working Group for Human Rights and Minorities within the ICFY, proposed a special census to be supervised by its "Group of Experts" and funded by the Council of Europe. However well intentioned, the proposal created a prolonged conflict concerning the desirability of another census, the composition of the municipal census administration, and whether to count Albanian refugees.[76] Despite significant European assistance, Macedonia's 1994 census became an additional source of tension. The Accord altered the political context of the issue by linking its results to a larger settlement, but by 2004 the Accord itself seemed threatened.

In 2004, a petition to hold a referendum on the Accord's provisions concerning local government threatened several years of progress. Parliament had adopted a law which reduced the number of municipalities from 123 to 80, allowing a higher level of Albanian self-government and use of national symbols, including the equal use of the Albanian language.[77] Organizers of the referendum expected that a majority of Slavs would reject the law on decentralization, while Albanian Macedonians responded by again threatening their own referendum to declare a "state of Ilirida."[78] The result was a disappointment for the Accord's opponents in that the 26% share of the electorate who voted did not constitute a quorum sufficient to repeal the law. It has been suggested that the low turnout was less a consequence of European protest about the referendum than a result of the United States' coincident decision to declare its recognition of the "The Republic of Macedonia" rather than FYROM.[79] Regardless of the reason, the failed referendum was contrary to the forecasts of two independent polls suggesting a high turnout of Slavic voters.[80]

According to a 2007 assessment of administration by the OSCE Spillover Mission, the "process of decentralization continues to be satisfactorily managed in 2007. The number one concern remains the lack of financial resources, a general problem of all units of local self-government in the country."[81] In areas including "communal service, environmental protection, and urban planning," a greater share of citizen opinion perceived "some improvement" or "improvement" rather than "no improvement" in services.

The problem of police and local government was initially one of reaching agreement about shared responsibility for local police with the central government. But beyond improvements in procedure, training, and administration, the arrest and trial of former Interior Minister Ljube Boškovski amounted to the single most significant episode in improving the functionality of the police. Boškovski had been appointed Interior Minister in May 2001 and was elected to parliament from the VMRO–DPMNE list in 2002. He became associated with police violence, the paramilitary Fast Intervention Force ("the Lions"), and more specifically with the wrongful deaths of ten Albanians in August 2001 in the village of Ljuboten and the murder of seven illegal immigrants at Rostanski Lozija, whom Boškovsi had characterized as "international terrorists"[82] Following an investigation into the latter incident, the examining magistrate issued a warrant for Boškovski's arrest, and the Assembly stripped him of his immunity. Arrested in flight by Croatian authorities, Boškovski, a Croatian citizen, was extradited to The Hague and indicted as a war criminal.[83] Prosecution followed a year-long effort which identified armed confrontation arising from governmental efforts to abolish the paramilitary "Lions."[84] The arrest of Boškovski, once considered an "independent" presidential candidate, enhanced Macedonia's suitability as a partner for other European institutions.

However important, no single arrest could resolve the more general problems of bureaucratic control, organized crime, and official corruption. Although distinct, the three problems were rooted in weak government accountability and control. I have already mentioned the wiretapping episode, but the persistent problem of corruption and organized crime remained. The International Crisis Group identified "endemic" corruption at all levels of the state, adding " [it] had evolved from passive exploitation to active coercion, and acquired not only the capacity to retard economic progress, but [also the potential] to feed organized crime and, in turn, political and communal instability."[85] Macedonia's scandal-ridden system of party finance was seldom examined.[86] Macedonia has cooperated with European efforts to combat money laundering, as well as human and narcotics trafficking. Demands for success against government corruption have been explicit. EU Commissioner for Enlargement, Olli Rehn, linked successful anti-corruption outcomes and EU membership in warning that "promises will be to no avail unless they [the government] do something to improve Macedonia's current situation."[87] He dismissed "projects that remain on paper." Shortly after the statement, some eleven government agencies signed a new anti-corruption protocol coincident with new reports of malfeasance, including a draft law on energy in contravention of EU transparency guidelines.[88] In March 2008 Rehn stated that, later in the year, talks on Macedonia's admission could start on "eight key policy areas," including police and judicial reform along with the "fight against corruption."[89]

Some four years earlier, in 2004, the Ohrid agenda had broadened to one negotiated with a view to EU membership. On 22 March 2004, the government applied to the European Council for membership. The European Commission gave its opinion on Macedonia's application in 2005.[90] The report determined that "the rule of law is being gradually consolidated"; that "no major problems existed in the area of respect for human rights"; that "considerable efforts" had been undertaken to align Macedonian laws with Community *acquis*; and that "substantial progress" had been achieved in "completing the legislative framework related to the Ohrid Accord of 2001." Perhaps most important, the European Commission judged that Macedonia was a "functioning democracy." As already mentioned, the European Council established

"European Partnership" and in 2008 an "Accession Partnership" as an extension of the Stabilization Accord.[91] The 2008 agreement included a complex array of goals in most areas of public life. Some, such as improving prison conditions, prompted sharp criticism by European officials.[92] But prospects for membership in either NATO or the EU remained vulnerable, for different reasons.

At the April 2008 NATO Summit, Greece vetoed Macedonia's membership, an event prompting Prime Minister Gruevski to call early elections. A strengthened VMRO–DPMNE might have afforded Gruevski greater flexibility in negotiations, but his DUI partner strongly opposed such alternative state names as "Slavic Republic of Macedonia" and others. However, apart from its results, the 1 June elections occasioned violence between rival Albanian parties, and the need to hold new polling in affected districts. The event undermined Macedonia's democratic credentials as an EU candidate. Doris Peck, Chair of the European Parliament's Delegation for Southeastern Europe, lectured Albanians as though their behavior had overlooked the "good treatment" afforded them in the Ohrid Accord, expressing a "lack of perception on democracy among Albanians."[93]

The Macedonian media

Art. 16 of the constitution guarantees freedom of speech and of access to information. Journalists are also free to form professional associations and, among these, the Macedonian Institute for Media and the Association of Journalists of Macedonia are particularly important. In 2007, Reporters without Borders ranked Macedonia 36th out of 168 states in terms of press freedom, placing it higher than Albania, Bulgaria, or Serbia.[94] Although Macedonians enjoy a large range of print and electronic sources of information and literally hundreds of private broadcasting media, the three best-selling newspapers – *Utrinski Vesnik*, *Vest*, and *Dnevnik* – have been owned by the German media conglomerate, Westdeutsche Allgemeine Zeitung, since 2004. Some television stations are owned by presidents of certain political parties or their sons – such as A1 Television, owned by Velija Ramkovski, leader of the Party for Economic Renewal (SPM), and Sitel TV, owned by Goran Ivanov, son of Ljubisav Ivanov, President of the Socialist Party.[95]

In 2005, a new Law on Broadcasting was adopted, which provided for greater independence for the Broadcasting Council which supervises the broadcast media. The law was judged to be in line, for the most part, with European media standards.[96] In 2006, the Macedonian parliament abolished imprisonment for defamation and libel, but during 2007, some journalists were victims of violence or threats of violence.

Conclusion

Macedonian democratization has been compromised by fragile interethnic relations and a persistent distrust of government. A 2007 Eurobarometer survey captured a "democratic deficit" in Macedonian attitudes towards national institutions. Citizens held a clear idea of "democracy," but were significantly more likely to trust in EU institutions than in those in their own country.[97] Lacking earlier Eurobarometer polls, it cannot be decided if relative confidence in Macedonian government is improving; evidence of increasing confidence in Macedonian institutions could indicate a relationship between popular and elite democratic values. We might assume that since independence, elite values were expressed through improving electoral procedures, more effective parliamentary activity, and an increasingly responsible opposition. At present, data are insufficient to "bridge" elite and popular "democratic values" through institutional change, a more casual or tentative relationship between elite and citizen values may be possible.

Diamond, Linz, and Stepan distinguish a "functioning" from a "consolidated" democracy through the "legitimation" of "specific rules and constraints of the country's constitutional system [for it to become] internalized, practised and transmitted across generations."[98] The conditions suggest a seldom considered obstacle to democratization. In a 2007 interview, Chair of the opposition SDSM, Radmila Sekerinska, acknowledged her party's unpopularity and admitted, "[W]hen we were the leading party in the government, we, as the party leaders used to state the positions of the party with little consulting of the members' opinion [*sic*]. We rarely engaged in intra-party dialogue."[99] Sekerinska went on to identify her role with a fundamental change expressed by the slogan,"SDSM is each of its members." In a similar expression, Deputy Chair of the DPA–PDSh, Suliman Rushiti, also admitted a "mistake" of his party's minister in the transfer of police officers from Tetovo and Gostivar after the government came to power in 2006.[100] The episode had been an instance of patronage abuse in an area of civil service that remained of special concern to foreign NGOs and part of the Ohrid Accord. The source also acknowledged the absence of communication between the two significant Macedonian Albanian leaderships. These admissions acknowledge both the absence of intraparty democracy and the intense partisanship of Macedonian politics. While the problems of administrative capacity, judicial reform, and anti-corruption have been central to the EU's efforts to prepare Macedonia for EU membership, the SDSM and PDA–PDSh's comments suggest that what is understood casually as "democratization" cannot be completely identified with "democratic values." This also suggests the limits of "leverage," since the EU cannot guarantee democratic practice in Macedonian parties. Finally, it is likely that attention to Macedonia's largest minority has come without corresponding benefit to other minorities. A comprehensive inclusion of all Macedonian minorities is a generational problem, one addressed initially in common approaches to Balkan history recently introduced in school texts.[101]

Nevertheless, the several phases of Macedonia's democratization and Europeanization since 1991 indicate a certain dynamism accelerated by several constants. Despite perceptions of a pro-Albanian bias in foreign NGO involvement, Slavic Macedonian opinion favored neither rupturing relations with Serbia nor aligning with Serbia against Europe. Macedonia's Albanians have shown little inclination for unity with Albania or Kosovo. The diplomatic and material resources invested by Europe and the United States in Macedonia's stability reflect its geopolitical potential within the Balkans. Taken together, these considerations have raised expectations about the benefits of European cooperation and have diminished the appeal of violent nationalism. The decisions of the VMRO-DPMNE and the DUI leaderships to take part in electoral politics were critical in achieving stability in both creating coalition governments and progressing through the Ohrid Accord. Membership in the EU should insulate Macedonia from the threat of an unstable Kosovo. As of the late fall 2008, those prospects remain dimmed by the need for "significant further effors required" in realizing the Accession Partnership's "key priority of political dialogue."[102]

Timeline 1990–2009

11 November–9 December 1990	Election of multiparty legislative assembly
8 September 1991	Referendum on independence
17 September 1991	Declaration of Sovereignty and Statehood
17 November 1991	Macedonian Assembly adopts new constitution
11 December 1992	UN Security Council authorizes 700 peacekeeping troops to Serbian/Kosovo boundary
8 April 1993	Admission to United Nations as FYROM
16 October 1994	Kiro Gligorov elected president
16–30 October 1994	SDSM Alliance wins 95/120 Legislative seats
3 October 1995	President Gligorov seriously wounded in assassination attempt
18 October and 1 November 1998	VMRO–DPMNE wins plurality of legislature seats
13 October and 14 November 1999	Boris Trajkovski elected president
26 February 2001	Fighting at Tanušcevci initiates insurrection
13 May 2001	National Unity Government formed
13 August 2001	Ohrid Framework Accord signed
7 and 15 September 2002	"Together for Macedonia" Coalition wins legislative elections
26 February 2004	President Trajkovski dies in plane crash
14 April and 28 April 2004	Branko Crvenkovski wins presidential election
9 November 2005	Macedonia attains candidacy status with EU
5–12 July 2006	VMRO–DPMNE coalition wins legislative elections
22 March–6 April 2009	Georgi Ivanov wins presidential election

Fact sheet

Area	25,333 km^2
Population (July 2008 estimate)	2,061,315
Macedonian	64.2%
Albanian	25.2%
Turkish	3.9%
Roma	2.7%
Serb	1.8%
Other	2.2%
Urban population (2005)	60%
GDP *per capita* (2008 est.)	$9,000
Real GDP growth (2008)	4.6%
Inflation (2008)	8.4%

Sources: CIA, *The World Factbook – Macedonia,* at www.cia.gov/library/publications/the-world-factbook/geos/mk.html [accessed on 8 November 2008]; and "F.Y.R.O. Macedonia Facts and Figures," MSN encarta, at http://encarta.msn.com/fact_631504806/f_y_r_o_macedonia_facts_and_figures.html [accessed on 8 November 2008].

Parties in the Macedonian parliament (elections of 1 June 2008)	% of the vote	Number of deputies elected
Party		
VMRO–DPMNE	48.75	63
Sun Coalition for Europe (SDSM bloc)	23.64	27
DUI	12.82	18
DPA–PDSh	8.26	11
Party for a European Future	1.47	1
Other parties	5.03	0

Source: IFES at www.electionguide.org/about.php.

Short biography of Kiro Gligorov

Kiro Gligorov was born on 3 May 1917 in the Macedonian city of Štip and graduated from the Faculty of Law of the University of Belgrade. At the age of twenty, he was arrested by the Royal Yugoslav authorities for political opposition to the monarchy. Released before the Axis invasion in 1941, Gligorov joined the communist partisans' resistance. Although he did not join the Communist Party until 1944, he was a deputy to the Anti-Fascist People's Assembly of Macedonia (ASNOM). After the war he moved to Belgrade and was recognized for his expertise in economics and finance, attaining the position of Minister of Finance in the federal government during 1962–7, and was a member of the Central Committee of the League of Communists after 1964. Gligorov was associated with the economic reform of 1965. Although responsible for further reforms after Tito's death in 1980, he retained a durable base of support in Macedonia, and was chosen the first president of independent Macedonia. Partially blinded by an assassination attempt in 1995, Gligorov was succeeded as president by Boris Trajkovski, a leading figure in the VMRO–DPMNE party. He served as president of Macedonia from January 1991 until November 1999.

Source: MSN Encarta, at http://encarta.msn.com/encyclopedia_761579560/gligorov_kiro.html.

Notes

1. Sabrina P. Ramet, *The Three Yugoslavias: State-Building and Legitimation, 1918–2005* (Bloomington, Ind. and Washington, DC: Indiana University Press and Woodrow Wilson Center Press, 2006), p. 271.
2. Duncan M. Perry, "The Republic of Macedonia: Finding its Way," in Karen Dawisha and Bruce Parrott (eds.), *Politics, Power, and the Struggle for Democracy in South-East Europe* (Cambridge: Cambridge University Press, 1997), pp. 226, 251–6.
3. Elizabeth Pond, *Endgame in the Balkans: Regime Change European Style* (Washington, DC: Brookings Institution Press, 2006), p. 168.
4. Milada Anna Vachudova, *Europe Undivided: Democracy, Leverage, and Integration after Communism* (Oxford and New York: Oxford University Press, 2005) p. 63
5. The abundant documentation that forms the body of EU–Macedonian relations can be found at the Europa site (http://europa.org). A brief history of the relation is available at The Thessaloniki Agenda for the Western Balkans, 16 June 2003, http://ec.europa.eu./enlargement/enlargement_process/accession-process/how-does-a-cou [accessed on 4 November 2008]. The accession partnership is 208/212/EC: Council Decision of 18 February 2008 on the principles, priorities, and conditions contained in the Accession Partnership with the former Yugoslav Republic of Macedonia, at http://eur-lex.europa.eu/LexUriServ/LexUriServ.do?uri=OJ:L:2008:080:0032:01:EN:HTML [accessed on 4 November 2008].
6. Council of Europe, Legal Affairs Portal, at www.coe.int/.../legal_co-operation/police_and_internal_security/OHRID%20Agreement%2013august2001.asp – 83k [accessed on 4 November 2008].
7. Council of Europe, CM Documents "Recent Political Developments in the former Yugoslav Republic of Macedonia in the Context of Regional Stability, Parliamentary Assembly Recommendation 1705(2005)," at https://wcd.coe.int/ViewDoc.jsp?Ref=CM/AS(2005) Rec1705&Language=1anEnglish&Ver... [accessed on 4 November 2008].
8. UNPD/Macedonia, *Blue Ribbon Report,* at www.undp.org.mk/datacenter/publications/documents/Angliski.pdf [accessed on 4 November 2008].
9. MIA, "Macedonian Local Self-Government Minister, EU Envoy Discuss Devolution Process, 22 June 2007," *World News Connection*, 22 June 2007, Doc #200706221277.1–437f00363af92642.
10. UNDP, *Human Development Index-Macedonia, Going Beyond Income*, at http://hdrstats.undp.org/countries/country_fact_sheets/cty_fs_MKD.html [accessed on 4 November 2008].
11. UNDP, *Decentralization for Human Development; National Human Development Report 2004*, FYR *Macedonia*, at http://hdr.undp.org/en/reports/nationalreports/europethecis/macedonia/name,3280,en.html.

12. Maja Micevska, Dimitar Eftimoski, and Tatjana Petkovska Mircevska, "Economic Growth of the Republic of Macedonia: Experiences and Policy Recommendations," World Bank Global Research Project, *Explaining Growth*, 2002, at www.cerge-ei.cz/pdf/gdn/grp_final_macedonia.pdf [accessed on 4 November 2008]. GSP was a measure of the Macedoman economy when it was a component part of FRY (see http://en.wik.pedia.org/wiki/gross state).
13. World Bank, *FYR of Macedonia, Poverty Assessment for 2002–3* (18 October 2005), pp. 24, 29, 35, at www-wds.worldbank.org/servlet/WDSContentServer/WDSP/IB/2005/12/21/000090341_20051221144229/Rendered/PDF/343240MK.pdf [accessed on 4 November 2008].
14. The CPI is at www.transparency.org/policy_research/surveys_indices/cpi/2006 [accessed on 4 November 2008].
15. Andrew Rossos, "Macedonianism and the Macedonian Nationalism on the Left," in Ivo Banac and Katherine Verdery (eds.), *National Character and National Ideology* (New Haven, Conn.: Yale Center for International and Area Studies, 1995), pp. 251–2.
16. *A History of the Macedonian People*, ed. Institute of National History (Skopje: Macedonian Review Editions, 1979) pp. 367–71.
17. Gary K. Bertsch, *Values and Community in Multinational Yugoslavia* (Boulder, Colo.: East European Monographs, 1976), pp. 86–7.
18. MIA, "Cleric: Serbian Church Working on 'Eliminating' Macedonian, Nation, State, Church ..." (11 July 2007), *World News Connection*, News Edge 200707111477.1-a6d10004ab563eee8f.
19. "Public Communique from the Regular Meeting of the Serbian Orthodox Church's Holy Assembly of Bishops" (27 May 2006), at www.spc.yu/eng/public_communique_from_the_regular_meeting_of_the_serbian_orthodox_churchs_holy_assembly_of_bishops [accessed on 4 November 2008].
20. The Church's official webpage offers commentary on its canonical authenticity and the position of the diaspora, at www.m-p-c.org/History/history.htm [accessed on 4 November 2008].
21. MIA, "Gruevski: DPA is a Respectable Subject on the Macedonian Political Stage," 30 June 2007, *World News Connection* (30 June 2007), Doc. # 200706301477.1-d 93f 003121dd68ca. MIA, "PM Gruevski: NATO Membership -Top Priority of Macedonian Foreign Membership" (29 June 2007), *World News Connection*, # 200706291477.1_d8f800ae6bb207a0.
22. Janusz Bugajski, *Political Parties of Eastern Europe: A Guide to Politics in the Post-Communist Era* (Armonk, NY: M.E. Sharpe, 2002), p. 746.
23. *Večer* (Skopje) (23 September 1994), trans. in FBIS-EEU, 92–192 (4 October 1994), p. 50.
24. MIC, 20 November 1998, "FYROM: Gligorov Officially Asks VMRO to Form Government," in *World News Connection*, AFS Document DREEEU11231998000584.
25. Sabrina P. Ramet, *Balkan Babel: The Disintegration of Yugoslavia from the Death of Tito to Ethnic War*, 2nd edn. (Boulder, Colo.: Westview Press, 1996), p. 230.
26. *Radio Budapest* (9 September 1991), trans. in *BBC Summary of WorldBroadcasts* EE/1175/B/1 (12 September 1991), on *Lexis-Nexis Academic Universe*.

27. Angie N. Bello and Metodija A.Koloski, "Name Dispute Covers Up Real Macedonian Problem," *Journal Gazette* (Ft. Wayne, Ind.), 10 December 2007, at http://nl.newsbank.com/nl-search/we/Archives?p_multi=JG|&p_product=JGNP&p_theme=jgnp&p_action=search&p_maxdocs=200&s_ dispstring=Macedonian%20Problem&p_field_advanced-0=&p_text_advanced-0=(Macedonian%20Problem)&xcal_numdocs=20&p_perpage=10&p_sort=YMD_date:D&xcal_useweights=no [accessed 4 November 2008].
28. The programs of smaller Albanian parties such as the People's Democratic Party, the Republican Party, and the Albanian Democratic Union–Liberal Party, and results for the 1994 and 1998 parliamentary elections are in Bugajski, *Political Parties of Eastern Europe*, pp. 756–7 and 776; for subsequent elections, see *Fakti* (19 October 2005), *on Lexis–Nexis Academic Universe* (20 October 2005).
29. *US Helsinki Commission Delegation to Hungary, Greece, Macedonia and Croatia November 11–17, 1992*, at www.csce.gov/index.cfm?FuseAction=ContentRecords.ViewDetail&ContentRecord_id=118&Region_id=0&Issue_id=0&ContentType=R,G&ContentRecordType=R&CFID=5878075&CFTOKEN=75154359 [accessed on 4 November 2008].
30. Department of Justice, *Profile Series, Former Yugoslav Republic of Macedonia: Human Rights since 1990* (February 1995), INS Information Center, at www.uscis.gov/files/nativedocuments/macedo95.pdf [accessed on 4 November 2008].
31. Altin Raxhimi, "Gaining Ground," *TOL Report* (7 March 2001), at www.tol.cz/look/TOLrus/article.tpl?IdLanguage=1&IdPublication=4&NrIssue=20&NrSection=3&NrArticle=639 [accessed on 4 November 2008].
32. "Walking on Eggshells," *TOL Week in Review* (26 February–4 March 2001), at www.tol.cz/look/TOLnew/article.tplYNrArticle+636&ST1'body&ST-T1'wir&ST-ma [accessed on 21 August 2001].
33. Statement by J. de Beaufort Wijnholds, Executive Director of the IMF for Former Yugoslav Republic of Macedonia, 10 May 2000, at www.imf.org/external/np/a4pilot/2000/stm0076.pdf [accessed on 4 November 2008].
34. International Monetary Fund, *Former Yugoslav Republic of Macedonia: Staff Report for the 2000 Article IV Consultation* (23 June 2000), p. 41, at www.imf.org/external/pubs/ft/scr/2000/cr0076.pdf [accessed on 4 November 2008].
35. *Nation by Nation*, "Macedonia: Economy," at www.multied.com/NationbyNation/Macedonia/Economy.html [accessed on 4 November 2008].
36. International Monetary Fund, Juan Zalduendo, *Enterprise Restructuring and Transition: Evidence from the Former Yugoslav Republic* of *Macedonia*, WP/03/136 (June 2003), at www.imf.org/external/pubs/ft/wp/2003/wp03136.pdf [accessed on 4 November 2008].
37. MIA, "Macedonia Low on List of SEE States Receiving Direct Foreign Investment," BBC Monitoring Europe, 11 July 2005, on *Lexis–Nexis Academic Universe* (11 July 2005).
38. M-2 Presswire, "FCO Spokesman, Monday 24 October 1994 Elections in the Former Yugoslav Republic of Macedonia" (15 November 1994), on *Lexis–Nexis Academic Universe* (24 October 1994).
39. Staff Report of the Commission on Security and Cooperation in Europe, *Macedonia's Parliamentary Elections: 1 October and 18 November 1998*, p. 7, at

www.csce.gov/index.cfm?FuseAction=Files.Download&FileStore_id=255 [accessed on 4 November 2008].

40. OSCE/ODIHR, "ODIHR Election Observation Mission Former Yugoslav Republic of Macedonia: 1999 Presidential Elections-Second Round Re-runs 5 December 1999: Preliminary Statement," at www.osce.org/documents/odihr/1999/12/1399_en.pdf [accessed on 4 November 2008].
41. *Financial Times* (11 November 1993), on *Lexis–Nexis Academic Universe* (11 November 1993).
42. "Largest Albanian Party Splits in Two," *BBC Summary of World Broadcasts*, 16 February 1994, on *Lexis–Nexis Academic Universe.*
43. MIA News Agency, "OSCE Official Says Macedonian Elections Held in Line with European Standards," *BBC Monitoring Europe*, 9 September 2002, on *Lexis–Nexis Academic Universe.*
44. PDP spokesman Abdulrahman. Aliti supported the principle of proportional representation "at all levels of government." "Macedonian Albanians Prefer Proportional Representation to Territorial Division," Yugoslav Telegraph Service (Belgrade), 15 August 1994; *BBC Summary of World Broadcasts*, 17 August 1994, on *Lexis-Nexis Academic Universe.*
45. Human Rights Watch, *A Threat to Stability? Human Rights Violations in Macedonia* (New York: Human Rights Watch, 1996) p. 30.
46. See SPSEE's 2004 and 2005 *Annual Reports*, at www.stabilitypact.org/about/finalreport.pdf [accessed on 4 November 2008].
47. *Ibid.*, p. 14.
48. MIA News Bulletin, "OECD Commissioner Notes Progress in Human Rights in Macedonia," *BBC Summary of World Broadcasts* EE/D3040/A, 4 October 1997 on *Lexis–Nexis Academic Universe.*
49. Atilla Agh, "Processes of Democratization in the East-Central European and Balkan States: Sovereignty Related Conflicts in the Context of Europeanization," *Communist and Post Communist Studies,* Vol. 32, No. 3 (September 1999), p. 267.
50. Karin D. Karlekar, "Press Freedom in 2006: Growing Threats to Media Independence," Freedom House, at www.freedomhouse.org/uploads/fop/2007/fopessay2007.pdf [accessed on 4 November 2008].
51. Radio Macedonia, "FYROM Assembly Debates Commission Report on Wiretapping Affair" (21 February 2001), FBIS–EEU *Daily Report* (21 February 2001), AFS EUP20010222000012.
52. MIA, "FYROM Interior Minister Dimovska Details Reasons for Resignation" (16 February 2001), FBIS–EEU *Daily Report* (16 February 2001), AFS EUP20010216000243.
53. Radio Macedonia, "FYROM PM Georgievski Views SDSM Role in Wiretapping Affair" (21 February 2001), FBIS–EEU *Daily Report* (21 February 2001), AFS EUP20010222000013.
54. MIA, "FYROM: Daily Condones Public Discontent Over Assembly Deputies' Defection" (28 August 2000), FBIS–EEU *Daily Report* (28 August 2000), AFS EUP2000829000012.
55. Eurobarometer survey, *Central and Eastern Europe*, March 1996, at http:cc.europa.eu/public opinion/archives/ceeb/ceeb6/ceeb6_en.htm#1–4 [accessed on 4 November 2008].

56. Helsinki Committee for Human Rights, *Annual Report for Human Rights in Macedonia Cases and Relations,* Vol. 3, No. 10 (1996), p. 5.
57. Elainor Pritchard, "Amnesty Condemns Macedonian Police," *Central European Review,* Vol. 2, No. 26 (3 July 2000), at www.ce-review.org/00/26/Macedonianews26.html [accessed on 4 November 2008].
58. Agence France Presse (1 November 1998), on *Lexis-Nexis Academic Universe.*
59. Armend Reka, "The Ohrid Agreement: The Travails of Inter-Ethnic Relations in Macedonia," *Human Rights Review,* Vol. 9, No.1 (March 2008), p. 55.
60. Steven Teffert, *The Dissolution of Yugoslavia and the Badinter Commission* (Dartmouth: Ashgate, 2000), p. 160.
61. Human Rights Watch, "*A Threat to Stability? Human Rights Violations in Macedonia: Cases and Reactions*" (New York: Human Rights Watch, 1996), p. 21.
62. Kalina Trenevska Blagoeva (Sts. Cyril and Methodius University, Skopje), "NFR Statistics-Problems and Perspective in the Republic of Macedonia," p. 1, at http://isi.cbs.nl/iamamember/CD2/pdf/240.PDF [accessed on 4 November 2008].
63. "Kosovo Crisis Poses Food Security Threat for Rural Households in Albania and the Former Yugoslav Republic of Macedonia," FAO Special Alert, No. 292, 29 April 1999, at www.fao.org/docrep/004/x1874e/x1874e00.htm [accessed on 4 November 2008].
64. *The Independent* (17 April 2001), on *Lexis-Nexis, Academic Universe.*
65. *Macedonia: The Last Chance for Peace,* ICG Balkans Report, No. 113 (20 June 2001), at www.crisisgroup.org/library/documents/europe/113___macedonia__the_last_chance_for_peace.doc [accessed on 4 November 2008].
66. *Ibid.*, p. 2.
67. MIA, "NATO, EU Chiefs Hold Talks with Macedonian Leaders, Urge Dialogue" (27 March 2001), *BBC Summary of World Broadcasts* (28 March 2001), on *Lexis-Nexis Academic Universe* (28 March 2001).
68. MIA, "OSCE Chairman Announces Agreement on Cessation of NLA Armed Activities in Fyrom" (18 May 2001), *World News Connection* (21 May 2001), FBIS -EEU- 2001-0518, AFS # EUP20010518000430.
69. *Macedonia: The Last Chance for Peace,* p. 10
70. "Ali Ahmeti," *Wikipedia,* at http://en.wikipedia.org/wiki/Ali_Ahmeti [accessed on 4 November 2008].
71. Michael Evans, "Police Deal Opens the Way to Macedonia Peace," *The Times* (6 August 2001), on *Lexis-Nexis Academic Universe.*
72. The text of the Accord, at www.coe.int/t/e/legal_affairs/legal_co-operation/police_and_internal_security/OHRID%20Agreement%2013august2001.asp [accessed on 4 November 2008].
73. *Fakti* (12 December 2006), trans. in *BBC Monitoring Europe* (14 December 2006), on *Lexis-Nexis Academic Universe.*
74. MIA (12 August 2008), in English, in *BBC Monitoring Europe,* on *Lexis-Nexis Academic Universe* [13 August 2008].
75. Radio Skopje (1 December 2003), trans. in *World News Connection,* FBIS-EEU 2003-1201 AFS #EUP20031201000329.
76. Victor A. Friedman, "Observing the Observers: Language, Ethnicity, and Power in the 1994 Macedonian Census and Beyond," *New Balkan Politics,* Issue No. 3 (2001),

at www.newbalkanpolitics.org.mk/OldSite/Issue_3/friedman.eng.asp [accessed on 4 November 2008].

77. MIA," Macedonian Government Adopts 23 Essential Laws of Decentralization Package" (9 June 2004), on *Lexis-Nexis Academic Universe.*
78. Brankoe Jokie, "Albanian Referendum Could Spell the End of the Macedonian State," *Delo*, 4 August 2004, *BBC Monitoring Europe*, 24 August 2004, on *Lexis-Nexis Academic Universe.*
79. "A Narrow Squeak: Macedonia's Referendum," *The Economist*, 13 November, 2004, on *Lexis-Nexis Academic Universe.*
80. *Fakti* (7 October 2008), trans. in *BBC Monitoring Europe* (7 October 2008), on *Lexis-Nexis Academic Universe.*
81. Public Administration Reform Department, OSCE Spillover Monitor Mission to Skopje, "Survey on Decentralization 2007," at www.osce.org/documents/mms/2007/09/26526_en.pdf" [accessed on 4 November 2008].
82. "Hague Continues Investigation of Ljuboten Case," *South East European Times* (24 January 2005), at www.setimes.com/cocoon/setimes/xhtml/en_GB/features/setimes/features/2005/01/24/feature-02 [accessed on 4 November 2008].
83. "Hague Tribunal Reportedly Set to Indict Ex-Macedonian Interior Minister," B-92 Website in *BBC Monitoring International Reports*, 25 December 2004, on *Lexis-Nexis Academic Universe.*
84. *Lions Caged*, TOL Balkan Reconstruction Report, 27 January 2003, at www.tol.cz/look/BRR/article.tpl?IdLanguage=1&IdPublication=9&NrIssue=1&NrSection=1&NrArticle=8490&search=search& SearchKeywords=lions&SearchLevel=0 [accessed on 4 November 2008].
85. International Crisis Group, *Macedonia's Public Secret: How Corruption Drags the Country Down*, ICG Balkans Report, 133 (14 August 2002), p. ii, at www.crisisgroup.org/library/documents/europe/133___macedonia_corruption__14_08_02.doc [accessed on 4 November 2008].
86. Renata Treneska, "Party Funding and Campaign Finance in Macedonia," in Daniel Smilov and Jurij Toplax (eds.), *Party Finance and Corruption in Eastern Europe: The Transition Period* (Aldershot: Ashgate, 2007), pp. 105–21.
87. *Makedonija Denes* (14 December 2007), trans. in *BBC Monitoring Europe* (18 September 2007), on *Lexis-Nexis Academic Universe.*
88. MIA, "Macedonia: 11 State Institutions Sign Anti-Corruption Protocol" (25 December 2007), *World News Connection*, 25 December 2007, News Edge Document #2007122514771-c1470020d7277540 and *Makfax* "Macedonia: Corruption Watchdog Warns New Energy Law Contravenes EU Guidelines" (28 December 2007), News Edge Document # 200712281477.1-4950002838b06a26.
89. *EU Business,* "EU Says Macedonia Can Begin Accession Talks This Year" (6 March 2008), at www.eubusiness.com/news-eu/1204824732.82/ [accessed on 4 November 2008].
90. Communication from the Commission – Commission Opinion on the application from the Former Yugoslav Republic of Macedonia for membership in the European Union … celex-txt- 52005DC0562 at http://eur-lex.europa.eu/Notice.do?val=417112:cs&lang=en&list=417112:cs,&pos=1&page=1&nbl=1&pgs=10&hwords=&checktexte=checkbox&visu=#texte [accessed on 4 November 2008].

91. EC Council Decision of 30 January 2006 on the principles, priorities and conditions contained in the European Partnership with the Former Yugoslav Republic of Macedonia … celextxt-Doc32006D0057, at http://eur-lex.europa.eu/Result.do?code=32006D0057&Submit=Search&RechType=RECH_celex&_submit=Search [accessed on 4 November 2008].
92. "Council of Europe Warns Macedonia about 'Deplorable' Conditions in Jails," *Makfax* (Skopje), 10 September 2008, on *Lexis-Nexis Academic Universe*.
93. "Elections Events Show Macedonia Still 'Not Mature,'" MIA (2 June 2008), on *Lexis-Nexis Academic Universe*.
94. Vladimir Misev, "Macedonia," in Jeannette Goehring (ed.), *Nations in Transit 2008: Democratization from Central Europe to Eurasia* (New York and Budapest: Freedom House, 2008), p. 382.
95. *Ibid*., p. 382.
96. Zhidas Daskalovski, "Macedonia," in Jeannette Goehring (ed.), *Nations in Transit 2007: Democratization from Central Europe to Eurasia* (New York and Budapest: Freedom House, 2007), p. 460.
97. Eurobarometer 67, *Executive Summary, the Former Yugoslav Republic of Macedonia*, Spring 2007, at www.delmkd.ec.europa.eu/en/whatsnew/2007/16%20EuroBarometer%2067.htm [accessed on 4 November 2008].
98. *The Breakdown of Democratic Regimes* ed. Juan J. Linz and Alfred Stepan (Baltimore, Md.: Johns Hopkins University Press, 1978) as cited in *Consolidating Third Wave Democracies: Regional Challenges*, ed. Larry Diamond, Juan Linz, and Alfred Stepan (Baltimore, Md.: Johns Hopkins University Press, 1997), p. xvii.
99. Vladimir Secansky, interview with Mrs. Radmilla Sekerinska, *Euromonitor International* (31 May 2007), at www.euromonitor.com [accessed on 5 October 2008].
100. *Fakti* (20 November 2006), trans. in *BBC Monitoring Europe* (23 November 2006), on *Lexis-Nexis Academic Universe*.
101. "Macedonia's New View of History," *Balkan Insight* (21 January 2008), at http://balkaninsight.com/en/main/news/7469/ [accessed on 4 November 2008].
102. European Commission, "Former Yugoslav Republic of Macedonia 2008 Final Progress Report: Communication from the Commission to the European Parliament and the Council," SEC(2008)269.5 Final (5 November 2008), at http://ec.europa.eu/enlargement/press_corner/key-documents/reports-2008-en.htm [accessed on 5 November 2008].

Further reading

Brown, Keith. *Modern Macedonia and the Uncertainties of a Nation* (Princeton, N.J.: Princeton University Press, 2003)

Cowan, Jane. *Macedonia: The Politics of Identity and Difference* (London: Pluto Press, 2000)

Danforth, Loring. *The Macedonian Conflict: Ethnic Nationalism in a Transnational World* (Princeton, N.J.: Princeton University Press, 1995)

Pettifer, James. *The New Macedonian Question* (New York: St. Martins Press, 1999)

Poulton, Hugh. *Who Are the Macedonians*, 2nd edn. (Bloomington, Ind.: Indiana University Press, 2000)

Ramet, Sabrina Petra. *The Three Yugoslavias: State Building and Legitimation 1918–2005*. (Bloomington, Ind. and Washington, DC: Indiana University Press and Woodrow Wilson Center Press, 2006)

Rossos, Andrew. *Macedonia and the Macedonians: A History* (Stanford, Calif.: Hoover Institution Press, 2008)

Williams, Abiodun. *The United Nations and Macedonia* (Lanham, Md.: Rowman & Littlefield, 2000)

16

Kosova: resisting expulsion and striving for independence

FRANCES TRIX

In March 1989, Slobodan Milošević, the party chief in Serbia, engineered Kosova's[1] loss of status as an autonomous province within Yugoslavia and its absorption into the Republic of Serbia. The Kosovar Albanians, who constituted more than 90% of the population of Kosova, protested the Serbian takeover. Later that year, Kosovar Albanian intellectuals founded the Democratic League of Kosova (LDK) and elected Ibrahim Rugova as leader. Through the 1990s Serbian power in Kosova became steadily more oppressive as Kosovar Albanians moved from the passive resistance advocated by Rugova and the LDK to more active resistance, culminating in the war for Kosova of 1998–9. At the end of the war, in June 1999, Kosova became a UN protectorate, still officially part of Yugoslavia, and when Yugoslavia ceased to exist in 2003, part of Serbia, but ruled by the United Nations Interim Administration Mission in Kosovo (UNMIK).

Thus, the history of Kosova since 1989 can be divided into two periods: the period of Serbian rule and Albanian resistance, and the period under UNMIK. In this chapter, I will discuss the institutional transformations of the two periods, economic issues, and interethnic relations of Kosovar Albanians and Serbs. I will also contextualize major events and ongoing problems. As for the communist past of Kosova, concern for it has been overshadowed by ethnic issues, nationalism, and the war, although socialist expectations from that time continue to exert influence.

The chapter is framed with brief discussion on the land, the nationalist significance of Kosova, and the 1981 riots. The first period (1989–99) is divided into two sections: the institutional expulsion of Albanians and growth of parallel institutions, followed by progression to war. The second period (1999–2009) is divided into three sections: return from war and stagnation, March 2004 riots to the status talks, and stalemate to Kosova's declaration of independence from Serbia in February 2008.

Background on Kosova

Kosova is a landlocked region in the central Balkans, bordered on the south by Albania and Macedonia, on the east and north by inner Serbia,[2] and on the west by Montenegro. It is slightly smaller than Montenegro, but has more than four times Montenegro's population. In broader European terms it is half the size of Wales and, like Wales, known for mining: Kosova is said to have 45% of the lignite reserves in Europe.[3] It has been famous for its silver mines since pre-Roman times, for silver filigree in Ottoman times, and for lead, magnesite, nickel, chrome, and zinc in more recent times.

Strategic routes across southeastern Europe pass through Kosova. One goes north from the Mediterranean, up through Kosova, to central Europe. Another passes west through Kosova to the Adriatic. Topographically Kosova is made up of two plateaux partially defined by mountain ranges. On the west are the Dinaric Alps and in the south are the Sharr Mountains. There is good farmland in the central and eastern regions, while in the west there is lumber, dairy farming, and sheep herding. It is important to recall that Kosova was largely rural until the second half of the twentieth century, but at the same time the population density is one of the highest in Europe.[4]

Nationalist significance of Kosovo/Kosova and demographics

Albanians are an ancient Balkan people, most likely descended from the Illyrians. The Serbs are a Slavic people who migrated into the Balkans in the sixth and seventh centuries. The region of Kosova was fought over by the Byzantines, the Bulgarians, the Serbian Nemanjids, and the Ottomans. In 1389, Serbian King Lazar and Ottoman Sultan Murad fought against each other in the Battle of Kosovo, with Albanians fighting on the side of King Lazar. After the battle, the Serbs became vassals of the Ottomans and were ruled by them. In the nineteenth century, Serbian nationalists used Serbian oral narratives of the 1389 battle to define themselves. The romanticized memory of this battle, compounded by the presence of Orthodox Serbian monasteries from this era in Kosova, led to Kosova being seen as the "cradle of the Serbs."

During Ottoman rule many people in Kosovo converted to Islam, including many Albanian Catholics. In the late seventeenth century there was a migration of Serbs north out of Kosova. Then in the nineteenth century, Serbs pushed many Muslim Albanians, who lived in what became Serbia, south into Kosova. By the last decades of the nineteenth century, the majority of people in Kosova were Albanian Muslims.

In 1878, 300 Albanian delegates from four Ottoman *vilayets* or provinces gathered in the city of Prizren in the *vilayet* of Kosova to form the League of Prizren. The purpose of this League was to protect Albanians' lands against encroachment by Montenegro, Serbia, Bulgaria, and Greece. This was the first such organization, made up of both Muslim and Christian Albanians;[5] it heralded the beginning of the Albanian *rilindja* or "rebirth," the rise in Albanian nationalist consciousness. Thus, both Serbs and Albanians look to Kosova as a special heartland.

In 1912 Serbia conquered Kosova from the Ottomans. In the Treaty of London in 1913, against the wishes of the Albanian majority, the Great Powers sanctioned Serbia's claim to Kosova. To increase the Serb population in Kosova, Belgrade confiscated Albanians' land and brought in Serbian colonists in the 1920s and 1930s. During the Second World War the Serbian colonists were forced out, but after the war, Aleksandar Ranković, Tito's Minister of the Interior, reinstated anti-Albanian policies. Between 1946 and 1966 over 100,000 Albanians fled Kosova to Turkey. Then Yugoslavia moved to a policy of decentralization and Ranković was dismissed.

In 1968, Kosova was accorded more autonomous status in Yugoslavia. This was reinforced by the 1974 constitution in which autonomous provinces were accorded almost all the rights of republics in Yugoslavia; they were even allowed their own constitutions. The University of Prishtina was established and Albanians took positions of leadership in Kosova. Kosova still was the poorest region in Yugoslavia with only 30% of the national median income,[6] but family members could work in Western Europe and send funds back home. Albanians served in the Yugoslav military and the first generation of Kosovar Albanians had the opportunity for higher education.

The riots of March 1981

The riots of March 1981 in Kosova were a turning point. They began when an Albanian law student named Bahrije Kastrati dumped her plate of food in protest in the University of Prishtina cafeteria. Students who protested conditions at the university were joined by fans returning from a soccer match. The rhetoric changed to more general criticism of authorities and some students were arrested. Two weeks later, students and others gathered; many called for republic status for Kosova within Yugoslavia, while some called for unification with Albania. Several days later, crowds gathered again, including construction workers who had more specific protests. The military responded with tanks in the streets, but the demonstration spread to five other cities in Kosova. Security police from outside Kosova were ordered in and a state of emergency was declared across the province.

It is important to realize that such demonstrations had no place in Yugoslavia at that time. The Cold War was still going on, and the West, preferring Tito-style communism, had ignored Tito's *Udba*, the Yugoslav secret police, second in size only to the East German *Stasi*. Officially only ten people died in the riots, but local hospitals reported numbers in the hundreds. Over 2,000 Kosovar Albanians were arrested and many given prison terms. Underlying the March 1981 events were economic woes from mismanagement of Kosova's economy.[7] Funds had been channeled into large industrial projects which often failed economically. More basic needs could have been met with investment in agriculture and roads, or allowing investment of funds earned abroad in enterprises back home. But the official line from Belgrade was that

Kosovar Albanians had sought unification with Albania. Many Albanians felt that these slogans had been planted by undercover police; they also noted sadly that people from other republics such as Slovenia or Croatia had not supported them. Tito had died in 1980; it seemed as if the shared sense of Yugoslavia had died with him.

The 1981 riots intensified Serbian concern that the Albanians in Kosova had been given too much power. The demographics had continued to diverge. In the 1981 census, 77% of the population of Kosova was Albanian, while only 13% was Serbian. Part of this related to differential birth rates, for Kosovar Albanians had one of the highest birth rates in Europe. But Serbs in Belgrade asserted that Serbs in Kosova were being pushed out. Statistics do show about 90,000 Serbs leaving Kosova for other parts of Yugoslavia between 1961 and 1981, but the main reason for this was economic.[8] A Memorandum by the Serbian Academy of Sciences and Arts in 1985 asserted that Serbs were being hounded from Kosova by Albanians, although the allegation was not documented. The Belgrade media spread accounts of Serbian victimhood in Kosova, while Albanians were seen as perpetrators and dehumanized.

Economic conditions across Europe in the 1980s worsened. Did the growing Serbian and Croatian nationalisms in Yugoslavia distract people from their economic troubles? Was there a malaise, a sort of spiritual void, as communism as an ideology and Yugoslavia as a land of "brotherhood and unity" lost meaning?[9] Did the political leaders stir nationalist agendas to maintain power? By the end of the 1980s there was 200% inflation in Kosova, 50% unemployment, and tensions were high.[10]

First period, 1989–99

Institutional expulsion of Albanians and growth of parallel institutions

In February 1989, Albanian miners held a hunger strike underground in the Trepça mines to maintain the 1974 constitution and to protest Milošević's replacement of Albanian provincial leaders. Earlier, in November 1988, 2,000 Albanian miners had held a march from the mines south to Prishtina. It was a disciplined march and 6,000 Albanians joined in solidarity along the way. Unlike the events of 1981, these were well-organized demonstrations, non-violent, and focused on maintaining the 1974 constitutional framework. The president of Slovenia acknowledged that the Trepça miners were defending Yugoslavia by striking.

Nevertheless, after the miners' strike, Milošević sent in troops and moved to rescind Kosova's autonomy. He needed the Kosovo Assembly to pass an amendment repealing its own veto power. On the day of the vote, the Assembly was surrounded by tanks and filled with Serb security police. No roll-call was taken. Most Albanian members chose to abstain, knowing that a two-thirds majority was required. The amendment was nevertheless declared passed. On

28 March 1989, the Serbian Assembly passed amendments giving it control over Kosova's police, courts, educational policy, economic policy, and language. There were massive demonstrations in Kosova, and people were killed.

But during 1990, at the height of the Serbian regime's hate campaign against them, Kosovar Albanians responded with organized activism grounded in non-violence. Rugova explained the strategy as a pragmatic one in the face of overwhelming Serb military strength: "There is no choice but self-control when facing terror." But the Kosovar Albanian political scholar Maliqi offered a more anthropological perspective: his people were redefining themselves in contradistinction to the other. Where Serbs were warlike and oppressive, Kosovar Albanians would be peaceful and democratic.[11]

In December 1989, two Kosovar Albanian organizations were formed. Academics founded the Council for the Defense of Human Rights and Freedoms to document police abuse and human rights violations, which soon had branches in every community in Kosova. During the 1990s whenever incidents of human rights abuse occurred, volunteers would visit the scene, take careful notes, and pass these on to Prishtina. Documenting and naming the perpetrators of police violence and abuse had a transformative effect that helped move people from submission to a form of resistance. The second organization was the Democratic League of Kosova (LDK), with the Head of the Kosovo Writers' Union, Ibrahim Rugova, elected president. Within several weeks, it had several hundred thousand members. This would become the main Kosovar Albanian political party for the rest of the 1990s and into the 2000s. As for Serbs in Kosova, they joined branches of new Serbian parties from Belgrade.

Albanian delegates of the Kosova Assembly met in July 1990 and declared their wish for sovereignty. Belgrade responded by suspending the Assembly and bringing in more troops from inner Serbia. But the Assembly continued to meet in secret and in September promulgated the constitution for the Republic of Kosova. These actions would form the basis for Kosovar Albanians' claim to legitimate sovereignty. The following year, in September 1991, the Assembly, the LDK, and other Albanian parties organized a referendum on Kosova's independence. In this secretly organized poll, 89% of registered voters voted, of whom 99% favored independence. In 1992, there were elections for a new Assembly and Rugova was elected president of the self-proclaimed "Republic of Kosova."

Meanwhile Serbia had already begun "bureaucratic expulsions" of Albanians in Kosova.[12] In 1990, Serbia dismissed all Albanian workers and professionals who worked for the state, which in a socialist system was just about everyone. Albanian police were fired and an all-Serb police force brought in. Albanians who worked for the media, the courts, state enterprises, and clinics were dismissed. By 1991, Albanian high school teachers had been effectively fired, and Albanian students and faculty were forbidden entrance to the University of Prishtina.

The closing of high schools and the university to Albanians led to the establishment of a parallel school system. Classes were held in private homes, storerooms, mosques, and Sufi centers. This parallel school system served a significant number of Kosova's 400,000 Albanian students and was funded by a 3% tax that Kosovar Albanians levied on their own diaspora populations. The system functioned best in the first part of the 1990s, but it was still a remarkable achievement and kept students from losing an entire ten years of schooling.

Healthcare was also a problem since Albanians were no longer welcome in state clinics. By 1994 infant mortality was 17%, the highest in Europe and three times higher than it had been in the 1980s. Kosovar Albanians set up the Mother Teresa Association which opened clinics where healthcare was given free by volunteer staff. By 1997, this organization had ninety-one clinics and 7,000 volunteer staff.

Media were also targeted and the main Albanian daily, *Rilindja*, was shut down. First an Albanian agricultural weekly added political pages; later a new weekly, *Koha Ditore*, evolved until in 1997 it became a daily. But editors and reporters were routinely picked up by police, interrogated, and imprisoned. As for electronic media, all Albanian employees of the state radio and television were dismissed. To help fill the void, the LDK instituted the Kosova Information Center as an electronic source of news for diaspora papers and broadcasts.

With so many people out of work, many Kosovar Albanians turned to small trading businesses that built on contacts with other Albanians in neighboring Macedonia. They also got help from relatives working in Germany, Switzerland, or America, but it became increasingly difficult to receive these funds. Even with small businesses, there was frequent harassment from authorities and confiscation of goods.

Survival under these circumstances was remarkable. Rugova continued to reassure people that their passive resistance would eventually be noticed by international powers. His quiet demeanor and unwavering insistence on independence for Kosova gave people hope. Albanians' awareness of the war in Bosnia where so many Muslims had been killed and displaced also kept people in line. Albanians feared all-out destruction, and actions by Serbian police reinforced these fears. In 1994, the Council for the Defense of Human Rights and Freedoms documented 2,157 physical assaults on Albanians by the police, 3,553 raids on private homes, and 2,963 arbitrary arrests.[13] The raids on the homes were allegedly searches for weapons, but they were carried out late at night, involved the smashing of furniture, the traumatizing of children, and often arrests of male members of the family. Clearly they were instruments of terror.

Progression to war

From 1995 the situation in Kosova deteriorated. The war in Bosnia ended, but in the ensuing Dayton Peace Accords Kosova was not even mentioned despite its five years of non-violence. Many saw this as proof of the failure of Rugova's strategy of passive resistance. Serb paramilitaries who had operated in Bosnia moved to Kosova. Also by 1995 Albanians were worn down by their increasing poverty and vulnerability. New forms of harassment appeared. There was a campaign to wipe out mad cow disease and 4,000 head of livestock belonging to Albanians were killed, although no trace of the disease was ever found.

For Serbs in Kosova, 1995 saw the arrival of 16,000 Serbian refugees from the Krajina region in Croatia. They were bused to Kosova and then housed in empty Albanian high schools. These Serbs did not want to be in Kosova and their presence depressed the local Serbs. Was this what was in store for them too? But the arrival of Serb refugees also allowed for the entrance of international relief agencies. UNICEF was first allowed in by Belgrade to help with the refugees. More international agencies soon followed and in the last half of the 1990s provided desperately needed resources for Albanians as well.

There were attempts to change the cultural landscape. The Serbian Orthodox Church was central to Serbian nationalist identity and so Orthodox churches were built anew in largely Muslim Albanian areas. Locals termed these "Milošević churches," the most prominent being one begun in 1995 on University of Prishtina land next to the National Library. It was never finished or used for worship, but continues to stand.

Muslim clerics were frequently called in for interrogation and Orthodox crosses etched on doors of mosques. The Serb authorities tried to provoke them to support their contention that Albanians were "radical Muslims who threatened the heart of Europe" and thus should be removed. Most of the Albanians in Kosova were Muslim, but many were cultural Muslims, not particularly observant let alone radical. Later when war broke out in 1998, foreign Muslims offered to fight, but Albanian Muslim leaders refused. They had enough men and did not want the troubles the *mujahedin* had caused in Bosnia.[14]

There were growing challenges to Rugova. In 1997 Adem Demaçi, who had spent twenty-eight years in Serb prisons, put forward an idea for a three-republic Balkania (Serbia, Montenengro, Kosova), but it did not catch on. That same year, Albanian students sought a more active non-violence and held two large demonstrations in Prishtina and other cities. The police blocked these, then broke them up brutally. But most significantly, the Kosova Liberation Army (KLA), which had directly challenged Rugova's non-violence, appeared publicly in the fall of 1997, declaring it was the only force fighting for the freedom of Kosova.

Early KLA attacks targeted Serb police stations, especially in Drenice, a rural area of central Kosova where local KLA groups cleared villages of Serb security forces. But in February 1998 US envoy Robert Gelbard referred to the KLA as "terrorists." The next week the Serb military attacked the family compound of the Jasharis, KLA leaders in Drenice, where they killed fifty-one members of the family. This destruction of an entire extended family was a turning point for

Kosovar Albanians; it mobilized them to join the KLA, or at least to support it. Indeed some have seen the KLA as the most successful guerilla movement in modern history with its clear rural support base.[15]

The Serbian offensive began in western Kosova in May 1998. By the end of the summer over 200,000 Kosovar Albanians had been internally displaced by the fighting. American Ambassador Richard Holbrooke brokered a cease-fire with Milošević in October 1998 that called for unarmed Organization for Security and Cooperation in Europe (OSCE) verifiers in Kosova. In January 1999, Serb police killed and mutilated forty-five civilian Albanians from the village of Raçak. This was discovered soon after it had occurred by the head of the OSCE verifiers, US Ambassador William Walker, who immediately termed it a "massacre." Media accounts mobilized world attention.

There was an international attempt at a political solution in Rambouillet, France. The Albanians were pressured into signing the agreement, but the Serbs never signed. On 20 March Serbia resumed its military campaign in Kosova, and on 24 March 1999 NATO began its bombing campaign, but it was not able to protect Albanians on the ground.

The violence on the ground was a coordinated and systematic campaign to terrorize, kill, and expel Albanians, organized by the highest level of the Serb government at the time, and carried out through close cooperation of the military, police, and paramilitaries. Five hundred Albanian villages were destroyed, and an estimated 10,000 people killed, with particular targeting of intellectuals and professionals. There was a deliberate attempt to destroy evidence and remove bodies to mass graves in Serbia.

Milošević's plan was to both expel Albanians and destabilize the region. Indeed, 850,000 Albanians were expelled from Kosova at this time. On the way their documents were destroyed, their money and goods stolen, and women and girls were raped. The police told the refugees that they would have no way of proving that they had ever lived in Kosova and they would have no homes to return to. The media images of the refugees galvanized support for the NATO action and helped keep the NATO alliance together throughout the seventy-eight-day bombing campaign. Albania, the poorest country in Europe, took in 460,000 refugees, of whom 260,000 lodged with private families. Macedonia received 300,000 refugees, of whom 138,000 were taken in by Macedonian–Albanian households. Montenegro received 60,000 refugees of whom 30,000 were taken in by Montenegrin–Albanian households, and Turkey took 24,000 refugees, of whom 9,000 were taken in by families whose relatives had earlier been forced out of Kosova.[16]

NATO had expected Milošević to collapse quickly; when this did not happen, the bombing targets moved to inner Serbia. On 9 June 1999 Serbia signed the Military Technical Agreement, a negotiated compromise guaranteeing the withdrawal of Serb military and police from Kosova. The NATO bombing stopped on 10 June when the UN Security Council passed Resolution 1244 which allowed the entry of NATO troops into Kosova. It also made Kosova a

UN protectorate, still under the technical sovereignty of Yugoslavia but to be administered by the UN, with reference to the will of the majority in deciding final status. A profoundly ambiguous document, Resolution 1244 would cloud the following UN and international administration for years.

Second period, 1999–2009

Return from war to stagnation

International agencies tried to keep the expelled Albanians outside Kosova until conditions on the ground improved. However, the Kosovar Albanians returned rapidly in June and July 1999 in the largest spontaneous movement of refugees since the Second World War. International NGOs and locals worked together to meet basic humanitarian needs. Over 40% of Albanian homes had been destroyed, but with funds from relatives overseas, Albanians rapidly rebuilt their homes so that internationals who came after 2000 did not realize the extent of wartime destruction. Now Kosovars just needed security and jobs, a rebuilding of civic and economic networks, and clear political status. But despite significant international aid and the efforts of many international organizations over ten years, this did not occur. In fact, some deem the UNMIK experience an administrative failure.[17] Why did this happen?

The UN was slow to establish local security and appoint administrators. The international civilian police did not come for two months; it took over a year before they were up to strength. NATO troops, known as KFOR (Kosovo Force), were responsible for external security and arrived after six weeks, but were reticent to take police action. The UNMIK administrators were few in number and not well organized.

In the political vacuum, the KLA quickly installed mayors in all major towns. This made the remaining Serbs fearful and was resented by many Albanians as well. UNMIK was also in charge of the judiciary, but was slow to get started. With no working security and judiciary, there was no clear way to control the incipient violence. There was also internal displacement after the war as some Serbs moved into the northern sector of Kosova where Serbs became a majority, and Albanians in that sector were pushed out of their homes.

In all fairness, transition from war and a police state posed massive problems. But the initial lack of security and rule of law, compounded by the lack of clarity of the final political status of Kosova, gave clout to extremists of both groups. This further polarized Albanians and Serbs. Mitrovice, the main city in the north, became the "flashpoint" for ethnic violence. Kosova had been divided into five sectors where KFOR troops were led by different NATO nations. The French, long known for their sympathy with the Serbs, took the northern sector. French KFOR became known for "force protection." That is, they protected their own force. They allowed the Serbian "bridge-watchers" by the Ibar River in Mitrovice to harass Albanians for several months, and after a riot in February

2000 allowed the division of the city of Mitrovice, with the Serbs on the northern side of the river, and the Albanians on the southern side. This division of Mitrovice gave the Serbs an urban center, but it also reinforced the Albanians' fear that the long-term plan was for partition of Kosova with Serbia taking the northern section[18] and its mines.

UNMIK itself was made up of several international organizations – the UNHCR, the UN, the OSCE, and the EU – all led by the Special Representative of the Secretary General (SRSG). Responsibilities were assigned to different organizations, but in practice there was some overlapping and lack of clarity in accountability.

There were several early successes. One was the police training school that the OSCE established at Vushtrri. Another was the rebuilding of the traditional markets of both Peja and Gjakova. Half of the 500 mosques in Kosova had been significantly damaged, and many of these were rebuilt. There was also rebuilding of schools. The municipal elections that took place in October 2000 can also be seen as a success. Voter turnout was 78%, although not many Serbs voted. Interestingly Rugova's party, (LDK), won 58% of the vote, while Thaçi's party of former KLA members (PDK) won only 27% of the vote. Clearly the majority of Albanians did not want to be ruled by the people who had initially seized power at the end of the war.

By May 2001, a constitutional framework was agreed upon for Kosovo's Provisional Institutions of Self-Government. It provided for elections every three years for the Kosova Assembly which in turn would elect the president and prime minister. Of the 120-member Assembly, 100 members are elected by proportional representation, with 20 more to represent national minorities. But this Assembly was forbidden from taking actions to decide the final political status of Kosova; the SRSG retained major executive and legislative powers. Rather the Provisional Government was given power over education, health, agriculture, and public services.

The first election for the Kosova Assembly was held in November 2001. The voter turnout was 65%. Again the LDK won the most votes (47%), the PDK came in second (26%), while the next largest number of votes (11%) was won by the Serbian *Povratak* Coalition. The voting of Serbs in this election was a distinct accomplishment, although some north of the Ibar River were intimidated from participating. Serbia had established parallel institutions there and could cut off wages and pensions if the Serbs did not follow Belgrade's instructions.

But the municipal elections the following year in 2002 had only a 54% voter turnout, with almost no Serbs voting. This decline from 78% in 2000 reflected problems in Kosova. It was over three years since the war and the internationals still had veto power over all locally elected people. More crucially, UNMIK had not begun to work toward new status for Kosova. To buy time with the increasingly impatient Albanians, the fourth SRSG, Michael Steiner, came up with the slogan, "Standards before Status." The "standards" referred to eight benchmarks that Steiner had developed with other internationals to measure progress by the Kosova Provisional Government. These were supposed to give Kosovar leaders direction. Instead they created much frustration for they were vague and many could be negatively affected by pressure from Belgrade or intransigence by local Serbs.

Further, the economy had stalled. Initially there had been progress with adoption of the Euro, growth in the banking system, and the imposing of a 10% duty on all imports. But many Kosovar Albanians had paid into the pension system of Yugoslavia, only to lose all assets from it after the war. Property documents had been removed by Serbian officials in 1999 which made privatization more difficult. In addition, some international officials felt that privatization of socially owned assets, which included much land and all factories, was an issue that could only be taken up when sovereignty was settled. There were also ongoing problems with the utility that provided electricity for Kosova. In April 2002 it was discovered that the German who had been in charge of public utilities in Kosova had embezzled $4.5 million.[19]

Besides the occasional international official, a broader problem with corruption and smuggling had developed among local Kosovar officials as well. By October 2003 the internationals in charge of privatization were so convinced of local corruption that they totally stopped the process. Here, however, they were wrong, for local controls were working.

But by 2003 a sort of imperial condescension by internationals toward Albanians had developed. Partly it was the isolation of the internationals who lived on one hillside in Prishtina, spent most of their time with each other, and did not interact significantly with Albanians. Many of these internationals had earlier spent time in Bosnia which was more different than they realized; their emphasis on "rebuilding a multi-ethnic society" sounded more like Bosnia than Kosova. This lack of sensitivity to the society they were supposed to be serving surfaced when they were totally caught off guard by the events of March 2004.

March 2004: riots to status talks

Poverty in Kosova was widespread. Fully 50% of the population lived on about $1.65 *per capita* per day, while 12% were extremely poor, living on less than $0.80 *per capita* per day.[20] After the March 2004 riots, civil society leader Albin Kurti would note, "It was the economic crisis, precipitated by Kosova's unresolved political status, that was the root cause of the inter-communal tensions and resultant instability."[21]

Several events preceded the riots, including a bomb attack on Kosovar Albanian ministers, the exploding of a grenade outside President Rugova's house, and the planting of an explosive device next to UNMIK headquarters. There was a drive-by shooting of a seventeen-year-old Serb south of Prishtina. In retaliation, Serbs put up road blocks on the two main roads south from Prishtina that blocked all traffic for three–four days. Then, on 16 March 2004, three young Albanian boys drowned in the Ibar River. A fourth Albanian boy recounted in an interview broadcast that evening how they had been chased into the river by Serbs with a dog. Riots broke out across Kosova on 17–18 March 2004. Nineteen people were killed (eleven Albanians and eight Serbs), 950 were injured, hundreds of homes of Serbs were damaged or destroyed, and thirty-six Serbian Orthodox churches were damaged with three utterly destroyed. Many UNMIK vehicles were damaged as crowds made clear that UNMIK was a main target of their wrath and frustration.

Why were the internationals so unprepared? With over 16,000 KFOR troops in Kosova, why were they not able to control the crowds? One of their main duties was to protect cultural monuments, so why were Orthodox churches damaged? The SRSG did not appear, nor did he have any other UNMIK official appear on the news for twenty-four hours. Thus, there was no international leadership. Some KFOR troops were injured while trying to control crowds, but when local Kosovar police called for help from KFOR and UNMIK, they were refused assistance. Where were the leaders of the Provisional Government of Kosova? Bajram Rexhepi and Lutfi Haziri, both former mayors, bravely stood in front of crowds, trying to disperse them. But neither Rugova nor Thaçi appeared. Albanians' longstanding record of respect for others' places of worship was sullied. Some reported that young Albanian men had been told that it was their duty to burn churches. Others were convinced that this was the work of paid agents, for Serb intelligence continued to operate in Kosova. As for destruction of homes, these disproportionately belonged to recent Serb returnees, often recently built for them by internationals.

The riots of March 2004 were a disaster in many ways. Several thousand Serbs were displaced – more than had returned to Kosova in the past few years. The moral status of Albanians was damaged, and many internationals felt that their work had been in vain. A study contrasting places where violence had erupted and where it had been contained found that projects for inter-ethnic interaction had not made a significant difference. What did matter for controlling violence was the level of cohesion within Serb or Albanian communities.[22] But at the same time, the riots of March 2004 were a wake-up call for internationals and locals alike. The Provisional Government of Kosova gave funds for immediate repair of Serb churches and houses. The SRSG fired the international head of privatization. And the Secretary General of the UN asked Norwegian ambassador Kai Eide to go to Kosova and report back on the implications of the riots.

In his report Eide noted that the international community had failed to read the mood of the population, and understand the depth of the dissatisfaction of the majority and the vulnerability of the minorities. He found that UNMIK was without direction or internal cohesion, and that it had become a target of criticism from all sides. From the perspective of the Albanian majority, "the main cause of their growing dissatisfaction was not of an inter-ethnic nature, but more from what is rightly seen as a lack of economic opportunities and an absence of clear political perspective."[23] From the perspective of the Kosovar Serbs, "they are victims of a campaign to reduce their presence in Kosova to a scattered rural population."[24] This was a remarkably straight-talking report. Eide made five major recommendations: maintain pressure on Albanians and Serbs to work together in institutions, transfer more authority to the Kosovar government, revise the current unworkable "standards" policy, urgently initiate an economic development strategy, and stop postponing final status talks.

By August 2004, a capable new SRSG, Soren Jessen-Petersen, was sent in. By December there were new standards that were prioritized and easier to meet. In the spring of 2005 the first city, Gjilan, passed from international to local security control. By spring 2007 only Mitrovice remained under international control; all other areas had successfully moved to local Kosovar control.

In April 2005, the privatization process was allowed to move forward, for Kosova was desperately in need of investment in factories and businesses to provide jobs. By mid-2007, apart from politically sensitive entities like the Trepça mines or the Brezovice ski resort, 60% of the socially owned enterprises had been privatized, the successful ventures tending to be joint ventures with companies in Slovenia or Croatia. The main obstacles to investment remain undependable electricity and lack of clear political status. What would happen to an investment if Belgrade took over Kosova again? Need for long-term sustained investment was one of the strongest arguments for moving to conditional independence for Kosova.

High unemployment is a continuing problem. What used to be the release valve, namely work in western Europe, has been closed to Kosovars who did not have visas before the war. This includes most of the youth, of whom 63–85% are unemployed; in addition, women have a low employment rate, only 9%.[25] Agriculture could be more profitable, but it takes long-term investment, as does the mining industry. Kosova could be an exporter of energy to the region, but it would take skillful long-term investment to make this work. Meanwhile, the main export of Kosova in 2006 was scrap metal from equipment in old factories.[26] There is a 70% trade deficit, with donor funds drying up and remittances declining.

The media in Kosova diversified over the UNMIK period. There are nine major dailies and many radio and television stations. The electronic media were criticized after the March 2004 riots for broadcasting the interview with the young Albanian boy without corroboration, and new standards of reporting were adopted. Meanwhile a positive aspect of the Albanian media in Kosova since 2000 is the absence of the language of hate;[27] Albanians had endured so much of such language in the nationalistic press from Belgrade that they had become disgusted. The Serb media in Belgrade still engages in hate rhetoric, while the Serb media in Kosova is quite negative. Different ethnic groups have, however, recently begun working together in the OSCE-funded Kosovo Media Institute.

Another area of ethnic cooperation is criminal activity. This was the joke at a time when both Albanians and Serbs tired of the internationals' push for inter-communal dialogue, but there is truth to it. Smuggling has become a problem with the reduced economy, while drug trade and trafficking in women are regional problems.

A strength of Kosovar Albanian society has been the way family members support each other, which allowed Albanians to survive most difficult times. But it has now translated into nepotism with political parties taking on clan-like structures. The educated young hope to work against these older ways, but with the stress of recent times and the economic problems it will take time.

After Eide's first report in 2004, the UN Secretary General asked him to conduct a follow-up study, published in October 2005. Although Eide did not find that much progress had been made, he still made a strong argument for status talks to begin. The UN endorsed this and talks began in Vienna that continued for fourteen months.

Stalemate to declaring independence

In February 2007, Martti Ahtisaari, former President of Finland and leader of the talks, presented drafts to Prishtina and Belgrade for a settlement proposal that included protection of minority communities, decentralization of the government, protection of Orthodox religious sites, the creation of a Kosova Security Force, and the right for Kosova to apply for membership in international organizations and adopt national symbols. However, Prishtina would not compromise on independence, nor Belgrade on sovereignty. Ahtisaari concluded that as neither side would compromise, he would present his own proposal to the Security Council which became known as the Ahtisaari Plan.

In May 2007, several members of the Security Council circulated a draft resolution to replace Resolution 1244, endorse Ahtisaari's plan, and end the UN protectorate of Kosova after 120 days. Russia objected. NATO said it would continue to maintain security with KFOR, and the EU promised to continue policing and judicial oversight. The draft resolution was rewritten four times, but Russia refused to accept any resolution that was not acceptable to both Prishtina and Belgrade.

As for the Kosovar people, in March 2007 the UNDP published a survey that found that 96% of Kosovar Albanians favored independence, while 78% of Kosovar Serbs preferred to stay under Serbian sovereignty.[28] Yet Belgrade had not even acknowledged the human cost to Albanians of its policies in the 1990s.

More Kosovar Albanians came to support declaring unilateral independence. With Russia supporting Serbia, any UN-sponsored plan for conditional independence would be vetoed. At the same time there was growing criticism of the special status for the Serb minority provided for in the Ahtisaari Plan. Would this "decentralization" lead to partition of Kosova? The November 2007 elections went ahead with only 40% participation, the lowest in Kosova's recent history. For the first time, Thaçi's PDK won. Again there was talk of a unilateral declaration of independence by Kosova.

On 17 February 2008 Kosova declared independence from Serbia. There was a day and night of celebration in Prishtina, and in Kosovar communities around the world. Serbia and Russia protested immediately, but France, Italy, Germany, the United States, and Turkey supported Kosova's independence. According to the Ahtisaari Plan, there would be a 120-day transition period, after which the EU would assume an advisory role to the new government, with a special mission to strengthen the rule of law, while UNMIK's responsibilities would transfer to the Kosovar government.

Serbs in the north burned customs posts to show their disdain for the turn of events. In March Serbs took over a UN-administered courthouse in northern Mitrovice. When UNMIK tried to regain it, there was fighting and an UNMIK soldier was killed. Serbs also refused to cooperate with the EU scheduled takeover of judicial authority. Under UN control there was always the possibility of a Russian veto, not so with the EU. The result was lawlessness in the north and confusion over the transition from UNMIK to the EU. But the rest of Kosova was peaceful and the new national anthem had no words, only music, so as not to divide people by language.

Meanwhile Kosova sought recognition of its independence. Of the twenty-seven member nations of the EU, twenty-two recognized Kosova in 2008. To counter this and try to halt further recognitions, Serbia worked to bring the question of Kosova's unilateral declaration of independence to the ICJ, although its opinion would not be binding. In October 2008 Serbia succeeded in getting the simple majority required from the UN to bring the case to the ICJ, but the following day both Montenegro and Macedonia recognized Kosova. By mid-2009, sixty-two states had officially recognized Kosova.

After twenty years of strife and political limbo, there is hope in Kosova that the economy will finally receive the attention it so desperately deserves. Kosova was accepted as a member in the IMF and the World Bank – indications of integration into the global financial system. There is also hope that the EU will be less interfering than UNMIK, and that the Kosova government will rise to its greater responsibilities, building on strengths exhibited by its people in the early 1990s.

Timeline 1989–2008

Kosova under Serbian rule

March 1989	Kosova loses autonomy and is taken over by Serbia
December 1989	Albanians found LDK
7 September 1990	Albanian Assembly members proclaim constitution of Republic of Kosova
September 1990–1	Serbia dismisses Albanians in state positions
26 September 1991	Albanians vote 99percent for independence in referendum
26 March 1998	Serb military kill fifty-one members of Jashari family in central Kosova
May–August 1998	200,000 Albanians internally displaced

16 January 1999	Serb police kill Albanian civilians in village of Raçak; found by OSCE verifiers
24 March 1999	NATO begins bombing Serbian installations; Serb police, military and paramilitary, kill, burn, loot, and expel 850,000 Albanians from Kosova
9 June 1999	NATO and Serbia sign Military Technical Agreement to end fighting

Kosova as UN Protectorate

10 June 1999	UNMIK is established.
June–July 1999	Some Serbs in Kosova flee to Serbia; most expelled Albanians return
17–18 March 2004	Albanians riot across Kosova against Serbs and UNMIK
April 2007	Ahtisaari presents his plan for "supervised independence" of Kosova
17 February 2008	Kosova declares independence from Serbia

Fact sheet

Area	10,887 km^2 (4,203 sq. miles)
Population (2007)	2,430,000
Albanian	92%
Serb	5%
Major cities (2006)	
Prishtina/Pristina	562,586
Prizren/Prizren	165,229
Below the poverty line (EU 2006)	37% of population
Unemployment rate (EU 2006)	42–44%
GDP *per capita* (EU 2006)	1,100 Euros
Higher education (UNDP 2004)	1.65% of population

Parties in the Kosova Assembly (November 2007 election)

Parties and coalitions	*% of the vote*	*Number of seats*
Democratic Party of Kosovo (PDK)	34.3	37
Democratic League of Kosovo (LDK)	22.6	25
New Kosovo Alliance (AKR)	12.3	13
Albanian Christian Democratic Party of Kosovo (PSHDK)	10.1	11
Alliance for the Future of Kosovo (AAK)	9.6	10
Minority parties that actually won seats (see below)		4
		100

Notes:

There are 100 members elected.

There are 20 additional seats reserved for minorities: 10 for Serbs; 4 for Roma, Ashkali, and Egyptian; 3 for Bosnians; 2 for Turks; 1 for Gorani.

Party	Seats: won	reserved
Turkish Democratic Party of Kosovo (KDTP)	1	2
Democratic Ashkali Party of Kosovo (PDAK)	1	2
Coalition Vakat (Bosnian) (Vakat)	1	2
Independent Liberal Party (Serb) (SLS)		3
Serb Democratic Party for Kosovo and Metohija[a] (SDSKM)		3
Party of Democratic Action (Bosnian) (SDA)	1	1
Serb People's Party[a] (SNS)		1
New Democracy (Serb) (ND)		1
Civic Initiative of Gora (Gorani) (GIG)		1
Serb Kosovo–Metohija Party[a] (SKMS)		1
New Democratic Initiative of Kosovo (Egyptian) (IRDK)		1
Union of Independent Social Democrats of Kosovo and Metohija[a] (SNSKM)		1
United Roma Party of Kosovo (PRBK)		1
		20
Total voter turnout	628,630	40.1%

Note:
[a] After the election these Serb parties formed a coalition.

Short biography of Ibrahim Rugova

Ibrahim Rugova, Kosovar Albanian scholar, writer and politician, is best known for his commitment to achieving independence for Kosova through peaceful means. In 1998, he received the Sakharov Peace Prize from the European Parliament.

Rugova was born in 1944 in northwestern Kosova. His father and grandfather were executed by communists soon after his birth, and their land confiscated. Rugova grew up in poverty. He specialized in Albanian literature, studied literary theory with Roland Barthes in Paris, and received his doctorate in Albanology from the University of Prishtina. In 1988 he became head of the Kosovo Writers' Union.

In 1989 Rugova co-founded and was elected president of the Democratic League of Kosova (LDK), the political organization that led resistance to Serbian oppression by setting up parallel educational and social welfare institutions for Albanians in Kosova. He was elected president of the self-proclaimed "Republic of Kosova" twice; however, after 1995 his popularity waned as more active resistance took center stage.

After the 1998–9 war, Rugova's LDK won the first elections and Rugova was elected president of the Provisional Interim Government of Kosova in 2002 and 2004. He continued to work for the independence of Kosova, but in January 2006 died of lung cancer.

Notes

1. Since Albanians constitute the vast majority of the population, I use the definite Albanian form, "Kosova." The Serbian form is "Kosovo."
2. Serbia without Vojvodina and Kosova.

3. From a personal interview with mining engineer and Director of Privatization, Kirk Adams, in Kosova Trust Authority, Prishtina, Kosova, 18 June 2007.
4. According to the OSCE 2004, the population density is 200/km^2, about 500 sq. miles
5. There are Muslim, Roman Catholic, and Orthodox Christian Albanians. In Kosova, 95percent of Albanians are Muslim, 5percent Roman Catholic.
6. Tim Judah, *Kosovo: War and Revenge* (New Haven. Conn.: Yale Nota Bene, 2002), p. 46.
7. Noel Malcolm, *Kosovo: A Short History* (New York: New York University Press, 1998), p. 336.
8. *Ibid.*, p. 331.
9. Pedro Ramet, "Apocalypse Culture and Social Change in Yugoslavia," in Pedro Ramet (ed.), *Yugoslavia in the 1980s* (Boulder, Colo.: Westview Press, 1985), pp. 3–26.
10. I spent an academic year in Kosova, 1987–8, when these were the conditions.
11. Shkelzen Maliqi, *Kosova: Separate Worlds* (Peja: Dukagjini, 1998), p. 62.
12. Frances Trix, "Kosovar Albanians between a Rock and a Hard Place," in Sabrina P. Ramet and Vjeran Pavlaković (eds.), *Serbia since 1989: Politics and Society under Milošević and After* (Seattle: University of Washington Press, 2005), p. 311.
13. Cited in Malcolm, *Kosovo*, p. 320.
14. From a personal interview with Dr. Rexhep Boja, who was Director of the Headquarters of the Islamic Community in Kosova from 1990 to 2003, in the Faculty of Islamic Studies, Prishtina, Kosova, 30 May 2007.
15. Judah, *Kosovo*, p. xxvii.
16. Frances Trix, "Reframing the Forced Migration and Rapid Return of Kosovar Albanians," in Elzbieta Gozdziak and Dianna Shandy (eds.), *Rethinking Refuge and Displacement: Selected Papers on Refugees and Immigrants (Vol. VIII)* (Arlington, Va.: American Anthropological Association, 2000), pp. 250–75.
17. Iain King and Whit Mason, *Peace at Any Price: How the World Failed Kosovo* (Ithaca, NY: Cornell University Press, 2006) is written by two UNMIK staff who worked in Kosova from 2000 to 2004. The book is interesting but uneven; it is historically shallow and limited in local understanding, but rich in detail of actions by internationals.
18. For an argument against partition, including the fact that the majority of Serbs in Kosova live south of the Ibar River, see European Stability Initiative, "The Lausanne Principle: Multiethnicity, Territory and the Future of Kosovo's Serbs" (June 2004), at www.esiweb.org
19. King and Mason, *Peace at Any Price*, pp. 187–8.
20. "Kosovo's Internal Security Sector Review," Kosovar Institute for Policy Research and Development, KIPRED), March 2006, p. 31.
21. King and Mason, *Peace at Any Price*, p. 190.
22. Care International, "Has Peacebuilding Made a Difference in Kosovo?" (Care International, 2006), at www.careinternational.org.uk.
23. Kai Eide, "Report on the Situation in Kosovo," for the UN Secretary General (S/2004/932, 15 July 2004), p. 3.
24. *Ibid.*
25. "Governance and Competition in Higher Education," Kosova Institute for Policy Research and Development, KIPRED), (2007), p. 13.

26. From a personal interview with Shpend Ahmeti, Operations Officer and Economist, World Bank, Prishtina, 19 June 2007.
27. From a personal interview with Kelmend Hapçiu, Director and Editor in Chief of KosovaLive, and Director of Kosova Media Institute, Prishtina, 28 May 2007.
28. Kosovo Early Warning, report No. 14, UNDP (June 2006), at early.warning.ks@undp.org.

Future reading

Care International. "Has Peacebuilding Made a Difference in Kosovo?" (July 2006), at www.careinternational.org.uk

DiLellio, Anna. *The Case for Kosova: Passage to Independence* (London: Anthem Press, 2006)

European Stability Initiative. "Cutting the Lifeline: Migration, Families and the Future of Kosovo (September 2006), at www.esiweb.org

European Stability Initiative. "The Lausanne Principle: Multiethnicity, Territory and the Future of Kosovo's Serbs" (June 2004), at www.esiweb.org

Judah, Tim. *Kosovo: War and Revenge.* (New Haven, Conn.: Yale Nota Bene, 2002)

King, Iain and Whit Mason. *Peace at Any Price: How the World Failed Kosovo* (Ithaca, N.Y.: Cornell University Press, 2006)

Malcolm, Noel. *Kosovo: A Short History.*(New York: New York University Press, 1998)

McAllester, Matthew. *Beyond the Mountains of the Damned: The War inside Kosovo* (New York: New York University Press, 2001)

Pettifer, James. *Kosova Express: A Journey in Wartime*, (Madison, Wisc.: University of Wisconsin Press, 2005)

Trix, Frances. "Kosovar Albanians between a Rock and a Hard Place," in Sabrina P. Ramet and Vjeran Pavlaković (eds.), *Serbia since 1989: Politics and Society under Milošević and After* (Seattle: University of Washington Press, 2005), pp. 311–49

Part 5
Southeastern Europe

17

Romania: in the shadow of the past

LAVINIA STAN

Introduction

Romanians take pride in being the only East Europeans to speak a Latin language, and point to Roman Emperor Trajan's column in Rome as testimony to their Latin origins. In 102 and 106 CE, the Dacian king Decebal was defeated by Trajan's legions, which subsequently colonized Dacia, the territory north of the Danube River that became Romania. Over the next millennium the Dacians intermingled with the Roman legions to form the Romanian people. After the fall of the Roman Empire, the territory passed under Byzantine rule until the seventh century, when the Slavs settled south of the Danube. In the fourteenth century Wallachia and Moldova gained independence from the Hungarian Kingdom, which also included Transylvania. To delay Ottoman occupation, Wallachia and Moldova formed an alliance, but after the Hungarian Kingdom fell in 1526 they recognized the sovereignty of the Ottoman Empire. For three centuries, the principalities paid tribute in exchange for the right to preserve their political, administrative, and military structures. The *millet* system allowed Romanians to keep their Christian Orthodox faith.

In the eighteenth century the Ottoman Empire gave Transylvania away to the expanding Austrian Empire, which appointed a governor to rule it, while in Wallachia and Moldova it introduced the "phanariot system," by which the positions of rulers of each country were up for grabs to candidates offering the largest payment to the Ottoman Sultan. The system encouraged corruption, overtaxation, and a speedy turnover of the country's administrators, since the Sultan could gain more if he dismissed the administrators quickly, and successful candidates were under pressure to recover the payments made to the Sultan by imposing ever higher taxes on the impoverished peasant population. Unsurprisingly, when Ottoman power eroded following the 1828–9 Russo-Turkish conflict, Romanians protested little against the newly imposed Russian protectorate. That arrangement proved less felicitous than Romanians had expected, however, and in 1856 they applauded the guarantees offered by the Paris Treaty signatories. Three years later, Alexandru Ioan Cuza was elected as ruling prince of both principalities, which in 1862 took the name Romania.

Cuza's successor (in 1866) was Prince Carol Hohenzollern-Sigmaringen, who served his country well, winning its independence in the Russo-Turkish war of 1877. Four years later, in 1881, Romania was proclaimed a kingdom, and Carol I became its king. His rule was marked by stability and progress in all areas of life. At the end of the First World War, Carol's nephew, Ferdinand, realized the dream of all Romanians by uniting under his scepter Wallachia, Moldova, and Transylvania, but his death in 1927 plunged the country into deep crisis. His grandson Michael inherited the throne, but, in 1930, Ferdinand's son Carol II deposed his own son Michael to institute a corrupt dictatorship. In the pre-Second World War European alignment, Romania slid progressively to the right, forging – by necessity as well as choice – closer ties to Nazi Germany. Although his country joined the Allies in mid-1944 and paid a steep price in the Second World War, young King Michael was forced to leave the country by a communist-led government backed by the occupying Russian troops. Romania's fate was sealed.

The new leaders moved quickly to build the communist system by introducing collectivization of agriculture; nationalization of private property; censorship of the mass media; mass arrests of pre-communist state dignitaries, non-communist party members, opposition leaders, and clergy members; and mass surveillance by the secret political police. Following the death of Stalinist leader Gheorghe Gheorghiu-Dej, Nicolae Ceauşescu became the First Secretary of the Communist Party and the country's president. After his outspoken condemnation of Czechoslovakia's invasion by Warsaw Pact members, in 1971 Ceauşescu introduced a number of measures domestically to curtail the citizens' fundamental freedoms and liberties, and internationally to give the impression of independence from Moscow.

Of all communist Central and Eastern European countries, Romania remained the least reformed, the most likely to deny basic human rights, and the only one with a sultanist-cum-totalitarianist regime up to the moment when communism collapsed. The state controlled the population through its secret political police – the notorious Securitate – the Communist Party controlled the state through the *nomenklatura* list and cells present in every locality, factory and school, while Ceauşescu and his family controlled the party. Romanian communism was associated with village systematization, which led to the destruction of traditional Transylvanian villages, the scientific diet program which encouraged Romanians to eat little at a time when basic food staples were in short supply, the pro-natal program, which prohibited family planning and ordered women to have as many children as possible to enlarge the country's working force, and Ceauşescu's megalomanic projects, which destroyed the old downtown Bucharest to make room for the House of the People, the world's second-largest building. Ceauşescu was head of the state, head of government, leader of the party, and the person overseeing the Securitate's activity, and his wife Elena was a member of the Politburo, head of the Communist Party's cadre office, and vice prime minister, while their son Nicu was party leader of the Sibiu county and heir apparent to his father. The constant surveillance and crackdown on independent activity meant that no organized political opposition was constituted, and the country's few dissidents were isolated from each other and from the larger society.[1]

Given Ceauşescu's personalized rule, the local uncivic political culture and the widespread corruption and intolerance, the country's limited historical experience with democracy, and the bloody revolution of December 1989, it is not surprising that Romania faced serious challenges in its efforts to create a stable democratic system and to gain acceptance into the larger European family. After Ceauşescu and his wife were executed on Christmas day 1989, Romanians hoped to gain the political rights and economic prosperity they had been denied for forty-five years. But the weakness of civil society and the absence of an organized political opposition sealed the country's fate, as power reverted to second-echelon *nomenklatura* members, who rejected communism less than they rejected Ceauşescu. The first years of post-communist transformation in Romania tell the story of the former communists establishing control over the state apparatus, intimidating political rivals, rigging elections, and appropriating state resources through shady privatization deals. The country has yet to overcome that handicap, as its democratization and marketization unfolded at a slower pace than other countries in the region. Whereas in Central Europe the collapse of the communist regime brought the pro-democratic opposition to government, in Romania this happened only in 1996. Whereas in other countries economic stabilization, liberalization, and privatization were largely completed by mid-1990s, in Romania these processes extended almost to the end of the decade. Whereas Hungary, Poland, the Czech Republic, and Slovakia joined the EU in 2004, Romania did so only in 2007. The country will need more time to catch up with the other new EU member states.

This chapter adopts a chronological approach to discuss Romanian post-communist political, economic, and social developments. After examining Ion Iliescu's first two mandates as president (1990–6) and the rule of President Emil Constantinescu and his Democratic Convention of Romania (CDR) (1996–2000), it analyzes the reasons why Iliescu returned to the presidency in 2000 and the policies his Party of Social Democracy adopted as major ruling partner. After the 2004 elections the Social Democrats (PSD) became the official opposition, Traian Băsescu was sworn in as the new president, while a new Justice and Truth Alliance (DA) formed the government with the support of two junior partners. The chapter argues that both communist legacies and post-communist political choices explain why Romania's transformation has consistently lagged behind that of Central Europe.

The first Iliescu regime, 1990–6

Despite their strong ties to the Ceauşescu regime and open endorsement of a "third way" retaining key political and economic communist traits, Iliescu and his National Salvation Front (FSN) won the first post-communist elections of

May 1990, a position they used to shape the country's new democracy. The 1991 constitution recognized Romania as a French-style semi-presidential republic, where the executive powers were shared by a president directly elected in a run-off system for a maximum of two four-year terms and a cabinet led by a prime minister; the legislative powers rested with a bicameral parliament consisting of a lower house, the Chamber of Deputies, and an upper house, the Senate; the judiciary included a new Constitutional Court and a Supreme Magistrates' Council. The country opted for a multiparty system from which only the Communist Party was formally excluded, and a proportional representation system with a national threshold of 5% for individual parties and 8% for multiparty coalitions.

Several legal provisions boded well for the new democracy. Small ethnic minorities unable to gain votes above the national threshold were guaranteed representation in the Chamber of Deputies. The country formally upheld the separation of powers and the separation of Church and state, and guaranteed basic human rights denied by the previous communist regime (the right to travel inside and outside the country, to worship freely, to organize associations, and the inviolability of the domicile and correspondence). Censorship of the mass media and other publications was discontinued, and new privately owned newspapers and radio and television stations were allowed to function alongside the publicly owned media outlets.[2] New political parties could be set up by as few as 250 adherents, embrace a range of ideological and policy preferences, compete in local and national elections, and collect membership fees and donations from sympathizers. The new Constitutional Court could overturn legislation running counter to fundamental law, the powers of the Prosecutor General were drastically curtailed, and the citizens were allowed to approach the new ombudsman with complaints about governmental agencies. The secret state security services were placed under parliamentary oversight, and some agents involved in human rights abuses were retired.[3] Private property was guaranteed by the constitution, previously confiscated land was returned to initial owners, new Romanian and foreign-owned private firms were allowed to function, and some unprofitable industrial giants were privatized. Last but not least, the Greek Catholic Church, which the communists had suppressed in 1948, was relegalized, and the destruction of places of worship initiated by Ceaușescu in the mid-1980s was halted.

Other constitutional and policy choices were less fortunate. In line with the precommunist Romanian precedent, the new democracy was over-bureaucratized, centralized, wasteful, and inefficient. At the county level, public administration included government-appointed prefects alongside elected councils with overlapping responsibilities, while the smallest village was represented by as many as seventeen councilors. Strict centralization was retained, as was Bucharest's domination over regions and provinces in terms of fund allocation and distribution.[4] As they were too similar in terms of competencies and the way they were elected, the two legislative chambers unnecessarily prolonged the law-adoption process without making it more democratic. Proportional representation fragmented parliament, at a time when the country needed leadership and coherence to implement painful but necessary socio-economic restructuring programs. With its many politically appointed and corrupt judges, the judiciary was not truly independent from the executive, which continued to influence court decisions in areas such as property restitution. The secret state security services were accountable to the president, as chair of the Supreme Council for the Country's Defense, and as such they controlled parliament more than parliament controlled them through its oversight committees.

More importantly, the ease with which political parties were set up made for a fragmented party system, which numbered close to 180 different formations in the early 1990s. The party system was dominated by the FSN, which benefited from the Communist Party's huge membership, strict hierarchical structure, and unparalleled penetration at the local level. Fragmented, polarized, and inexperienced, lacking leadership and resources, the political opposition was unable to mount credible campaigns in the weeks leading up to the 1990 and the 1992 elections. It managed to gain parliamentary representation without the right to form the government. This modest result was due not only to its many weaknesses, but also to the FSN's undemocratic style of conducting politics. The 1990 poll was seriously tainted by the FSN's smear campaigns against the budding opposition, allegations that the opposition was ready to deprive ordinary Communist Party members of their political rights and to reinstate interwar social inequalities, and insistence that Romanians should unite around the FSN if they wished to prevent the country's disintegration in the face of Hungarian demands for the return of Transylvania, a former province of the Austro-Hungarian Empire which Romania had acquired in 1918. An important intimidation factor was the so-called *mineriade*, the descent on Bucharest of angry Valea Jiului miners encouraged, organized, and condoned by Iliescu and his FSN. Shock troops of hundreds of miners came down on the capital in January, February, and June 1990, and again in September 1991, ransacking the headquarters of opposition parties, and physically assaulting opposition leaders.[5] Ironically, the *mineriada* of 1991 also led to Premier Petre Roman's resignation, and the split of the FSN into the more reformist FSN led by Roman, and the more conservative Democratic National Salvation Front (FDSN) led by Iliescu. The *mineriade* greatly divided the Romanian electorate, damaged the country's international reputation, and isolated it within Europe.

The 1992 elections reaffirmed Iliescu as the president (with only 61.4% of the vote in the second round compared to nearly 80% in the first round in 1990) and allowed his FDSN to form a government under the leadership of Nicolae Văcařoiu, an economist who had made a career in the communist planning system. Eight parties were represented in the new parliament. To the left of the political spectrum were the two Front offshoots mentioned above together with the Socialist Party of Labor (PSM) and the Agrarian Democratic

Party (PDAR), heirs to the Communist Party. The center-right Democratic Convention (CDR) united two parties active in the inter-war period, the National Liberal Party (PNL) and the National Christian-Democrat Peasant Party, supported by former political prisoners and anti-communist dissidents. To the extreme right stood the chauvinistic Greater Romania Party (PRM) and the Party of Romanian National Unity, two new formations gathering former communist secret agents and apparatchiks. The Democratic Union of Magyars in Romania (UDMR) represented the interests of the 2 million-strong Transylvanian Hungarian community (table 17.1).

From 1992 to 1996, the country gained some political stability, and as a result it received some international recognition, though Western governments remained critical of Iliescu and Văcařoiu, their ties to the former communist regime, their strong endorsement of key communist principles, and their reluctance to effect resolute reforms. In 1993, Romania became an observer to

Table 17.1 Parliamentary elections, 1992 and 1996

	1992				1996			
	Chamber of Deputies		Senate		Chamber of Deputies		Senate	
Party	Seats	(%)	Seats	(%)	Seats	(%)	Seats	(%)
Democratic National Salvation Front[a] (Frontul Democrat al Salvarii Nationale, FDSN)	117	34.3	49	34.2	91	27.7	41	28.6
Democratic Convention of Romania (Conventia Democrata din Romania, CDR)	82	24	34	23.7	122	35.5	53	37
National Salvation Front[b] (Frontul Salvarii Nationale, FSN)	43	12.6	18	12.5	53	16.1	23	16
Party of Romanian National Unity (Partidul Unitatii Nationale Romane, PUNR)	30	8.8	14	9.7	18	5.4	7	4.9
Democratic Union of Magyars in Romania (Uniunea Democrata a Maghiarilor, UDMR)	27	7.9	12	8.3	25	7.6	11	7.6
Greater Romania Party (Partidul Romania Mare, PRM)	16	4.6	6	4.1	19	5.7	8	5.5
Agrarian Democratic Party of Romania (Partidul Democrat Agrar din Romania, PDAR)	–	–	5	3.4				
Socialist Party of Labor (Partidul Socialist al Muncii, PSM)	13	3.8	5	3.4				
Ethnic minorities[c]	13		–	–	15		–	–
Total	341	100	143	100	343	100	143	100

Notes:

[a] In 1996, it ran as the Romanian Party of Social Democracy (Partidul Democratiei Sociale din Romania, PDSR).

[b] In 1996, it ran as the Social Democrat Union (Uniunea Social Democrata, USD).

[c] Ethnic minorities other than the Hungarians are each allotted a deputy seat.

Source: Central Electoral Bureau.

the Council of Europe, and in 1994 it joined the NATO Partnership for Peace. Within months, however, the momentum behind the country's international opening was lost when nationalists were coopted into the government.

Politically, the country's leaders gradually accepted the role of the constitutional opposition, renounced the most violent intimidation tactics (the *mineriade*), continued the institutional reform of the judiciary by agreeing to the irremovability of judges, strengthened the counties' autonomy relative to Bucharest, and pledged to observe fundamental human rights and to refrain from using the secret intelligence services against their political rivals. Political decisions were no longer adopted in the streets, under the pressure of the mob, but through negotiations between formations represented in parliament. In April 1993, the government created the Council for Ethnic Minorities to tackle the problems of the country's fourteen minority groups, but the protection of minorities was grossly undermined from 1994 to 1996, after Văcařoiu refused to strike a partnership with the CDR, preferring instead to coopt the PRM and the Party of Romanian National Unity (PUNR) to government, a move giving the nationalists increased legitimacy, visibility, and influence. Ethnic clashes flared between Romanians and Hungarians or Roma, with some reports claiming that by 1995 there had been thirty-seven interethnic clashes in which six Roma were killed and dozens of Roma homes destroyed.[6] The nationalists incessantly promoted an irredentist agenda calling for the integration of the independent Republic of Moldova into a resurrected Greater Romania, and for ethnic minorities' rights to be limited to allow Romanians to be "true masters of their own land."[7] Popular attitudes toward ethnic minorities remained generally negative, despite the availability of civic education programs encouraging tolerance and inclusiveness.

Economically, the country made progress, without bridging the gap separating it from Central Europe. Hyperinflation was slowly brought under control; the agricultural collectives were dismantled and peasants received small land plots; the currency was stabilized at a significantly depreciated rate relative to the dollar; and new markets were identified to compensate for the massive loss of business with former communist countries. The most difficult problem revolved around the state's devolution in the economy, as in communist times over 95% of economic activity had taken place in state-owned units, one of the highest percentages in the region. As unemployment remained high, closing the unprofitable state-owned industrial giants (petrochemical refineries, aluminum processing plants, coal and rare metal mines) was not an option. Given the foreign investors' lack of interest and the domestic investors' lack of resources, the government opted for the management–employee buy-out and the mass voucher privatization programs, which transferred property rights to managers and/or workers and granted shares in large industrial plants to all Romanian adult citizens. Privatization largely benefited former communist party officials and enterprise managers, who had insider information about profitable ventures, connections to political decision-makers, raw material providers and retailers, and previous managerial experience. As the Roman and Văcăroiu governments did little to open the system to outsiders, the former communists became Romania's most important and successful businessmen.[8]

The Constantinescu regime, 1996–2000

The 1996 victory of the pro-democratic opposition, united under the banner of the CDR, was much anticipated both domestically and internationally.[9] For the first time, religion featured prominently in the electoral race. The highlight of the presidential campaign was a televised confrontation during which CDR candidate Constantinescu took incumbent Iliescu, a self-avowed atheist, by surprise by asking him to state whether he believed in God. Constantinescu, a University of Bucharest geology professor, won the second round of presidential elections with 54% of the vote. Only six coalitions and parties entered parliament. The government was formed by the CDR, together with the UDMR and the Social Democrat Union, which included the Democratic Party (Roman's former FSN). The opposition consisted of the Party of Social Democracy (Iliescu's former FDSN), the PRM, and the PUNR. Dissensions within the CDR and between it and the Social Democratic Union meant that three premiers, all representing the Christian Democrats, were appointed from 1996 to 2000. Former trade union leader and Bucharest Mayor Victor Ciorbea was forced to resign in April 1998, being replaced by academic Radu Vasile, who in turn lost his party's support in late 1999 in favor of economist Mugur Isărescu, the National Bank governor.

The participation in government of the UDMR greatly improved the minorities' input into the public decision-making process, and as a result some of the most restrictive laws on minority rights were amended and the number of ethnic clashes greatly diminished. As the nationalists and the Social Democrats controlled a significant number of parliamentary seats, and some government partners were particularly sensitive to arguments advanced by the country's religious majority, the Romanian Orthodox Church, accommodation of sexual and religious minorities came at a slower pace. It was only in 2000, hours before the deadline imposed by the Council of Europe, that homosexual behavior was legalized, amid the protests of Christian Democrat deputy Emil Popescu, who claimed that "incest was preferable to homosexuality, since at least the former preserved the chance of procreation."[10] At the same time, the position of the Orthodox Church relative to other religious denominations was further strengthened. The Church was tacitly allowed to control the way religious instruction was delivered in public schools, received support from special governmental funds, and in 1999 Premier Radu Vasile even agreed to recognize it as a national, state Church (a proposal abandoned before parliament could debate it). Meanwhile, no new religious group that entered the country after 1989 received official recognition, making Romania one of the most restrictive countries in the region in this regard. Although the communist state had transferred Greek Catholic property to the Orthodox Church, the post-communist authorities refused to settle the property-restitution issue. This position gave the Orthodox Church the upper hand, forcing some Greek Catholic congregations to organize demonstrations in parks or in the street.[11]

The new government promised a lot, but delivered relatively little. Penal Code stipulations that punished press offences, calumny, insult, and defamation of the country, were finally lifted, years after the Council of Europe had voiced its concern about the lack of guarantees for genuine independence of the mass media. Over the years, several journalists had been jailed for calumny or defamation, and only one freed by President Constantinescu. Steps were taken toward decentralizing public administration, fighting high-level corruption and organized crime, closing unprofitable mines at Valea Jiului and professionally retraining miners who lost their jobs in the process, creating a viable private banking system, and selling off public utilities and state monopolies to strategic foreign and domestic investors. The new rulers made accession to NATO and the EU their utmost priority, taking steps to reform the army, police and intelligence services, protect the rights of minorities, and create a functional market economy.

However, governmental portfolios were divided according to a political algorithm where positions were proportional to the votes obtained in the 1996 general elections. To satisfy the demands of its constituent parties, the ruling "coalition of coalitions"[12] increased the number of ministerial and deputy ministerial posts and agreed to a pernicious rotation of cadres whereby the same seat was subsequently occupied by many individuals, some appointed only for weeks. From 1996 to 2000, four different politicians served as Ministers of Health Care, while the Minister of Finance had no fewer than thirteen different deputies.[13] President Constantinescu's claim that the new coalition had 15,000 specialists ready to fill governmental positions at all levels was mocked when it became apparent that the "specialists" lacked familiarity with the domains they supervised, had been appointed for their loyalty to party leaders more than for their training and expertise, and were encouraged to think of the interests of their party more than those of the country. With limited time at their disposal, cabinet members could not understand their departments, identify and prioritize objectives, or implement long-term programs. Inefficiency was not the only problem the new rulers faced. The inability to explain their goals to the population; the unwillingness to take seriously the concerns of the impoverished population; the propensity to fight with other coalition partners rather than with the opposition; the tendency to eschew responsibility for mistakes and to blame the Social Democrats for socio-economic problems; and the lack of feasible reform targets with clear deadlines greatly eroded public confidence in the government. Predictably, the main ruling partner, the Christian Democrats, gained no parliamentary representation in 2000. Constantinescu unexpectedly withdrew from the presidential poll, and has been unable to revive his political career ever since.

The new rulers lost many hard-core supporters due to their refusal to launch transitional justice. During the presidential race Constantinescu supported lustration as a method to block the access of former communist officials and secret agents to political office, but after assuming the office he insisted that the results of the 1996 poll amounted to elite renewal, since younger, untainted specialists could replace Social Democrat public officials.[14] In practice, this elite renewal was superficial, affecting central more than local government. Looking for milder ways to come to terms with the past, the CDR turned its attention to the opening of the secret Securitate archives, but its commitment to that process was equally lukewarm. In December 1999, parliament granted Romanian citizens access to files compiled on them by the Securitate, and entrusted a National Council for the Study of Securitate Archives with the task of investigating the past of elected and nominated public officials, including the president, members of parliament and cabinet, prefects, county and municipal councilors, ambassadors, presidents of public universities, heads of public mass media outlets, managers of state-owned enterprises (SOEs) and utilities, religious leaders and priests. Because the law was not a lustration law, individuals unmasked as former secret agents were not asked to renounce their public office, but their names were published in the official gazette. The intent was to clarify the criteria used for distinguishing between angels and villains, to force the intelligence services to be more transparent and accountable, to prevent public scandals resulting from the uncontrolled release of sensitive information, and to end the manipulation of secret files by politicians seeking to discredit their rivals. In 2000 for the first time the Council investigated electoral candidates. But the benefits of both secret file access and identification of former spies from among post-communist politicians were meager, given the Information Services' refusal to open the Securitate archive, the Council's lack of independence *vis-à-vis* political parties, and the legislative loopholes permitting spies to plead not guilty of engaging in "political police" activities infringing human rights.[15] Equally notable have been changes to history books presenting the communist period in a more critical manner, describing the waves of arrests of the late 1940s and the 1950s, and reassessing Romania's partnership with the Nazi regime during the Second World War. Pre-university teachers could choose among several textbooks approved by the Ministry of Education, and university students could enroll in either public or private higher education institutions offering an unprecedented variety of degrees and specializations. While still struggling to protect their autonomy, universities were rocked by scandals of plagiarism, misconduct, and corruption involving their teaching and administrative staff.[16]

The second Iliescu regime, 2000–4

As the main parties on both the left and the right side of the political spectrum were discredited by poor governmental performance – the Social Democrats before 1996 and the CDR after 1996 – many Romanians supported the nationalists in the 2000 general elections. In the second round of the presidential elections, the PRM chauvinist leader Corneliu Vadim Tudor, a poet known as a Ceauşescu sycophant, confronted Iliescu, and only a concerted effort on the part of more liberal elements in society succeeded in preventing his election as president of Romania. Consolidation of the party system, and the disappearance of most unviable small formations, meant that only five coalitions and parties entered parliament. The new government was formed by the Party of Social Democracy (PDSR) (renamed the Social Democratic Party, PSD) and the UDMR. The opposition was represented by the PRM, the Democratic Party, and the PNL, formations that seldom saw eye to eye on policy matters. Social Democrat Adrian Năstase, a legal scholar with personal connections to the former communist *nomenklatura*, became the new prime minister.

Under Năstase's leadership, Romania took additional steps to fulfill the EU pre-accession requirements, although by 2000 it was clear that its admission would have to be postponed because of its inability to close the important chapters on agriculture, justice, and home security. A new anti-corruption bill asked public officeholders and candidates to disclose their assets, income, and interests when assuming and renouncing governmental posts. A new nationwide electronic system allowed state agencies and public utilities, banks, enterprises, schools and universities to accept bids from companies in order to conclude the most advantageous tender. A new law on transparency compelled governmental agencies to disclose unclassified information to interested citizens, and to update and maintain websites detailing their composition and activity. In 2004, Romania was welcomed into NATO, and soon thereafter started to send troops to Afghanistan and then Iraq and allowed the United States to set up a military base near the Black Sea port of Constanta. After a decade of economic contraction, Romania registered economic growth in 2000, which had reached unprecedented levels by 2004. Compared to the chronic cabinet instability of the 1996–2000 period, most of Năstase's ministers fulfilled their four-year mandates and enjoyed the support of local governments dominated by the Social Democrats.

Despite these positive signs, the Social Democrats were unable to make the most of their rule. Soon after Năstase assumed the premiership it became apparent that his tolerance of corruption and patronage was high even by Romanian standards, and that he regarded public resources as his own private assets. Although Năstase's conspicuous consumption, lavish display of possessions, arrogance, and cronyism were bitterly criticized by President Iliescu, many high-ranking Social Democrat ministers, deputy ministers, senators, deputies, and prefects continued to enrich themselves under Năstase's patronage. Notwithstanding promises made to the EU and the Romanian electorate, the fight against corruption lost its momentum, no high-ranking politician was brought to trial, and no action was taken against public officers who refused to declare their assets. Journalists probing into the connections of Social Democrat leaders with organized crime groups were threatened, censored, or intimidated, even after the opposition introduced a motion of no-confidence and the country's freedom of press ranking was downgraded from "partly free" to "not free."[17] Fearful that investigations could taint the reputation of their Social Democrat colleagues, the cabinet members obstructed the work of the Council for the Study of Securitate Archives, pressuring it into hiding the identity of former spies turned Social Democrat politicians. Dissensions between Iliescu and Năstase seriously fragmented the party, which faced the 2004 general elections at an unprecedented low.

The Băsescu regime

The 2004 presidential poll was the first in which Iliescu, the veteran of Romanian post-communist politics, did not run. In the second round of presidential elections Premier Năstase confronted Traian Băsescu, a ship's captain turned Democratic Party leader who served as Minister of Transportation in 1991–2 and 1996–2000, member of the Chamber of Deputies in 1992–6, and Bucharest Mayor in 2000–4. The highlight of the campaign was a televised debate in which Băsescu candidly admitted that Romanians had to choose between two candidates with a communist past, alluding to the fact that until 1989 both he and Năstase had occupied leadership positions or had benefited from the *nomenklatura*'s protection. That remark apparently helped Băsescu to win the first five-year presidential mandate, but his support of only 51.2% of the national vote reflected the electorate's apathy and division. The parliamentary poll allowed four coalitions and parties to gain seats. Although the PSD and the Humanistic Party (PUR) together gained a plurality of seats in each chamber and PSD leader Năstase voiced his readiness to assume the premiership, Băsescu refused all cabinet formulas which would have excluded his DA, which united the Democrats and the Liberals. Liberal Călin Popescu-Tăriceanu, a wealthy businessman, became the premier of a cabinet representing the DA, the UDMR and the Humanistic Party (later renamed the Conservative Party, PC). The Social Democrat Party and the PRM formed the opposition.

The new government was responsible for Romania's final leg of EU accession, arguably the most important stage of the process. Politically independent lawyer Monica Macovei assumed the Minister of Justice portfolio, and set out to re-launch the fight against political corruption, reform the Supreme Magistrates' Council, restructure the prison system, and align the Penal Code to European legislation. The control of mass media activity imposed by the Năstase government was lifted, and the government refrained from harassing journalists. The cabinet's concerted efforts resulted in sufficient progress to convince the EU leaders to accept Romania as a member in January 2007, with the expectation that further reforms would be carried out after accession. But the Romanian political landscape became increasingly unstable due to divergence among government partners, and between the president and the prime minister. In a development reminiscent of the CDR rule of 1996–2000, in 2004–8 government allies fought each other more than they fought the opposition, and proved unable to transcend the logic of the electoral campaign to focus on the business of running the country. Within weeks of the 2004 poll, President Băsescu voiced support for early elections, which he hoped would alter the balance of power within the Alliance, transforming it from a partnership of equals into a union where his Democrats could tower over the Liberals. More importantly, the president hoped that early elections would bring the Alliance the clear parliamentary majority it needed to dispense with the support of the Conservatives, siding with the opposition Social Democrats in key policy options. Led by the controversial Dan Voiculescu, a self-declared "media magnate" and one of Romania's richest businessmen, the party withdrew support from the government when its ministers were placed under investigation for corruption in 2006. Băsescu disliked not only Voiculescu and his Humanists, but also Popescu-Tăriceanu and his Liberals, whom he called "oligarchs" in an effort to draw attention to their involvement in corruption, abuse of power, and considerable wealth not fully accounted for (table 17.2).

Politically, the country experienced a profound crisis, and even some of the small advances made by the governments of 1996–2004 were rendered meaningless. By 2007, the legal requirement for public officials to disclose assets was ignored with impunity by all politicians, and the fight against corruption was brought to a standstill by the new Minister of Justice Teodor Chiuariu, himself placed under investigation. The number of young ministers increased, but their lack of managerial experience affected governmental performance. Even before losing the Conservatives' support, the government was a minority one, due to the lukewarm commitment of the Democrats, who wanted a share of governmental portfolios without assuming responsibility for governmental policy. In 2007, Popescu-Tăriceanu lost his Democrat ministers, but not the premiership, although his cabinet was supported by only 15% of parliament members. Despite Băsescu's insistence on early elections, his Democrats refused to see their mandates cut short and give up their lucrative local administrative positions when the party joined the opposition. The war of all against all placed Romania in an irresolvable deadlock, prompting its political class to waste time in debates lacking direction and on initiatives lacking real chances of success. On 19 April Parliament suspended President Băsescu at the request of a parliamentary commission led by Voiculescu, without explaining the reasons for the suspension. A month later, however, a popular referendum reinstated Băsescu as head of the state in a bitter victory which only deepened the estrangement between him and his Democrats, on the one hand, and Premier Popescu-Tăriceanu and his Liberals, on the other. This open conflict degenerated into personal insults traded during prime-time televised programs, and led to the death of the DA which had helped the two parties win the 2004 poll.

The political climate was also destabilized by the frequent public scandals surrounding revelations that prominent politicians had worked for the Securitate. In an unprecedented step in 2006, Băsescu ordered the Romanian Intelligence

Table 17.2 Parliamentary elections, 2000, 2004, and 2008

	2000				2004				2008			
	Chamber of Deputies		Senate		Chamber of Deputies		Senate		Chamber of Deputies		Senate	
Party	Seats	(%)	Seats	(%)	Seats	(%)	Seats	(%)	Seats	(%)	Seats	(%)
Social Democrat-Conservative National Union (Uniunea Nationala Partidul Social Democrat-Partidul Conservator, PSD–PC National Union)					132	39.7	57	41.6	114	34.1	49	35.7
Social Democrat Party (Partidul Social Democrat, PSD)	155	44.9	65	46.4								
Justice and Truth Alliance (Alianta Dreptate si Adevar, DA)					112	33.8	49	35.8				
Democrat Liberal Party (Partidul Democrat Liberal, PD–L)	31	8.9	13	9.2					115	34.4	51	37.2
National Liberal Party (Partidul National Liberal, PNL)	30	8.7	13	9.2					65	19.4	28	20.4
Democratic Union of Magyars in Romania (Uniunea Democrata a Maghiarilor din Romania, UDMR)	27	7.8	12	8.5	22	6.6	10	7.3	22	6.5	9	6.5
Greater Romania Party (Partidul Romania Mare, PRM)	84	25.6	37	26.4	48	14.5	21	15.3				
Ethnic minorities[a]	18				18				18			
Total	345	100	140	100	332	100	137	100	334	100	137	100

Note:
[a] Ethnic minorities other than the Hungarians are each allotted a deputy seat.
Source: Central Electoral Bureau.

Service to surrender the bulk of the secret archive to the Council for the Study of Securitate Archives, including files on prominent politicians, set up the Presidential Commission for the Study of Communist Dictatorship in Romania to investigate communist crimes, and officially condemned the communist regime and its abuses. By doing so, Băsescu promoted transitional justice as no other Romanian post-communist president before him. The Liberal government also furthered the process by creating a research institute, promoting lustration legislation, and initiating court trials against communist prison guards suspected of human rights abuses. The file opening showed the unsavory past of popular Liberal Minister of Culture Mona Muscă, Central European University vice-president Sorin Antohi, Braşov Mayor and Liberal leader Ioan Ghişe, Social Democrat leaders Rodica Stănoiu and Serban Mihăilescu, former Minister of Economic Reform Mircea Coşea, Conservative Party leader Dan Voiculescu, Romanian Academy member Constantin Bălăceanu-Stolnici, Orthodox Bishop of Alba Iulia Andrei Andreicuţ, Orthodox Metropolitan of Banat Nicolae Corneanu, former Orthodox Patriarch Teoctist Arăpaşu, and journalists Valentin Hossu-Longin, Carol Sebastian, and Dan Ciachir, among others. According to archival evidence, these individuals had provided the Securitate with information on their relatives, friends, neighbors, co-workers or students, but the Council failed to name them as former secret agents, claiming that they carried out no political police activities infringing fundamental human rights. Even President Băsescu and new Orthodox Patriarch Daniel Ciobotea were suspected of having engaged in secret collaboration, though no files detailing their spying activity have been found. With the exception of Muscă and Corneanu, none of those unmasked as former spies publicly apologized or gave up their public offices.

Economically, the country registered diminished growth rates, reduced inflation and unemployment, and increased productivity levels. A currency stabilization drive helped the Leu gain strength relative to the Euro, and made the country more appealing to foreign investors. A flat income tax replaced the progressive tax to discourage small businesses and employees to hide revenues, and the tax collection process was streamlined to make it more customer-friendly. The government encouraged entrepreneurship and sold the old Oltcit small car manufacturing plant to Ford, thus avoiding its closure and the ensuing lay-offs. After 2005 the country faced several unusually hot summers, mild winters and floods that spoiled harvest and destroyed dwellings, roads and bridges, prompting the government to grant limited aid to affected families. Despite commitment to classical liberal values, the Liberal government raised pensions and wages to government employees, refrained from reducing the number of public offices, and retained most social programs (including two-year-long maternity leave, "food tickets" to governmental employees, a governmental allowance for every living child, heating subsidies for the poorest families, and lower public transportation fees for pensioners and students). This governmental aid neither made the country more attractive to Romanians living abroad nor slowed down the migration of Romanian workers to Western Europe in the hope of more lucrative jobs. The sharp increase in the number of Romanians working abroad generated unprecedented social problems, as the 170,000 children left behind by their parents struggled with psychological problems, and were more likely to commit suicide, use drugs, and engage in criminal and gang activity.[18] With as much as 25% of its population living below the poverty line, Romania remains the poorest member of the EU.[19] It is also the Union's most corrupt country, where bribes, demanded by and offered to most governmental employees to do their job, account for some 20% of the ordinary citizens' income.[20]

The 2008 general elections were the first to employ a mixed-member-majority system allowing Romanians to vote for individual candidates rather than political parties. Candidates run in single-member colleges, in a college a candidate can represent only one political party, and a party can support only one candidate. Candidates who muster a simple majority of the vote in the college win the seat, all other colleges are allocated to candidates in proportion to the votes their respective parties receive at district and national levels. As parliament has remained one of the country's least-trusted institutions, the electoral reform sought to make the legislature more efficient and accountable to electors, correct for the legislators' rampant absenteeism, prevent them from crossing the floor, and ultimately lead to the emergence of a new, reform oriented political elite. But the poll revealed the shortcomings of the new system: political parties remained stronger than individual candidates, and the system worked for large, consolidated parties and against independent candidates and smaller and newer formations. As a result, Romanian political parties intend to enact electoral changes in the near future.

The 2008 elections further consolidated the Romanian party system. For the first time since 1990, the nationalists did not enter parliament, but the Social Democrats (running together with the Conservative Party) garnered the largest number of votes, as in all other previous polls. President Băsescu's Democratic Liberals (PD–L, the former Democrats) garnered the most seats, followed closely by the Social Democrats. The Liberals and the UDMR also gained parliamentary representation (see table 17.2). While the elections seemed likely to bring the Democrat Liberals to government, and their arch-enemy Social Democrats to opposition, the two parties unexpectedly formed the government together. The new government, which enjoys the support of more than 70% of all members of parliament, is led by Democrat Liberal leader Emil Boc and includes twenty ministers equally divided between the two parties. An initial Social Democrat promise to extend the social safety network was scuttled and, instead, the government undertook to protect the country against the international economic crisis by controlling inflation, monitoring budgetary spending, and reducing the national deficit.

Romania as an EU member

Keenly supported by the political elite, the civil society, and the general public, accession into the EU in 2007 was regarded as a long-overdue recognition of Romania's rightful place among European states from a geographic, historic, political, and cultural viewpoint. To date, the small group of Euroskeptics, led by the nationalist Greater Romania Party and the traditionalist Romanian Orthodox Church, has remained marginalized, but it could attract new adherents if the promised advantages of accession fail to materialize in the future.[21] For now, ordinary Romanians, together with the Bulgarians, are content to enjoy the benefits of being the youngest members of the European family. Many Romanians travel freely to Western Europe for either pleasure or for work, and are proud that a growing number of the citizens of neighboring countries visit Romania. The hope is that the income gap between them and the other EU citizens will close soon, and Romanian children will be able to study in European schools.

Despite the Romanians' positive attitude towards the EU project, the political leaders have proven less ready to adapt their mores to European standards. In fact, the Romanian political elite does not seem to take the EU recommendations, deadlines, and warnings seriously. After waiting longer than their neighbors to join the Union, the Romanian politicians have lost interest in the issue, and seem convinced that, no matter how little they work towards fulfilling the accession and integration criteria, the Union will never punish them drastically by rescinding the country membership. While steps have been taken to ensure the independence of the judiciary, Romanian politicians are still able to influence the outcome of trials and to avoid prosecution by intimidating or buying out judges. The investigative anti-corruption departments have acquired little space for maneuver relative to the government, which can restructure and dismantle them when the accused are friends of the government, not opposition leaders. The decision of the Popescu–Tăriceanu government to postpone the country's first Euro elections met with little resistance from the political class. Some of this apathy could stem from the fact that the Union still treats Romania as a second-class member. Romania has therefore proven incapable of accessing the bulk of the funds the Union set aside to improve infrastructure, upgrade education, or revive agriculture and tourism. President Băsescu has talked about a Bucharest–London–Washington axis, and the country seems closer to the United States than to the EU in its foreign policy and military strategy.

When the country was asked to name its EU commissioner, its first choice was rejected for trivial reasons. Leonard Orban was appointed commissioner, receiving the portfolio of multiculturalism, an administrative more than a political position requiring him to oversee the translation of official EU documents. Critics have argued that the post's minor importance reflects the limited importance given to Romania by the EU leaders.

Conclusion

A Balkan country with a tortuous communist past and a bloody regime change, Romania has faced many roadblocks on its way to effect successful post-communist transition. The unreformed communist regime prevented the formation of opposition groups capable of wresting power from the Ceaușescu family. Its greedy and largely unrestrained communist elite retained considerable political clout, dictating the rules of the game, allowing liberalization only when it benefited its interests, and even outwitting naïve and impatient EU leaders. The Romanian public remains despondent, apathetic, and ignorant of its political rights and of political mechanisms. However, since the 1990s Romania has made significant strides toward establishing liberal democracy and a market economy and gaining acceptance into the larger European family. While corruption remains pervasive, the country has effected political change peacefully through elections and nationalist sentiment has declined considerably since EU accession. Citizens and politicians alike need to continue to work toward bridging the gap that separates the country from its neighbors.

Timeline 1989–2007

25 December 1989	Nicolae and Elena Ceauşescu are executed
20 May 1990	Following first post-communist general elections, Ion Iliescu wins presidency, and National Salvation Front secures a majority of seats in parliament.
13–15 June 1990	Valea Jiului miners descend upon Bucharest, ransacking University of Bucharest classrooms and terrorizing residents, Iliescu later thanks them
24–28 September 1991	Premier Petre Roman steps down after miners return to Bucharest at Iliescu's request.
4 October 1993	Romania joins Council of Europe
November 1996	Emil Constantinescu becomes president, and Democratic Convention secures majority of seats in parliament in the first alternation of power in Romania in fifty years
20 January 1999	Some 10,000 Valea Jiului miners move toward Bucharest, but are stopped at the Cozia monastery, where an agreement is signed by cabinet and miners' representatives.
November 2000	Ion Iliescu returns as president, while Social Democrats form the government
29 March 2004	Romania joins NATO
November 2004	Traian Băsescu becomes president, and Justice and Truth Alliance (DA) forms government
18 December 2006	President Băsescu officially condemns communist regime
1 January 2007	Romania joins EU

Fact sheet

Area	237,500 km^2
Population (July 2008)	22,246,862
Romanian	89.5%
Hungarian	6.6%
Roma	2.5%

Ukranian	0.3%
German	0.3%
Russian	0.2%
Turkish	0.2%
Other	0.4%
Major cities	
Bucharest (January 2006)	1,930,390
Iasi (July 2004)	317,812
Cluj (January 2007)	311,391
Timisoara (July 2004)	307,365
Below the poverty line (June 2007)	25% of population
Unemployment rate (October 2006)	7.6%
GDP *per capita* (January 2007)	$8,800
Higher education (2006)	12% of population
Literacy rate (2003)	
Adult male	0.9%
Adult female	2.3%

Source: Wikipedia.

Political parties represented in parliament (September 2007)

Party	Chamber of Deputies	Senate
Social Democratic Party (PSD)	113	46
National Liberal Party (PNL)	64	28
Democratic Party (PD)	48	21
Greater Romania Party (PRM)	48	21
Democratic Union of Magyars in Romania (UDMR)	22	10
Conservative Party (PC)	19	11
Minorities	18	–
Total	332	137

Source: Chamber of Deputies.

Short biography of Ion Iliescu

No other politician has dominated the Romanian post-communist landscape more than Ion Iliescu, a fact attesting to the ambivalent and protracted nature of the country's transformation. Iliescu, president of Romania from 1990 to 1996 and from 2000 to 2004, is credited with stabilizing the country, helping it to join NATO and the EU, and teaching his former communist collaborators to peacefully renounce their positions after being voted out. His critics accuse him of retaining communist convictions, tolerating corruption, opposing an honest re-evaluation of the communist past, and engaging in crimes against humanity and abuse of power during the revolution of December 1989 and his 1990–1 rule.

Born on 3 March 1930 in the small town of Olteniţa, Iliescu was the son of a rail worker with communist views who spent the 1930s in the Soviet Union before returning to Romania to die in prison. Iliescu studied fluid mechanics at the Bucharest Polytechnic Institute and Moscow University, where he also served as secretary of the Association of Romanian Students. Upon his return to Bucharest he joined the Communist Party in 1953, becoming secretary of the Central Committee of the Union of Communist Youth in 1956, member of the Central Committee of the Communist Party in 1965, and Minister of Youth in 1967. While initially supportive of Iliescu's career, in 1971 Ceauşescu removed Iliescu from all major political offices to thwart the ascension of a contender viewed as his heir apparent. Iliescu served as vice-president of the Timiş county (1971–4) and president of the Iaşi county (1974–9), but was further sidelined in the 1980s, as Ceauşescu's rule became more personalized, megalomaniac, and erratic. After being excluded from the Central Committee in 1984, Iliescu served as head of the party-controlled Editura Politică until 1989.

His political career got a new lease of life in December of that year, when he emerged as leader of the anti-Ceauşescu camp, but not of the anti-communist forces. He was elected as Romania's first post-communist president by a landslide in 1990, and then again in 1992 and 2000, although by the constitution a person could occupy the office only twice in a lifetime. Iliescu opposed radical political and economic reforms, including the restitution of abusively confiscated property, the ban on communist decision-makers engaging in post-communist politics (lustration), and the dismantling of agricultural collectives. In June 1990 and September 1991, he asked the Valea Jiului miners to come to Bucharest to "defend" his government from peaceful anti-communist protesters dissatisfied with the pace of reforms. In 1990 the miners ransacked the University of Bucharest, beat up onlookers, and shouted "We work! We don't think!," while in 1991 they forced Premier Petre Roman to resign. After losing the 1996 presidential campaign to Emil Constantinescu, Iliescu represented the Social Democrats in the Senate. He helped the party to consolidate its social base, and win the 2000 poll. While still honorary president of the Social Democrats, in the spring of 2005 he was succeeded as party leader by the much younger, but less experienced, Mircea Geoană.

Notes

1. The weakness of civil society is discussed in, and the sultanism-cum-totalitarianism label was proposed by, Juan J. Linz and Alfred Stepan, *Problems of Democratic Transition and Consolidation: Southern Europe, South America, and Post-Communist Europe* (Baltimore, Md.: Johns Hopkins University Press, 1996), pp. 344–65.
2. Peter Gross, *Entangled Evolutions: Media and Democratization in Eastern Europe* (Washington, DC: Woodrow Wilson Center Press, 2002).
3. Kieran Williams and Dennis Deletant, *Security Intelligence Services in New Democracies: The Czech Republic, Slovakia and Romania* (Houndmills: Palgrave, 2001).
4. Lavinia Stan, *Leaders and Laggards: Governance, Civicness and Ethnicity in Post-Communist Romania* (Boulder, Colo.: East European Monographs, 2003).
5. In January 1999 the miners were unable to reach the capital. See John Gledhill, "States of Contention: State-Led Political Violence in Post-Socialist Romania," *East European Politics and Societies*, Vol. 19, No. 1 (2005), pp. 76–104.

6. "Chronology for Roma in Romania" (College Park, Md., 12 September 2007), at www.cidcm.umd.edu/mar/chronology.asp?groupId=36003.
7. Tom Gallagher, *Romania after Ceaușescu* (Edinburgh: Edinburgh University Press, 1995).
8. Lavinia Stan (ed.), *Romania in Transition* (Aldershot: Ashgate, 1997).
9. Robert D. Kaplan, "The Fulcrum of Europe: Romania Longs for the West, and the West Needs Romania more than it Knows," *The Atlantic Monthly* (September 1998).
10. *Evenimentul Zilei* (15 May 1998), p. 4.
11. Lavinia Stan and Lucian Turcescu, *Religion and Politics in Post-Communist Romania* (New York: Oxford University Press, 2007).
12. Michael Shafir, "The Ciorbea Government and Democratization: A Preliminary Assessment," in Duncan Light and David Phinnemore (eds.), *Post-Communist Romania: Coming to Terms with Transition* (Houndmills: Palgrave, 2001), pp. 84–90.
13. Lavinia Stan, "Comparing Post-Communist Governance: A Case Study," *Journal of Communist Studies and Transition Politics*, Vol. 18, No. 3 (September 2002), p. 85.
14. Emil Constantinescu, *Timpul darimarii, timpul zidirii* (Bucharest: Editura Du Style, 2002).
15. Lavinia Stan, "Spies, Files and Lies: Explaining the Failure of Access to Securitate Files," *Communist and Post-Communist Studies*, Vol. 37, No. 3 (September 2004), pp. 341–59.
16. Lavinia Stan and Lucian Turcescu, "Politicians, Intellectuals and Academic Integrity in Romania," *Problems of Post-Communism*, Vol. 51, No. 4 (2004), pp. 12–24.
17. See Press Freedom Rankings 2001, World Audit (n.p., 3 October 2007), at www.worldaudit.org/press.htm.
18. Georgiana Toth, Alexandru Toth, Ovidiu Voicu, and Mihaela Stefanescu, *Efectele migratiei: copii romani acasa* (Bucharest: Fundatia Soros, 2007).
19. "Population below Poverty Line," *CIA World Factbook* (14 July 2007), at www.nationmaster.com/graph/eco_pop_bel_pov_lin-economy-population-below-poverty-line.
20. *Diagnostic Surveys of Corruption in Romania* (Washington, DC: World Bank, 2001).
21. Lavinia Stan and Razvan Zaharia, "Romania," *European Journal of Political Research*, Vol. 46, No. 7–8 (December 2006), p. 1088.

Further reading

Carey, Henry F. (ed.). *Romania since 1989: Politics, Economics and Society* (Lanham, Md.: Lexington Books, 2004)

Gallagher, Tom. *Modern Romania: The End of Communism, the Failure of Democratic Reform, and the Theft of a Nation* (New York: New York University Press, 2005)

Romania and the European Union: How the Weak Vanquished the Strong (Manchester: Manchester University Press, 2009)

Georgescu, Vlad. *The Romanians: A History* (Columbus, Oh.: Ohio State University Press, 1991)

Iliescu, Ion with Vladimir Tismaneanu. *Communism, Post-Communism and Democracy: The Great Shock at the End of a Short Century* (Boulder, Colo.: East European Monographs, 2005)

Phinnemore, Davis (ed.). *The EU and Romania: Great Expectations* (London: The Federal Trust, 2007)

Roper, Steven. *Romania: The Unfinished Revolution* (London: Routledge, 2000)

Siani-Davies, Peter. *The Romanian Revolution of December 1989* (Ithaca, NY: Cornell University Press, 2007)

Tismaneanu, Vladimir. *Stalinism for All Seasons: A Political History of Romanian Communism* (Berkeley Calif.: University of California Press, 2003).

18

Bulgaria since 1989

MARIA SPIROVA

As a small Balkan country on the edge of the European continent, Bulgaria attracts little international attention. It has not seen any of the violent conflicts that have troubled most of the rest of Southeastern Europe, nor has it been among the best political and economic performers in the region during the post-communist era. Nonetheless, in 2007, Bulgaria is substantially different from the Soviet satellite it was in 1989. Today, the country is a member of both NATO and the EU, and has a stable democracy and a functioning market economy.

But if Bulgaria's transition from one-party communist rule to a multi party political system was not violent, the country had difficulty in adjusting to the challenges of a free-market economic system, most of which were the result of its recent history. Prior to 1989, the country was characterized by prolonged periods of foreign domination, dependence on its trading partners in the Soviet bloc, and several non-democratic regimes, with only brief periods of democratic development. Consequently, when the political system opened up to allow for the establishment of democratic values and institutions, Bulgaria experienced numerous, and often daunting, challenges in reforming or replacing its existing political, economic, and social systems.

Despite these difficulties, the transformation of the country since 1989 has been impressive. Bulgaria's transformation consisted of three distinct, but often interrelated, processes: the dismantling of the pre-1990 one-party state, the establishment of a multiparty democracy, liberal society, and a market economy; and the gradual adoption of European norms, policies, and practices. Although distinct, these processes tended to reinforce one another; so as the Bulgarian commitment to EU integration solidified and negotiations got underway, the impact of the EU became increasingly felt and in many ways undistinguishable from the domestic process of change. In 2007, Bulgaria was admitted into the EU, confirmation that its people had established a stable democracy with a functioning market economy, the rule of law, protection of human rights, and guarantees for the country's minorities.

Bulgaria until 1989

Bulgaria's history has been characterized by long periods of foreign domination. Having been founded in the late seventh century, the first Bulgarian kingdom reached it highest point in the ninth century, under the rule of Kings (Tsar) Boris I and Simeon I. It was during that time that Christianity was adopted and the Cyrillic alphabet was created and introduced and territorial expansion was at its highest. However, by 1018 Bulgaria had been overtaken by Byzantium and remained under its rule until the late twelfth century. The independence of the second Bulgarian Kingdom was also short-lived – 1396 marked the defeat of the Bulgarian King Shishman by the Ottoman Empire. Bulgaria spent the next 500 years as a subjugated nation under Turkish rule, a period that has left its legacy on Bulgarian culture, politics, and everyday life.

The Bulgarian national revival was a movement for both political and ecclesiastical autonomy that developed during the nienteenth century as a response to the decay of the Ottoman Empire and the national liberation movements in Greece and Serbia. In 1876, it organized a national uprising which was not only limited in scale but also violently put down by the Ottomans. Bulgarian liberation from Turkish rule came as a result of the Russian–Turkish War of 1877–8. The Berlin Peace Treaty established half of the country as an autonomous state and left the other half as a sovereign territory in the Ottoman Empire. The country was unified following a war with Serbia in 1885, and in 1908 Bulgaria became an independent state. Politically, Bulgaria was set up as a monarchy with a parliament and active political parties. The Saxe-Coburg-Gotha dynasty assumed the throne in 1887.

The early twentieth century saw the country engulfed in several wars – two Balkan Wars were fought over territory disputes among the Balkan nations, and Bulgaria allied with Germany during the First World War in an effort to re-claim some of the territories lost during the Balkan Wars. Following the defeat in 1918, Bulgaria experienced a high level of political turmoil: a military coup took place in 1923, followed by peasant- and communist-led uprisings, and in 1934 King Boris II abolished political parties and imposed authoritarian rule.

Bulgaria joined the losing side again during the Second World War, and afterwards, with the help of the Red Army, the "fatherland front" forces (i.e. the parties that opposed the King and his regime) in the country took power. The Bulgarian Communist Party (BKP) quickly usurped control over the politics of the new government and by the late 1940s it had virtually established a one-party state and was on the path to building a collective economy. Bulgaria spent most of the second half of the twentieth century as the most loyal ally of the Soviet Union. The political and economic systems were re-structured accordingly and no major challenges to the regime emerged until the late 1980s.

Transition to democracy

As in most of the region, the end of the Bulgarian one-party political system came in November 1989. However, unlike other countries of the region, such as Czechoslovakia or Poland, in Bulgaria this happened through what has been called "an internal coup within the Bulgarian Communist Party (BKP)."[1] This provided for the dominance of the BKP during the initial stages of the liberalization and democratization of the regime. Initially, the political opposition in Bulgaria was scattered, poorly organized, and without any coherent programs. The Round Table Talks (RTT) that established some of the first democratic institutions in the country were therefore organized by the BKP, and although the talks legitimized the first fledgling opposition groups, the first free elections were won by the BKP.

Opposition groups were slow to emerge in Bulgaria. The most prominent among them were the environmental group "Ekoglasnost" and the "Club in Support of Glasnost and Perestroika in Bulgaria." Although they had gained some visibility by the summer and fall of 1989, the pressure for reform that they exercised was relatively insignificant. Some additional pressure came from the Bulgarian intelligentsia – in the spring of 1989 professional organizations of writers, journalists, and actors began to express their dissatisfaction with the developments in the country, which were falling short even of the *perestroika* and *glasnost* reforms in the USSR.[2]

The biggest challenge to the regime initially came from the Turkish minority rather than from neoliberal parties. For years the Communist Party had carried out assimilation campaigns against the citizens of ethnic Turkish origin, culminating in the forced changing of their names and surnames to Bulgarian equivalents in the summer of 1985. Four years later, the Turkish minority, organized by the clandestine Turkish National Liberation Movement in Bulgaria (NOD), staged public protests, some of which were put down violently. These led to international outrage and domestic criticism, and the ethnic Bulgarian intelligentsia, which had until then been quiet, began to call for the respect of minority rights in the country. In an attempt to silence both, the BKP opened up the Bulgarian borders and "allowed" the Bulgarian Turks to "choose their homeland."[3] Taking this invitation more as encouragement to leave than a free choice to remain in Bulgaria or emigrate to Turkey, over 300,000 of Bulgaria's ethnic Turks left the country, taking as many of their possessions as they could, leaving Bulgaria in political, economic, and social disarray.[4]

Partially in response to challenges from the Turkish minority and an embryonic opposition, dissatisfaction among growing segments of the intelligentsia, and embarrassment at the adverse publicity attendant on the coerced emigration of 300,000 ethnic Turks, reformers within the BKP engineered the resignation of its General Secretary, Todor Zhivkov, on 10 November 1989, which allowed for the initial liberalization of the regime. The new BKP General Secretary and party leaders, among them Petar Mladenov, Andrey Lukanov, and Alexander Lilov, called for the rehabilitation of political prisoners and blamed Zhivkov for the economic, financial, and political crisis in the country. But they did not appear to offer any serious promise of democratization. Although party leaders were prepared to liberalize the political and economic systems of the existing communist regime, they were not ready to question the leading role of the BKP or socialist economic principles. Radical change of the sort already underway in Poland and Czechoslovakia thus seemed unlikely.

At this point, developments in the country took on a momentum of their own. Historic parties that had been banned in the mid-1940s, such as the Democratic Party (DP) and the Social Democratic Party (SDP), re-emerged after 1989 and new political groups were created. The Union of Democratic Forces (SDS), formed on 7 December 1989, united most opposition groups under an umbrella organization. On 14 December 1989, the BKP leadership introduced an amendment to the Bulgarian constitution that removed the provision about the leading role of the BKP, and the Bulgarian parliament promulgated legislation that allowed the Turkish minority to reclaim their Turkish names. The RTT between the BKP (renamed the Bulgarian Socialist Party, BSP) and the opposition were held from January until May 1990. Although chaired and controlled by the BSP, the talks legitimized the newly formed SDS as the main opposition party and led to agreements regarding multiparty elections.

The decisions taken at the RTT set the stage for the first democratic elections in Bulgaria. Scheduled for June 1990, they were to elect 400 members of a Grand National Assembly. Unique among the countries of the region whose statehood had not been interrupted, the primary task of the first democratically elected Assembly was to draft and approve a new constitution for democratic Bulgaria. Bulgaria was also unique in that the first democratic elections returned the BSP to power, despite the high hopes of the SDS. Dissatisfaction with the results and allegations of irregularities during the elections led to massive protests organized by the SDS and joined by university students and Sofia residents throughout the summer of 1990 which the government was not able to control. Following an attempt to set the old BKP party headquarters on fire in late August, Petar Mladenov resigned as president, further evidence of the inability of the BSP to govern in the face of widespread public discontent.[5]

The Grand National Assembly convened in the summer of 1990, signaling the beginning of Bulgarian democratic decision-making. Several features made its position difficult. While it was given the crucial task of formulating basic political principles and creating an entirely new institutional structure for the country, it was also expected to act as a normal national assembly and to pass a wide range of urgently needed legislation. However, its legitimacy was compromised because the parties gathered in the SDS continued to employ non-parliamentary means to achieve their ends, and the governing BSP was either unable or unwilling to prevent them from doing so. Nonetheless, despite the opposition's criticisms and the BSP's tenuous grip on power, which created an atmosphere of institutional and political instability, the new legislation adopted by the Grand National Assembly, and the institutions created during 1990 and 1991, set the stage for the democratic political development of the country over the following decades.

Building democratic institutions

Political parties

Political parties developed in a polarized environment for most of the 1990s, gravitating toward either the BSP or the SDS, which tended to occupy the extreme ends of the political spectrum. The BSP remained relatively unreformed until 1995, so in terms of both support for market reform and European integration the party lagged substantially behind most of its post-communist counterparts. Although it lost the 1991 parliamentary elections, its defeat was not serious enough to succeed in bringing about real change in the party. Having narrowly won the 1991 elections, the SDS could not govern without the support of the third party in Parliament, the Turkish-dominated Movement for Rights and Freedoms (DPS). When interparty problems led to the withdrawal of DPS support in late 1992, the BSP politicians were probably the biggest winners, because the "expert" government that was subsequently formed could survive only with the BSP's support. The early elections in late 1994 again returned the BSP to power, and they continued to govern until 1997, when the BSP Prime Minister Videnov was forced to resign in the wake of a dramatic economic and financial crisis. In the process, the BSP lost its legitimacy and was forced to reconsider its ideological and policy positions. By the early twenty-first century, the BSP had come to advocate a social-democratic platform, embracing the principles of a market economy, and supporting a pro-EU and pro-NATO foreign policy.[6]

At the other end of the spectrum, the anti-communist opposition had gathered within the SDS. Founded in 1989 as a single political entity within which eleven diverse parties maintained separate organizations, the SDS proved fissiparous and soon began to experience a chronic factionalism. The first rift appeared as early as late 1990, when some SDS MPs began to cooperate with the BSP majority in the Grand National Assembly while some refused and maintained their extra-parliamentary opposition of the ruling party. The 1991 elections thus saw three different SDS splinter groups compete with the original SDS for the anti-communist vote. Not surprisingly, only the original SDS made it into parliament, while the others contributed to an extremely high level of vote wastage at the 1991 election.[7] Factionalism continued to plague the party through the early 1990s, and not until 1996–7 did its leadership realize that the only way to achieve a stable position in Bulgarian politics was by building unified structures and formulating a clear ideology. During 1997 and 1998, as the BSP was suffering a loss of legitimacy, the SDS registered itself as a single political party and began to behave as such.[8] From its formation in 1989, the SDS had been consistent in advocating the country's integration into the Western European and North Atlantic communities, and by the mid-1990s it had adopted a center-right domestic political platform.

Although the BSP and SDS dominated Bulgarian politics during the 1990s, a number of smaller political parties struggled for "survival between the poles."[9] The most important of these was the DPS, a *de facto* ethnic party representing the relatively well-mobilized Turkish minority. Because ethnic parties are banned by the 1991 Bulgarian constitution, the legality of the DPS was questioned at numerous times during the early 1990s. However, by not having an openly stated ethnic platform and by including ethnic Bulgarians in both its membership and its leadership, the DPS managed to maintain a stable base among voters and to deflect charges that it was primarily an ethnic party, even though it clearly represented the interests of the Turkish minority in Bulgaria.[10]

The 2001 elections transformed the bipolar nature of the Bulgarian party system with the successful entry of a major new contender in the electoral lists, the National Movement Simeon the Second (NDSV).[11] The NDSV was built around the personality of the Bulgarian ex-monarch, Simeon Saxe-Coburg-Gotha, but most of its policies focused on economic and financial issues, and its leader urged the Bulgarian people to abandon partisanship and to unify around "historical ideas and values."[12] The NDSV swept the 2001 elections and in alliance with the DPS took over the government of the country. In the meantime, the SDS experienced a new wave of internal fissures, and the BSP transformed itself into a social-democratic party.

The increasing pluralism of the party system was evident in the results of the 2005 elections, which sent seven parties to parliament and created the most potentially unstable political situation in the sixteen-year history of Bulgarian democracy. In addition to the NDSV, DPS, BSP, and SDS, three new parties and alliances contested elections and won seats in parliament (see table 18.1 for the election results). One of the new contestants, the Bulgarian National Union (BNS), was a centrist alliance of parties which had previously been part of, or allied with, the SDS. The other new parties were Democrats for a Strong Bulgaria (DSB), a conservative splinter from the SDS, and Ataka, a right-wing populist party. Since no party had a working majority in parliament, the socialist BSP, the liberal NDSV, and the ethnic DPS formed a three-party coalition cabinet.

By 2007, the Bulgarian party system was clearly in flux. With the exception of the BSP and DPS, none of the other parties seemed to have stable electoral bases and clear links to specific sectors of Bulgarian society, raising questions regarding their ability to maintain themselves as viable political parties; factionalism and fractionalization continued. During the May 2007 elections for the European Parliament, and local elections in October, yet another "populist party," Citizens for European Development of Bulgaria (GERB),

Table 18.1 Bulgarian election results, 2005 elections (40th National Assembly)

Party/Alliance	% of the vote	Number of seats	% seats
Bulgarian Socialist Party (BSP) and alliance	30.95	82	33.98
National Movement Simeon II (NDSV)	19.88	53	21.80
Movement for Rights and Freedoms (DPS)	12.81	34	14.07
Ataka	8.14	21	8.93
Union of Democratic Forces (SDS) and alliance	7.68	20	8.44
Democrats for a Strong Bulgaria (DSB)	6.40	17	7.07
Bulgarian National Union (BNS)	5.19	13	5.70
Others	8.95	240	100

emerged as a major – and successful – contender for power. GERB continued to grow and swept the 2009 national elections, promising (once again) to bring new faces into politics. The elections continued the trend of fluidity and volatility begun in 2001; faced with continued and increasing criticism from Brussels about the level of corruption and clientelism, two of the incumbent parties lost heavily. The BSP won a little under 18% of the votes, while the NDSV did not even make it into parliament. The DPS maintained its traditional vote base and secured some 14% of the votes and a comfortable parliamentary presence. A new party – Order, Lawfulness, Justice (RZS) – edged its way into the National Assembly with 4.13% of the votes, while the center-right unified into the Blue Coalition (SK) and emerged as the most likely coalition partner of GERB with some 7% of the votes. These developments clearly raised questions concerning the stability of the system and its ability effectively to channel and represent popular interests, particularly given that, with the exception of the BSP and DPS, Bulgarian parties tend to be strongly elitist and often lack specific and consistent principles, ideas, and policies.

Electoral rules

One of the peculiar developments of Bulgarian politics since 1989 has been the increase in the number of political parties. Unlike other countries in the region, the number of entrants in the electoral competition, as well as the number of successful competitors, has not declined over the years. Both the electoral and the parliamentary arena have seen a consistently high number of parties competing for office. The explanation for this peculiar development lies at least in part in the electoral rules of the country, which encourage a large number of competing political parties.

Since the 1991 parliamentary elections, Bulgaria has used a system of proportional representation (PR). The 1990 elections to the Grand National Assembly had used a mixed system which allowed for half of all seats to be elected in majority, single-member districts and the other half to be chosen from regional PR lists. However, as agreed upon during the RTT, this system was to be used only for electing the Grand National Assembly, and a new system was adopted by the Assembly and remained in use until 2001.

The electoral system used between 1991 and 2001 introduced thirty-one regional districts that were based on the country's territorial units. Each of the country's twenty-eight administrative regions also represented an electoral district, and the capital city of Sofia was divided into three additional districts. Parties ran lists of candidates in each region, but the distribution of seats was based on results at the national level. Despite some attempts to tinker with the level of the threshold and the perennial attempts of electoral reform, this "relatively unusual" system remained in effect until 2001, when a new electoral law was introduced.[13] However, the main features of the electoral procedure – in terms of threshold, counting method, and distribution method – have remained the same.[14]

Seats are now allocated only to parties that pass a 4% national threshold, and there are no special requirements for electoral alliances and coalitions.[15] Any "surplus" percentage points that have been won by parties which failed to surmount the 4% threshold are then redistributed proportionally to the parties which did manage to surmount the threshold. But proportionality is preserved at the national level, so each party gets as many seats in parliament as its national electoral share dictates. The more successful contenders there are, the more complicated the system of allocation becomes, and occasionally parties trade votes from different regions. As a result, the connection between elected and electors, already tenuous in a party-list system, becomes even more so, as people see their votes translated into seats in a way that is as dependent on the bargaining among the national headquarters of the various parties as on the popular vote.

Another unusual feature of the Bulgarian PR system is its permissiveness. In fact, the system was introduced precisely because its relatively low threshold and the D'Hondt counting method used to distribute the remaining votes after full quotas have been distributed to the parties promised to allow the representation of smaller parties in parliament (it is one of the most proportional, and thus gives the least advantage to the big parties). Encouraged by the low threshold, new parties form while factions from established ones often choose to split from the main party and run independently. Because the electoral system applies the same electoral threshold for all electoral contestants, there are no disincentives for parties to form alliances.[16] Parties therefore tend to try to bring their votes together "mechanically" by forming pre-electoral alliances that rarely survive more than one electoral cycle. This tendency has led to the further distancing of parties and their leaders from their supporters, because a party's leadership is often perceived as devoid of both ideological principles and consistent policies. The Bulgarian electoral system has thus been seen as encouraging the proliferation of unsuccessful parties and the formation of disparate and short-lived alliances during electoral campaigns.

Governmental system

The 1991 constitution established a parliamentary form of government with a unicameral legislature and a directly elected, but relatively weak, president. The president acts as a head of state, while the government, which exercises the executive functions of governing, is led by a prime minister. The constitution also set up an independent judiciary and a Constitutional Court to safeguard the rule of law and the constitutional principles in the country.

The Bulgarian constitution has not been amended as the result of domestic pressure, but it has been amended as a result of EU accession. The European Commission was particularly concerned to assure the independence, efficiency, and transparency of the judiciary in Bulgaria, and prior to 2006 the country's constitution was amended to strengthen the independence of high judicial officers. Another amendment has given foreigners the right to own land in Bulgaria and, on the urging of the EU Commissioner, Bulgaria in 2006 again amended its constitution to increase the powers of the Prosecutor General and the ombudsman, and to transfer some powers from the Supreme Judicial Council to the Ministry of the Judiciary.[17]

As the parliamentary nature of the political system suggests, the government in Bulgaria is directly accountable to the 240-member parliament, whose support the government needs to remain in power. Between 1990 and 1997, Bulgaria's fissiparous party system and the constant flux within the political system as a whole resulted in substantial variations in the composition of successive parliaments and a certain instability of governing cabinets. During this period, no parliament or government completed its constitutional term. Six quite different cabinets governed the country during this period, introducing haphazard reforms and reversing each other's policies. As a result, economic and social reforms proceeded slowly and fitfully (see table 18.2 for a list of Bulgarian cabinets and their parliamentary support and opposition since 1990).

Since 1997, both parliamentary and governmental stability have improved substantially. Ironically, as table 18.2 demonstrates, the *decrease* in instability happened despite an *increased* number of parties in parliament over the past decade. This trend can be explained, at least partially, by a moderate political climate and the adoption of relatively bland policies during the late 1990s by most parties, which succeeded in taming or ridding themselves of their most extreme factions and moving toward the center of the political spectrum. The BSP accepted the inevitability of a liberal market economy and a pro-European and pro-NATO foreign policy; the SDS came to accept the BSP as a normal political partner and gave up its extreme anti-communist posture of the early 1990s; and the NDSV's platform and policies differed little from those of the SDS. During the early 2000s, as Bulgaria came closer to realizing its goal of joining both NATO and the EU, direct and indirect external pressure further encouraged moderation and helped to complete the transformation of Bulgaria's political system and the parties within it to conform to Western European norms.

Table 18.2 Bulgarian parliaments and cabinets, 1990–2007

Parliament	Government period and prime minister	Parties in government and seat share in parliament (%)	Parties in opposition and seat in parliament (%)
Grand National Assembly (1990–1)	1990 Lukanov (BSP)	BSP 211 (53)	SDS 144 (36) MRF 23 (5.75) BZNS 16 (4)
	1990–1 Popov (IND)	Caretaker	
36th National Assembly (1991–4)	1991–2 Dimitrov (SDS)	SDS 110 (46) DPS[a] 24 (10)	BSP 106 (44)
	1992–4 Berov (IND)	DPS 24 (10) BSP 106 (44)	SDS 110 (46)
	1994 Indjova (IND)	Caretaker	
37th National Assembly (1994–7)	1995–7 Videnov (BSP)	BSP 125 (52)	SDS 69 (28), BZNS–DP 18 (7.5), DPS 15 (6.3) BBB 13 (5.4)
	1997 Sofianski (SDS)	Caretaker	
38th National Assembly (1997–2001)	1997–2001 Kostov (SDS)	ODS 137 (57)	BSP 58 (24) DPS 19 (8) EvroLef 14 (5.8) BBB 12 (5)
39th National Assembly (2001–5)	2001–5 Sakskoburggotski (NDSV)	NDSV 120 (50) DPS 21 (8.75)	ODS 51 (21.25) BSP 48 (20)
40th National Assembly (2005–)	2005–9 Stanishev (BSP)	BSP 82 (34) NDSV 53 (22) DPS 34 (14)	Ataka 21 (8.75) ODS 20 (8.3) DSB 17 (7) BNS 13 (5.4)

Note:
[a] The DPS supported the SDS cabinet in parliament but did not participate in the actual government.

Safeguarding democracy: media freedom and minority rights

The media

Multiple sources of information free of state control were among the first demands of the Bulgarian opposition after the fall of Zhivkov in 1989. While the liberalization of the print media happened quickly, the end of the state's monopoly of the electronic media came much more slowly. However, despite the privatization of Bulgaria's media and constitutional guarantees, freedom of both the print and electronic media have remained somewhat problematic through 2007.

The first issue of *Demokratsiya* (Democracy), a newspaper published by the SDS, came out in February 1990. Other independent media followed, and by 1992 there were 920 newspapers with a total circulation of 1,098,000. However, the pressures of the free market proved to be as strong a constraint on the proliferation of media as state control, and by the late 1990s economic realities had forced more than half of these newspapers to close. By 2005, there were only 423 newspapers in Bulgaria with a circulation of 310,000, a third as many as in 1992.[18] State influence over the press has virtually disappeared, but most newspapers are now affiliated with a handful of corporate groups, so the print media is once again controlled by a small elite, who can, and apparently do, prevent divergent views from being reported. According to both domestic and international observers, press freedom in Bulgaria has slumped substantially since the mid-1990s, and in 2006 Bulgaria ranked 51st in the world in terms of press freedom, substantially lower than other EU members.[19]

In the broadcasting sector, change came more slowly, owing to the absence of appropriate legislation. Radio and television therefore enjoyed less freedom than the print media until the promulgation of a new law on the electronic media in 1996 which created the National Radio and Television Council (NRTC). The NRTC, which later became the Council for Electronic Media (CEM), oversees media operations and elects the heads of state radio and television. However, since the council is selected by the Parliamentary Committee for Radio and Television, the government, led by the most powerful political party, still effectively exercises oversight of state-owned radio and television stations, a situation that has led to repeated allegations of political control over both the personnel employed in the state-owned media and political influence on the content of its programming.

In the private sector, licensing of radio and television frequencies is also in the hands of politically elected bodies, while the stations themselves are increasingly concentrated and subject to the influence of particular economic groups. Consequently, although by 2003 there were eighty-nine radio and ninety-eight television stations in Bulgaria, the majority of these were owned by a few corporations, most of which were foreign-owned. There are still only three national broadcast television stations and three national radio stations. Of these, one television station and two radio stations are state-owned. Overall, although the electronic media is substantially freer than in 1989, it continues to be subject to economic and political interests, so there is relatively little competition and the points of view presented in the media are more limited than they might be.[20]

Minority rights

Although Bulgaria is not as ethnically heterogeneous as some of the other Balkan states, it is not as ethnically homogenous as countries such as Hungary or Poland. About 15% of the Bulgarian population do not consider themselves to be ethnically Bulgarian. Ethnic minority groups officially recorded by the Bulgarian Census Bureau are listed in table 18.3, the two most important are the Turks and the Roma. Until 1989, Bulgaria's record in respecting minority rights was generally dismal. For most of the twentieth century, Bulgarian citizens of Turkish, Roma, Jewish, Armenian, and other ethnic origins were repeatedly subjected to coercive policies of assimilation, from being forced to adopt Bulgarian names and surnames and to endure having their cultures suppressed, to being forcibly resettled and encouraged to leave the country.

Since 1989, Bulgaria has had a better record in ensuring minority group rights. Domestically, the constitution prohibits the restriction of the rights of people because they belong to a particular race, nationality, or ethnic group. Bulgaria has also become a signatory to all international documents that are pertinent to this issue, including the European Convention on Human Rights and the Framework Convention for the Protection of National Minorities. In addition, as minority protection was been made part of the EU conditions for membership, special policies and programs were implemented to address minority problems. Nonetheless, issues remain.

One of the more controversial issues regarding Bulgaria's minority policy is the constitutional ban on ethnic political parties. Article 11 of the 1991 constitution prohibits "political parties on an ethnic, racial or religious basis." This restriction is in line with the general spirit of the Bulgarian constitution, which avoids the mention of the word "minority" and does not provide for any collective rights.[21] However, the presence of a constitutional ban has not prevented the formation of political parties that are effectively advocates for a

Table 18.3 Minority groups in Bulgaria, 2001[a]

Ethnic group	Size of minority	% of total population
Turks	746,664	9.42
Roma	370,908	4.68
Russians	15,595	0.20
Armenians	10,832	0.14
Vlachs	10,566	0.13
Others	29,722	0.38

Note:
[a] National Statistical Institute, Official Census of the Republic of Bulgaria, 2001, at www.nsi.bg/Census/Ethnos.htm.

particular ethnic or national group, but which have been able to participate in the political process by not openly registering as ethnic political organizations.

The biggest and most visible of these parties is the DPS which, in reality, if not formally, represents the Turkish minority in Bulgaria. Comprising approximately 9% of the population, the Bulgarian Turks live chiefly in the northeastern and southwestern parts of the country, where they constitute a majority. As table 18.2 illustrates, the DPS has been in every parliament since 1990, and since 2001 has participated in the government of the country. In addition, it played the role of a power-broker in at least two other governments. The DPS has consistently controlled the Ministry of Agriculture, a key economic sector for its electorate, as a result, it has been able to build and maintain a solid system of benefits for its members and supporters. The Turkish minority has thus been able to address most of the issues it considers important and to resolve many of the problems it has identified through the representation of the DPS in the policy-making process. This has led to some backlash among ethnic Bulgarians, many of whom believe that Turkish regions and Turkish agricultural businesses have benefited disproportionably from the EU agricultural subsidies in Bulgaria and who are in general unhappy with the high-profile role played by the DPS in Bulgarian politics.

In contrast to the Turkish minority, the second largest minority in Bulgaria, the Roma, have not been politically well organized. Representing about 5% of the Bulgarian population according to official figures and up to 8% according to expert estimates,[22] unlike the Turks, who are concentrated in certain areas, the Roma are scattered around the country and most suffer high levels of poverty, unemployment, and illiteracy, making them more severely disadvantaged both socially and economically than either most members of the Turkish minority or the majority of ethnic Bulgarians.[23] Nor have the Roma had an easy time organizing to protect their interests and improve their situation. Immediately after 1989, the Democratic Union of Roma (DSR) was denied registration as a political party because of its openly ethnic platform. Not until 1997–8 did Roma organizations again establish a notable political presence. Encouraged by international support for greater minority rights in Bulgaria, twenty-one Roma political organizations were founded between 1997 and 2003. Using various mechanisms to bypass the constitutional ban on ethnic parties, they managed to secure registration to run in elections. However, the heterogeneity of the Roma population and infighting among its political leaders prevented a unified Roma party from emerging, and none of the various Roma parties has been able to achieve representation in parliament.

As a result, until 2001, none of the Bulgarian governments made a conscious effort to resolve the Roma's socio-economic problems. Even if policies were adopted, they were never implemented, and the Roma remained enmeshed in a vicious cycle of discrimination, deteriorating living conditions, lower school attendance rates, and high levels of anti-social and small-scale criminal behavior. As in other areas where reforms lacked political will and social support, it was not until the EU began to use its annual progress reports on Bulgaria to criticize the country's Roma record that the government took the task to heart. Specific policies to improve the condition of the Roma began to be implemented in 2001–2, leading to some improvements in their socio-economic situation by 2004. However, attention to Roma problems in the context of generally decreasing standards of living for the lower socio-economic strata of Bulgarian society led to some hostile responses in the media and public discourse generally, both of which assumed a strong anti-Roma position in 2005–6. Since 2005, this dissatisfaction has also been expressed politically by the nationalist, and openly anti-Roma, Ataka party.

Challenges to democracy: economic development and corruption

Economic development

As with its political development, the economic development of Bulgaria since 1989 can be divided into two main periods – until 1997, and since then. The first period was characterized by political instability, which translated into short-term, and short-sighted, economic policies. While the short-lived SDS government of 1991–2 attempted to introduce some liberal policies, successive cabinets dominated by the BSP tried to preserve a social market economy. Privatization proceeded slowly and fitfully, and no large-scale privatization occurred until 1995; foreign investment was haphazard and all but absent; corruption was widespread; and links between the grey economy and the politically powerful thrived while unemployment and inflation soared. The bad debt of the uncompetitive SOEs combined with the lack of financial support from the international community to lead to the financial and economic crisis of 1996–7. During this period, inflation reached 550%, about two-thirds of the banks became insolvent, and the country's economy spiraled into total chaos.

In 1997, the new SDS government quickly introduced a variety of economic reforms, and the Bulgarian economy has since achieved respectable levels of macroeconomic stability. The Kostov government after 1997 lifted price controls, rescheduled part of the external debt, and allowed an international currency board to monitor the country's financial development. Bulgaria's currency, the lev, was finally stabilized by pegging it to the German mark (later, the Euro), and a severe financial discipline reduced inflation from 670% in 1997 to 9% in 1998.

Since then, inflation has been kept at about 5%, with peaks of 10% in 2000 and 6.1% in 2004. Personal savings accounts of up to 10,000 lev are guaranteed by the state, easing the anxiety of the average Bulgarian regarding the reliability of the country's banks following several failures during the early 1990s. Between 1997 and 2001, the SDS government also encouraged large-scale privatization, and most of the major industries in the country were privatized, which most analysts believe helped to achieve an annual economic growth rate of about 5%. As Bulgaria's macroeconomic indicators have stabilized and shown signs that the country's economy is growing, FDI has increased exponentially – from approximately US$600 million in 1997 to US$4 billion in 2006.[24] Trade has also increased: exports have tripled since 1997, and in 2006, approximately half of Bulgaria's exports and two-fifths of its imports were with the EU.[25]

While these indicators provide a picture of stable economic development, the repercussions of economic reform were strongly felt by the Bulgarian people. In 2000, about 18% of the workforce was unemployed. While this had declined to 8% in 2006, it remained a major reason for dissatisfaction with the economic reforms carried out by the SDS between 1997 and 2001. Although the current level of unemployment is comparable to the average in European countries, the collapse of the welfare system in Bulgaria that accompanied market reforms has made unemployment a more serious problem than it is in countries such as the Netherlands or Germany. So while economic reforms have fueled economic growth, they have also caused a significant amount of social dislocation and personal suffering, even for those with jobs, and Bulgaria remains far behind not only Western European countries, but behind some Eastern European countries as well. GDP *per capita* at purchasing power parity (PPP) was only US$8,630 in 2005, the lowest of all EU member states. In comparison, GDP *per capita* (at PPP) was $20,140 in the Czech Republic and about $17,000 in Hungary. In addition, the long-term economic problems have led to a high rate of immigration from Bulgaria. Close to a million people have left the country to live and work in Western Europe and the United States, leading to a substantial brain drain and demographic problems.

Corruption

Corruption has been one of the major problems in Bulgaria's democratic development since 1989. Allegations of corrupt links between the governing BSP and the grey economy played an important role in the social discontent against the Videnov cabinet in the winter of 1996–7. Similar accusations proved crucial for the SDS government that succeeded it, suggesting that corruption was endemic to the political system and not the monopoly of a particular party. Despite the success of the Kostov cabinet in bringing about reforms in many areas of government, alleged corrupt privatization deals led to widespread discontent with the behavior of the SDS cabinet. Successive governments sought also to curb corruption in various areas, but its persistence was the key hindrance to Bulgaria's entry into the EU. Even after Bulgaria became a member of the EU, it has continued to be monitored by the European Commission in an effort to increase the country's efforts to limit corruption and punish those guilty of corruption and malfeasance.

The relatively high levels of corruption in Bulgaria are illustrated by the rankings of Transparency International. According to their studies, Bulgaria has consistently ranked among the more corrupt countries on its CPI, the country's position varying between 2.9 and 4.1 on a scale of 10 (no corruption) to 0 (pervasive corruption). While positive change was recorded from 1999 to 2002, the level of (perceived) corruption seems to have reached a plateau since then and resisted further reform.

Official efforts to curb corruption have been made since the late 1990s, but results have been disappointing and slow. For example, charges of corruption and promises to end it dominated the electoral campaign in 2001, with the NDSV, the major contender for power, promising sweeping reforms. However, once elected, the NDSV failed to deliver, confirming the belief of some observers that the fight against corruption remained a useful election tool but not a realistic possibility, given Bulgaria's political system.[26] Indeed, while the government focused on small-scale fraud, it appeared unable or unwilling to address high-level political corruption.

Corruption continued to be high on the public agenda during the electoral campaign of 2005, but the electorate seemed to reward, rather than punish, those who tacitly admitted having engaged in what appeared to be corrupt behavior. The DPS, whose leader publicly acknowledged the presence of a "circle of companies" that provided the party with the resources needed to run its electoral campaign in exchange for public procurement contracts, was the biggest winner in the elections. In reality, in Bulgaria the presence of political-cum-business networks linked to political parties had become an accepted fact of political and business life. This period also saw political corruption shift from "privatization and illegal trafficking to the spheres of concessions, public procurement, and the use of EU funds."[27]

What is particularly worrying about these developments in Bulgaria is that the 2005–9 government has failed to address the issue of high-level political corruption, despite clear indications from the EU that progress in this area is needed in order for Bulgaria to become a full member. Instead, attention has been limited to curbing corruption in the high-profile judiciary and the police sectors. In these areas, once again, it appears that the efforts of successive Bulgarian governments have been aimed more at satisfying EU demands rather than at implementing real change.

Conclusion: democracy in Bulgaria after twenty years

Twenty years after the collapse of communism, Bulgaria is a transformed country. Most of the elements of the old political, economic, and social systems have been dismantled and replaced, and the country is now a member of both the EU and NATO. However problems remain. These include an inequitable distribution of the country's wealth and questions regarding who has benefited from increasing economic prosperity; the effects of corporate control on the independence of the country's media; strained interethnic relations; a persistent and apparently pervasive corruption; and a judiciary still in process of reform.

Besides the challenges these problems themselves bring to the daily struggle of the average Bulgarian to earn a living and raise a family, there are also unsettling implications for the political legitimacy of democratic governance. While the Bulgarian people are in general very supportive of democracy, they are not yet certain that it can work.[28] Results from popular surveys have repeatedly reported that more Bulgarians are dissatisfied than satisfied with the current state of democracy in their country. Indeed, not until late 2006 did the proportion of Bulgarians who believed that the country was changing for the better compared to pre-1989 rise to 30% and reached the same percentage as those who thought that the country was changing for the worse.

Timeline 1989–2007

1989	
10 November	General Secretary of the Bulgarian Communist Party, Todor Zhivkov, resigns
1990	
10 June and 17 June	First democratic elections, BSP wins clear victory, forms Lukanov cabinet
	Opposition leader Zhelyo Zhelev elected first president of the Republic by Grand National Assembly
1991	SDS wins elections and forms Dimitrov cabinet with support of the DPS
1992	DPS withdraws support from government, Dimitrov cabinet resigns
	Popov cabinet sworn in with support of DPS and BSP
1994	BSP wins early parliamentary elections and forms Videnov cabinet
1996	SDS leader Stoyanov wins presidential elections
	Financial and economic crisis, Videnov cabinet resigns, President Stoyanov schedules early elections
1997	
April	SDS wins elections in alliance with several other parties, forms Kostov government
1998	EU negotiations start
	NATO negotiations start
2001	Ex-monarch Simeon Saxe-Coburg-Gotha becomes prime minister after party sweeps the regular June elections
	NATO membership
2005	BSP wins plurality of votes in June elections, forms coalition Stanishev cabinet with BSP and NDSV
2007	
1 January	Bulgaria becomes member of EU

Fact sheet

Area	110,910 km^2
Population (July 2007 estimate)	7,322,858
Major cities	
Sofia	1,173,988
Plovdiv	338,302
Varna	320,668
Bourgas	209,479
Below the poverty line (2003 estimate)	14.1% of population
Unemployment rate (2006 estimate)	9.6%
GDP *per capita* (2006 estimate, PPP)	$10,700
Higher education (2001 census)	9.8% of population
Illiteracy rate	1.8% of population

Sources: CIA, *The World Factbook* and Bulgarian National Statistical Institute.

Short biography of Simeon Saxe-Coburg-Gotha

Born on 16 June 1937, Simeon Saxe-Coburg-Gotha served as King (Tsar) of Bulgaria from 1943 to 1946. Exiled in 1946, he spent most of his adult life in Spain. After 1989, Saxe-Coburg-Gotha's personality became a subject of popular interest and political speculation. Simeon II, as he is known in Bulgaria, returned to the country for the first time in 1996 when he was met by excited crowds. However, he publicly proclaimed that he had no desire or interest to resurrect the monarchy or get involved in Bulgarian politics. However, he was somewhat involved with the creation of the Union for National Salvation (UNS) alliance in 1997, which was built around the DPS. In April 2001, Simeon II returned to Sofia and openly proclaimed his desire to join the political process. His party, the NDSV, swept the 17 June elections and he became prime minister. Although he fulfilled his promise to "bring new faces to politics," his populist pledges to improve the lives of the Bulgarian people "in 800 days" never materialized. His popularity declined dramatically during his tenure as Prime Minister. In the 2005 elections, the NDSV received just under 20% of the vote and joined a coalition government with the BSP and the DPS.

Notes

1. Juan Linz and Alfred Stepan, *Problems of Democratic Transition and Consolidation: Southern Europe, South America, and Post-Communist Europe* (Baltimore, Md. and Washington, DC: John Hopkins University Press and Woodrow Wilson Center Press 1997), pp 338–9.
2. Evgenija Kalinova, and Iskra Baeva, *The Bulgarian Transitions: 1944–1999* (Sofia: Tilia, 2000), p. 146.
3. *Ibid.*, 148.
4. For more on this topic, see Ali Eminov, *Turkish and Other Muslim Minorities of Bulgaria* (London: C. Hurst & Co. and New York: Routledge, 1997).
5. Kalinova and Baeva, *The Bulgarian Transitions*, p. 160.

6. Jeffery Murer, "Mainstreaming Extremism: The Romanian PDSR and the Bulgarian Socialists in Comparative Perspective, " in Andras Bozoki and John Ishiyama (eds.), *The Communist Successor Parties of Central and Eastern Europe* (Armonk, NY: M.E. Sharpe, 2002), p. 392.
7. At the 1991 elections, only three parties – the BSP, SDS, and DPS – managed to enter parliament, leaving around 25% of the popular vote unrepresented in the legislature.
8. Georgi Karasimeonov, "The New Party System in Bulgaria: Current Situation and its Future," *Razum*, Vol. 1, No. 2 (2003).
9. Michael Waller and Georgi Karasimeonov, "Party Organization in Post-Communist Bulgaria," in Paul Lewis (ed.), *Party Structure and Organization in East-Central Europe* (Cheltenham: Edgar Elgar, 1996), p. 140.
10. Maria Spirova, *Political Parties in Post-Communist Societies: Formation, Persistence, and Change* (New York: Palgrave Macmillan, 2007), p 74.
11. Karasimeonov , "The New Party System in Bulgaria," p. 54.
12. M.A.G. Harper, "The 2001 Parliamentary and Presidential Elections in Bulgaria," *Electoral Studies*, Vol. 22, No. 2 (2003), p. 336.
13. Sarah Birch, Frances Millard, Kieran Williams, and Marina Popescu, *Embodying Democracy: Electoral System Design in Post-Communist Europe* (Houndmills: Palgrave Macmillan, 2002), p. 121.
14. Radka Tzenova, "The Electoral System and the Fragmentation of the Party System in Bulgaria 1991–2001," University of National and World Economy Research Papers (Sofia: UNSS), at www.unwe.acad.bg/research/?id=505.
15. The counting method is the D'Hondt formula.
16. This is in sharp contrast to the electoral systems in countries such as the Czech and Slovak Republics, Poland, Romania, Latvia, and Estonia which have different provisions for electoral alliances or at least electoral alliances of certain type: Spirova, *Political Parties*, p. 151.
17. Maria Spirova, "Bulgaria: Political Data Yearbook," *European Journal of Political Research*, Vol. 46, No. 7–8 (2007), pp. 901–8.
18. Bulgarian Statistical Institute, *Bulgarian Statistics Yearly* (Sofia: Bulgarian Statistical Institute, 1995 and 2006).
19. Reporters Without Borders, *Worldwide Press Freedom Index 2006*, at www.rsf.org/article.php3?id_article=19388; Bulgarian Helsinki Committee Annual Report 2006, at www.bghelsinki.org/upload/resources/hr2006_bg1.doc.
20. Bulgarian Helsinki Committee Annual Report 2006, at www.bghelsinki.org/upload/resources/hr2006_bg1.doc.
21. Rosen Vassilev, "Post-Communist Bulgaria's Ethnopolitics," *Global Review of Ethnopolitics*, Vol. 1, No. 2 (December 2001), p. 43.
22. UN Development Program, *Faces of Poverty, Faces of Hope*, at vulnerability.undp.sk.
23. For a discussion of the conditions in which Roma in Bulgaria live, see Maria Spirova and Darlene Budd, "The Roma: A European minority? The EU Accession Process and the Roma Minority in New and Soon-to-be Member States," *Comparative European Politics*, Vol. 6, No. 1 (April 2008), pp. 81–101.
24. Bulgarian National Bank, *Foreign Direct Investment Flows in Bulgaria*, at www.bnb.bg/bnb/home.nsf/vWebPagesByADOptionEN/3E4C52F8CF03636FC2256F78003EB3D3?OpenDocument&count=-1&EN.

25. Bulgarian National Bank, *Foreign Trade in Bulgaria*, at www.bnb.bg/bnb/home.nsf/fsWebIndex?OpenFrameset.
26. Coalition 2000, *Corruption Assessment Report 2000*, at www.anticorruption.bg/eng/news/events.php&event=0&id=11643&place=3&lang=en, p. 65.
27. Coalition 2000, *On the Eve of EU Accession: Anti-Corruption Reforms in Bulgaria*, at www.anticorruption.bg/eng/news/events.php?event=0&id=7298&place=3&lang=en, pp. 20–4.
28. John S. Dryzek and Leslie Holmes, *Post-Communist Democratization: Political Discourses in Thirteen Countries* (Cambridge: Cambridge University Press, 2002), pp. 206–21.

Further reading

Coalition 2000. *On the Eve of EU Accession: Anti-corruption Reforms in Bulgaria*, at www.anticorruption.bg/eng/news/events.php?event=0&id=7298&place=3&lang=en.

Crampton, Richard. *Bulgaria* (Oxford, Oxford University Press, 2007)

Dimitrova, Antoaneta. "Europeanisation and Administrative Reform in Central and Eastern Europe," in Frank Schimmelfennig and Ulrich Sedelmeier (eds.), *The Europeanization of Eastern Europe* (Ithaca, NY: Cornell University Press, 2005)

Eminov, Ali. *Turkish and Other Muslim Minorities of Bulgaria* (London: C. Hurst & Co. and New York: Routledge, 1997)

Ganev, Venelin I. "History, Politics, and the Constitution: Ethnic Conflict and Constitutional Adjudication in Postcommunist Bulgaria," *Slavic Review*, Vol. 63, No. 1 (Spring 2004), pp. 66–89

Preying on the State: The Transformation of Bulgaria after 1989 (Ithaca, NY: Cornell University Press, 2007)

Karasimeonov, Georgi, Kay Lawson, and Andrea Rommele. *Cleavages, Parties, and Voters: Studies from Bulgaria, the Czech Republic, Hungary, Poland, and Romania* (Newport, Conn.: Praeger, 1999)

Kolarova, Rumyana and Dimitr Dimitrov. "The Roundtable Talks in Bulgaria," in Jon Elster (ed.), *The Roundtable Talks and the Breakdown of Communism* (Chicago, Ill.: University of Chicago Press, 1996)

Spirova, Maria, *Political Parties in Post-Communist Societies: Formation, Persistence, and Change* (New York: Palgrave Macmillan, 2007)

19

Albania since 1989: the Hoxhaist legacy

BERND JÜRGEN FISCHER

When Enver Hoxha, Albania's long-time Stalinist dictator, was buried with honors under the socialist realist statue of Mother Albania in the Martyrs' Cemetery in Tirana, the date of his death was omitted from his tombstone. Ramiz Alia, who followed Hoxha as party secretary, was responsible for the omission, arguing that such a man could never die. Unfortunately for Albania, still mired in its transition and heavily influenced by its Stalinist past, Alia may have been right. Certainly the most brutal aspects of the Hoxha regime, including its state-of-siege isolation, its political murders, its prisons, its forced labor camps, and the hardships of long internal exile are gone. But aspects of its intolerant authoritarianism, the general disregard for the well-being of its people and the best interests of the state on the part of the elite, brutal uncompromising politics, and lack of a rule of law, have obstructed the path to Albania's broadly articulated goals of establishing a functioning democracy and market economy, and Euro-Atlantic integration.

The Hoxha regime

That the Hoxha period left a profoundly negative impression on post-communist Albania is clear. Still, some historians have credited him with achievements in specific areas such as health, education, and women's rights. Despite grinding poverty, he did diversify the economy and society through a program of Soviet-style industrialization, he raised the standard of living, and he reduced the impact of divisive factors on Albanian society, such as regional and clan loyalties, the traditional north–south division, and the occasional tension associated with the presence of four distinct religious groups. And he did defiantly and doggedly defend Albania's territorial integrity and independence.[1]

But while some Eastern European dictators mellowed with age, Hoxha became more extreme, building his regime on terror administered by his extensive security apparatus – positioned around the dreaded Sigurimi, the secret police – which allowed Hoxha and his state into not only the homes but also the minds of Albanians. They were cowed into a fearful state of conformism and apathy, with their thoughts kept secret, and like their leader, paranoid and suspicious of all around them, losing their sense of personal dignity and responsibility. The Albanian Party of Labor (APL) and its members fared little better, for Hoxha ruthlessly eliminated his colleagues – no communist regime experienced such repeated purges and decimations. Ultimately power was restricted to a small group bound together by traditional ties of family or clan loyalty, and their common complicity in the continuing murderous purges.[2] But even these people were not safe, and as a result little in the way of active dissent could be found anywhere in the country.

The collapse of communism in Albania

When Hoxha died in 1985 he was succeeded by his protégé Ramiz Alia who, among other challenges, was immediately faced with increasingly serious economic and social problems. These resulted in part from the usual plague of overcentralization, persistent often inept interference from the center, further complicated by high birth rates, overcrowding in the countryside and increasing unemployment. Albania's economic woes were further exacerbated by inefficient enterprises, widespread corruption and constant shortages of basic goods. In the midst of this looming disaster, Albania entered the television age with over 200,000 sets by 1985, affording Albanians the opportunity of a glimpse of the outside world via Yugoslav, Greek, and Italian stations and adding to the growing disaffection. By the late 1980s, as the repressive aspects of the regime were gradually reduced, alienated segments of society became slightly bolder. Alia, who recognized the growing political, social and economic crisis, did not handle this increasingly complex situation very well. His response was always reactive, tinkering with the structure when it was already too late. To his credit, he lessened his reliance on the Sigurimi, but he was pushed into reforms in fits and starts, which prevented him from developing anything like a cohesive program. Perhaps his biggest problem was his goal, which was to preserve the system while instituting minor technical adjustments. Events, including the expanding revolutions elsewhere in Eastern Europe – in particular the rapid fall and execution of Nicolae Ceauşescu of Romania – stimulated the Albanian leadership to push this grudging minimalist reform further.[3] But the communists slowly lost control as disenchantment amongst the population found more active expressions, including spontaneous strikes and demonstrations, while the government became increasingly reluctant to use its still extensive security apparatus. At the emergency 9th plenum of the party in January 1990 the leadership voiced criticism of Mikhail Gorbachev and refused to consider political pluralism, hoping to contain the situation with baby steps in terms of minor economic decentralization.

That this was not working and that a degree of panic was setting in is indicated by the rapid convocation of the 10th plenum in April that took more dramatic steps. At this important meeting, the party essentially reversed the 1967 degree which had abolished religion in Albania, reinstituted the ministry of justice which Hoxha had dissolved in 1966, after declaring that the ideal of "socialist justice" had been achieved, and removed the 1976 restriction on foreign investment.[4] Alia continued to hope that communism could be saved through gradual change but, as with others like him in Eastern Europe, he underestimated the seriousness of the crisis and was overwhelmed by the momentum of the growing revolt.

By the spring of 1990, with little hope of an economic turnaround, Albania was faced with a slow decline in public discipline. More and more workers, those who were still employed, failed to show up for work. Peasants, who still made up the vast majority of the population, refused to deliver food to the cities and stole state-owned animals. People took revenge on the state through the destruction of state property, including government offices and schools. By July the regime's very legitimacy was called into question when it was faced with the spectacle of thousands storming western embassies in Tirana seeking asylum, while thousands more commandeered rusty boats in Durrës harbor and fled to Italy.

The next months saw the development of an increasingly radical, violent, and confrontational street culture of a random and anarchic character that took hold in almost all of Albania's cities and towns. The final push towards political pluralism, and with it the eventual end of the regime, came from students, particularly those from Albania's only university in Tirana who, unlike the majority of intellectuals, were willing to risk open defiance of the government. Alia was concerned enough to send Dr. Sali Berisha, who had been one of the first to openly advocate political pluralism and was assumed, therefore, to have some standing with the students, to act as a mediator. Berisha very skillfully used his role to commandeer and then direct the protests, which by December had finally pushed Alia to give up Europe's last political monopoly and schedule new elections. On 12 December, once such a thing had become legal, the Democratic Party (DP), with a rather ill-defined ideology but based generally on democracy, a market economy and national reconciliation, was born, with Berisha in a leading role.

But it required two difficult elections, during which the country nearly fell apart, before Alia was finally ousted and the transition could begin. Albania had no experience with pluralist elections and no tradition of political parties on which to draw. The new DP had little organizational experience, minimal external political contacts, and severely limited financial resources.[5] On the eve of Albania's first multiparty election in March 1991 the party was not only without a clearly articulated program – no clear policy on land reform, and vague notions about visas to Europe and admission to the EC – it was also without the means to spread these ideas. The party had only eight automobiles. The APL, conversely, despite rapidly deteriorating conditions, had well-entrenched national organizations, control of all radio and television, and the support of Albania's conservative peasants who had little in common with the DP leadership and its urban supporters.

In an atmosphere of tense anticipation, the APL won two-thirds of the seats in parliament. Fatos Nano, a young economist and protégé of Hoxha's wife who seemed to favor the party's new moderate forces, was appointed prime minister. In increasingly difficult circumstances, Nano was responsible for some important achievements, including continuing to open Albania to the world, a policy begun by Alia, and the adoption of a provisional constitution which endorsed political pluralism and freedom of religion, guaranteed human and civil rights and, in a symbolic move, reduced the name of the country to simply the Republic of Albania.[6] The energetic Nano also saw the need for significant changes within the APL itself and he took the opportunity to do so at the 10th party congress in June. Under Nano's guidance the party renamed itself the Socialist Party (SP). Nano was elected party president and proclaimed a new program based on the principles advocated by West European social democratic parties. He declared himself dedicated to a gradual transition to a market economy while strengthening international ties. As a concrete and symbolic gesture of change, Nano dissolved the Sigurimi in July.

Despite these significant political changes taking place in Tirana, the country in general simply continued to degenerate into chaos. The security apparatus, particularly the underpaid demoralized army, continued to disintegrate, basic services collapsed, food production and distribution lagged, both internal and external immigration continued, while violent demonstrations and destruction of property increased. Cities became unsafe, particularly at night. Alia had ordered the removal of the last statue of Stalin in December 1990. In February 1991 demonstrators destroyed the larger-than-life size golden statue of Hoxha in the main square in Tirana, while others repeated the process in smaller towns. The old guard resisted by organizing and arming the so-called Enver Hoxha Voluntary Activists Union which, along with some elements of the security apparatus, organized pro-Hoxha rallies throughout the country and managed to detain and occasionally torture hundreds of the most outspoken critics of the regime.[7] There appeared to be a threat of civil war.

These conditions were exacerbated by a virtual economic collapse – by mid-1991 only some 25% of the state's productive capacity was operational.[8] In May the already paralyzed government was faced with a nationwide strike, organized by newly independent labor organizations. The government appealed for foreign help and received some in the form of Operation Pelican, a coalition of the willing spearheaded by Italy which was having trouble coping with the massive influx of refugees. The operation, led by 750 Italian troops, provided up to 90% of Albania's basic food needs until the end of December 1993 when the mission was declared complete. While starvation, which had become a tangible threat, was averted, the general decline continued, making it impossible for the Alia–Nano regime to stabilize. In June, soon after the party congress, Nano was replaced by Ylli Bufi and a "Government of National Stability" which included seven DP ministers. The new government had a very limited mandate, which included attempting to deal with the economic crisis and preparing for new elections, which the DP had been demanding for some time. The first goal proved beyond the government's capacity and the internal situation deteriorated further. A particularly severe winter gripped the country in 1991, there was no fuel – and no real functioning economy – and serious disturbances continued. In December 1991 Bufi was replaced by the more able Vilson Ahmeti who called together some independent technocrats and did at least adopt a new electoral code and finally scheduled new elections for March 1992.

This time the DP, which had withdrawn from the coalition government in December, had had time to prepare, having received both advice and funding from the increasingly active, anti-communist, diaspora. During the campaign, Berisha as always was perhaps too lavish with his promises. Among other things, he suggested that a DP victory would result in a massive influx of foreign aid as well as increased quotas for visas to the West[9] – ironically very much in line with what he continues to promise today. His platform also called for radical political and economic reform and the restoration of law and order. All of this was delivered with Berisha's dynamic campaigning and personal tenacity. In the end, in a generally fair and honest election, the DP won a substantial victory. The party gained some 65% of the popular vote, doing well in both urban and rural constituencies. Ramiz Alia resigned in April and the new parliament elected Sali Berisha as Albania's first post-communist president.

President Berisha in power, 1992–7

Sali Berisha's task was more than daunting and he attacked it with energy and uncompromising determination. At least in the initial period, he was able to achieve some far-reaching political, economic, and social reforms. Berisha began by rapidly dismantling some aspects of the previous one-party state. He removed communist symbols from the coat of arms and the flag, and banned the APL. Wide-ranging purges were carried out in all of the ministries and remaining security organs.

Early economic and social change was much more profound. The process of privatization had begun prior to the Berisha presidency but significantly accelerated under the new government which enthusiastically adopted the IMF macroeconomic stability package, or the "shock therapy" approach. This program, which had done well elsewhere, included rapid privatization, removing restrictions on imports, abandoning price controls, and phasing out subsidies to unprofitable or even marginal businesses. These policies, supplemented by nearly $1 billion in foreign assistance (1992–5) and $350 million in immigrant remittances, did push GDP into positive numbers again by 1993. But the costs of these programs were heavier than they were elsewhere. First, the economic turnaround was based principally on consumption rather that on manufacturing and agriculture, resulting in a massive foreign trade deficit. The cost to the average Albanian included extensive unemployment and for the tens of thousands who had become dependent on government subsidies and government services, which were cut significantly in line with IMF instructions, even deeper poverty. While some of course thrived, for most the concepts of democracy and a free market economy became synonymous with insecurity and hardship.

The social changes accompanying this upheaval were also profound. Seemingly overnight, Albanians were released from one of the most restrictive and isolated social structures in Europe. New-found personal freedoms were perhaps best exhibited through automobiles, televisions, and simple mobility. During the Hoxha years, private automobiles had been outlawed so that by 1989 there were no more that 200 cars in the entire country. Once the restrictions were lifted, used cars, many of them stolen, were imported by the tens of thousands so that, by 1992, Albanians were driving 120,000 private vehicles.[10] The lifting of Albania's draconian travel restrictions not only allowed hundreds of thousands to flee abroad,[11] but also resulted in extensive internal migration with entire poverty-stricken northern villages resettling in hastily constructed squalid shanty towns near Tirana and other cities. Even the past was changed, with history cleansed by the new leadership at the Albanian Academy of Sciences which oversaw the production of new textbooks focused on the contribution of the nationalist forces during the Second World War.[12] Religious freedom was confirmed and while there was periodic tension, and Berisha's adherence to the Islamic Conference in 1994 raised some concern abroad, religious issues did not become major political issues.[13]

While some of these social changes can be considered at least partially positive, others were decidedly not. New-found freedom led to a rapid rise in both organized and random petty crime, in a country that had been relatively free of it. Albania proved ideal for the rise of international criminal organizations, it was a poor area in a chaotic state surrounded by wealthy countries, with a legacy of clans which provided organization and codes of conduct, and many unemployed former secret policemen with special talents and networks for sale. These new criminal organizations were able to take advantage of the breakdown of the law-enforcement system, porous borders, a growing diaspora and migrant labor population which often served as a vehicle. The insecurity in the Balkan region in general – in particular the collapse of Yugoslavia and the sanctions imposed on what remained – offered unique smuggling opportunities, similar perhaps to the period of prohibition in the United States. Individuals in these brutal organizations maintained their old contacts with the political class to the extent that the state became further ensnared.[14] Violence was further increased by the revival of blood feuds, which continue to be a scourge in the north of Albania.

The end of communism also brought in its wake a significantly deteriorated status for Albania's women. While Hoxha, at least in theory, held to the Marxist concept of gender equality, with the beginning of the transition even the fiction of equality disappeared. During the Hoxha years rural women especially did see some benefit. For the first time they had access to medical care and education for their children. They could leave the house to meet with other women, participate in politics and own property. With the collapse of communism traditional attitudes and actions resurfaced, often returning women to the role of chattel. With the coming of significant unemployment, women were always the first to lose their jobs; they found themselves once again confined to the house, producing many of the family's basic needs. To be sure, the new Albania provided women some benefits, including freedom of contraception, eased abortion and divorce restrictions, and enhanced mobility. But much of this was offset by the return of patriarchal predominance, the virtual disappearance of women from politics, and new dangers including pornography and crime, and abduction for purposes of sex trafficking and rape – the latter being ills generally new to Albania which continue to be concerns today.[15]

Still, social and economic trends could be said to be moving in a generally positive direction. The same can not be said of politics which remains a major problem. The authoritarian and intolerant nature of Albania's elite precluded the negotiation and compromise which was desperately needed for Albania's new political forces to move steadily in the direction of democracy. Despite his singular courage during the last stages of the old regime, Berisha seemed unable to distance himself from an unhealthy political culture. He ultimately proved to be the poster child of old-school politics with the DP becoming his personal vehicle for increased power. He refused to allow any internal dissent within the party, and when his policies were questioned and the continuation of his presidency challenged, he struck out with everything at his disposal – willing to use violence and prepared to undermine Albania's fledgling democracy in the process.

President Berisha's political honeymoon was rather short-lived. Although the DP won the local elections of July 1992, it polled only 43 % of the vote, down from 65% in April. This outcome resulted generally from continuing, even growing, insecurity, popular disappointment with the pace of economic recovery and reform, discord within the ranks of the DP and overconfidence on Berisha's part.[16] Progressive elements within the party accused him of ignoring socio-economic problems, of cronyism in order to augment his power base and attempting to mask his failure and growing authoritarianism through the settling of old scores and vengeance against former communists.

Much of the criticism was justified. Berisha was increasingly influenced by former political prisoners who were uninterested in the original DP platform of national reconciliation. Although a former low-ranking communist functionary himself, Berisha found revenge against former communists useful in distracting the population. It was to be expected that many former communists would be replaced but Berisha launched a wholesale purge of the security organs, the ministries, and state administrative structures. Since there were not nearly enough qualified DP militants to fill the vacancies, Berisha required that the University of Tirana construct a six-month "how to be a judge or prosecutor" training course which enrolled many who had no legal background whatsoever. Those within the party who objected to this procedure were simply removed. With his new judges in place Berisha targeted, among others, former politburo members like Alia and Hoxha's widow. Their trials had many of the attributes of traditional communist show trials, including television coverage and young unqualified judges humiliating older defendants.[17] Nano, too, was arrested on corruption charges and in what many observers saw as primarily a political trial was sentenced to twelve years in prison.

As Berisha's authoritarianism intensified, Albania's fledgling new media became a target as well. Given the lack of an underground or dissident press during the Hoxha period upon which to build, the construction of a free press was complex. With radio and television remaining under state control, Albania's first independent print reporters were challenged by the concept of press responsibility. Press outlets themselves tended to be the mouthpieces of political parties and therefore highly partisan. Employing invective reminiscent of the Hoxha era, much of the press became increasingly critical of Berisha. The president struck back with violence and through his courts. Policemen and thugs, often interchangeable, attacked the offices of the opposition press as well as individual reporters. A restrictive press law was passed in 1993 which instituted high taxes, allowed for heavy fines and imprisonment, and did much to cow the press into silence or self-censorship, which in turn encouraged the people to question the value of print media, reducing readership. Even today Albania has many newspapers but remarkably low circulation rates.

With every election, the president came under greater pressure and in response became more authoritarian. By 1994 the Berisha regime had finally prepared a new draft constitution which would have further augmented the power of the president. Lacking sufficient support in parliament, Berisha referred the constitution to a popular referendum, but despite extensive manipulation lost by a wide margin. Stunned and angered, the president became even more determined and began planning early for the upcoming parliamentary elections of May 1996, with which he intended to cement his power.

Albania had degenerated into an illusion of democracy with an isolated authoritarian president, facing no effective parliamentary opposition, supported by an overly large highly politicized security apparatus. While some in the West continued to support him as the road to stability – Italian politicians referred to him as "the good doctor" – the important support of the United States was effectively undermined by the heavily manipulated elections of 1996. With the electoral defeat of 1994 fresh in his mind, in 1996 Berisha was leaving nothing to chance. Preparations began in 1995 with the introduction of the so-called "Genocide Law," which barred former top-ranking APL and state officials, as well as communist-era secret police informants from holding political office until 2002. After selectively releasing files, Berisha was able to disqualify 142 parliamentary nominees, only three of whom were Democrats. A series of other changes in the electoral law also clearly favored the DP.

The campaign itself was reminiscent of communist-era propaganda with Berisha branding the opposition, whom he accused of terrorism, as the "Red Front" subsidized by Albania's traditional enemies the Serbs and the Greeks.[18] Security forces and thugs were used to disrupt opposition political meetings, harass and physically attack opposition supporters and candidates, and the press. On the day of the election, the situation deteriorated further to the extent that the Socialists withdrew from the election two hours prior to the closing of the polls claiming, with some justification, that the DP was perpetrating a massive fraud.

President Berisha was elated with his victory – the DP now controlled 87% of the seats in parliament, was in firm control of the police and the courts, and had cowed the media. The principle of the one-party state had been reconstructed. The cost of this victory, however, was enormous. The election was roundly condemned by the United States, the EU, various human rights organizations like Helsinki Watch, and monitoring groups like the OSCE. The United States, which until this point had been Berisha's strongest supporter, suggested that the entire election be re-run, while members of the opposition compared the election to a coup. The 1996 election was viewed as a litmus test of Albania's commitment to democracy and speedy reform and Berisha had failed.[19] Despite the progress for which he was responsible, Berisha's domestic and international credibility was badly tarnished by this episode and has yet to fully recover.

The popular revolt of 1997

Before the president could even attempt to deal with the outcome of the 1996 election, he did much to create an even more serious crisis which not only eventually swept him away, but caused what could be considered Europe's first successful popular armed uprising since the nineteenth century.

In the existing atmosphere of political tension and stalled social and economic reform, it likely would not have taken much to push Albania over the edge. The crisis began with the collapse of a series of pyramid investment schemes. In many ways, Albania was ripe for such activity given its cash economy, the large amounts of currency controlled by criminal elements, and the considerable immigrant remittances which continue to make up some 15% of GDP. The schemes began rather slowly in the 1990s but by the summer and fall of 1996, as those who had invested early began realizing massive profits of up to 50% a month, they expanded dramatically ultimately involving 65–75% of all Albanian families. The funds likely collected at least $1 billion. Many impoverished Albanians sold everything they had including homes, farms, livestock and personal belongings fully expecting to live off of their investments for the rest of their lives.[20]

The schemes expanded because there were so few areas of legitimate investment in Albania and because scheme managers effectively argued that they had diversified and had essentially become successful investment bankers. They also expanded because of the astonishing failure of the leadership on all sides, with both the DP and the SP benefiting directly from specific schemes. Senior government officials ignoring, albeit belated, IMF warnings called the schemes good business and attacked those few in the media who were critical.

Inevitably, as pyramids do, the schemes began to falter. As they did so, by January 1997 popular panic set in and protests, which quickly became violent, broke out in Tirana and some southern cities. In Vlorë, Lushnjë and Berat, angry investors attacked and set fire to government buildings, including city halls, courts, police stations, land registry offices, and DP offices.[21] The police attempted to curtail this escalating violence but to no avail, as it became increasingly clear that hundreds of thousands faced financial ruin. The situation took a major turn for the worse when the large Gjallica fund collapsed in Vlorë in early February. The predominately Socialist seaport town erupted in violence and for days Berisha's security forces battled the citizens before having to abandon the town.

The growing unrest spread rapidly to other southern towns where the Socialists were strong, often with the direct involvement of high-ranking SP officials. With this crisis many Socialists and other party members saw an opportunity to finally be rid of Berisha. Many who had fled abroad, fearing Berisha's vengeance, returned to help organize the resistance around disaffected former military and secret police officers, people whose experience with the concept of Hoxha's long-practised militia strategy would confound the government's attempt to restore order by force.

By the beginning of March, spreading unrest had degenerated into full-scale rebellion. On 2 March, Berisha finally proclaimed a state of emergency and issued a shoot-to-kill order, to be administered by the feared SHIK, the new secret police, which had already arrested hundreds in the capital. On the very next day, in a move condemned by the internationals and both domestic opponents and supporters, Berisha had his now puppet parliament re-elect him to an additional five-year term as president, after which parliament ceased to meet.

Berisha's situation took a decided turn for the worse when the army began to disintegrate. Technically a force of 55,000 with hundreds of armored vehicles, the army proved to be less than useless to Berisha. The president had purged the officer corps, replacing trained personnel with the usual party militants.[22] This served to further demoralize the troops who already suffered from miserable pay and very poor living conditions. Rather than fire on civilians, soldiers simply went home, abandoning well-stocked armories. The population, particularly in the south where Hoxha had stockpiled most of his weapons in anticipation of an invasion from Greece, quickly raided the weapons depots, eventually making off with close to 1 million Kalashnikov assault rifles[23] with hundreds of millions of rounds of ammunition, tanks and artillery pieces and sophisticated Chinese surface-to-air missiles. While much of the latter was thankfully unusable, almost anyone can fire a Kalashnikov, allowing insurgents to take and hold large southern towns in which banks and government offices were sacked, shops looted, and prisons thrown open. Ultimately every prison in the country was opened, releasing all of Albania's convicted criminals, as well as those who were considered to be political prisoners including Nano, whom Berisha quickly pardoned.

The criminals rapidly armed themselves and added to the chaos and terror. By mid-March at least 15,000 Albanians had fled to Italy and an estimated 2,000 had been killed. The country was being ransacked. Nearly every industrial and manufacturing plant was looted and destroyed – even schools and hospitals were not spared. Spartak Ngjela, the minister of justice, announced with considerable candor that "All structures of the state have failed. In this moment we are in a natural state, if you know your Hobbes."[24]

Still, Berisha had been able to hold on to Tirana – in part through SHIK terror, whose headquarters was guarded by six tanks. He was also able to maintain control of much of the north, where ardent supporters had also broken into armories and swore to defend the president. As the insurgents began moving on Tirana, a full-scale bloody civil war drawn along traditional north–south lines became increasingly likely. Although Berisha had pledged never to negotiate with "red terrorists," once it became clear to him that he could not rely upon foreign military intervention he was forced into a humiliating compromise with those opposition leaders still at large in Tirana. On 9 March 1997, an agreement was reached which included the construction of a so-called national reconciliation government, the proclamation of a general amnesty for rebels, and new parliamentary elections, accompanied by a referendum on the restoration of the defunct monarchy of King Zog, both of which were scheduled for June. The latter was likely intended by Berisha to deflect at least some attention away from his own failure.

Although significant disorder continued, this political agreement and the arrival of foreign troops helped to avert the threatened civil war and an uneasy stand-off ensued.[25] Albania's neighbors, fearful of yet another massive wave of unwelcome refugees, put together Operation Alba which commenced in April 1997. Finally responding to desperate pleas from Berisha, 6,300 European troops, with the Italians in the lead, dispersed throughout the south and central lowlands on what was billed a humanitarian mission. Although Alba troops did not intervene in the fighting or attempt to disarm the now heavily armed population, they did create at least a modicum of calm during which another seriously flawed election took place.

Following some procedural agreements, including revision of the "Genocide Law," the vicious and violent campaign led to possibly the least democratic election in post-communist Eastern Europe.[26] The campaign process was marred by bomb attacks and several assassination attempts against Berisha who at one point was caught in a gun battle which wounded at least eight people.[27] Actual campaigning was impossible for one party or the other in much of the country. There was little debate, with Nano, despite occasional vaguely progressive rhetoric, simply running against Berisha and rather disingenuously promising to compensate pyramid scheme victims. Berisha just ran against the communists. An added feature was the sight of the nearly 7 ft tall pretender to the throne, Leka, campaigning with his small private army. Immediately after learning that the monarchy had been rejected, Leka declared the election to be stolen and attempted an armed uprising. Dressed in fatigues, accessorized with pearl handled revolvers and grenades, Leka led a group of several hundred armed supporters along the principal boulevard in Tirana. To the surprise of no one, shooting eventually erupted and after one of his militants was killed, the pretender fled back into exile.[28]

Berisha and the DP paid a heavy price for their adherence to the old ways, for their arrogance and incompetence, their intolerance and corruption. Albanians overwhelmingly voted against Berisha as opposed to for the SP, which was rewarded with 101 out of 155 seats in parliament. On 23 July, President Berisha resigned in disgrace. Despite the appalling example of democracy which produced this result, the international community had no choice but to sign off on the outcome.

Berisha had started with such hope – declaring to a large crowd in 1992 "Hello Europe, we hope we find you well." And Europe had responded. But he had squandered the goodwill of the international community and the nation with his inability to move past Albania's political culture of authoritarianism and rigidity. Perhaps it was too much to ask of him, or of any Albanian politician so soon after the collapse of Stalinism. But the damage brought on by this failure of leadership was enormous not only to the state and the well-being of the people, but also to the very concept of democracy and a market economy. Albanians who had yet to really experience either, found themselves wondering whether these goals were indeed worth achieving.

The Nano years, 1997–2005

Nano had walked out of an unguarded cell in the middle of March 1997 and by the end of June he was again prime minister with a powerful mandate – it had been a remarkable political come-back and could have been used to accomplish much-needed reform, reconstruction, and national reconciliation. But like Berisha, Nano was a creature of his age and was immured in Albania's political culture of revenge and authoritarianism. Rather than attempt to diverge from that culture, Nano in many ways was its embodiment. Nano, who had gained prominence as an economist at the Institute of Marxist–Leninist Studies, was considered a dedicated communist. While he was perhaps more open to reform than some of the dinosaurs on the politburo, he had opposed real pluralism and a market economy until the very end of one-party rule.[29] But his native intelligence allowed him to rise quickly in the rapidly disintegrating APL and, as we have seen, he served briefly as prime minister in 1991 while still in his thirties. He surrounded himself with some of the old hardliners, sidelined many dedicated reformers, and left little room for internal party discussion. His rhetoric in the run-up to his second stint as prime minister, like that of Berisha, envisioned meeting the needs of the population, establishing a free-market economy based on fiscal discipline, reducing corruption, and enhanced respect for human rights.[30] The reality which Nano created was something quite different.

Nano set his tone early and, like Berisha's, it tended to be dogmatic, confrontational and, initially at least, focused on the settling of scores. Like Berisha, Nano did much to undermine the notion of a civil service by initiating a broad-ranging purge of the security apparatus, the judiciary and the state administration, and almost all ambassadors and generals. Albania's recent historical past was once again rewritten under the close supervision of new university rectors and new leadership at the Academy of Sciences. SP militants replaced DP militants. Once the judiciary was secure, Nano ended the ongoing trial of some thirty former communists, dropped the remnants of the "Genocide Law," and arrested prominent DP members from among those who had not fled the country. The prime minister, ignoring many of the reformers and foreshadowing later party splits, quickly constructed a government comprising many from the former communist regime and almost all from the south, not bothering to obtain party approval beforehand.[31]

Nano quickly turned his attention to restoring some semblance of order, and was able to calm the south with the help of pro-Socialist criminal bands, who continued to play an important role in the SP government for years to come. The north was more problematic but by the end of November, stability was returning allowing Nano to focus on other critical issues, often simply continuing the policies of the previous regime. Certainly, slow progress on some issues was registered. Albania continued haltingly toward democratic consolidation, establishing the framework for a market economy and international integration. Nano proved less oppressive when it came to press freedom and slowly growing civil society organizations.

Privatization continued, with the industrial base and banking system privatized by 2005.[32] This helped to set up at least the basic conditions for market-driven competition. Annual economic growth remained at about 5% during the SP years due mainly to construction, small businesses, and the service sectors, but Albania had of course started from a rather low level in 1991. The Bank of Albania reported that *per capita* income had reached $2,883 in 2006[33] but because distribution was extremely uneven, rural poverty remained a major problem with fully a quarter of Albanians living below the poverty line. It is likely that close to 50% of GDP came from criminal activities but the large influx of cash tended to keep the lek, Albania's currency, quite stable.[34] Unemployment officially hovered around 15% but with the near-subsistence farming in reality was likely higher than 30%, exacerbated by under-employment. FDI remained very low and the business climate, restricted by a permanent energy crisis marked by daily disruptions in the supply of electricity and drinking water, serious environmental problems, extensive corruption, and a still-developing concept of a rule of law, remained unattractive. With a high internal state debt and negative trade balance, economically Albania did little more than continue to creep forward.

Part of both the cause and effect of this painfully slow level of economic advance was the continuing problem of the "brain drain." Although the various crises of course accelerated the process, even during periods of relative stability, Albanians continued to flee their country in astonishing numbers. A total of 720,000 Albanians are estimated to have emigrated between 1989 and 2001, representing well over 30% of the total population.[35] Naturally, this number included many of the best and the brightest whose talents were very much needed. The professions, particularly health care and education, suffered. While under the Hoxha regime Albanians had been afforded some basic universal health care, with social collapse village clinics were often destroyed, and the medical personnel assigned there often left for Tirana or abroad. Even in the cities, however, there was a significant degeneration of the system. Apart from the shortage of trained personnel and limited resources, the chairman of the parliamentary health committee estimated in 2006 that the level of medical technology was at least forty years behind Albania's Balkan neighbors. He suggested that health care in general was in a state of crisis, hobbled by a communist centralized bureaucracy pressured by a rudimentary market economy. This clash of systems resulted in extensive corruption, endangering the health of many.

Education, which had been touted as another success story under Hoxha, suffered from related problems. Apart from the lack of adequately trained personnel and resource problems, education – in particular the field of history – became a political battleground. Central to the struggle was the issue of resistance and collaboration during the Second World War, an event which continues to dominate the national psyche. The war remained something of a *leitmotiv* during the communist period, conferring legitimacy on Hoxha and the party who labeled as traitors all those who failed to participate in partisan resistance. When the DP came to power, personnel and textbooks were replaced, with the new leadership of the Albanian Academy producing a new version of the war intended to "make science free of indoctrinated, political party tactics."[36] Instead, science was captured by different indoctrinated political party tactics and new textbooks were produced reflecting DP reinterpretations of the war. Once the SP came to power, predictably, those books were withdrawn and replaced, moving Albania back to a view of the war somewhat closer to the original APL version. The topic remains a major issue to this day, while standards deteriorate and illiteracy, which had been effectively eradicated during the Hoxha years, is again on the rise. The education system in general remains in crisis.

Most of the socio-economic problems of the Nano period were exacerbated by the continuation of poisonous, often murderous politics, precipitated by the continuing inability of Albania's elite to distance itself from its Hoxhaist past. The tone was set immediately in 1997 when the DP boycotted what Berisha called the new "parliament of Kalashnikovs." Berisha escalated the usual invective by frequently referring to Nano as a criminal and a drug addict, while DP militants often degenerated into terrorist gangs. Following a DP rally, one such gang, consisting of dozens of heavily armed thugs, attacked Shkodër in February 1998, looting and burning the state bank and the university.[37]

Later in 1998 Berisha took one step beyond his noisy obstructionism and attempted a coup. Political tension in Tirana increased during the summer of 1998 and then exploded in September with the assassination of the DP leader Azem Hajdari on 12 September 1998. While there remains considerable confusion concerning who was responsible, the immediate aftermath constituted another serious political crisis. Berisha saw the opportunity and seized it, leading some 2,000 militants, many of them armed, into the streets with Hajdari's coffin which was used to pound against the doors of Nano's office. One group of demonstrators attacked and occupied the state-run television studios broadcasting the message that "we have taken over" while others looted central Tirana, shouting "death to Nano." The prime minister panicked and fled to Macedonia leaving President Rexhep Meidani to call in the troops and disperse Berisha's ragtag militia. Following three days of chaos, along with eight dead and nearly 100 injured, basic order was restored.

Nano's behavior during the crisis, as well as the animosity of President Meidani who disliked the prime minister's excessive drinking and high living, undermined him to the benefit of a young group of reformers within the party. Nano was forced to resign on 28 September 1998 and was replaced by the relatively untainted SP secretary general, Pandeli Majko. The thirty-one-year-old new prime minister was faced not only with the continuing challenge of crime, violence, and public disorder, but was also forced to deal with the deteriorating situation in Kosovo and Macedonia.

In the midst of these challenges, Majko did manage to oversee the adoption of a new constitution. With no functioning opposition and despite a DP boycott and general obstructionism, and with considerable assistance from internationals and popular input, he approved a relatively progressive constitution which vested power in the prime minister and the cabinet, securing its implementation through a national referendum in November 1998. Majko was also in part responsible for Albania's receiving much-needed international approval for its moderate stance and cooperative attitude on the Kosovo war of 1998–9 and the Macedonian violence of 2001, despite the DP playing the nationalist card and portraying the SP as un-Albanian and pro-Slav. Although these conflicts were not crucial factors in Albanian internal politics, internal instability was further challenged as Albania was inundated with refugees, principally fleeing Kosovars, who swelled Albania's population by nearly 17% in a two-month period in 1999.[38] Demonstrating remarkable selflessness, Albanians shared what little they had with the refugees and along with extensive foreign assistance, the Majko government was able to avoid what could have become a major humanitarian crisis – and both Nano and Majko were able to avoid war with Serbia. In general, Albania has avoided any serious long-term tensions with its neighbors since 1989.

Despite these successes, the hostile relationship between the two major parties and growing instability at the top of the SP power structure continued to complicate Albania's road forward. In October 1999 Nano, who had maintained the loyalty of a large group of SP deputies, was re-elected leader of the SP, defeating Majko who had hoped to solidify his position. Majko subsequently resigned as prime minister and was replaced by Deputy Prime Minister Ilir Meta, like Majko a former student leader, and a leading figure in the "reformist" group. Nano continued to intrigue behind the scenes, forcing the resignation of a number of Meta supporters in the cabinet and blocking the appointment of their successors. Unable to resolve the crisis, an embittered Meta resigned in early 2002 to be replaced by Majko. Within days, however, Nano had convinced the SP steering committee to combine the positions of party leader and prime minister, which effectively forced Majko's resignation. Nano's return as prime minister began with some promise, as the DP and SP had given in to European pressure and in July 2002 elected a consensus president in Alfred Moisiu, who proved to be quite effective in his limited role. But the period of reconciliation was short-lived and Nano soon returned to monopolizing power in the party and government.

The SP of course also continued to battle the DP in parliament, on those occasions when the DP was not boycotting the body, in the streets, and in a series of bitterly contested elections in 2000, 2001, and 2003. These elections, although not as flawed as that of 1996, were accompanied by intimidation, violence, and manipulation. Party militants confronted each other in the streets, threatened voters at the polls, while party officials occasionally altered civil registries and stuffed or stole ballot boxes. These and other problems resulted in frequent re-voting and protracted battles in Albania's politicized courts, delaying the announcement of the results. None of these elections fully measured up to international standards, giving the opposition reason to question not only the legitimacy of the ballots but also that of the governments they produced.

Once again, as a result of the enormous energy which these parallel struggles consumed, real progress was slow during the Nano years. While many lived in poverty, criminal organizations acted with impunity, having infiltrated government at every level. Albania gained an unenviable reputation as a haven for traffickers who turned the state into both a major transit and a major source country.[39] The police and the courts remained politicized, inefficient, and corrupt; Albania was labeled one of the worst states in the world in this regard.[40]

Nano, who seemed comfortable with the status quo, likely would have remained the prime minister had it not been for a major split in his party in

2004. Ilir Meta, who had considered defecting as early as 1996, finally decided that he could no longer work with Nano and organized one of many new parties, the Socialist Movement for Integration, just before the parliamentary elections of July 2005. Nano certainly had other disadvantages going into the election. Corruption was growing, his lifestyle increasingly became an issue, and he seemed unconcerned as the nation struggled with several tragedies resulting in significant loss of life. And the DP ran an effective, generally professional campaign emphasizing an anti-corruption, or "clean hands" platform. But many Albanians were still wary of Berisha. It was the defection of Meta which resulted in the narrow SP defeat and a peaceful transfer of power, in what was one of the fairest elections Albania had ever experienced. Following the construction of a coalition, Berisha returned to power, this time as prime minister, taking office on 3 September 2005.

Conclusion

It is clear that Albania continues to move in a positive direction; in particular, the economy and the business climate continue to improve. While there is perhaps no "new" Sali Berisha, he has abjured much of the violence and extremism that characterized his presidency. In addition new younger politicians, like celebrated Tirana mayor Edi Rama who became the new leader of the SP, are offering Albanians real policy choices for the first time. There has even been some agreement between the two main parties, including a hastily passed constitutional amendment which introduced a regional–proportional electoral system effectively disenfranchising most of the smaller parties. The parliamentary elections of June 2009, which saw Berisha hang onto power with a much-reduced majority, were deemed an improvement by international monitors.[41] This slow but steady progress has been noted by internationals, as evidenced by the signing of the SAA with the EU in 2006 and by Albania's invitation to join NATO in April 2008 and subsequent admission a year later.

But it is also clear that the old ways linger. Too much of Berisha's energy in 2005–6 was dedicated to enhancing his own power through increased control of ostensibly independent administrative institutions and local government units, and preparing to dominate the local and presidential elections of 2007. In February 2007 Albania conducted local elections which both international and domestic observers labeled as a step backward, followed soon after by the July 2007 election of the fifty-year-old Bamir Topi as president. While he has shown promise, Topi is seen by many as a non-consensus DP president. Both elections were preceded by invective and lengthy political crises which postponed work on needed reforms. Although the 2009 parliamentary elections were marginally better than those of 2005, they were still marred by some pre-election violence, politicization of technical aspects, family voting and reports of voter intimidation and, as a result, did not fully meet international standards. The Berisha regime has been further buffeted by a series of unseemly scenes in parliament and high-profile scandals which have undercut its corruption-fighting credentials. The most serious of the latter involved a deadly explosion at a munitions de-commissioning plant in the suburbs of Tirana which exposed not only the hiring of women and children for dangerous work, but arms trafficking that implicated individuals near to and within the government.[42]

These disappointments, too, were noted by domestic and international observers who continue to call for urgent action on electoral and judicial reform, increased attention to government corruption and government connections with organized crime, and the strengthening of the rule of law. That the legacy of the Hoxha regime, with its history of failed political leadership, has demonstrated resilience seems evident given that nearly two decades after the fall of communism, Albania is still struggling to realize its democratic transition.

Timeline 1985–2009

April 1985	Enver Hoxha, Albania's long-time Stalinist dictator, dies
November 1989	Pressure on government of Ramiz Alia to reform
July 1990	Thousands of desperate Albanians storm Western embassies in Tirana
December 1990	Beginning of political pluralism in Albania; Democratic Party (DP) is founded
March 1991	Albania conducts first multiparty parliamentary elections, communists win
June 1991	Albanian Party of Labor renames itself the Socialist Party (SP) under Fatos Nano
March 1992	DP wins fair parliamentary elections in landslide
April 1992	Alia resigns, Sali Berisha elected president
November 1994	Berisha fails to pass constitutional referendum
May–June 1996	DP wins flawed parliamentary elections
March 1997	Pyramid scheme crisis precipitates armed revolt; Sali Berisha is re-elected president
June 1997	Special parliamentary elections, although marred by extensive violence and irregularities, lead to landslide victory for the Socialist Party (SP); monarchist referendum fails
July 1997	Berisha resigns; parliament elects Rexhep Meidani president; Nano takes office as prime minister
September 1998	Azem Hajdari assassinated; Berisha attempts armed coup, Nano flees to Macedonia and subsequently resigns as prime minister
October 1998	Pandeli Majko becomes prime minister
November 1998	New constitution approved by referendum

March–September 1999	Nearly 500,000 Kosovar refugees driven into Albania by Serbian forces
October 1999	Ilir Meta becomes prime minister
June–July 2001	Flawed parliamentary elections result in SP victory
February 2002	Majko replaces Meta as prime minister
July 2002	Alfred Moisiu elected by parliament as consensus president
July 2002	Nano returns as prime minister
September 2004	Ilir Meta deserts SP and forms Socialist Movement for Integration
July–August 2005	Improved parliamentary elections see SP defeated by DP who emphasize corruption
September 2005	Sali Berisha becomes prime minister
October 2005	Nano replaced by Tirana mayor Edi Rama as leader of SP
June 2006	Albania signs SAA with EU
February 2007	Flawed local elections result in SP victories in most major cities
July 2007	Bamir Topi, deputy head of DP, elected as president following lengthy political crisis
April 2008	Albania invited to join NATO
June 2009	Improved but still flawed parliamentary elections weaken Berisha regime

Fact sheet

Area	28,748 km^2
Population (July 2008)	3,639,453
Albanian (1989 estimate)	95%
Greek (1989 estimate)	3%[a]
Other (1989 estimate)	2%
Urban population (2007)	47%
Below the poverty line (2004 estimate)	25% of population
Unemployment rate (2008 estimate)	12.5%[b]
GDP *per capita* (2008 estimate)	$6,000
Real GDP growth (2008 estimate)	6.1%
Inflation (2008 estimate)	4%

Notes:

[a] In 1989 other estimates of the Greek population ranged from 1% (official Albanian statistics) to 12% (from a Greek organization).

[b] This is the official rate, but unemployment may exceed 30% due to the preponderance of near-subsistence farming.

Sources: CIA, *The World Factbook*, at www.cia.gov/library/publications/the-world-factbook/geos/al.html/www.cia.gov/library/publications/the-world-factbook/fields/2046/html [accessed on 7 April 2009]; and unicef-Albania, at www.unicef.org/infobycountry/albania _ statistics.html [accessed on 7 April 2009].

Parties in parliament results of the 2005 elections

	Constituencies	PR[a]	Total
Democratic Party of Albania (DP)	56		56
Socialist Party of Albania (SP)	42		42
Republican Party of Albania (DP)[b]		11	11
New Democratic Party (DP)		4	4
Christian Democratic Party (DP)		2	2
Liberal Democratic Union (DP)		1	1
Social Democratic Party		7	7
Socialist Movement for Integration	1	4	5
Environmentalist Agrarian Party		4	4
Democratic Alliance Party		3	3
Social Democratic Party		2	2
Union for Human Rights Party		2	2
Non-partisan		1	1

Notes:
[a] PR = Proportional representation.
[b] DP and allies (as indicated) control 81 seats.

Parties in parliament (results of the 2009 elections)

Party	Seats (out of a total of 140)
DP-controlled "Alliance for Changes"	
Democratic Party	68
Republican Party	1
Party for Justice and Integration	1
Total	**70**
SP-controlled "Unification for Changes"	
Socialist Party	65
Unity for Human Rights Party	1
Total	**66**
Socialist Movement for Integration	4

Short biography of Sali Berisha

Sali Berisha is the most prominent post-communist politician in Albania. Born in the mountainous northeastern region of Tropojë, he studied medicine at the University of Tirana and became the country's leading cardiologist. Although a communist party member for some twelve years, Berisha was one of the first of Albania's intellectuals to call for the establishment of political pluralism. Berisha became one of the founders and head of the DP in December 1990 and was elected president in 1992. Although he initiated many important reforms, his penchant for authoritarianism made him increasingly unpopular. He was ousted in 1997 following an armed revolt, caused in part by a vast pyramid scheme swindle which he had mishandled. Indicative of his non-constructive role as leader of the opposition, he launched an unsuccessful coup attempt in 1998. Following a split in the ruling SP, as well as increasing corruption, Berisha was returned to power as prime minister in 2005 and has since produced a mixed record.

Notes

1. James O'Donnell, *A Coming of Age* (New York: Columbia University Press/East European Monographs, 1998), p. 239.
2. Miranda Vickers *The Albanians: A Modern History* (London: I.B. Tauris, 1995), p. 189.
3. Elez Biberaj *Albania in Transition: The Rocky Road to Democracy* (Boulder, Colo.: Westview Press, 1998), p. 33.
4. *Ibid.*, p. 39.
5. Nicholas Pano, "Albania," in Karen Dawisha and Bruce Parrott (eds.), *Politics, Power and the Struggle for Democracy in South-East Europe* (Cambridge: Cambridge University Press, 1997), p. 307.
6. Albania had been officially known as the People's Socialist Republic of Albania.
7. Biberaj, *Albania in Transition*, p. 91.
8. Pano, "Albania," p. 315.
9. *Ibid.*, p. 319.
10. Derek Hall, *Albania and the Albanians* (London: Pinter, 1994), pp. 90–3.
11. It is estimated that 300,000 left between 1990 and 1993.
12. For more on the Second World War in Albania, see Bernd J. Fischer, *Albania at War, 1939–1945* (London: C. Hurst and Co., 1999). For the Socialist Albanian perspective, see the four-volume collective work produced by the Institute of Marxist–Leninist Studies at the Central Committee of the Albanian Party of Labor, *Historia e Luftës Antifashiste Nacionalçlirmtare të popullit shqiptar*.
13. While the old statistics with regard to religious make-up in Albania, which reported 70% Muslim, 20% Orthodox, and 10% Catholic, are outdated, Albania is still a majority Muslim state.
14. UN Office of Drugs and Crime, Crime and Stability in the Balkans, draft document, October 2007.
15. Hall, *Albania and the Albanians*, pp. 87–90.
16. Pano, "Albania," p. 322.
17. Miranda Vickers and James Pettifer, *Albania from Anarchy to a Balkan Identity* (London: C. Hurst & Co., 1997), p. 258.
18. Pano, "Albania," pp. 341–2.
19. Biberaj, *Albania in Transition*, p. 306.
20. *Ibid.*, pp. 316–18.
21. *Ibid.*, p. 319.
22. James Pettifer and Miranda Vickers, *The Albanian Question: Reshaping the Balkans* (London: I.B. Tauris, 2007), p. 26.
23. Many of the Kalashnikovs, which at one point could be purchased for as little as $4, were smuggled to Kosovo.
24. As quoted in Biberaj, *Albania in Transition*, p. 326.
25. Pettifer and Vickers, *The Albanian Question*, p. 54.

26. *Ibid.*, p. 82.
27. Biberaj, *Albania in Transition*, p. 334.
28. Leka was eventually sentenced to prison *in absentia* on a charge of inciting a revolution. He was ultimately pardoned and returned to Albania in 2002, briefly becoming involved in politics.
29. Biberaj, *Albania in Transition*, p. 351.
30. *Ibid.*
31. *Ibid.*, pp. 340–1.
32. Adelheid Feilcke-Tiemann, "Albania: Gradual Consolidation Limited by Internal Political Struggles," *Southeast European and Black Sea Studies*, Vol. 6, No. 1 (March 2006), p. 31.
33. US Department of State, Background Note, September 2007.
34. International Crisis Group Report 2003, Albania, State of the Nation.
35. "Albanian Emigration 1989–2001," Paper submitted by INSTAT, Albania to UNECE and EUROSTAT, Seminar on Migration Statistics, Geneva, 21–23 March 2005.
36. Daniel Perez, "Rewriting History after Communism: Negotiation and Debate at Albania's Institute of History, 1993–1997," unpublished manuscript, p. 1.
37. Pettifer and Vickers, *The Albanian Question*, pp. 113–14.
38. *Ibid.*, p. 218.
39. UN Office of Drugs and Crime, World Trafficking Survey, 2006, at www.unodc.org/unodc/en/human-trafficking/index [accessed 20 September, 2007].
40. Transparency International, World Corruption Survey, 2006, at www.transparency.org/policy-research/surveys-indices/gcb/2006 [accessed 14 September, 2007].
41. As of this writing (July 2009), Meta and the Socialist Movement for Integration had agreed to join the Berisha government, although final details of the new government's makeup were not expected to be announced until September 2009.
42. The massive explosion at Gerdec on 15 March 2008 left 26 dead, 300 injured, and some 5,000 structures destroyed or damaged.

Further reading

Biberaj, Elez. *Albania: A Socialist Maverick* (Boulder, Colo.: Westview Press, 1990)
Albania in Transition: The Rocky Road to Democracy (Boulder, Colo.: Westview Press, 1998)

Fischer, Bernd J. *Albania at War, 1939–1945* (London: C. Hurst & Co., 1999)
(ed.). *Balkan Strongmen: Dictators and Authoritarian Rulers of Southeastern Europe* (London: C. Hurst & Co., 2007)

Halliday, Jon. *The Artful Albanian: The Memoirs of Enver Hoxha* (London: Chatto & Windus, 1986)

Pano, Nicholas. *The People's Republic of Albania* (Baltimore, Md.: Johns Hopkins University Press, 1968)

Pettifer, James and Miranda Vickers. *The Albanian Question: Reshaping the Balkans* (London: I.B Tauris, 2007)

Prifti, Peter. *Socialist Albania since 1944* (Cambridge, Mass.: MIT Press, 1978)

Schwandner-Sievers, Stephanie and Bernd J. Fischer (eds.). *Albanian Identities: Myth and History* (Bloomington: Ind.: Indiana University Press, 2002)

Vickers, Miranda. *The Albanians: A Modern History* (London: I.B. Tauris, 1995)

Vickers, Miranda and James Pettifer. *Albania from Anarchy to a Balkan Identity* (London: C. Hurst and Co., 1997)

Part 6
Former Soviet republics

20

The Baltic states

HERMANN SMITH-SIVERTSEN

In August 1991, following the abortive conservative attempted coup in the Soviet Union, Estonia and Latvia declared their complete independence, following Lithuania, which had declared independence the previous year. With these declarations, the three Baltic states restored the independence they had enjoyed in the years 1918–40. The last Russian troops left the Baltic states in August 1994. Ten years later, all three republics gained entrance into both the European Union (EU) and NATO.

Historical background

The first human settlers came to the Baltic region in the tenth millennium BCE. By the end of the twelfth century Northern Europe was generally Christianized, except for the area of today's Baltic states and some remote Arctic areas and Prussia. Finland had just been Christianized by the Swedes and the core of today's Russia was Christianized even before that from the ancient *Rus* capital of Kyiv. The areas of Prussia and today's Latvia and Estonia were Christianized by force mainly by German crusaders (the Order of the Brethren of the Sword and the Teutonic Knights, later merged as the Teutonic [or German] Order). Livonia was the historical name of the Order state covering today's Latvia and Estonia (named after the tribe – Livs – who lived in the coastal areas near Riga). The territory of Livonia was easier to access from the sea and the rivers than the areas of future Lithuania. Estonia was under foreign rule beginning in 1227, while Latvia came under foreign rule in the twelfth century. At the battle of Saule in 1236 the Teutonic Order was defeated by the Lithuanians, who avoided the forced Christianization and the German-speaking upper class; Lithuania was, in fact, the last nation in Europe to convert to Christianity, accepting that religion only in 1385. Subsequently, in 1410, a joint Polish–Lithuanian army inflicted a more decisive defeat on the Teutonic Knights at the Battle of Grünwald. The destiny of the indigenous tribes in Livonia was not shared by the Lithuanians, who succeeded in creating their own medieval monarchy. By 1309 all the areas of future Latvia were conquered by the Order, and in 1346 the remaining parts of future Estonia were acquired.[1] Medieval Livonia was a feudal state with German-speaking landowners, clergy, and merchants. The peasantry spoke Latvian dialects in the south and Estonian in the north. In the Livonian area the linguistic situation remained broadly the same for about 600 years, changed by democratization in 1918 making German a minority language, and finally by the removal of the Baltic Germans during the Second World War.

Under different multinational empires

Around 1621 most of Livonia[2] fell under Swedish rule, lasting for a century. Eastern Latgale remained under Polish rule, and Lutheran Christianity accordingly did not get the upper hand in that smaller part of Livonia, but in the bulk of Livonia (Courland included) it did. Apart from Latgale, the territories of future Estonia and Latvia were managed by the Baltic–German elites, while different empires shifted in demanding allegiance from the Baltic Germans. Roman Catholicism dominated in Lithuania and Latgale, Lutheranism in the rest of Livonia. In Lithuania the landowning elite and clergy spoke Polish (because of the process of "Polonization"[3]) and the peasants Lithuanian, while in Livonia the peasants spoke Latvian or Estonian while the elites spoke German.

After the great Nordic War the Swedish part of Livonia became a part of the Romanov empire (imperial Russia), to be followed seven decades later by the other Baltic provinces, when the third partition of Poland–Lithuania took place in 1795. After the partitions of Poland–Lithuania the whole territory of today's Estonia, Latvia, and Lithuania was within the Russian empire. The Baltic nations experienced the national awakening of the nineteenth century and early industrialization under a single multinational empire. Still, these processes evolved differently. Lithuania remained agricultural throughout the nineteenth century, while the harbor cities of Livonia, especially Riga and Tallinn, experienced growing industry and trade in the century up to 1914. This changed the ethnolinguistic situation, Russian speakers started to move in to get jobs, and indigenous people moved to the Livonian cities for the same reason. The Baltic Germans diminished in prominence in Riga and Tallinn. The national awakening was different, too. In future Estonia and Latvia, it was about indigenous-language interests facing the claims of the local elites and the russophone interests of the center of the empire. In most of Lithuania the linguistic fronts were broadly similar as the cleavage between landowners and clergy versus peasants. The Polish-speaking nobility in Lithuania had been involved in the Polish rebellions of 1830–1 and 1863 against the Tsar. In Latvia and Estonia the emphasis was on collecting samples of popular culture; thousands of folk songs were recorded on paper. The song festivals became ethno-linguistic manifestations during the nineteenth-century national awakening, and increasing the cultural influence of the indigenous languages in the major cities became an important task.

National independence was proclaimed in 1918 at the end of the First World War, and the first years of statehood were marked by struggles among Bolsheviks, German forces, and forces of the three Baltic nations. The heirs of the Livonian territories had to define their borders with Soviet Russia while the Republic of Lithuania faced Poland and Germany. The interwar regimes of Estonia, Latvia, and Lithuania were rather similar at the outset, with strong parliaments and presidents appointed by the legislature. The percentages of the titular nationalities in the republics varied from 77% (Latvia) to 86% (Estonia). Most compact with regard to religion was Lithuania, with 81% Roman Catholics, while Estonia had 78% Lutherans. Latvia was most divided ethnically and religiously, having 56% Lutherans, 24% Roman Catholics and three other significant minorities – Orthodox Christians, Mosaic, and the orthodox Old Believers.[4] Also here we can notice the relevance of history: if somebody observes that among the Baltic nations of our time Estonia is culturally the most like the Nordic countries, Latvia is most divided culturally, and Lithuania is the most culturally Central European, this was the case for these territories also at the beginning of the nineteenth century, probably even before that.

The end of parliamentary rule

Proportional representation without electoral thresholds contributed to fragmented parliaments in the new republics during the 1920s. Latvia, for example, always had at least twenty parties in the legislature of 100 deputies (Saeima). Still, parliamentary rule lasted longer in Latvia than in Estonia or Lithuania. The breakdown of representative democracy happened rather early in the latter case, in December 1926. The parliamentary elections that year had produced victory of a leftist coalition, and the new government established diplomatic relations with the USSR. By the end of that year the extreme right had succeeded in a coup d'état that was a collaboration between the army and right-wing leaders, notably the nationalist leader Antanas Smetona, against the cabinet of ministers and the majority of the Seimas (the legislature of Lithuania). The collapse of the democratic regime occurred later and was different in Estonia and Latvia. In these countries it was the president or prime minister – an agrarian – who led a coup d'état in 1934 as a pre-emptive action against the far right.

An important policy issue in the interwar era was the redistribution of agricultural land from the estates to the landless and smallholders, creating family farms. In Estonia and Latvia these policies were radical and swift, and the former estate owners got little or no compensation. In Lithuania, such policies were slow and less radical.

The end of independence

The secret protocols of the Molotov–Ribbentrop Treaty of August 1939 defined the Baltic states as lying within the Soviet sphere of influence. The Baltic states were pressured to accept Soviet military bases in their territories that autumn; an occupation was carried through in the summer of 1940, and mock elections were staged in the summer for republic assemblies. Candidates not loyal to the USSR were barred from running in these unfree elections. Shortly after being convened, the assembly of each state applied for membership in the USSR, which was ratified in August 1940. Thus, the Baltic states had been Soviet republics for eleven months when Hitler's troops arrived in 1941; the German occupation lasted three years. As a result of the massive USSR deportations of Baltic inhabitants (to Siberia), the flight of local people before the victorious Red Army in 1944, the ejection of the Baltic Germans (and many Lithuanian Poles), as well as the Nazi Holocaust against the Baltic Jews, the ethno-linguistic situation had changed fundamentally by 1945, and was soon to change even more. The harbors, railways, and industry-friendly infrastructure of Latvia and Estonia made industrialization attractive and this resulted in the post-war influx of large numbers of Russian-speaking workers. Lithuania was more agrarian at that time and had post-war anti-communist guerilla fighting up to the mid-1950s, making it less attractive for the establishment of large Soviet factories. This partly explains why the ethnic balance in Lithuania did not change so much during the post-war decades. The censuses of 1989 showed that there were 61.5% Estonians in Estonia, 52% Latvians in Latvia, and 80% Lithuanians in Lithuania. Lithuania was also the exception with regard to territory: thanks to the USSR it had regained the ethnically mixed Vilnius area from Poland as well as the Klaipeda region (the city of Memel and its vicinity until 1918 and again from the spring of 1939). Estonia and Latvia lost territory in the east when they entered the USSR, territories they never regained.

Also at the elite levels the Soviet era was not quite similar in each of the Baltic republics. During Stalin's reign policies were rather similar, but the communists had different cadres at hand. Significant groups of red Estonians and Latvians had stayed in the USSR since around 1920 and could be sent back to their native lands in order to build socialism there on behalf of the USSR regime. There were very few Lithuanian communists at hand in 1944. The party cadres of the titular nationality had to be recruited from 1944 onwards, this meant that the influence of Stalinism was stronger in Estonia and Latvia compared to Lithuania. During the post-Stalin era, developments within the republic communist parties differed in some regards. In Latvia, national communists tried to win leadership during the late 1950s but met resistance from Communist Party headquarters in Moscow. During 1959–60 Latvian national communists were purged in large numbers, their demand that communist officials working in Latvia should learn the Latvian language was subsequently ignored. Officially the republic had two languages, but Russian got the upper hand in industry, central government, and the cities. In Lithuania national communism managed to keep a low profile, but the percentages of Lithuanians in the republic communist party increased, rising from 66% in 1968 to 71% in 1989, while the Russian share was only 17% in the latter year. The share of ethnic Latvians in the republic communist party of Latvia was 45% in 1967 and 40% in 1989, and in 1989 as many as 43% of the party members were Russians. Estonia was the "middle case" in this regard. These developments during the 1960s and 1970s became relevant in 1989, when the communist party organization in Lithuania separated from the Communist Party of the Soviet Union (CPSU) and voted for national independence in the spring of 1990. In Latvia, the opposite was the case. Pro-independence Latvians had to leave the republic communist party in 1990, because the communists rejected independence from the USSR. The reformed, pro-independence Lithuanian ex-communists even won the parliamentary election of 1992, while the ex-communist party members in Latvia were dispersed politically and most were marginalized.

System rebuilding

Lasting from the summer of 1987 to the autumn of 1991 the independence struggle in the Baltic states turned out as crucial – not only in terms of the actual achievement of independence from the USSR, but also for the post-1991 political developments in the Baltic countries. The configuration of the competing political elite groups as well as the mass mobilization of the populations occurred in the special context of the independence struggle. During this period – not before – there was a relatively open and free competition in the political field, which allowed the elites and citizens to start developing political allegiances in competitive politics. Former communists got the chance to distinguish themselves in the independence conflict (striving to achieve independence from the USSR), thus blurring any subsequent communist–anti-communist cleavage.

The early electoral mobilization of the Baltic opposition forces occurred in the spring of 1989 for the elections to the USSR Congress of People's Deputies. Candidates supported by the popular fronts (see below) won at least 75% of the seats of each Baltic republic. These elections were perceived as overwhelming victories.[5] However, in all three Baltic states, it was mainly the seats in the republic supreme soviets (republic councils) that the early competitive elections were about. In every Baltic state it was the republic soviet that passed the declaration of independence in 1990. Still, the legal continuity with the Soviet Union was broken in these countries through the symbolic or real re-adoption of the last constitution of the interwar republic. In Lithuania this re-adoption only lasted for a few hours on 11 March 1990, because the prewar constitution was an authoritarian one from 1938.[6] Vytautas Landsbergis, a professor of music, was elected chairman of the Supreme Council of Lithuania (an office which was later renamed "President of the Republic"). Lithuania passed a new constitution in 1992 (approved by a referendum of 25 October 1992), with a semi-presidential executive and a strong unicameral parliament.

The new constitution of Estonia was prepared by a Constitutional Assembly[7] and adopted in a referendum on 28 June 1992, enjoying the support of 91.2% of the voters. The 1992 constitution was modeled on the Estonian interwar constitutions.[8] Lennart Meri, a dramatist and novelist, took office as president. The president – appointed by parliament – has a ceremonial role, while the unicameral parliament is the dominant public institution. This is also the case for

Latvia. There, the constitution from 1922 with amendments from 1933 was again in full force from 1993 onwards. Resurrecting that constitution underlined the claim that post-communist Latvia was not first and foremost the heir of a Soviet republic, but in reality the heir of an independent nation state that had been a member of the League of Nations in the interwar era. This was possible in Latvia because the authoritarian regime of Kārlis Ulmanis (1934–40) had not changed the formal constitution of the republic. Guntis Ulmanis, grandnephew of Kārlis Ulmanis, was elected president of Latvia in 1993.

Politics and governance

During the independence struggle, the popular fronts were important in the Baltic states. In Estonia, the front was called Rahvarinne, in Latvia Latvijas Tautas Fronte (LTF) and in Lithuania it was called Sajudis. Rahvarinne was mostly centrist already in the beginning, having a big independence movement outside it (to the right of Rahvarinne) organizing the citizens' committees (representing pre-war citizens and their descendants). To the south of Estonia LTF was by contrast very encompassing, probably because the small Latvian ethnical majority in the republic made it hard to achieve a two-thirds majority in the republic soviet for independence. The Lithuanian Sajudis was more right-leaning than left-leaning in 1990, since the bulk of the communists in Lithuania supported independence already while remaining a unified group in a reformed party (LDDP) led by Algirdas Mykolas Brazauskas.

Accordingly, after 1991 the remnants of these fronts did not find similar placements inside the new party systems that emerged in the post-transition parliamentary elections. In Estonia the significant parties of a centrist and slightly-left-of-center orientation emerged from the popular front (the Center party and the Moderates/Social Democrats), while in Lithuania the bulk of the popular front transformed to be the main right-of-center party (The Homeland Union, TS–LKD). In Latvia a host of parties are offshoots of the popular front, from center-left, to centrist, to rightist parties.

Electoral systems

Independent Estonia has a complicated electoral system for parliamentary elections. The system is proportional and *de facto* dominated by party lists. In the polling booth the voter must cast their vote for an individual candidate. But most often this candidate will be on a party list of candidates, so the votes for the candidates of that party will be counted as party votes also. In the first round of counting, personal mandates may be won, but this is not the usual way politicians get elected. In the second counting, the mandates are distributed proportionally among the parties in eleven regional multiseat constituencies, not rewarding those parties getting fewer than 5% nationally. The remaining seats are distributed in the third round of counting, which is at the national level using the modified d'Hondt system and a 5% threshold; now mandates are distributed to candidates of national party lists. Many MPs are elected at the national level, which implies weak voter support in specific constituencies for these individual MPs. This feature, however, increases the autonomy of the political elites.

The system for parliamentary elections in Latvia is simpler and also based on proportional representation. Every member of the Saeima is elected in a regional multiseat constituency. These constituencies are rather significant in size: constituencies having 14–26 seats to distribute – combined with St. Lagüe's divisors – ensure a high level of proportionality between the party share of votes and the party share of seats (the divisors are 1, 3, 5, 7, and so on). However, the high level of proportionality is only relevant for those electoral parties passing the 5% threshold at the national level. The sole change after the 1993 election was the adjustment of the threshold from 4% to 5% in 1995. The most important difference from the Estonian system is that the Latvian one makes it harder for the parties to elect less popular persons to parliament. The reasons are that there are no seats at the national level to distribute and, more importantly, the voters may give candidates (on the party list of candidates) an extra vote or even a minus vote, while the parties may not list important candidates twice on a single ballot in one constituency. This weakens party autonomy.

Since 1992, the Lithuanian Seimas has been composed of 71 seats elected in single-seat constituencies, where a system resembling the French one has been used to decide when a second-round election is necessary. The other 70 Seimas seats are distributed proportionally in a single nationwide constituency in a system resembling the Dutch electoral system, but with an electoral threshold. The major features of this electoral system have been stable since 1992, but some small adjustments did occur.

Party systems

In Lithuania during the 1990s the party system was dominated by two big blocks that alternated as the majority alternative. Either the LDDP – the heirs of the previous pro-Lithuanian communists – or the Sajudis heir The Homeland Union (TS–LKD) together with the weaker Christian Democrats – had the majority in the Seimas. In 2000, several middle-size (more or less) liberal parties emerged between these older blocks. In the 2004 election a brand-new populist party (Labor Party) outside the blocks suddenly won the plurality, but lacked the support to form a cabinet on its own. In both 2000 and 2004 three middle-size (more or less) liberal parties were elected to parliament, as well as the Farmer's Union. The dominance of the old blocks of the 1990s was brought to an end.[9]

The party systems of Estonia, Latvia, and Lithuania are significantly more fragmented than the average for Western Europe, although Lithuania used to have a (lower) fragmentation level closer to the West European average. The 2004 Seimas election produced a result of 6.14 effective parties in Lithuania (calculated from party seats), while the post-communist average for this country was 4.1. In Latvia the 2006 election resulted in 6.00 effective parties (calculated from party seat, slightly above the post-communist average for Latvia of 5.8. Despite electoral thresholds in these countries, the party system fragmentation in these systems is stable and high or increasing and high. On average, Estonia has a party system fragmentation placed between the levels of the two other Baltic states.[10] This feature of the party systems prompts the dominance of coalition governments.

The measures of stability should also be considered. Net electoral volatility in 1991–2005 was higher in Estonia, Latvia, and Lithuania compared to the countries of Central Europe, while the latter had a higher average volatility than the West European average during the 1990s.[11] From 1992 to 2002, Latvia had a somewhat higher rate than Lithuania with regard to volatility. This was mainly because Lithuania showed a modest electoral volatility in the mid-1990s; this reduced the Lithuanian average volatility (in 1992–2002) to a lower level than those of the other Baltic states. In 2005, the Estonian average volatility was the lowest among the Baltic states, while the average levels of the two other Baltic states were rather similar. This implies a somewhat higher level of stability in the Estonian party system.

In Lithuania the alternation of ruling power between competing parties has been observed since the early 1990s, featuring a system in which all parties of some significance – more than 8% of the votes – have participated in the cabinet of ministers for some of the time. No middle-size or bigger parties have over time been excluded from participation in the ruling coalition.

After 1990, other relations of party cooperation developed in Latvia. There the pattern is that such parties which are understood as left-of-center never participate in the cabinet of ministers. The only exception is that the Democratic party Saimnieks – helped by its significant size at the time – participated in the grand coalition from December 1995 until April 1998. But this party was not regarded as far from the center and was never thought of as being an ideological party.

The main pattern of Latvian coalitions after 1993 is that some center-right and rightist parties rule together with a few weaker centrist parties. Alternation of rule in Latvia happens in this way: new center-right and rightist parties are elected to parliament and enter the cabinet of ministers, while other center-right and rightist parties become weaker or even drop below the 5% electoral threshold. The weaker form of alternation of rule is that a new prime minister with a slightly changed coalition is installed. New center-right and rightist parties of Latvia are not similar – some are more preoccupied with ethno-linguistic and national issues than others, some are more preoccupied with the economy and the market, some are more rurally oriented, some are more open to Christian interests. But these parties never disclose their center-right and/or rightist party orientation, and they are all dominated by ethnic Latvian politicians.

To the left of the center the social democrats participated for four years (1998–2002) in the Saeima with a caucus of middle size, and were never invited to join the coalition, even if they were pro-regime and dominated by ethnic Latvians. Left of center we find as a stable parliamentary party, the Harmony Party (TSP), with an electoral basis of Russian speakers who supported Latvia's secession from the USSR. TSP is a fully fledged pro-democracy party that is now in the multiparty faction Harmony Center (the socialist party LSP is in that faction, too.) TSP too was never included in the ruling coalition. On the left wing we find a group that has always been in the Saeima since the transition to democracy: Equal Rights, which is a left party representing the heirs of those who did not wish Latvia to leave the USSR (LSP also represents such heirs). Since 2003, Equal Rights has been the biggest group behind the parliamentary faction PCTVL – For Human Rights in a United Latvia. The huge political distance between Equal Rights (and Latvia's Socialist Party LSP) and the rightist parties implies that Latvia has a party system with more polarization than that of Lithuania and Estonia. However, the left pole is weak in Latvia, but permanently in the Saeima (although the name of the parliamentary caucus is now PCTVL, while these leftist forces were earlier in factions such as Equal Rights or LSP).

Considering the incentives the electoral system offers to political actors, the effects of the electoral system are crucial. In Lithuania it is very important to become the largest party, while in Latvia political influence can be secured by becoming a middle-size party with good potential for coalitions. Estonia is closer to Latvia than to Lithuania in this respect.

Cleavages

The Lithuanian political scientist Mindaugas Jurkynas claims that the lines of conflicts and alignments in Lithuania have not yet stabilized, and that so far we should talk about "issue divides," related to particular issues. I would propose that cleavages can explain why the parties to the left of the center are a more fragmented group in Latvia than in Lithuania. Old and new conflicts about citizenship and language policies, as well as conflicting views on the secession from the political center in Moscow, are cutting much deeper through the parties to the left of the center in Latvia than in the other Baltic states.

In Lithuania there was for a long time less conflict about citizenship and language than in Latvia, and the resistance against secession from the USSR was much weaker in Lithuania (and Estonia) than in Latvia. The significant conflict within the center-left in Lithuania was about how to assess the regime in Soviet Lithuania. This divide was overcome nine years after the country's independence. At that time, the two social democratic parties – the small western oriented one and the large post-communist one (LDDP) – were merged. After 1990 Latvia had parties center-left that were more profoundly divided – and with more cleavages – than in the country south of Latvia. The parliamentary left pole is further away from the political center in Latvia compared to any other Baltic state. The total effect that cleavages have on voters' behavior can be estimated by multivariance methods, provided that one has at hand reliable survey data about the party voters' placement in the social structure and the individual voters' relation to various social groups and possibly relevant cleavages. But there is a lack of such data sets. In the best available, that from Latvia in the 1998 election, data on religion are missing.

Frode Berglund and I did a regression analysis of the 1998 voters' survey in Latvia, with 860 party voters willing to reply. The analysis showed that voting center-left was determined by three variables: being non-Latvian in ethnicity, being male, and having a low income ("low" in the context of Latvian economic circumstances). In the lower-income brackets 43.8% of the voters voted center-left as compared to 28.6% in the higher-income brackets. Looking only at the ethnic Latvians in the sample, for those with low income 35.2% voted center-left while 23.3% did so in higher-income groups. The level of education had the same covariance. Those with higher education tended more to vote center-right than voters with more limited education.[12]

The disadvantaged strata versus the managing, occupational elites is an emerging cleavage that I have observed in Latvian mass politics, and I believe it will be relevant for Lithuania, too. This cleavage can explain the support for left-of-center parties and protesting populists as a single phenomenon (regardless of whether these populists seem centrist or right-of-center). The supporters backing Arnold Rüütel for president of Estonia may be defined by a similar cleavage (or divide). He was a high-ranking Communist Party official in Soviet Estonia who served as chairman of the supreme soviet of Estonia elected in free elections in 1990 and that passed the independence resolutions.

Some would explain party support by the popularity of the party leaders and not by cleavages or issue divides. However, there are also examples of parties elected to parliament in several elections without any really popular leader (for example, For Fatherland and Freedom/LNNK (TB/LNNK) and the Harmony party (TSP) in Latvia). Surveys in Latvia show that many of the voters select their candidate list on the basis of their personal situation or interests, or the social group to which they belong. I would claim that the general patterns of cooperation and conflict within these party systems is better explained by cleavages than by elite politics. However, when developments in shorter time spans are explained, or details in these party systems accounted for, elite politics prove to be a significant variable.

Concerning controversies about lustration, former KGB officers are banned from political office and from running as candidates for parliament in the Baltic states. This has prompted discussions about exactly what should be regarded as "KGB" in the Soviet era. The Soviet border guards were under the umbrella of the KGB, so should people who served with them be banned, a question facing deputy J. Adamsons in Latvia in the 1990s. In 2005, the Lithuanian foreign minister A. Valionis admitted that he had served in the KGB reserves, and two other senior officials faced similar allegations. However, the former reservists were deemed exempt from the legal requirement that former KGB agents must disclose their past to the public.[13]

The party systems of the Baltic states are different, as I try to show in table 20.1 covering all three countries. Only Lithuania has a party system in which the center-left parties enjoy significant support in the post-communist era. In this country, the center-left even had the prime minister for most of the time after 1992. Still, in all the Baltic countries the center-right parties are on average the strongest group, in Estonia and Latvia every prime minister from 1990 until now has been centrist or rightist. I would explain this Lithuanian exception

Table 20.1 Voter support for categories of parties

a Estonian Riigikogu elections, 1992–2007[a]

Electoral alternative	1992 (%)	1995 (%)	1999 (%)	2003 (%)	2007 (%)
Center-right and rightist parties	47.4	34.1	34.4	50.7	47.4
Centrist parties	22.0	52.4	46.2	32.4	43.8
Center-left and leftist parties	15.2	5.9	15.4	15.8	8.4
Others[b]	15.4	7.6	4.0	1.1	0.4

Notes:
[a] The votes of failed electoral alternatives are included.
[b] Tiny electoral alternatives.

b Latvian Saeima elections, 1993–2006[a]

Electoral alternative	1993 (%)	1995 (%)	1998 (%)	2002 (%)	2006 (%)
Center-right and rightist parties	71.4	40.6	56.9	60.5	52.9
Centrist parties	4.8	16.7	11.3	10.2	16.7
Center-left and leftist parties	20.5	17.0	27.4	26.0	26.0
Populist lists[b]	–	22.1	2.2	–	–
Others[c]	3.3	3.6	2.2	3.3	4.4

Notes:
[a] The votes of failed electoral alternatives are included.
[b] The Peoples' Movement for Latvia (Siegerist) and The Unity Party of Latvia.
[c] Tiny electoral alternatives.

c Lithuanian Seimas elections, 1992–2004[a]

Electoral alternative	1992 (%)	1996 (%)	2000 (%)	2004 (%)
Center-right and rightist parties	40.0	57.3	38.4	38.8
Centrist parties	4.7	17.4	28.5	38.8
Center-left and leftist parties	50.0	22.0	31.6	20.7
Others[b]	5.3	3.3	1.5	1.7

Notes:
[a] Votes for party lists only; the votes of failed electoral alternatives are included.
[b] Tiny electoral alternatives.

historically: the stronger the national communist movement was during the 1960s and 1970s, the stronger the center-left parties became after 1990. Latvian national communism was severely suppressed by the extensive purges in the Republic Party in 1959–60,[14] making the remaining communists mainly pro-Russian in 1990. Lithuanian national communism was never weeded out during the post-Stalin era of the USSR.

Latvia has the strongest group of center-right parties in the Baltic area, probably facilitated by mainstream popular nationalism. This is generally pro-Western and broadly identifying individualism and conservatism with non-Russian national allegiance. In Lithuania we saw that the mass support for centrist parties has grown significantly since the early 1990s. This probably implies that the divide between Lithuanian national communists and anti-communists has lost its significance since the early 1990s. The party system in Lithuania has become less deviant from the other Baltic party systems, while still retaining a stronger democratic left than the two other countries. It should also be noted that the center-left is marginalized in Estonia and Latvia – in Estonia because center-left parties are too weak; in Latvia they are stronger but they are generally not accepted as coalition partners. The stronger emphasis on nationalism and current lack of inclusion of leftist parties in Estonia and Latvia can also be explained further back in history. For centuries the peasants there faced a local upper class that was perceived as colonialist and non-indigenous. Later, the communist elites were perceived in a similar vein. This translates popular anti-elite sentiments into popular ethnic nationalism. In Lithuania the peasants faced local nobles of Lithuanian heritage, only "polonized" linguistically and the communist elites were mainly indigenous, too. The latter situation may more easily translate into class consciousness.

The role of the media

Since the 1990s the main media situation in each Baltic country has been relatively free. There are several national TV channels, of which one is state-owned and the others are in private hands. There are also a host of independent newspapers. Freedom of the press and free speech are respected by the authorities, although in Latvia it has been reported that many media outlets frequently report rumors and ill-founded accusations. Some media outlets are also suspected of being under the control of elite members who are both politicians and major business owners.[15]

In Estonia, a new Broadcasting Act was passed in 1994 and amended several times subsequently; Estonia does not have a law governing the print media, but the constitution prohibits censorship and provides assurances of freedom of speech and of writing. Latvia adopted a new law on the mass media in 1996 and a law on broadcasting in 1997. A commentator for the Cardozo School of Law expressed concern at the time that the law governing Latvian mass media might prove "unworkable" and "impossible to administer," and that it did not provide a reliable guarantee of freedom of the press,[16] but in 2004, criminal liability for the defamation of government officials was effectively abolished.[17] In 2006, Latvia's First Party (Latvijas Pirmas Partia, LPP) introduced a bill in parliament to ban any mention of homosexuality in the mass media; the bill was defeated by a narrow vote, however. Lithuania passed a new media law in 1996, covering both print and broadcast media. Subsequently, a Law on the Provision of Information to the Public was passed in 2000. In 2002, the Constitutional Court of Lithuania ruled that journalists should have to reveal their sources, if issued a court order. Although a policy paper reported, in 2001, that the Lithuanian media continued "to perpetuate discrimination and hostility against ethnic and sexual minorities,"[18] Freedom House ranked the Estonian press as the freest in the post-communist region, and the Lithuanian press as second freest (tied with the Czech Republic), with the Latvian press ranked fourth freest in the region.[19] In a global context, Estonia was ranked in 16th place in terms of press freedom (tied with Germany, Ireland, the United States, and others), Lithuania was ranked in 29th place (tied, as already indicated, with the Czech Republic), and Latvia was ranked in 31st place (tied with the United Kingdom).[20]

The printed media are privately owned, and, in Estonia and Latvia Russian-language media are available. Latvians tend to ignore the Russian-language press, while local Russians tend to ignore the Latvian-language press, although the situation with broadcasting is less polarized. This results in Latvians and Russians living in Latvia reading different news articles. In Lithuania, by contrast, the four main Russian-language newspapers in circulation in 2003 consisted of a mixture of articles translated from the Lithuanian press and of articles carried over from newspapers published in Russia.[21] There is some foreign investment in Baltic media. For example, the Bonnier Group of Sweden is the largest shareholder in the Latvian newspaper, *Diena*, which appears in both Latvian- and Russian-language editions, while TV3, one of four national broadcasting stations in Lithuania, is owned by Scandinavian Modern Times.[22] Foreign investment in the media is the most extensive in Latvia where, since 2007, almost all private Latvian-language media are foreign-owned.[23] Some broadcast media are state-run, and some are owned by local private businessmen. Internet use is already increasing.

Economic issues

In the three Baltic states the planned economy familiar from Soviet times prevailed throughout the 1980s, making the economic transition in the early 1990s rather traumatic. These countries experienced hyperinflation in the years 1991–2 (in Lithuania, it lasted well in to 1993). Since 1995 inflation rates have been moderate, and real GDP has started to grow again.[24] With regard to economic and monetary reform policies Estonia was the extreme case. The center-right government taking office after the 1992 election abolished tariffs, freed prices, made taxation simpler, pegged the currency to the German mark and sold large parts of industry to foreigners. This course was continued by the succeeding governments, emphasizing a balanced budget and introducing a flat tax on income.[25] By the end of 1997, Estonian political scientists reported a lack of domestic opposition to the cornerstones of Estonian economic policies, the latter being within "the consensual area" of Estonian politics.[26] By 2004 it was clear that Estonia had become the most successful of all post-communist countries in attracting direct FDI in the post-communist era, when measured *per capita*.[27]

Concerning Latvia, the European Commission reported in 1997 that privatization of large-scale industrial enterprises was remarkably slow as compared to the swift privatization of the agricultural sector and small-scale businesses. One of the few victories of the combined Latvian center-left forces pertained to the Latvenergo company of power plants. In 2000, as many as 307,000 voters signed a proposal for a legal act that would halt the partial privatization of Latvenergo. In order to prevent a referendum over this proposal, parliament had to pass the proposed act. In Lithuania it was the privatization of big companies that evoked the most conflict. The sale of Mazeikiu Nafta to the American company Williams International in the late 1990s was very controversial, and contributed much to the severe defeat of the conservative ruling Homeland Union (TS–LK) in the Seimas election of 2000: the party dropped from 70 to 9 seats!

Criminality and corruption

According to Transparency International's CPI, Estonia has a lower degree of perceived corruption than the two other Baltic states. Estonia is on the level of Portugal and Slovenia. Latvia and Lithuania are close to Slovakia and Greece. Estonia and Slovenia are actually regarded as the least corrupt of all post-communist counties, while Latvia and Lithuania are more favorably rated than Poland.

In Lithuania a host of high-profile corruption scandals made headlines from 2004 to 2006. The most famous was about incumbent President Rolandas Paksas who was impeached for corruption in 2004. His actions were investigated by a parliamentary committee and its report treated in the Constitutional Court. Paksas was found guilty of having unlawfully granted citizenship to the shady businessman who financed his presidential campaign, a businessman also linked to organized crime and foreign intelligence services.

In Latvia the reported oligarchs Andris Šķēle, Aivars Lembergs, and Ainārs Šlesers made headlines before and during 2007. What they share is that they mixed the roles of big business owners with roles in political leadership. Šķēle began as deputy minister for agriculture in the early 1990s, then appeared as the owner of much of Latvia's food processing facilities in the mid-1990s, moving on to be prime minister for a broad coalition in 1995–7, then founding his own center-right party in 1998 (the People's Party, TP), serving one year as prime minister for this party and then retreating from institutional politics. Even after this Šķēle is said to be the real power center in the TP, which emerged as the winner after the elections of 1998 and 2006. Aivars Lembergs was from the 1980s the mayor of Ventspils city, and is also an important business owner, as well as the sponsor of the electoral and parliamentary union of two parties: the Latvian Farmers' Union (LZS) and the Green Party (LZP). From the spring of 2007 until February 2008, Lembergs was under arrest, suspected of corruption. Ainārs Šlesers is both the chairman of a middle-size centrist party (LPP/LC) as well as transport minister and an important business owner. During the autumn of 2007 there was significant popular mobilization in Latvia against the political influence of the oligarchs. An anti-corruption official (Loskutovs) was making problems for Šķēle and the TP, and the prime minister of this party tried to have him dismissed. The end of the story was that the TP lost the post of prime minister and Loskutovs remained in his job.

Coming to terms with the past

In Latvia and Estonia, the controversies regarding the past are mainly between the mainstream groups within the titular nationality and the less anti-Soviet groups among the Russian speakers. The main disagreement is what happened really in 1940 when the Baltic states were annexed to the USSR. There have also been efforts to try and convict persons guilty of crimes against humanity during the communist era. In one example, an Estonian court found an eighty-one-year-old former Soviet security police agent guilty, in 2002, of crimes against humanity for his role in deporting forty-one people, including children, to Siberia after the Soviet occupation of Estonia.[28]

In Lithuania the controversies about the past are more between Lithuanians and ethnic Poles. The latter were owning extensive land around Vilnius before the Second World War, when that area was under Polish administration. After 1990 the ethnic Poles living in that area had problems in proving their pre-war ownership of the land. The political expression of this is the stable presence of the Polish minority party (LLRA) in the Seimas. Their deputies get elected in single-seat constituencies from the region around Vilnius city.

The revival of religion in the Baltics

In the Baltic states the popular national identity is more connected to language than to religious affiliation, which helps to explain why religious issues are only modestly important in the political life of these countries. Estonia is mostly Lutheran, Lithuania overwhelmingly Roman Catholic, while Latvia has four main groups: Lutherans, Roman Catholics, Russian Orthodox, and non-believers. The (orthodox) Old Believers are a religious minority that is significant for Latvia; they arrived several centuries ago, escaping church reforms in Russia. Since 1991, Protestant Churches based in the United States and Western

Europe have sent missionaries to the post-communist states and, as of 1994, there were forty-five non-indigenous Protestant missionaries working in Estonia, twenty-nine in Latvia, and four in Lithuania.[29] Some non-traditional, non-Christian associations have also been present in the region, such as the Sri Radmish Mystical Cult in Latvia, the Maharishi Association of the Vedic Sciences, which promotes transcendental meditation, in Estonia,[30] and Scientology and the Hare Krishna in Lithuania.[31]

About 60% of Estonians do not belong to any religious community, but almost 29% of the population belong to Christian denominations, with the Estonian Evangelical Lutheran Church being the largest single religious community with about 180,000 members.[32] The Estonian Orthodox Church has about 170,000 members, while the Estonian Apostolic Orthodox Church has about 25,000 members. The Roman Catholic Church has 6,000 adherents in Estonia. Other religious groups have smaller memberships and include Jews, Muslims, Buddhists, Baptists, Jehovah's Witnesses, Pentecostals, Old Believers, and Methodists, among others. The restitution of religious properties confiscated by Soviet authorities has been largely completed. A new Law on Churches and Congregations came into force in 1993, placing all religious communities on an equal footing; every religious community is required to register with the authorities, and a religious body must have at least twelve members in order to qualify for registration.[33]

In Latvia, Roman Catholics are the largest religious denomination, comprising some 22% of the country's population (about 500,000 members); the Lutheran Church is the second-largest congregation, comprising some 20% of the population (about 435,000 members). Orthodox Christians make up 15% of the population (350,000 members). There are also Baptists (7,089), Seventh-Day Adventists (3,900), Old Believers, Mormons, Methodists, Pentecostals, evangelical Protestant groups, and (as of 2008) 334 Muslims. There were also 10,168 persons defined as ethnically Jewish living in Latvia in 2008, but only 247 persons registered as religiously Jewish.[34] Under legislation passed in 1995, any group of twenty citizens or other persons over the age of eighteen, who have been recorded in the register of population, may apply to register a religious association. Under current legislation, religious associations defined as "traditional" enjoy rights and privileges not accorded to non-traditional ones. In 2003, two religious bodies – the Confessional Lutheran Church and the Autonomous True Orthodox Church – were denied registration on the grounds that, under Article 7, part 3, of the law of 1995, "Congregations of the same denomination may establish only one religious association [Church] in the country."[35] Efforts were subsequently made to change this provision of the law.[36]

Among Lithuanians, Roman Catholics comprise 79% of the country's population of 3,565,205 (July 2008) – or about 2,816,500.[37] Among traditional faiths – defined as religious associations which have existed in Lithuania for at least 300 years – there are also about 140,000 adherents of the Eastern Orthodox Church, 27,000 Old Believers, 20,000 Lutherans, 7,000 members of the Evangelical

Reformed community, 4,000 members of the Jewish community, 2,700 Sunni Muslims, an estimated 300 Greek-Rite Catholics, and 250 Karaites. Fewer than 5% of Lithuania's population belongs to non-traditional religious communities; among these are the Full Gospel Word of Faith Movement, Pentecostals/Charismatics, Jehovah's Witnesses, Baptists, Seventh-Day Adventists, the Church of Jesus Christ of Latter-Day Saints (Mormons), the New Apostolic Church, and, as already mentioned, Scientology and Hare Krishna.[38]

Aside from these religious bodies, one may also note that "there still remain pockets of pagan beliefs and practices" which have survived the centuries of Christian rule and the decades of communist rule.[39] Moreover, since the achievement of independence, the neo-pagan movement has established roots in Lithuania, and there have also been some manifestations of Satanism in the republic, especially after the publication of Anton Sandor La Vey's *Satanic Bible* in 1999.[40] At the same time, the Christian Church enjoys the highest degree of trust in Lithuania, where 74.4% of respondents in the most recent European Values Study (1999) said that the Church could "contribute significantly to solving the moral, family, spiritual, and social problems of society," compared with 52.8% of respondents in Latvia and 38.5% of respondents in Estonia.[41]

Nationalism and interethnic relations

Issues of internationality relations in the Baltic region may be understood to involve essentially relations between the local Baltic peoples and Slavs (mostly Russians). Estonia and Latvia were more affected by Russian immigration during the Soviet years than was Lithuania. During the half-century which began in 1940, Russians moved in large numbers to these republics and, as the share of Russians in the Baltic republics increased, the proportion of members of the titular nationalities decreased. Thus, whereas the shares of the titular nationality in the populations of Latvia and Estonia stood, in 1935, at 75.5% and 90%, respectively, by 1989, Latvians comprised only 52% of the population of Latvia, while Estonians comprised just 61.5% of the population of Estonia.[42] By 1989, most of the rest were Russians. Since independence, the proportion of the titular nationality has risen in both republics and the proportion of Russians has declined. As of 2006, Russians comprised 25.7% of the population of Estonia, for example.

By contrast, 79.6% of the residents of Lithuania in 1989 were Lithuanians (according to the last Soviet-era census), with Russians making up 9.4% and Poles 7.0%. According to the census of 2001, Lithuanians comprised 83.45% of the population of the republic in that year, with Russians accounting for 6.31% and Poles 6.74%. In neither census did any other nationality comprise 2% or more of the population.[43]

Of the three republics, Estonia probably had the most sensitive interethnic relations during the 1980s. After achieving independence, Estonia defined its citizens as the inhabitants of Estonia in 1940 and their descendants. Other residents could qualify for naturalization. The naturalization rules imposed the requirement that only persons who could speak Estonian could gain Estonian citizenship and this resulted in many Russians becoming stateless (with others holding Russian citizenship). Most non-Estonians live in the larger cities of the republic, especially Tallinn (where they constitute 46% of the city's population) and Ida-Virumaa (80%); these two municipalities are home to 84% of non-Estonians living in Estonia.[44] As of 1992, however, 23% of non-Estonians living in Estonia had no knowledge of the Estonian language, and 39% had only a poor knowledge of it.[45] The Estonian authorities have wanted permanent residents of the country to learn Estonian, but some Russians have seen any effort to teach Russian children Estonian as an effort to suppress their Russian identity and culture, meanwhile, schooling in Russian continued. In 2007, the Estonian authorities introduced a language reform, requiring that high schools using Russian as the language of instruction teach Estonian literature in Estonian, rather than in Russian, and announced that the proportion of classes taught in Estonian in Russian schools would rise to 60% by 2011.[46] Although this new policy has proven controversial, in October 2008 Education Minister Tonis Lukas suggested that, in time, Russian-language schools should be phased out of existence; his announcement provoked fresh charges that the government in Tallinn was discriminating against local Russians.[47]

In neighboring Latvia, as in Estonia, there were frictions between local Russians and members of the titular nationality in the years immediately following independence; in Latvia as in Estonia, local Russians who had, for the most part, neglected to learn the local language, suddenly found themselves faced with the necessity to do so. As of July 2004, Latvians comprised 58.7% of the population of their republic – an increase of nearly 7% since 1989 – while Russians still constituted 28.8% of the population. As in the case of Estonia, most of Latvia's Russians live in major urban centers.[48] Mastery of Latvian is a condition for citizenship and, as of 1994, 85% of the 673,400 non-citizens living in Latvia were Russian-speakers.[49] In 1995, the government introduced elements of bilingual education, modeled on programs already in use in Canada and the United States, in order to promote greater fluency in Latvian among non-Latvians; under this program, the minority language remained the language of instruction in minority schools, but Latvian was introduced as a supplement. Three years later, legislation was adopted in Riga aiming at increasing the number of subjects for which Latvian would be used as the language of instruction in minority schools. In 2004, parliament approved an amendment to the law, reducing the amount of instruction in non-Latvian languages for minority high-school students: local Russians marched outside the Ministry of Education in protest.[50] As of 1 October 2006, about 400,000 persons living in Latvia – mostly Slavs – were still classified as non-citizens.[51]

For Lithuania it was much easier to give citizenship to the Russian-speaking population that had arrived in the USSR era, since the generous granting of citizenship would not threaten the language policies of the future. Discrimination and ethnic intolerance have also been problems, although laws prohibiting discrimination are on the books. The small Romani community, which numbers about 3,000 persons, has "experienced discrimination in education, employment, health care, housing services, citizenship, and in contacts with the police" and there have been reports of police mistreatment.[52] The US government revealed that "reports of racial or ethnic violence and intolerance [in Lithuania] increased in 2007," with some violent incidents between Lithuanians and African students.[53]

The resilience of history

The Baltic states are good examples of how hard it is to escape historic memories. The Baltic Germans' conquests during the medieval ages, religious divisions of Europe during the seventeenth century, the invasion of the Bolsheviks in 1918–19, the brief independence in the interwar era, the Molotov–Ribbentrop Treaty, the Soviet occupation in 1940, the deportations to Siberia, Russification during the USSR era, the massive settlement on occupied territory 1944–89: the memory of all such matters are very much alive. The strong ethno-linguistic awareness in the Baltic states, and even policies of today (concerning language and education), are influenced by such memories.

Looking at these three countries, the stable feature seems to be that Lithuania is the most deviant case. This may be traced back to medieval times. Estonia and Latvia are more similar to each other. So, when Estonia reformed faster after 1990 than Latvia, how could it be explained? Estonia was less divided than Latvia on several dimensions: the divide between left and right, the linguistic divide, the religious divide, and the domestic regional divide. Less division probably facilitated swift policy-making processes in Estonia during the early 1990s, however, the other Baltic countries have been catching up during the 2000s.

Timeline 1944–2004

1944	Soviet re-conquest of the Baltics
1950–2	Purge of native communists in Estonia
1959–60	Purge of native communists in Latvia
14 June 1987	Riga, Latvia: first successful public mass demonstration in the Baltic states after the Second World War, marking the anniversary of the Soviet deportations of 1941
1988	Popular mobilization in the independence struggle in all Baltic states: Popular Fronts are organized, the first parties, and also the pro-Soviet campaigns

March 1989	Elections to the USSR Congress of People's Deputies; Popular Fronts emerge as victors in every Baltic republic
23 August 1989	The "Baltic Way" demonstration of 2 million Balts forming a continuous human chain from Vilnius through Riga to Tallinn, demanding independence on the anniversary of the Molotov–Ribbentrop Pact of 1939
24 February–10 March 1990	Elections to republic soviet of Lithuania clearly won by Sajudis; first multiparty elections in the USSR
11 March 1990	Republic soviet of Lithuania votes overwhelmingly in favor of declaration of independence
18 March 1990	Elections to republic soviets of Estonia and Latvia, with run-offs in March and April, elections clearly won by pro-independence forces
Late March and early May 1990	Estonia and Latvia declare independence after vote in the republic supreme soviet with an over two-thirds majority for independence
January 1991	Soviet attacks in Vilnius
March 1991	Pro-independence referendums in Baltic republics
August 1991	Communist reactionary coup in Moscow fails, first Western states recognize full independence of the Baltic states
Spring 2004	Estonia, Latvia, and Lithuania become full members of NATO and the EU

Fact sheet

Estonia

Area	45,226 km^2
Population (July 2008)	1,307,605
Estonian (2000 census)	67.9%
Russian (2000 census)	25.6%
Ukrainian (2000 census)	2.1%
Belarusian (2000 census)	1.3%
Finn (2000 census)	0.9%
Other (2000 census)	2.2%
Urban population (2005)	70%
Below the poverty line (2003)	5% of population
Unemployment rate (2007)	4.7%
GDP *per capita* (2007)	$21,800
Real GDP growth (2007)	2.1%
Inflation (2007)	6.6%
Literacy rate (2000)	99.8% of population

Sources: CIA: *The World Factbook – Estonia*, at www.cia.gov/library/publications/the-world-factbook/geos/en.html#Geo; and "Estonia – Population," at www.studentsoftheworld.info/pageinfo_pays.php3?Pays=EST&Opt=population [both accessed on 1 November 2008].

Latvia

Area	64,589 km^2
Population (2008)	2,276,282
Latvian (2006)	59%
Russian (2006)	28.4%
Byelorussian (2006)	3.8%
Ukrainian (2006)	2.5%
Polish (2006)	2.4%
Lithuanian (2006)	1.4%
Other (2006)	2.5%
Urban population (2005)	67.9%
Below the poverty line (2007)	21% of population
Unemployment rate (2007)	5.7%
GDP *per capita* (2007)	$17,700
Real GDP growth (2007)	10.3%
Inflation (2007)	14.1%
Literacy rate (2000)	99.9% of population

Sources: Center of Demography, University of Latvia; CIA: *The World Factbook - Latvia*, at www.cia.gov; and "Poverty risk index declines in Latvia in 2007," *WSE InfoSpace* (26 November 2008), at www.gpwinfostrefa.pl/ [all accessed on 14 December 2008].

Lithuania

Area	65,300 km^2
Population (2007)	3,371,000
Lithuanian (2001 census)	84.6%
Polish (2001 census)	6.3%
Russian (2001 census)	5.1%
Byelorussian (2001 census)	1.1%
Other (2001 census)	2.9%
Urban population (2005)	67%
Below the poverty line (2003)	4% of population
Unemployment rate (2007)	3.5%
GDP *per capita* (2007)	$16,800
Real GDP growth (2007)	8.8%
Inflation (2007)	5.7%
Literacy rate (2001)	99.6% of population

Sources: www.president.lt/lithuania/; and CIA: *The World Factbook - Lithuania*, at www.cia.gov.

Short biography of Algirdas Mykolas Brazauskas

Born in 1932, he was the first leader of the Lithuanian Democratic Labor Party (LDDP) from 1990 to 1993, then president of Lithuania from 1993 to 1998 and prime minister from 2001 to 2006. Brazauskas was born in Rokiškis, Lithuania, and graduated 1956 from Kaunas Polytechnic Institute with a degree in engineering. He had different positions as a minister and top jobs in the Communist Party from 1965 to 1987, the last ten years as Secretary of the Central Committee of the Communist

Party of Lithuania, promoted to First Secretary in 1988. He led the divorce between the bulk of the Lithuanian communists and the Communist Party of the USSR by the end of 1989. Brazauskas chaired the ruling Social Democratic Party of Lithuania (LSDP) until 19 May 2007, a party that was the result of the merger of the post-communist LDDP and the LSDP.

Notes

1. Denmark held the Tallinn area during 1219–1346, and sold it to the Teutonic Order in 1346. The meaning of "Tallinn" is "Danish castle" (Ole Nørgaard and Lars Johannsen, with Mette Skak and René Hauge Sørensen, *The Baltic States after Independence*, 2nd edn., Cheltenham: Edward Elgar, 1999), p. 49.
2. Please notice that Livonia comes in two definitions. Medieval Livonia (the Order state) covered the areas of what is modern Estonia and Latvia. From the eighteenth century onwards there is also a smaller concept of Livonia: the region covering Northern Latvia (neither western Courland nor eastern Latgale) and also southern Estonia. I use the medieval concept of Livonia in this text.
3. Anatol Lieven, *The Baltic Revolution. Estonia, Latvia, Lithuania, and the Path to Independence* (New Haven, Conn.: Yale University Press, 1994), pp. 46–9.
4. Richard Crampton and Ben Crampton, *Atlas of Eastern Europe in the Twentieth Century* (London: Routledge, 1996).
5. Romuald Misiunas and Rein Taagepera, *The Baltic States: Years of Dependence, 1940–1990*, expanded and updated edn. (London: C. Hurst & Co., 1993), p. 323.
6. Joachim Tauber, "Das politische System Litauens," in Wolfgang Ismayr (ed.), *Die politischen Systeme Osteuropas*, 2nd edn. (Wiesbaden: VS Verlag für Sozialwissenschaften), p. 156.
7. Half of the assembly was appointed by the republic's supreme Soviet, the other half came from the Citizens' Congress (representing only pre-war citizens and their descendants).
8. Mikko Lagerspetz and Konrad Maier, "Das politische System Estlands," in Ismayr (ed.), *Die politischen Systeme Osteuropas*, p. 73.
9. The preliminary results of the first round of the 2008 Seimas election confirm this impression, adding even more new parties to the Seimas. The most significant new party is the National Revival Party, a centrist party putting forward celebrity figures such as major TV and pop music personalities as candidates.
10. Elisabeth Bakke (ed.), *Sentral-Europa og Baltikum etter 1989* (Oslo: Samlaget, 2002), p. 254.
11. *Ibid.*, p. 257.
12. Hermann Smith-Sivertsen, "Latvia," in Sten Berglund, Joakim Ekman, and Frank H. Aarebrot (eds.), *The Handbook of Political Change in Eastern Europe*, 2nd edn. (Cheltenham: Edward Elgar, 2002), p. 115.
13. Freedom House country reports about Lithuania, 2002–7.
14. Misiunas and Taagepera, *The Baltic States*, n. 3, pp. 140–6.
15. Freedom House country reports about Latvia, 2002–7.
16. "Latvian Mass Media Act," in *Post-Soviet Media Law & Policy Newsletter* (Cardozo School of Law), Issue 30–31 (30 May 1996), at www.vii.org/monroe/issue30_31/act.html [accessed on 1 November 2008], p. 1.

17. Juris Dreifelds, “Latvia,” in Jeannette Goehring (ed.), *Nations in Transit 2006: Democratization from Central Europe to Eurasia* (New York: Freedom House/ Aguincum Publishing, 2006), p. 361.
18. Arturas Tereskinas, “Ethnic and Sexual Minorities in the Lithuanian Mass Media: Images and Issues,” Policy Paper (Budapest, 2001), at www.policy.hu/tereskinas/ policypaper.html [accessed on 1 November 2008].
19. “Freedom of the Press 2007: Press Freedom Rankings by Region,” Freedom House, at www.freedomhouse.org/uploads/Chart112File157.pdf [accessed on 1 November 2008].
20. “Freedom of the Press 2007: Global Press Freedom Ranking,” Freedom House, at www.freedomhouse.org/uploads/Chart110File156.pdf [accessed on 1 November 2008].
21. Monika Frėjutė-Rakauskienė, “Dimensions of Ethnicity in Mass Media: Lithuanian Press in the Russian Language on the Membership in the European Union,” *Lietuvos Etnologija* (Lithuanian Institute of History, 7 September 2006), at www.istorija.lt/le/ rakauskiene2005en.html [accessed on 1 November 2008].
22. Juris Dreifelds, “Latvia,” in Jeannette Goehring (ed.), *Nations in Transit 2007: Democratization from Central Europe to Eurasia* (New York: Freedom House, 2007), p. 403; and Aneta Piasecka, “Lithuania,” in Goehring (ed.), *Nations in Transit 2007*, p. 430.
23. Juris Dreifelds, “Latvia,” in Jeannette Goehring (ed.), *Nations in Transit 2008: Democratization from Central Europe to Eurasia* (New York: Freedom House, 2008), p. 339.
24. Ole Nørgaard and Lars Johannsen with Mette Skak and René Hauge Sørensen, *The Baltic States after Independence*, 2nd edn. (Cheltenham: Edward Elgar, 1999).
25. Hans P. Svege and Christer D. Daatland, “Estonia,” in Frank Aarebrot and Terje Knutsen (eds.), *Politics and Citizenship on the Eastern Baltic Seaboard: The Structuring of Democratic Politics from North-West Russia to Poland* (Kristiansand: Nordic Academic Press, 2000).
26. Mikko Lagerspetz and Henry Vogt, “Estonia,” in Sten Berglund, Tomas Hellén, and Frank Aarebrot (eds.), *The Handbook of Political Change in Eastern Europe* (Cheltenham: Edward Elgar, 1998).
27. Eva Sarfi, “Den økonomiske overgangen – ulike veier til samme mål,” in Bakke (ed.), *Sentral-Europa og Baltikum*, n. 8, p. 213.
28. *The Independent* (London), 1 November 2002, at www.independent.co.uk/ [accessed on 1 November 2008].
29. Sabrina P. Ramet, *Nihil Obstat: Religion, Politics, and Social Change in East-Central Europe and Russia* (Durham, NC: Duke University Press, 1998), p. 266.
30. *Ibid.*, p. 331; and “Religion – Buddhism in Estonia,” *Culture Estonica*, at www. estonica.org/eng/lugu.html?kateg=41&menyy_id=101&alam=56&leht=12 [accessed on 1 November 2008].
31. “Cults and New Religious Movements in the Former Soviet Union,” *What’s News*, Vol. 3, No. 3 (29 July 1999), at apologia.gospelcom.net/mainpages/WhatsNews/ WN990729.html [accessed on 1 November 2008].
32. “International Religious Freedom Report 2008 – Estonia,” released by the Bureau of Democracy, Human Rights, and Labor, US Department of State (19 September 2008), at www.state.gov/g/drl/rls/irf/2008/108444.htm [accessed on 20 October 2008], p. 1.

33. Ringo Ringvee, "Religious Freedom and Legislation in Post-Soviet Estonia," *Brigham Young University Law Review* (2001), at findarticles.com/ [accessed on 20 October 2008], p. 2.
34. "International Religious Freedom Report 2008 – Latvia," released by the Bureau of Democracy, Human Rights, and Labor, US Department of State (19 September 2008), at www.state.gov/g/drl/rls/irf/2008/108454.htm [accessed on 20 October 2008], p. 1.
35. Quoted in Felix Corley, "Latvia: Registration: 'refusedniks' to challenge 'discriminatory' law," *Forum 18 News Service* (Oslo), 30 April 2003, at www.forum18.org/Archive.php?article_id=42&printer=Y [accessed on 20 October 2008].
36. Felix Corley, "Latvia: New hope to change religion law?," *Forum 18 News Service* (17 September 2003), at www.forum18.org/Archive.php?article_id=140&printer=Y [accessed on 20 October 2008].
37. CIA, *The World Factbook–Lithuania*, at www.cia.gov/library/publications/the-world-factbook/geos/lh.html [accessed on 1 November 2008].
38. "International Religious Freedom Report 2008 – Lithuania," released by the Bureau of Democracy, Human Rights, and Labor, US Department of State (19 September 2008), at www.state.gov/g/drl/rls/irf/2008/108456.htm [accessed on 1 November 2008], p. 1.
39. "Pagan Lithuanian Folk Beliefs," at www.geocities.com/athens/delphi/3501/lecture.html [accessed on 1 November 2008], p. 1.
40. Renatas Delis, "The Neo-Pagan Movement in Post-Soviet Lithuania – Constructing an Alternative Lithuanian Identity as a Response to the Conditions of Modernity?," *Lietuvos Etnologija* (Lithuanian Institute of History, 5 February 2008), at www.istorija.lt/le/delis2006en.html [accessed on 1 November 2008]; and Milda Alisauskiene, "Manifestations of Satanism in Catholic Lithuania: The Case of www.satan.lt," *CESNUR Center for Studies on New Religions* (Vilnius, Lithuania), 2003, at www.cesnur.org/2003/vil2003_alisauskiene.htm [accessed on 1 November 2008]. See also "Introduction to Lithuanian Paganism," at www.druidry.org/obod/deities/lithuanian_paganism.html [accessed on 1 November 2008].
41. Nonka Bogumilova-Todorova, "Reflections on the Contemporary Religious 'Revival,'" *Journal for Social Research/Časopis za Društvene Nauke* (Sofia), Issue 4 (2003), p. 518.
42. Aadne Aasland and Tone Flotten, "Ethnicity and Social Exclusion in Estonia and Latvia," *Europe–Asia Studies*, Vol. 53, No. 7 (November 2001), p. 1028.
43. "Lithuania," at ec.europa.eu/education/policies/lang/languages/langmin/euromosaic/lith_en.pdf [accessed on 1 November 2008], section 2.
44. Elvira Küün, "The Ethnic and Linguistic Identity of Russian-Speaking Young People in Estonia," *Trames*, Issue 2 (2008), p. 184,
45. Raivo Vetik, "Ethnic Conflict and Accommodation in Post-Communist Estonia," *Journal of Peace Research*, Vol. 30, No. 3 (August 1993), p. 274.
46. *International Herald Tribune* (3 September 2007), at www.iht.com/ [accessed on 20 October 2008].
47. *Baltic Times* (15 October 2008), at www.baltictimes.com/news/articles/21537 [accessed on 1 November 2008].
48. Nils Muizneiks, "Russians in Latvia – History, Current Status and Prospects," *Ministry of Foreign Affairs of the Republic of Latvia*, at www.am.gov.lv/en/policy/464|/4642/Muznieks/?print=on [accessed on 20 October 2008], p. 3.

49. *New York Times* (1 March 1994), at query.nytimes.com/ [accessed on 20 October 2008].
50. Elizabeth Celms, "Latvia: Quiet Revolution in the Classroom," *Transitions Online* (31 October 2006), at www.ceeol.com, pp. 1–2. For further discussion, see Artemi Romanov, "The Russian Diaspora in Latvia and Estonia: Predicting Language Outcomes," *Journal of Multilingual and Multicultural Development*, Vol. 21, No. 1 (2000), pp. 58–71.
51. "Country Reports on Human Rights Practices – 2006, Latvia," released by the Bureau of Democracy, Human Rights, and Labor, US Department of State (6 March 2007), at www.state.gov/g/drl/rls/hrrpt/2006/78822.htm [accessed on 20 October 2008], p. 9.
52. "Country Reports on Human Rights Practices – 2006, Lithuania," released by the Bureau of Democracy, Human Rights, and Labor, US Department of State (6 March 2007), at www.state.gov.g/drl/rls/hrrpt/2006/78824.htm [accessed on 20 October 2008], p. 11.
53. "Country Reports on Human Rights Practices – 2007, Lithuania," released by the Bureau of Democracy, Human Rights, and Labor, US Department of State (11 March 2008), at www.state.gov/g/drl/rls/hrrpt/2007/100569.htm [accessed on 1 November 2008], p. 10.

Further reading

Bennich-Björkman, Li. "The Cultural Roots of Estonia's Successful Transition: How Historical Legacies Shaped the 1990s," *East European Politics and Societies*, Vol. 21, No. 2 (2007), pp. 316–47

Clark, Terry and Diana Jurgeleviciute "'Keeping Tabs on Coalition Partners': A Theoretically Salient Case Study of Lithuanian Coalitional Governments," *Europe–Asia Studies*, Vol. 60, No. 4 (June 2008), pp. 631–42

Dreifelds, Juris. *Latvia in Transition* (Cambridge: Cambridge University Press, 1996).

Fritz, Verena. *State-Building: A Comparative Study of Ukraine, Lithuania, Belarus, and Russia* (Budapest: Central European University Press, 2007)

Jeffries, Ian. *The Countries of the Former Soviet Union at the Turn of the Twenty-First Century: The Baltic and European States in Transition* (New York: Routledge, 2004)

Johnson, Jeff. *The New Theatre of the Baltics: From Soviet to Western Influence in Estonia, Latvia, and Lithuania* (Jefferson, NC: McFarland & Co., 2007)

Jungerstam-Mulders, Susanne (ed.). *Post-Communist EU Member States – Parties and Party Systems* (Aldershot: Ashgate, 2006)

Krupavicius, Algis. "The Post-Communist Transition and Institutionalization of Lithuania's Parties," in Richard Hofferbert (ed.), *Parties and Democracy: Party Structure and Party Performance in Old and New Democracies* (Oxford: Blackwell, 1998)

Lieven, Anatol. *The Baltic Revolution: Estonia, Latvia, Lithuania, and the Path to Independence* (New Haven, Conn.: Yale University Press, 1994)

Misiunas, Romuald J. and Rein Taagepera. *The Baltic States: Years of Dependence, 1940–1990*, expanded and updated edn. (London: C. Hurst & Co., 1993)

Nørgaard, Ole and Lars Johannsen, with Mette Skak and René Hauge Sørensen. *The Baltic States after Independence*, 2nd edn. (Cheltenham: Edward Elgar, 1999)

Plakans, Andrejs. *The Latvians – A Short History* (Stanford, Calif.: Hoover Institution Press, 1995)

Rozenvalds, Juris. *How Democratic is Latvia: Audit of Democracy* (Riga: LU Akadeiskais apgads, 2005)

Skapars, Janis. *The Baltic Way to Freedom: Non-Violent Struggle of the Baltic States in a Global Context* (Riga: Zelta grauds, 2005)

Smith, David J., Artis Pabriks, Aldis Purs, and Thomas Lane. *The Baltic States: Estonia, Latvia and Lithuania* (London and New York: Routledge, 2002)

Smith-Sivertsen, Hermann. "*What Kind(s) of Political Parties Emerged and Why? Comparing the Parties of Latvia and Lithuania of the Late 1990s by their Organizations, Policies and Surroundings*," PhD dissertation submitted to the Faculty of Social Sciences (University of Oslo, 2005)

Steen, Anton. "The Elite Network State," in Anton Steen (ed.), *Between Past and Future: Elites, Democracy and the State in Post-Communist Countries. A Comparison of Estonia, Latvia and Lithuania* (Aldershot: Ashgate, 1997)

21

Moldova since 1989

STEVEN D. ROPER

As the borders of European institutions such as the EU and NATO dramatically changed during the 1990s and early 2000s, the question of identity became part of the larger debate over expansion and integration. These debates occurred not only in Brussels but also in various post-communist states in which the expression of a European identity was not necessarily a given nor embraced by all segments of society. Among central and southeastern European states, there was a general consensus among political elites and civil society regarding the economic virtues of EU membership and integration in European institutions. However, acceptance of European democratic values, including freedom of the press, religion, and assembly, has been more problematic. Moldova presents an interesting case study of the potential and the pitfalls of Europeanization and democratization for two reasons. First, Moldova contains a breakaway region not under central government authority in which communist-era symbols, institutions and leadership endure. Second, as the opening decade of the 2000s closes, Moldova is unique among central and southeastern European states in re-electing a parliament composed of a majority of communists (who subsequently elected a communist president). However, unlike the communists of old, these politicians were chosen in generally free and fair elections and, with varying degrees, advocate European integration and democracy – if not in actions, then at least in words. Moldova is at the crossroads of post-communist Europe and the former Soviet Union and provides us not only with an interesting case study of transition politics in southeastern Europe but also with a glimpse into efforts at Europeanization and democratization in former Soviet republics. In order to understand Moldova's path since 1989, this chapter begins by exploring Moldovan political development during the twentieth century. Moldovan identity politics of the 2000s, which includes issues such as dual citizenship, language, and education as well as relations with Romania and Russia, must be placed within contemporary Moldovan history.

Creation of a Moldovan nation and state

The area of present-day Moldova has been historically, culturally, and geographically situated as a crossroads between east and west. Moldovan nation- and state-building projects have involved the push-and-pull of various empires and political elites. While the Moldovan language is essentially Romanian, Moldovan political culture has been fundamentally shaped by two centuries of Russian influence. Following the Russo-Turkish War in 1812, the eastern area of Moldova, between the Prut and the Dniester River (known as Bessarabia), was annexed by Russia and was administered as a part of the Russian Empire until the First World War. The war, combined with the Russian Revolution, provided Moldovan pan-Romanian nationalists with an opportunity to press their claims for Romanian integration. By the end of 1918, Moldovan Bessarabia joined with the territories of Bucovina and Transylvania to form "Greater Romania." Moldovan Bessarabia was thus an integral territorial part of Romania during the interwar period.

In August 1939, Germany and the USSR signed the Molotov–Ribbentrop Pact including the secret protocols conceding Bessarabia to the USSR. By the summer of 1940, Moldovan Bessarabia had been joined with Northern Bucovina and the six counties which formed the Moldovan Autonomous Soviet Socialist Republic on the left (east) bank of the Dniester River (present-day Transnistria) to form the Moldovan Soviet Socialist Republic (MSSR).[1] The newly constructed MSSR inherited a large Russian-speaking community, and Russian once again became the language of interethnic communication, higher education, and public life. Van Meurs argues that the Soviet mythology regarding Moldovan identity consisted of four parts: an independent Moldovan nation, state, culture, and language (the Moldovan alphabet was changed from Latin to Cyrillic by Soviet authorities).[2] By the early 1960s, Soviet linguistic policy was focused on the delineation of a distinct Moldovan language separate from Romanian as a basis of Moldovan identity. Although Romania and the MSSR were both socialist states, Moldovan intellectuals were instructed to find differences between the two languages as a basis for the interpretation and re-interpretation of Moldovan history.[3]

As occurred elsewhere in the Soviet Union, reforms introduced by Mikhail Gorbachev in the mid-1980s created conditions in which long-standing resentment against Soviet assimilation policies could be expressed. In 1987, Moldovan intellectuals organized informal discussion groups that focused on promoting the use of the Moldovan language. By mid-1988, these intellectuals had formed the Democratic Movement in Support of Re-structuring (later renamed the Popular Front or PF) to address discriminatory practices imposed upon the titular ethnic Moldovan majority population. The prospect of ethnic Moldovans gaining political power provoked an immediate response from Russian-speaking minorities. Many non-ethnic Moldovans supported the Internationalist Movement for Unity (*Edinstvo* or PSMUE), a pro-Russian movement, which found its strongest support in Transnistria as well as in the southern region of Moldova known as Gagauzia (home to the largest concentration in southern Europe of ethnic Gagauz, a Turkic Christian people).[4]

Nationalism, romanization, and secession

By 1989, the PF had become the leading Moldovan opposition force, proposing a strong Romanian and unionist agenda. In August, the Moldovan parliament proclaimed Moldovan (using the Latin alphabet) as the state language. In response, Russian speakers began a wave of strikes to protest the language law as a form of "reactive nationalism" as they struggled to maintain the pre-eminence of the Russian language as well as their political and economic influence.[5] Moldova's last Soviet-era parliament, elected in March 1990, was also the country's first post-independence parliament. Therefore, there was a direct institutional link between Moldova's communist past and democratic future. At this time, the Moldovan Communist Party was sharply divided between a reformist and conservative wing – many conservatives ultimately left the capital, Chişinău, and consolidated their control over Transnistria. The reform communist faction cooperated with the PF, and collaboration between these two groups extended into the electoral arena where one could find the names of ranking Communist Party members among the nominees of the Front.[6] Following the March 1990 elections, the PF entered into a parliamentary coalition with several other parties which held over 66% of the seats. The parliament confirmed a government composed almost entirely of ethnic Moldovans and also re-elected Mircea Snegur as its chairman and, later, president. During this period, Front MPs and the government of Prime Minister Mircea Druc pursued a pro-Romanian and pro-unionist agenda which alienated the Russian minority.

By May 1990, the ethnic minority elites who controlled the city governments of Tiraspol, Bender (Tighina), and Rîbniţa refused to accept the legitimacy of the new parliament and asserted sovereignty over all local institutions.[7] Tiraspol, the capital of Transnistria, organized several referenda throughout the region in which voters overwhelmingly chose local autonomy from Chişinău. Just a few months previously in September 1989, Gagauz leaders had proclaimed the creation of an independent republic in the southern part of the country. Therefore, by mid-1990, the Moldovan central authorities were facing the possibility of two secessionist movements at the same time as the country was grappling with a transition to democracy and market economics. During the next two years, the status of Transnistria was the single most important domestic and foreign policy issue facing the Moldovan government and formed a backdrop to various institutional choices made during the early transition process. Even in 2008, Transnistria had lost none of its salience as an important factor in Moldovan discussions concerning European integration, economic reforms, and general security issues for the EU and NATO.

Transnistria

The August 1991 Soviet coup clearly demonstrated the division between Moldova and Transnistria. While the Moldovan leadership denounced the coup leaders, the Transnistrian leadership, including future president Igor Smirnov, supported it. Following the coup and Moldova's announcement of independence on 27 August 1991, relations with Transnistria further deteriorated. A week after the announcement, on 2 September, Transnistria declared its independence from Moldova and formed its own separate republic. One of the reasons why Transnistria was so opposed to the agenda of the Front-led Moldovan government was that the region's ethnic composition was unlike the rest of Moldova. In Transnistria at this time, approximately 55% of the population were ethnic Ukrainians and ethnic Russians, and aside from Bender and a few right-bank villages, the region had never been part of Romania. While the conflict between Transnistria and Moldovan central government authorities involved issues of identity and ethnicity "it is a gross simplification to present the conflict as a showdown between ethnic Moldovans and the 'Russian-speaking' part of the Moldovan population ... the conflict is essentially political in character."[8]

During 1991 and 1992, several clashes occurred between the Moldovan military and Transnistrian paramilitary units which greatly benefited from equipment and personnel provided by the Russian 14th Army based in Tiraspol. As the Transnistrian separatists consolidated their position, nationalists inside the Moldovan legislature became increasingly militant. This brought intense pressure on President Snegur to undertake decisive action to resolve the conflict. In late March 1992, a state of emergency was declared and an effort was made to disarm the separatist militia by force. This attempt met with violent resistance, and by May the conflict had escalated into a full-scale civil war. The heaviest fighting occurred in the cities of Dubăsari and Bender. There are various estimates of the number of casualties, but perhaps as many as 1,000 people died during this period. The violence in Bender compelled the Russian government to actively intervene in the conflict. In July 1992, Russian President Boris Yeltsin and President Snegur signed a cease-fire agreement which established a Joint Control Committee to observe the military forces in the security zone and maintain order.[9] The cease-fire ended the hostilities but provided no lasting mechanism for resolving the stalemate.

The "frozen conflict" in Transnistria has had several lasting effects on Moldovan domestic and foreign policy. First, the fighting in Bender became part of the mythology of Transnistria.[10] Those who were associated with the conduct of the war, such as Smirnov, his advisor Valeri Litskai (later named Transnistrian foreign minister), Grigore Mărăcuță (speaker of the Transnistrian parliament until 2005), and Vladimir Atamaniuk (later named Transnistrian deputy minister of defense) were viewed as heroes and were able to maintain their influence over Transnistrian policies during a period in which Moldova had four different governments. Second, resolving the status of Transnistria is one of the key dilemmas facing Moldova as the country integrates into European institutions. Moldova's relationship with the EU places the resolution of the conflict as a key objective in order to enhance EU security. Third, the Transnistrian conflict created significant financial burdens for Moldova. During the Soviet period, the Transnistrian region accounted for almost 40% of Moldova's industrial base and employed 25% of the country's industrial workers. Moldova lost important industrial plants such as the Moldova Steel Works (based in Rîbniţa) and the Cuchurgan Power Station (located in Dnestrovsk).

Party politics in the 1990s

Even before the civil war, political support for the Front had essentially vanished. By the start of the civil war in May 1992, the Front held only thirty parliamentary seats compared to over 140 the previous year. President Snegur also began to distance himself from the Front, and in the first direct election for the presidency in December 1991, he ran unopposed as Front loyalists boycotted the election. The civil war, and particularly the violence in Bender, had an immediate impact on Moldovan domestic politics. In July 1992, almost all of the members of the Front-dominated government resigned, and Snegur began to form alliances with other MPs and consolidate his power within parliament. In December 1992, Snegur delivered a speech to parliament in which he laid out a Moldovan foreign policy based on the pursuit of national independence. He warned against extremism associated with Romanian unification as well as reintegration into a Russian political sphere.

As a consequence of this speech in January 1993, the chairman of the parliament, Alexandru Moşanu, resigned and was replaced by Petru Lucinschi. During this time, party labels and affiliations were fluid, and many MPs resigned from their parties as new alliances were created. The Communist Party was banned in August 1991 so rural agricultural elite as well as former communist *apparatiks* formed the Agrarian Democratic Party (PDA), which maintained the principle of Moldovan independence from Romania and Russian political institutions while allowing for greater integration into Russian and CIS markets.[11] By 1993, defections within parliamentary groups, the formation of new parties, and the re-positioning of political elites stymied MPs' efforts to pass critical legislation.

The parliament was dissolved and early elections were held in February 1994 for elections to the 13th parliament.[12] The results of the first entirely post-communist election marked a sharp reversal from the politics of the 1990 transition one. Nationalist and pro-Romanian forces were overwhelmingly rejected in favor of those supporting Moldovan independence and accommodation with ethnic minorities. The PDA won 43% of the vote and received 56 of the 104 seats in the parliament.[13] Another 28 seats were won by the socialist bloc (the Socialist Party and the Movement Unity *Edinstvo*/PSMUE) which received 22% of the vote. The pro-Romanian parties suffered a severe setback. The Front, which two years earlier led the coalition government, received only 7.5% of the vote and 9 seats. Members of the PDA controlled all the leadership positions in parliament, and Lucinschi was re-appointed chairman.

The new parliament faced three crucial issues: first, a new constitution had to be passed. Second, the status of Gagauzia had to be finalized, and third economic reform, including privatization and foreign investment, had to be further implemented. One of the first issues which the new parliament had to address was the creation of Moldova's post-Soviet constitution. The PDA-dominated Constitutional Commission crafted a constitution which was ethnically inclusive and did not refer "to any specific ethnic group as the locus of state sovereignty,"[14] referring to the "Moldovan people" rather than a specific ethnic group. In addition, Art. 111 allowed for the creation of a special autonomous status for Transnistria and Gagauzia, and, as a reversal from the Frontist policies of the early 1990s, the constitution named the official state language "Moldovan" with no reference to Romanian.[15] Moreover, unlike most other post-Soviet republics, Moldova adopted a form of semi-presidentialism which restrained presidential powers.[16] Parliamentary chair Lucinschi was also head of the Constitutional Commission and sought to deny Snegur the type of power other post-Soviet presidents wielded. While PDA MPs were aligned with Snegur, these MPs did not want to surrender their authority to the executive branch.

Settling one conflict at a time: Gagauzia's negotiated autonomy

The constitution provided that Transnistria and Gagauzia would be granted a special autonomous status with the passage of a parliamentary law. Given the continuing presence of the Russian 14th Army in Transnistria as well as Russian political and economic support to Transnistrian elites, resolving this conflict was always going to be a long and a complicated affair. Although Gagauzia had declared independence from Moldova even before Transnistria, several features of this secessionist movement made conflict resolution much easier than with Transnistria. First, Gagauzia was almost entirely agricultural and rural while Transnistria was highly industrialized, with several urban areas. Thus, Gagauzia had none of the economic advantages Transnistria possessed. Second, Transnistria also benefited from Russia's "near-abroad" policy of defending ethnic Russians while Gagauzia had no titular state to champion its cause.[17] While the Gagauz were heavily Russified to the point that the majority could not speak or read the Gagauz language, the Gagauz elite were not as closely linked to former Soviet political and economic institutions. Thus, the negotiations toward a Gagauz settlement were bilateral while from the beginning, the Transnistrian talks involved Russia, the OSCE, and later Ukraine.[18]

In December 1994, the Moldovan parliament approved a special law on the status of Gagauzia. The legislation provided that Gagauzia was an "autonomous territorial unit with a special status for the self-determination of the Gagauz people." In addition, the legislation stated that "in case of a change of the

Republic of Moldova's status as an independent state, the Gagauz people have the right to external self-determination." Thus, the Moldovan parliament acknowledged that it had no right to cede the Gagauz territory to another state without the agreement of the Gagauz people. At the same time, this provision recognized that Gagauzia was a "constituent part of the Republic of Moldova." Moldovan, Gagauz, and Russian serve as the official languages, and Gagauzia can use its own symbols together with those of Moldova.

The legislation defines the territory of Gagauzia as those localities in which the Gagauz constitute more than 50% of the population. Those localities in which the Gagauz are fewer than 50% are included if a majority decides in a local referendum that it wants to link itself to the Gagauz territory. Some outlying Gagauz settlements are included in Gagauzia even though they are not contiguous to the main area of the autonomous region. Gagauz were an absolute majority in only two of the five counties (*raions*) that were to be included in Gagauzia, and ethnic Moldovans and ethnic Bulgarians formed majorities in the other counties and most of the villages in the region. Thus, part of the problem in creating this special administrative area for the Gagauz involved the special demography of southern Moldova. Ultimately, Gagauzia incorporated thirty settlements, including three large towns (Comrat, Ceadir-Lunga and Vulcaneşti) and twenty-seven villages. The Popular Assembly was designated as Gagauzia's representative authority, elected every four years. The chief executive was the Başkan who is also elected for a four-year term and is a member of the Moldovan government. Moldovan central government authorities hoped that the special status accorded the Gagauz would serve as an example for those in Transnistria. However, paradoxically, many Transnistrians were unwilling to accept territorial autonomy precisely because of the example of Gagauzia. Most Transnistrians and many Gagauz believed that Gagauzia did not truly enjoy an autonomous status within Moldova. As a consequence, throughout the 1990s and into the 2000s, the Gagauz leadership persisted with demands for greater local autonomy, which only demonstrated to the Transnistrians that territorial autonomy was a poor substitute for the status quo.

Economic reform: promises made and broken

The third major issue confronting the 1994 parliament was to continue to work with the Moldovan government by passing economic reform legislation. By the mid-1990s, Moldova was regarded by international financial organizations (IFIs), such as the World Bank and the IMF, as one of the success stories of the former USSR. Owing to its pursuit of a strict monetary policy, the Moldovan currency, the leu, was one of the most stable in the region. Although the country experienced hyperinflation in the early 1990s, the Moldovan Central Bank worked to contain inflation which, by the mid-1990s, was the lowest of all the former Soviet republics. In addition, many privatization policies begun during the early years of the transition had been finalized by the mid-1990s.[19] After the 1994 parliamentary elections, Moldovan MPs and members of the government turned their attention to policies aimed at attracting greater foreign investment and reducing unemployment. While the turnover in the parliament following the 1994 election was rather high, there was considerable continuity in the government. Andrei Sangheli, first elected prime minister in 1992, continued to serve throughout the first years of the 13th parliament, and Leonid Talmaci has been the head of the Moldovan Central Bank since its inception. While Moldovan macroeconomic policy was in far better shape than most former Soviet republics, the loss of industry in Transnistria, combined with a growing trade deficit with West Europe and the need for Russian energy imports, eventually caused severe strains on the Moldovan budget.

As a consequence of the budget deficit, the World Bank and the IMF urged the Moldovan parliament to pass legislation which would increase tariffs for electricity as well as the retirement age. By 1996–7, the parliament was split over the pace and substance of economic reforms. Moreover, challenges to President Snegur's authority by Prime Minister Sangheli and parliamentary chair Lucinschi contributed to fractured economic policy-making. While the PDA began the first session of the 13th parliament with a clear majority, several key members defected from the parliamentary majority. With presidential elections in 1996 and parliamentary elections scheduled for 1998, no one in the parliament or government was willing to make bold reforms. Muddling through became the preferred political alternative to decisive decision-making.

Political musical chairs

By the time of the 1996 presidential election (the first multicandidate presidential election in the country's history), the internal divisions within the PDA had become part of the public debate over the direction of the country. While Sangheli maintained his party affiliation with the PDA, Snegur formed the Party of Rebirth and Conciliation of Moldova shortly before the presidential election, and Lucinschi ran as an independent with no specific party affiliation. There were few policy issues which separated the three candidates. While Snegur once again adopted a pro-Romanian position and campaigned for more rapid economic reform and Lucinschi advocated closer ties with Russia and pledged to work to resolve the Transnistrian conflict, the election occurred in the absence of clear policy differences.[20] In the second-round presidential election between Snegur and Lucinschi, Lucinschi received 54% of the vote and promised to work with a parliament dominated by his former party.

Party membership was quite fluid at this point as MPs attempted to find new party identifications. In 1997 and 1998, Lucinschi was able to play off different party factions and at the same time remain above party politics as an independent. As parliamentary elections in early 1998 drew near, the fortunes of the Party of Communists of the Republic of Moldova (PCRM) had a huge impact on Moldovan electoral and party politics. The PCRM had previously been banned and while re-legalized before the 1994 parliamentary elections, the Party chose not to field candidates in the election. While the PCRM did well in the 1995 local elections and PCRM leader Vladimir Voronin came in third on the first ballot in the 1996 presidential election, the 1998 parliamentary elections were the first significant test for the Party. The PCRM claimed to be the direct heir to the Communist Party of Moldova and adopted the symbols of the hammer and the sickle. Not surprisingly, so-called reform parties attempted to portray a victory by the PCRM as a return to Soviet-era communism and a rejection of European values. However, as March notes, "although the party's opponents are quick to brand the Communist party as authoritarian or even totalitarian, the picture is more complex."[21]

A unified and cohesive PCRM, which just a few years earlier had been banned, received a plurality of the vote and parliamentary seats. Center and right forces joined together to block the party, and immediately after the elections Lucinschi's parliamentary supporters created a coalition called the Alliance for Democratic Reform (ARD), which was composed of the Bloc of the Democratic Convention of Moldova, the Bloc for a Democratic and Prosperous Moldova (BMDP), and the Party of Democratic Forces. The coalition controlled approximately 60% of the seats with the remaining seats controlled by the PCRM. The BMDP was a pro-presidential party formed by Lucinschi's supporters after the 1996 elections. Although part of the coalition, the BMDP was clearly first among equals. It was expected that with the BMDP in power, Lucinschi would be able to dominate the legislative process. Immediately after the election, the parliament once again confirmed Ion Ciubuc as prime minister, but less than a year later in February 1999 tensions in the coalition prompted the resignation of his government. President Lucinschi nominated Ion Sturza as prime minister, and his government was considered much more pro-reform than the two previous Ciubuc governments and enjoyed real popular support. Perhaps because of Sturza's popularity, conflict with Lucinschi and the parliament resulted in his removal from office in November. In December 1999, Dumitru Braghiş was confirmed as prime minister.

The conflict between Sturza and Lucinschi formed part of the larger conflict between the parliament and the president. While the disagreements were ostensibly over economic reform, the reality was that Lucinschi simply did not have a significant parliamentary party organization to provide support. The BMDP was part of a coalition that began to splinter and eventually voice disagreements with the president. In addition, the BMDP itself began to fragment and lose members. In March 1999, Lucinschi issued a decree to conduct a consultative referendum in which he proposed the creation of a "presidential regime."[22] Over 50% of the voters approved the referendum, although, exact figures were never published by the Central Election Commission. After the referendum, Lucinschi proposed a draft law which would have provided the president with the sole authority to appoint and to remove cabinet ministers. Most of Moldova's political forces spoke out against the draft. The Council of

Europe's Venice Commission also expressed its concern over the constitutional change. However, Lucinschi maintained that a presidential regime would allow him the ability to assume greater responsibility for the country's economic performance rather than a diverse group of parliamentarians and government officials.

By the summer of 2000, Lucinschi's support within the parliament was at its lowest point in almost four years. His attempts to strengthen the presidency caused the parliament in July 2000 to approve a series of constitutional amendments which created a parliamentary regime, stipulating that the president would be elected – and, if necessary, dismissed – by the parliament. The amendments passed by a vote of 92 to 4. Although the parliament was united in its opposition to Lucinschi, the process of voting for a new president underscored the significant differences between party factions and political elites. As a result of the inability to elect a president, Lucinschi was able to dissolve the parliament and announce early parliamentary elections in February 2001.[23] In these elections, the PCRM received 50% of the vote and 71 seats (out of a total of 101) in the parliament. The only other parties to obtain seats were the Braghiş Alliance (formed by the former prime minister) and the Christian Democratic People's Party or PPCD (the reformed Front), as few parties could pass the increased electoral threshold of 6%. With a super-majority of over 70% of the seats, Voronin was elected president in April 2001 and subsequently nominated Vasile Tarlev prime minister.[24]

Thus, by the early 2000s, the PCRM controlled the executive and the legislative branches, which caused many to fear that the Communists would begin to dismantle Moldova's nascent democracy. As the only European country led by communists, Moldova seemed out of step with the changes which had swept the rest of post-communist Europe. However, the party platform in the 2001 elections rejected totalitarianism, embraced political rights and freedoms, and affirmed the Party's commitment to a parliamentary republic.[25] Moreover not only was the PCRM not opposed to private property and a market economy, but President Voronin's son, Oleg, was one of the most prominent businessmen in Moldova. While one could argue that the Moldovan electorate chose the PCRM in 2001 as a form of post-Soviet nostalgia for economic security due to the deteriorating economy, the reality was that the squabbling and the fighting among the political elite had made the PCRM the one clearly united party.[26]

Resolving the status of Transnistria: before and after the Kozak Memorandum

Following the presidential and the parliamentary elections in 2001, there was optimism that a conclusive status could be negotiated for Transnistria. During the last two years of the Lucinschi presidency, negotiations had basically stopped as the Transnistrian political elite had advocated a "two-state" approach in which Transnistria was to have equal status with Moldova.[27] In the 2001 parliamentary election campaign, the PCRM proposed making Russian a second state language and addressed the possibility of Moldovan membership in the proposed Russian–Belarusan Union. The hope was that the support of the Moldovan leadership for such issues would satisfy the large pro-Russian population in Transnistria. Moreover, because Voronin had been born there, he had a personal interest in settling the conflict. Initially, the negotiations between Voronin and Smirnov were successful. In May 2001, Transnistria released the Romanian–Moldovan nationalist, Ilie Ilaşcu, from a Transnistrian jail, a long-standing demand of the Moldovan government. While Voronin and Smirnov met on subsequent occasions to negotiate on a wide range of issues, by late 2001, Voronin concluded that Smirnov had no real interest in ending the status quo and suspended the talks.

In order to revive negotiations, ambassadors from Russia, Ukraine, and the OSCE submitted in 2002 a new proposal to Moldova and Transnistria which was the most detailed and far-ranging draft so far presented by the international mediators. The document envisioned the federalization of Moldova with Transnistria exercising local power over a range of issues subordinate to Moldovan central administration. Although the 2002 draft was very detailed, there were several key issues which required further elaboration and generated considerable debate. Principally, the definition and the implementation of federalism proved problematic, especially on issues concerning the division of political power, the structure of the judiciary, and finance and tax authority. President Voronin invited the Transnistrians to form a Joint Constitutional Commission (CCM) in February 2003 to discuss possible constitutional arrangements. At the same time, a new government agency was created to coordinate activity between Moldova and Transnistria, and Vasile Şova was named the Minister of Reintegration.

Discussions within the CCM failed to resolve critical differences between Chişinău and Tiraspol. Indeed, the CCM became increasing irrelevant as Voronin centralized negotiations within his presidential administration as well as the Ministry of Reintegration. While Voronin was publicly committed to the OSCE-approved constitutional process, he secretly entered into negotiations with Russia without the participation of other international negotiators. Russian Deputy Head of Administration, Dmitri Kozak, was appointed by President Vladimir Putin to mediate between Moldova and Transnistria and produce a memorandum that would serve as the basis of a new constitution. Throughout the summer and early fall of 2003, Kozak was engaged in shuttle diplomacy between Moscow, Chişinău, and Tiraspol.

In November 2003, Russia gave the OSCE and Ukraine a final draft which has become known as the "Kozak Memorandum." Much of the draft focused on a re-structuring of the political system. For example, the document provided for a Senate in which 50% of the members would be chosen by Transnistria and Gagauzia. This was extremely important because the upper house had become the most important veto locus within the federal institutional framework. Organic laws, requiring a change in the constitution, had to be confirmed by a three-fourths Senate vote, which gave the Transnistrians an effective veto.

In addition, the Constitutional Court was appointed by the Senate as well as all cabinet members.[28] These institutional features were designed to provide Transnistria with a veto over any legislation that would threaten the leadership. In addition, the Memorandum included clauses that could have been interpreted in such a way as to easily dissolve the federation. For example, the Memorandum allowed for subjects of the federation to have the right "to leave the federation in case a decision is taken to unite the federation with another state and (or) in connection with the federation's full loss of sovereignty."[29]

Moldovan civil society and opposition groups felt that the Memorandum was a betrayal of the state and reinforced the feeling that federalization was an anti-Moldovan plan orchestrated by Russia. The international community was equally concerned about the document. Voronin very quickly realized that the Memorandum had virtually no domestic or international support (aside from Russia) and therefore refused to formally sign. In all respects, the Memorandum was a failure that set back negotiations, but one of the consequences of this failure was a change in Moldovan foreign policy. Upcoming parliamentary elections combined with a more unified, pro-West civil society forced the once all-powerful PCRM to become more pragmatic and flexible in its dealings with Europe, the EU, and the United States. Indeed after Voronin's *volte-face*, Moldovan relations with Russia soured. President Vladimir Putin, who was to visit Moldova for the formal signing ceremony, immediately canceled his trip. Using economic tools to undermine Moldova's re-defined European foreign policy, Russia also later enacted a ban on Moldovan agricultural goods.

At the same time that Moldova was re-orienting its foreign policy, the borders of European institutions such as NATO and the EU were also changing. Romania became a member of NATO in March 2004, and the EU formally fixed Romania's date of accession later that year. As Europe's borders changed, Moldovan relations became more important for Europe as NATO and EU member states were concerned about Moldovan emigration as well as the status of Transnistria. This policy re-orientation from Russia toward the EU and Europe was accompanied by a steady increase in public support for EU membership. While Moldovan foreign policy became more aligned with Europe, economic considerations, especially concerning gas imports from Russia, forced Moldova to attempt to balance competing needs and foreign policies. President Voronin often spoke of the special relationship between Moldova and Russia, trying to avoid making foreign relations among Russia, Europe and Moldova a zero-sum game.

Leading up to the 2005 parliamentary elections, the Moldovan leadership intensified discussions with the EU concerning economic and political coordination. Before the elections, the EU and the Moldovan government announced an EU/Moldova Action Plan in February 2005, designed to facilitate the coordination of Moldovan legislation with EU norms and to encourage Moldova's further integration into European markets.[30] Indeed, the trade between Moldova and the EU steadily increased over the 2000s. By 2005, Moldovan exports to the

EU had overtaken Russia, and imports from the EU were three times greater than those from Russia (however, Russian exports of energy and imports of wine and tobacco were vital). While Moldova re-oriented its trade, the country failed to enact several of the economic reforms that had been part of the Action Plan. Moldova also refused to accept negotiations with the IMF which would have required economic reform. One of the reasons that Moldova did not have to significantly re-structure the economy was due to the large influx of migrant worker remittances. By 2007, Moldova tied for first in the world in terms of transferred remittances as a percentage of GDP. The remittances of Moldovan migrant workers constituted over a third of Moldovan GDP which, for a time, sustained the economy without the need for IMF loans or serious economic reform.[31]

Old challenges, new realities

The March 2005 parliamentary elections were the first national test for the PCRM. While opposition forces coalesced into new political groups, the PCRM's leadership remained virtually the same. Having control of the executive and the legislative branches provided the PCRM with the opportunity to appoint individuals to several key positions in the state media. Indeed, one of the negative trends during the 2000s in Moldova had been the limiting of freedom of the press and the use of state media outlets for political advantage. For example when the PCRM came to power in 2001, Freedom House, a US-based NGO, described the Moldovan press as "partly free"; by 2004, it had changed the rating to "not free." Restrictive media laws were enacted by the government in 2003, and in 2004 all staff members of the former public broadcaster, Teleradio-Moldova, were dismissed by the government (accusations were made that the new and re-hired employees faced a political litmus test). In addition, the licenses of several private broadcasters were suspended, which restricted the media space.

The 2005 parliamentary elections confirmed these trends. In its final report, the OSCE Election Observation Mission noted several shortcomings with the electoral process. The report noted that the "state television, *Moldova 1*, the only Moldovan broadcaster with countrywide coverage, displayed a clear bias in favor of the ruling party and failed to meet its obligation as a public media. Restrictive and, at times, ambiguous regulations on campaign coverage in broadcast media further impeded voters access to information and resulted in undue self-restraint in campaign coverage."[32] While there were no accusations of voter fraud, the manipulation of the electronic media called into question the fairness of the results. Indeed, only the PCRM, the Moldova Democratic Bloc (BMD, which comprised three parties and alliances), and the PPCD passed the threshold. The PCRM won 46% of the votes cast (56 seats), the BMD received 28.5% (34 seats), and the PPCD obtained 9% of the vote (11 seats). The PCRM held an absolute majority of seats but was still 5 seats short of being able to re-elect Voronin as president. After negotiations with the PPCD and other parliamentary factions, Voronin was re-elected president in April 2005 and subsequently re-appointed Tarlev prime minister.

While many of the negative trends in domestic politics have continued throughout the period since these elections, foreign policy has ebbed and flowed as Moldova has attempted to balance competing political and economic demands from Europe and Russia. Following the creation of a new EU-assisted customs regime along the Moldovan border in 2005, the Russian authorities imposed a punitive ban on Moldovan wine imports (as well as a significant hike in natural gas tariffs). These economic pressures undermined Moldova's pro-European policies so that by 2008 the government could point to very few concrete foreign policy successes with the EU. While a Common EU visa center was created by summer 2007, economic pressure led President Voronin once again to resume bilateral talks with Russia over the status of Transnistria and the possible resurrection of a Kozak-like agreement. Undoubtedly, the economic retaliation of Russia in 2006 and 2007 has significantly influenced the negotiation process between Moldova and Transnistria, as well as the country's wider foreign policy.

In addition, relations between Romania and Moldova have fluctuated from indifference to hostility. In January 2005, the newly elected president of Romania, Traian Băsescu, visited Moldova and declared his support for the country's aspirations to eventually accede to the EU. Since then, however, the issues of dual citizenship, religion, and language have complicated the relationship. By late 2007, the Romanian authorities claimed that approximately 800,000 Moldovans had applied for citizenship. In addition, by December 2007 talks over signing a Basic Political Treaty and Border Treaty broke down between the two countries over the name of the language in which the two treaties were to be signed. The issue of religion has also remained a highly divisive issue between Moldova and Romania. In 1992, the re-established Bessarabian Orthodox Metropolitanate, which was recognized by the Romanian Orthodox Church, applied for legal recognition in Moldova. A year later, its application had received no reply and instead the Metropolitanate of Chişinău and All Moldova, which was under the authority of the Russian Orthodox Church, was legally recognized.[33] Eventually, the Bessarabian Orthodox Metropolitanate sued the Moldovan government at the European Court of Human Rights and won in December 2001. In July 2002, after a deadline established by the Court, the Moldovan government finally registered the Bessarabian Orthodox Metropolitanate. Since then, however, priests of this Church traveling from Romania to Moldova to administer to their parishes have been denied entry into the country, and President Voronin has even gone so far as to call for the possible cancellation of the Church's registration. By 2008, Moldova's relationship with Romania was at its lowest point since the PCRM came to power.

Indeed as the end of the 2000s approaches, Moldova is confronted with the same issues that have plagued the country since even before independence in

1991. The politics of identity and location are just as important today, and while Moldova has embraced a much more pro-European foreign policy in the last decade, linguistic and cultural issues still figure prominently in relations with Russia and Romania. Russia's vital markets, as well as energy exports, provide the country with an important influence over Moldovan politics. All these issues play out in the conflict resolution possibilities between Moldova and Transnistria. While negotiations have ebbed and flowed, there has been very little agreement between the two sides on the fundamental issues necessary to end this "frozen conflict." Until the country is able to come to terms with all these critical issues, European integration efforts will always be promises unfulfilled.

Timeline 1989–2005

31 August 1989	Moldovan supreme Soviet adopts a law in which Moldovan with the Latin script is proclaimed state language
25 February 1990	Elections to Moldovan supreme Soviet held
19 August 1990	Gagauzia declares independence
2 September 1990	Transnistria declares independence
27 August 1991	Moldova declares independence from the USSR
8 December 1991	Mircea Snegur elected president
21 July 1992	Peace agreement signed between Moldova and Transnistria, ending the civil war
27 February 1994	Elections held to the Moldovan parliament
28 July 1994	Moldova adopts new constitution
23 December 1994	Parliament passes a law granting Gagauzia autonomy
1 December 1996	In second round of voting, Petru Lucinschi elected president
22 March 1998	Elections held for parliament
28 July 2000	Constitutional amendments transforming Moldova from semi-presidential to parliamentary regime enacted
25 February 2001	Elections held for parliament
4 April 2001	Vladimir Voronin elected president by parliament
18 November 2003	Kozak Memorandum announced
6 March 2005	Elections held for parliament
4 April 2005	Vladimir Voronin re-elected president by parliament

Fact sheet

Area	33,800 km^2
Population (2006)	3.4 million[a]
Urban population (2007)	45%
GDP *per capita* (PPP) (2007)	$2,200
Real GDP growth (2007)	6%
Inflation (2007)	12.5%

Note:
[a] Not counting Transnistria.
Sources: Eastern Europe, Russia and Central Asia 2008, 8th edn. (London: Routledge, 2007); *CIA: The World Factbook*, at www.cia.gov/library/publications/the-world-factbook/geos/mj.html [accessed on 8 February 2008]; Population Reference Bureau, at www.prb.org/Datafinder/Geography/Summary.aspx?region=213 [accessed on 8 February 2008].

Parties in the Moldovan Parliament (results of the 6 March 2005 election)

Deputies	% of the vote	Number of deputies elected
Party of Communists of the Republic of Moldova (PCRM)	45.98	56
Moldova Democratic Bloc (BMD)	28.53	34
Christian Democratic People's Party (PPCD)	9.07	11

Short biography of Vladimir Voronin

Vladimir Voronin was born on 25 May 1941 in the village of Corjova in the county (*raion*) of Dubăsari in the MSSR. From 1961 to 1971, he worked in a bread factory in the town of Criuleni and eventually head of the bread factory in Dubăsari. From 1971 to 1985, he worked in the state administration of the MSSR. Between 1985 and 1989, he worked as first secretary in the Bender (Tighina) Town Committee of the Communist Party. In 1989 and 1990, he was the Minister of Home Affairs of the MSSR. He was also a member of the Supreme Soviet of the MSSR for the 10th and 11th parliaments. In 1994, Voronin was elected first secretary of the PCRM. He ran for president in 1996 and in the first round received the third highest amount of votes. In 1998, he was elected a member of the parliament and was re-elected in 2001. He was elected president in April 2001 and was re-elected in April 2005.

Source: en.wikipedia.org/wiki/Vladimir_Voronin [accessed 8 February 2008].

Notes

1. For an excellent discussion concerning the creation of the MSSR and its use as a propaganda tool of the Soviets against Greater Romania, see Charles King, "Ethnicity and Institutional Reform: The Dynamics of 'Indigenization' in the Moldovan ASSR," *Nationalities Papers*, Vol. 26, No. 1 (March 1998), pp. 57–72.
2. Previously, Moldovan was written with the Cyrillic alphabet. See, Wim van Meurs, "Carving a Moldavian Identity out of History," *Nationalities Papers*, Vol. 26, No. 1 (March 1998), p. 50.
3. King notes that while political elites attempted to maintain the distinctiveness of Moldovan from Romanian, linguistic reforms ironically led to an increased influence of Romanian on the Moldovan language so that by the 1980s there were few

differences, aside from the alphabet, between the two languages. See Charles King, *The Moldovans: Romania, Russia and the Politics of Culture* (Stanford, Cant.: Hoover Institution Press, 2000), pp. 107–8.

4. For a discussion of the ethnography of the Gagauz, see Jeff Chinn and Steven D. Roper, "Territorial Autonomy in Gagauzia," *Nationalities Papers*, Vol. 26, No. 1 (March 1998), pp. 87–90.
5. The term "reactive nationalism" was coined by William Crowther to describe the attempts of ethnic minorities in Moldova to maintain the status quo. William Crowther, "The Politics of Ethno-National Mobilization and Reform in Soviet Moldavia," *Russian Review*, Vol. 50, No. 2 (April 1991), pp. 183–202.
6. William Crowther and Steven D. Roper, "A Comparative Analysis of the Institutional Development in the Romanian and Moldovan Legislatures," in David M. Olson and Philip Norton (eds.), *The New Parliaments of Central and Eastern Europe* (London: Frank Cass, 1996), p. 144.
7. While the city of Bender (Tighina) is under the control of Tiraspol, it is actually located on the right bank of the Dniester River and was part of Romania during the interwar years.
8. Pål Kølsto, Andrei Edemsky, and Natalya Kalashnikova, "The Dniester Conflict: Between Irredentism and Separatism," *Europe–Asia Studies*, Vol. 45, No. 6 (1993), p. 975.
9. For a more complete discussion concerning the events which led to the summer 1992 civil war, see Steven D. Roper, "From Frozen Conflict to Frozen Agreement: The Unrecognized State of Transnistria," in Tozun Bahcheli, Barry Bartmann, and Henry Srebrnik (eds.), *De Facto States: The Quest for Sovereignty* (New York: Routledge, 2004), pp. 102–17.
10. King, *The Moldovans*, p. 197.
11. For an excellent overview of the PCRM, see Luke March, "Socialism with Unclear Characteristics: The Moldovan Communist in Government," *Demokratizatsiya*, Vol. 12, No. 4 (Fall 2004), pp. 507–24.
12. The 12th parliament was elected for a five-year term in 1990.
13. The size of the parliament had been drastically reduced from 380 seats, see William Crowther and Steven D. Roper, "A Comparative Analysis," pp. 133–60.
14. King, *The Moldovans*, p. 169. As King notes, Moldova's inclusive ethnic minority policy was well received by European states and institutions. Indeed, Moldova was the first post-Soviet state to become a member of the Council of Europe, in 1995.
15. The 1989 "Law on the Official Language" declared the language of the state Romanian rather than Moldovan. This was also noted in Moldova's declaration of independence in 1991.
16. Matsuzato attributes the choice of semi-presidentialism to the influence of the Council of Europe's Venice Commission as well as to the influence of the Romanian constitution. Others such as Way argue that the institutional design of the Moldovan constitution had less to do with the conscious choice of a "Romanian model" and more to do with the nature of party politics. See Kimitaka Matsuzato, "Differing Dynamics of Semipresidentialism Across Euro/Eurasian Borders: Ukraine, Lithuania, Poland, Moldova, and Armenia," *Demokratizatsiya*, Vol. 14, No. 3

(Summer 2006), pp. 317–45; Lucan A. Way, "Pluralism by Default in Moldova," *Journal of Democracy*, Vol. 13, No. 4 (October 2002), pp. 127–41.

17. Throughout this period, the Gagauz and Transnistrian elites colluded against the Moldovan central government.
18. Romania initially participated in the peace talks between Moldova and Transnistria. See Chinn and Roper, "Territorial Autonomy in Gagauzia," p. 93.
19. Steven D. Roper, "The Politics of Economic Reform in Moldova," *Balkanistica*, Vol. 12, No. 1 (June 1999), pp. 95–118.
20. King, *The Moldovans*, p. 161.
21. March, "Socialism with Unclear Characteristics," p. 510.
22. Because the Moldovan president would nominate the prime minister subject to a vote of confidence, the proposed change was in fact a continuation of the semi-presidential regime.
23. The law stated that if no candidate was elected after three rounds of voting, the president had the right to dissolve parliament. As a consequence, Lucinschi was able to dissolve the parliament under Art. 78 of the constitution and call for new elections.
24. The law requires a three-fifths majority to elect the president (61 votes) which the Communists easily secured.
25. March, "Socialism with Unclear Characteristics."
26. The 1998 collapse of the Russian economy devastated Moldovan exports, especially in the all-important wine and tobacco sectors. By 2000, GDP had contracted by more than 10%, intensifying the amount of emigration from the country.
27. Going back to the ill-fated 1997 Memorandum signed by both parties, the concept of a "common state" was interpreted by Transnistria as an indication of equality within a confederal Moldova.
28. The Kozak Memorandum provided for a Constitutional Court composed of eleven judges (four chosen by Transnistria) in which a decision required the consent of nine judges (until 2015).
29. Not surprisingly, the full text of the Kozak Memorandum can be found on a web site maintained by the Transnistrian authorities, at www.pridnestrovie.net/kozak_memorandum.html.
30. For more discussion on Moldova's re-orientation in foreign policy, see Steven D. Roper, "Post-Soviet Moldova's National Identity and Foreign Policy," in Oliver Schmidtke and Serhy Yekelchyk (eds.), *Post Soviet Foreign Policy and Europe* (New York: Palgrave, 2007).
31. Moldova tied with Tajikistan – in 2007, both countries registered remittances as 36.2% of GDP. See, Dilip Ratha, Sanket Mohapatra, K. M. Vijayalakshmi, and Zhimei Xu, "Migration and Development Brief 3: Development Prospects Group, Migration and Remittances Team," available at siteresources.worldbank.org/EXTDECPROSPECTS/Resources/476882-1157133580628/BriefingNote3.pdf [accessed on 12 February 2008].
32. "OSCE/ODHIR Election Observation Mission Final Report," ODHIR.GAL/42/05 (3 June 2005), p. 1.
33. For an excellent discussion of the religious and political issues surrounding the registration of the Bessarabian Orthodox Metropolitanate, see Lucian Turcescu and Lavinia Stan, "Church–State Conflict in Moldova: The Bessarabian

Metropolitanate," *Communist and Post-Communist Studies*, Vol. 36, No. 4 (December 2003), pp. 443–65.

Further reading

Ciscel, Matthew H. *The Language of the Moldovans: Romania, Russia, and Identity in an Ex-Soviet Republic* (Lanham, Md.: Lexington Books, 2007)

Crowther, William. "Ethnic Politics and the Post-Communist Transition in Moldova," *Nationalities Papers*, Vol. 26, No. 1 (March 1998), pp. 147–64

Hill, Ronald J. "Moldova Votes Backwards: The 2001 Parliamentary Election," *Journal of Communist Studies and Transition Politics*, Vol. 17, No. 4 (December 2001), pp. 130–9

King, Charles. "Minorities Policy in the Post-Soviet Republics: The Case of the Gagauzi," *Ethnic and Racial Studies*, Vol. 20, No. 4 (July 1997), pp. 738–56

Kølsto, Pål (ed.). *National Integration and Violent Conflict in Post-Soviet Societies: The Cases of Estonia and Moldova* (Lanham, Md.: Rowman & Littlefield, 2003)

Kølsto, Pål and Andrei Malgin. "The Transnistrian Republic: A Case of Politicized Regionalism," *Nationalities Papers*, Vol. 26, No. 1 (March 1998), pp. 103–27

Lewis, Ann (ed.) *EU and Moldova: On a Fault-Line of Europe* (London: Kogan Page, 2007)

Protsyk, Oleh. "Federalism and Democracy in Moldova," *Post-Soviet Affairs*, Vol. 21, No. 1 (January–March 2005), pp. 72–90

Quinlan, Paul D. "Back to the Future: An Overview of Moldova Under Voronin," *Demokratizatsiya*, Vol. 12, No. 4 (Fall 2004), pp. 485–504

Roper, Steven D. "From Semi-Presidentialism to Parliamentarism: Regime Change and Presidential Power in Moldova," *Europe–Asia Studies*, Vol. 60, No. 1 (January 2008), pp. 113–26

Way, Lucan A. "Weak States and Pluralism: The Case of Moldova," *East European Politics and Societies*, Vol. 17, No. 3 (August 2003), pp. 454–82

Weiner, Robert. "The Foreign Policy of the Voronin Administration," *Demokratizatsiya*, Vol. 12, No. 4 (Fall 2004), pp. 541–56

Part 7
Present and future challenges

22

Regional security and regional relations

RICK FAWN*

Central Europe's regional security and regional relations today are unimaginably different from those of 1989. The Warsaw Treaty Organization (WTO) and the Council for Mutual Economic Assistance (CMEA), the principal intergovernmental bodies to which these states belonged, were not devised so much for their own mutual benefit as to give a legalistic veneer of multilateralism and, foremost, to ensure their loyalty to Moscow.[1] No socialist country that remained a member of those organizations practised what could be considered an independent foreign policy. The geopolitical orientation of these countries, regardless of any popular self-perceptions or desires otherwise, was to the East.

By 2007, ten post-communist states were members of NATO and of the EU (including six which had lacked statehood in 1989),[2] and by 2009 Albania and Croatia had been admitted to the Alliance.

This chapter argues that the overall transformation of the region – in terms of regional self-perception, outside perceptions, and institutional memberships – was due to a significant extent to regional cooperation initiatives originating from within this region. By that we mean bodies created by these states and for these states, rather than any broader regional cooperation that may have stemmed, and belatedly so, from Western intergovernmental initiatives.[3] Of course, Western institutional membership – foremost in the EC/EU and in NATO – became a primary foreign policy aim of these former Soviet satellite states. As this chapter also covers security, a final section addresses how NATO enlargement occurred.

There are now a considerable number of groupings involving states covered by this volume, as well as several other post-communist initiatives whose member states are mostly or entirely beyond its scope.[4] Three groupings involving many post-communist states originated outside the region but were intended to foster cooperation within it. The first is the Council of the Baltic Sea States (CBSS), stemming from a Danish–Swedish proposal in 1992, and which includes all ten littoral states of the Baltic Sea, the European Commission, and the (officially called) "exception" of far-removed Iceland, which was admitted in March 1995. A second is the Organization for Black Sea Economic Cooperation (BSEC), a Turkish initiative launched formally in 1992 and arising from Turkish political and economic ambitions to extend influence in the south of the former Soviet Union and back into (perhaps coincidentally) its former Ottoman holdings in Southeastern Europe. Whatever the motivations, unlike the CBSS, BSEC extends far beyond the littoral states of the Black Sea to include both Balkan and Caucasian states, such as Albania and Armenia, that do not lie on that body of water. A third regional grouping is the eighteen-member Central European Initiative (CEI), launched in another form by Italy in November 1989. It receives specific attention because so many of its member states are addressed in this volume, even though CEI's membership extends beyond that remit, to include also Belarus and Ukraine.

Initiatives such as the CBSS and BSEC are limited by two related factors. One, they are each very functionally based – that is, concentrating not on high-security but low-political issues that are meant to be win–win, such as on transportation, energy, and the environment. Indeed, the CBSS even specifically excluded security from its mandate, presumably realizing that trying to address any such issues with such diverse membership, including the Russian Federation, could paralyze any other initiatives. Of course, even low-political functional issues can and do become politicized and even influence national security. It therefore is not surprising that the second consideration – membership – has also limited these groupings, both regarding their stipulated (and limited) mandates and also in elevating them to higher objectives that might fundamentally change the geopolitical and geocultural orientation of their region. The CBSS and the BSEC initiatives have homogenous memberships – NATO and EU members, former communist regimes and former Soviet republics, and the Russian Federation. Officials and analysts say that Russia particularly hampers working relations in these bodies.

The most important grouping, however, in the view of this chapter has been Visegrád cooperation of then-Czechoslovakia, Hungary, and Poland. As much of this chapter will indicate, it changed the nature of regional relations at the core of former Eastern Europe, and thereby managed to contribute significantly to changing Western perceptions of the region and to open the region to Western integration. Visegrád furthermore provided inspiration for cooperation as well as for an enduring, tangible policy toward the region, in the form of the Central European Free Trade Agreement (CEFTA), which now ironically no longer includes any of its original signatories but ten Balkan entities (including Kosovo, even before the declaration of independence, through its international administrator, the UN Mission in Kosovo, UNMIK). Because of its particular salience to Visegrád, and its relevance also to so many of the countries covered in this volume, it too receives attention.

The chapter proceeds by giving background to the CEI and then concentrates on Visegrád, including its origins, the challenges it has faced, its endurance past EU accession, and also its legacy in bequeathing CEFTA to Southeastern Europe.

The Central European Initiative (CEI)

Like the CBSS and BSEC, the CEI maintains a predominantly functionalist agenda, working on low-political issues of (ideally) mutual benefit, such as transportation, technology, and tourism, as well as, more recently, some security issues such as coordination on combating transnational crime and on developing minority rights protection. The CEI, which started with only one member in the EU (Italy), and now has twelve of its members in that supranational entity, developed as its principal aim to bring its members "closer together" and to assist their accession to the EU.[5]

That said, the CEI's importance and utility remain questionable. Its greatest achievement may simply be its existence, having overcome one death and serious challenges since. Its precursor was founded in 1978 on the basis of some existing dialogue among, importantly, substate entities of Austria, Germany, Italy, Hungary, and Yugoslavia. Thus talks among Austrian, Hungarian, and Italian provinces, Bavaria, Slovenia, and Croatia (when the latter two were still republics of federal Yugoslavia) occurred in the forum of the Alpen–Adria Working Group. This group took advantage of the relative decentralization of Yugoslavia, which permitted subfederal units to engage in foreign relations (relations being lower than foreign policy) and the very limited but still unusual freedom of movement in communist Hungarian foreign policy.

At the initiative of Italy this subnational grouping was moved up to the national level in 1989, as change swept Eastern Europe. Reflecting one interpretation of those changes, this new grouping became not only the first post-communist regional cooperation initiative, but also the only one to be established with an explicit reference to traditional power politics. The group was formed on 11 November 1989, just two days after the opening of East Germany's border crossings, including its most famous crossing in central Berlin.

The driving force behind the cooperation, Italian Foreign Minister Gianni de Michelis, saw this grouping of Austria, Italy, Hungary, and Yugoslavia as a means to "contribute to a more even balance of power" after the changes to Europe's political landscape following German unification,[6] which perhaps suggested a more *Realpolitik* motivation behind this regional grouping than the others. Indeed, Germany was excluded from becoming a national-level successor to Alpen–Adria. That some Italians might have continued to think in *Realpolitik* terms about Germany after the Cold War was indicated by Italian scholarly works that advocated a project that was described as seeking to make Serbia "the bastion against German hegemonism [in the Balkans]" as it was the "only regional power strong enough to prevent a German sphere of influence [from] taking root in the Balkans."[7] In addition, a foreign observer could write "For Italy, a controlling interest in Albania is almost a prerequisite to the success of its new *Ostpolitik* which has gradually evolved since the downing of the Berlin Wall."[8]

Regardless of the group's original purposes, its membership was expanded in March 1990 first to Czechoslovakia (whose foreign policy was highly creative and keen to try new diplomatic constructions) and then in 1991 to Poland. Because neither new member had any reasonable claim of geographical proximity to the Alps or the Adriatic, the formation was renamed the *Pentagonale* and then *Hexagonale*; it used the Italian phraseology in deference to the national pedigree. But just as the group seemed to gather greater membership and better prospects for influence, its momentum ceased with the outbreak of war in Yugoslavia.

The grouping was rekindled at a Vienna Summit in July 1992, at which the Yugoslav successor states of Slovenia, Bosnia-Herzegovina, and Croatia gained membership. It also adopted the new name (in English, and with English as the working language) of the CEI. Considering that it had not used such a name before and that its membership was still predominantly Balkan/southeast European and/or Adriatic, the choice seemed to signal an attempt at geocultural relocation. Indeed, as will be mentioned also regarding Visegrád, several southeast European countries were keen to change the outward perceptions of their geocultural location by shedding reference to themselves as "Balkan," much as the former "East Europeans" were intent on banishing that term. In 1993, the CEI admitted Macedonia (using that name). At its Trieste Summit in 1994 the CEI developed its "Association Council" for Belarus, Bulgaria, Romania, and Ukraine, and included Albania a few months later. At the Warsaw Summit the CEI decided to upgrade all associates into members; Moldova sought and received membership in 1996, raising participation to sixteen. The Federal Republic of Yugoslavia (Serbia and Montenegro), however, remained outside until the fall of Serbian leader Slobodan Milošević, being admitted only in November 2000. Once it separated peacefully in 2006 from the short-lived union of Serbia and Montenegro, Montenegro became the eighteenth – and, to date, final – member state.

Despite claims, as outlined at the start of this section, that the CEI is useful for functionalist purposes within the region and for further EU integration, the overall ability of the group to function is questionable. The diversity of its membership – from the pariah dictatorship of Belarus to what have become member states of the EU and NATO – seems to disadvantage the workings of the grouping, rather than providing for a means of increased mutual understanding. Some of the diplomats attending its meetings have said that not all member states bother even to send delegations.[9]

By contrast, the one grouping that has had a profound impact on the geopolitical reorientation of its members, and to a significant but underappreciated extent also on the transformation of European security, is Visegrád. It deserves careful attention for the role it has played in achieving the leading foreign policy aims of its members and in changing the overall dynamics of post-communist regional relations and security.

Visegrád

To make consideration of Visegrád more salient, it is beneficial to outline its main achievement: NATO and EU membership. With accession now well past (and an outcome often taken for granted by younger observers!) we must not lose sight of what an achievement it was. Simply put, NATO and the EC responded to the revolutions of 1989 with no indication whatsoever that eventual membership for the newly freed Soviet satellite states might be a possibility. As but one of those involved in that process, Magda Vašáryová, a post-communist Czechoslovak ambassador and then Slovak ambassador and Slovak Secretary of State for Foreign Affairs, reminds us, the goals of NATO and EU membership in 1991 "seemed virtually impossible to achieve."[10]

What role did Visegrád play? Various Central European political leaders involved in the NATO and EU accession processes are clear that Visegrád was central to attaining that outcome. By way of brief example, post-communist Polish president Lech Wałęsa called membership of NATO and the EU the "tangible fruits" of Visegrád cooperation.[11] A senior Hungarian diplomat wrote that Visegrád cooperation could claim "historic success in its efforts to win the trans-Atlantic community's embrace."[12] And the leading foreign policy advisers in post-communist Czechoslovakia have said that Visegrád was "a powerful negotiating tool" in securing NATO membership, irrespective of what may have been said by member governments, and that it was precisely Visegrád's "close and coordinated work ... that compelled American and Western European politicians to open the doors of the Atlantic alliance to us."[13]

Apart from that, Visegrád was important in several other respects. It offered – and has been seen both by outside observers and regional practioners – a new form of relations for the region, one of sustained cooperation rather than short-term, specific interest-serving activity. Likewise, they saw Visegrád as the most successful post-communist regional cooperation initiative.[14] Visegrád was also particularly important because it changed how its members were perceived by outside powers and how they ultimately realigned their economic, political, and security responsibilities. Visegrád also spawned a second grouping in the form of CEFTA which, having completely transferred its membership to another set of post-communist countries, continues today. As will be illustrated, Visegrád has had, and continues to have, an impact on other regional groups and dynamics. How did Visegrád arise?

Visegrád: origins

Visegrád was unquestionably strongly rooted in both communist-era dissident values and in the limited but important physical cooperation among them.[15] None of the other post-communist regional cooperation initiatives possesses such heritage, one fundamental in my view to Visegrád's unique successes.

That said, differences exist on its origins. Solidarity leader and post-communist Polish president Lech Wałęsa writes that Visegrád was the "fruit of the idea" of the Polish Solidarity movement.[16] The former dissident and post-communist deputy prime minister of Czechoslovakia Ján Čarnogurský states that the idea for such post-communist cooperation came from the group advising Czech dissident and post-communist Czechoslovak president Václav Havel and unambiguously credits Havel with specifically initiating it, as does post-communist Czechoslovak ambassador to Hungary Rudolf Chmel.[17] Several former Czech dissidents with whom I have spoken suggest that the inspiration, at least, was jointly from Polish and Czech dissidents who had cooperated in the late 1970s and 1980s and that the practical implementation both grew from that and required their input. By contrast, Hungary's first post-communist Foreign Minister Géza Jeszenszky counters "the many versions in circulation" regarding Visegrád's origins. He writes that "as probably the closest witness," it was Hungarian Prime Minister József Antall who, at the November 1990 Conference on Security and Cooperation in Europe meeting, invited the Czechoslovak and Polish leaders to Hungary.[18]

Whatever the exact origins, within days of having become Czechoslovak president, Havel made speeches in both the Polish and Hungarian parliaments in January 1990 and called on the three populations to remember their mutual support in the dark times of communism and to use that to combine efforts to rejoin "Europe," which they could achieve better and faster together than by working at cross-purposes. Havel then convened a meeting in April 1990 in Bratislava, to which the leaderships of Hungary and Poland were invited, with Austrian, Italian, and Yugoslav Foreign Ministers as observers.

The importance of former dissidents to regional cooperation can be seen in the failure of that first initiative to produce concrete results.[19] I would adapt Timothy Garton Ash's famous term, "refolution," by which he described domestic change in late-communist Poland and Hungary as the result of reform from above and revolutionary pressure from below. We can see refolution in early Central European foreign policy – that old communists still had retained important posts in Poland and Hungary and had no interest in cooperation with ex-dissidents.[20] Such cooperation was a dead initiative until that old guard was replaced by more ex-dissidents, as happened in the course of 1990. As one former Czech dissident participating in the meeting recounted, his fellow Hungarian and Polish ex-dissidents wished not to be represented by communists. And while it was clear that Wałęsa and Havel did not work well on a personal level,[21] the former's replacement of communist-era General and President Wojciech Jaruzelski was important for progress. Nevertheless, the irony of Hungary's evolutionary process of change in the late 1980s meant that its foreign ministry was nevertheless the best able of three ministries to organize the Visegrád meeting in 1991.[22] But even that was not enough, as developments outside the region also seemed to compel cooperation.

First, to reiterate more specifically, the EC made no membership overtures to the Central Europeans in the early 1990s. The most general form of EC terms for any future membership, and with no guarantees even of that possibility, came only in 1993 with the Copenhagen Criteria. NATO offered no more than interparliamentary discussions through the North Atlantic Cooperation Council (NACC) in 1990–1. Its Partnership for Peace (PfP), launched on 1 January 1994, was open to almost all post-communist and post-Soviet states and was therefore the opposite of the security guarantee that NATO membership signified. Rather than a possible antechamber to future membership, the Central Europeans saw PfP even as a "threat" because NATO could thereby forgo enlargement entirely.[23] The Central Europeans therefore understood in the early 1990s that they had little alternative but cooperation among themselves.[24] Second, although writings by participants of Central European regional cooperation do not make much reference to the Baltic events of January 1991, when Soviet forces killed unarmed peaceful protestors in Latvia and Lithuania, interviews suggested that this Soviet backlash was deeply alarming and prompted further regional cooperation. Certainly, post-communist Czechoslovak Foreign Minister and former dissident Jiří Dienstbier said that the resignation of Soviet Foreign Minister Eduard Shevardnadze prompted the Three to cooperate on ending the Warsaw Pact,[25] although Shevardnadze had stepped down (citing pressure from "hardliners") in December 1990, before the Baltic violence. In any case, regional cooperation really started in February 1991 – within days of the disturbing events in the neighboring Baltic republics.

The three leaders of Czechoslovakia, Hungary, and Poland met at the Hungarian town of Visegrád, used previously to crown Hungarian kings, and announced their cooperation with the Visegrád Declaration of 15 February 1991. The declaration made positive, though to my mind at least, very selective, use of common history, to underline that the three countries were departing from the region's history of interethnic tension and mistrust and were now reasserting values that were fundamentally European and would thereby not only contribute to, but be an essential part of, the ongoing integration of "Europe."[26] Symbolism for both the Central Europeans and their absent West European interlocutors was intended in the choice of summit location. As former dissident and leading post-communist Czech politician Petr Pithart wrote: "Those three kings back in 1335 knew very well why they chose that place to meet, on a solid outcrop high above the Danube. They did so because they wanted the majesty of the silent and powerful river to remind them that there are values that stand above the daily conflicts and squabbles of neighbors."[27] If also unintended at the time of formation, this Visegrád provides contrast to another Visegrád only a few hundred km south, where interethnic violence occurred in Yugoslavia.

Tangible Visegrád cooperation pushed forward. While the three states diverged in 1990 (remarkably) on how to deal both with the Soviet military on still their soil and with the WTO and CMEA, by 1991 they had achieved the formal end of both institutions. Fears of the Soviet Union re-emerged with the August coup against Gorbachev, at which time joint meetings of Visegrád defense ministers were held and which also contributed to the holding of Visegrád's second presidential summit, in Kraków, and the emergence of the three states' clear, unified intentions to seek NATO membership.[28] Visegrád also demonstrated to the EC that the three countries could cooperate. They secured individual, but identical Association Agreements with the Community in December 1991, which were also signed at a joint ceremony. Czechoslovak Foreign Minister Dienstbier credits the rapid achievement of the Agreements to the coordination provided by Visegrád, while Hungary's then-Foreign Minister said that they were "a very visible endorsement of the Visegrád model."[29]

Within months Visegrád had secured a distinctive identity for the region. Apart from the attainment of the Association Agreements, the Three also secured important policy changes by major Western governments, such as the lifting of visa regimes and of bans on Western arms purchases. Western governments also began adopting the terminology that the Central Europeans wanted–so that, for example, the British Foreign Office changed its "Eastern Europe" section to "Central Europe and Eastern Adriatic." Other post-communist countries began to recognize Visegrád's success and sought membership, a further sign of its success. But Visegrád was already aware of its achievements and sought to keep membership exclusive, even though it has never expressly stated that, and in fact has claimed to remain open. Indeed, Visegrád has continued to be the only post-communist regional cooperation initiative not to expand beyond its original membership (excluding the Czech Republic and Slovakia as successor to Czechoslovakia).

Other states saw the group as a way of propelling themselves away from the backwardness of association with the former "Eastern Europe" and the "Balkans." Visegrád had thus quickly attainted a symbolic standard, within both the former socialist bloc and the West. Sensing this development, "Romania tried to join the group at an early stage. The door was firmly closed in its face" due to its failed democratization.[30] Romania's post-revolution prime minister, Petre Roman, expressed concern that Visegrád was creating an artificial division among post-communist countries into "Central Europe" and "Eastern Europe."[31] For Bulgaria's post-communist President Zheliu Zhelev, success for his country would be measured by "whether Bulgaria will no longer be apart from the three central European countries – Poland, Hungary, and Czechoslovakia."[32] Bulgaria and Romania saw their exclusion from Visegrád as "implicitly exclud[ing] them as primary candidates for integration with the West."[33]

Visegrád was important also to Croatia. Franjo Tudjman's electoral success in 1990 was presented as a "fulfillment of the nationalist myth of 'Croatia's return to the West' after some kind of a Babylonian captivity in the multiethnic federation dominated by atheistic communists and Orthodox Serbs."[34] As part of Croatia's intended geocultural reorientation, a Croatian Foreign Ministry official told me that Croatian membership of Visegrád would have signaled that the country was no longer Balkan but instead "Central European" and thus successful.[35]

Despite such interest in Visegrád by other post-communist states, the group continued with its original membership. On 6 May 1992 at the Prague Summit, Visegrád was demonstrating its ambition: not only did its leaders jointly and clearly declare their intention to join NATO, but they also signed the CEFTA that would come into effect at the end of the year. Czechoslovakia's June elections produced a fatally divided federal parliament when the ultra-market (or so in rhetoric) Václav Klaus won in the Czech lands and nationalist Vladimír Mečiar won in Slovakia. Visegrád suffered from the temporary eclipse of Havel, a driving force behind the cooperation but who resigned as Czechoslovak president, and from the antagonistic policies of Klaus and Mečiar.

Visegrád's questionable middle age

While Visegrád continued in 1993 after the split of Czechoslovakia and was colloquially rechristened the "Visegrád Four" or the "Visegrád Square," or V4, the Klaus and Mečiar leaderships challenged, in different ways, its capacity to operate. Klaus saw Visegrád as at best economic cooperation and was seen as deliberately undercutting and even insulting its meetings by sending inappropriately low-ranking officials and apparently refusing to partake in cooperation other than economic. He declared during the 25 November 1994 meeting of Visegrád Prime Ministers in Poznán, "Now the Czech Republic, in its dictionary, literally translates 'Visegrád' as 'CEFTA.'"[36] But even with deliberate efforts to weaken Visegrád, Klaus still – when former dissidents most supportive of it thought it had collapsed – weighed in to say that it was alive.[37] He also came to realize that Visegrád would not hold back the Czech Republic, the region's presumed frontrunner, from entering the EU.[38]

The challenge to Visegrád from Slovakia was also ideological, but with different content. The nationalistic Mečiar anatagonized his Hungarian minority, damaging relations with Budapest; his regime's foreign policy also moved from Euro-Atlanticism and even made surprising overtures to Russia, including consideration of the purchase of a Russian air defense system. Slovakia generally put itself outside Visegrád during Mečiar's government of 1994–8,[39] although an exact date for when fourway Visegrád cooperation seems to have died remains unclear.[40]

But even in this nadir, the value of the grouping remained, as did several of its activities. Trilateral meetings at different levels continued throughout the mid-1990s, particularly on coordination of positions towards EU and NATO accession. And despite Slovakia's relative isolation, Mečiar nevertheless wanted Visegrád, stating, or perhaps pleading, "Our foursome is being buried prematurely. In the end, sooner or later we will have to cooperate together."[41]

Furthermore, Slovak officials reacted with anger when in 1996 Polish President Aleksander Kwaśniewski stated that only the "three," excluding Slovakia, would enter the EU.[42]

In any case, Visegrád's arguably most successful product – CEFTA – not only continued throughout this period but attracted membership interest from Slovenia, Romania, Bulgaria, and Croatia, while FYROM and Ukraine attended as observers. The first four entered CEFTA in 1996, 1997, 1999, and 2003, respectively; CEFTA became the only sector of Visegrád activities into which new full members were allowed.

By 1997, the Czech Republic, Hungary, and Poland were clear frontrunners among post-communist states when measured by their certain entry into NATO (effective in 1999), and, with Estonia and Slovenia, the announcement of EU accession negotiations. The fall of Klaus later that year and Mečiar in 1998 allowed for the immediate and energetic resumption of fourway Visegrád cooperation. A series of fourway meetings were held, culminating in a prime ministerial summit on 14 May 1999 which launched what has become known as "Visegrád II." Far from having suffered a blow, the group's formal reintegration of Slovakia and the renewed joint efforts at Euro-Atlantic integration became Visegrád's "finest hour."[43]

The new cooperation also included very specific fostering of regional cultural cooperation, particularly through the Visegrád Fund, headquartered in Bratislava. But the rebirth did not mean the absence of problems. Cooperation almost broke down in 2002 when the Czech and Slovak governments boycotted a prime ministerial-level meeting of Visegrád after Hungarian Prime Minister Viktor Orban called for the post-Second World War Beneš decrees to be revoked. The decrees, sanctioned by the Allies, allowed for the expulsion, sometimes violently and even fatally, of both Germans and Hungarians. Despite any moral questions about the decrees, they have been untouchable political issues (though some humanist Czech dissidents thought differently). While Visegrád had become a vehicle for diplomatic protest, it did not cease to function. In fact, a Visegrád meeting of culture ministers occurred soon after. Hungarian proponents of early Visegrád cooperation responded to wider concerns in the group about Orban's apparent intentions to scuttle cooperation and differences were reconciled.[44]

That incident reveals perhaps the most essential feature of Visegrád cooperation. It is not an institution – although some outside observers mistakenly so claim; and although it possesses some attributes of an intergovernmental organization, such as regularized meetings at all levels of government, an annual high-level summit, a rotating chairmanship with an annual set of goals, and so on, it has never created institutional rules that then force its members to juxtapose cooperation against (supposed) national priority. This practise came in part from earlier post-communist idealism, whereby its dissident-era supporters "wanted to avoid the creation of new bureaucratic offices, organs and officials that would be remote."[45] These unconventional operating principles certainly provide considerable flexibility which can keep cooperation functioning.

Visegrád's importance continues also in its influence on wider regional relations. Visegrád has been clearly recognized as the inspiration of the Vilnius Group, ten other post-communist countries that aligned to lobby for NATO accession. Still more importantly, CEFTA was taken over by the EU as part of its Stability Pact for Southeastern Europe, and in 2006 ten entities were signed to it, including Kosovo, through its overseer UNMIK. Visegrád thus became a working platform in international efforts to kindle economic integration in the postwar Balkans.

With all four members of Visegrád having obtained both NATO and EU membership by 2004, future cooperation among them specifically through the Group may have seemed terminal, a victim perhaps of its own success. Visegrád may not be immortal; but the new institutional circumstances of EU membership have, rather, given it new life.

Rumors of another death: post-EU accession

Because Visegrád's primary aims of EU and NATO accession were achieved, we might therefore reasonably expect that its importance in each member's foreign policy would disappear or, worst, that cooperation would be downgraded from, for example, a "priority" in Polish foreign policy to "important."[46] Magda Vašáryová said that, after entry to the EU, Visegrád remained a stable priority in Slovakia's foreign policy.[47] The passing of competition over accession to the EU and NATO and the consequent "none-too-gentlemanly horse-race" has removed a major cause for disruption.[48] Apart from that, and to dispel any doubt, Visegrád leaders specifically agreed on the Group's continuation beyond EU membership. The Visegrád leaders, on 12 May 2004, therefore deliberately issued a sequel declaration at Kroměříž in the Czech Republic, explaining that the Group would continue to contribute to the development of European values.[49] That was reiterated two years later, on the fifteenth anniversary of Visegrád's 1991 foundation, by Visegrád ambassadors abroad who jointly wrote of the Group's success and continuation.[50]

Declarations are one thing; actions another. Further evidence of Visegrád's longevity comes from its integration into regular governmental activity. A senior Hungarian diplomat responsible for regional cooperation told me that every level and every sectoral department of the Hungarian Foreign Ministry has dealings with Visegrád.[51] Vašáryová similarly wrote that "Visegrád cooperation is a daily reality in the work of all government and state institutions."[52] In addition, since 2004 Visegrád has embarked on a new level of cooperation among regions formed within each country, and now has a Forum for Regions of V4 Countries. Much of the Forum's intended work concerns coordination of V4 policy within the EU.[53]

In addition, according to regional diplomats, Visegrád has become a brand-name and a trademark with recognition overseas, and in international business activity, particularly in east Asia, helping to make its members appear a coherent investment area.[54] One of Slovakia's principle foreign policy architects, Pavol Demeš, similarly called V4 "a tried and true foreign policy trademark" which could last another fifteen years.[55] The value of the name is not immortal but certainly extends beyond EU accession.

Still more importantly, the Visegrád countries have shared interests in the EU. Many Visegrád activists, such as Havel, believe that membership itself does not preclude cooperation when it serves the Group and in addition, based on such interests, that regional groupings exist within the EU and that Central Europe constitutes one of them.[56] The issues pertaining to membership that Visegrád was coordinating before accession continue to be common to them and generally to prompt a common stand, such as access to Structural and Cohesion Funds, voting rights, and Commission seats. As Czech Prime Minister Jiří Paroubek wrote on the fifteenth anniversary of Visegrád's establishment, "Fears that the activities of [the] Visegrad Group would flag after the member countries joined the EU have proven unfounded."[57] Rather than diminishing, Hungarian diplomat and parliamentarian Gábor Hárs asserts that Visegrád cooperation has grown stronger in the context of EU membership.[58] As one practitioner from the region noted, "on repeated occasions it [the Visegrád Group] has been able to present a more or less united position within the European Union."[59] This is perhaps an exaggeration, but some argue that the V4 have "brought a new dynamism to the EU."[60] Their entry has also made the EU fundamentally different and almost certainly ensures that the Union can never approximate a federation.[61] Regardless of how Visegrád may secure its members' interests within the EU or affect the internal development of the current Union, Visegrád is very likely to influence EU policy on its relations with other post-communist states and even on further enlargement. Visegrád cooperation has consequently been called by its sponsors an "engine of a more dynamic EU policy towards Eastern and South-Eastern Europe," one able to export democracy and freedom throughout the region.[62] As Wałęsa commented after accession: "Cooperation between the Visegrad Group and other countries, especially those of Eastern Europe, has become an important assignment ... We can play an essential role as a bridge" between the post-communist states not currently in the EU and NATO and those intergovernmental bodies.[63]

While some involved in Visegrád thought that the Group neglected its collective duty to support Ukraine's "Orange Revolution," much coordinated activity has nevertheless been undertaken to support democratization in that country, as several Visegrád prime ministers have asserted, as well as in other former communist states outside the EU.[64] The International Visegrád Fund proudly announces that it is the single largest provider of scholarships for foreign study to and in Ukraine. Indeed, Vašáryová writes that Visegrád's "engagement with Ukraine, Moldova and other neighboring states has increased the scope of the Visegrád Group's activities far beyond the border of simple regional cooperation."[65]

While NATO and EU accession were principal goals behind Visegrád, accession to the latter has created reasons for the Group to continue. Furthermore, the post-communist member states want a role in the EU, and that includes democratization and human rights promotion among their immediate post-Soviet neighbors. To be sure, Visegrád countries will have different views on how to approach these matters; nevertheless, the V4 agree on both general and specific cases and can and will act in unity. Visegrád is serving as a vehicle both for its member states to pursue more effectively their own interests within the EU and to prompt the EU to take a different, even more proactive line on democratization and Europeanization further East.[66]

As important as post-communist regional cooperation initiatives have been, in terms of security, NATO membership quickly became the ultimate objective of most of the countries covered in this volume (and certainly for the Baltic states and Croatia) and therefore requires specific attention.

NATO membership: the "real" security in regional relations?

As this chapter has indicated, NATO (and the EC/EU) had no intention initially to extend membership to post-communist states. Rather, the leaderships of these countries, particularly those in Visegrád, lobbied diligently and often creatively to change Western mindsets. While sympathetic interlocutors were found, considerable opposition to opening NATO came from within parts of the US political system, from within the NATO Alliance, and from the Russian Federation.

Since coming to power and throughout the 1990s, the Central European leaderships certainly recognized the importance of other pan-European structures, and the EC/EU held particular importance for its markets and socio-economic benefits, as well as providing an institutional reiteration that the post-communist countries were rejoining "Europe." Despite some foreign policy experimentation immediately after the collapse of communism, by 1991 the Central European leaderships had realized that their states required a full security guarantee, which only NATO could furnish. This was in part due to the continuing turmoil and threats emanating from the Soviet Union, including the use of violence against civilian protesters and the August coup by military–security hardliners, but also because the Central European leaders began to view NATO membership as even a moral and political right, an opinion that some Western leaders then absorbed to enhance their own arguments for enlargement.

To be sure, even before the end of the USSR, NATO was adapting to the monumental changes brought by the collapse of communism in Eastern Europe. At its Rome Summit in November 1991, NATO issued the Declaration on Peace and Cooperation, which included discussion of partnership and cooperation with the countries of Central and Eastern Europe and established the Alliance's first institutional outreach through the NACC.

Although novel, such initiatives fell short of what post-communist governments sought. Specific lobbying for Central European entry into NATO can be dated to the presence of these leaders in Washington, DC, in April 1993, for the opening of the Holocaust Museum.[67] Each leader seized the opportunity to impress personally upon US President Bill Clinton the importance of NATO membership. The first Western public figure, however, to voice the idea of inclusion of post-communist governments in NATO was German Defense Minister Volker Rühe, who asserted that the Alliance could not remain a "closed shop" and that no good reason existed for denying membership.[68] NATO's collective response was the launch of the PfP, which was opened to, and accepted by, almost all post-communist countries, starting in early 1994 (although some war-torn countries, such as Bosnia, were excluded), as well as European neutrals such as Austria, Finland, and Switzerland. Central European leaderships, however, deemed PfP insufficient and even counter-productive, fearing that it was a measure to pacify Russia while continuing to leave them vulnerable.[69]

Indeed, many in the Clinton Administration and several European governments were concerned not to alarm Russia with any appearance of NATO encroachment on its borders; in addition, Russian President Boris Yeltsin, the West's preferred political partner on the (perturbingly) extensive Russian political spectrum, referred to his tenuous domestic position from Russian perceptions of the malevolence of NATO expansion. Particularly as a result of the popularity of more extreme Russian politicians, Clinton's speeches regarding NATO's future in 1993 remained "highly ambiguous" as well as "extremely cautious."[70] Nevertheless, continuing Central European pressure, a growing US domestic lobby, coming partly from Republicans and from descendants of Central Europeans, and a growing recognition of the need to transform NATO for its own sake, encouraged US President Bill Clinton to embrace enlargement. Just days after PfP's initiation, Clinton travelled to the Central European capitals. In Prague on 12 January 1994, in front of the four Visegrád presidents, Clinton announced that NATO enlargement was no longer a question of whether, but rather of when.

But who would have membership, on what basis, and when, remained unanswered. NATO, while still a military organization, had already given clear indications that it sought from its partners a general spirit of cooperation, and the domestic transformation of their political and economic systems, including the unquestionable establishment of democratic polities. It was also clear that the contributions of the post-communist states' GDP to defense spending would remain below the NATO average. Detractors of enlargement argued that any new members – quite apart from possibly drawing NATO into conflicts, provoking Russia, and undermining the credibility of the Alliance's collective defense – would simply cost the United States too much.[71]

For their part, however, the Central Europeans were keen to prove that they were not only reliable but also physically able to assist the Alliance in some of its newer, and very demanding operations, particularly in the Balkan conflicts.

Thus. they partook in joint peacekeeping in Bosnia (with Russian forces also, an activity which Western pro-enlargement politicians such as Clinton used to illustrate that both that NATO had changed from being a Cold War military alliance and to emphasize the scope for NATO–Russian military cooperation). Donald Blinken, US Ambassador to Hungary in the mid-1990s, captured Hungary's efforts to impress upon the Alliance its utility by making available its facilities for Balkan operations, to the extent that rather than Hungary joining NATO, he quipped, NATO was joining Hungary![72]

That longer-term evidence of political transformation was a requirement for NATO membership was also evident when Slovakia, during the Mečiar government of which adopted anti-Euro-Atlantic policies and antagonized its minorities, was excluded from the first round of accession.[73] Similarly, when Romania's government changed in 1996 and sought to demonstrate the country's commitment to reforms, American officials replied to Romania's pursuit of NATO membership that it had undertaken reforms for only a few months, in contrast to Poland's efforts over several years. The decision agreed at NATO's Madrid Summit in July 1997 to admit the Czech Republic, Hungary, and Poland was still not undertaken by clear criteria; indeed, which specific post-communist countries were to be invited to join the Alliance remained unresolved in the preceding weeks.[74]

Keeping NATO's door open after the Madrid Summit became the Alliance's next challenge. The Russian Federation opposed further enlargement, especially to the Baltic states, while other post-communist governments, particularly in the Baltic and Slovenia, feared their permanent exclusion from NATO as part of what they (mistakenly) suspected was a secret agreement between Washington and Moscow to placate the latter over the Central European accession.[75] At NATO's Washington Summit in April 1999, which also commemorated the Treaty's fiftieth anniversary, the Alliance spelled out more concrete requirements for joining under the Membership Action Plan (MAP). Prospective members were to demonstrate commitment to resolving disputes peacefully, to the rule of law and human rights, and to democratic oversight of their militaries, and the capacity, though unspecified, to add to the Alliance defense and mission capabilities; to assign national resources to their armed forces to fulfil membership requirements; to undertake means to safeguard sensitive information; and to make domestic law compatible with NATO requirements. Prospective members would have to have to supply NATO with annual reports on these requirements and could receive Alliance assistance in meeting them.

The Alliance thus sought not simply, perhaps not even foremost, new members on the basis of their military or strategic value, but rather ones that were stable, democratic, and peaceable. At the same time, they were also told, such as by the fervent supporter of enlargement US Secretary of State Madeleine Albright, that NATO was not a charity but a military alliance. Much as Hungary did in the mid-1990s, so did Southeast European governments calculate during NATO's war with Yugoslavia in 1999 that they needed to demonstrate their commitment to the Alliance. Public opinions in those countries heavily opposed both the war and their governments' assistance to NATO; yet all the surrounding countries facilitated NATO's operations.[76]

By 2002, NATO had issued membership invitations to seven further countries: Bulgaria, Estonia, Latvia, Lithuania, Romania, Slovakia, and Slovenia, all of which entered the Alliance on 29 March 2004. Though that was the Alliance's largest enlargement, the process continued. At NATO's Bucharest Summit in April 2008, Albania and Croatia received invitations to join NATO; Macedonia was refused on the basis of continuing Greek objections to the country's name; Macedonia also remained the only country in late 2008 working on the basis of MAP. Other countries, such as Montenegro, and some countries outside the scope of this volume, have expressed interest in NATO membership. Enlargement in south-eastern Europe may continue but the Alliance's possible expansion to post-Soviet states such as Georgia and Ukraine is already proving profoundly challenging to wider Russian–Western relations, something that the Alliance, with difficulty and talent, managed nevertheless to maintain, thereby crafting new security relations that would have been unimaginable in and for the Eastern Europe of 1989.

Conclusion

We should not overestimate the role of post-communist regional cooperation initiatives – they were not and are not aims in themselves, but stepping stones. That said, their roles have been generally misunderstood (sometimes objectively incorrectly by otherwise erudite region-watchers) and their contributions to changes within their region and in wider Europe has been undervalued. They have transformed the geopolitical face of what was communist Eastern Europe. Groupings such as CBSS, BSEC, and CEI created cooperation and allowed established Western democracies and market economies to assist in the transition process. They have also created forums in which countries with strained or even non-existent relations still meet (such as among several Balkan states in the CEI, and between Armenia and Turkey, and Armenia and Azerbaijan in BSEC).

Foremost, Visegrád helped to project a new image of Central Europe as one of stability, reliability and, some relatively brief policy divergences notwithstanding, countries that are committed to Euro-Atlantic political values. Visegrád particularly helped to extract its members from Soviet instruments of control and eased some of the strains of the transition process. Perhaps most importantly, if increasingly less appreciated as time moves on, Visegrád helped to project the term "Central Europe" on to Western policymakers and to generate a positive image of the region as peaceful and progressive. The end result has been the more general reference to the region as simply part of the "West." From the standpoint of 1989, these are remarkable achievements.

Post-communist regional cooperation initiatives

These are outlined in table 22.1.

Table 22.1 Regional cooperation initiatives

Group	Date of formation	Original membership	Current numbers and membership	Type of member states
Visegrád	15 February 1991	3 – Czechoslovakia, Hungary, Poland	4 – original plus Czech Republic and Slovakia as Czechoslovak successors	All post-communist
Organization of the Black Sea Economic Cooperation (BSEC)	25 June 1992 (Charter creating international legal basis came into effect on 1 May 1999)	11 – Albania, Armenia, Azerbaijan, Bulgaria, Georgia, Greece, Moldova, Romania, Russian Federation, Turkey, Ukraine	12 – original plus Serbia (after the dissolution of Serbia and Montenegro, Montenegro submitted an application for observer status but is not a member)	Mixed: • NATO • EU • Post-communist • Post-Soviet
Council of the Baltic Sea States (CBSS)	5–6 March 1992	11 – European Commission and 10 states: Denmark, Estonia, Finland, Germany, Latvia, Lithuania, Norway, Poland, Russian Federation, Sweden	12 – original plus Iceland	Mixed: • European Commission • NATO • EU • Post-communist • Post-Soviet • Neutral
Central European Initiative (CEI)	By that name, July 1992	As "Quadragonal," 11 November 1989: Austria, Hungary, Italy, Yugoslavia; as CEI: those four and Czechoslovakia, Poland, Bosnia and Herzegovina, Croatia, Slovenia	18 – Albania, Austria, Belarus, Bosnia and Herzegovina, Bulgaria, Croatia, Czech Republic, Hungary, Italy, Macedonia, Moldova, Montenegro, Poland, Romania, Serbia, Slovakia, Slovenia, Ukraine	Mixed: • NATO • EU • Post-communist • Neutral
CEFTA	May 1992, in effect on 21 December 1992	Czechoslovakia, Hungary, Poland	Czech Republic and Slovakia; then Bulgaria, Croatia, Romania – due to EU accession of original members, as well as all pre-CEFTA 2006 members	All post-communist, Central European
CEFTA 2006	19 December 2006	10 – Albania, Bulgaria, Bosnia and Herzegovina, Croatia, Moldova, Montenegro, Romania, Serbia and FYROM, UNMIK/Kosovo	8 – Bulgaria and Romania renounced their membership on 31 December 2006, in advance of joining the EU on 1 January 2007	All post-communist, southeast European

Timeline 1989–2008

9 November 1989	Berlin Wall opens.
11 November 1989	Governments of Italy, Austria, Hungary, and Yugoslavia sign agreement for cooperation that would become, with expanded membership, the CEI
2 October 1990	German unification; former East Germany automatically becomes a member of EC and NATO
15 February 1991	Start of Visegrád cooperation
1 July 1991	Already defunct in practice, WTO formally disbanded at its final summit, in Prague
7 and 8 November 1991	NATO's Rome Summit launches NACC, which meets for first time on 20 December 1991, as outreach to non-member states
5–6 March 1992	CBSS launched
6 May 1992	Prague Summit of Visegrád., launch of CEFTA and clear declaration that three countries sought full membership of NATO
1 January 1993	Formal end of Czechoslovakia; Czech Republic and Slovakia come into existence
22 April 1993	Official opening of Holocaust Memorial in Washington, DC, attended by Central European leaders who press US President Clinton to open NATO membership
24 August 1993	Russian President Boris Yeltsin says on an official visit to Poland that Russia did not oppose NATO's enlargement, but issued conflicting views thereafter (see 5 December 1994)
10–11 January 1994	Partnership for Peace (PfP) launched at NATO's Brussels Summit. The cooperation initiative carries no specific indications of eventual membership
12 January 1994	In a landmark statement, Clinton announces in the presence of the presidents of the Czech Republic, Hungary, Poland, and Slovakia that NATO enlargement is no longer a question of "whether" but "when"
5 December 1994	To the shock of Clinton Administration, Yeltsin attacks the idea of NATO enlargement and says a "Cold Peace" now threatens.
27 May 1997	In Paris, Russian and Allied leaders conclude NATO–Russia Founding Act on Mutual Relations, Cooperation and Security, and establish Permanent Joint Council which sought to include Russia more deeply in NATO's activities, Russia opens a diplomatic mission at NATO heaquarters a year later
29 May 1997	Euro-Atlantic Partnership Council created as a successor to NACC as a more intensified form of cooperation between the Alliance and post-communist states, and which was to coexist with PfP

8–9 July 1997	At the Alliance's Madrid Summit membership invitations issued to the Czech Republic, Hungary, and Poland; even close to the summit date which specific countries would be invited remained unclear
12 March 1999	Czech, Hungarian, and Polish foreign ministers sign accession protocols bringing their countries into NATO
April–June 1999	NATO at war against Yugoslavia over treatment of Kosovo's Albanian population; neighboring post-communist states, either joining NATO or so intent, made contributions to facilitating the war effort
24–25 April 1999	NATO's Washington Summit commemorates Alliance's fiftieth anniversary and is the first in which new members of the Czech Republic, Hungary, and Poland participate; among initiatives is launch of MAPs which establish specifics for Alliance membership of other countries
21–22 November 2002	NATO's Summit in Prague issues membership invitations to Bulgaria, Estonia, Latvia, Lithuania, Romania, Slovakia, and Slovenia
29 March 2004	NATO's largest enlargement, seven post-communist states become NATO members
12 May 2004	Leaders of the V4 issued Kroměříž Declaration, reaffirming their countries' cooperation even after entry into the EU
19 December 2006	CEFTA 2006 launched among southeastern states; none of the original members, having attained EU membership, remain
3 April 2008	Albania and Croatia receive invitations to join NATO at Alliance's Bucharest Summit

Notes

* Thanks are due to the Carnegie Trust for the Universities of Scotland for funding research trips concerning Visegrád, and to various officials of Visegrád ministries of foreign affairs who kindly gave their time and insights.

1. At times the WTO member states could make some initiatives, but there cannot be any comparison between them and, say, the multilateralism of the EC. The WTO even became the first military alliance to attack a fellow member, when five member states participated in the military intervention against the Czechoslovak communist reform movement of 1968.
2. The three Baltic states, Estonia, Latvia, and Lithuania; the two successor states to Czechoslovakia, the Czech Republic and Slovakia; and one successor of Yugoslavia, Slovenia. The other EU and NATO entrants by 2007, and which had statehood in 1989, were Bulgaria, Hungary, Poland and Romania.
3. By these, I mean for example, the Associate membership that was granted in the Western European Union (WEU), or in NATO's PfP, or, eventually, membership in the EU and NATO themselves. As part of its response to postwar Balkan

reconstruction, the EU launched its Stability Pact. Again, because the Stability Pact was inspired from outside the region it is not considered in this chapter.

4. These would include the cooperation among the three Baltic states; the Commonwealth of Independent States (CIS); GUAM (Georgia, Ukraine, Azerbaijan, Moldova) which is sometimes seen as a counterweight within the CIS of countries that have, or fear, Russian involvement in secessionist regions; and the more recent Shanghai Cooperation Council.
5. See "1.1 Objectives" at www.ceinet.org/main.php?pageID=17 [accessed 1 November 2007].
6. See Gianni de Michelis, "Europe: A Golden Opportunity not to be Missed," *International Herald Tribune* (26 March 1990).
7. Carole Hodge, "Albania, Italy and Greece: Some Geopolitical Considerations," in Brad K. Blitz (ed.), *War and Change in the Balkans* (Cambridge: Cambridge University Press, 2006), p. 228.
8. Hodge, "Albania," p. 226.
9. Interviews with various foreign ministry officials responsible for regional cooperation and organizations.
10. Magda Vašáryová, "The Optimal Format for Regional Cooperation," in Andrzej Jagodziński (ed.), *The Visegrád Group: A Central European Constellation* (Bratislava: International Visegrad Fund, 2006), p. 77.
11. Lech Wałęsa, "From Solidarność (Solidarity) to Cooperation and Integration," in Jagodziński (ed.), *Visegrád*, p. 81.
12. András Simonyi, "Visegrád Cooperation: A 15-Year-old Successor Story," in Jagodziński (ed.), *Visegrád*, p. 96.
13. Michal Žantovský, "Visegrad between the Past and the Future," in Jagodziński (ed.), *Visegrad*, p. 80. Žantovský was a senior foreign policy figure in post-communist Czechoslovakia and the Czech Republic. Alexandr Vondra, "Visegrad Cooperation: How Did It Start?," in Jagodziński (ed.), *Visegrád*, p. 80.
14. For a practioner's view, see Simonyi, "Visegrád." For earlier analytical views, see Adrian Hyde-Price, *The International Relations of East-Central Europe* (Manchester: Manchester University Press, 1996), p. 122 and Joshua Spero, "The Budapest–Prague–Warsaw Triangle: Central European Security after the Visegrád Summit," *European Security*, Vol. 1, No. 1 (Spring 1992), p. 58.
15. See, for example, Andrej Ananicz, "From the Anti-Communist Underground to NATO and the EU," in Jagodziński (ed.), *Visegrad*. The present author is also working on a study of how communist-era dissident, values were translated into post-communist foreign policy.
16. Wałęsa, "From Solidarność," p. 81.
17. See Jan Čarnogurský, "Visegrad Today," and Rudolf Chmel "Visegrád Question," in Jagodziński (ed.), *Visegrad*.
18. Géza Jeszenszky, "The Origins and Enactment of the 'Visegrád Idea'," in Jagodziński (ed.), *Visegrad*.
19. See Rudolf L. Tökés, "From Visegrád to Kraków: Coup, Competition, and Coexistence," *Problems of Communism*, Vol. 40, No. 6 (November–December 1991), pp. 100–14.
20. Timothy Garton Ash, *We the People* (London: Granta, 1990).

21. Ex-dissidents brought into foreign policy immediately after the 1989 revolutions have informed me quite graphically of the differences between Havel and Wałęsa, and how they tried desperately to get the latter to meet with the former on his visit to Poland. For an account of early wrong footing by Wałęsa with Hungarians and its effect on regional cooperation, see Ákos Engelmayer, "Fanfare and Frictions," in Jagodziński (ed.), *Visegrád*, pp. 46–7.
22. Vondra, "Visegrád Cooperation."
23. Andrej Ananicz, "From the Anti-Communist Underground to NATO and the EU," in Jagodziński (ed.), *Visegrád.*
24. For an overview, see Milada Anna Vachudova, "The Visegrád Four: No Alternative to Cooperation?," *RFE/RL Research Report*, Vol. 2, No. 34 (27 August 1993).
25. Jiří Dienstbier, "Visegrad: The First Phase," in Jagodziński (ed.), *Visegrad.*
26. The Declaration is available in the original and English translation, at www.visegradgroup.eu/main.php?folderID=940&articleID=3940&ctag=articlelist&iid=1. I have addressed this issue briefly in the context of reviewing a Czech-language book on Visegrád which forwent the opportunity to assess the use of the medieval Visegrád meeting in the post-communist era. See Rick Fawn, "Enlarging (The Debate on) Central Europe," *Slavonica*, Vol. 13, No. 2 (November 2007), pp. 168–75.
27. Petr Pithart, "The Firm Rock of Visegrád," in Jagodziński (ed.), *Visegrád*, p. 73. An analysis of "symbolism" in Havel's foreign policy can be found in Rick Fawn, "Symbolism in the Diplomacy of Czech President Václav Havel," *East European Quarterly*, Vol. XXXIII, No. 1 (March 1999), pp. 1–19.
28. For an account of this impact, see Vondra, "Visegrad cooperation."
29. Dienstbier, "Visegrad," and Jeszenszky, "Origins," p. 62.
30. Timothy Garton Ash, "The Puzzle of Central Europe," *The New York Review of Books* (18 March 1999).
31. See the commentary in Chmel, "Visegrád Question."
32. *Demokratsiya*, 24 June 1991, *Foreign Broadcast Information Service. Eastern Europe*, 1 July 1991.
33. Andrew Cottey, "The Visegrád Group and Beyond: Security Cooperation in Central Europe," in Andrew Cottey (ed.), *Subregional Cooperation in the New Europe* (London: Macmillan, 1999), p. 83.
34. Vjekoslav Perica, *Balkan Idols: Religion and Nationalism in Yugoslav States* (Oxford: Oxford University Press, 2002), p. 187.
35. Interview, Croatian Foreign Ministry, Zagreb, 8 April 2005.
36. Cited in V. Todres, "Czechs Reject Political Ties Within Free-Trade Agreement," *Prague Post*, 6 December 1994.
37. Cited in Tomáš Vrba, "Breakfast with a Billionaire, or a Central European Dream," in Jagodziński (ed.), *Visegrad*, p. 37, citing *Středoevropské noviny* (August 1995).
38. For such an assessment of Klaus' changed opinion, see Gábor Hárs, "Visegrad – A Personal Memoir of Cooperation," in Jagodziński (ed.), *Visegrad.*
39. See Simonyi, "Visegrád Cooperation."
40. See Zoltan Barany, "Visegrád Four Contemplate Separate Paths," *Transition*, 11 August 1995.
41. Mečiar's interview in *Wprost*, 13 February 1994, cited in George Kolankiewcz, "Consensus and Competition in the Eastern Enlargement of the European Union," *International Affairs*, Vol. 70, No. 3 (1994), p. 477.

42. See "The Visegrád Three ...," *The Economist*, 9 March 1996.
43. Žantovský, "Visegrad," p. 85.
44. See Engelmayer, "Fanfare."
45. Čarnogurský, "Visegrad Today," p. 34.
46. For a comment, see Barbora Gábelová and Juraj Marušiak, "Foreign and Security Policy Priorities of Poland," in Tomáš Valášek and Olga Gyárfášová (eds.), *"Easternization" of Europe's Security Policy* (no location given: Institute for Public Affairs, 2004), p. 56.
47. Vašáryová, "The Optimal Format."
48. Vrba, "Breakfast," p. 130.
49. See the Kroměříž Declaration, at www.visegradgroup.eu.
50. See *National Post*, 15 May 2006.
51. Interview, Hungarian Foreign Ministry, Budapest, 8 November 2004.
52. Vašáryová, "The Optimal Format," p. 78.
53. An enthusiastic version of the creation of this dimension of V4 cooperation is given in Ladislav Snopko, "A European Crossroads Worn by Centuries of Use," in Jagodziński (ed.), *Visegrad*.
54. Interview with a Hungarian diplomat, Hungarian Foreign Ministry, Budapest, 8 November 2004.
55. Pavel Demeš, "Visegrád Dreams," p. 39.
56. Václav Havel, "The Visegrád Dream Still Relevant Today," in Jagodziński (ed.), *Visegrád*.
57. Jiří Paroubek, "Visegrad Group Celebrates its Fifteenth Anniversary," in Jagodziński (ed.), *Visegrad*, p. 14.
58. Hárs, "Visegrad," p. 50.
59. Čarnogurský, "Visegrád Today," p. 35.
60. Simonyi, "Visegrad Cooperation," p. 96.
61. For such a view, see Jan Zielonka, *Europe as Empire: The Nature of the Enlarged European Union* (Oxford: Oxford University Press, 2006).
62. Simonyi, "Visegrad Cooperation," p. 97.
63. Wałęsa, "From Solidarność," p. 82.
64. See Martin Dangerfield, "The European Union and Post-Communist Europe: One Approach or Several?," *Journal of Communist Studies and Transition Politics*, Vol. 23, No. 4 (2007), p. 494.
65. Vašáryová, "The Optimal Format," p. 78.
66. I have sought to demonstrate how post-communist governments advocate democracy promotion and human rights advocacy towards post-Soviet governments more than "older" members of the EU within EU structures, in Rick Fawn, "Bashing about Rights? Russia and the 'New' EU States on Human Rights and Democracy Promotion," *Europe–Asia Studies*, Vol. 61, No. 10 (December 2009), pp. 1777–1803.
67. In what is a very detailed academic work that also benefits from policy-making experience and access to official sources, Ronald Asmus pays particular attention to this process in impressing upon the Clinton Administration the importance of NATO enlargement. See Ronald D. Asmus, *Opening NATO's Door: How the Alliance Remade Itself for a New Era* (New York: Columbia University Press, 2002).

68. See his International Institute for Strategic Studies Alastair Buchan Memorial Lecture, 26 March 1993, an edited version of which appeared as "Shaping Euro-Atlantic Policies: A Grand Strategy for a New Era," *Survival*, Vol. 35, No. 2 (Summer 1993), quotations at p. 135.
69. Powerful examples of Central European presidential views are given in Asmus, *Opening NATO's Door*, pp. 54–5, 66.
70. James M. Goldgeier, *Not Whether But When: The US Decision to Enlarge NATO* (Washington, DC: Brookings Institution Press, 1999), p. 45.
71. For one such view of the financial dimension in particular, see Amos Perlmutter and Ted Galen Carpenter, "NATO's Expensive Trip East: The Folly of Enlargement," *Foreign Affairs*, Vol. 77, No. 1 (January–February 1998), esp. pp. 2–6.
72. Donald Blinken, "How NATO Joined Hungary," *European Security*, Vol. 8, No. 4 (Winter 1999), pp. 109–29.
73. As Asmus writes, "Prime Minister Vladimir Mečiar's strong-arm authoritarian tactics had taken Slovakia out of the running," Asmus, *Opening NATO's Door*, p. 212.
74. See Asmus, *Opening NATO's Door*, book VII, and esp. pp. 214–21.
75. See, for example, Asmus, *Opening NATO's Door*, p. 233.
76. I try to offer some detail in "Perceptions in Central and Southeastern Europe," in Mary Buckley and Sally N. Cummings (eds.), *Kosovo: Perceptions of War and its Aftermath* (London and New York: Continuum, 2001), pp. 136–55.

Further reading

Regional Cooperation

Cottey, Andrew (ed.). *Subregional Cooperation in the New Europe: Building Security, Prosperity, and Solidarity from the Barents to the Black Sea* (Houndsmills, UK: Palgrave Macmillan in association with the East–West Center, 1999)

Dangerfield, Martin. *Subregional Economic Cooperation in Central and Eastern Europe: The Political Economy of CEFTA* (Aldershot: Edward Elgar, 2000)

Dangerfield, Martin. "Subregional Integration and EU Enlargement: Where Next for CEFTA?," *Journal of Common Market Studies*, Vol. 44, No. 2 (2006), pp. 305–24

Fawn, Rick. "The Elusive Defined? Visegrád Cooperation as the Contemporary Contours of Central Europe," *Geopolitics*, Vol. 6, No. 1 (Summer 2001), pp. 47–68

Jagodziński, Andrzej (ed.). *The Visegrad Group: A Central European Constellation* (Bratislava: International Visegrád Fund, 2006)

Rhodes, Matthew. *Visegrád Turns Ten* (Pittsburgh, Penn.: Center for Russia and East European Studies, University of Pittsburgh, Carl Beck Papers in Russian and East European Studies, No. 1701, March 2003)

NATO enlargement

Asmus, Ronald D. *Opening NATO's Door: How the Alliance Remade Itself for a New Era* (New York: Columbia University Press, 2002)

Barany, Zoltan. *The Future of NATO Expansion: Four Case Studies* (Cambridge: Cambridge University Press, 2003)
Goldgeier, James M. *Not Whether But When: The US Decision to Enlarge NATO* (Washington, D.C.: Brookings Institution Press, 1999)
Grayson George W. *Strange Bedfellows: NATO Marches East* (Lanham, Md.: University Press of America, 1999)

Further links

Central European Initiative, at www.ceinet.org/home.php
Council of the Baltic Sea States, at www.cbss.st
Organization for Black Sea Economic Cooperation, at www.bsec.organization.org
Visegrád, at http://visegradgroup.eu

23

The EU and democratization in Central and Southeastern Europe since 1989

ULRICH SEDELMEIER

A distinctive feature of the democratic transition in Central and Southeastern Europe after 1989 has been its close link to the process of accession to the EU. There are certain similarities to the transition to democracy in Greece, Portugal, and Spain, but in these cases the EU was much less explicit and direct in its attempts to influence democratic reforms. Transition studies have been reluctant to take account of this distinctive characteristic of the process of democratization in East-Central Europe. Instead, analyses have focused predominantly on domestic factors to explain its outcome.[1] Those transition scholars who have focused on the international dimension of democratization generally consider European integration a beneficial influence on the consolidation of democracy.[2] However, the link between European integration and democratization is not straightforward:[3] first, it is not clear to what extent the EU actually had a causal influence and how its influence varied across countries and issues; second, even if the EU did have a causal impact, it is not obvious that its influence was always entirely positive for democracy in ECE.

There is little doubt that the EU can exercise a tremendous influence on the domestic politics of Central and Southeastern Europe. One of the most striking examples of the EU's ability to make a government do what it would not have done otherwise – even with regard to one of the most sensitive questions of statehood – is the decision of the Montenegrin leadership to set the threshold for the success of the referendum on independence at 55 rather than 50%. Another often-cited example outside the area of democracy is the June 1999 session of the Hungarian parliament that passed 152 of 180 laws without any debate since they concerned EU legislation.[4] While the EU can thus be a pervasive force in the domestic politics of would-be members, there are also plenty of examples of the limits of the EU's influence. The EU's efforts to influence domestic politics continue to have little effect in Belarus, just as they were unsuccessful in Slovakia under the government of Vladimír Mečiar, in Croatia under Franjo Tudjman, and in Serbia under Slobodan Milošević. At the same time, it appears rather questionable that, say, Poland, Hungary, or the Czech Republic would not have democratized without the EU. The key questions that this chapter pursues are, therefore, how much the EU has influenced democratization and how we can explain variation in its influence.

Research on the effects of the EU on democratization in post-communist Europe has advanced to the point that it is no longer "a topic that remains mostly unexplored."[5] A number of studies agree that while the EU can play a powerful role in the domestic politics of would-be member states, its influence depends on a favorable constellation of domestic factors.[6] In fact, the impact of the EU on the general pattern of democratization in ECE might have been restricted to a specific subset of countries: fragile democracies that experienced alternations in power between governments composed of nationalist/authoritarian parties on the one hand and of liberal-democratic parties on the other. The chapter first provides an overview of the instruments through which the EU can promote democracy in its European neighborhood. The most powerful instrument is political conditionality, linked to the incentive of membership in the EU. I then discuss the explanatory factors for the success of EU democracy promotion that are identified in literature analyzing the EU's influence in the region. The final section considers the adverse effects that the EU can have on democracy in would-be members as well as the sustainability of democratic reforms after accession is achieved and conditionality is no longer applicable.

EU instruments for promotion of democracy in ECE

The EU has a range of instruments through which it can promote democracy. The first mechanism was particularly prominent in the context of the Mediterranean enlargements of the 1980s when Greece, Portugal, and Spain joined the EU. Membership in the EU was seen both by the EU and the then-candidate countries as an opportunity to anchor the fragile democracies that emerged from authoritarian rule in a prosperous and democratic international community. This mechanism, which operates primarily after accession to the EU, remains relevant in the case of the EU's eastern enlargements. In addition, however, the EU also adopted much more explicit instruments to promote democracy in the candidate countries of ECE *prior* to their accession.

One EU instrument in non-members is financial support for activities that foster democracy. Since 1994, the EU has had a specific budget line for democracy promotion – the European Initiative for Democracy and Human Rights (EIDHR) – but it established its first assistance program for democratization in the context of its policy toward Central and Southeastern Europe after the fall of the Berlin Wall. Initially, the EU's financial assistance program – the Pologne Hongrie: aide à la restructuration économique (PHARE) program – supported only market economic restructuring. In 1992, the European Parliament inserted into the EU budget a specific budget line within the PHARE program in order to finance support for the consolidation of democracy. This "Democracy Program" provided funding for civil society organizations that engaged in activities to promote an inclusive, pluralist, and participatory political culture.

The most prominent EU instrument is political conditionality. It consists of offering target states certain benefits – that can range from financial assistance, market access, to membership – for their compliance with specific conditions, such as democratic principles or human rights. If these benefits are sufficiently large, conditionality can change the incentive structure for non-member states in such a way as to trigger domestic changes that would not have occurred otherwise.[7]

Evolution of the EU's conditionality in promotion of democracy

The EU's eastern enlargement policy is the context in which it developed an explicit, and expanding, conditionality with regard to democracy and human rights. The EU's founding treaties specified only one condition that a state had to fulfill in order to apply for membership: it had to be European. The EU made the first reference to political membership conditions in the context of its Mediterranean enlargements. Elements of a democratic conditionality were visible in the EU's rejection of an application by General Franco's Spain for an association agreement in 1962, or the freezing of the association agreement with Greece in 1967 following the Colonels' coup.[8] The most explicit statement of the political conditions of EU membership was the "Declaration on Democracy" at the European Council in Copenhagen in 1978. It confirmed that "respect for and maintenance of representative democracy and human rights in each Member State are essential elements of membership."[9] Although the occasion for the declaration was the impending first direct election to the European Parliament, it was also intended to provide the EU with a safeguard in case the candidate countries might revert to authoritarian rule after obtaining membership.[10] The risk of a return of authoritarianism was then arguably more salient than later in Central and Southeastern Europe where there was no dramatic challenge to democratic consolidation such as the attempted putsch in Spain in 1981, but it did not lead the EU to codify the political conditions of membership in its treaty.

The EU's use of conditionality with regard to human rights and democracy developed significantly in the context of eastern enlargement. PHARE aid was only provided to post-communist countries once they had achieved progress in democratic transition (which is also the reason why the acronym refers only to Poland and Hungary). By the same token, the EU suspended aid for Romania in 1990 (along with negotiations for a trade agreement), for Yugoslavia in 1991, and for Croatia in 1995. The EU also started to apply conditionality to trade agreements with post-communist states. The start of negotiations for "Europe Agreements" reflected differences in democratization across Central and Southeastern Europe. The EU took one step further in the context of negotiations with Romania. Concerns about democracy in Romania led the EU to discuss the inclusion of a suspension clause into the agreement to allow one party to terminate it in reaction to violations of democracy and human rights in the other party. However, partly in order to point the finger less directly at Romania, the Council agreed in May 1992 that henceforth all cooperation and association agreements with CSCE members should contain such a suspension clause. In May 1995, the Council extended the suspension clause to agreements with any non-member state. In addition to this expansion of the use of conditionality in the EU's external relations with regard to trade and aid, the European Council in Copenhagen in June 1993 made a first direct statement of the political conditions for membership. The European Council declared for the first time that countries in Central and Southeastern Europe that so desired might eventually become members. To make this step acceptable to the member states that had been reluctant about an eastern enlargement, the European Council formulated a number of broad conditions that would-be members had to meet. In addition to the ability to apply EU legislation upon accession, a successful transition to a market economy, as well as the EU's own ability to absorb new members, the political conditions specified the need for "stable institutions guaranteeing democracy, the rule of law, human rights and respect for and protection of minorities."[11]

On the basis of these "Copenhagen criteria," political conditionality broadened considerably in its subsequent application by the Commission and the European Council. For example, the Commission's annual monitoring reports that formed the basis of decisions by the Council about starting accession negotiations included issues such as language training for non-citizens and prison conditions in Latvia, or the conditions of state-run orphanages in Romania. A more recent example of the wide-ranging political conditions are the "benchmarks" that the Commission established in 2008 for Macedonia to start accession negotiations, which included improved dialogue with political parties, reforms of the police, the legal sector, and of public administration, the fight against corruption, and electoral law reform. The EU's political conditions are most extensive with regard to the successor states of Yugoslavia, where they include issues related to the violent breakup of Yugoslavia and ethnic conflict, such as cooperation with the ICTY, the return of refugees, or regional cooperation.

The scope of the EU's political conditionality goes far beyond the rules covered by the EU treaty and in which EU institutions have leverage over its member states. This discrepancy has led to accusations of double standards in the treatment of candidates and full members. Partly as a result of the EU's vulnerability to such criticism, partly to increase the leverage of EU institutions over new members if democratic standards should slip after accession, the member states agreed to strengthen EU competences in these areas. An amendment in the Treaty of Amsterdam in 1997 stated that "the principles of liberty, democracy, respect for human rights and fundamental freedoms, and the rule of law" are preconditions for membership. It also specified procedures to suspend membership of a country for serious and persistent breaches of these principles. Yet even with this treaty change, pre-accession conditionality still extends far beyond the principles codified in the EU treaty.

Conditions for the EU's influence through conditionality

Studies of the conditions under which the EU has been able to influence European non-member states share one main finding, namely that the EU's influence depended primarily on target governments' cost/benefit calculations in response to the incentives provided by the EU. Moreover, there is also a fairly large consensus on which particular factors are most important for such cost/benefit calculations and hence for the effectiveness of conditionality: the size of the EU's incentives, the credibility of the EU's conditionality, and, crucially, the domestic adjustment costs for target governments.[12] The first two factors are primarily in the hands of the EU, while the last one is not; it largely explains which countries were susceptible to EU influence.

Size of the EU's rewards

The EU's incentives include aid, such as the PHARE program, market access – for example, through association agreements – and full membership. The size of these incentives is lowest in the case of aid, and highest for membership. The EU's influence increased the closer it came to offering accession as a reward for meeting its conditions. Candidate countries often complied with domestically contested issues only in the final stages of the accession process, when such issues were the main remaining stumbling block on the road to membership – such as in the case of the Latvian election law with regard to language requirements for candidates.

A key challenge for the EU is that for many target countries its most sizable incentive – membership – is too far off to provide a tangible incentive for domestic change. The EU has therefore started to identify intermediate benefits, or intermediate conditional steps on the road to market access or EU membership. For example, the EU has made distinctive demands with regard to various steps towards market access through association agreements. These subsequent steps include the start of negotiations, the initialing of the agreement, the formal signing of the agreement, the implementation of an interim agreement (through which the trade aspects of the agreement can enter into force without national ratification by the member states), and finally the ratification of the agreement. With regard to EU membership, distinctive steps that form conditional rewards are a formal recognition as an EU "candidate country," the opening of accession negotiations, the opening and closing of negotiations on specific issue areas, the signing of the agreement, the ratification agreement, as well as – most recently in the cases of Romania and Bulgaria – a separate decision whether accession will take place on the envisaged date or be postponed by one year.

In addition to breaking down the offer of its more traditional incentives into separate steps, the EU has identified new incentives as rewards for compliance with its conditionality. The most prominent of these incentives is a facilitation of the visa regime, or a progressive lifting of visa requirements. However, the EU has not offered concessions on the visa regime as direct rewards for progress with democratization, but has linked it to meeting additional criteria, such as the signing of a Readmission Agreement for asylum seekers, or cooperation on improving border controls and combating cross-border crime.

Credibility of conditionality

The offer of membership is the EU's most sizable incentive, but the offer alone is not enough for the EU to have influence. The offer – and its conditional nature – have to be *credible*. Credibility implies both that a target country has to be certain that the EU will deliver on awarding the promised benefits, and that these benefits will be delivered only in response to compliance with the conditions set. How can the EU increase the credibility of its incentives? Generally, the literature agrees that key elements are a consistent and merit-based application of conditionality and clear and consensual messages from EU actors about what target states need to do in order to obtain their reward.[13]

By and large, the EU has applied democratic conditionality fairly consistently. Some questions have been raised as to whether the EU has been consistent in its criticisms of undemocratic practices. For example, EU representatives did not criticize Sali Berisha's autocratic style and alleged rigging of the 1996 Albanian election due to his perceived contribution to maintaining stability in the country.[14] However, the EU has been fairly consistent with regard to making fulfillment of democratic conditions the precondition for opening accession negotiations. The best-known example was the decision by the European Council to exclude Slovakia from the group of countries opening accession negotiations in 1998 – despite sufficient progress with economic and legal adjustment – due the shortcomings of democracy under the Mečiar regime. Another example was the EU's postponement of opening accession negotiations with Croatia scheduled for March 2005. It stated that the postponement was due to the government's failure to cooperate fully with the ICTY in the arrest of General Ante Gotovina who had been indicted for war crimes during the military operations that expelled the Krajina Serbs in 1995. After the ICTY's then Chief Prosecutor, Carla Del Ponte, confirmed that the Croatian government had fully cooperated, the EU opened accession negotiations in October 2005 (and Gotovina was arrested in December 2005 with the active assistance of Croatian security agencies).[15] By contrast, the decision to include Bulgaria and Romania in accession negotiations in 2000 cast doubts about the merit-based application of conditionality, since it arguably owed more to their support for NATO's intervention in Kosovo than their progress with meeting the EU's conditions. However, the two countries' shortcomings in compliance concerned primarily legislative alignment, rather than political conditions.

The credibility of conditionality in specific issue areas was low if the EU failed to make it subject to clear conditionality. For example, between 1997 and 1999 the EU did not attach explicit conditions to changes in Estonia's controversial language requirements for candidates in national elections, in contrast to the criticism from the OSCE High Commissioner for National Minorities, as well as to the EU's conditionality with regard to citizenship for stateless children.[16] In other areas, credibility was weakened when EU actors sent out contradictory signals about the necessary requirements. For example, with regard to regional policy, some parts of the Commission initially promoted a far-reaching agenda of regionalization, partly because the EU considered decentralization beneficial for democracy.[17] However, EU legislation only requires the establishment of statistical regional units to calculate financial allocations through the EU's regional policy, rather than an actual delegation of powers to the regional level. Moreover, the Commission subsequently recommended that the central government should manage regional funds, which appeared more efficient. These contradictory messages undermined the EU's influence on regionalization in Central and Southeastern Europe. Another example is the area of social policy, because some actors in the Commission's Directorate General for Enlargement informally indicated that some problems of alignment in this area would not be a major stumbling block for accession – much to the dismay of the Directorate General for Social Policy.[18]

More generally, a factor that threatened to undermine the credibility of the EU's membership incentive were doubts in candidate countries about the consensus among the EU member states on enlargement. At one level, these doubts made the EU's conditionality more credible, as it made it highly unlikely that the EU would admit a country that had not met the conditions. However, the reluctant and incremental nature in which the EU's policy on eastern enlargement evolved in the face of strong reservations in many EU member states, also brought into question the EU's ability to agree unanimously on the accession of a country even once it had met all the conditions.

In view of these doubts about the member states' willingness to enlarge, the main act that made the membership perspective credible to candidate countries was the opening of accession negotiations.[19] Officials in the Commission suggest that opening accession negotiations is the most important stage of the enlargement process, "because opening them implies a willingness to conclude them."[20] The importance of accession negotiations for the credibility of conditionality also explains why the candidate countries carried out difficult adjustments if the EU made the opening of accession negotiations conditional on the fulfillment of specific political conditions. Examples include the cooperation of the Croatian government with the ICTY over the arrest of General Gotovina, which had been the main obstacle to the start of negotiations, or the revision of the Latvian state language law in conformity to EU demands.

Another example of the importance of the credibility of the threat of exclusion is the case of Cyprus. The EU's promise not to make accession dependent on the unification of the island was meant to deprive the Turkish Cypriot leadership of a *de facto* veto over Cypriot membership. Instead, it undermined the credibility of any pressures on the Greek Cypriot community to compromise over a settlement, leading it to reject the Annan Plan for the unification of the island. It was therefore to little avail that the credible threat of exclusion worked on the Turkish Cypriot community, which supported the plan despite its long-standing resistance to international pressures for doing so.

More recently, the EU has undermined the positive effect of starting accession negotiations on its conditionality. Prior to the opening of negotiations with Turkey in 2005, some member state governments, particularly in France and Austria, and actors in the Commission argued that negotiations might not necessarily lead to accession, but to another form of "privileged partnership." Moreover, subsequent amendments to the French constitution required all EU enlargements (after Croatia) to be approved by referendum, or a three-fifths majority of both houses of parliaments meeting in congress. These developments greatly reduce the credibility of the EU's promise to grant accession if Turkey met the conditions, and by extension the incentive for the Turkish government to do so.

Domestic adjustment costs and the EU's influence on democratization

A credible conditionality is therefore a necessary condition for the EU to influence democratization, but it is not sufficient, even if it is linked with a membership perspective, the most sizable incentive at the EU's disposal. If the EU offers a credible membership incentive, the impact of its political conditionality still depends crucially on factors outside its control, namely favorable domestic conditions in the countries concerned. The main domestic conditions are the adjustment costs of compliance with EU conditionality for target governments. For example, with regard to issues such as minority rights, domestic adjustment costs depend on the strength of nationalist parties in parliament.[21] With regard to democratization, the EU's influence varies according to domestic party constellations, for which the literature distinguishes among liberal, illiberal, and mixed party constellations.[22]

Democratic frontrunners with liberal party constellations

The democratic frontrunners in ECE – Hungary, Poland, the Czech Republic, Slovenia, Estonia, Latvia, and Lithuania – generally followed a liberal trajectory[23] and were characterized by a liberal party constellation in which the major parties agreed on liberal reforms and integration into Western international organizations. These countries began to democratize and to consolidate democracy without EU pressure and it is highly doubtful that they would not have democratized without the EU. In these countries, the EU was therefore without much causal influence on the broad patterns of democratic development.[24]

At the same time, the EU might still have an impact in these countries. First, EU membership can be an international anchor for longer-term democratic stability, similar to the role of the EU in post-authoritarian Spain, Portugal, and Greece. Second, the EU still tried to influence specific aspects of democracy in these countries – especially with regard to questions of minority rights. Although the adjustment costs in such areas were still considerable, the general agreement on democratic principles among the main parties meant that, for governments in these countries, the adjustment costs were usually not so prohibitively high that they threatened the basis of their power.

The main examples here are Estonia and Latvia with their sizable Russophone minorities. In these countries the EU was able to overcome even strong domestic opposition to reversing discriminatory policies by using conditionality – such as in the case of the Latvian citizenship and language laws – while discrimination prevailed in areas where the EU did not make use of its conditionality, such as the election and education laws in Latvia.[25] Examples in other countries range from the adoption of reforms in the Czech judicial system to the question of the segregation of the Roma population in the Czech town of Usti Nad Labem that the EU raised in 1999, or EU criticism of the freedom of the media in Hungary in the early years after the fall of communism.

Authoritarian/nationalist governments in illiberal party constellations

At the other end of the spectrum are countries that were dominated by nationalist, authoritarian, or populist regimes, or where governments relied on authoritarian practises to stay in office. There are not many countries in East-Central Europe in which such regimes have held power uninterruptedly since 1989. Belarus is probably the only case, while in other countries – such as Slovakia under Mečiar, in Croatia under Tudjman, or Serbia under Milošević – nationalist/authoritarian regimes were in power only temporarily.

In such domestic party constellations, the EU also had very little impact on democratization while such parties were in power. For authoritarian and nationalist governments the political adjustment costs of complying with the EU's political conditions could be prohibitively high.[26] As the EU's conditions could have undermined the very basis of their rule, the leadership of such countries was immune to EU pressure. In the case of Belarus under President Aleksander Lukashenko, the EU combined the positive incentives of democratic conditionality with negative sanctions, such as a freezing of high-level political contact between the EU and Belarus in 2004, a visa ban and freezing of assets of the country's main leaders, or the suspension of the Generalized System of Preferences (GSP) on trade. After the release of political prisoners in 2008, and some democratic improvements, the EU temporarily suspended some of the sanctions and resumed political dialogue. It remains to be seen how much influence the EU will have on further democratization beyond these initial and rather limited steps.

Fragile democracies with mixed party constellations

Arguably, the EU's impact on democratic consolidation was most pronounced in those states in which nationalist or authoritarian forces lost power to liberal forces, such as in Slovakia, Croatia, Romania, or Bulgaria. Once more liberal opposition parties assumed power, the EU's conditionality – if combined with a credible accession perspective – had a lock-in effect that endured subsequent changes in government.[27]

For democratic, reform oriented forces that had been in opposition, the compliance costs with regard to the EU's political conditionality might still have been high, but they did not threaten their very power basis. If these forces formed the government and adopted reforms demanded by the EU, and the EU rewarded compliance with further steps towards integration, the political opportunity structure for subsequent governments changed. As long as the electorate expected benefits from EU membership, future governments faced costs if they attempted to roll back the democratic reforms of their predecessors and thereby slow down progress on the path to European integration. By the same token, progress towards EU membership through democratic reform also created incentives for nationalist parties to moderate their platform. In order to win re-election, they had to reassure the electorate that they would not endanger the progress made.

Examples of such dynamics include Romania, where democratization improved significantly after a reform coalition replaced the first post-communist government of Ion Iliescu following the 1996 elections, but where democratic performance was maintained after Iliescu and his PDSR returned to power in 2000. Maybe the clearest example is Slovakia, after Mečiar and the HZDS lost the 1998 elections to a broad coalition of liberal democratic parties. The new government, led by Mikuláš Dzurinda, rapidly complied with the EU's democratic conditions that corresponded to its own priorities for political reform. It met the EU's demands for municipal elections, a charter for municipal self-government, direct elections of the president, and involvement of opposition parties in parliamentary appointments. In the area of minority rights, it established a parliamentary committee and a government council, and passed a law on the use of minority languages, which was the last precondition for EU accession negotiations that subsequently started in 2000.[28] The 2006 elections brought to power Robert Fico's *Smer* in coalition with the nationalist Slovak National Party and Mečiar's (renamed) L´S–HZDS (People's Party–Movement for a Democratic Slovakia). However, despite some of the rhetoric, there has not been a significant democratic backsliding in practice, even if the sanctions available to EU institutions after Slovakia's accession are much more blunt.[29]

A similar example is Croatia after Tudjman's death and the defeat of the HDZ in the 2000 election. The liberal democratic coalition government formed by Ivica Račan made strong progress towards starting EU accession negotiations, although some of the EU's conditions still imposed high costs – notably cooperation with the ICTY and the extradition of generals indicted for war crimes that large parts of the population considered to be heroes. The HDZ returned to power after the 2003 elections, but had moderated its platform in opposition. It eventually removed the last remaining obstacle to EU accession negotiations by cooperating with the ICTY, leading to the arrest of General Gotovina.

The key common point in all these examples is that changes in democratization patterns in response to EU demands required a prior change in government for the EU to have an impact; "European designing of democracy follows rather than precedes the establishment of and first efforts in creating new liberal democracies."[30] Debate persists on whether the EU was able to influence the electoral defeat of nationalist/authoritarian governments.

Some authors argue that the EU's causal influence on national elections has been extremely limited.[31] In this view, since the EU's influence is limited to the intergovernmental channel, it was powerless when faced with an authoritarian/nationalist leadership. Its inability to mobilize societal actors and voters against such governments restricted it to waiting for favorable developments in domestic politics that would bring to power liberal-democratic parties for which the EU's political conditions did not impose prohibitive costs. Rather than EU influence, the outcome of such "watershed elections" then reflected domestic factors, such as party strategies on electoral pacts in Slovakia's 1998 election,[32] or voter dissatisfaction with the government's record on the economy and corruption in Croatia.

However, even if the EU did not directly influence voters' choices and the outcome of elections, it might have influenced domestic politics indirectly.[33] By contributing to the creation of more competitive political systems in illiberal states, it pushed them towards a liberal political trajectory. The EU empowered liberal reformers by informing electorates about the implication of their choices for the country's accession prospects. The EU could also influence successful electoral strategies. It fostered cooperation among a hitherto fragmented opposition by providing a common platform. The need for such a platform also induced a moderation of opposition forces through the alignment of their programs with the EU's agenda of democratization. In this way, the EU also influenced the nature of the elites that won power in watershed elections.

Maybe one of the clearest attempts by the EU to influence the outcome of key elections is its change of strategy with regard to conditionality *vis-à-vis* Serbia. The EU initially made the signing of an association agreement conditional on full cooperation with the ICTY. It subsequently implemented its threat to suspend the ongoing negotiations if the Serbian government failed to extradite Bosnian Serb General Ratko Mladić. After the pro-European Boris Tadić won the presidential election in January 2008, the EU signed the agreement in April (while keeping its implementation conditional on cooperation with the ICTY). This move was intended to signal to the electorate the tangible benefits of a victory for Tadić in the parliamentary elections in May, which he had framed as a referendum on Serbia's European integration.

Adverse effects of the EU on democracy in ECE

While the EU can thus have a powerful impact on democratization, its use of accession conditionality can also have more ambiguous or even detrimental effects on democracy in its candidate countries.[34] For example, a domestic consensus about European integration has a de-politicizing effect that "hollows out" political competition.[35] In the context of accession conditionality and post-communist transition this effect is exacerbated and arguably particularly detrimental to democratic developments. The EU "could have a debilitating effect, arresting party developments by excluding from political competition those substantive, grass-roots, ideological policy conflicts around which western European party systems have evolved."[36] Similar criticism has been leveled against the impact of the EU on the development of domestic civil society organizations. Some authors argue that EU attempts to strengthen NGOs in the ECE have actually undermined them by usurping their agenda and divorcing them from grass-roots support and activism,[37] although other authors have observed a more symbiotic relationship between global links and local roots of NGOs in ECE.[38]

Another ambiguous effect of the EU on democratic consolidation in the candidates – which has been also observed in the member states – is the strengthening of executives *vis-à-vis* parliaments.[39] As Wojciech Sadurski puts it:

> Enactment of EU-related laws was often fast-tracked, with little or no serious parliamentary discussions, and with the executive controlling the process throughout. This was perhaps no bad thing, given the notorious inefficiency and incompetence of parliamentary institutions in post-communist states, and was arguably the only way to ensure that the enormous body of EU law was transposed into domestic legislation … [However], it strengthened the executive bodies over their parliamentary equivalents, a secretive procedure over fully transparent ones, and the quick-fix pace of decision-making over comprehensive deliberation. [The goal of accession] gave the executive more power to by-pass parliament and to justify the centralization of decision-making by the emergency-like circumstances.[40]

Conclusions

The conditional promise of EU membership has been a powerful tool for the Union to promote democratization in Central and Southeastern Europe since

1989. At the same time, the influence of the EU has varied considerably over time, across issues, and across countries. A consistently applied link between a credible membership perspective and democratic reforms has been generally a precondition for the EU's influence. At the same time, the influence of conditionality has depended crucially on favorable domestic constellations. The EU had only a very limited impact in countries with authoritarian and nationalist leaderships whose hold on power was threatened by its demands. It had its most significant impact once such governments were replaced by reform oriented parties for which compliance was less costly. In these cases, the EU appears to have locked in democratic reforms even after a subsequent reversal in government.

Although the leverage of EU institutions decreased after most of the ECE achieved EU membership in 2004 and 2007, there has so far been no evidence of democratic back-sliding. By contrast, the power of EU conditionality in the remaining candidate countries in southeastern Europe might be more limited than in ECE, since the circumstances are generally less favorable. With the exception of Croatia, which started accession negotiations alongside Turkey in October 2005, for most of these candidates the membership perspective is far more distant and less credible than it has been in ECE. Economic reforms and legislative alignment are generally less advanced, which makes EU accession a more distant prospect, even if all the political conditions have been met. The credibility of the membership perspective has suffered from signs of an "enlargement fatigue" in the EU after the 2007 enlargement, as reflected in the debate on the EU's "absorption capacity." At the same time, the EU's political conditionality generally implies much higher domestic adjustment costs in southeastern Europe than in ECE. In many areas, the EU's demands touch directly on questions of national identity and statehood, and its demands more directly threaten the political support of governments.

Beyond southeastern Europe, the EU has employed conditionality in its relations with the European successor states of the Soviet Union that are included in its "European Neighborhood Policy" and more specifically the more recently created "Eastern Partnership." However, the EU's ability to wield influence through conditionality is even more circumscribed in these countries. The most powerful incentive that the EU has on offer – membership – is explicitly not on the agenda. Moreover, since democratization is generally much less advanced than in Central and southeastern Europe, the high domestic adjustment costs of complying create much less conducive circumstances for the EU to have influence.

Thus, the EU faces a challenge if it wants to continue to play as important a role in promoting democratization in the remaining candidate countries of southeastern Europe and the European successor states of the Soviet Union as it played in some of the countries of ECE. To meet this challenge, the EU has to adjust its practice of using conditionality as an instrument of democratization in its European neighborhood, as well as the balance of offering conditional incentives and alternative means of external influence.

Notes

1. See, for example, Valerie Bunce, *Subversive Institutions: The Design and Destruction of Communism and the State* (Cambridge: Cambridge University Press, 1999); Jon Elster, Claus Offe, and Ulrich Preuss, *Institutional Design in Post-Communist Societies: Rebuilding the Ship at Sea* (Cambridge: Cambridge University Press, 1998); Juan Linz and Alfred Stepan, *Problems of Democratic Transition and Consolidation: Southern Europe, South America, and Post-Communist Europe* (Baltimore, Md. and Washington, DC: Johns Hopkins University Press and Woodrow Wilson Center Press, 1996); and Michael McFaul, "The Fourth Wave of Democracy and Dictatorship: Noncooperative Transitions in the Postcommunist World," *World Politics*, Vol. 54, No. 2 (2002), pp. 212–44.
2. Phillipe Schmitter, "The International Context of Contemporary Democratisation," in Geoffrey Pridham (ed.), *Transitions to Democracy: Comparative Perspectives from Southern Europe, Latin America and Eastern Europe* (Aldershot: Dartmouth, 1995); and Laurence Whitehead, *The International Dimensions of Democratization: Europe and the Americas* (Oxford: Oxford University Press, 1996).
3. Geoffrey Pridham, *Designing Democracy: EU Enlargement and Regime Change in Post-Communist Europe* (Houndmills: Palgrave, 2005), p. 3; and Frank Schimmelfennig and Ulrich Sedelmeier, "Introduction: Conceptualizing the Europeanization of Central and Eastern Europe," in Frank Schimmelfennig and Ulrich Sedelmeier (eds.), *The Europeanization of Central and Eastern Europe* (Ithaca, N.Y.: Cornell University Press, 2005), p. 3.
4. Jeffrey Kopstein and David Reilly, "Geographical Diffusion and the Transformation of the Postcommunist World," *World Politics*, Vol. 53, No. 1 (2000), p. 27, citing *Magyar Nemzet* (19 June 1999).
5. *Ibid.*, p. 25.
6. Wade Jacoby, "Inspiration, Coalition, and Substitution – External Influences on Postcommunist Transformations," *World Politics*, Vol. 58, No. 4 (2006), pp. 623–51; Judith G. Kelley, *Ethnic Politics in Europe:, The Power of Norms and Incentives* (Princeton, N.J.: Princeton University Press, 2004); Pridham, *Designing Democracy*, pp. 9–11; Frank Schimmelfennig, Stefan Engert, and Heiko Knobel, *International Socialization in Europe: European Organizations, Political Conditionality and Democratic Change* (Houndmills: Palgrave, 2006); Schimmelfennig and Sedelmeier (eds.), *The Europeanization of Central and Eastern Europe;* and Milada Anna Vachudova, *Europe Undivided: Democracy, Leverage, and Integration after Communism* (Oxford and New York: Oxford University Press, 2005).
7. Heather Grabbe, *The EU's Transformative Power: Europeanization through Conditionality in Central and Eastern Europe* (Houndmills: Palgrave, 2006); Kelley, *Ethnic Politics*; Paul J. Kubicek (ed.), *The European Union and Democratization* (London: Routledge, 2003); Pridham, *Designing Democracy*; Schimmelfennig, Engert, and Knobel, *International Socialization*; Schimmelfennig and Sedelmeier, *The Europeanization of Central and Eastern Europe*; Karen Elizabeth Smith, "The Use of Political Conditionality in the EU's Relations with Third Countries: How Effective?," *European Foreign Affairs Review*, Vol. 3, No. 2 (1998), pp. 253–74; and Vachudova, *Europe Undivided.*

8. Pridham, *Designing Democracy*, pp. 31–2; and Daniel C. Thomas, "Constitutionalization through Enlargement: The Contested Origins of the EU's Democratic Identity," *Journal of European Public Policy*, Vol. 13, No. 8 (2006), pp. 1190–1210.
9. European Council in Copenhagen, 7–8 April 1978, EC Bulletin 3/1978, p. 6.
10. William Wallace, *Opening the Door: The Enlargement of NATO and the European Union* (London: Centre for European Reform, 1996), p. 16.
11. European Council in Copenhagen, 21–22 June 1993, Conclusions of the presidency, SN 180/93, p. 16.
12. Grabbe, *The EU's Transformative Power*; J. Hughes, G. Sasse, and C. Gordon, *Europeanization and Regionalization in the EU's Enlargement to Central and Eastern Europe: The Myth of Conditionality* (Houndmills: Palgrave, 2004); Kelley, *Ethnic Politics*; Kubicek, *The European Union and Democratization*; Schimmelfennig, Engert, and Knobel, *International Socialization*; Schimmelfennig and Sedelmeier, *The Europeanization of Central and Eastern Europe*; and Vachudova, *Europe Undivided.*
13. Grabbe, *The EU's Transformative Power*; Hughes, Sasse, and Gordon, *Myth of Conditionality*; Schimmelfennig and Sedelmeier, *The Europeanization of Central and Eastern Europe*; and Vachudova, *Europe Undivided.*
14. Pridham, *Designing Democracy*, p. 59.
15. At the same time however, the opening of negotiations in October 2005 prior to the actual arrest of Gotovina appeared to undermine the credibility of conditionality, especially since it appeared that the Austrian government had made its consent to the opening of accession negotiations with Turkey conditional on also starting them with Croatia. However, the EU argued that by then the Croatian government had already cooperated fully with the ICTY contributing to Gotovina's eventual arrest in Spain.
16. Schimmelfennig, Engert, and Knobel, *International Socialization.*
17. Martin Brusis, "Between EU Requirements, Competitive Politics, and National Traditions: Re-Creating Regions in the Accession Countries of Central and Eastern Europe," *Governance*, Vol. 15, No. 4 (2002), pp. 531–59; Hughes, Sasse, and Gordon, *Myth of Conditionality*; and W. Jacoby, *The Enlargement of the European Union and NATO: Ordering from the Menu in Central Europe* (Cambridge: Cambridge University Press, 2004).
18. Beate Sissenich, *Building States without Society: European Union Enlargement and the Transfer of EU Social Policy to Poland and Hungary* (Lanham, Md.: Lexington Books, 2007).
19. Schimmelfennig and Sedelmeier, *The Europeanization of Central and Eastern Europe.*
20. Graham Avery and Fraser Cameron, *The Enlargement of the European Union* (Sheffield: Sheffield Academic Press, 1998), p. 27.
21. Kelley, *Ethnic Politics*, pp. 47–53.
22. McFaul, "Fourth Wave"; Frank Schimmelfennig, "Strategic Calculation and International Socialization: Membership Incentives, Party Constellations, and Sustained Compliance in Central and Eastern Europe," *International Organization*, Vol. 59, No. 4 (2005), pp. 827–60; Schimmelfennig, Engert, and Knobel, *International Socialization;* and Vachudova, *Europe Undivided.*

23. Vachudova, *Europe Undivided.*
24. Schimmelfennig, Engert, and Knobel, *International Socialization*, pp. 246–7.
25. Kelley, *Ethnic Politics*, pp. 73–93.
26. Kelley, *Ethnic Politics*, pp. 50–1; and Schimmelfennig, Engert, and Knobel, *International Socialization*, p. 248.
27. Schimmelfennig, "Strategic Calculation"; Schimmelfennig and Sedelmeier, *The Europeanization of Central and Eastern Europe*; and Vachudova, *Europe Undivided.*
28. Geoffrey Pridham, "The European Union's Democratic Conditionality and Domestic Politics in Slovakia: The Mečiar and Dzurinda Governments Compared," *Europe-Asia Studies*, Vol. 54, No. 2 (2002) pp. 203–27.
29. Geoffrey Pridham, "Status Quo Bias or Institutionalisation for Reversibility? The EU's Political Conditionality, Post-Accession Tendencies and Democratic Consolidation in Slovakia," *Europe-Asia Studies*, Vol. 60, No. 3 (2006), pp. 423–54.
30. Pridham, *Designing Democracy*, p. 61.
31. Tim Haughton, "When Does the EU Make a Difference? Conditionality and the Accession Process in Central and Eastern Europe," *Political Studies Review*, Vol. 5, No. 2 (2007), pp. 233–46; Schimmelfennig, Engert, and Knobel, *International Socialization.*
32. Schimmelfennig, Engert, and Knobel, *International Socialization*, pp. 127–8.
33. Vachudova, *Europe Undivided.*
34. See also Pridham, *Designing Democracy*, pp. 226–7; and Vachudova, *Europe Undivided*, pp. 225–7.
35. Peter Mair, "The Limited Impact of Europe on National Party Systems," *West European Politics*, Vol. 23, No. 4 (October 2000), pp. 27–51.
36. Abby Innes, "Party Competition in Postcommunist Europe – The Great Electoral Lottery," *Comparative Politics*, Vol. 35, No. 1 (2002), pp. 101–2. See also Anna Grzymala-Busse and Abby Innes, "Great Expectations: The EU and Domestic Political Competition in East-Central Europe," *East European Politics and Societies*, Vol. 17, No. 1 (February 2003), pp. 64–76.
37. Adam Fagan, "Taking Stock of Civil-Society Development in Post-Communist Europe: Evidence from the Czech Republic," *Democratization*, Vol. 12, Issue 4 (August 2005), pp. 528–47.
38. David Stark, Balazs Vedres, and Laszlo Bruszt, "Rooted Transnational Publics: Integrating Foreign Ties and Civic Activism," *Theory and Society*, Vol. 35, No. 3 (2006), pp. 323–49.
39. Klaus Goetz, "The New Member States and the EU: Responding to Europe," in Simon Bulmer and Christian Lequesne (eds.), *The Member States of the European Union* (Oxford: Oxford University Press, 2005), pp. 254–84; Grabbe, *The EU's Transformative Power*; and Kristi Raik, "Bureaucratization or Strengthening of the Political? Estonian Institutions and Integration into the European Union," *Cooperation and Conflict*, Vol. 37, No. 2 (2002), pp. 137–56.
40. Wojciech Sadurski, "Introduction: The Law and Institutions of New Member States in Year One," in Wojciech Sadurski, Jacques Ziller, and Karolina Zurek (eds.), *Après Enlargement: Legal and Political Responses in Central and Eastern Europe* (Florence: European University Institute, 2006), p. 7.

Further reading

Grabbe, Heather. *The EU's Transformative Power: Europeanization through Conditionality in Central and Eastern Europe* (Houndmills: Palgrave, 2006)

Jacoby, Wade. "Inspiration, Coalition, and Substitution – External Influences on Postcommunist Transformations," *World Politics*, Vol. 58, No. 4 (2006), pp. 623–51

Kelley, Judith G. *Ethnic Politics in Europe: The Power of Norms, and Incentives* (Princeton, NJ: Princeton University Press, 2004)

Kubicek, Paul J. (ed.). *The European Union and Democratization* (London: Routledge, 2003)

Pridham, Geoffrey. *Designing Democracy: EU Enlargement and Regime Change in Post-Communist Europe* (Houndmills: Palgrave, 2005)

Schimmelfennig, Frank, Stefan Engert, and Heiko Knobel. *International Socialization in Europe: European Organizations, Political Conditionality and Democratic Change* (Houndmills: Palgrave, 2006)

Schimmelfennig, Frank and Ulrich Sedelmeier (eds.). *The Europeanization of Central and Eastern Europe* (Ithaca, NY: Cornell University Press, 2005)

Vachudova, Milada Anna. *Europe Undivided: Democracy, Leverage, and Integration after Communism* (Oxford and New York: Oxford University Press, 2005)

24

Facing the twenty-first century: lessons, questions, and tendencies (a conclusion)

AUREL BRAUN

This is both an ambitious and a necessary volume. It is vastly more than a regional study, though the contributors seek to provide a comprehensive and probing assessment of developments in a politically and strategically crucial area. In an attempt to conduct what, in effect, is a 360° examination, with the benefit of being able to look at two decades of transition, this collective work also transcends the false dichotomy between area and comparative studies. Moreover, it is not bound by the old regional geographical limitations that had defined what was called "Eastern Europe." Going beyond historical analysis, both regional and country-specific, this volume thus evaluates overarching issues within a larger analytical context as well as particular political, economic, and cultural factors. In a sense, this effort entails a melding of theory and considerations of practical developments. As such, the dynamic analysis that the editor invited and the contributors produced gives us not only a better opportunity to understand causality, but also a chance to search for patterns and divine lessons.

Drawing lessons though, is both difficult and risky. It is also tempting to see patterns and conclude that our social science tools will allow us to identify them with a high degree of confidence. These social science tools, however, proved rather inadequate during the Cold War (certainly when it came to prediction) and though we have a far greater degree of transparency in the region, it would be prudent to exercise considerable skepticism and perhaps speak more about trends or tendencies. Further, though it is of course desirable to learn lessons for the future, perhaps even more importantly we should make certain that we learn the right ones. In that sense, we may need to think of the richness of the analyses of the many contributors in terms of first principles and use an "Occam's razor" approach to focus on the essentials.

The above caveats are not meant to minimize the opportunities that students, analysts, and policy-makers in the region and beyond have to understand and learn from this remarkable transition. And it is not surprising that the fall of communism in Central and Southeastern Europe drew the attention of so many scholars in a variety of fields, who had previously had little interest in the region, but who understood that the transition also provided chances to test and adapt ideas and programs that have for long preoccupied political philosophy, democratic jurisprudence, and economic conceptualization. Though it was only natural that there would be misunderstandings and disappointments in this process, the "outside-in" and the "inside-out" analyses (incompatible or tense at times, as they may have been) have allowed us, I believe, to overcome at least some of the scholarly analytical weaknesses that were so evident during the Cold War. Still, in the attempt to identify overarching issues as well as trends or tendencies, we need to continually challenge assumptions and be prepared to think counter-intuitively. We should also be aware of the changing configuration of the region as the addition of such states as Estonia, Latvia, and Lithuania, for instance, may be supplemented by Ukraine and Georgia. Equally, we need to continue to pay attention to both the centrifugal and centripetal forces that drive key developments. And, perhaps most of all, we need to search for the right questions, as the contributors to this volume have done, so that we may identify and understand the crucial forces driving the transition during the past two decades and those likely to shape future developments.

It is by posing certain questions that we can situate and evaluate developments, engage in a dynamic type of analysis, try to identify trends or tendencies, and potentially arrive at useful lessons. Perhaps the first question then should relate to the standards that we apply in judging past, current, and future developments. The second question is made up of multiple parts, or at least leads to several others. It involves defining success but, as noted, it contains or leads to several others. These include judging legacy; evaluating transition risks; asserting the role of elite persistence; weighing the impact of economic policies; assessing civil society; judging corruption; situating the role of the state; and examining the impact of nationalism and ethnicity. Last, we need to assess the problems and prospects of external security and the attendant questions within the context of the centrifugal and centripetal forces of the region.

What standards?

In any assessment of developments, even before entertaining notions of success or failure, we need to clarify the standards according to which judgments are to be made. Perhaps the early writers on transitions (often focusing on or incorporating assessments of transitions in South America) raised strong expectations by looking at the problem as a kind of inverse analysis where entities which had experienced a democratic breakdown were to restore what eventually would be recognized as consolidated democracy. Linz and Stepan, in their *Breakdown of Democratic Regimes*,[1] but also others, including Guillermo O'Donnell, Philippe Schmitter, and Lawrence Whitehead[2] and Enrique Baylora[3] in certain ways did raise expectations that have influenced those who have analyzed the specific issues of transition in Central and Southeastern Europe.

There have been obvious differences, though, between the problems and dilemmas confronting the people in the latter region, on the one hand, and those associated with the transition in South America and Spain and Portugal, on the other. Emerging from communism, where the damage to civil society, political society, market economy institutions, and the rule of law had been so enormous, the countries of Central and Southeastern Europe had no roadmap to follow and the possibilities for transition to democracy and markets were even more uncertain than elsewhere. Consequently, some analysts, such as French political scientist, Guy Hermet, rightly contend that post-communist states should not be judged by the standards of established democracies.[4] It is not that Hermet thinks that human rights abuses, the excesses of majority rule, or the persistence of barely reformed communist elites in key positions of power were insignificant. Rather, he is worried that by setting the standards too high, the governments pushing for fundamental change put themselves at risk and endanger the sustainability of the process of transition.[5] And, indeed, there were risks, especially in the early years. Adam Przeworski, for instance, persuasively argued that both Poland and Hungary embarked on a transition to market economy, "without having even a plan to protect individuals from the vicissitudes of the market economy."[6] Thus, concern with sustainability is both understandable and prudent.

Yet, there is also a risk of selling short the post-communist states in general, and those in Central and Southeastern Europe, in particular. After all, since the fall of the communist regimes the governments in the region have professed their goal to be the construction of political democracy and the establishment of a market economy as quickly as possible. Blithely lowering the bar can certainly discourage the fulfillment of these professed goals. So what, then, should be the standard?

In view of such competing impulses, and in order to clarify viable expectations, it may be useful to go back to some key notions of democracy. In particular, it is worth noting that democracy, according to the Jeffersonian axiom, is a process which needs continual improvement rather than a state or condition. A more radical interpretation of Jefferson's conception of democracy even suggests a "permanent revolution."[7] At the very least, then, democracy should be seen as evolving and the states in the region should not be held to a fixed or unattainable standard. An intent to truly transform the system and a genuine movement toward democratic goals – goals which themselves continue to evolve in certain respects in consolidated democracies – should allow for both sustainable transition and the fulfillment of basic goals.

It should also be understood, though, that despite continuing evolution, democracy as a concept or theory is not infinitely elastic. Limitations of power, protection of basic human rights, and the rule of law, among others, are still pivotal requirements. It is little wonder then that Russia's former finance minister, Boris Federov, a committed democrat, warned Western policy-makers and scholars some years ago that when it came to post-communist states, "Don't pretend that democracy is one thing in the West and something else in Russia."[8] By this he did not mean a simple replication of

Western democracy but rather spoke to standards. Others, such as Paul Marer, argued that, for his part, he took as a standard the average or the median performance of democratic governments around the world.[9] Perhaps an approach that used democracy as a process, as something dynamic, and incorporates the notion of average or median performance of consolidated democracies, possibly offers the best way to ensure that the difficulties and achievements of the Central and Southeastern European states are not minimized but that there is a standard that requires that the transition be truly meaningful.

Defining success?

If finding the appropriate "standard" is difficult, assessing transitional success in the region may be outright risky. Mere snapshots of ongoing and changing processes may be inadequate or even misleading. Transitions themselves are multifaceted and complex. Further, as Samuel Huntington argued two decades ago, democratizing states could possibly (and unexpectedly) reverse course and democratic achievements might disappear.[10] Still, students, scholars, and policy-makers need to assess success and failure if they are to understand not only what has happened in Central and Southeastern Europe since 1989, but also if they are to learn at least some of the right lessons for the future. Contributors to this volume themselves engage, in part, in such assessments. Since we are looking at multifaceted and complex processes, it would be helpful, I would suggest, to unpack and to look individually at several of the key elements or areas involved, while keeping in mind the overarching issues and the motor forces for change during the transition.

Foreshadowing/legacies

Though this volume is about the post-1989 era, the contributors do look at the past. Carol Skalnik Leff (chapter 8) alludes to the Czech Republic's democratic past, Lavinia Stan (chapter 17) refers to the "sultanist-cum-totalitarianist" rule, and András Bozóki and Eszter Simon (chapter 10), for instance, point out that in Hungary it was not a *return* to democracy in the post-communist era but rather a case of building democracy for the first time. That the past has influence, and that we need to learn from it, is obvious. Does it, however, tell us to what extent it predetermines the present or the future in the case of this region? Philippe Schmitter and Adam Przeworski, for example, were profoundly concerned about legacy and expressed considerable trepidation about the prospects for democratic progress due to the difficult impact of the specific past problems.[11]

Yet, it is important to treat the past cautiously, contextually, and even skeptically. The past is rich with possibilities and, as Stephen Holmes has argued, it is possible to find foreshadowing of just about anything that comes to pass.[12] He rightly warns against confusing *analogy* with *causality*.[13] Nonetheless, he does admit that certain legacies or preconditions do have an effect. The issue here, then, is how to find the right balance. Determinism would be a mistake, but so it would be to ignore the past. It is essential to look at the specifics of each case.

Even when we examine particular cases and specific conditions, though, there may be differing interpretations. For instance, when it came to Hungary's transition, some analysts like Anna Seleny[14] have given a very positive assessment of certain pre-1989 legacies, while Paul Marer[15] has suggested that misguided communist economic policies made Hungary more vulnerable in the post-communist era. Further, even when legacies may have a positive effect on success, they hardly guarantee that the latter will be sustained. Leff, for example, points out in chapter 8 that even though the Czech Republic successfully democratized and marketized, this has not been wholly favorable and that there has been some retrenchment. The past ought therefore, to be treated not only with caution in terms of legacy influences but there is a need to continue to balance competing forces that are part of the complex set of inputs that may constitute causality.

Transition risks

Unpredictability is a key characteristic of transitions, in part because of the volatility of the process. As some key elites resist fundamental change and the consequent possibility or likelihood that they would lose power, they may be tempted to engage in dangerous behavior. As Edward Mansfield and Jack Snyder have shown, incomplete democratization combined with weak institutions give elites "ample opportunity to engage in reckless foreign policy gambles in order to promote their own rise or forestall their downfall."[16] Such policy gambits often promote crises and war. We have seen this specifically in the case of the War of Yugoslav Succession. Though there were multiple causes here, incomplete democratization and the threats that Slobodan Milošević, for instance, saw to his power during transmission, were factors.

Mansfield and Snyder in fact refer specifically to Serbia and we can see evidence of some of the above problems in Sabrina Ramet's chapter on Serbia and Montenegro. As Yugoslavia fell apart, the ruling elites had the opportunity to control what was broadcast on television and leaders such as Milošević and Franjo Tudjman used this to their advantage. Milošević had Serbian television paint an inflammatory picture of Albanian threats to Serbs in Kosovo and Tudjman used the media in a similar way to claim threats by Serbs to Croatian interests.[17] There has also been violence since the start of the transition in Moldova, Macedonia, and countries that in the future might come to be viewed as part of the region we are examining, Georgia and Armenia. What is remarkable in some ways, though, is that so far, in most transitions in the region, there has been an absence of violence of this type, which indicates that other factors have successfully dampened down a possible tendency for reckless gambles by elites during incomplete democratization.

Elite persistence

Once totalitarian regimes no longer have the ability or confidence to use force, and especially when they are viewed as having been imposed by outside forces, as was the case in this region, they disintegrate very quickly. In some cases, the elites will try to persist, sometimes changing their outward appearance via cosmetic programs and declaratory statements supportive of change. Transition, however, is to a significant degree characterized by a degree of elite persistence and by the continuities and changes in elite relations. As John Higley has contended, elite persistence and behavior have a profound impact on the success of transition.[18] He argues persuasively that transitions that involve significant change in elite composition and elite relations (there is usually some elite persistence) differ importantly in their processes and outcomes from cases in which elites are mainly unchanged.[19] Higley points to the absence of much elite circulation and changed elite relations in Bulgaria, Romania, and Slovakia during several years after the beginning of the 1989 transitions. In this volume, Maria Spirova (chapter 18), Lavinia Stan (chapter 17), and Erika Harris (chapter 9) also give evidence of the persistence of former communist elites in key positions in Bulgaria, Romania, and Slovakia, respectively. Elite persistence, again, is but one factor in determining the course of transition, but it seems an important one. If we look at such success indicators as the level of democratization and transparency, the rule of law, media freedom, and the health of civil and political society, then it may be hardly surprising that Bulgaria under Zheliu Zhelev, Romania under Ion Iliescu, and Slovakia under Vladimír Mečiar were laggards. Bulgaria and Romania, moreover, still continue to struggle.

Economic transition

That economics play a vital role in transitions and form a crucial element of what constitutes success is evident not only in Karl Kaser's chapter in this volume but also in those of many of the other contributors. Different elements of economic transition, from creating markets to privatization, impact not only economic progress and stability, but also on social well-being and political legitimacy. We can see some of these linkages in chapter 10 by Bozóki and Simon, chapter 8 by Leff, and chapter 20 by Smith-Sivertsen, among others. Bozóki and Simon in their discussion of reform and revolution helpfully point out that transitions are closer to revolutionary forms of change than to reform (or "refolution"). In economics, in fact, the change is meant to be fundamental. Markets, for instance, even when there is a significant involvement of government through the creation of a "thick" social safety net, are driven by an ideology that is radically different from that of Marxist–Leninist economics.

At a basic level, for example, even reformist "Goulash communism" had little in common with the Social Democrat Olaf Palme's market economy in Sweden.

The magnitude of the change is one of the reasons why genuine economic transitions are, as János Kornai suggested, invariably painful.[20] Fundamental economic change does not, however, mean that the states in the region had to mimic *mutatis mutandis* the American or a particular West European model of economic development. The level of state ownership, the "thickness" of the social safety net, and monetary or fiscal policies could vary. Certainly, economists have argued about which particular market model might provide the best prospects for growth, and political scientists have differed as to the effect on political stability. What has been crucial, though, is the commitment to a genuine market economy, the depoliticization of ownership, ensuring that money becomes active and replaces commands (through market contracts), the evolution of a business legal system, and the end/or limitation of rent-seeking.[21] This is necessary for both internal and external reasons. First, states in the region lack the massive natural resources such as oil which have allowed some OPEC states and Russia to attempt to at least temporarily defy "the economic laws of gravity." Second, as the states in the region tried to integrate themselves within the world economy (after the restrictions of the CMEA that they had been forced to live under during the Soviet era), marketization has proven to be crucial to their international competitiveness.

It may also be worth noting that as the states in the region begin to gain membership in the EU, they are required to live by EU rules and adopt the overarching EU economic model, including the vast set of rules coming from Brussels. The exceptions to this might be somewhat perturbing. Lavinia Stan pointed out in chapter 17 that Romanian political elites have ignored a number of EU obligations with impunity – but then this, it seems, is because the Union has not taken Bucharest seriously. Therefore, the centripetal forces that should help this region integrate within the larger European family are diminished when countries like Romania ignore obligations and the EU in turn does not find such new members sufficiently important to merit the effort to enforce Brussels' own rules.

Last, questions of the speed of transformation and the rate of privatization also need to be treated with extreme caution, as should the term "shock therapy." Even comparing the early "success stories" – Poland, the Czech Republic, Hungary, and Slovenia – is risky, as Paul Marer has noted.[22] Speed has to be applied to specifics, and *semi-privatization* cannot be meaningfully compared to *real privatization*. What is crucial to successful marketization, though, has been momentum and determination.

Perils of corruption

Probably no country is entirely corruption-free (although the Nordic countries come close), regardless of how high its ranking by Transparency International might be. The standard for success, then, cannot be an absolute absence of corruption. Rather, we look at the extent and the deleterious character of corruption in particular states during specific epochs in order to judge just how corrosive it may be and to what extent it might damage political legitimacy and stability, inhibit economic growth, or provoke violence. What is quickly apparent in this volume is that, during a period of transition, when economic progress and building legitimacy are so vital to transcending the old economic and political order, corruption does create a particular vulnerability. It drives away investments, it destroys business confidence, it reinforces a perception of unfairness and a sense of victimization among vast segments of the population, and it breeds the kind of cynicism that is profoundly destructive when it comes to efforts to build political legitimacy.

We see the damage that corruption has caused throughout the region, whether in Serbia and Montenegro as Ramet shows in chapter 13, or as evidenced in chapter 20 on the Baltic States (particularly in Lithuania) by Smith-Sivertsen, or in Romania as Stan shows in chapter 17, or in Albania, as discussed in Bernd Fischer's chapter. Poland, too, has experienced serious problems of corruption in the post-communist era, as Konstanty Gebert notes in chapter 7, while in Croatia, as Ramet's chapter on that country reveals, the Račan and Sanader governments have made energetic efforts to roll back the extensive corruption which developed in the years that Franjo Tudjman was president. In Slovenia, by contrast, corruption has been a lesser problem, as Danica Fink-Hafner outlines in chapter 11. Furthermore, judicial corruption not only inhibits economic development but can also dangerously blur the important distinction between legality and legitimacy that Bozóki and Simon describe in chapter 10. Last, corruption can also impede the centripetal forces that can help the regional states join and then thrive within the EU. The level of corruption in Bulgaria and Romania – which were ranked in terms of the 2007 CPI of Transparency International at 64 and 69, respectively (among the worst in the region)[23] – has caused considerable amount of disillusionment among the established EU states. Skeptical EU members are questioning the decision to let the two nations join the Union and some are pressing Brussels to impose sanctions.[24] In the case of Romania, not only is the EU treating the country as a second-class citizen by at times not even bothering to press for the enforcement of certain regulations, but in 2008 the newly elected Italian government unveiled plans to make illegal immigration a crime which, in a non-too-subtle way, was directed at Romanians who arrived in Italy via Schengen states.[25] What makes this particularly sad is that corruption is certainly not preordained in the region. Estonia and Slovenia, for example, both managed highly respectable rankings with Transparency International in 2007.[26]

Civil society

With the fall of communism in 1989 scholars began to pay considerable attention to civil society – perhaps even viewing it as a fashionable exercise.[27]

Though a "rediscovered" concept, civil society, disturbingly, has been endowed at times (during the transition) with excessive explanatory powers, even if it does not have a commonly accepted definition. Grzegorz Ekiert, almost two decades ago, recognized some of the conceptual problems (and this has been understood by many in the scholarly community) and concluded that civil society, in essence, is made up of two categories: on the one hand, the notion of "domestic society" which includes the range of primary and secondary social groups within society, and on the other hand, the category of "political society" which includes the voluntary associations and social movements that we see comprise the political community that is active within a society.[28]

What we have seen in various chapters in this volume, and particularly chapters 7, 10, and 8 on Poland, Hungary, and the Czech Republic, is that civil society in its totality does make a difference. A better-developed civil society in the late communist era appeared to give some advantage in the early days of transition and the politics of civil society *tends* to be a significant component both throughout the transition period and during democratic consolidation. Yet, civil society is not a panacea. It does not invariably contribute to long-term democratic legitimacy, its level of institutionalization may be low, and there is the risk, as Andrew Arato warned, of the development of anti-political movements and initiatives.[29] He rightly cautioned that for democracy to be successful, civil actors of all types also need to learn the art of political self-limitation. Paradoxically in a sense, although a well-functioning civil society may help democratic development, the former may very much need the presence of a well-formed, strong, democratic state that would encourage political self-limitation and inhibit extremism.

The role of the state, and elections

Part of the communist legacy was widespread fear of the state among much of the population in the region. In 1989, mistrust was understandable in light of the recent memory of the repression that had endured for several decades, but a weak state also presented problems if democracy and markets were to succeed. Though democracy is, to a significant degree, about limitation of power, a well-functioning state is needed to ensure the protection of law, the collection of taxes, the administration of social security, and the fostering of a secure environment within which civil society can thrive. In a number of instances, a weak state thus turned out to be quite a significant problem. In the case of Bosnia and Herzegovina, for example, as Florian Bieber shows in his chapter 14, a weak state was one of the many difficulties plaguing that entity, and it was only between 2000 and 2005–6 that state-building started to become effective.

Whether a state is strong or weak in a transition period cannot be measured, however, in terms of the power of its coercive instruments. The latter may give a state some temporary advantage but it is not sustainable in the long term when there are demands for and movement towards democracy. To a significant degree, therefore, a strong state is predicated on legitimacy, whether that is understood in the Weberian or Habermasian sense. One of the early ways to achieve such legitimacy in the region was through elections. Certainly, there is far more to legitimacy than elections, but the latter offer highly visible and instantly attractive means. Therefore, elections had a great deal of visibility in the region though they were not always well understood. Elections, in fact, involve a complex and vulnerable process, as we have seen in various chapters in this volume. They can and have been undermined in a number of instances. Some of the elections in Romania (chapter 17) illustrate starkly how they may be democratic in form without substantive content, particularly in the case of the manipulated 1992 parliamentary votes.[30] Elections, then, are a fragile but necessary part of creating legitimacy and building a viable democratic state. Ensuring that elections are fair and meaningful remains a part of an ongoing and difficult struggle in the region,[31] an important one in terms of building a capable and legitimate state. The latter is not only a domestic requirement throughout the region but it is also needed if the populations are to benefit from the centripetal forces that are drawing them towards integration within the EU. The requirements for entry into the latter and meaningful membership are difficult to meet, as we have seen, unless there is a legitimate and strong state to implement the vast body of Union regulations and policies.

Addressing nationalism and ethnicity

Marxist–Leninist systems are by nature universalistic – or at least, so they claim. The regimes in the region therefore asserted that they had relegated nationalism to the bourgeois past and that ethnicity was to disappear with the rise of "socialist man." Indeed, the *Pax Sovietica* for decades camouflaged nationalist tensions among regional states, and the various regimes contended that ethnic minority differences had long been resolved. As we can now see, such claims were considerably removed from reality. With the fall of communism (which had allowed tensions to fester under the surface while assiduously creating a portrait of harmony) many of the chapters in this volume demonstrate that nationalism and ethnic tensions re-emerged – and, if anything, in even an more virulent form.

Though nationalism, particularly in its civic form, may be beneficial in restoring pride and a sense of security and justice, it may also be a profoundly negative factor.[32] Elites, who oppose or wish to slow down democratization, might, as we have seen, employ nationalism to exaggerate external threats and create a diversion. Further, as Robert Dahl long ago suggested, such elites may also employ nationalism as a justification for curtailing the rights of potential domestic opponents.[33] In light of the current avid use of nationalism in the region, few if any of the post-communist states are likely to render ethnicity legally and politically irrelevant.

We have seen deadly interplays of nationalism and ethnicity in several of the chapters in this volume. Bieber (chapter 14) writes about the vast loss of human life in Bosnia; Zachary Irwin (chapter 15) highlights the armed violence in Macedonia in 2001 and the continued fragility of interethnic relations; and Steven Roper discusses nationalism and ethnic tensions in his chapter 21 on Moldova, the violence in the case of the breakaway region of Transnistria, and the way in which identity politics fed the centrifugal forces of ethnic divisiveness. We can see these problems in various forms in many of the other chapters, where ultra-nationalism and inadequate respect for or sufficient sensitivity to ethnic diversity and communal rights encourage a sense of majority victimology and ethnic minority dissatisfaction. Extremist movements or institutions continue to feed tensions, whether it is *Romania Mare* (Greater Romania) in Romania, the more recently formed *Magyar Garda* (Hungarian Guard) in Hungary, or the virulent nationalistic and anti-Semitic broadcasts of Radio Maryja in Poland. Though nationalistic and ethnic extremism are not the norm in the region, much work remains to be done in the case of all of the states as they try to consolidate democracy. It would thus be imprudent to underestimate the continued risks that remain.

Searching for security

Prior to 1989 it would have been rather difficult to understand developments in the region unless one had also studied Soviet policies and interests: In a sense, these states were the Soviet Union's borderlands. Insofar as much of the region is integrating into the EU and NATO, there may be a tendency currently to think of the area as Western Europe's borderlands, with Russia receding into the past. Yet, in many respects, this is a region that is *sui generis*. It has an opportunity to build security along all horizons as long as the states in the region are able to both identify and effectively address the security issues and opportunities. It should also be worth pointing out at the beginning that security here too involves political and economic as well as military factors.

As Rick Fawn very persuasively shows in chapter 22, a number of states in the region took an early but vital initiative that sent a message of self-definition and of a larger vision to NATO and the EU – Visegrád. Through that 1991 initiative and the specifics of regional cooperation, Poland, Hungary, and Czechoslovakia (later the Czech Republic and Slovakia) were able to project an image of stability and reliability that later did so much to facilitate not only their own but also that of several other states' entry into NATO and the EU.

Similarly, Ulrich Sedelmeier, in chapter 23 on the region's relations with the EU, paints a picture that is both complex and cautionary. Exogenous factors are not insignificant and the promise of EU membership and the accompanying conditionality, he argues, have produced some positive results in the case of Eastern European aspirants, particularly in reversing certain discriminatory policies. Yet, as he rightly points out, there is no simple causality or a clear link between EU integration and democratization. The EU may even produce some adverse effects on democratization and the Union, as he notes, may be starting to suffer from enlargement fatigue. Exogenous factors thus have intrinsic limitations in the integrative and democratization processes.

In short, what the regional states do domestically and among themselves makes a profound difference in terms of enhancing the centripetal forces that allow them to become part of the integrative process within the EU that is so vital to their economic security and political stability. Similarly, NATO membership has been dependent to a great degree on what the regional states do themselves.

Still, the relationship between the states of Central and Southeastern Europe on the one hand, and Western Europe, Canada, and the United States on the other, is not simply a dyadic one. Though the Soviet Union has disintegrated, the military relationship that the Warsaw Pact embodied has been dismantled, and trade relations with Russia have been drastically reduced and reformed, Russian regional influence has not disappeared and may well grow in importance again. And although one might say that current overall regional relations with Moscow are relatively peaceful and stable, there are significant issues that could pose major security problems.

Russia, for instance, has been unhappy about NATO enlargement, with the Kremlin leaders repeatedly stating that they view it as both unnecessary and hostile to Moscow. It may also be said that, at times, the states in the region have been less than sensitive to Russian security concerns, economic interests, and national pride. None of the latter obviates Russian foreign policy responsibilities, however, just as, for their part, the states in the region need to try to improve relations with Moscow in order to bring greater security to all states, from Vancouver to Vladivostok. To achieve that, however, the states in the region confront a number of dilemmas.

First, the large gap in democratization between Russia on the one hand, and most of the states on the other, has been growing significantly. As Timothy Colton pointed out, in the first half of this decade Russia began sliding backwards in terms of freedom – so much so that by 2005 Freedom House, in its taxonomy, moved it from its "Partly free" into its "Not free" category.[34] By 2007, moreover, Transparency International ranked Russia, in terms of corruption, at a new low of 143rd, one of the worst states in the world.[35] To further complicate matters, despite such political retrenchment, Russia – which by the summer of 2008 was flushed with energy revenues – had become an ever-larger supplier to West European states, and increasingly more assertive politically and militarily. Vladimir Putin, who continues in power now as prime minister, is seeking to enhance Russian regional power, while his (so far) rather powerless, hand-picked successor in the presidency, Dmitry Medvedev, though in a seeming diarchy, still largely parrots his patron's policies, even if using more moderate, liberal language. This can only make the regional states less secure. Yet the latter have few options in changing Russian domestic developments or ending West European energy dependence.

Second, there is a worrying continuity in Russia's aspirations, at least during the past several years, where a foreign policy and security/military establishment has been influenced by ideas first articulated in a comprehensive fashion by the former Russian prime minister, Yevgeny Primakov – himself drawing on the nineteenth-century Russian foreign minister, Aleksandr Gorchakov.[36] It envisions a Russian restoration to superpower status if it can manipulate and control its smaller neighbors while it rebuilds domestically. It is, however, also a *Weltanschauung* that mistakenly, I believe, holds that there is a shortcut to power and international respect and that clever maneuvers and manipulation and compressed (if unidimensional) economic development will not only succeed but also avoid negative repercussions. Nonetheless, a newly confident Russia has readily pressured the states in the region, using its energy influence with major West European states to undercut them within NATO and stirring up "frozen conflicts," such as that in Transdniester, as leverage.[37] In October 2007, then-US Secretary of State, Condoleezza Rice, commented that she thought it was a mistake, "if Russia uses its great wealth, its oil and gas wealth, as a political weapon, or if it treats its independent neighbors as some old sphere of influence."[38]

In August 2008, whatever the proximate causes of conflict, Moscow used a well-planned massive military campaign to crush Georgian military forces and fully occupy Georgia's lightly-populated but strategically important separatist regions of South Ossetia and Abkhazia.[39] The Russians who, during the conflict, made a point of having their massive forces rest on top of Georgian energy lines taking fuel to Europe,[40] not only quickly recognized the independence of the two separatist regions – contemptuously ignoring the strong East European support for Georgia and Georgian territorial integrity – but successfully persuaded energy-dependent Western Europe (especially France) to pressure Tbilisi to agree to the terms of a cease-fire that heavily favored Moscow.[41]

Similarly, in December 2008 Moscow again used energy supplies to pressure a neighbor – in this case, NATO aspirant, Ukraine. Demanding sharply higher natural gas payments and accusing Ukraine of stealing from the transit pipelines, the Kremlin cut the flow, leaving significant parts of Eastern Europe without or with drastically reduced energy supplies just as temperatures plunged.[42] EU mediation helped reach a one-year settlement, but recipients of Russian gas were badly shaken.

Third, both NATO and the EU impose responsibilities and create difficulties for the regional states, as well as opportunities. NATO itself suffers from something of an identity crisis (drifting between collective security and collective defense) that Moscow has only been too keen to exploit. The regional states have insisted on "hard security guarantees" that collective defense and ultimately only American military commitment could provide.[43] This can create friction within the alliance and it is thus particularly important for the regional states to contribute. This involves not only increased military spending and modernization, but also steps that unfortunately anger Russia.

The deployment of a missile defense is a prime example. At the Bucharest summit in April 2008, NATO, despite Russian objections, agreed on the deployment of a thin missile shield and its Secretary General strongly urged the Czech Republic and Poland to allow the installation of missiles on their territory.[44] With the Russian invasion of Georgia, Poland and the Czech Republic indicated that they would not be cowed and approved deployment.[45] Actual deployment, though, will depend on the outcome of the review of the missile shield that US President Barack Obama ordered, and on his final decision.

It is true that-with the worldwide recession hitting Russia especially hard as oil and gas prices plunge, as its currency reserves dramatically contract, and as its economic growth evaporates,[46] Moscow no longer has the same power to intimidate as it did in August 2008. Nonetheless, the Kremlin has yet to curtail its ambitions to dominate or at least marginalize Eastern Europe and new NATO aspirants. The regional states need counter-weights, and therefore have to tread a fine line in both drawing benefits from and in making contributions to the alliance, just as they need to do within the EU if they are to build multiple, sustainable relations that will enhance their military, political, and economic security.

Conclusion

There is much to be optimistic about in the region. In most of the states democratization and marketization, despite flaws and some setbacks, are little short of remarkable when we look at the 1989 starting point. Despite the persistence of centrifugal forces in some of the states, centripetal ones point to strong integrative movements within the European family. There is, moreover, considerable potential to continue these positive trends and to enhance overall military, political, and economic security.

Nonetheless, if there are lessons to be learned, we need to continually ask probing questions, and these states need to balance hopes and risks. It is essential to identify the early warning signs of trouble. We have seen how corrosive corruption can be in the region, and how essential it is to address minority and individual rights. We can also understand that there are no shortcuts to effective transformation and "clever" short-term solutions generate very heavy long-term costs. As in the case of Western consolidated democracies, with all of their own imperfections, the states of Central and Southeastern Europe need to appreciate that they have committed themselves to a continuing struggle to ensure the rule of law, the balancing of power, and the safeguarding of rights when they choose the road of democratization and marketization. Equally, in joining NATO and the EU, and in the case of those who aspire to do so, they have to understand that the benefits also come with serious commitments and responsibilities. Ignoring such responsibilities again incurs major long-term cost. Finally, achieving long-range security will involve a continuing struggle, balancing various interests and concerns, and sustained efforts. There is no reason why the regional states should not be successful in the twenty-first century; there are, however, no guarantees.

Notes

1. Juan Linz and Alfred Stepan (eds.), *The Breakdown of Democratic Regimes*, 4 vols. (Baltimore, Md.: Johns Hopkins University Press, 1978).
2. Guillermo O'Donnell, Philippe C. Schmitter, and Lawrence Whitehead (eds.), *Transitions from Authoritarian Rule*, 4 vols. (Baltimore, Md.: Johns Hopkins University Press, 1986).
3. Enrique Baylora (ed.), *Comparing New Democracies: Transition and Consolidation in Mediterranean Europe and the Southern Cone* (Boulder, Colo.: Westview Press, 1987).
4. Guy Hermet, "Rethinking Transitology," in Aurel Braun and Zoltan Barany (eds.), *Dilemmas of Transition: The Hungarian Experience* (Lanham, Md.: Rowman & Littlefield, 1999), pp. 35–44.
5. *Ibid.*
6. Adam Przeworski, "Economic Reforms," in Luiz Carlos Bresser Pereira, Jose Maria Maravall, and Adam Przeworski, *Economic Reforms in New Democracies: A Social-Democratic Approach* (Cambridge and New York: Cambridge University Press, 1993).
7. Richard K. Matthews, "The Radical Political Philosophy of Thomas Jefferson: An Essay in Retrieval," *Midwest Studies in Philosophy*, Vol. 28, No. 1 (September 2004), p. 48. Even if Matthews overstates the case somewhat, Jefferson made it very clear that he envisioned continuing change and struggle. He spoke, for instance, about a constitution as an "experiment to be amended hereafter when time and trial shall show where it is imperfect." Thomas Jefferson to Comte de Moustier, 1790. ME 8:108, in *Thomas Jefferson on Politics & Government*, at http://etext.virginia.edu/jefferson/quotations/jeff1770.htm [last accessed on 3 February 2009].
8. Boris Federov, in interview with the author, Berlin, 26 August 1994, Aspen Institute Congressional Program Conference, Berlin, Germany (August 1994).
9. Paul Marer, "Economic Transformation, 1990-1998," in Braun and Barany (eds.), *Dilemmas of Transition*, pp. 157–61.
10. Samuel P. Huntington, *The Third Wave: Democratization in the Late Twentieth Century* (Norman, Okla.: University of Oklahoma Press, 1991), pp. 17–20.
11. Philippe C. Schmitter, "Dangers and Dilemmas of Democracy," *Journal of Democracy*, Vol. 5, No. 2 (April 1994), pp. 57–74; and Adam Przeworski, *Democracy and the Market* (Cambridge: Cambridge University Press, 1991).
12. Stephen Holmes, "Cultural Legacies or State Collapse? Probing the Post-Communist Dilemma," in Michael Mandelbaum (ed.), *Post-Communisn: Four Perspectives* (New York: Council on Foreign Relations, 1996), p. 27.
13. *Ibid.*
14. Anna Seleny, "The Foundations of Post-Socialist Legitimacy," in Braun and Barany (eds.), *Dilemmas of Transition*, pp. 131–54.
15. Marer, "Economic Transformation," pp. 159–64.
16. Edward D. Mansfield and Jack Snyder, "Electing to Fight: Emerging Democracies and International Instability," in Aurel Braun (ed.), *NATO–Russia Relations in the Twenty-First Century* (London: Routledge, 2008), p. 15.
17. *Ibid.*, p. 17; and Mark Thompson, *Forging War: The Media in Serbia, Croatia, Bosnia and Herzegovina*, rev. edn. (Luton: University of Luton Press, 1999), *passim*.

18. John Higley, "Transitions and Elites," in Braun and Barany (eds.), *Dilemmas of Transition*, pp. 47-57.
19. Braun and Barany (eds.), *Dilemmas of Transition*, p. 47.
20. János Kornai, "Paying the Bill for Goulash Communism: Hungarian Development and Macro-Stabilization in a Political Economy Perspective," Discussion Paper 1748 (Cambridge, Mass.: Harvard Institute for Economic Research, Harvard University, 1996).
21. See for instance, Anders Åslund, "Post-Communist Economic Transformation," in Braun and Barany (eds.), *Dilemmas of Transition*, pp. 71–84.
22. Marer, "Economic Transformation," pp. 166–7.
23. Transparency International, Corruption Perceptions Index 2007, at www.transparency.org/layout/set/print/policy_research/survey [last accessed on 3 February 2009].
24. *New York Times* (10 May 2008).
25. "EU: Italy Targets Romanian Immigrants With Plan to Suspend Schengen," Radio Free Europe/Radio Liberty (hereafter RFE/RL), 13 May 2008, at www.rferl.org/featuresarticleprint/2008/05/df977d72-aca2-49 [last accessed on 3 February 2009].
26. Transparency International, Corruption Perceptions Index.
27. Adam B. Seligman, *The Idea of Civil Society* (New York: Free Press, 1992) and pertinent articles by Colin Powell, E.J. Dionne, Jr., Jean Bethke Elshtain, Theda Skocpol, and others in *The Brookings Review*, Vol. 15, No. 4 (Fall 1997), pp. 2–41.
28. Grzegorz Ekiert, "Democratization Processes in East-Central Europe: A Theoretical Reconsideration," *British Journal of Political Science*, Vol. 21, No. 3 (July 1991), pp. 299–300.
29. Andrew Arato, "Civil Society, Transition, and Consolidation of Democracy," in Braun and Barany (eds.), *Dilemmas of Transition*, pp. 243–45.
30. Henry F. Carey, "Irregularities or Rigging: The 1992 Romanian Parliamentary Elections," *East European Quarterly*, Vol. 29, No. 1 (Spring 1995), pp. 43–88.
31. Jørgen Møller, "Wherefore the Liberal State?: Post-Soviet Democratic Blues and Lessons from Fiscal Sociology," *East European Politics and Societies*, Vol. 21, No. 2 (Spring 2007), pp. 294–315.
32. Stefan Auer, "Nationalism in Central Europe – A Chance or a Threat for the Emerging Liberal Democratic Order?," *East European Politics and Societies*, Vol. 14, No. 2 (Spring 2000), pp. 213–45; and Venelin I. Ganev, "History, Politics and the Constitution: Ethics, Conflict and Constitutional Adjudication in Post Communist Bulgaria," *Slavic Review*, Vol. 63, No. 1 (Spring 2004), pp. 66–90.
33. Robert A. Dahl, *Polyarchy: Participation and Opposition* (New Haven, Conn.: Yale University Press, 1971), p. 44.
34. Timothy J. Colton, "Post-Postcommunist Russia, the International Environment and NATO," in Braun (ed.), *NATO-Russia Relations*, pp. 25–6.
35. Transparency International, Corruption Perceptions Index.
36. Yevgeny Primakov, "Russia in World Politics: A Lecture in Honour of Chancellor Gorchakov," *International Affairs* (Moscow), Vol. 44, No. 3 (1998), pp. 7–12.
37. RFE/RL *Features*, "Voronin Says Russian Troops in Moldova Illegally," RFE/RL (24 March 2006); and RFE/RL *Features*, "Moldovan President Says Transdniester Solution in Sight," RFE/RL (6 November 2007). Russia, in fact, is involved in a number of these "frozen conflicts," including those in South Ossetia and Abkhazia,

located in Georgia, which it has not hesitated to use to manipulate or punish that NATO aspirant.

38. As quoted in *New York Times* (25 January 2008).
39. *New York Times* (24 January 2009); *New York Times* (16 September 2008); "Russia Plans Base in Georgian Breakaway Region," RFE/RL (26 January 2009), at www.rferl.org/articleprintview/1374903.html [last accessed on 3 February 2009]; *New York Times* (18 December 2008).
40. *New York Times* (29 January 2009).
41. EurActiv.com, "Sarkozy, Solana in Russia to Clarify Georgia Ceasefire" (2 February 2009), at www.euractiv.com/en/enlargement/sarkozy-solana-russia-clarify-georgia-ceasefire/article-175176 [last accessed on 3 February 2009]; and Daisy Sindelar, "OSCE to Dissolve Georgia Mission After Russia Blocks Extension," RFE/RL (22 December 2008), at www.rferl.org/articleprintview/1362355.html [last accessed on 3 February 2009].
42. *New York Times* (1 January 2009); and Chloe Arnold, "In Short Term, the One with the Gas Wins," RFE/RL (23 January 2009), at www.rferl.org/content/In_Short_Term_The_One_With_The_Gas_Wins/1374062.html [last accessed on 3 February 2009].
43. Daniel Braun, *NATO Enlargement and the Politics of Identity* (Martello Paper, No. 31, Kingston, ON: Queen's Centre for International Relations, 2007), pp. 43-9.
44. RFE/RL *Features*, "NATO: Alliance Chief Calls Missile Defense a Key Element for Security," RFE/RL (5 May 2008), at www.rferl.org/featuresarticleprint/2008/05/67b2f4d2-e589-4 [last accessed on 3 February 2009].
45. BBC News, "US and Poland Seal Missile Deal" (20 August 2008), at http://news.bbc.co.uk/go/pr/fr/-/2/hi/europe/7571660.stm [last accessed on 3 February 2009]; Agence France Presse (AFP), 7 August 2008, and 29 October 2008.
46. Josh Calder, "Challenging the Assumptions About Russia's Future," RFE/RL (2 January 2009), at www.rferl.org/articleprintview/1365602.html [last accessed on 3 February 2009]; *New York Times* (2 February 2009); and *Moscow Times* (2 February 2009), at http://themoscowtimes.com/articles/detail.php?ID=374139&p [last accessed on 3 February 2009].

Index

Abdić, Fikret 263
Adžić, Blagoje 119
Agh, Attila 339
agrarian parties 81
Ahmeti, Ali 342
Ahtisaari, Martti 371
Albania 3, 4, 9, 15, 16, 18, 20, 28, 46, 98, 421, 437–9
communist regime 421–2: collapse 422–5
constitution 428, 435
corruption 11, 426, 436
economic reforms 425: brain drain 104, 434; industrial transformation 96; privatization 433
education 434
electoral system 68, 70
EU and 524
factual information 439
health care 434
media 428
political parties 67, 71, 423, 424, 429, 436: ethnic minority parties 83; trajectories of the left 75
popular revolt (1997) 429–32
poverty 105, 433
president 68
pyramid investment schemes 429–30
social changes 426
unemployment 433
women in 426
Alexander I, Tsar 44
Alia, Ramiz 422
American Bar Association Central and East European Legal Initiative (CEELI) 4, 30
Antall, József 224, 500
Austria 50, 212
Austro-Hungarian Empire 43, 44, 182, 205
auto-centric development 16
Baković, Anto 260
Balcerowicz, Leszek 145, 154
Balkan Wars (1912–13) 45, 287
Bánffy, Desiderius 182
Băsescu, Traian 390, 391
Belarus
corruption 20
EU and 527
Beneš decrees 62n, 166, 167, 174, 177
Berisha, Sali 423, 425, 427, 428, 430, 431, 432, 435, 437, 440
Bielecki, Jan Krzysztof 149
black markets 21
Bohle, Dorothee 92
Boškovski, Ljube 344
Bosnia-Herzegovina 4, 30, 55, 311, 322–3
before the Yugoslav war 311–13
constitution 314–15
corruption 11, 20
economic reforms 92, 100, 318–19: privatization 319
electoral system 312
EU and 317–18
factual information 324
media 320
parliament 67
political parties 72, 312, 316–17: conservative parties 80; nationalist parties 82
poverty 105
president 312, 315
state entities 314–15
war in 111, 290: Bosnian revival and road to Dayton Accord 129–33, 314; dealing with the past 321–2; genocide claims against Serbia 302; Muslim–Croat conflict 127–9, 264, 313; Serbia's assault 123–7, 290, 302, 313

brain drain 104
Albania 104, 434
Bulgaria 104
Macedonia 104
Brazauskas, Algirdas Mykolas 467
Brezhnev Doctrine 53, 54
Bulatović, Momir 9
Bulgaria 3, 16, 17, 20, 401, 416
constitution 406, 409
corruption 11, 20, 415–16, 543
creation of 45
economic reforms 106, 414–15: brain drain 104; industrial transformation 96; internationalization and transnationalization 94; privatization 98, 414; "shock therapy" 97; women and 103; workforce's reactions 101
electoral system 13, 68, 407–8
ethnic minorities 10, 83, 403, 406, 409, 412–14
EU and 524
factual information 412
foreign investment in 419
historical background 402
international community and 29
Macedonia and 329
media 410–11
parliament 404–5, 407–8
political parties 67, 71, 74, 403–4, 405–7, 409: agrarian parties 81; conservative parties 79; ethnic minority parties 83, 413; liberal parties 79; miscellaneous parties 84; nationalist parties 83; trajectories of the left 75, 77
president 68, 405–7, 409
unemployment 98, 415
Visegrád Group and 501, 502
Bush, George H. 143
Butković, Davor 273
Buzek, Jerzy 154

Čarnogurský, Ján 194
Carrington, Lord 58
Ceauşescu, Elena 16, 17, 380
Ceauşescu, Nicolae 16, 17, 144, 380
Central European Initiative (CEI) 497
Cimoszewicz, Włodzimierz 153
civil society 65–7, 543–4
Clemenceau, Georges 48
Clinton, Bill 508
communist/socialist parties 75–7
see also under individual countries
Congress system 41, 42
conservative parties 77, 79–80
Constantinescu, Emil 386, 387
constitutions *see under* individual countries
corruption 11, 19–21, 542–3
see also under individual countries
Council for Mutual Economic Assistance (COMECON) 3, 495
Council of Europe 10, 29–30, 337
Council of the Baltic Sea States (CBSS) 495, 496
crime 21
see also corruption
Croatia 4, 9, 20, 55, 258, 274–6
constitution 68, 260
corruption 11, 20, 259–61
economic reforms 106
electoral system 68, 269
EU and 275, 521, 524, 525, 529
factual information 278
historical background 258–9, 276–7
media 272–4
NATO and 275
Nazi regime and 50
political parties 67, 72, 266–72: agrarian parties 81; conservative parties 81; liberal parties 79; nationalist parties 83; pensioners' parties 83; regionalist parties 83; trajectories of the left 75, 77
president 68, 268
tensions in Yugoslavia and 116
Visegrád Group and 502
war in 27–8, 117–19, 120–3, 130–1, 133, 261–6, 290, 313: genocide claims against Serbia 302
Crvenkovski, Branko 329
Cyprus
EU and 526
Czech Republic 3, 5, 20, 55, 59, 72, 162, 175, 540
civil society 65
constitution 168, 170
corruption 174
economic reforms 174: industrial transformation 96; privatization 22, 170–1
economy 171
electoral system 70, 169–70
EU and 175, 527
factual information 176
historical background 162–8, 176
international community and 29
media 170
NATO and 549

parliament 67, 168, 169
political parties 67, 73, 74, 169: conservative parties 80; dilemma of unstable parliamentary majorities 171–5; liberal parties 78; regionalist parties 83; trajectories of the left 75, 172, 173
president 168–9
Roman Catholic Church and 167
Czechoslovakia 3, 10, 15, 16, 18, 52, 53, 162
communist regime 163, 164, 184
creation of 47–8
crime 21
dissolution 165–6, 184–5
economic reforms: privatization 22, 98, 170–1; "shock therapy" 97
German relations with 166–7
historical background 162–8, 183
lustration 164, 165
Nazi regime and 50, 51, 166, 183
political parties 71
Visegrád Group and 500, 501

democratization 538
EU and 191, 519–20, 530–1: adverse effects 530; conditions for influence through conditionality 523–6; credibility of conditionality 524–6; domestic adjustment costs 526–30; EU instruments for democracy promotion 520–1; evolution of EU conditionality in democracy promotion 521–3; rewards 523–4
see also under individual countries
Divjak, Jovan 130
Djindjić, Zoran 292, 295, 296, 297
Drašković, Vuk 292, 293
Drnovšek, Janez 247
Dubcěk, Alexander 184
Duroselle, Jean-Baptiste 39, 40
Dyba, Karel 170

economic reforms 73, 91–2, 99–101, 541–2
brain drain 104
informal sector 101–2
key factors for emergence of differences and similarities 93–4: industrial transformation 96–7; internationalization and transnationalization 94–5; weaker and stronger transformative state power 95–6
labor unions and 102–3
pathways into global economy 99
privatization 9, 21–3, 97, 98–9
results 104–7
"shock therapy" and gradualism 97–8
women and 103–4
workforce's reactions 101
see also under individual countries
education
Albania 434
Hungary 220–1
Kosova/Kosovo 363
Slovenia 248
Eide, Kai 369, 371
electoral system 68–70
see also under individual countries
elite persistence 541
Engels, Friedrich 40
environmental issues
Green parties 81
Estonia 3, 4, 5, 16, 20, 72, 465, 468
cleavages 456
coming to terms with the past 461
communist regime 450
constitution 451
corruption 460
economic reforms 459–60: privatization 22
electoral system 452
ethnic minorities 463–4
EU and 525, 527
factual information 466
historical background 447–51
independence 451
media 458–9
political parties 72, 74, 452, 453–5, 457–8: agrarian parties 81; conservative parties 79; liberal parties 79; trajectories of the left 75
president 25, 451
religion 461, 462
ethnic minorities 73
ethnic minority political parties 83
poverty and 105
see also under individual countries
EU 4, 10, 14, 28–9, 64, 94, 495, 501, 502, 542, 546
Albania and 524
Belarus and 527
Bosnia and 317–18
Bulgaria and 524
Croatia and 275, 521, 524, 525, 529
Cyprus and 526
Czech Republic and 175, 527

EU (cont.)
democratization and 191, 519–20, 530–1: adverse effects 530; conditions for influence through conditionality 523–6; credibility of conditionality 524–6; domestic adjustment costs 526–30; EU instruments for democracy promotion 520–1; evolution of EU conditionality in democracy promotion 521–3; rewards 523–4
Estonia and 525, 527
Hungary and 212, 216, 521
influence on state formation in East-Central Europe 57–9
institution building and 95
Kosova/Kosovo and 4, 58
Latvia and 522, 526, 527
Macedonia and 329, 333, 342, 345, 347, 348, 522
Moldova and 476, 484
Montenegro and 296
Poland and 154, 521
Romania and 381, 389, 390, 394–5, 521, 522, 524, 528
Serbia and 298, 302, 529
Slovakia and 191, 524, 528, 529
Slovenia and 240
Turkey and 526
Visegrád Group and 505–7
war in Yugoslavia and 120, 122, 128
European Initiative for Democracy and Human Rights 520

federalism 71
Federov, Boris 538
Fico, Robert 77, 83, 190, 191
Finland 212
First World War 41
foreign investment 106
Bulgaria 419
Hungary 92
France
Kosova/Kosovo and 366
war in Yugoslavia and 126, 131
Freedom House 19
Furet, François 39

Georgia 4, 548
Georgievski, Ljubco 334
Geremek, Bronislaw 154
German Democratic Republic (GDR) 3, 16
Germany 497
borders 145
Nazi regime 49
relations with Czechoslovakia 166–7
war in Yugoslavia and 122
Gheorghiu-Dej, Gheorghe 16
Giordano, Christian 91
Girault, René 44
Gligorov, Kiro 328, 334, 336, 349
Göncz, Árpád 229
Gorbachev, Mikhail 16, 55
Gotovina, Ante 275
government and the state
economic reforms and transformative state power 95–6
role of 544–5
Granić, Mate 259, 269
Greece 4
creation of 43, 44, 45
EU and 520, 521
Macedonia and 329, 335, 346
green parties 81
Greskovits, Béla 92
Gross, Jan T. 155
Gruevski, Nikola 332

Habermas, Jürgen 14
Hadžić, Goran 299, 302
Halili, Nevzat 334
Halilović, Sefer 129
Havel, Václav 4, 9, 59, 163, 168, 177, 500, 501
health care
Albania 434
Kosova/Kosovo 363
Serbia 291
Helsinki Watch 340
Henlein, Konrad 51
Hermet, Guy 538
Higley, John 541
historical legacies and historical memory 13–17
dealing with the past: Bosnia 321–2; Estonia 461; Latvia 461; Lithuania 461
Hlinka, Andrej 183
Hobsbawm, E.J. 14
Holy Alliance 44
homosexuality 29, 250
Hooghe, Liesbet 175
Horn, Gyula 225
Howard, Marc Morjé 65
Hoxha, Enver 15, 16, 421–2
Hraba, Joseph 171

Hudelist, Darko 264
human trafficking 21
Hungary 3, 5, 9, 15, 16, 17, 20, 204, 226–7, 540
Austro-Hungarian Empire 43, 44
communist regime 206–8
constitution 25
corruption 219–20
democratization 208–10, 519
economic reforms 100, 216–19: industrial transformation 96; informal sector 102; privatization 22, 98, 219; "shock therapy" 97; workforce's reactions 101
education 220–1
electoral system 68, 213–14
ethnic minorities 222–5
EU and 212, 216, 521
factual information 228
foreign investment in 92
gender issues 221–2
historical background 204–6
international community and 29
NATO and 212, 509
Nazi regime and 206
parliament 213
political parties 71, 73, 74, 214–16, 227: agrarian parties 81; conservative parties 79, 80; liberal parties 78; trajectories of the left 75
political values and visions 210–13
poverty 105
religion 225–6
Visegrád group and 500, 501
Huntington, Samuel 539
Husák, Gustáv 184

Iliescu, Ion 9, 72, 381, 385, 386, 397–8
industry *see* manufacturing sector
inflation
Romania 98
Serbia 291, 292
informal sector 101–2
institution building 23–4, 95
in conditions of war 27–8
parliamentary 24–6
presidentialism 26
see also political parties
international community 28–31
International Court of Justice (ICJ) 321
International Criminal Tribunal for the former Yugoslavia (ICTY) 4, 295, 298, 299, 302, 321, 522, 529
International Monetary Fund (IMF) 97
Macedonia and 337
internationalization 94–5
investment
foreign investment 106: Bulgaria 419; Hungary 92
pyramid investment schemes 429–30
Israel 146, 150
Italy
Central European Initiative (CEI) and 497, 498
unification of 44
Izetbegović, Alija 9, 129, 263, 265, 311, 325

Janša, Janez 20, 237, 238, 239
Jaruzelski, Wojciech 18, 140, 144, 148
John Paul II, Pope 150
Jović, Borisav 117, 289
Jowitt, Ken 15

Kaczyński, Jaroslaw 149, 151, 155
Kaczyński, Lech 149, 151, 155, 157
Kádár, János 207
Kadijević, Veljko 117, 119, 121
Karadžić, Radovan 124, 265, 299, 302
Kasza, József 303
Kavan, Jan 165
Kitschelt, Herbert 163, 164
Klaus, Václav 10, 166, 168, 170, 175, 503
Klitgaard, Robert 19
Kornai, János 171
Kosova/Kosovo 4, 30, 286, 372
conflict in 58, 112, 133, 363–6: post-conflict period 366–8
constitution 362, 367
education 363
electoral system 68
EU and 4, 58
expulsion of Albanians and growth of parallel institutions 361–3
health care 363
historical background 359–60
independence 55, 57, 58, 300, 301, 329, 371–2
media 363, 370
miners' strike (1989) 361
Orthodox Church 364
parliament/assembly 361, 362, 367
poverty 368
privatization 368, 370
riots (1981) 288, 360–1
riots (2004) 368–70

Kosova/Kosovo (cont.)
Serbian coercion of 115, 116, 288, 299, 362
Serbian minority 361, 364, 366, 369, 372
UN protectorate 365, 366, 367, 373
unemployment 370
Koštunica, Vojislav 294, 295, 296, 297–300, 302
Kožený, Vladimir 171
Krzaklewski, Marian 155
Kučan, Milan 239, 254
Kundera, Milan 163
Kuron, Jacek 153
Kwasniewski, Aleksander 147, 153, 155

labor markets
economic reforms and 101
migrant labor 102, 105: brain drain *see* brain drain
unemployment 98, 105: Bulgaria 98, 415; Kosova/Kosovo 370; Romania 98
women in 103–4
labor unions 65
economic reforms and 102–3
Latvia 3, 4, 5, 16, 20, 72, 465, 468
cleavages 455
coming to terms with the past 461
communist regime 450
constitution 452
corruption 460
economic reforms 459–60: privatization 22, 460
electoral system 68, 453
ethnic minorities 463, 464
EU and 522, 526, 527
factual information 467
historical background 447–51
independence 451
media 458–9
political parties 72, 74, 449, 452, 453–5, 456, 457–8: agrarian parties 81; conservative parties 79; ethnic minority parties 83; liberal parties 79; miscellaneous parties 83; trajectories of the left 75, 77
president 25
religion 461, 462
League of Nations 48
Leiden University 30
Leka, Prince 432
Lenin, Vladimir Ilyich 41
Lepper, Andrzej 155, 157
liberal parties 77–9
Lipski, Jan Józef 143
Lithuania 3, 4, 5, 9, 16, 20, 146, 465, 468
cleavages 455
coming to terms with the past 461
communist regime 164, 450
corruption 460
economic reforms 459–60: informal sector 102
electoral system 68, 453
ethnic minorities 463, 465
factual information 467
historical background 447–51
independence 451
lustration 456
media 458–9
political parties 72, 74, 452, 453–5, 457–8: agrarian parties 81; conservative parties 79; liberal parties 79; miscellaneous parties 83; trajectories of the left 77
president 25, 67
privatization 22
religion 461, 462–3
Lloyd George, David 48
Lucinschi, Petru 480, 481, 482
lustration 10–11
Czechoslovakia 164, 165
Lithuania 456
Macedonia 10
Poland 11, 153, 156
Romania 11

Macedonia 4, 9, 20, 45, 55, 133
before independence 331–2
conflict in 112
constitution 335–6, 341
corruption 11, 345
democratization 332–4, 346–8
economic reforms 337: brain drain 104; privatization 337
electoral system 68, 70, 339: fraud 338
ethnic minorities 329, 334, 336, 337, 338, 341–2, 343, 348
EU and 522
factual information 349
historical background 328–9, 348–9
independence referendum 334
international context 329–30
local government 344
lustration 10
media 346
Ohrid Framework Accord 342–3, 344, 345, 347
Orthodox Church 331
parliament 340
police 344

political parties 72, 332–3, 347: conservative parties 81; ethnic minority parties 83
president 68
Majko, Pandeli 435, 436
manufacturing sector
industrial transformation 96–7
outward processing trade 94
Marer, Paul 539
Marković, Mihajlo 124
Marx, Karl 40
Masaryk, Tomás 162, 163
Mazowiecki, Tadeusz 144, 148, 149, 151
Mečiar, Vladimír 10, 72, 77, 166, 185, 188–9, 196–7, 200
media *see under* individual countries
Meidani, Rexhep 435
Mesić, Stipe 27, 122, 269
Meta, Ilir 436, 437
Michnik, Adam 144
migrant labor 102, 105
see also brain drain
Mihailović, Draža 287, 296
Milczanowski, Andrzej 153
Miller, Leszek 147
Milošević, Slobodan 9, 23, 26, 51, 72, 111, 115, 117, 119, 121, 122, 126, 262, 263, 274, 286, 288, 291, 293, 295, 306, 312, 321, 365
Mladić, Ratko 299, 302
Moldova 3, 4, 9, 13, 473, 485–7
constitution 68, 478
creation of nation and state 473–4
economic reforms 479–80: industrial transformation 96
electoral system 68
EU and 476, 484
factual information 487
Gagauzian autonomy 478–9
media 485
nationalism, Romanization, and secession 475
parliament 68
political parties 71, 477–8, 480–2: agrarian parties 81; conservative parties 80; liberal parties 79; third parties 81; trajectories of the left 75
poverty 105
president 68, 478
Transnistria 475–7, 482–5
Montenegro 4, 20, 31, 55, 58, 286, 290
corruption 11
electoral system 68
factual information 305
historical development 287
independence 293–4, 296, 297, 300–1, 519
political parties 72: trajectories of the left 75, 77
privatization 23

Nagy, Imre 207
Nano, Fatos 424, 428, 432–3, 435, 436
Napoleon III, Emperor 44
Năstase, Adrian 389
nation-states 39–42, 59
end of communist regimes and proliferation of new states 55–7
formation in Age of Empires (nineteenth century) 42–6
influence of EU on state formation in East-Central Europe 57–9
Nazi System 49–52
Versailles State System 46–9
Yalta State System 40, 41, 52–4
nationalism 82–3, 545–6
Nazi System 41, 49–52
Croatia and 50
Czechoslovakia and 50, 51, 166, 183
Hungary and 206
Poland and 50, 142
Romania and 388
Slovakia and 50, 183, 194
Slovenia and 244
Yugoslavia and 50, 287
Nonaligned Movement 287
North Atlantic Treaty Organization (NATO) 3, 10, 29, 495, 501, 502, 547, 548
Croatia and 275
Czech Republic and 549
Hungary and 212, 509
Kosovo campaign 57, 365
Macedonia and 329, 342
Partnership for Peace (PfP) 4, 508
Poland and 151, 154, 549
regional relations and 507–10
Romania and 389, 509
war in Yugoslavia and 130, 132
Novotný, Antonín 184

Olesky, Józef 153
Olszewski, Jan 151
Onyszkiewicz, Janusz 154
Orenstein, Mitchell 174
Organization for Black Sea Economic Cooperation (BSEC) 495, 496

Organization for Economic Cooperation and Development (OECD) 94
Organization for Security and Cooperation in Europe (OSCE) 30, 315
Orthodox Church
Kosova/Kosovo 364
Macedonia 331
Moldova 486
Romania 386
Ottoman Empire 43–4, 45
outward processing trade 94

Panić, Života 119
parliamentary systems 24–6, 67, 530
see also under individual countries
parties *see* political parties
Pavelić, Ante 267
Pawlak, Waldemar 151
Pejovnik, Stane 247
pensioners' parties 83
PHARE program 28, 520, 521
Piłsudski, Józef 142, 160n
Pithart, Petr 169
Poland 3, 9, 15, 16, 17, 20
abortion issue 11
borders 145
civil society 65
communist regime 142–40, 146, 149
constitution 25, 68, 153
corruption 11, 19
crime 21
economic reforms 92, 100, 144, 147–8: industrial transformation 96; informal sector 102; privatization 22, 98, 140, 144; "shock therapy" 97; women and 104
elections of 1989 139, 140, 143–4
electoral system 70
EU and 154, 521
foreign policies 145–6, 150, 151, 156
historical background 141
international community and 28, 29
lustration 11, 153, 156
NATO and 151, 154, 549
Nazi regime and 50, 142
parliament 67, 150
political parties 67, 71, 73, 74, 84, 147, 148–9: agrarian parties 81; conservative parties 79, 80; liberal parties 78; miscellaneous parties 83; Solidarity movement 139, 140, 143, 144, 146, 148, 152, 154–5; trajectories of the left 77, 152–4, 155–6
president 67, 140: Wałęsa 149–52
relations with Russia 145, 150
Roman Catholic Church in 150, 151, 155
security services 147
Visegrád group and 500, 501
political parties 64, 84
civil society and 65–7
electoral system 68–70
overview of development 70–4
party families and origins 74: agrarian parties 81; conservative parties 77, 79–80; ethnic minority parties 83; Green parties 81; liberal parties 77–9; nationalist parties 82–3; regionalist parties 83; third parties 80–4; trajectories of the left 75–7
see also under individual countries
Pond, Elizabeth 329
Pop-Eliches, Grigore 162, 163
Portugal
EU and 520
post-socialist development 12, 19, 31–2, 536–7, 549
corruption/crime and 19–21
defining success 539–46
democratization *see* democratization
dilemma of synchronicity 12–13
economic reforms *see* economic reforms
elite persistence 541
historical legacies and historical memory 13–17
institution building 23–4: in conditions of war 27–8; parliamentary 24–6; presidentialism 26
see also political parties
international community and 28–31
patterns of breakdown and re-creation of political rule 17–18
security and 546–9
standards for judgment 537–9
transition risks 540–1
see also individual countries
poverty 105
see also under individual countries
presidents 26, 67
see also under individual countries
Primakov, Yevgeny 548
privatization 9, 21–3, 97, 98–9
see also under individual countries
Putin, Vladimir 547

Radoš, Ivica 264
Rašković, Jovan 262, 289

regional security and regional relations 495–6, 510
see also individual organizations
regionalist parties 83
Rehn, Olli 345
religion *see* Orthodox Church; Roman Catholic Church
Renouvin, Pierre 39
Ribičič, Mitja 248
Rokkan, Stein 70
Roman Catholic Church 150, 151
abortion issue 11
Czech Republic 167
Hungary 225, 226
Poland and 150, 151, 155
privatization and 21
Slovakia 194–5
Slovenia 244, 249
Romania 3, 9, 16, 17, 20, 32, 484, 486
communist regime 380–1
constitution 382
Constitutional Court 382
corruption 20, 389, 391, 394, 543
creation of 45
economic reforms 106, 385, 387, 389, 393: industrial transformation 96; informal sector 101; internationalization and transnationalization 94; privatization 385–6; women and 103; workforce's reactions 101
electoral system 13, 382, 383, 394
ethnic minorities 10, 83, 224, 382, 385–6
EU and 381, 389, 390, 394–5, 521, 522, 524, 528
factual information 397
historical background 379–81, 395–6
inflation 98
international community and 29
judiciary 383
local government 382
lustration 11
media 387
NATO and 389, 509
Nazi regime and 388
Orthodox Church 386
parliament 67, 382
political parties 71, 72, 382, 383, 386, 388, 390, 391, 394: conservative parties 79, 80; ethnic minority parties 83; liberal parties 79; trajectories of the left 75, 77
poverty 393
president 382
Securitate 388, 392–3
unemployment 98
Visegrád Group and 501, 502
Rugova, Ibrahim 362, 363, 374
Rusko, Pavol 83
Russia 20, 30, 99
corruption 11, 19, 20
crime 21
democratization 547
NATO expansion and 509, 547
Polish relations with 145, 150
privatization 22
regional power 547–8
Rydzyk, Tadeusz 155

Sadurski, Wojciech 530
Sanader, Ivo 270
Saxe-Coburg-Gotha, Simeon 406, 418
Schuster, Rudolf 83
security 546–9
Sekerinska, Radmila 347
Serbia 4, 9, 20, 51, 55, 275, 286–7, 540
break with Montenegro 293–4, 296, 297, 300–1
constitution 293
corruption 11, 20, 286, 291, 298
creation of 43, 45
creation of Yugoslavia and 46–7
economic reforms: privatization 23; women and 103
electoral system 68, 292
ethnic minorities 224, 303
EU and 298, 302, 529
factual information 305
health care 291
historical development 112, 113, 114, 115–17, 287–8, 288–90, 303–5
inflation 291, 292
loss of Kosovo 288, 300, 301
media 303
political parties 72, 290, 291, 292, 297–300: conservative parties 81; nationalist parties 82; trajectories of the left 75
president 68, 293, 294
re-integration into international community 295–6
war in Yugoslavia and 11, 18, 27–8, 51, 290: armed conflict begins in Croatia 117–19, 313; assault on Bosnia-Herzegovina 123–7, 290, 302, 313; genocide claims against Serbia 302

Šešelj, Vojislav 292, 311
Shamir, Yitzhak 146
Siegerist, Joachim 83
Šimonović, Ivan 263
Skubiszewski, Krysztof 145
Slánský, Rudolf 184
Slovakia 3, 5, 55, 59, 72, 197–8
  communist regime 184
  corruption 195–6
  democratization 186–8, 519: consolidated 197; democratic consolidation or Europeanization 190–3; first phase (1989–93) 186; second phase (1994–8) 186, 188–9; third phase (1998–2004) 186, 189–90
  economic reforms 103: industrial transformation 96; privatization 22, 195
  economy 171
  electoral system 68, 70
  ethnic minorities 83, 224
  EU and 191, 524, 528, 529
  factual information 197
  industrialization 193
  international community and 28
  media 196–7
  from nationhood to statehood 182: Slovak national question (1918–1989) 182–4
  NATO and 509
  Nazi regime and 50, 183, 194
  parliament 26
  political parties 72, 73, 74, 199: conservative parties 80; ethnic minority parties 83; liberal parties 78; miscellaneous parties 83; third parties 81; trajectories of the left 75, 77
  Roman Catholic Church in 194–5
  Visegrád Group and 503, 505, 506
Slovenia 5, 11, 20, 27, 55, 98, 235, 250
  abortion issue 11
  citizenship 248
  civil society 65, 241
  constitution 237, 239, 240, 249
  corruption 246
  economic reforms 100: industrial transformation 96; privatization 23, 246, 247; state power and 96
  education 248
  electoral system 241
  EU and 240
  factual information 242
  historical background 235–7
  homosexual people 250
  institutional transformation 238–41
  media 245
  Nazi regime 244
  parliament 67, 239, 240
  political parties 71, 241–7: conservative parties 79, 80; liberal parties 77; pensioners' parties 83; trajectories of the left 75, 77
  poverty 248
  refugees in 248
  Roman Catholic Church 244, 249
  tensions in Yugoslavia and 116
  war in Yugoslavia and 117, 119–20, 290–2
Snegur, Mircea 477, 480
socialist/communist parties 75–7
Solidarity movement 139, 140, 143, 144, 146, 148, 152, 154–5
Soviet Union 3, 18, 53
  break-up 54, 55
  see also Russia
Spain
  EU and 520, 521
Špegeli, Martin 118, 120, 121
Stability Pact for South Eastern Europe (SPSEE) 339
state *see* government and the state; nation-states
Stoklosa, Henryk 143
Strøm, Kaare 173
Suchocka, Hanna 151
Šušak, Gojko 128
synchronicity, dilemma of 12–13

Tiso, Jozef 183, 194
Tito, Josip Broz 114, 287
Tocsik, Marta 219
Tőkés, Rudolf 13
Topolánek, Mirek 168
trade unions *see* labor unions
Trajkovski, Boris 329
transition *see* post-socialist development
transnationalization 94–5
Transparency International 5
Tudjman, Franjo 9, 26, 72, 117, 120, 121, 122, 128, 259–61, 262, 263, 264, 265, 266, 268, 274, 278, 289
Tudjman, Nevenka 271
Turkey
  EU and 526
Tusk, Donald 155, 157
Tymiński, Stan 149

Ukraine 4, 146
corruption 11, 20
dispute with Russia 548
unemployment 98, 105
Bulgaria 98, 415
Kosova/Kosovo 370
Romania 98
unions *see* labor unions
United Kingdom
war in Yugoslavia and 126
United Nations 58
Development Program 337
High Commission on National Minorities 30
Kosova/Kosovo protectorate 365, 366, 367, 373
war in Yugoslavia and 120, 126, 128, 130–1
United States 55
war in Yugoslavia and 130, 131, 132
Uspaskich, Viktor 83

Vachudova, Milada 175
Vance, Cyrus 122
Versaillles State System 46–9
Vienna Congress (1815) 41, 42
Visegrád Group 496, 499, 503–5, 546
origins 499–503
post-EU accession 505–7
Voiculescu, Dan 391
voluntary organizations (civil society) 65–7
Voronin, Vladimir 483, 484, 488

Wachowski, Mieczyslaw 149
Wałęsa, Lech 4, 9, 17, 140, 148, 159, 500, 501
as president of Poland 149–52
Warsaw Treaty Organization (WTO) 3, 495
Williams, Kieran 164
Wilson, Woodrow 41, 48
women
Albania 426
economic reforms and 103–4
Hungary 221–2
workers *see* labor markets
World Bank 94
World Trade Organization (WTO) 94

Yalta state system 40, 41, 52–4
Yugoslavia 3, 10, 18, 41, 52, 53
creation of 46–7, 48
economic reforms: privatization 22; "shock therapy" 97
history 112–15, 287, 288–90: Serbian rebellion against Titoism 115–17
Nazi regime and 50, 287
political parties 72
war in 11, 13, 18, 27–8, 30, 51, 72, 111–12, 290, 540: Bosnian revival and road to Dayton Accord 129–33, 314; conflict in Croatia 27–8, 117–19, 120–3, 130–1, 133, 261–6, 290, 313; conflict in Slovenia 117, 119–20, 290–2; Muslim–Croat conflict 127–9, 264, 313; Serbia's assault on Bosnia-Herzegovina 123–7, 290, 302, 313
see-also individual republics

Zeman, Miloš 84
Zhelev, Zheliu 9
Zhivkov, Todor 17
Župljanin, Stojan 299, 302
Zuschlag, János 219